History of Colonial America

A Captivating Guide to the Colonial History of the United States, Puritans, Anne Hutchinson, The Pilgrims, Mayflower, Pequot War, and Quakers

Free Bonus from Captivating History (Available for a Limited time)

Hi History Lovers!

Now you have a chance to join our exclusive history list so you can get your first history ebook for free as well as discounts and a potential to get more history books for free! Simply visit the link below to join.

Captivatinghistory.com/ebook

Also, make sure to follow us on Facebook, Twitter and Youtube by searching for Captivating History.

Contents

Part 1: Colonial America

A Captivating Guide to the Colonial History of the United States and How Immigrants of Countries Such as England, Spain, France, and the Netherlands Established Colonies

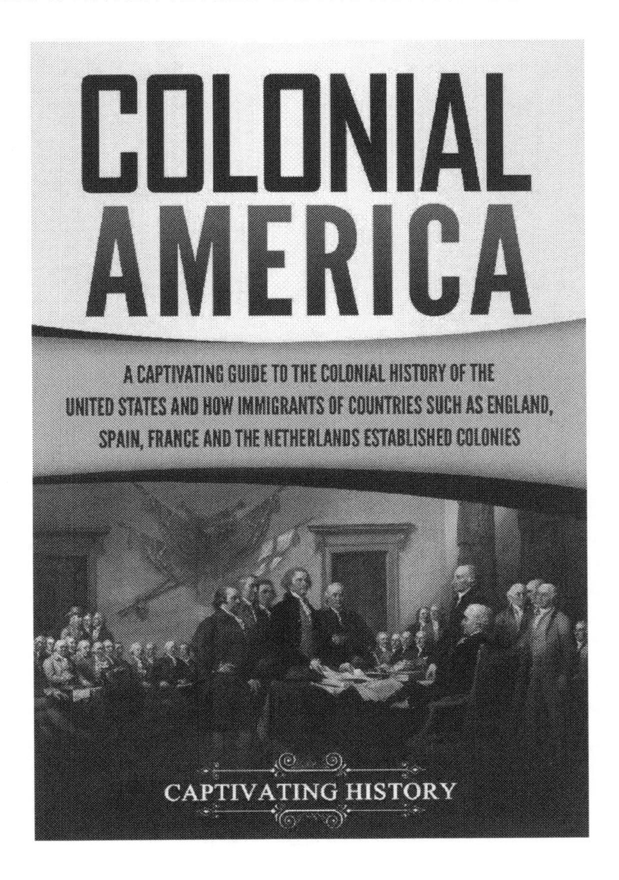

Introduction

The colonial period of American history lasted almost three hundred years. It saw discoveries, revolution, and the shaping of a future country. From 1492 to about 1763, several countries made their play for the land. France, Spain, and England all attempted to plant their flag on the North American continent.

Each country staked a claim, but it seems that England was the true victor, at least in regards to the modern United States. But ultimately, the pioneering, inventive, and scrappy colonists earned their freedom and rights to the land. The road to revolution began in 1763. To their credit, the colonists attempted to compromise with Britain before rebelling against it.

However, to fully understand colonial America and the colonists' road to revolution, it's important to cover what happened before even Jamestown was settled in 1607.

Spain first made inroads in North America. Its territories in what would become the United States of America consisted of the southern portion, such as Florida, New Mexico, and California. France was the next to enter the picture, but it never held much compared to Spain and England, which was the next large power to arrive on the scene.

Once the door opened for the English to sail to the New World, religion became a big reason Englishmen risked their lives on the seas. As the Puritan movement gained steam and the Church of England grew in opposition to it, the new land turned into an opportunity for the bravest of souls.

By 1790, the British population in the United States was quite large. It stood at 66.3 percent with just over 2.6 million people. After that, there were the German, Irish, Dutch, and French, who were all in the single digits percentage-wise. In terms of religion, the makeup depended on the location. By 1775, 575,000 individuals identified as Congregationalists in New England. The Quaker population stood at forty thousand, and the vast majority of them lived in Pennsylvania, New Jersey, and Delaware.

In time, the Kingdom of Great Britain (which was established in 1707, replacing the Kingdom of England) realized that settling the colonies and protecting the colonists was an expensive task. To raise funds to cover its debts, Britain raised taxes on the colonists. Britain had the right to do this; after all, it had protected its interests and the colonists against the French,

Spanish, other mercenaries, and Native Americans. However, the colonists had tasted freedom, and they enjoyed it. They had become accustomed to their new way of life, and they had put in the effort to build their infrastructure. To them, they were as independent and free as the Englishmen who still roamed England.

When Christopher Columbus sailed the ocean blue, it's doubtful that even he knew what would come after him. He was going to unleash a flurry of explorations, battles, and a republic that still stands as the world's beacon of freedom today.

Explore American history with us. Dive into the colonial period one more time, and remember where the United States got its start.

Chapter 1 – The Beginning

Before the land became the United States, it was known as the Thirteen Colonies. Those colonies first took shape in the early 1600s with the settlement of Jamestown in 1607, which was a part of the Colony of Virginia. The Thirteen Colonies would continue to take shape throughout the 17th and 18th centuries, with Georgia being the last colony to be founded in 1732.

However, before the Thirteen Colonies were even established, the land was up for grabs. Several powers attempted to claim it, including even the Netherlands and Sweden, although their power did not last as long as the heavy-hitters, such as England and France.

It's fair to extend American colonial history to 1492, as this will help the reader understand why the establishment of Jamestown didn't solidify England as the world's superpower. In 1607, when Jamestown was founded, France, Spain, and England were still competing for that title.

In addition, although Britain dominated the settling of the land that would one day become the United States, the battles within Britain and against France and Spain never stopped. Britain stood as the world's top dog, but the other powers never stopped attempting to topple it. France likely knew that the most impactful thing it could do was take its rival deeper into debt, which it did. France never missed an opportunity to poke at Britain financially and defense-wise. After all, it was France that funded the Thirteen Colonies during the Revolutionary War.

A lot of exploring took place between the late 1400s and the early 1600s that is relevant to colonial America. France, England, and Spain, among other countries, had economic reasons for attempting to expand their empires. For example, Spain sought to amplify its trade capacity and spread the Catholic religion. What follows is a brief snapshot of what took place during the Age of Discovery.

The Early Days of the Age of Discovery

Trade between Europe and the East, which included countries like China and India, had been on the rise since the mid-13th century. Individuals started to see new textiles, goods (namely spices), and cultures, and they wanted more. To improve trade, one Italian explorer named Christopher Columbus aimed to find a better trade route to the Far East by sailing west.

Christopher Columbus set sail on August 3rd, 1492, with financial help from the Spanish Crown. That October, he stepped foot in the Bahamas—he had found the Americas. However, he did not know this; he believed he had found East Asia. On his third voyage to the New World, he would take his first steps on the North American mainland, namely Venezuela in South America. (It should be noted that Columbus did not discover mainland North America in the literal sense. The Viking Leif Eriksson had landed on the continent five hundred years earlier.)

When Columbus made it back to Spain, others saw that it could be done. Discovering new lands was possible. This set off the rivalry between Spain, England, and France.

Italian John Cabot attempted his first trip in 1497 under the sponsorship of King Henry II of England, landing on the coast of what is believed to be Newfoundland. He claimed the land for England, although, at the time, both Cabot and Columbus thought they were looking at the land of Asia. Cabot returned to North America again in 1498, but his fate after this remains unknown.

Amerigo Vespucci gets the credit for realizing that the land these explorers were looking at was not Asia. It is believed that he realized this in 1501 when he landed in Brazil. A cartographer in 1507 called these new lands South and North America, giving Amerigo the credit for making this discovery.

Vasco Núñez de Balboa was inspired by Christopher Columbus, and he first explored the New World in 1500. However, his best-known achievement happened in 1513. Balboa, a Spanish conquistador, was the first European to see the Pacific Ocean from this new land. Although his trip did not receive royal sponsorship, he claimed the ocean (then called the South Sea) for Spain. Like other Spanish explorers, Balboa was interested in finding gold.

Juan Ponce de León also searched for gold, as well as the Fountain of Youth, at least according to stories told about him. He was an avid explorer of North America, and he even traveled with Columbus on one of his expeditions. In 1513, Ponce de León led an official exploration of what is now Florida. In fact, he gave the state its name, as he called it La Florida. He also became the first governor of Puerto Rico. Ponce de León shows a common theme among the explorers of this era. The expeditions were often funded to find gold and other riches; however, the explorers tended to run into new lands and natives.

The exchanges between natives oftentimes turned hostile during this period of time, but there were occasions when peaceful communication took place. For instance, Juan Ponce de León used the natives as a source of slave labor, which was something explorers often did back then. This likely stemmed from the fact that the natives did not practice the same religion as the explorers and that their ways seemed "backward." The French, on the other hand, tended to befriend the Native Americans while exploiting their rivalries with other tribes to their advantage. It is also important to note that disease devastated the Native American population since they did not have immunities to European diseases. It is thought that beginning with Columbus's arrival in the New World, around 90 percent of Native Americans died, with most of that being due to epidemics of smallpox, cholera, and other diseases, although violence certainly played a role as well.

One of the greatest voyages that took place during the Age of Discovery was when Portuguese Ferdinand Magellan sought to circumnavigate the globe. He was tasked by the Spanish Crown to find a new route to the East Indies, and he set sail in 1519. It's no secret that Magellan embarked on this voyage to gain fame and notoriety for his accomplishments; however, he died in 1521 before he could make it back to Spain to be lauded for his achievement.

In 1524, Italian Giovanni da Verrazzano set sail on behalf of King Francis I of France. He ended up exploring the eastern coastline of the United States. He started in what is today North Carolina and made his way up the coast as far north as Newfoundland.

King Francis I was in a heated rivalry with Charles V of the Holy Roman Empire (he also ruled as the king of Spain and Germany, the archduke of Austria, and the lord of the Netherlands). Charles V wanted a universal monarchy, which means he wanted to be the supreme ruler over all the major states of Europe. As you can see, he was well on his way to doing so. Francis I was not willing to let his territories go without a fight, and the two powerful kings duked it out on the battlefield. But this rivalry spread into other spheres, such as exploration.

Jacques Cartier helped the French Crown gain footing in the North American continent. He set sail in 1534 to discover the alleged Northwest Passage to Asia. The French mariner explored the Gulf of St. Lawrence and parts of Canada, namely Newfoundland, parts of the Labrador Peninsula, and some of Canada's islands. On future journeys, he would sail the St. Lawrence River. He receives credit for naming Canada, which comes from the Huron-Iroquois word *kanata*.

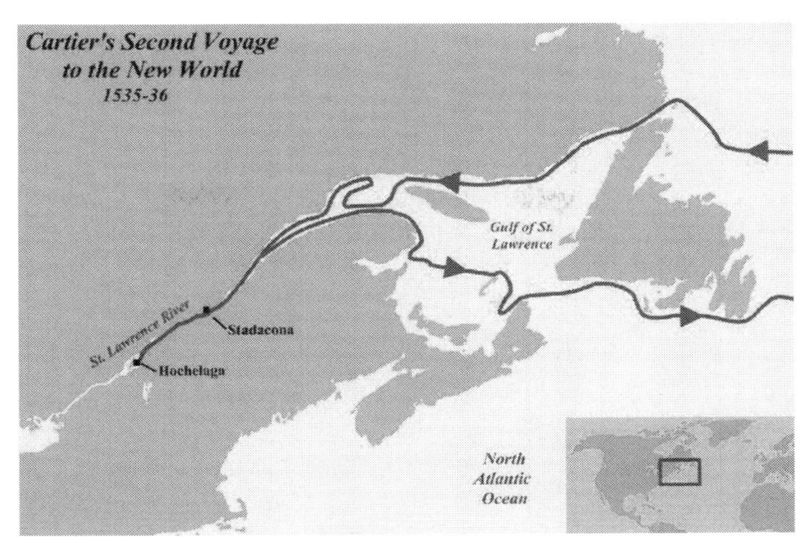

Jacques Cartier's second voyage, which took place from 1535 to 1536.
(Source: Jon Platek; Wikimedia Commons)

King Charles I of Spain (the same Emperor Charles V of the Holy Roman Empire) funded the infamous explorer Hernán Cortés, who would go on to conquer the Aztec Empire in 1521. He also funded Francisco Pizarro, who, in turn, conquered another existing civilization. Pizarro made his way to Peru and successfully defeated the Inca. His success helped him claim Peru on behalf of Spain in 1532. As mentioned above, some of the Europeans' success in conquering the native people had to do with the spread of diseases, to which the natives had no immunity. It absolutely devastated their populations, although the enslavement of the people and the sheer brutality in which the wars were fought did not help. Many historians also believe that the Europeans had better weapons than the natives, which is likely true, although some contend that the natives had just as strong weapons as the Europeans.

Conquistador Hernando de Soto participated in conquering Peru on behalf of Spain. In 1539, he made his way to Florida and traveled through the Southeast. In 1541, he crossed the Mississippi River, making him the first European to do so.

Francisco Vázquez de Coronado traveled to Mexico in 1535. Five years later, he set out on a grand expedition, making his way north to the American Midwest; he also explored the Southwest. Coronado searched for gold, treasure, and other valuables. Instead, he spotted natural landmarks, such as the Grand Canyon and the Colorado River.

Portugal

Although Portugal didn't end up being a power in what would become the United States, it deserves a special mention for its contributions to the Age of Discovery. As France and Spain tried to outdo each other, Portugal remained a player in the game too. Before the Portuguese made inroads in the New World, word of Columbus's travels and discoveries reached them. On June 7th, 1494, the Treaty of Tordesillas was signed between Spain and Portugal. Portugal planned to make major inroads in the New World, and Spain agreed to the treaty, knowing its fleet could not match Portugal's. The Treaty of Tordesillas divided the world, with Portugal taking control of undiscovered lands east of the line, while Spain would take the lands that were west of it. Lands that had already been claimed by either country would remain theirs because they believed that they could profit by establishing trading posts in coastal Africa. This agreement was, for the most part, respected by Spain and Portugal, but the other countries did not recognize it.

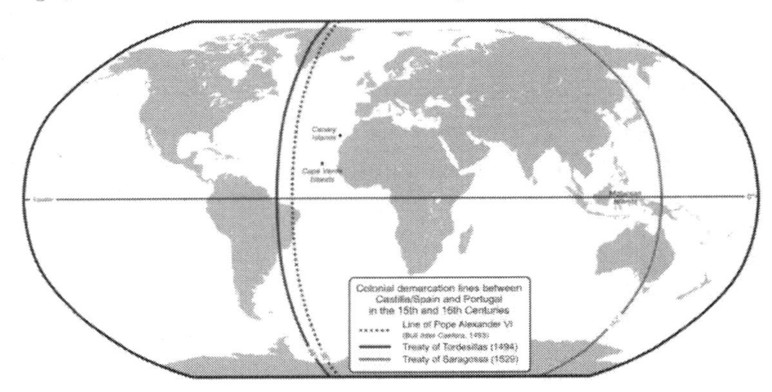

The western line is from the Treaty of Tordesillas, while the eastern line is from the Treaty of Zaragoza (Saragossa), which was the median that split the Far East between the two countries. (Source: Lencer; Wikimedia Commons)

Nevertheless, Portugal saw its own heyday. For instance, the Portuguese captured Ceuta in North Africa in 1415. They soon realized that improved ships would improve their ability to travel. The Portuguese made several contributions to maritime technology, including advanced ships, navigation techniques, and collecting oceanography data. It should also be noted that Columbus spent around a decade training in Portugal before he received financing for his voyage from Spain. In fact, he first sought funding from the Portuguese Crown before turning to Spain.

In 1488, before Columbus set sail, Portuguese explorer Bartolomeu Dias became the first European to travel around the southern tip of Africa, which was no doubt an inspiration to many explorers. The Portuguese also sailed to

Africa, India, China, and other areas of Asia, with their travels beginning in the early 1400s. During the 15th century, trade increased, becoming global. Moreover, Portugal faced no competition until the Spanish Crown funded Columbus, allowing it to become a wealthy power.

In 1517, when Martin Luther started the Protestant Reformation, things began to change. During the European Age of Discovery, religion remained a present factor in why people moved to the Americas. But all good things come to an end, and they did for Portugal as well. The world power suffered significant military defeats in Africa under King Sebastian. In 1580, King Henry of Portugal, Sebastian's great uncle, passed away. This meant that the throne had a vacancy. Philip II of Spain claimed it for himself, stating he had a right to it because he had Portuguese blood.

Portugal attempted to regain its independence and began to break away in 1640. England, Holland, and France used the idea of the Black Legend to strip Spain and Portugal of lands left in their control. The Black Legend was anti-Spanish propaganda that the other major countries disseminated. The propaganda claimed that the Spanish were cruel and intolerant. It is interesting to note that the other major European powers pointed out how cruel the Spanish were to the Native Americans when all of them were guilty of doing so. As far as we know, Spain was the first country to pass laws that protected the natives, something that was, of course, not mentioned in this propaganda. In addition, the Spanish Black Legend made the Spanish discoveries seem minor, even though they were ground-breaking, and it diminished the Catholic Church.

The Competitors for North America: England and Spain

When you study history, it's easy to see how power shifted from one empire to another. While you're living history, though, it's tough to see the forest for the trees.

Then there was the relationship between England and Spain.

England and Spain remained allies for several years. However, the low-key rivalry heated up after Queen Elizabeth I took the throne in 1558. As a Protestant, she differed from Catholic Spain, and as a result, the relationship between England and Spain was strained. However, Protestantism unified England. The arts flourished during Elizabeth's rule, and moreover, England found a way to defeat the Spanish Armada in 1588.

History shows that the Spanish overplayed their hand. Up to this point, England remained the underdog. Thanks to the queen's financing choices, the Royal Navy remained healthy. In fact, in the process, they established the greatest navy the world had seen at that time. The fleet saw new life as shipbuilders placed large guns on them. Queen Elizabeth's investment in the navy allowed the country to build up its defense. Without pushing back against Spain, the English travels to the New World would have seen further delays and opposition.

Francis Drake marked the beginning of England's efforts to push back against the Spanish Empire. He circumnavigated the globe, with his expedition lasting around three years (1577–1580). His travels took him to the West Indies. When he neared Mexico, he attacked Spanish settlements and ships, taking the plunder back to England. Although the Spanish arrived at the Pacific Ocean first, Drake became the first Englishman to see it.

Queen Elizabeth greatly favored Drake for his work on the high seas, granting him a knighthood in 1581. Mayorships and governorships were also common rewards conquistadors and explorers received for their successful trips, and in that same year, Drake became the mayor of Plymouth, England. Although there were plenty of lands to still explore, the conquistadors and explorers wanted to get there first.

Thus, the rivalry between England and Spain intensified. When the English arrived in parts of the New World where the Spanish were already exploring, skirmishes broke out. In 1586, Elizabeth I prepared to push back against Spanish retaliation. With an estimated thirty ships, Drake took care of the Spanish at Cádiz for over thirty-six hours. Researchers believe that Britain felt that a war with Spain could not be avoided. Thus, they struck first. Drake entered Cádiz and surprised the Spanish who stood guard. By raiding Spanish resources, the English successfully weakened the Spanish position. When the Spanish Armada reached the English Channel in 1588, it was considerably weaker.

Defeating the Spanish Armada marked the turning point for England. The English could journey to the New World without the Spanish acting as a barrier. Plus, the English landed in the north, whereas the Spanish explored the southern areas of the Americas.

Sir Humphrey Gilbert receives credit for his ability to develop tactful plans of colonization. He served under Queen Elizabeth I as early as 1566. A year later, Gilbert began developing plans to colonize Ireland. Then he was tasked with attempting to colonize America. However, he was unable to make any permanent settlements in the Americas, although he did claim Newfoundland for England.

Sir Walter Raleigh, who was related to Gilbert, also served under Queen Elizabeth I. He accomplished several feats, including becoming the governor of Jersey, a small island off the coast of Normandy. In many ways, Raleigh set up the first English settlement in the New World: Roanoke. He entrusted the settlement to an explorer and cartographer named John White, but unfortunately for England, the settlement did not work out (this settlement will be explored in more depth in the next chapter).

These explorations paint the broad strokes of what would become the future Thirteen Colonies. To understand colonial America, it's important to understand the rivalries that took place between England, France, and Spain. Had the English not pushed back against Spain, North America might look very different today.

Part of the desire to expand to the New World came from the growing populations in Europe. For instance, by 1600, England had a population of over four million. The growing population led to unemployment, lack of sufficient food supplies, and crowded lands. This led to tensions between the people, which was only exacerbated by religion.

London saw their countrymen turn into beggars on the streets. Plus, the cards were stacked against families that had more than one son. By law, only the eldest son inherited the family's land and estate. Therefore, the younger males had to fend for themselves in other ways.

Exploring the New World provided a viable solution. It also meant that they could compete on the world stage.

However, the English could not have imagined what awaited them. They also could not have imagined what their explorations would unleash.

Chapter 2 – The Thirteen Colonies: A Brief Overview

The Spanish conquistadors conquered their way through the land that became Mexico and other parts of Central America. They also made their way through the modern United States of America's southern regions, which included California, Texas, and Florida, to name a few.

While England watched Spain spread out and take control of these new lands, it is likely its people felt envious. Some believe that it pressured the English to stake out some fresh soil too. It didn't help that England made several attempts to settle in the new land and failed.

Sir Walter Raleigh finally gave England something to celebrate, albeit only for a time. Although the English had attempted to settle the island of Roanoke in 1585, the settlement failed. In 1587, the English gave it another shot. John White and his crew landed on the island, which is located off modern-day North Carolina. The expedition was backed by Raleigh. The settlement soon ran into trouble, and White returned to England in 1588 to bring back more supplies. However, he was forced to stay in the country due to the breakout of the Anglo-Spanish War. When he arrived back at the island, everyone was gone. Nothing was left behind but the word "CROATOAN" on a fence. It is likely the settlers moved to Croatoan Island, where they mixed with the natives, but this cannot be confirmed for certain.

As mentioned in the prior chapter, the tide changed in England's favor in 1588 when it defeated the Spanish Armada. The win gave the English newfound hope and confidence. England had at last gained leverage over Spain. The Spanish Empire had finally met its match, and the defeat forced the county to pull back. It opened the road for England to establish the Thirteen Colonies, as the Atlantic Ocean posed less of a threat, at least in terms of Spanish ships looking to bring down the British.

The Treaty of London was signed in 1604 between Britain and Spain, ending the nearly twenty-year Anglo-Spanish War. The treaty didn't change anything in regards to land. However, both countries made pledges to stop capturing ships on the Atlantic. Spain also stated that it would stop seeking to install Catholicism in England. The English hated the treaty, while the Spanish celebrated it. Regardless of their feelings, peace between the two countries lasted until 1625.

King James I of England had started his rule over a year before the signing of the treaty in 1603 after Queen Elizabeth passed away. Even though the country had new leadership, England's need to continue its explorations did not fade. To finance the voyages to the land across the Atlantic, King James I authorized charters for new settlements. Once a company's trip received approval, the members had leverage to raise money to finance it.

List of Kings and Queens of the Kingdom of England (1558-1707)

The various civil wars and throne changes can be confusing to follow. We have provided a handy list here of who was in charge at what time. This chapter is divided into sections, and there is some jumping around in the timeline to properly cover the history of the colonies. It should be noted that colonial history extends past this list, but the colonies, except for Georgia, were established during the Kingdom of England, which means the names of later kings and queens are not mentioned as often in this chapter.

- Elizabeth I (1558-1603)
- James I (1603-1625)
- Charles I (1625-1649)
- The Royal Interregnum (1649-1653; when England was ruled directly by the Parliament)
- Oliver Cromwell as Lord Protector (1653-1658)
- Richard Cromwell as Lord Protector (1658-1659)
- Charles II (1660-1685)
- James II (1685-1688)
- Mary II (1689-1694)
- William III or William of Orange (1689-1702; ruled alongside his wife, Mary)
- Anne (1702-1707)
- The Kingdom of England becomes the Kingdom of Great Britain in 1707.

The Colony of Virginia

In 1606, the Virginia Company of London received its charter to establish a colony in the New World. Around 104 men and boys headed to found England's first permanent colony. The colony was officially founded in 1607 at Jamestown, Virginia. It received additional charters in 1609 and 1612. In 1624, Virginia was made a royal colony, and by 1775, the colony still had its royal status.

A colony could have different statuses. It could be under royal, proprietary, or charter rule. A royal colony was under Crown rule. Representation came from an appointed governor and council. Those that were under Crown rule received official acknowledgment, and they oftentimes had more of a military presence. A proprietary colony was one that had charters granted by England; the land belonged to the Crown, but the proprietors could choose who would lead. A charter colony was one that had a royal charter but did not experience direct interference from the English government.

The Virginia Company of London named Jamestown after England's king. The ships landed at this site on purpose. Those funding the voyage knew that the land had a few special characteristics that would make a settlement prosper. The settlement was located on a peninsula, which would allow the English to defend it against the Spanish if necessary. In addition, the area was free of natives—they didn't inhabit this part of Virginia because the land was unfavorable for producing crops. It turns out the natives knew best; the land was isolated, and there was no good source of fresh water nearby.

However, it was in England's interest to settle in the New World, and Jamestown would end up persevering, despite the severe drought the English suffered that first year. On top of that, the men had arrived too late in the year to plant crops. Two-thirds of the colonists died before ships came back with supplies the following year. Nevertheless, the men got to work and built a fort to protect themselves against potential threats. Soon after the fort was completed, Captain Christopher Newport went back to England to pick up additional supplies.

Life in the colonies before solid infrastructure was built was rough. The colonists consumed water that was filled with bacteria, which led to diseases and infections that caused many deaths. And if the first settlers didn't die from diseases, they likely passed away from a lack of food.

The relationship between the settlers and the local natives, in this case, the Powhatans, remained strained. The year 1609 through 1610 (known as the Starving Time) proved difficult for the settlers. Due to the lack of food and water and their inability to depend on the Powhatans for such things, the winter became challenging. Estimates show that only around 10 percent of the original settlers lived. In their desperation, the people turned to cannibalism to stay alive.

In May of 1610, ships arrived from Bermuda. Sir Thomas Gates, who had made his way to Jamestown with more supplies from England, got caught in a terrible hurricane that pushed his ships down to Bermuda. When he arrived in Jamestown, he found it in such bad condition that the decision was made to abandon the settlement. The arrival of another ship, led by Thomas West, the baron of De La Warr ("Delaware"), encouraged the colonists to head back to Jamestown and give it another chance. A more in-depth look at the Colony of Virginia, whose story includes such famous figures as John Smith, John Rolfe, and Pocahontas, can be found in Chapter 6.

Mass grave found under a building at Jamestown. (Source: Sarah Stierch; Wikimedia Commons)

The Colony of Massachusetts

Although the expeditions to the New World became more organized over time, a surefire path to success didn't exist. Some settlers were veered off course, such as the Pilgrims.

By several accounts, the Pilgrims intended to land near the Hudson River in modern-day New York. Weather veered the *Mayflower* to Cape Cod, where they landed on November 11th, 1620. Before the Pilgrims created their colony, the men agreed to sign the Mayflower Compact on November 21st, 1620. Although it took a few months of exploring, they eventually established Plymouth Colony (named after Plymouth, England). The site was cleared, and the nearby hills provided defense. However, this site was cleared because it once belonged to the Wampanoag; the village had suffered a smallpox outbreak, and they abandoned the village.

In the process of finding a place to settle, the Pilgrims came across Native Americans, including Squanto, who had been captured by the English previously but later became an ally of the Pilgrims. Their interactions with the natives were not peaceful, as both sides antagonized the other. The natives had encountered the English before; for instance, Squanto was taken prisoner sometime around 1614.

In Edward Winslow's letter to a friend in England, Winslow details finding food in caves that belonged to nearby natives. The letter also helped establish when the first traditional Thanksgiving took place—November 1621.

Edward Winslow, who played a key role in establishing Plymouth Colony, had made his way to Holland in 1617 as part of the Separatist movement. Separatists played a major role in the development of the United States. They believed that the state had no say in how their churches were run. Unlike the Puritans, they did not want to work with the Church of England; they wanted to completely separate.

Winslow and his wife were among the passengers of the *Mayflower*. However, she passed away shortly after they landed. He remarried in 1621 to Susanna White, who gave birth to Peregrine White in 1620 while on board the *Mayflower*. Peregrine White was the first European baby born in that part of North America (the first European baby to be born in North America was Virginia Dare, who was a part of the failed Roanoke colony). In addition, Winslow's marriage to Susanna was the first on colonial soil.

Since Winslow was not a Founding Father, it is probably why his name gets lost in the shuffle of American history. However, he is a key figure and served as the governor of the colony several times. When he didn't serve as governor, he served as a member of the governor's council. Moreover, he later served as the Massachusetts Bay agent, which allowed him to represent the colony. Like other colonial icons and the Founding Fathers, Winslow left behind several writings. In many ways, American history comes from them.

Like the inhabitants of Jamestown, Winslow detailed that the first winter presented harsh experiences. In March 1621, the settlers made formal contact with the local natives. Although the Native Americans were apprehensive about the newcomers at first, they eventually decided to aid them. Squanto played a key role in this; since he had been captured by the English, he could speak their language. He taught them how to farm the land, which was a good thing for the Pilgrims, as their seeds were not fit for the soil.

The first traditional Thanksgiving was celebrated that same year, and the meal consisted of waterfowl, fish, and deer. It is believed the first Thanksgiving might have taken place earlier in 1619, but this took place on board a ship and was a smaller affair.

Although Plymouth became an English colony, no official charter was issued to it since it wasn't the intended landing spot for the Pilgrims. However, it still operated as a charter colony. In 1691, Massachusetts Bay Colony absorbed it.

Massachusetts was one of the most important colonies. After all, this was where the Boston Massacre and Boston Tea Party took place, two important events that fueled the fire of revolution. The official formation of the Massachusetts Bay Colony began in the late 1620s. In 1628, a land grant was given to a group of investors. The territory was mostly settled by the Puritans, who were seeking religious reform that was not possible in England.

The Puritans played a large role in the formation of the land that now makes up part of the United States of America. They had become disenchanted with the Church of England. The Puritan movement started because they felt the church had adopted too many Catholic practices. Those with economic bones to pick with the English government also latched onto the Puritan movement. In 1691, Massachusetts became a royal colony. A more complete story of the founding of Massachusetts will be told in Chapter 4.

Maine

Maine became a state in 1820, but it was never an official colony. Sir Ferdinando Gorges helped fund Popham Colony in 1607, but it failed. He then received a land grant for territory in Maine in 1622. Gorges attempted to build the land with an aristocratic mindset, but needless to say, his attempt did not succeed. In 1677, Massachusetts purchased the land.

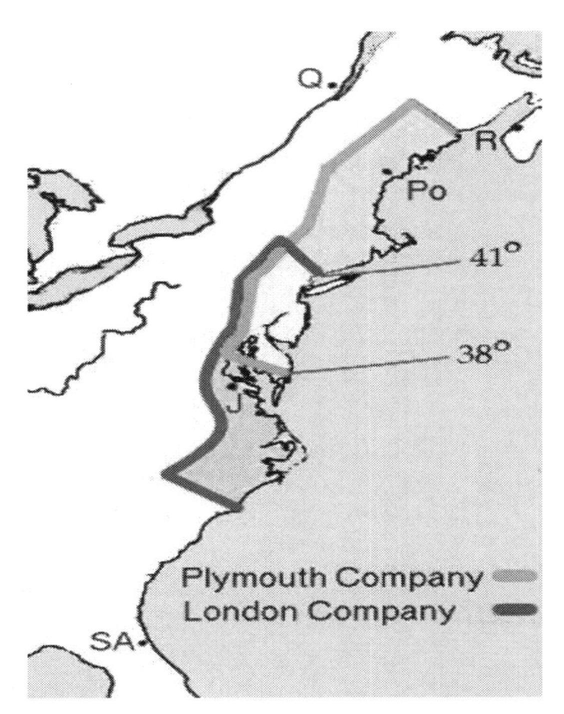

"Po" is where Popham Colony was located; "J" is where Jamestown was located. (Source: Wikimedia Commons)

The Colony of New Hampshire

New Hampshire was settled by John Mason and Ferdinando Gorges in 1623 and became a royal province in 1679. During these early years, the land boundaries remained fluid. Before receiving its charter and royal status, Massachusetts absorbed jurisdiction of the land from 1641 to 1679.

Keep in mind that border disputes were common while the original Thirteen Colonies took shape. Even today, some citizens of the United States don't realize that borders among the colonies were blurry sometimes. As the colonists worked to establish infrastructure, proprietors, leadership members, and representatives knew that access to water was essential. Access to ports was vital too.

The border dispute between New Hampshire and Massachusetts was bitter, as Mason's heirs sought to claim their inheritance. These disputes eventually led to the colony receiving its own leadership again in 1679. In 1691, New Hampshire became a royal colony.

The people who settled in New Hampshire started an economy based on fishing and trading. They had access to whales, timber, fur, and fish. Even though the colony experienced the typical harsh winters of New England, they were able to set up some agricultural practices. They did not grow enough for trade, but they did grow their own crops that provided sustenance. Common crops included squash, wheat, corn, rye, and beans. The trees found in the colony were used to build ships.

While the Puritans, Catholics, and Quakers sought a place to live in the New World that would provide them the freedom to practice their religion as they saw fit, those who traveled to New Hampshire were often searching for riches. They knew that the fish, fur, and timber trade with England would net them handsome profits.

The colony experienced its fair share of disputes. It seemed to be caught in a tug of war with Massachusetts Bay Colony. Between 1699 and 1741, its governor was often the same as the governor of Massachusetts. In 1741, Benning Wentworth became the governor of New Hampshire, ending the practice of being overseen by Massachusetts. He holds the record for having the single longest tenure as a colonial governor.

Other issues New Hampshire faced were boundary issues with New York. Wentworth began selling land grants, which New York contested, claiming they belonged to New York. Wentworth ignored them, saying that he would only stop if a royal decree was made in New York's favor. In 1764, the British government ruled in favor of New York, upholding the original grant that was given to New York. The Connecticut River became the official boundary. Those who had bought land grants from Wentworth lost their land, although New York representatives were willing to sell them the land again at a much higher price.

The Colony of Maryland

George Calvert, an English politician, sought to establish a space in the New World for Catholics. In 1623, he founded Avalon, which was located in Newfoundland, with the intent to provide a safe haven for Catholics facing persecution in England. Soon after this, though, he resigned from his government posts. He had supported a marriage alliance between England and Spain, and when that fell through, he publicly declared that he was a Catholic. He had been loyal to the king, so Calvert did not lose his favor with him; rather, he was given the title of Baron Baltimore in Ireland.

Lord Baltimore wished for another safe haven for Catholics in the New World after experiencing hostility from the colonists in Jamestown due to his religion in 1629. He received the charter to what is now Maryland in 1632. However, he died the same year, and the charter was inherited by his son, Cecil, also often known as Cecilius Calvert. To help set up the colony, he made his brother Leonard the first governor of Maryland.

Interestingly, Cecilius was very hands-on in regard to the colony's affairs. He gave Leonard instructions for setting up the colony called "Instructions to the Colonists by Lord Baltimore." His main concern was religious freedom for Catholics and Protestants since the Puritans had difficulty accepting those of a different faith.

Many of the early settlers were, oddly enough, Protestants, and they did not run into many issues with the local tribes. In fact, the early colonists of this region owe much of their success to the Native Americans, as they taught them how to plant crops and showed them where to find seafood. To encourage settlement, men willing to eke out a living in the colony were given fifty acres of land for each person they brought, whether that was another family member or a slave.

Cecilius never set foot in Maryland. Since King Charles I (r. 1625–1649) faced so much adversity, the situation in England remained unstable. A change on the throne could easily undo anything that Charles I had set down. Thus, Cecilius remained in England to protect his interests, which were also his family's interests.

It turns out that he had reason to worry, although the problems occurred across the ocean. A privateer named Richard Ingle attacked the capital of the colony and took prisoners in 1644. Leonard fled to Virginia. The brothers managed to retake control of Maryland two years later. Leonard passed away in 1648.

William Stone became Maryland's new governor in 1649. The conflict in Maryland didn't end with him. As a Protestant, he signed the Religious Toleration Act of 1649, which granted religious tolerance to all Christian denominations. The Puritans in the colony thought it was too Catholic in nature. They had to swear allegiance to Calvert, a Catholic, and they believed that, in turn, made them obedient to the pope.

That same year, Charles I was executed; he was accused of treason. He refused to instate a constitutional monarchy, and many viewed him as being too Catholic. He was not actually Catholic, but his wife was. His eldest son, who was also named Charles, took the throne, although he would also face many difficulties as well.

In 1654, the act was repealed. This took place shortly after the end of the Third English Civil War, which saw Scotland absorbed by England. More importantly, at least in regards to Maryland, those fighting for a constitutional monarchy (the Roundheads) won the day, creating the short-lived English Commonwealth. Members of this faction rose up against Stone in 1654 and removed him from power.

Stone attempted to reassert his control at the Battle of the Severn in March of 1655. However, he failed and was taken prisoner in the process.

As you can see, the colonies were an extension of England. What happened in the Motherland impacted them. After Oliver Cromwell, the leader of the Roundheads, passed away in 1658, Charles II was restored to the throne, although he would only do so in 1660. This led to Stone receiving his freedom. The Calvert family rewarded Stone with land granting him Charles County, Maryland. Stone passed away that same year.

In 1729, the city of Baltimore was established, and it was named after Cecil Calvert. Baltimore became an important port that shipped tobacco and grain. Flour milling became an important economic activity in the area.

In regards to Maryland's status as a colony, it was initially a proprietary colony that was overseen by Cecilius Calvert. In 1689, the colony was overseen by the Crown, as the aftereffects of the Glorious Revolution, which was another internal conflict that saw a change on the English throne, saw Cecilius's son removed from power. In 1715, the colony was returned to proprietary rule once George Calvert, 5th Baron Baltimore, stated he was a Protestant.

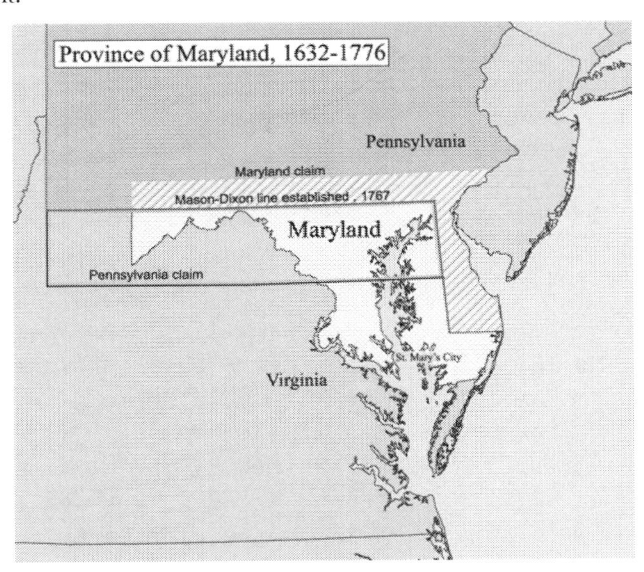

Map of the Province of Maryland. (Source: Karl Musser; Wikimedia Commons)

The Colony of Connecticut

In 1636, Thomas Hooker, a Puritan minister, and John Haynes, the governor of Massachusetts Bay Colony, founded Connecticut. In the early years, the colony governed itself, but in 1662, it received an official charter.

Hooker is known as the Father of Connecticut. He began his career by preaching in England. Over time, his beliefs began to be more and more suppressed. In the late 1620s, he fled England after being summoned to appear before the Court of High Commission for his Puritan sympathies. From Holland, he emigrated to Massachusetts Bay Colony.

Thomas Hooker was not the only settler who started in Massachusetts and sought refuge somewhere else in the New World for religious reasons. John Cotton, an influential preacher who lived in Massachusetts, was one of the reasons Hooker and his supporters left the colony. Cotton did well at his position in St. Botolph's in England, but when Cotton became the second pastor of the First Church of Boston in 1633, he quickly turned into a controversial figure. For instance, he helped to banish Roger Williams, who would go on to establish Rhode Island.

Several debates involving American history exist, including whether or not the Founding Fathers, colonists, or settlers favored separating church from state. Although Thomas Hooker did not hold the same stern views on religion as the Puritans, he did not advocate for the separation of church from state. Back then, men could only vote if they had been formally admitted to the church. Instead, Hooker extolled the idea that all freemen deserved voting rights. He believed that individuals had the God-given right to determine their leadership. His works helped shape the Fundamental Orders of Connecticut, the first written constitution in what would become the United States.

Another interesting part of Connecticut's colonial history involves the failed New Haven Colony. A Puritan minister named John Davenport led emigrants from Massachusetts in 1638 to New Haven. The aim was to establish a utopia with Christians through economic self-sufficiency. New Haven refused to take in colonists who were not Puritans, which might be nice for the religious side of things. However, running a colony takes more than just faith. They needed people who knew how to farm the soil and how to trade with others.

The colony had other problems as well. For instance, it never received an official charter. Connecticut had one, though, and it was willing to use whatever means it could to incorporate New Haven. The towns of New Haven Colony began to join with Connecticut, and by 1664, all of them had submitted.

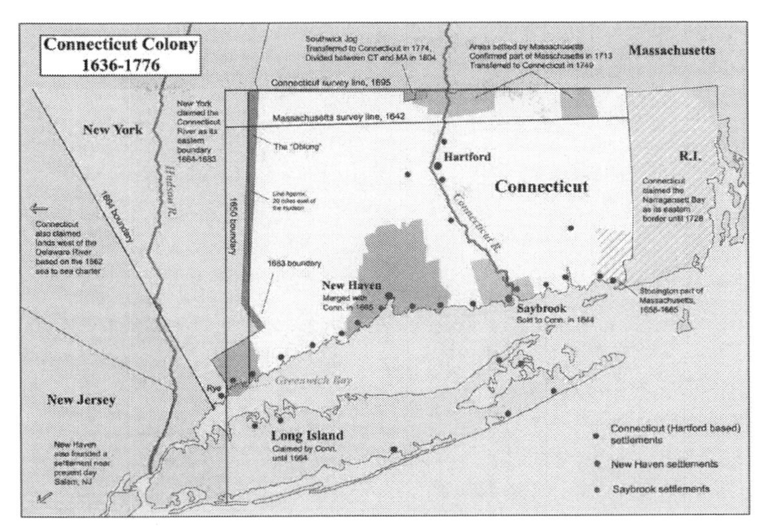

Map of the Colony of Connecticut. (Source: Wikimedia Commons)

The Colony of Rhode Island

Some colonies, such as Virginia, were founded by investors. Others were founded as a result of disputes among the colonists. Rhode Island is one example of the latter. Roger Williams founded Rhode Island in 1636 after his banishment from Massachusetts.

In order to achieve cohesion among the colonists, they each had to conform to basic principles. To those in charge, Boston succeeded economically as a society because it became a homogenous population. Those who refused to adhere to Anglican Puritan principles received banishment.

The civil authorities took action against Williams and his dangerous views. He believed that land ownership titles meant nothing if they came from England. Instead, the natives needed to grant them to make them official. His vocal opinions on the king and who the land rightfully belonged to, among other things, led to his banishment in 1635. However, he was sick at the time; since winter had arrived, the court agreed that he could stay a while longer if he stopped publicly speaking on these issues. He did not. In early January 1636, the sheriff came to escort him out of the colony, but Williams had already left. That same year, he purchased land directly from the Narragansett. Providence became a place for those who differed from the Puritan ethos, such as the Quakers.

The Quakers got their start in England too. It started as the Religious Society of Friends, and it was founded by George Fox, who believed that faith was more important than rituals. The Quakers kept worship simple. Others made their worship ceremonies ornate and lavish, but the Quakers did not believe that was needed to have a close connection to God.

George Fox left his home in England and traveled, visiting the colonies in the early 1670s to spread his beliefs. He believed that God rested within every individual, while other religions stated that God lived in the church. This mindset got him in trouble. Anyone who questioned the church was subject to imprisonment. Despite this, he managed to form chapters. On the other hand, between 1649 and 1673, Fox was imprisoned eight times.

Over time, laws were enforced that detrimentally impacted the Quakers. For instance, in 1658, Quakers were banished from Massachusetts upon pain of death. Nonetheless, Fox encouraged his followers to continue meeting consistently, and Rhode Island proved to be a safe haven. The Toleration Act of 1689 gave relief to the Quakers in England, as it repealed the laws that had once discriminated against them. Fox passed away in 1691, preaching his views of God until the end.

The Colony of Rhode Island is remembered as being perhaps the most progressive of all the colonies. It even passed the first law against slavery in the 1650s; however, slavery still remained rather popular, so it is likely the law was not enforced. Despite this, the colony is remembered for its peaceful relationships with the Native Americans and its religious tolerance.

The Colony of Delaware

Delaware was initially established by the Swedes in 1638, and it was known as New Sweden. Swedish King Gustavus Adolphus authorized the charter in 1626. He passed away in 1632, but his daughter, Christina, continued the administration of it. Her chancellor finalized the plans, and the company made its move to the New World. The crew landed in Delaware in 1638 at Wilmington. The first settlement was named after Queen Christina. Although the Swedes were not in control of the region for very long, they had enough time to leave their mark. They built the Old Swedes Church, also known as the Holy Trinity Church. It is one of the oldest churches in the United States that still receives worshipers.

In 1655, the colony fell to the Dutch, who annexed it to their colony of New Netherland. Around ten years later, in 1664, the British took control of the region. It was an incorporated county under Maryland between 1669 and 1672. However, the land was attractive to William Penn, among others. In 1682, Penn negotiated a merger between it and Pennsylvania, leasing some of the lands for several years. The merger benefited Pennsylvania because it gave it access to the Atlantic Ocean. In 1701, the leased Delaware lands and

Pennsylvania shared the same governor, a situation that lasted for over seventy years.

Even as a colony, Delaware was small. In modern America, it's the second-smallest state but among the most densely populated. It is believed that Thomas Jefferson had an affinity for the tiny colony. Supposedly, Jefferson gave it the nickname of the Diamond State. Jefferson apparently alluded to it as being a jewel. Many believe it has to do with its location next to the Eastern Seaboard. The colonists (and really any explorer to a new land) wanted to establish settlements near water sources. When colonies weren't situated near rivers, lakes, bays, or the ocean, it made setting up their infrastructure a bigger challenge. Luckily for them, there was no shortage of bodies of water in the United States.

The Colony of North Carolina and the Colony of South Carolina

Although the English certainly made South Carolina their home, they were not the first to land in the Carolinas. The Spanish landed there first. In 1526, they established the first European settlement in what is now the United States, but it did not last long. In 1562, French Huguenots arrived in the area. (The Huguenots were a group of French Protestants that had Calvinist leanings. The areas where the Huguenots lived in France were heavily Catholic, so the Huguenots were persecuted.) They spent less than a year on Parris Island before they moved on.

In 1629, King Charles I of England granted a patent to the land, but he placed a restriction on it: land could only be given to members of the Church of England. Since the man who had been granted the patent, Robert Heath, wanted to use the land for French Huguenots, he gave the patent away to William Berkeley, who would play an important role in the founding of other colonies, particularly Virginia. King Charles I would be executed in 1649. Heath's heirs sought the patent for themselves, but Charles II stated their claim to the grant was invalid.

Initially, North Carolina and South Carolina were one colony; it was known as the Province of Carolina. Carolina is named after King Charles II, even though the first land grant in the Carolina area had been administered by King Charles I.

In 1663, Charles II issued a charter for the land. The Spanish had been making inroads in the region, and Charles II hoped fortifications in the area would put a stop to them. The men who had the charter were known as the Lords Proprietors, with several of these men being involved with the formation and running of other colonies. Although the province had a governor and a council, the Lords Proprietors held the most power. They even controlled who was chosen to be on the council!

The land of the province changed over time, and it was much larger than present-day North and South Carolina today. In 1665, it stretched all the way into Florida. The settlers moved around the land until they found the most suitable areas. This led them to Charleston, which was settled in 1670 as Charles Town. It soon became the seat of government for the province.

Although there was only one seat of government, the northern and southern halves of the province operated independently, for the most part. In 1669, the province was divided into two provinces: Abermarle in the north and Clarendon in the south. In 1691, a governor was appointed to oversee the whole province.

People still referred to the colonies as being separate, though. And eventually, the two would separate. This happened in 1712 after several conflicts, including Cary's Rebellion (an uprising over who would be deputy governor of North Carolina), the Tuscarora War (a war between the Tuscarora, who were upset about the Native American slave trade and the encroaching settlers, and the settlers and their native allies), and the Yamasee War. It was clear to see that the Lords Proprietors were losing their grip on the colonies.

These conflicts all played a major role in the history of the Carolinas, and the two wars deserve a special mention. Due to the Tuscarora War, South Carolina began to better control its slave trade, at least when it came to the Native Americans. The Yamasee War was fought for a number of reasons, of which the slave trade was one. The Native Americans, which included the Yamasee, Cherokee, and Shawnee, just to name a few, devastated South Carolina, killing about 7 percent of its settlers. The Yamasee War was the tipping point that the Carolinas needed to be split into two. It also led to the creation of Georgia, as the Yamasee withdrew from that area after the conflict.

Although South Carolina and North Carolina had two separate governments in 1712, this would not be officially recognized until 1729, which was when the two became royal colonies.

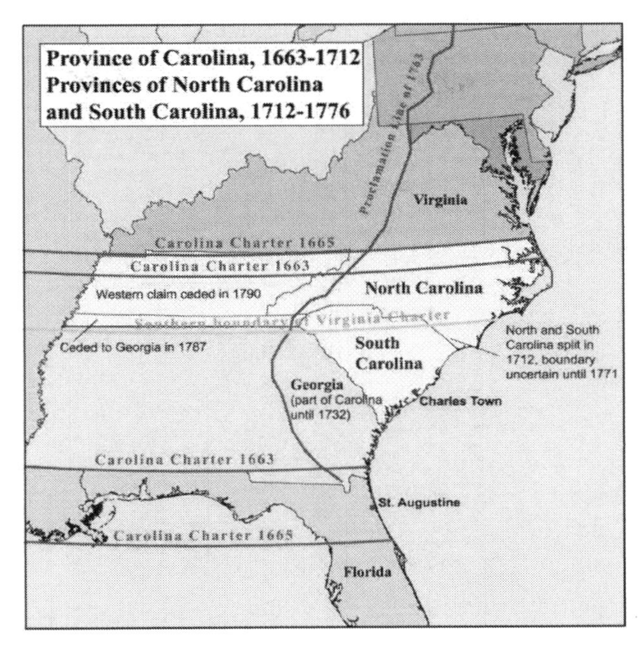

A map of South and North Carolina from 1663 to 1776. (Source: Wikimedia Commons)

New Netherland

In the early 1600s, the Dutch East India Company set out to explore North America, as it believed a passage existed there that would connect to Asia. Henry Hudson, an English explorer, made inroads in New York for the company, seeking the famous Northwest Passage. He did not find it, but he claimed the lands he discovered for the company. His name might sound familiar to some; Hudson River and Hudson Bay are named after him.

In 1614, New Netherland was established, although it would take some time for the colony to expand and be settled. A year later, the Dutch would create their first settlement in the Americas: Fort Nassau. This was located near present-day Albany, New York. New Netherland would grow to include parts of New York, New Jersey, and Delaware, just to name a few. Some of the regions it claimed, such as Pennsylvania, were not heavily populated and held only a few outposts.

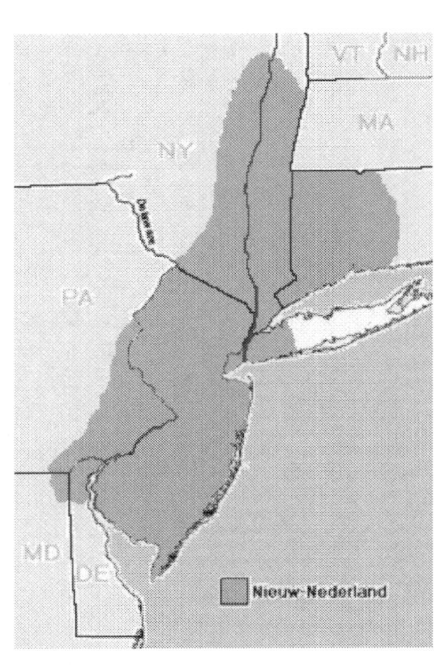

Area settled by the Dutch in the 1660s. (Source: Red4tribe; Wikimedia Commons)

The first Dutch colonists arrived in 1624, and they settled the land and constructed forts. In the 1650s, the Dutch began pushing for even more land, overtaking what was left of New Sweden in 1655. This included Fort Christina, which is now Wilmington, Delaware.

In 1664, the English moved in. Peter Stuyvesant, the director of New Netherland, knew his forces could not face the English without being slaughtered. He ceded the colony to them, although it is important to note that, on paper, the Dutch held the territory until 1674, the year that the Third Anglo-Dutch War ended.

King Charles granted his brother, James, Duke of York, the lands of New Netherland and Maine. New Netherland would then become the Colony of New York and the Colony of New Jersey.

The Colony of New Jersey

James, Duke of York, gave away part of his new territory in late 1664. Sir George Carteret had given the duke help when he was exiled during England's political turmoil in the 1650s when Charles was fighting for his right to the throne after his father died. George's name might sound familiar to some; Carteret County, North Carolina, and Carteret, New Jersey, were both named after him. (He was one of the Lords Proprietors of Carolina.) The other part of New Jersey was sold to a friend of the duke, Lord Berkeley of Stratton.

In 1665, Carteret helped draft the Concession and Agreement, which stated that those who lived in New Jersey could practice whatever religion they wished. They also gave out land to attract settlers, but to obtain this land, they had to pay taxes on it. Many refused to do so, saying their land came from the governor of New York, not New Jersey. To recoup New Jersey's losses, the governor had to sell West Jersey, which the Quakers bought.

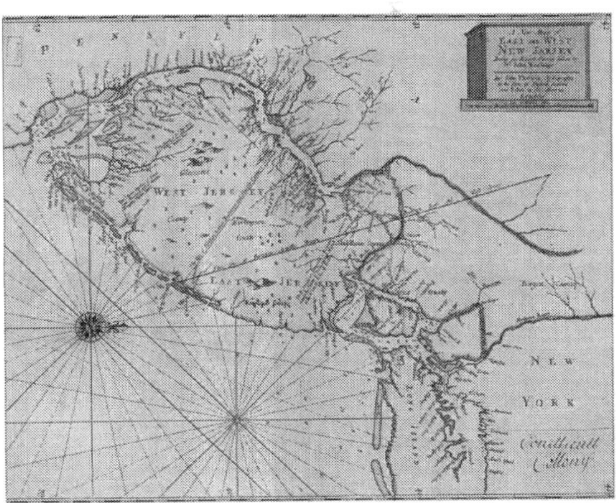

Map of East and West Jersey (1706) by John Worlidge. (Source: Wikimedia Commons)

Eventually, New Jersey was divided into two: West Jersey and East Jersey. They had their own governors and even their own constitutions. In 1680, Edmund Andros, the governor of New York, sought to control East Jersey, a territory that was overseen by his own cousin. Despite their friendly, familial relationship, Andros had his cousin imprisoned. However, he was unable to gain the territory. This would not be the last time New York and New Jersey jostled over land.

But before getting into the next major conflict between the two territories, we should note that until 1702, New Jersey was a proprietary colony. That changed when the two halves were united. Queen Anne (r. 1702–1707) made it a royal colony, with Edward Hyde becoming the first governor. He was seen as immoral and corrupt. Author Shelly Ross believes that the articles of impeachment in the US Constitution were written due to Hyde's actions. He allegedly liked to cross-dress, which would have been scandalous back then (so scandalous, in fact, that it seems very unlikely that he would have done so in public as some state). There are firsthand accounts of him opening the New York Assembly while dressed as a woman, but historians today contend that it is possible these writers were trying to assassinate his character. Hyde also accepted bribes, embezzled, and poorly managed funds, just to name a few.

No one seemed to care for him, and no one seemed to be upset when he was recalled to England in 1708. Well, perhaps they were a little upset. Once Hyde left, New Jersey was overseen by the governor of New York. In 1738, a separate governor for New Jersey was installed.

While these events were going on, New Jersey and New York were poking at each other in the New York-New Jersey Line War (1701-1765). Many colonies engaged in border wars, but this is thought to be the largest one; around 210,000 acres were at stake. In the end, the border was established at the confluence of the Delaware and Neversink Rivers.

The Colony of New York

New York's beginning sounds a lot like New Jersey's. In 1664, James, Duke of York, was given New Netherland, of which New York was a part. Unlike New Jersey, though, James did not sell New York. So, when he took the throne in 1685, James II's territory became a royal colony.

James II would be removed from the throne in 1688 due to the Glorious Revolution, which saw his daughter, Mary II, and her husband, William of Orange, take the throne. Again, the internal conflicts in England could be felt in the Americas. At the time, Edmund Andros was serving as the governor of the Dominion of New England, a short-lived government venture. This will be talked about more in a future chapter, but to briefly summarize, the Dominion oversaw a large portion of New England, including New York and New Jersey, which means these colonies no longer had their own governor.

Edmund Andros was overthrown, and New York began its process to restore its former government, something that was seen throughout all of the former Dominion of New England. Francis Nicholson, a captain in the English navy who had served as the lieutenant governor of the Dominion, took charge of New York. In the summer of 1689, he headed to England, and Jacob Leisler, a German-born merchant, took the opportunity and installed himself as the leader of the southern part of New York. He collected taxes and even attempted to take control of parts of Canada. In 1691, the royally appointed governor, Henry Sloughter, arrived. He had Leisler arrested, and he was later tried and executed.

The Colony of Pennsylvania

In 1681, Pennsylvania received its official charter. It was granted to William Penn by Charles II, who was restored to the throne on May 29th, 1660. Penn, a writer and a firm believer in Quakerism, sought to establish a space for Quakers.

As a Quaker, William Penn faced jail time for not shying away from his religious beliefs. In his writings, he criticized Catholics, Anglicans, and others. He wrote *No Cross, No Crown,* one of his most important works, while in jail. Penn gained influence in legal matters too. He helped free Quakers and political prisoners from prison.

Penn maintained a friendship with Charles II and his brother, James, Duke of York. In 1681, Penn, along with eleven other Quakers, bought the rights to the eastern side of New Jersey. Afterward, he received present-day Delaware from the duke of York. Despite this, Penn sought to buy the land from the Lenape, who already lived on the land.

William Penn used the opportunity to design laws based on the Quaker mindset. Residents received the freedom to practice their religion, and all Christians were welcome. Plus, their rights as Englishmen remained protected. In addition, Penn influenced the beginnings of Philadelphia, which was founded in 1682 and served as the seat of the province's government. A more complete history of colonial Pennsylvania can be found in Chapter 5.

The Colony of Georgia

Georgia was the last of the Thirteen Colonies to be established. It was first established in 1732, but it would receive royal status in 1752. In many ways, it was a special colony. King George II was involved in its establishment, as he signed the charter for it, and it was named after him. James Oglethorpe, who served as a minister in British Parliament, was granted authority over the project. He would be the governor of Georgia for over a decade.

George II's rule is notable for several reasons, including the Seven Years' War against France. When he passed away, his grandson, George III, took the throne. He had to deal with the tail end of that very same war, which manifested on the North American continent as the French and Indian War.

After James Oglethorpe secured the charter for Georgia, he aimed to turn it into a colony that gave individuals a second chance. He spent time in London helping individuals who could not pay off their debts, and he also worked with the poor. Once a person fell into debt in Britain, there was not much they could do to gain their position back. Given that the economy experienced severe fluctuations, there was no real way out of poverty for most individuals. Oglethorpe came up with the idea of shipping these two groups of people to the New World to give them a new start.

He led a crew of over one hundred settlers to the New World, landing in what is now Savannah. None of the trustees received land from the charter. Georgia was set up more as a charity, not for making a profit. The Georgia trustees saw how South Carolina had developed. The colony contained large tracts of land and many indentured servants and African slaves. Therefore, the Georgia trustees placed a size limit on the parcels of land.

The trustees also kept the colony's leadership to themselves. They did not establish a representative assembly. The goal was to achieve social control. In the leaders' eyes, the people who were shipped to Georgia were poor, and there was no way to know if they had the capacity to govern themselves. After all, many had already gotten themselves into trouble with debt.

History tells that the proprietors used a lot of idealism to establish the colony. They outlawed slavery and heavy drinking, and they also granted religious freedom. Georgia had fertile land, but without the extra labor, it was difficult to churn out enough products to meet demand in those early days when the population was low.

Oglethorpe's time in office ended in 1743, and the trustees began to lose interest in the colony. The colony started to see changes as a result. In 1749, it was decided that the ban on slavery would be lifted. The economy also remained weak, and Georgia placed a focus on exporting lumber. To pick things up economically, Georgia started to resemble South Carolina. Otherwise, it would require constant subsidies. African slaves did make their way to Georgia eventually, but the colony did not become exactly like South Carolina. There was variation within the population. By the time Georgia became a state, it had the most plantations. This was probably a result of the land limits being removed.

In the mid-1700s, many Spanish still resided in Florida. Their closeness to the settlers in Georgia led to renewed tensions between the two powers. The Georgia settlers, with Oglethorpe's leadership, successfully established the border between the two territories.

In 1755, Georgia was no longer a proprietary colony; instead, it became a royal colony.

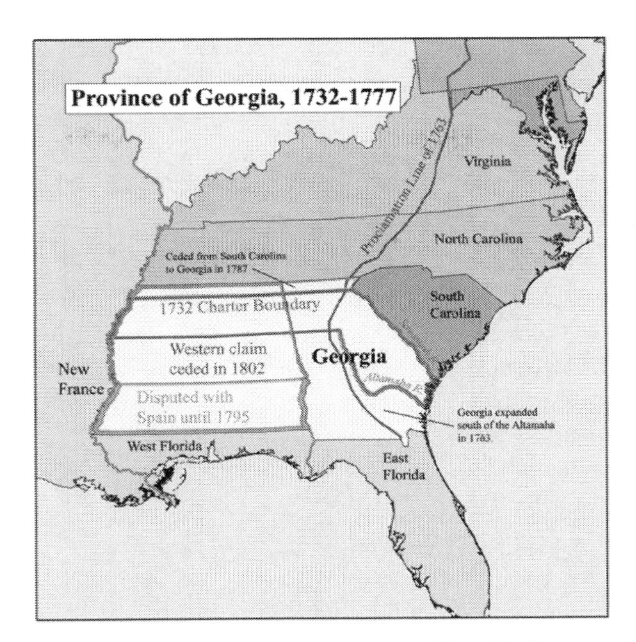

Map of Colony of Georgia. (Source: Wikimedia Commons)

Chapter 3 – The Three Regions of the Colonies

The Thirteen Colonies can be divided into three regions: New England, Middle, and Southern. Each region had different demographics and natural resources to utilize. Each settlement had to build shelter, procure food, and clothe its people, but as time went on, this became easier and easier to do. In the beginning, the settlers would either find their path on their own and/or depend on assistance from Native Americans.

New England Colonies

The New England Colonies included Massachusetts Bay, Rhode Island, New Hampshire, and Connecticut, as well as some other smaller ones. This area was great for fishing, hunting, and procuring lumber. However, it consisted of hills and rocky soil, which made it challenging to grow crops on a large scale. The settlers in this northernmost region of the Thirteen Colonies did grow things, though, such as squash, beans, and corn.

When the colonists first arrived in the region in the early 1600s, there were many Native American tribes already living there, such as the Wampanoag, Pequot, and Narragansett, just to name a few. Although the natives and the colonists traded with each other and even assisted one another, there were a lot of conflicts. The tensions between the Europeans and Native Americans tended to develop over time. In the mid- to late 1600s, wars broke out, such as the Pequot War (1636-1638) and King Philip's War (1675-1678). Both wars were deadly, with the Pequots being wiped out nearly to extinction. And while King Philip's War saw many Wampanoag and other natives killed or enslaved, the European population of Plymouth and Rhode Island was decimated. It is believed they lost one-tenth of their fighting men.

Many people know of the horrors Africans faced in the colonies, but some may be unaware of the enslavement of Native Americans. Many Native American slaves were sold to plantations in the West Indies, where the conditions were notoriously difficult and harsh. And while some people might point out that Native Americans kept slaves themselves, their form of slavery tended to be less oppressive.

Speaking of slavery, New York had an astounding number of slaves. By 1703, over 42 percent of New York homes had slaves, putting New York behind only Charleston, South Carolina, in regards to the slave population.

Middle Colonies

New York was not a part of the New England Colonies; it belonged to the Middle Colonies. The Middle Colonies also included Delaware, New Jersey, and Pennsylvania.

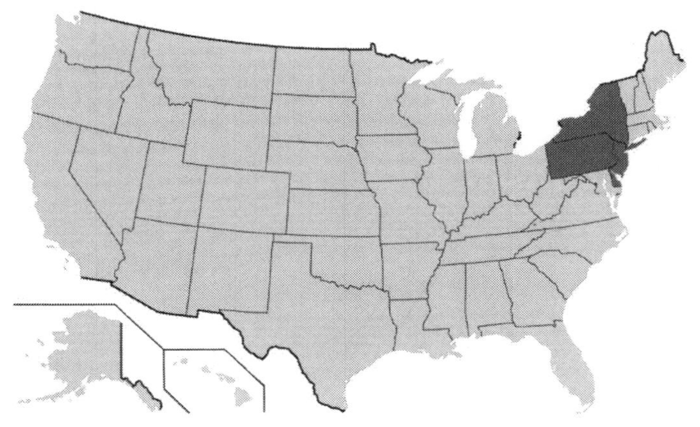

Where the Middle Colonies were located. (Source: Kevin Payravi; Wikimedia Commons)

These colonies had more fertile soil than the New England Colonies, which tended to be rockier. The Middle Colonies grew and exported many grains, such as hemp, wheat, and flax. They exported so many grains that it became known as the Breadbasket Colonies. In addition to this, the region was heavily forested, leading to the establishment of the lumber industry. Pennsylvania was successful in the textile and iron industries as well.

Before the colonists arrived, the region was inhabited by Native American tribes, including but not limited to the Mohawks, Lenape, and Mohicans. The colonies embraced diversity, and there were times when peace with Native Americans was the norm.

Due to this diversity, which included not only different ethnicities (such as Scottish, Irish, German, English, French, Dutch, etc.) but also different religions (such as Methodism, Quakerism, Calvinism, Lutheranism, etc.), the Middle Colonies tended to be more socially tolerant. This was very different than the New England Colonies, where Puritanism tended to reign supreme. In the Middle Colonies, though, immigrants were welcomed with open arms, although part of this might be due to the fact that these colonies had a hard time keeping up with demand.

Indentured servitude was common. Men, women, and sometimes even teenagers wanted to make their way to the New World but had no money. A deal would be struck where they would be provided free passage in return for working on a farm or learning a trade for a certain number of years. They would work off their debt, meaning they would be free after it had been worked off. Between the 1630s and the 1790s, it is believed that around one-half to two-thirds of European immigrants came to the colonies as indentured servants.

Slavery did exist, which is apparent by the high number of African slaves in New York. The major cities tended to depend on slave labor more, and they were usually used as domestic slaves. The Middle Colonies didn't rely on slaves for their economy as much as the Southern Colonies did, though.

Southern Colonies

The Southern Colonies consisted of Virginia, North and South Carolina, Georgia, and Maryland. It would eventually grow to include the colonies of Florida, but the United States held them for only around twenty years (1763-1783), so their history is not touched on much in this book. The Spanish maintained control over Florida for most of colonial America. Today, Florida is a part of the United States; it was finally gained in 1819 due to the Adams-Onis Treaty.

The Southern Colonies had incredibly fertile soil, access to waterways, and a warm, agreeable climate most of the year. Even their winters were (and still are) fairly mild. It is no surprise that these colonies produced most of the crops that were exported. They grew many things, but the most profitable were tobacco, rice, and indigo. Cotton was grown, but it would not become an important crop until the invention of the cotton gin in 1793. Fewer people inhabited the towns in the Southern Colonies in comparison to New England because the bulk of the land was used to grow crops.

Native Americans, such as the Powhatan, Cherokee, and Tuscarora, just to name a few, called these colonies home long before the colonists arrived. The settlers' initial interactions with the natives were, for the most part, peaceful. But like in the other colonies, these interactions tended to turn violent over time. Colonists in all three regions continued encroaching on the natives' land and ignoring promises that had been made. In addition, the colonists sought to "civilize" the Native Americans by imposing their religion and customs on them. Interactions with the Europeans benefited the Native Americans to an extent, but it also saw the deterioration of their own cultures in the process. Unfortunately, due to the European mindset back then, this outcome was likely inevitable for the Native Americans, and it remains a tragic part of United States history.

Another tragic part of US history is, of course, slavery. And the Southern Colonies utilized this practice the most of the three major regions. It took time for slavery to take hold, as many people started out at the bottom and had to work their way to the top. The cash crops of tobacco, indigo, and rice began to be highly demanded, but these crops are labor-intensive to plant, grow, and harvest. To keep up with demand, the colonists turned to the African slave trade. The Africans, similar to the Native Americans, were seen as "lesser." More often than not, their lives were incredibly hard, with punishing hours and even more punishing masters.

The Southern Colonies began to rely so heavily on slavery that the people could see no other way to keep the economy afloat. Today, people think of large plantations with many slaves as being the norm, but that was not the case. The South consisted of many small farms, which would typically have at least one slave. This changed over time, though, as most things do. By the time of the Civil War (1861–1865), buying a slave was incredibly expensive due to the more restrictive slavery laws, so smaller farms often did not have slaves unless they had been inherited or gifted.

Since the Southern Colonies had so many individuals working as slaves, they outnumbered the non-labor (really, the white) population. Due to this, there was a great fear of revolts breaking out. In 1739, their worst fear did take place. This was a slave revolt in South Carolina known as the Stono Rebellion or Cato's Rebellion.

In early September, a slave named Cato led a group of slaves to Spanish Florida in hopes they could live in freedom. On the first day of the revolt, they stormed down the street, killed two shopkeepers, and raided their stores. On their way to Florida, they gathered slaves; it is believed they gathered around eighty of them. They also burned plantations and killed around thirty European colonists.

However, the residents of South Carolina did fight back. They managed to catch up to the slaves, and in the confrontation, around twenty colonists and nearly fifty slaves were killed. The ones who survived continued to flee toward Florida, but they were tracked down. Most of them were executed, while the others were sold to the West Indies, which was deemed to be one of the worst places to be enslaved due to the terrible working conditions and hot environment.

This rebellion led to the Negro Act of 1740. To ensure rebellions would not be commonplace, plantations had to maintain a ratio of one white to every ten Africans. Slaves could not grow their own food, assemble in groups, earn money, or learn to read. It also ensured that slaves would not be brutally punished by imposing penalties on those colonists who engaged in such behavior. Of course, this still happened. Few cared if such things happened, and on top of that, slaves could not testify against a white person.

South Carolina was the largest importer of slaves in North America, with over fifty-eight thousand Africans entering the colony between 1750 and 1775. Almost all of the slaves that came to the New World passed through Charleston (Charles Town) first. During the colonial period, the transatlantic slave trade ensured that slaves continued to arrive on the shores of the Southern Colonies. Traders would bring Africans over on large ships, where they were subjected to terrible conditions. Between 1500 and 1866, it is estimated that nearly two million out of 12.5 million slaves were killed on the long voyage. Not all of these slaves went to what would become the United States, though. In comparison to other areas, the intake of slaves was rather minor. According to Henry Louis Gates, Jr., the director of the Hutchins Center for African and African American research, around 388,000 of the 12.5 million slaves who came to the New World went to North America. Most slaves that came to the New World went to the Caribbean and South America. However, the trade would continue until 1808 when it was banned, and it continued on after that, albeit illegally.

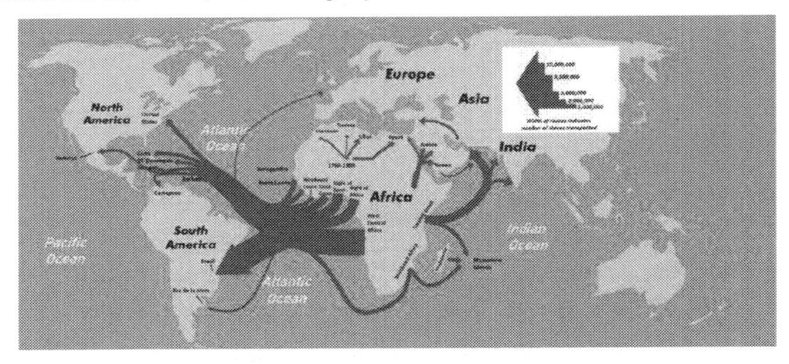

Slave trade between 1500 and 1900. (Source: KuroNekoNiyah; Wikimedia Commons)

The slave trade played a key role in what was included in the Declaration of Independence, a document that was written in 1776 to declare the colonists' independence from Great Britain. Thomas Jefferson, who was the primary author of it, condemned the practice of slavery in an early draft. Although he owned slaves himself (it is estimated he owned more than six hundred throughout his life), he saw the institution as being evil, foisting most of the blame on King George III. Jefferson wrote, "He [King George] has waged cruel war against human nature itself, violating its most sacred rights of life & liberty in the persons of a distant people who never offended him, captivating & carrying them into slavery in another hemisphere or to incur miserable death in their transportation thither."

Jefferson stopped short of calling for the ban of slavery altogether (though he would later put together such a plan in the early 1800s), but even so, this passage was stripped from the Declaration of Independence. One-third of the signers had a vested interest in the practice, and alienating them would be too hard of a blow.

The issue of slavery was still debated during the American Revolution and afterward, but the institution was left intact to please the Southern Colonies, with more restrictions being placed on the practice over the years. Slavery in the United States would only end after the Civil War in 1865.

Chapter 4 – A Closer Look: Massachusetts

Colonial Massachusetts played a large role in the founding of the United States of America, so it bears a closer look. As the largest colony in the New England area, it indirectly helped found Rhode Island and Connecticut. Boston was also one of the most important colonial cities. It became a center for trade, innovation, and politics.

The first colonial college was established in Massachusetts; this was none other than Harvard, and it was established in 1636. In those days, colleges educated clergy. Thus, the colonial colleges had a denomination. For Harvard, it was Congregational. Congregationalists, a Protestant denomination, believe that each congregation should be run autonomously, not by a higher church official.

Massachusetts Bay Colony was not the first colony the English established in the New World, but it was certainly the most prosperous of the New England Colonies.

Its beginnings go back to the Pilgrims. These were Separatists who were seeking a different way to worship their religion. They disagreed with the Church of England and its mandates. The Separatists first made their way to Holland in 1608, where they were allowed to worship and flourish. As their families grew, they worried about the Dutch influence on their children. Even though they had fled England, they wanted to remain Englishmen and women. Thus, they wanted to raise their children in that culture too.

From their base in Holland, the Separatists negotiated with the Virginia Company. They intended to land near the Hudson River, which at that time was considered to be part of northern Virginia. After some setbacks and delays, 102 men, women, and children boarded the *Mayflower* in 1620. It set sail and spent sixty-six days at sea. The winds veered them away from their intended settlement, instead sailing the ship toward Cape Cod, which is located in modern-day southeastern Massachusetts.

The Embarkation of the Pilgrims *(1857) by Robert Walter Weir. (Source: Wikimedia Commons)*

Once they found a shoreline on which to land, they didn't deboard immediately. They wanted to find the Hudson River, which was where they were supposed to settle. While they sailed about looking for a good place to call their own, the passengers acknowledged that there was no charter ruling over them or the way they were going to live. As a result, the leadership put together the Mayflower Compact. The Mayflower Compact was one of the earliest governing documents in what would become the United States. Other colonies would follow its example.

After sixty-six days at sea, tensions were high among the passengers. Not everyone on board was a Separatist. When those who had different views than the Pilgrims realized that they were outside the jurisdiction of their destination, it caused some chaos. Since the people were no longer bound to a charter due to the fact they were not landing in Virginia, they wanted to leave the group and settle on their own. Although they may not have realized it on the *Mayflower*, they needed each other. The numbers were not on their side.

The Mayflower Compact was only around two hundred words long. William Bradford and William Brewster, men who would play an integral role in the shaping of Plymouth Colony, helped draft it. The document established a government that bound each of the members on board the ship. To keep the group afloat, they agreed that laws and regulations for the good of the colony applied to each member. It was a voluntary way to self-govern. Forty-one adult male passengers signed it.

William Bradford was the governor of Plymouth Colony for a combined total of about thirty years. During his time in office (and even while not in office), he had great influence over the shaping of the colony. Bradford was part of a Separatist group that traveled to Holland in 1609. When the economic opportunities for the Separatists began to wane, he helped organize the expedition from Holland to the New World that set sail in 1620.

Thanks to Bradford, the colony got off to a good start. He helped establish the principles of self-governance. Impressively, he also set down guidelines that helped nonbelievers assimilate to the colony's culture.

William Brewster helped lead the Separatist migration from England to Amsterdam. He maintained a leadership role during their time in Holland. Brewster printed Puritan books that the English government had banned. The English authorities found out in 1619 and seized them. Brewster managed to escape before they could arrest him, and he became part of the Virginia Company. Brewster sailed on the *Mayflower* with the Pilgrims in 1620. Thanks to his education, he became the senior elder of the church, and he helped shape its customs.

The passengers would eventually land in what is now Plymouth, Massachusetts. Funding for the *Mayflower*'s voyage came from John Carver, who was a deacon in the Netherlands. After the formation of Plymouth Colony, he was elected as its first governor. Carver also managed to strike peace between Wampanoag Chief Massasoit in 1621, with their treaty lasting for over fifty years.

New England winters were (and still remain) harsh. Americans had to learn how to survive them as they established their infrastructure, which was made easier after formal contact with the local tribes. The Pilgrims weren't prepared for the elements, especially that first winter. Only 44 of the original 102 survived. As they got hold of their bearings, they learned how to find, pick, and store food, with their techniques being greatly enhanced by the Native Americans, namely Squanto.

The Massachusetts Bay Colony charter was issued in 1629, establishing the colony as a charter colony. A fleet of ships carrying over seven hundred settlers set off for the colony in 1630. This was just one of the many voyages that took place during what is known as the Great Puritan Migration. Several more fleets followed, with most of them arriving by 1640. Although Puritans came after 1640, the number of those who dared to cross the ocean greatly dwindled. They headed for Massachusetts, as well as to modern-day Maine, New Hampshire, Rhode Island, Connecticut, Virginia, and Maryland. Puritans also headed toward the Caribbean islands, such as Barbados and St. Kitts.

In Massachusetts, John Winthrop, the leader of the fleet in 1630, became one of the notable heads of the colony. Although Winthrop led a life according to Puritan values, he had enjoyed a good life in England. On his voyage to Massachusetts, he composed a sermon called "A Model of Christian Charity," which he delivered aboard the *Arbella* on April 8th, 1630.

In 1629, Winthrop was voted as the governor of the new colony; this was before he even set sail for the New World. Also, in 1629, Winthrop and Thomas Dudley, among others, signed the Cambridge Agreement in August 1629. Essentially, it stipulated that those who went to the New World could buy shares from shareholders who stayed behind in England. It also stated that Massachusetts Bay Colony would be ruled by a local power in New England instead of being controlled by the shareholders in the Old World. Dudley served as a deputy governor and governor for a total of seventeen years. He contributed as a civil servant and was a leader in education. Dudley helped establish Roxbury Latin School, and he signed Harvard's new charter in 1650. His daughter, Anne Bradstreet, was one of the earliest American poets.

Although Dudley made important contributions to the colony, they are often overshadowed by Winthrop, who was quite popular among the freemen of Massachusetts. Winthrop served as governor from 1631 to 1649, off and on. All the colonies and colonial territories found ways to govern themselves since they were so far from England. In Massachusetts, only members of the Congregational church received the right to vote. The irony is that under this system, more men received a voice than they did in England. Property owners also received a voice in town affairs.

Since Winthrop ruled with an iron fist, his popularity waned, although he always remained somewhat beloved. During his time in charge, opposition grew toward Puritanism. Individuals, such as Roger Williams and Anne Hutchinson, had different ideas about how people should relate to God. Winthrop led the charge against Anne Hutchinson. Somehow, she managed to take a leadership role in the community in regard to religion. She hosted local meetings, inviting men and women to discuss sermons, something that was discouraged back then. A minister's sermon was to be taken at face value, not debated about behind closed doors.

After becoming mired in the Antinomian controversy, Hutchinson was accused of heresy. Put very simply, Anne Hutchinson was a free grace advocate. She believed that people do not have to do good works to attain salvation; rather, good works were a part of being a Christian. Eternal life was free to any who believed. These ideas were heretical at the time, especially in Puritan-controlled Massachusetts. Anne Hutchinson was excommunicated from the colony in 1638.

A drawing of Anne Hutchinson on trial by Edwin Austin Abbey. (Source: Wikimedia Commons)

Another prominent figure in early colonial Massachusetts was John Cotton. Cotton fled England due to the persecution of his non-conforming beliefs. He was an avid Puritan. He became embroiled in controversy in the New World as well since he encouraged Anne Hutchinson's beliefs. However, during her trial, he had to reprimand her for not conducting herself properly. Back then, the colonies did not practice democracy. Men like Winthrop and Cotton believed that laws were meant to enforce God's will and religious rules.

John Endecott held these same beliefs as well, and no chapter on Massachusetts history would be complete without at least mentioning him. He is thought to be one of the Fathers of New England, and he was the longest-serving governor of Massachusetts Bay Colony. He was a firm believer in Puritanism, but he also firmly believed in Separatism, which was not a popular belief among the Puritans. Regardless, Endecott did not think men should be able to make decisions if they did not have Puritan interests at heart.

Increase Mather and his son, Cotton Mather, also played an important role in religious affairs. Both father and son were Puritan clergymen, and they both played an important role in the Salem witch trials. Between February 1692 and May 1693, more than two hundred people, both men and women, were accused of witchcraft. In Salem Village (present-day Danvers, Massachusetts), the daughter and niece of Samuel Parris, the reverend, began to have fits. In time, the number of those afflicted grew.

The girls accused three women of causing their odd behavior. One of these women, Tituba, was a slave, and she corroborated what the young girls were saying, that someone had put an enchantment on them. She even said that there were more witches living among them. The two other women, Sarah Good and Sarah Osborn, were likely targeted because of their oddities. Good was homeless, and Osborn was incredibly reclusive. In other words, all three women were seen as outcasts.

Hysteria swept the town and the neighboring villages. Upstanding citizens started to be accused, which led to even more paranoia. If people who bettered the community could be witches, then anyone could be one.

Of course, it is highly unlikely that there were actually witches. It is not known what exactly caused the trials to occur, but it is likely a combination of factors, such as family feuds, bored/hysterical children, and politics within the church. Some scholars have even proposed that the teenage girls ate moldy bread, which caused hallucinations, and that mass panic set in once people started taking the accusations seriously.

The people who were accused were put under tremendous pressure to confess. And this is meant literally. Giles Corey was pressed to death for his refusal to plead guilty. In total, nineteen people were hung for the crime of witchcraft, with at least five other people dying in jail.

Cotton Mather and Increase Mather believed in witchcraft, but they also believed that the people deserved a fair trial. Spectral evidence had been allowed in court proceedings. A person was allowed to say that they saw the apparition of the person afflicting them. Some believed that the Devil needed a person's permission to use their visage, which is why the court allowed this kind of evidence. Almost all of the evidence submitted in court was spectral evidence, which is not surprising, considering how hard it was to disprove. Cotton Mather even said, "Do not lay more stress on pure spectral evidence than it will bear...It is very certain that the Devils have sometimes represented the shapes of persons not only innocent, but also very virtuous." Increase Mather shared the same beliefs, saying, "It would better that ten suspected witches may escape than one innocent person be condemned." This kind of evidence was allowed until October 1692.

The Salem witch trials are still remembered today as a dark period of US history. However, there were many positives, especially in Massachusetts Bay Colony. In terms of the colony's economy, John Winthrop the Younger (the son of John Winthrop) established the Saugus Works in 1644. The system had a dam that provided water. It connected to a smelting furnace, forge, and rolling mill, complete with a slitter. It had the capability to produce two types of iron: pourable and pig. This is described as the beginning of the colonial iron industry. The Saugus Works helped spawn an estimated 175 more plants across the colonies. Since England made great use of the products these ironworks churned out, they eliminated custom duties on it.

For the most part, in the early days of the colony, Massachusetts lived in relative peace. The majority of the freemen retained similar values, and there were no major issues to disagree on until people like Anne Hutchinson and Roger Williams began popping up. Tensions rose even more when the Quakers started showing up in 1656. The Quakers also ventured to the new land from England. Since their religious views differed from the Puritans, they rocked the boat. To keep the peace, the leadership banished the Quakers, Anabaptists, and individuals like Roger Williams and Anne Hutchinson.

The residents of Massachusetts had their rebellious side, though, and England recognized it. The colony's charter was revoked in 1684 for several reasons. Violations included trading with other countries; the Navigation Acts, which were instituted throughout the 1600s, prevented this. The colony was also caught melting English coins to create their own money that did not have the image of the king on them. Perhaps most damning, the residents of Massachusetts Bay Colony created laws that did not fit with what was established in England, particularly laws based on religion.

England spent a good amount of time and funds keeping the colonies in line. In 1686, the royal authority created the Dominion of New England to enforce the Navigation Acts. These acts helped bolster England's shipping, trade, and fleets, and they restricted the colonies from depending on other foreign goods. As the colonies developed their own economies and trading abilities, they started trading with countries outside of England's circle. England had to put a stop to that, as the wars it participated in against the other European powers greatly drained its coffers. And at the end of the day, the colonies belonged to England to serve the Crown. Any goods they produced needed to benefit England first.

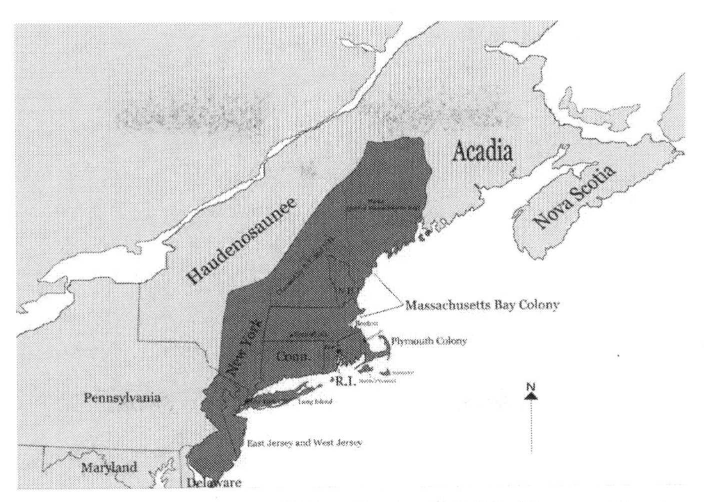

A map of the Dominion of New England, 1688. (Source: Tpwissaa; Wikimedia Commons)

The Dominion set up shop in Boston, Massachusetts. The Dominion got off to a rocky start, with the local officials refusing to acknowledge it. In late 1686, Sir Edmund Andros, the governor of New York, took control of the Dominion. He was pro-Church of England while Boston remained set in its puritanical ways. He made it clear that the colonists had no rights as Englishmen since they did not live in England. Laws were made that aligned more closely with that of England's, but Andros had a hard time getting the colonists to follow them. Landowners needed to receive land patents, and local taxes rose. The soldiers who accompanied Andros were far from saints too, which only exacerbated tensions.

In essence, Andros made attempts to quench the colonists' thirst for independence. In some ways, the Dominion of New England foreshadowed what was to come in the 1760s. The Declaration of Independence and the United States Constitution stem from English culture and laws. When Britain felt like it was losing its grip on the colonies, it tightened its grip on them. For instance, Andros began canceling town meetings, placing restrictions on the courts, and revoking land titles. Restrictions on the press and schools were also put into place.

During Andros's time serving as governor of the Dominion, the British Crown experienced instability. Every time England experienced problems at the royal level, it allowed the colonies to breathe easier again. In this case, it was the Glorious Revolution, which took place from 1688 to 1689. The Glorious Revolution saw James II, a Catholic, dethroned. William III of Orange and James's daughter, Mary II, became the king and queen. William was a Protestant Dutchman, while Mary was an Anglican Englishwoman.

The change in power caused the Dominion of New England to tumble. Once the colonists found out, it gave them the confidence to rebel. They reasserted their power in their respective colonies. Andros attempted to flee, but the colonists caught him, along with the other leaders sent by the Crown. They were held in captivity for ten months with no trial before being put on a ship back to England.

When the Dominion dissolved, Massachusetts and Plymouth Colony were in a weird spot. If you can recall, Plymouth never had an official royal charter, and Massachusetts had lost theirs. Without a charter, there was no reason for these colonies to even exist. The leaders of Massachusetts worked hard, and in 1691, the charter was restored, but it was far from the original. It also established that Plymouth and parts of the Province of New York would become part of the colony.

The new charter caused chaos for the Puritans. It did away with tying voting rights to church membership. Massachusetts's new royal status delivered a new royal governor. The colonists no longer filled the positions of authority; British appointees filled them instead.

The colonies became important for England, especially during the many conflicts that England was facing. They provided England with lumber, tobacco, and dried fish, among many other things. Trade with Britain, in turn, gave the colonies manufactured goods and textiles.

Massachusetts Bay Colony started as an agricultural economy. Farmers grew corn and raised cattle. Keep in mind that the colonists learned a lot through trial and error. As the population of Massachusetts grew, they overused the soil. When they realized that the soil was depleted of its nutrients, they had to find other ways to keep the economy alive. Their proximity to the Atlantic Ocean meant that they had access to maritime activities, so they balanced their economy with fishing. Their access to timber allowed them to build fishing vessels. In turn, this gave birth to merchants, tradesmen, and craftsmen.

Massachusetts continued to flourish, even after the American Revolution. The colony played an important role in the war, as it became the site of the first military engagements of the revolution: the Battles of Lexington and Concord.

Chapter 5 – A Closer Look: Pennsylvania

The famous Quaker William Penn named Philadelphia, one of the most influential cities of colonial America, in Pennsylvania. Philadelphia is the combination of two Greek words: *phileo* and *adelphos*, or "beloved" and "brother." That's why Philadelphia is known as the City of Brotherly Love.

Although Penn was a student at the University of Oxford, he rejected the Anglican teachings. In 1662, he was expelled for nonconformity. Two years later, Penn came across Thomas Loe, a Quaker missionary, for the second time in his life. This time, Penn made his membership in the Society of Friends permanent.

Penn left behind many books, treatises, and pamphlets. When he received an opportunity to preach his Quaker principles to a group of people, he did. Penn's nonconformity got him in trouble on several occasions. In 1668, he was imprisoned for his beliefs. Two years later, England banned religious public meetings of more than five people. Penn and his friend William Mead ignored this and were arrested for preaching at a Quaker meetinghouse in London. During his trial, Penn showed his ability to defend himself. He asked for a copy of the charges that were being levied against him, but the judge refused. On top of this, the judge wouldn't let the defense present their case. The jury found Penn not guilty, and they were punished for it. They were imprisoned and fined.

Jury tampering was commonplace at this time. The Crown and its representatives expected to receive their desired verdict every time. Sometimes they rigged the juries. Other times, the juries experienced threats to coerce them into giving the proper verdict.

As time passes, it's easy to forget why the Founding Fathers integrated the Bill of Rights. Today, Americans expect to receive a fair trial and a jury of their peers. In colonial America, this was often not the case. Today, American citizens also receive the right against unlawful searches and seizures.

Back in Penn's time, though, the jury should have acquiesced to the judge. However, they refused and filed what is known as Bushel's Case. The case established that juries could not be punished for not delivering a certain verdict, although jury members could be fined or imprisoned if they behaved inappropriately.

Many of the most famous American colonial historical figures maintained journals. Without their writings, American history would be a guessing game. Penn's day in court was published in *The People's Ancient and Just Liberties Asserted* in 1670.

When Penn's father, an admiral and politician, passed away in 1670, he inherited the estates. In 1671 and 1677, Penn undertook missions to Holland and Germany. There, he made contact with people who would help him populate Pennsylvania.

The year 1681 began Penn's journey toward proprietorship. With eleven Quakers, he purchased the rights to East New Jersey from Sir George Carteret's heirs. Penn put together the pieces of the land, and he named the colony after his father. Charles II got the ball rolling, but the duke of York granted Penn the Lower Counties, which today make up Delaware.

The Birth of Pennsylvania *(1680) by Jean Leon Gerome Ferris. (Source: United States Library of Congress Prints and Photographs)*

Penn saw the colony as a religious experiment. He assembled the Frame of Government, with his goal being to write a set of rules that would prevent future leaders from "doing mischief" with their power. Penn integrated his Quaker and Whig ideas into the framework. Whigs did not believe in an absolute monarchy; rather, they wanted a constitutional monarchy.

The first city that Penn's crew assembled was Philadelphia. Penn asked them to lay it out in a grid pattern. The pattern made it easy to hand out parcels of land. In time, Pennsylvania became the largest shipbuilding colony. Thanks to the colony's success, it attracted notable men, such as Benjamin

Franklin. Franklin was born in Boston, but he spent so much time in Philadelphia that the people claim him as his own.

Franklin moved there at the tender age of seventeen. A few years later, in 1729, he started publishing *The Pennsylvania Gazette*. In 1731, Franklin founded the Library Company of Philadelphia. This library continues to collect important historical documents that tell the story of America. The library has also become a research center. It boasts a collection of 500,000 books. The collection includes rare books, prints, photographs, manuscripts, and pamphlets. It makes sense that the library collects so many printed items; after all, Franklin championed the printing press in Philadelphia.

Promoting the written word was just one of Franklin's many accomplishments. During the colonial period, fires threatened homes, as open fires were common in colonial America. The colonists used them for warming their homes during the winter and for burning trash. In Philadelphia, fires were a particular problem. In 1736, Benjamin Franklin established the first volunteer fire department in colonial America. Groups of thirty men put out fires, and they also met regularly to discuss issues impacting their area. The fire department led to the establishment of the first insurance company in the United States.

By 1770, Philadelphia grew to hold a population of around thirty thousand. This is quite impressive, as only twenty years before, the population was twenty-five thousand. In 1776, the population of the Thirteen Colonies reached 2.5 million. The largest city was Philadelphia, with forty thousand people. New York, Boston, and Charleston followed with twenty-five thousand, fifteen thousand, and twelve thousand, respectively. Although the first official census didn't take place until 1790, these estimates are thought to be close.

These population numbers include slaves. Since the inhabitants of Pennsylvania were mostly Quakers, they had to reconcile several realities in regards to slavery. Some of the original inhabitants, including William Penn, tolerated the act. Slavery was already present in the region by the time they arrived, as the Dutch and Swedes brought slaves with them and/or bought them after becoming established. However, as time passed, many Quakers did their best to protest the act. The 1688 Germantown Petition Against Slavery was the first protest against slavery in the New World. The petition placed emphasis on the Golden Rule ("Do unto others as you would have them do unto you").

Francis Daniel Pastorius drafted the petition with three local Quakers. Pastorius helped found Germantown in Pennsylvania. He was of German descent, and he was an author, humanitarian, and educator. The German

Quakers signed him as an agent of the Frankfurt Land Company in 1683. Right off the bat, he purchased fifteen thousand acres from Penn. This became Germantown. In 1707, Germantown lost its charter. It would become a part of Philadelphia in 1854.

Historians haven't decided if the four men who drafted the petition expected any real action. They knew that abolishing slavery in the whole colony would have been almost impossible. However, the document played an important role in the abolition movement in the mid-1800s. Its wording likely influenced the Declaration of Independence, which sought to create fairness for all men (although it should be noted that this wasn't necessarily the case).

Pennsylvania didn't have a great need for slaves. Their economy consisted of exporting and importing iron goods. The colony had access to iron ore, and they produced tools, plows, nails, and kettles. Pennsylvania had an agricultural economy as well, producing crops like wheat and corn. The people raised livestock, which means they had access to dairy products. In addition to manufacturing iron goods, the residents of Pennsylvania also produced paper goods and textiles. Their proximity to bodies of water helped them become worthy shipbuilders too.

Chapter 6 – A Closer Look: Virginia

Although Jamestown was the first permanent English settlement in what would become the United States, it almost didn't turn out that way. The Virginia Company of London received its charter in 1606 and founded the settlement a year later. However, due to the colonists' late arrival, they were unable to plant crops. It also didn't help that many who went on the voyage were not used to hard labor. Before ships arrived in 1608 to aid in the relief effort, two-thirds of the settlers had died. More people were brought on these relief ships, exacerbating the issues the colony was already facing. In addition to this, the investors of the Virginia Company were unhappy with the profits. The task to turn the colony around fell on Captain John Smith.

A lot of lore surrounds Captain John Smith. The captain was undoubtedly an adventurer, soldier, and explorer. He was also an author. His family rented a farm from a local lord, and he was able to attend school, where he learned how to read, write, and do arithmetic. Legend has it that he ran away from home at the age of thirteen. He wanted to become a sailor; however, his father found him before he got too far.

When Smith's father passed away in 1596, he left home. In 1598, he became a mercenary for the French, who were fighting against the Spanish in the Netherlands. The experience helped sow the seeds for his fighting and exploring tendencies. Supposedly, Smith even killed three Ottomans in duels. He also managed to escape enslavement by beguiling his mistress. His life is filled with other legendary exploits, so it is hard to know what is fact and what is fiction.

In 1606, Smith became involved with the Virginia Company's venture. However, on his way to the New World, he was charged with mutiny and placed under arrest. He was supposed to be executed upon their arrival, but a letter from the company saved him, as the letter stated that he was to become one of the leaders. In 1607, Jamestown was founded. Smith helped secure food and resources for the first Virginians. He also created maps, which greatly benefited the settlers.

In late 1607, Smith was captured by the Powhatans. It is hard to know exactly what happened, as Smith's testimony is the only source on the following events. According to him, Pocahontas, the chief's daughter, risked her own life to save his. Some scholars think that perhaps his life was never in danger and that what took place was an adoption ceremony.

In 1608, Captain John Smith had to make some bold moves to ensure the survival of the colony. He mapped the shoreline that ran along the Chesapeake Bay, searching for food. In 1609, before the Starving Time (the winter where nearly all of the settlers of Jamestown perished), Smith was gravely injured in a gunpowder explosion and was shipped home to England. He would return to the New World, but he would never go back to Virginia.

Despite the departure of John Smith and the terrible winter of 1609/10, the settlement survived. This was due to the arrival of the relief ships that had become stranded in Bermuda. On board one of these ships was John Rolfe, who would greatly influence the future of the colony. John Rolfe receives credit for starting the tobacco industry in the colonies. Rolfe possessed tobacco seeds from the West Indies, and in 1611, he became the first person to grow tobacco commercially. He started to experiment with growing and planting them in Jamestown. The colonial leadership had spent a lot of time searching for successful goods to export. Tobacco became the first.

Keep in mind that the colonists experienced a lot of trial and error. They didn't realize that growing one crop year-round on the same soil would drain it of its nutrients. As the Virginia soil started to suffer, they had to find other ways to support their economy.

In 1619, the Virginia General Assembly began setting down rules to maximize the crop's profitability. They set up ports and warehouses, which then led to the settlement of Norfolk, Alexandria, and Richmond. The colonists shipped tobacco to England, where England's agents distributed it. Since Virginia and England relied so heavily on the crop, it reached the point where they did overgrow it. Shipping disruptions also became an issue. Remember that England never stopped being involved in conflicts. The events of the early 1700s caused tobacco prices to fluctuate. They stabilized from 1740 to 1750, but the tobacco market didn't return to its glory days. It continued to deteriorate in the 1760s and 1770s.

Tobacco growers had to adjust to the market, so they started to plant other crops. It made more sense to focus on growing food-related crops such as wheat. When the Revolutionary War broke out, the colonists were in a better position to grow food due to this move. Plus, it helped restore the soil in areas where it was drained.

John Rolfe is notable for another reason as well. Like John Smith, Rolfe encountered the famed Powhatan chief's daughter. In 1613, the English captured Pocahontas by tricking her into thinking they could make an alliance. They demanded several things from her father, and while he gathered them, Pocahontas lived with the Europeans in Virginia. While she was there, she met John Rolfe.

Rolfe's wife and child had passed away on the voyage to the New World, leaving him a widow. However, although he loved the chief's daughter, he had a hard time justifying his marriage to her; in his eyes, she was a heathen. Practically everyone in the settlement would have had the same opinion. By that point in time, though, Pocahontas had become a Christian, taking on the name Rebecca. In 1614, Rolfe put aside his moral dilemma and married her.

The Baptism of Pocahontas *(1840) by John Gadsby Chapman. (Source: Architect of the Capitol)*

During ancient and colonial times (and even today to some extent), marriages helped two sides gain something politically or even financially. It does not seem as if this particular arrangement was political; by all accounts, they actually cared for each other. Nevertheless, their marriage helped to establish peace between the inhabitants of Jamestown and the natives.

In early 1615, the two had a son named Thomas. Later that year, their small family headed to England. Pocahontas (now Rebecca) was presented to the court in England. She was treated like royalty, but there is no doubt she was also seen as an oddity. They paraded her around like a princess, even though her culture did not recognize her as such. The couple was set to return to the colonies in 1617, but she passed away before seeing Virginia again.

Rolfe married yet again in 1619. Unfortunately, he didn't have the opportunity to spend the rest of his life with her. In 1622, he died, likely of natural causes. However, it is possible that he died in the Jamestown massacre. This massacre occurred due to the tensions between the Powhatans and the European settlers. Although the marriage of Pocahontas helped create peace while her father was alive, once the throne was taken by his younger brother, Opechancanough, around 1620, things changed. In March 1622, the Powhatans attacked, killing around four hundred colonists, which equates to about a third of their population. They attacked not only Jamestown but also other nearby settlements.

The conflicts between the Powhatan and the English were rough for both sides. Both sides killed the other, even women and children, and the English no longer saw the land as belonging to the Powhatan. In fact, the massacre gave the English the perfect justification for continuing to take their land. British historian Betty Wood states that "As far as the survivors...were concerned, by virtue of launching this unprovoked assault, Native Americans had forfeited any legal and moral rights they might previously have claimed to the ownership of the lands they occupied." More wars took place, such as the Third-Anglo Powhatan War of 1644. Many settlers died, but it also saw the death of Opechancanough. His death caused the end of the Powhatan uprisings. By 1684, the Powhatan Confederacy no longer existed, and the Powhatans instead lived on reservation lands.

Jamestown residents, as well as residents in all Thirteen Colonies, became the victims of many things other than Native American attacks, including the weather, disease, and food shortages. In addition, some sailed to the New World to hunt for gold. Since they focused on riches, they didn't focus on finding ways to sustain themselves.

Smith is quoted as saying, "There was no talk, no hope, no work but dig gold, wash gold, refine gold, load gold—such a bruit of GOLD that one mad fellow desired to be buried in the sands, lest they should by their art make gold of his bones!" Smith also famously said, "He that will not work shall not eat."

In addition to gold, England needed lands to expand. It needed to provide for its growing population at home. On top of this, England needed to compete with France and Spain. England had to expand trade to help the economy. The country also sought to spread its religion. Spain spread theirs in Mexico; England could do the same.

In 1642, Sir William Berkeley became the governor of Virginia. This was the year the First English Civil War broke out. While the conflict raged in England, the supporters of Charles I fled to Virginia, bringing their ideas to the colony. When Charles I was beheaded for treason in 1649, British Parliament turned on Berkeley, as he supported the Crown. From 1652 to 1659, he was forced out of the governorship. He spent that time on his Virginia plantation. In 1660, he was restored as governor.

Sir William Berkeley's time as governor experienced other problems. For example, Nathaniel Bacon led a rebellion against him. Berkeley was not responding to attacks by Native Americans efficiently enough. In addition, the economy was in a slump, the crops ceased to grow successfully, and the taxes went up. The people had had enough. In 1676, Bacon, who was Berkeley's cousin, led an attack against an Occaneechi village, killing most of the men, women, and children who lived there.

Although reforms were passed to placate Bacon and his followers, it was not enough. Bacon then led five hundred followers to Jamestown to demand the establishment of a militia in order to deal with the threat the Native Americans posed. The rebellion was a bloody moment in Virginia's history. During the rebellion, which lasted several months, buildings in Jamestown were burned to the ground. Eventually, the rebellion was subdued, with Bacon dying of dysentery in October of 1676 before the Royal Navy could arrive as backup. Berkeley returned to Jamestown at the beginning of 1677. He was relieved of the governorship and ordered to return to England to answer for his actions and the chaos that took place in Jamestown. That summer, he passed away.

Despite this stain on his time in office, Berkeley managed to accomplish several important things during his governorship. Since he was an educated man, he had an instinct for running the colony. He helped the colony experiment with crop diversification, and he also encouraged manufacturing and expansion. In addition, he had to deal with the aggressions posed by the Dutch and Native Americans, with his efforts to tamp down those aggressions slowing down as he grew older.

In the 1700s, the Virginians decided to expand their lands. The governors of Virginia during this time, which lasted from the 1730s to the 1770s, believed this was a great idea. By having settlers in the backwoods area, they would act as a buffer zone against Native American attacks. It is thought that by the 1740s, ten thousand Europeans lived in the Shenandoah Valley, a valley bounded by the Blue Ridge Mountains, the Potomac River, and the James River. As time passed, the Virginians continued pressing for more land, such as the Ohio Country. Their efforts to gain this land helped lead to the French and Indian War, which will be discussed in more detail in Chapter 8.

Shenandoah Valley *(1859-1860) by William Louis Sonntag Sr. (Source: Virginia Historical Society)*

Several leaders of the American Revolution War hailed from Virginia, including George Washington. It was also the site of the First Continental Congress. At the Second Virginia Convention, Patrick Henry gave his famous "Give me liberty or give me death!" speech in 1775.

Chapter 7 – Life in the Colonies

Sometimes individuals who take a glance at American colonial history make assumptions. It takes time to study and understand everything that happened in the span of about three hundred years. To fully appreciate American colonial history, it's also important to take off the glasses through which we view the world today.

Colonial America didn't have cars, phones, or the internet. However, it did have ingenious, scrappy individuals and great thinkers. Colonial life in America was far different from life in the 1900s and 2000s. Thanks to Benjamin Franklin, individuals who wanted to read books could read them at the first circulating library in Philadelphia. Services like this were free for members, but even those who were not members could check out books; they just had to leave behind the money for the book, which they would get back when they returned it.

Of course, things like libraries took time to develop. Also, some educational opportunities were reserved for certain occupations and genders. Women, for instance, were often only taught enough to read the Bible in the early days of the colonial period. But everyone had a purpose, especially at this point in history. The majority of the individuals traveling to the New World were male. For several decades, the population saw an imbalance between males and females. Therefore, women were in high demand. When the settlers started having children, the ratio improved but remained unbalanced. The first census numbers show that men easily outnumbered women six to one. This makes sense. Many men were unattached when they made their way to the Americas, as the new lands supposedly promised riches and stability; it was a place where they could start and raise a family of their own.

To boost the female population, they were offered free passage to the New World. Between 1619 and 1622, tobacco brides were sent to Jamestown. In total, 144 women traveled to America, and once they got there, they were auctioned off for around 150 pounds of tobacco each, with the price going to the company who shipped the women. However, only around thirty-five of these women survived their first six years in the colonies.

Regardless, the female population increased as the Pilgrims, Puritans, and other settlers started having children on American soil. By the time the 1700s rolled around, the ratio of men to women improved; it was now three to one.

A woman's place became her home, and she was surrounded by her children. This was especially the case in New England, which makes sense since this region was mainly inhabited by the Puritans. Since women birthed the babies, it was logical that her contribution to her household and society was bearing and raising children in the Christian way. Researchers estimate that a healthy woman bore ten children in her lifetime. Evidence shows that women bore children until they reached menopause. If she could birth them, she would have them. It is believed that one out of eight women died giving birth to children.

Although modern America has a different view on motherhood and a woman's place in society, Puritan women didn't see anything wrong with how they lived. Today, we would see their position as being inferior to men, but mothers were still celebrated back then. She played an important role as the gatekeeper of her children and family. Women were also still loved, at least for the most part, by their husbands. However, they did have few rights in regard to the law and had to listen to her husband in almost all matters.

Puritan women maintained the home. They looked after the children, cooked, and cleaned. Women also had the job of weaving clothes. Men worked the land or engaged in craftsmanship. The eldest children helped look after their younger siblings, did chores, and attended church. There was not much socializing for children back then, as the Puritans were rather strict. They wanted children to be obedient, and if they stepped out of line, they would often be beaten. However, this was not done out of hate. The Puritans believed firm discipline was needed at a young age so children would grow up to be adults with a firm belief in the way God wanted the world to work. Schools were set up for children, and all children knew how to read. Typically, though, only boys learned how to write.

Some of the colonists, especially in the North and even the South, lived in the backwoods of America. For some, it might be easy to write them off as uneducated "hillbillies," a derogatory term used to refer to people in the United States who live in rural areas. The truth is the exact opposite. The colonists built their homes, worked the land, and gave birth to the next generation. Many of them were indeed educated, and the Puritans began an effort to continue that tradition in the New World.

Religious leaders did their best to make sure everyone adhered to a high moral standard. There was a tendency to drink even among the Puritans, but the degeneracy was kept to a minimum. The Puritans allowed divorces (in fact, they had the most liberal divorce laws in all of the Thirteen Colonies), but they did not happen very often. Back then, people didn't divorce for the lack of love in a marriage; rather, they could only do so in cases of infidelity or desertion. Remarrying was also common for men since they tended to outlive their wives. Several of the Founding Fathers and colonial icons remarried.

The living situation varied from region to region, but in colonial America, religion always played an important role in the lives of colonists. Women did not work alongside their husbands in New England, but in the Middle Colonies, it was common to see women working in the fields. Overall, though, women were expected to listen to their husbands, raise the children, and take care of the household.

In the early colonial period, there was not much time for extraneous activities since the colonists had to remain vigilant of potential threats to their well-being. Although the settlers encroached on the lands of the Native Americans, many of them did their best to establish peace with them. Of course, not all of the settlers did so, and not all of the natives accepted their terms of peace. The battles that took place between the natives and settlers are common events that take place when any group comes into a new land.

The colonists faced other dangers besides Native American attacks. If they didn't die from starvation, they passed away from disease. If they survived starvation, disease, and outside attacks, they still had to deal with the wildlife that lived in the New World too.

Having an educated populace to counter the problems they faced was of the utmost importance. In 1636, the Great and General Court of Massachusetts Bay Colony received a significant grant. They established Harvard in Cambridge, Massachusetts, although it would only get its name a year later. Harvard is the oldest educational institution in America. All the Ivy League educational institutions had a religious slant. Harvard's denomination leaned toward Congregational. Harvard's purpose was to educate the clergy, and its early model was based on English universities. Most of the ministers who attended Harvard went to preach in Puritan churches. Estimates show that seventeen thousand Puritans had migrated to the New World by 1636. Thus, the population needed religious leadership.

Despite competition from other universities, Harvard still remains one of the most prestigious in the United States. However, the purpose of Harvard has changed. It stopped being a place to educate clergymen and evolved into producing entrepreneurs and America's top leaders. Even today, in many cases, Harvard's dropouts have the same caliber as those who graduated, as many of them enter the technology sector.

The next colonial college in what is now the United States was not established until 1693. William and Mary College was an Anglican college, and it resided in Williamsburg, Virginia. King William III and Queen Mary II approved the charter that established the college. They deemed that the institution's purpose was to create a place for studying, philosophizing, and learning languages. This school has stayed true to its original purpose. Today, its commitment is research and learning. It also still retains ties with the British Crown.

In 1701, the Connecticut legislature helped establish Yale. Like Harvard, it leaned toward Congregational. Its religious origins could explain the intense rivalry that still takes place between Harvard and Yale in all aspects of education, from sports to student performance. Unlike Harvard, Yale moved locations a few times. Yale remained true to its Orthodox Puritan ideals, with its studies focusing on the classics. In the early 1800s, the school branched out its studies. It established its medical school in 1810. The school of divinity and theology arrived in 1822. Finally, the school established its law school in 1824.

Education in colonial America focused on the things that the communities needed. As the needs of the colonies evolved, education did too. The next school that was established was Princeton in 1746. It started as the College of New Jersey, and it leaned Presbyterian. Nine colleges were founded during the colonial period. Some of the other colleges that were built included the University of Pennsylvania in 1751, Columbia in 1754, Brown in 1764, Rutgers in 1766, and Dartmouth in 1769.

North America was established primarily by the English. Therefore, the culture that thrived throughout the colonies was English. However, many immigrants called the Thirteen Colonies home, with the most diverse populations of settlements residing in the Middle Colonies. Regardless of their differences, the colonists all held education in high regard. Thus, it makes sense that they began to establish schools. In the colonial days, education at a university level was reserved for the upper crust of society, and only men could attend. Typically, universities had around two hundred young men in attendance, which is much lower than admittance today.

Although schools were available for younger children, wealthy families often used private tutors to educate their young. This was often the case in the Southern Colonies, regardless of wealth. Its makeup was different from its New England and Middle Colonies counterparts. Since the Southern Colonies focused heavily on agriculture, the parcels of land were separated from each other. They had large cities, but oftentimes, the people would be spread out more, making them more isolated from each other. This made community schools, for the most part, impossible, so children would either be taught by their parents or tutors.

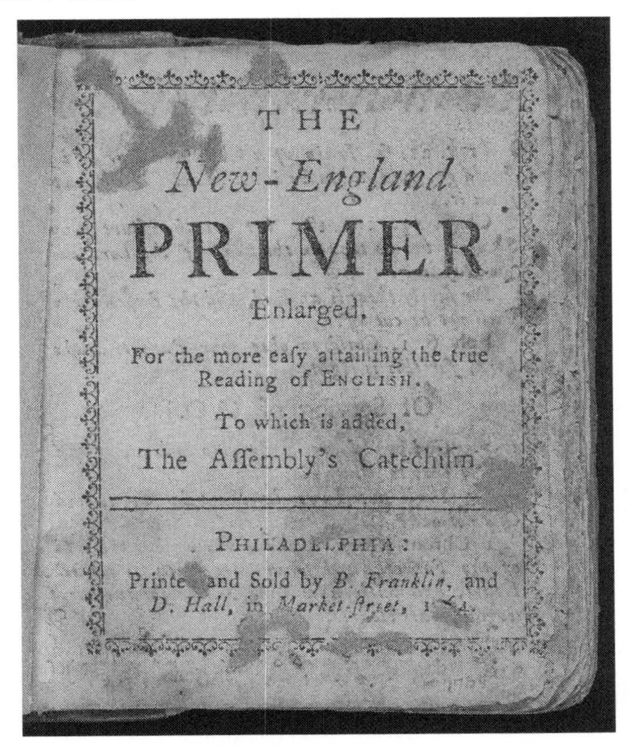

THE

New-England

PRIMER

Enlarged.

For the more eaſy attaining the true Reading of ENGLISH.

To which is added,

The Aſſembly's Catechiſm.

PHILADELPHIA:

Printe[illegible] and Sold by *B. Franklin*, and *D. Hall*, in *Market-ſtreet*, 1[illegible]

A copy of the New England Primer*, which was the most popular primer to teach reading in the late 17th and 18th centuries. (Source: Beinecke Rare Book & Manuscript Library)*

The colonists throughout the New World didn't have a lot of spare time. They spent their days working the land, turning textiles into products, and preparing meals from scratch. However, there was some time for fun. Even the Puritans played games and had celebrations. Some of the most popular pastimes in the Thirteen Colonies were dancing, singing, sharing stories, and having quilting bees. Horse races were a huge source of entertainment in Virginia. Racing horses were reserved for the wealthy, as it was expensive to maintain a healthy racing horse. But everyone enjoyed the spectacle, and the landed gentry enjoyed showing their horses off. Children would play games like hopscotch, marbles, tag, and hide-and-seek. Young girls would also dress up dolls made out of corn husks.

But again, things started to change as the Europeans settled into their new home. The first generation spent their time figuring things out. The second generation learned from the first. They had the opportunity to improve the processes established by the original generation. Thus, life improved for the colonists. They accumulated land, wealth, and knowledge. They set down roots in the New World, and they influenced other parts of the world. And as time passed, people were able to focus on the arts. There were several individuals who made contributions to the arts during the colonial period.

For instance, there was John Trumbull (1756–1843). He had a diverse set of skills; he became a painter, author, and architect. Trumbull is the artist responsible for capturing the signing of the Declaration of Independence in art. He studied with Benjamin West, another influential artist of the Revolutionary period. Trumbull balanced his art with serving as a public servant. In 1794, he became John Jay's secretary; in fact, he was present when the Jay Treaty was signed. The Jay Treaty helped to avert more warfare between the United States and Great Britain.

Trumbull finally settled in New York City from 1815 to 1837. There, he maintained a small art studio. The United States Congress commissioned him to paint four paintings that would sit in the Capitol Rotunda. The paintings included *General George Washington Resigning His Commission, Surrender of Lord Cornwallis,* and *Surrender of General Burgoyne.* His *Declaration of Independence* was painted in 1818. In 1831, Benjamin Silliman set up the Trumbull Gallery at Yale, which was the first gallery established at an American educational institution.

The Declaration of Independence, July 4, 1776 *(1832) by John Trumbull. (Source: Yale University Art Gallery)*

Charles W. Peale also painted portraits that focused on moments from the Revolutionary War. Like most American colonial icons, Peale had a modest beginning. He gained skills as a saddler, watchmaker, and silversmith. His first exposure to art was trading a saddle for painting lessons. Peale later met and received advice from John S. Copley. He even received sponsorship and had the opportunity to study under Benjamin West in London. In 1775, he moved to Philadelphia and saw his demand increase in the Middle Colonies. When the Revolutionary War broke out, he served in the militia. He saw his career suffer when he advocated for the Whigs in 1789.

Estimates show that Peale painted 1,100 portraits. His subjects included the Founding Fathers, such as George Washington, Thomas Jefferson, and Benjamin Franklin. Since he settled in Philadelphia, he had access to these great men. Peale wrote an essay in 1812 called "An Essay to Promote Domestic Happiness." Some individuals make a connection between the essay and how he posed his subjects.

Washington at Princeton *(1779) by Charles Wilson Peale. (Source: Yale University Art Gallery)*

Benjamin West was well regarded in the art circle. Both Charles W. Peale and John S. Copley studied under him. West painted under George III, and he helped to found the Royal Academy in 1768. Before this, West studied painting in Philadelphia in 1756, and he found success painting portraits in New York City. As neoclassicism caught on, he found sponsors who helped him travel to Italy to see the art trend for himself. George III provided Benjamin West with financial support, which meant that he didn't need to make a living painting portraits anymore. Once he received this financial support, West didn't return to the United States. However, colonists traveled to London to learn from him. Thus, his influence was felt outside of London.

Self-portrait of Benjamin West *(1776). (Source: National Gallery of Art)*

John S. Copley was perhaps the best painter in colonial America. He painted portraits and historical subjects. It is believed that he picked up basic skills in art from his stepfather, but no one knows for sure because there aren't many records.

Copley found that his skills lay in portraits. He posed his subjects with objects from their daily life. The technique gave more insight into the subject. For example, Copley painted the portrait of Paul Revere that is commonly found in American history textbooks. In this painting, Revere is holding a silver teapot. It was a great artistic choice. Instead of depicting the man in a heroic pose on top of a horse, Revere is portrayed as any American. He is holding one of the pots he had crafted himself.

Paul Revere *(1768) by John Singleton Copley. (Source: Museum of Fine Arts, Boston)*

Those who commissioned portraits from Copley were often from the upper class. This isn't surprising, as portraits like this were quite expensive. The artist decided that he wanted to branch out, and he entered art shows. He showed *Boy with a Squirrel* at the Society of Artists in London in 1766. The portrait received high praise from Copley's peers.

The artist ended up leaving the colonies before the American Revolution broke out. His father-in-law was involved in the Boston Tea Party, though. In 1776, Copley established his home in London. In 1778, he started painting people and nature, such as his *Watson and the Shark.* He entered the Royal Academy in 1779, and he gained a foothold in the Romantic art movement. Some believe that his paintings in Boston were superior to those he painted in London. His deteriorating health probably played a role in the quality of the portraits.

Paintings were not only the artistic forms found in the colonies. In terms of music, it depended on the region. The people who inhabited the colonies brought their culture and customs with them. The English, French, Dutch, Swedes, and Spanish brought their music with them. Even the German population that settled in Pennsylvania integrated their customs with their surroundings. Since the British were the majority population by 1776, their culture was the most prominent.

Drumming was perhaps the most common form of music after singing. Since the colonies were all fairly religious, they often sang the Psalms. Other instruments that found their way to the colonies included the flute and fife. Most people have seen images of the drum and fife corps that marched with the soldiers during the Revolutionary War. Wooden instruments were also common, such as the recorder. Brass instruments also became prevalent, which included the trombone, trumpet, and French horn. String instruments found their way to the colonies from Europe as well. Most instruments were reserved for men. If women wanted to play instruments, they chose the harpsichord, which is an instrument similar to the piano.

A chapter on colonial life wouldn't be complete without talking about the economy. As mentioned in this book, the colonies were an extension of England (later known as Great Britain). They were not independent even though they sat an ocean away. England dictated the terms of trade. The colonists had the freedom to establish representation to help them complete daily activities, but England set down the rules in regard to major decisions.

The colonies produced crops and other items that were shipped to England. The colonists could only receive raw materials and products from England. This situation led to what is known as the triangular trade.

Although the cargo sometimes changed, essentially, English/British ships would sail to Africa with textiles, rum, and other manufactured goods. In return for these goods, the merchants would receive slaves, which they would then take to the West Indies or Thirteen Colonies. The slaves would then be exchanged, and the ships would be loaded with items for England. The triangular trade made good use of the ships and maximized resources.

Mercantilism and the triangular trade ensured that the colonies had several restrictions placed on them. They could have traded with France for better profits. However, England's military on the ground ensured that this didn't occur. Nevertheless, contraband was smuggled both in and out of the colonies. The colonists were a shrewd people and bribed customs officials to look the other way.

Chapter 8 – Threats and Conflicts That England Faced: The Lead-up to the American Revolution

During the colonial period, many major wars took place. Some of them have been mentioned above, such as the English Civil Wars. The wars covered in this chapter took place later, with the first one taking place in the late 17th century. The Nine Years' War, also known as the War of the League of Augsburg or the War of the Grand Alliance, took place from 1688 to 1697. This conflict was between France on one side and England, the Netherlands, and the Austrian Habsburgs, to name just a few, on the other. King Louis XIV of France continued his attempts at expansion across the Rhine. He sought to pressure the Holy Roman Empire but was met with pushback from England.

Although many powers faced off against France, Louis XIV's men fought well. However, in 1696, the country was suffering from a poor economy. The other powers were also tired of the fighting and suffering on the economic front. Peace was agreed to in 1697. However, the Treaty of Ryswick didn't completely end the ill feelings the countries had toward each other.

The conflict continued between the English and French and between the Habsburgs and the Spanish Bourbons. During this period, who took the throne mattered. Alliances were still formed through marriage; thus, some heirs carried French blood while others carried Spanish. This became a problem because King Charles II of Spain (r. 1665-1700) didn't produce any heirs.

This culminated in another major war: the War of the Spanish Succession. The war lasted from 1701 to 1714. When Charles II passed away, the throne was open. It essentially boiled down to either a Habsburg or a Bourbon taking the crown. Before his death, Charles named Philip of Anjou, Louis XIV's grandson, who was a Bourbon, as his heir. If he did not accept, Charles II wanted the throne to go to Archduke Charles, the son of Holy Roman Emperor Leopold I. The issue was made complicated due to the various treaties that had been signed in the decade prior to Charles's death. War would have likely happened no matter who took the throne. Britain entered the war because it feared French expansion.

The French did well at the beginning of the war, but they began to lose their grip by 1706. The British forces managed to win battles against France, and the French started losing their strongholds in lands outside its borders. For instance, France found itself forced out of the Low Countries and Italy. Nevertheless, Philip was still made king. In 1711, Archduke Charles, the other contender for the throne, became the Holy Roman emperor. There was no need to continue the war, so peace talks were soon sought. In 1713, the countries agreed to the Treaty of Utrecht. Philip was acknowledged as the king of Spain. Britain, on the other hand, received territories like Gibraltar and gained trade agreements in the Spanish colonies in the New World. Due to these developments, Britain was now the leading commercial power.

The War of the Austrian Succession was another conflict between the Bourbons and Habsburgs. It took place from 1740 to 1748. This time, it was Holy Roman Emperor Charles VI (the same Archduke Charles involved in the War of the Spanish Succession) who passed away. His daughter, Maria Theresa, was in line for the throne, but other powers, such as France and Prussia, saw a chance to challenge the Habsburgs' power. This was because the original pact of succession saw the throne first going to the female heirs of Charles's older brother, Joseph I. The opposing powers used this as a pretext to start a war.

Frederick II of Prussia invaded Silesia in December 1740, kicking off the war. Many European powers got sucked into the conflict. The French and Spanish sided with the Prussians against the Austrians, who had the support of the British and the Dutch. France made inroads in the Austrian Netherlands, but Austria was able to stop the Spanish from spreading into Italy again. In the meantime, the Royal Navy had blockaded the French, creating dire economic conditions in regard to trade.

The Treaty of Aix-la-Chapelle, which was signed in 1748, ended the conflict. It allowed Maria Theresa and her husband to take the throne as planned. Prussia got to keep Silesia, but most of the other territories that had been taken during the war were returned to their previous owners.

These succession wars took place in Europe. But at times, they spread over into the Thirteen Colonies. For instance, during the War of the Spanish Succession, Queen Anne's War took place. In 1701, the three big powers of England, Spain, and France began asserting their control over North America. The British won the war in 1713, with the French ceding several of their territories in the north to Britain, such as Hudson Bay and Newfoundland.

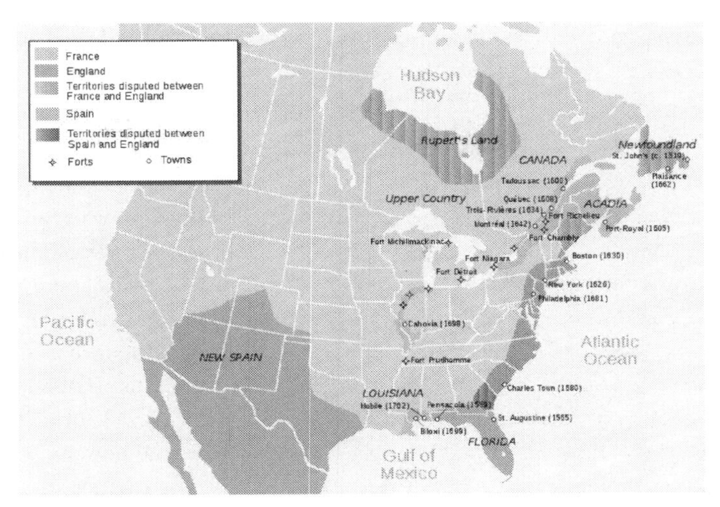

What European occupation looked like at the beginning of Queen Anne's War. (Source: Magicpiano; Wikimedia Commons)

During the War of the Austrian Succession, the North American continent saw King George's War break out. In 1744, once France heard of the war taking place in Europe, it soon acted out against the nearby British. Both sides raided the other's villages and forts. Like in Queen Anne's War, the colonists were assisted by Native Americans. This war ended in 1748 with the Treaty of Aix-la-Chapelle; everything went back to the way it had been before the war.

But perhaps the best-known American colonial war is the French and Indian War, which started in 1754. This is considered to be the North American theater of the Seven Years' War, which actually began two years later in 1756. It was a significant war, as it allowed Britain and its colonies to obtain the Canadian areas that the French had settled, as well as Florida from Spain.

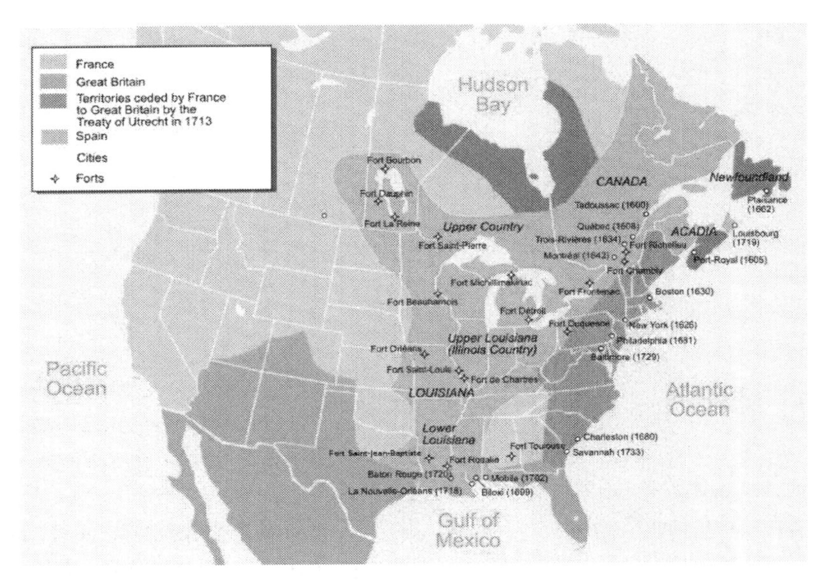

Map of European occupation in 1750. (Source: Pinpin; Wikimedia Commons)

The French presence has not been touched on much in this book, but they had a strong foothold in present-day Canada. As time passed, they spread westward, going as far as Wisconsin and parts of North Dakota. The French also laid claim to Louisiana, which was a highly desired territory due to its access to the Mississippi River.

Water sources were important for everyone settling in the New World. As such, the Ohio River became a focal point of conflict. In 1753, a young George Washington (who would become the first president of the United States) was sent to Ohio to protect British interests. The French were unwilling to engage in diplomatic talks, so Washington moved back south to inform the British of what he had seen.

In 1754, the first conflict of the war broke out. Both sides relied on Native Americans to augment their forces, but France certainly depended on them more. Population-wise, the British outnumbered the French by over one million; the British had around two million people, while the French had sixty thousand.

That same year, George Washington suffered his first defeat at Fort Necessity in what is today Pennsylvania; in fact, it was the only battle in which he ever surrendered. The weather, lack of equipment, and the likelihood that no reinforcements were going to arrive to aid the battle all led the young major to surrender the fort to the Canadians.

The war ebbed back and forth at the beginning, but by 1757, the British settlers were doing rather poorly. William Pitt helped turn things around. Pitt, who was the Leader of the House of Commons and the Secretary of State, understood the importance of defending the colonies against all invaders. He requested a lot of money to finance the British side of the battle. In regards to the war in Europe, Pitt began financing the Prussian forces. In regards to the war in North America, he sent forces to help conquer Canada. France, on the other hand, did not want to waste their valuable resources by sending them to the New World.

The British managed to beat the French in several key spots in Canada. They gained the most momentum when they defeated the French in Quebec in 1759. In 1760, Spain joined forces with France in the French and Indian War to protect its interests in the New World. However, it was not enough, as the British ended up winning the war.

The Treaty of Paris ended this war and the Seven Years' War in 1763. Spain lost Florida, but France gave it Louisiana instead. France lost all of its territories east of the Mississippi River.

Although the fighting with France and Spain subsided, it didn't stop with others. Immediately after the French and Indian War, the colonists near Ohio experienced Pontiac's War. Chief Pontiac from the Odawa tribe managed to unite several groups of natives. They destroyed forts and killed civilians. For instance, in 1764, a school teacher and ten children were scalped in a terrible massacre. However, the British were guilty of atrocities as well, including the killing of civilians. They offered rewards for the scalps of Native Americans for anyone above the age of ten, including women.

It was also during this war that the legendary smallpox blanket infection took place. At the Battle of Fort Pitt, which took place in 1763, the colonists were looking at a defeat. Some of the leaders thought about sending infected blankets to lower the number of Native Americans at their doors. William Trent, the commander of the fort, wrote, "We gave them two Blankets and an Handkerchief out of the Small Pox Hospital. I hope it will have the desired effect." However, the items that were sent to the natives most likely didn't have the desired effect Trent was hoping for. Still, scholars point to this incident as proof that colonists deliberately infected Native Americans throughout the colonization period. Whether this actually occurred is unknown.

This war ended in 1766 in a stalemate. Boundary lines were redrawn, recognizing the Native Americans' rights to the land, while the Native Americans recognized British sovereignty. However, this led to resentment in the colonists; they had just fought a hard war against the French for the lands in the Great Lakes region; now, they could no longer settle them? It is believed the results of this war helped contribute to the breakout of the American Revolution.

All of this fighting continued adding to Britain's debt. They leaned heavily on British bankers for financing. King George III made the decision that the Thirteen Colonies would have to provide resources to pay down the debt. After all, they had become safer as a result of Britain's victories. Logically, some of the debt belonged to them too.

Chapter 9 – The Road to Revolution

The colonists officially declared their independence from Britain on July 4th, 1776. On that day, they became Americans and formed the United States of America.

However, the path to freedom wasn't easy. The debates over whether to separate from the Motherland lasted several months. Communication was slow. Letter writing and traveling on horseback dominated these days, not smartphones, the internet, and cars.

The seeds for independence were planted fairly early on. In 1651, the Navigation Acts were passed to curtail trade. In those days, the Dutch controlled maritime trade, and England sought to change that by ensuring only ships that were manned with mostly Englishmen could transport goods from the American colonies. Historians believe the economic impact of these acts was minor but that they were the start of political tensions between the colonies and England.

The colonists learned how to survive on their own without help from the English, which created a separate identity from the mainland. The English sought to get rid of this kind of thinking, which was one of the reasons why the Dominion of New England was created. As you now know, the Dominion ultimately wasn't successful, as the colonial governments took back control.

In 1733, Britain passed the Molasses Act. The act imposed a tax on molasses and sugar that arrived from colonies that were not owned by Britain. It had to protect its sugar interests in the West Indies, as the sugarcane growers faced intense competition from the French. Thankfully, this act was not enforced well. New England depended on molasses to make rum, which was a large industry in that region. Smuggling increased, and the colonists simply refused to pay the tax.

About thirty years later, the Sugar Act was enacted. Although this act lowered the tax on molasses and sugar, it increased the enforcement of the law. At this point, the Thirteen Colonies were in a depression, and it was easy for the colonists to point to the law as a way to keep them dependent on Britain.

Both Britain and the colonies were feeling the effects of the Seven Years' War and the French and Indian War. It is easy to see why Britain demanded so much from the colonists. To the British government, the colonies were an investment, and an investment should show returns. It was costly to protect the colonists from the Native Americans, French, and Spanish. It was only right that the colonists helped share that burden.

However, the Thirteen Colonies were separated from Britain by an ocean, which allowed the colonists to develop a form of independence that the Crown could not have imagined. In 1764, though, the colonists were not as concerned about taxation without representation as they were about the negative impact the act would have on their industries.

The Sugar Act introduced an indirect tax, which means that molasses had the tax added to it by the time it reached the market. The Stamp Act, however, introduced a direct tax. It was passed in 1765, and it is safe to say the colonists did not approve of the measure. Any paper product had to have a stamp on it–including playing cards. And it could not be paid for in colonial money; it had to be paid for in British currency.

This time around, it was not the tax itself that upset the colonists; it was the fact that they had no representation in British Parliament. Even though these restrictions angered them, many of the colonists still attempted to make amends with Britain. Thomas Jefferson wrote a list of grievances, as he hoped Britain would offer some compromises. However, it couldn't compromise on the taxes since the country was in debt from fighting battles on several fronts.

On top of this, the Quartering Acts were passed later that year. British soldiers were still being stationed in the colonies even though there were no real threats to the colonists at this point. Britain ordered the colonists to provide them with housing and food.

The Stamp Act led to riots and stamp burning. It also led to the harassment of British officials. The colonists were so serious about protesting the Stamp Act that it led to the creation of the Sons of Liberty. In an ironic twist, the colonists took their group name from a speech given by Isaac Barré in British Parliament in 1765. He called the colonists who wouldn't cooperate with the new taxes the "sons of liberty." He believed the people in the Americas were as loyal as any other subject but that they sought liberties that had been denied to them for so long.

The colonists managed to organize themselves in secret extremely well. They knew that getting caught was not an option. If they did, they would find themselves in prison without bail or a fair hearing. Researchers believe that the Sons of Liberty was an offshoot of the Loyal Nine. In 1765, nine Bostonians formed the Loyal Nine in secrecy to protest the Stamp Act. These nine men all joined the Sons of Liberty. The Sons of Liberty counted Samuel Adams (who founded the group), Benjamin Edes, John Hancock, Paul Revere, Charles Peale, and Benedict Arnold as members. It also had a few chapters, with the two biggest ones found in Boston and New York. The Boston chapter was the first one, and its members met in Hanover Square next to what was dubbed the Liberty Tree.

An illustration of the Liberty Tree (1825). The Liberty Tree was felled by Loyalists in 1775. (Source: Houghton Library)

Remember that the colonists who resisted Britain's rule didn't have access to the internet, computers, or vehicles. Instead, they used pamphlets, petitions, and assemblies to share their thoughts. Some say that the colonists used propaganda to motivate their peers. In addition, some historians view the Sons of Liberty as extremists. However, revolutions are rarely civil.

It is true that the Sons of Liberty resorted to extreme civil disobedience. For example, Andrew Oliver received a letter asking him to present himself at the Liberty Tree. Oliver was the new collector of stamps, and the colonists immediately asked him to resign in public. The letter stated that as long as he resigned, he would be treated with respect, leaving one to wonder what would have happened if he had not resigned. A crowd of two thousand people showed up at the Liberty Tree. When Oliver resigned, the public cheered and left him alone. The Sons of Liberty also burned records and looted officials' homes to make their point.

The Sons of Liberty made the colonists realize that the issue at hand wasn't about taxes; it was the fact that Britain had too much control over the colonists, who had proven time and again that they could handle themselves. Something had to change, and the Sons of Liberty were a cog that made that happen. In 1766, the Stamp Act was repealed. At the same time, the Declaratory Act was passed, which asserted Britain's right to pass binding laws on its colonies. Nevertheless, the colonists were happy with their progress.

Their happiness did not last for long. The Townshend Acts were passed only a few months later. The mastermind behind the Townshend Acts was Charles Townshend. There is no doubt that Townshend had a solid financial mind. However, he lacked political tact. Townshend also had the ability to give beautiful speeches even while drunk. According to legend, he once gave a speech while drunk on champagne in 1767. Townshend passed away a few months after Parliament passed his four resolutions (one of the Townshend Acts, the Vice Admiralty Court Act, was passed after his death). Thus, he didn't receive the opportunity to see his resolutions unfold.

The first Townshend Act was the New York Restraining Act. As the name hints, this act was aimed at New York. The colony refused to comply with the Quartering Act of 1765. Under this new act, the New York Assembly could not gather until the Quartering Act was honored. Before the act could be implemented, though, New York began paying for the soldiers.

The next resolution was the Revenue Act, which was designed to help put money into Britain's coffers. The Revenue Act placed taxes on glass, paper, paint, and tea. In addition, a person's private property could be searched to see if there were any smuggled goods. Not even people living in Britain were subjected to such violations, so the colonists protested against this measure.

The following act was the Indemnity Act. The British East India Company saw reduced taxes on exports of tea to Britain. Britain could then export the tea to the colonists at a lower price. The Dutch were a formidable trade competitor to Britain when it came to tea. They smuggled tea into the colonies, so Britain sought to put a stop to it. The act was supposed to make British tea more attractive to the colonists than tea from other countries.

The final Townshend resolution was the Commissioners of Customs Act. A new customs board was created in the colonies, which was supposed to enforce taxes and shipping regulations. Before this, Britain had to oversee these kinds of things from Europe. With a direct presence in the colonies, it made it harder for the colonists to skip out on paying taxes.

Eventually, the Townshend Acts led to a British military buildup in the Thirteen Colonies. These troops only added tension among the colonists, who saw the troops as a threat. This led to the pivotal incident of the Boston Massacre.

In early March 1770, a mob gathered around the Boston Custom House. Around fifty people gathered around the small British presence. They threw objects and shouted and taunted the soldiers standing guard. One of the soldiers was knocked down, and he angrily shot into the crowd. This was followed by several more volleys, which were never ordered by the captain. Five colonists died, with two of them dying afterward.

A 19th-century lithograph of Paul Revere's engraving. (Source: US National Archives and Records Administration)

That same year, British Parliament did away with all of the extra taxes except for the one on tea. This helped appease the colonists somewhat, although the Sons of Liberty continued to agitate for independence.

One of the most influential Sons of Liberty was Samuels Adams, who remains one of the most important figures of colonial America and the Revolutionary War. He was a cousin of John Adams (the second president of the United States), but the two differed in their approach toward independence. John Adams was determined to remain civil, and he worked within the law.

Although Samuel Adams was an agitator and a fan of mob violence, he did attend Harvard and studied law for a brief time, so he understood the underlying issue the American colonists were facing: no representation in Parliament. He attempted to become an entrepreneur but ended up becoming a tax collector instead. However, he often refused to complete the duties of his job and didn't collect the new taxes. Samuel Adams also served as a Continental Congress delegate and signed the Declaration of Independence.

Other well-known members of the Sons of Liberty include John Hancock, Paul Revere, and Benedict Arnold.

John Hancock was a threat to British power. He successfully riled up crowds against the taxes. His efforts led him to become one of the signers of the Declaration of Independence; in fact, he was the first one to sign it.

When John Hancock's uncle passed away, he inherited his shipping business. He led a lavish lifestyle, but he was also generous with his money. Hancock first entered the political fray in 1765. Around this time, the taxes started to hit home for the colonists. It makes sense that Hancock was so opposed to the British taxes since he would have experienced the effects firsthand due to his shipping business. Thus, protests got under way. Boston became the "Cradle of Liberty." The Boston Tea Party, the Boston Massacre, and the seizure of Hancock's ship all gave the colonists a common cause around which to rally.

In 1775, Hancock was voted as the president of the Continental Congress, which met in Philadelphia. The Continental Congress chose George Washington to serve as its commander of the Continental Army. Hancock's wealth came in handy here, as he used it to fund the army and Congress.

Paul Revere is best known for his famous "Midnight Ride" in April 1775. However, both he became involved in the Sons of Liberty, he was a prosperous silversmith and engraver, and he continued his rise into the upper ranks of society during the American Revolution. He was unable to become a part of the gentry, but his Midnight Ride ensured that his name lasted to the modern age.

Revere's mission to deliver news of the British movements was secret, so he never shouted the famous words, "The British are coming!" He rode through the night, with around forty men joining him by the end of it. Revere reached Lexington around midnight, and after discussing matters with Samuel Adams and John Hancock, they decided the British would attack Concord first. Revere headed out, but he was captured along the way. One of the three riders who made the trip to Concord, Samuel Prescott, managed to elude capture and made it to Concord. (The other rider, William Dawes, was not captured, but he did not complete the ride due to falling off his horse.)

In many ways, the most famous colonists were ordinary men who did extraordinary things. Americans remember Paul Revere's ride thanks to Henry Wadsworth Longfellow's poem, which is not historically accurate. For instance, the poem says that the lanterns hung in the Old North Church were placed there for Revere to begin his ride. In reality, he was the one who had the lantern system set up.

Perhaps the most infamous Son of Liberty was Benedict Arnold. Most Americans today have heard of this man. If someone uses the name, they're referring to the word traitor. But Arnold actually started off as a hero to the colonists. It seems like his ego got in the way. Other men continued to win the hearts and minds of the colonists, such as George Washington. Thus, they started to receive glory and promotions. Arnold was passed up for promotions, and he felt like he was not being recognized for his services.

It perhaps did not help that Arnold's second marriage was to a woman whose father was loyal to the British cause. He started to communicate with the British through her family's contacts, with those contacts asking him to surrender West Point in New York, of which he had command, in 1780. However, the colonists captured Major John André, a British spy, who had papers revealing Arnold's plans of surrender. Arnold then received a commission with the British army, and after the war, he spent the rest of his days in England.

Before Arnold's betrayal, George Washington greatly admired the man. Although Washington was not a part of the Sons of Liberty, he deserves a special mention, as he was not only the commander of the Continental Army during the Revolutionary War but also became the first president of the United States. He did not approve of what the British were doing in the colonies, and he accepted the roles that were thrust upon him.

The number of things that Washington accomplished after the Revolutionary War are many. He wasn't an inventor like Benjamin Franklin, and he wasn't a prolific writer like Thomas Jefferson. However, he contributed as a leader. He set the bar for leadership and the number of terms a US president should serve. Washington passed away at the age of sixty-seven, but he lived a full life. He had military accomplishments and leadership accomplishments of which many leaders could only dream.

Benjamin Franklin was another Founding Father who wasn't involved in the Sons of Liberty. He had perhaps the most communication with British Parliament. Franklin was in Britain as a diplomat when some of the restrictive measures, like the Stamp Act, were being passed. He testified against this act, saying, "Suppose a military force sent into America; they will find nobody in arms; what are they then to do. They cannot force a man to take stamps who chooses to do without them. They will not find a rebellion; they may indeed make one." Shortly after the American Revolution began, Franklin cut his ties to Britain and headed home to aid in the war. He served on the Continental Congress and helped draft the Declaration of Independence.

These men all played an important role in the lead-up to the war. But it must be noted that the war effort would have never succeeded if it weren't for the many ordinary people who sought independence. Perhaps the most famous act of civil disobedience that took place during the road to the Revolutionary War was the Boston Tea Party in 1773. This was a result of the

Tea Act, which was passed to deal with the problem of smuggling. The British East India Company could now ship tea directly to the colonists, but the people still had to pay the tea tax. The people did everything they could to protest this.

On the evening of December 16th, 1773, a group of colonists, mainly men from the Sons of Liberty, dressed as Native Americans and destroyed ninety-two thousand pounds of tea at Boston harbor. The loss would equate to about one million dollars today. The British tea stained the water, and the colonists found themselves in hot water. However, they didn't care about the feelings of the British anymore. Most of them had already made up their minds.

An engraving titled Boston Tea Party *(1789). (Source: Wikimedia Commons)*

After the Boston Tea Party, British Parliament passed the Intolerable Acts in 1774, directly retaliating against the colonists for their rebellion. Parliament started with the Boston Port Act. Since Boston was ground zero for the destruction of so much tea, they received the harshest punishment. The port was closed until the tea that was destroyed was repaid. Next, Parliament passed the Massachusetts Government Act. This made the colony a crown colony, which meant that the people could no longer represent themselves. The colony's leadership was replaced with appointed representatives from Britain. Only one town meeting could take place a year unless the people had the approval of the governor.

The Administration of Justice Act helped get English troops and officials out of trouble. Some of them behaved in careless ways; thus, the colonists had the right to put them on trial. However, this act allowed the troops to travel to England and face trial there. Obviously, this was a way to help them avoid punishment. However, it was rare for a British official to face an unfair trial. Even those involved in the Boston Massacre had fair representation. Many, including George Washington, called this the "Murder Act," as it essentially let the British in North America get away with murder.

The Intolerable Acts also introduced another Quartering Act. The previous one had been mostly ignored, but this one stated that the governor should house soldiers in buildings that were unoccupied. A popular myth is that the British made the colonists take soldiers into their own private homes. The act did not require such a thing to occur, and this only happened on a small scale.

One other act proved "intolerable" to the colonists, although it was not officially a part of the previous acts. The Quebec Act was passed by British Parliament in 1774. Its goal was to expand the Province of Quebec into much of what is now the Midwest. This essentially voided the colonists' hard-won French and Indian War, as it granted concessions to the French still living there. It also limited the Ohio Company's claims on the land, which it utilized for the fur trade industry. In addition, it restored the power of the Catholic Church in the region. The colonists saw how generous British Parliament was to the French while they were being oppressed as British subjects.

Later that year, the First Continental Congress met, and the rest is now history. The following year, the colonists faced off against the British in the Battles of Lexington and Concord, kicking off the American Revolutionary War. This war is heavily featured in many history books, so we will end the period of American colonial history here. However, some scholars push the end date of colonial America to the Declaration of Independence, which declared America's independence from Britain. Some even go as far as the end of the American Revolution, which concluded in 1783.

Conclusion

Over four hundred years ago, Jamestown was founded. It is astounding to see how much progress has been made in that city and throughout all of what is now the United States. The United States of America saw several demographic changes during the 1900s. Its economy, value system, and laws have seen several changes too.

In fact, for Americans today, it's difficult to imagine that such disputes occurred between a country that is often seen as the greatest ally of the US. By taking a look at American colonial history, it's possible to understand the sacrifices that were made by the Founding Fathers and the other colonists. Hundreds of thousands of men volunteered to fight for independence, and many risked jail time to get out from under the thumb of the British Crown.

However, their actions would not have been possible without the early colonists, those men and women who established infrastructure and government systems that allowed the colonies to flourish into a place where revolutionary ideals could take hold. These men and women had to learn how to adapt to their environment, which was filled with enemies and diseases that claimed many lives. American colonial history also shows the ingenuity of the colonists who left the comforts of home behind. They set down the foundation for the Industrial Revolution, future infrastructure, and innovations.

Even though the colonists engaged in reprehensible acts, especially when looking at them from a modern viewpoint, it is clear to see that they achieved many impressive accomplishments. Studying this fascinating period of history allows people to not only acknowledge past mistakes but also to find inspiration from the dedication and ingenuity of the early European settlers of the United States of America.

There is so much more to learn about colonial America, and we highly encourage you to look at the list of suggested reading to continue your education on this captivating time period.

Part 2: The Puritans

A Captivating Guide to the English Protestants Who Grew Discontent in the Church of England and Established the Massachusetts Bay Colony on the East Coast of America

Introduction: A Puritanical Recipe

The Puritans. The very name invokes images of the religiously strict and austere. Those puritanical purists who considered all other religions null and void in comparison to their own. The very word "puritanical," in fact, is derived from this group of religious zealots. And zealot here is not being used in the pejorative sense but rather as a very apt description of the manner in which the Puritans lived their lives.

The Puritans believed very strongly in their religious sensibilities, and they were willing to do just about anything to see them be carried out. As was often the case with new religious movements, the title of "Puritan" was not one that the Puritans themselves came up with. It was a nickname given to them by opponents of the religious movement who ridiculed them as being unrealistic purists. Those labeled with this title took it to heart, and they took up the challenge that it meant, declaring that they were indeed Puritans, just as their adversaries had charged.

In the beginning, the Puritans were simply religious reformers who sought to separate English Protestants from the last vestiges of Roman Catholic tradition. England entered the Reformation a little bit later than continental Europe, and the initial cause of the English Reformation was much different. Initially, it was due to a falling out between King Henry VIII and the pope, which led the British king to separate from the mother church and declare himself the head of a brand-new church, the Church of England. In many ways, the Church of England was Catholic in all but name. Many of the same doctrines and rituals of the Catholic Church carried over into the Church of England. Perhaps the biggest difference was that the pope in Rome no longer had any authority over the British.

At any rate, this act opened up the floodgates, and a religious reformation began to take hold in Britain. The Puritans were against the Catholic Church and sought to "purify" their pews of any and all Catholic teachings. As they progressed as a Protestant faith, the Puritans became even more puritanical, and soon, they rejected just about all other Protestant faiths that differed from their own teachings.

But as much as the Puritans were lambasted as being hypocritical by their opponents, they did indeed try to practice what they preached. They firmly believed that if they openly lived what they deemed to be a righteous life, they could persuade others by their very example. Through their own self-sacrifice, they wished to serve as a living testament of what Christian believers should be like. But as was often the case in the aftermath of the Reformation, this interpretation of what Christians should be like was almost always a recipe for strife and conflict. The Puritans sincerely believed that it was their duty to be that "shining city on a hill" that would set the example for others. They attempted to live a life that was set apart, almost as if it would be a testimony to the world that one could follow in the goodness of God. Their intentions were good, but as often is the case with even the best-laid plans of both mice and men, such things are often easier said than done.

Chapter 1 – Before the Puritans

"That man is truly humble who neither claims any personal merit in the sight of God, nor proudly despises brethren, or aims at being thought superior to them, but reckons it enough that he is one of the members of Christ, and desires nothing more than that the head alone should be exalted."

-John Calvin

In order to really understand the religious movement known as the Puritans, you really need to understand what went on before the Puritans came about. The Puritans, of course, were successors of the Protestant Reformation that shook the Catholic Church to its core. The Reformation was sparked by a Catholic monk named Martin Luther, who began questioning official church teachings. It was Luther who, on October 31st, 1517, nailed his *Ninety-five Theses* to the doors of an abbey called All Saints' Church.

Luther ignited a dialogue that led to new thought among Christians, and soon, new denominations began to spring up. Prior to the Reformation, the Catholic Church, whose very name, "Catholic," is the Latin derivative of a Greek word meaning "universal," had positioned itself as the one true universal church in the land. After the Reformation, however, there were several denominations in Europe that competed with each other to gain faithful converts.

Martin Luther, of course, became a primary leader of the Reformation, but he was not the only one. Close on the heels of Martin Luther's rise to prominence was a man named John Calvin. John Calvin is crucial to the history of the Puritans, as it was upon his subsequent doctrine of Calvinism that many Puritan beliefs and thoughts would be based.

John Calvin was a French reformer who, after being driven out of his native France, set up shop in nearby Switzerland, where he preached his beliefs on predestination. Calvin, just like Luther before him, stressed the need for faith in order for Christians to achieve salvation. Just like Luther, he believed that salvation was not something someone could earn through good works; rather, it was something one could only achieve through faith in God.

But—and this is a big but—Calvin proclaimed that God had already preordained who would be open to having faith in him and who would not. Basically, he believed that the story of life had already been written long ago, and the author of creation—God—had already created all of the parts that we would incredibly end up playing. Imagining God to be the ultimate producer/screenwriter/director of reality, Calvinists would tell you that we're all simply playing out the role we have been given. That everything that we do has been predestined and preordained.

John Calvin preached that whether we come to have faith in God or go astray and turn our backs on grace and faith, all of it had already been predetermined in advance. This viewpoint would become an important fixture in the life of the Puritans. The concept of predetermination is still a hot-button issue among Christians even today. Many Christians view such concepts as absolute anathema, feeling as though it negates the central Christian tenant of free will. Most Christians would agree that man has free will and chooses whether to do good or bad. The Calvinist idea that some are doomed to darkness while others are destined to go toward the light seems to contradict the very notion that we have free will. Then again, even Christians aghast at the Calvin doctrine of predestination would be hard-pressed to explain how a God, whom they will readily admit is omnipotent and all-knowing, would not know what our futures have in store. If God knows everything and can see the past, present, and future all at once, as most Christians would tell you, then how could He not know what our ultimate outcome would be? Some Christians, however, might contend that it's not so much that God predestined or preordained our choices but that it's just His nature to know how everything is going to play out. This wouldn't be so much predestination as rather just knowing everything in advance. Predestination, of course, is a very complicated theological concept, and it can be analyzed, viewed, and argued from a wide variety of angles, as one can see.

John Calvin's notion of "the elect," or the idea that it was a chosen few whom God had chosen to be saved, also resonated with the Puritans, who would truly come to believe that they were a people set apart. One of the great Puritan leaders of the 1600s, John Winthrop, would liken the Puritan movement to being a "shining city on a hill" for all the world to see. Winthrop did not invent this phrase; these words were gleaned from the New Testament of the Bible itself. The verse can be found in Matthew 5:14, in which Jesus declared to his followers, "You are the light of the world. A city set on a hill cannot be hidden." The Puritans would take these words to heart, and they would take it to mean that they were indeed the elect that God had set apart to fulfill his divine will.

Another Calvinist doctrine that would come to greatly influence the Puritans was the notion that all church members should be equal and that there should be no centralized authority figure to rule over them. The Catholic Church, of course, was (and still is) a highly organized and hierarchical body, in which the pope is on top with cardinals and other high-ranking members branching out below. John Calvin wanted nothing to do with any of this. The Puritans agreed, and when their movement eventually kicked off in England, they were steadfastly against the Church of England's hierarchical archbishops and bishops. The Puritans declared that they did not want these religious authorities telling them what to do.

Another tenant of Calvinism that the Puritans wholeheartedly embraced was the notion of the separation of church and state. John Calvin declared that the state government had no right to interfere or dictate matters of the church. The Puritans passionately agreed on this matter as well, and they ultimately brought this concept to America. It was in the New World that the Puritans would leave one of their most lasting legacies, as the separation of church and state would eventually become a hallmark of the later United States.

John Calvin first arrived in Switzerland in 1536, and by the 1540s, many of his ideas had firmly taken root in the region. The English, in the meantime, had been fairly inoculated from the Reformation that was sweeping the European mainland. Prevented from having such expressions of thought by stern Catholic rulers, the most anyone could do was to sit back and watch what was occurring across the English Channel and wait. Since 1509, England had been in the grip of King Henry VIII, who began his career as a staunch Catholic. In his advocacy for the Catholic Church, he initially set himself up as an opponent of the Reformation and even wrote a treatise in defense of Catholicism called the *Defence of the Seven Sacraments*. King Henry didn't have very many kind things to say about Martin Luther either; at one point, he likened Luther to a snake whose words were like "viper's venom." The pope over in Rome wholeheartedly approved of Henry's thoughts and actions, and at one point, he even proclaimed King Henry to be a "defender of the faith."

But this great defender of the faith would prove somewhat fickle and would only support the pope when he was allowed to get his way. And as it pertains to England, the break with the Roman Catholic Church came not over religious disagreements but rather because King Henry was upset with the pope for not fulfilling his request to have his marriage annulled. Divorce was out of the question in those days, so the next best thing was to get an annulment, as it would declare the marriage to have been null and void in the first place.

Henry had been married to Catherine of Aragon for over two decades, and he was quite distressed that she had not been able to produce a male heir to the throne. Henry, feeling that his very legacy was at stake, decided he needed a new wife. Since England was Catholic, this meant that this supposedly sovereign king had to first consult with the pope. And when the pope refused to fulfill his wishes, an infuriated King Henry broke with the pope and the Catholic Church outright. However, Henry was still very much Catholic in his beliefs. He did not want to get rid of Catholic tradition; he just wanted to get rid of papal authority. It's for this reason that he created his own state-run church, the Church of England, of which he would be the head. The pope would no longer be in charge of religion for the English; now, it would fall upon their own king's shoulders to dictate to them the correct modes of religious worship and thought.

Although King Henry VIII took over England's church, he left most of the Catholic traditions and trappings intact, and it was these vestiges of the old Catholic Church that progressive-minded reformers within the Church of England sought to do away with. In a sense, they wanted to "purify" the Church of England of all former links to Roman Catholicism. It was from this mindset that the concept of Puritanism came forth.

Before the Puritans, England's pseudo-Reformation had been deemed by many to be woefully incomplete. How could any self-respecting Protestant and Calvinist believer (as many English Protestants were) tolerate the donning of Catholic-styled priestly vestments and readings from a book of prayer that harkened back to the mother church in Rome? For many, these holdovers of Catholicism were intolerable. It was as if the door to religious freedom had been cracked open ever so slightly, but no one was allowed to open it the rest of the way.

Britain's Protestants longed to have the religious freedoms that had been won by their Protestant brethren in strongholds such as Switzerland and Germany. Some fervently prayed and waited for that day to come; others, however, were willing to couple their prayers with action.

Chapter 2: The First Puritans

"It is God's will through His wonderful grace, that the prayers of His saints should be one of the great principal means of carrying on the designs of Christ's kingdom in the world. When God has something very great to accomplish for His church, it is His will that there should precede it the extraordinary prayers of His people; as is manifest by Ezekiel 36:37. And it is revealed that, when God is about to accomplish great things for His church, He will begin by remarkably pouring out the spirt of grace and supplication."

-Jonathan Edwards

Those who ended up being the founders of Puritanism did not have the intention of starting a new religious movement but of simply purifying the Protestant Church of England of all latent vestiges of the Catholic Church. King Henry VIII broke from the Catholic Church in 1534, and although his actions led to reform, King Henry VIII was not himself a reformer. Ironically enough, he began his career as a staunch supporter of the Catholic Church, which was perhaps why he kept so many of the traditions of the Catholic Church intact in his new state religion, the Church of England.

Even though the king had split with the Roman Catholic Church for temporal rather than spiritual reasons, Protestants were grateful. However, they were not excited about the continued presence of the Catholic Church in the country. Later English Protestants would work to slowly reform these aspects of the Church of England from the inside out. One of these early English reformers was Thomas Cranmer, an archbishop of the Church of England.

Cranmer championed the cause of the Church of England adopting the Protestant belief in "justification by faith" rather than "justification by works." It was perceived by the Protestants of this time that the Catholic Church was too focused on doing good works rather than simply having faith in God. Protestants knew that both good deeds and faith were important, but they wished to stress the belief that it was only through faith in God that one could gain salvation.

Archbishop Cranmer and his supporters also refused to recognize the Catholic belief in "transubstantiation," which held that Jesus was literally transformed into bread and wine during communion. Even today, it's still a strange concept for Catholics to have to explain. Transubstantiation teaches that while Christ is not in any way perceived by the physical senses during the rite of communion, a transformation does indeed take place. Although the bread and wine still look and taste just like bread and wine, the substance of the sacraments transforms into a non-physical manner during that brief moment of taking the Eucharist. Yes, even once explained, it's a hard concept for some to fathom.

Cranmer and his Protestant allies were quick to discard this often confusing and hard-to-grasp aspect of the Catholic faith. But even though King Henry VIII had broken with the Catholic Church, the king was slow to accept many Protestant beliefs. Furthermore, there was a growing conservative wing in the Church of England who did not wish to lose the old teachings of the mother church. These conditions made the English Reformation a much slower process than the rapid reform that had taken place in other countries on the European continent.

In England, political reversals often led to religious reversals, and much of the gains that the English Protestants had made could be quickly overruled. After King Henry VIII passed in 1547, power was given to his then nine-year-old son, Edward. Although he was certainly not old enough to lead on his own, Protestants were assured that his eventual reign would be friendly to their faith.

However, King Edward VI unexpectedly perished in 1553, and with him, much of the Protestant cause perished as well. For it was after his demise that Edward's sister, Mary, who was a staunch Catholic, came to the throne. Yes, ironically enough, despite all of King Henry VIII's efforts to produce a male heir to succeed him, it was ultimately his eldest daughter Mary who would come to hold real power over England.

Mary I, who would go on to develop the nickname of "Bloody Mary," would put on a full reversal of all Protestant reforms. Suddenly, it was a crime to engage in religious practice outside of Catholicism. Before Mary took her place on the throne, allegiance to the pope and Roman Catholicism was considered anathema, but once she took power, the Catholic rites were once again in fashion. Cranmer himself fell victim to this sudden reversal, and he was subsequently burned at the stake for holding fast to the reforms that had once been deemed acceptable.

However, in England, what was acceptable as it pertains to religion had almost become anyone's guess, as the shaky sands of British religious doctrine continued to shift under everyone's feet. Queen Mary I angered Britain's Protestants even further when she married the Catholic stalwart Philip, the king of Spain, in 1554. Close on the heels of this marriage was the announcement that Catholicism in England would be officially restored. Then, in 1555, Mary went a step further by putting Catholic laws regarding heresy back in place. It was this renewed push against heresy that would cost Protestant reformers, such as Cranmer, their lives.

Many more reformers, realizing that England would no longer tolerate their beliefs, made the decision to flee to Switzerland. At this point in time, Switzerland—the land of Calvinism, no less—had become a refuge for many English Protestants. And soon enough, those who could be called "Puritans" were flocking to Swiss cities such as Geneva and Zurich in droves.

Some sense of stability did not arise until Queen Mary I abruptly perished from what is thought to be cancer in 1558, allowing her half-sister, Elizabeth, to come to the throne. Queen Elizabeth I was a Protestant, and she set in motion a trend toward basic Protestant ethos that would remain in place thereafter. But whether Protestant- or Catholic-leaning, British monarchs quickly realized that they had to placate both the reformers, who sought new ways of dealing with religion, and the conservatives, who wished to maintain old traditions.

It was this ideological dichotomy of Britain that often persuaded British monarchs to take the middle of the road, so to speak. They allowed for some Protestant reform, but they also did not want to take things too far. Due to the monarchs' reluctance to fully shift the religion of the country, there were always some among the Protestants who felt that England's move toward Protestantism wasn't going far enough. This was where the Puritans came in.

Of particular early interest for those who would become Puritans was the issue of the priestly vestments used by the clergy in the Church of England. The Puritan Protestants wished to get rid of this tradition since it seemed to harken back to the Catholic Church. Instead of elaborate dresswear, Puritans recommended modest black gowns that were less flashy and ostentatious. It might seem like a minor detail today, but the dress code of the priests of the Church of England was a big deal back then.

The Puritans were downright ashamed of the slow pace of the reformation within the Church of England. This sentiment was perhaps summed up best in the anonymous tract *Admonition to the Parliament,* which was authored in 1572. The tract proclaimed its disdain, stating, "We in England are so far off from having a church rightly reformed, according to the prescript of God's word, that as yet we are not come to the outward face of the same." English-based Puritan Protestants could only look with envy at the more robust Protestant reforms taking place on the European continent.

Queen Elizabeth was indeed a middle-of-the-road reformer when it came to domestic affairs, and she was very much a stickler for keeping the status quo. But while she sought to maintain the slow pace of English reforms at home, she was quite progressive when it came to her Protestant policies abroad. Queen Elizabeth became a kind of Protestant crusader when it came to taking on Catholic Spain. It is rather ironic that her former brother-in-law, King Philip, would become her archnemesis, but this is essentially what the state of affairs was like in Elizabethan England.

Like master chess players, both of these leaders watched the other very carefully as they engaged in their own personal holy war, and whenever one made a move, the other was sure to attempt a move to directly counter their efforts. Most notably, Queen Elizabeth was a staunch supporter of the Protestant-leaning Netherlands, which King Philip was actively trying to bring back into the Catholic fold. King Philip, who had inherited the region from his father, Holy Roman Emperor Charles V, had been waging war with his proxies in the southern reaches of the Netherlands against the Protestant stronghold in the north. In 1580, after a long, protracted struggle between these factions, King Philip sent one of his loyal commanders, Alessandro Farnese, also known simply as the Duke of Parma, to try and put the Protestants of the northern Netherlands to rest.

The Protestants of the north, in the meantime, had formed the so-called Union of Utrecht, for they had pledged to band together to ward off any foreign invasions. They managed to hold their own after several incursions, but in the summer of 1585, the defenders appeared to be on their last legs right when the Duke of Parma was getting ready to unleash an all-out invasion of the northern Netherlands.

All seemed just about lost when British troops suddenly arrived on the scene, sent at the behest of Queen Elizabeth herself. As the British soldiers stepped foot in the Netherlands, the queen was signing into law an official pledge to aid the Protestants. This aid was the Treaty of Nonsuch, which declared that the queen wouldn't hesitate to use military force to defend her Protestant allies in the Netherlands. These two daring moves were enough to convince the Spanish Crown to back off, and the northern Netherlands were left in peace.

The queen's actions indicate that although she was very careful to walk a tightrope between the various factions within her own country, when it came to the larger international showdown between Catholics and Protestants, she was more than ready to go on the offensive. At home, though, she was always careful not to antagonize her own citizenry and potentially spark a rebellion by giving too much to the reformers.

On the international stage, this strong stance against Catholicism actually prompted Spain to try and invade England in 1588. But despite all of Spain's power, the Spanish Armada was successfully beaten back by the British navy.

Many Protestants and Puritans alike viewed this success as a sign of divine providence at work. They truly believed that God was on their side.

At any rate, Queen Elizabeth I certainly seemed to be adept at stifling the spread of Catholic power. Even in the Americas, Queen Elizabeth was ready to take on the Spanish at every turn. Although England had yet to create a viable colony at this point, the queen was sure to employ privateers, which is basically just a fancy word for pirates, to roam the high seas near Spanish possessions in the Caribbean and beyond. These private sailors were tough as nails, and they were more than willing to seize Spanish treasure ships and haul the silver, gold, and jewels they acquired from them back to England.

Overall, as it pertains to Protestants far and wide, Elizabeth wasn't a bad ruler to have. After Elizabeth's passing in 1603, the more Puritan-minded faithful became somewhat hopeful in regard to her successor, James Stuart. James Stuart was a champion of the Protestant sect known as the Presbyterians. The Presbyterians hailed from Scotland, and prior to James Stuart being crowned in England, he was the king of Scotland, known as James VI (he became James I after the union of England and Scotland in 1603). As such, he was obviously quite familiar with these Protestants. And upon his arrival to the English throne, the idea that James I would be helpful in the Protestant cause quickly took hold.

Soon enough, Puritan Protestants put together an official petition to get the king to consider their reforms. These efforts resulted in the so-called Hampton Court Conference. King James I proved to be uninterested in most of their notions, although he did agree on one important point—there should be a new English translation of the Bible.

The Puritans were key in getting the king to set in motion the great translation project that would result in the King James Version of the Bible. This was welcomed with open arms by the Puritans, who had been calling for an English version of the Bible for all to be able to freely read for many years. The Puritans, however, did not have the favor of the king when it came to their battle against priestly vestments, and many puritanical Protestants ended up getting booted out of the church simply for declining to wear them.

Some of those belonging to the Puritan wing of the Church of England were influential enough that local clergy secretly made certain compromises just to keep them on board. But such things could not go on forever, and like oil and water, the Puritans in the Church of England soon found themselves separating entirely and creating their very own religious movement. The most assertive of these puritanical faithful began to hold secret meetings in their own homes. These meetings were considered illegal at the time, and the fact that these Puritans did not attend the officially sanctioned Church of England was considered a crime in itself. All it took for one to be prosecuted was for a nosy neighbor or former church member to report their absence, and they would be subjected to punishment. Some even lost their lives, as was the case with reformer Henry Barrow, who was executed in 1593.

Nevertheless, despite the push to conform to the Church of England, King James was a Calvinist, and he supported Calvinist teachings. This support was clearly demonstrated in 1618 when the leading Calvinists of the day held a conference in the Netherlands. The main purpose of the meeting was to discuss the work of one Jacob Arminius. Jacob Arminius hailed from Utrecht, the same part of the Netherlands in which the Protestants of the northern Netherlands had banded together and forged the Union of Utrecht in the face of Catholic aggression. The reason why Jacob Arminius became a matter of debate was over his view that the choices of human beings could shape their destiny and that they did indeed play an active role as it pertained to whether or not they were saved. These views, although perhaps quite commonplace in other Christian groups, absolutely rubbed Calvinists the wrong way. John Calvin's teachings on predestination were quite clear, and Calvinists were to believe that God was the author and finisher of the human story, with men and women being completely unable to change the course of their destiny on their own. Nevertheless, this "reformed Calvinist," as it were, managed to gain a substantial following with his modified teachings of Calvinism, and his unique point of view was dubbed Arminianism.

Yes, once again, there was yet another variation of Christian thought springing forth. And no sooner than it did, critics and detractors came out of the woodwork. Jacob Arminius himself passed away in 1609, but in the ensuing years, his teachings continued to catch on. In order to tackle the so-called Arminianism controversy that had been emerging in Protestant circles, the great minds of Calvinism came together in the Netherlands in 1618.

King James I was sure to send his own representatives to the conference to argue for the complete rejection of Arminianism. Such efforts were most certainly pleasing to those of a Puritan bent. Even though they were not happy with the remnants of Catholic tradition in the Church of England, the knowledge that the overall Calvinist doctrine was being embraced would most certainly have been encouraging.

These positive developments were enough to keep the more vocal voices of the Puritans down, and many were content just to engage in what they called "practical divinity." These efforts focused on teaching the average person Puritan ideals by example without actually going so far as to openly disobey the Church of England.

In that same fateful year of 1618, however, some Puritans felt it expedient to circumvent the will of their king when King James I decided not to back his own son-in-law, Frederick, the king of Bohemia, in his struggle against Catholic forces during the Thirty Years' War. Some Puritans began to raise and send funds of their own accord to this potential Protestant potentate.

However, besides some clandestine efforts such as these, most Puritans were willing to tolerate King James as long as he, in turn, tolerated the main tenants of Calvinism. This mutual toleration of sorts would last for much of King James I's reign. It was at times an uneasy alliance, but it seemed to serve its purpose.

King James positioned himself as the steward of Calvinism, and he stressed that the clergy should be careful not to confuse the laity with the complexity of the doctrine. In 1622, he even went so far as to issue a command that only those who held "a Bachelor of Divinity or higher" would be permitted to teach on predestination in order to safeguard the public from further confusion.

Perhaps King James, who had witnessed plenty of upheaval over various interpretations of predestination, meant well enough, but this directive struck many as an intolerable overreach. Protestants were growing concerned that their religious rights were beginning to be taken away. Without the ability to speak freely and have an open dialogue, what would this mean for spiritual growth? The Puritans, for one, were not going to allow any sovereign to handcuff their faith.

When King James allowed his son Charles to wed a French Catholic princess, many Puritans sensed further trouble lay ahead. And when Charles I came to the throne in 1625 and began practicing Catholicism openly, they felt that their worst fears had been confirmed. It was the arrival of King Charles, in fact, that led many Puritans to seek somewhere farther afield to plant their faith—as far afield as the other side of the Atlantic, to a little-known place called America.

Chapter 3 – How the Puritans Came to America

"For we must consider that we shall be as a city upon a hill. The eyes of all people are upon us. So that if we shall deal falsely with our God in this work we have undertaken, and so cause Him to withdraw His present help from us, we shall be made a story and a by-word throughout the world."

-John Winthrop

Most Americans know the story of the Pilgrims who came to America on a ship called the *Mayflower* and how they made their home in Plymouth in 1620. But many are unaware of just how much religious piety drove these settlers to leave their old world for a completely new one. It wasn't in search of gold or land that the Puritan Pilgrims embarked on this dangerous voyage. Their quest was for religious freedom and the chance to build a society marked by the ideals that they held dear.

Plymouth Colony was only the second successful English colony in America, coming after the previous settlement of Jamestown in what is now the state of Virginia. The wooded backdrop of Plymouth would end up being famously commemorated in America on the Thanksgiving holiday, in remembrance of a time when puritanical Pilgrims and their Native American allies sat down during the fall harvest to have a meal together and give thanks to God.

Although we now know Plymouth to be a city in Massachusetts, it was initially a part of the general colony of New England before separating off into the Massachusetts Bay Colony. The Puritans who settled Plymouth were led by a man named William Bradford. Before even stepping foot on land, the Puritans famously signed the Mayflower Compact, in which they dictated how both the colony and their own individual lives should be run. This document would prove pivotal in the shaping of America itself. It was cited by philosopher John Locke, who made his famed "social contract," which then later influenced the very creation of the Declaration of Independence that gave birth to the United States of America itself. So, to say that the words of the Mayflower Compact were influential would be a bit of an understatement.

Upon landing, the Puritans got to work building up their settlements and putting their principles to practice. Further waves of Puritan migration were in the works in Britain, and by 1630, a Puritan leader named John Winthrop was leading the so-called "Great Migration" of a large Puritan flock to the Massachusetts Bay Colony. It was named as such because of the fact that the colonization enterprise was funded by a group of London-based financiers called the Massachusetts Bay Company.

The amount of money that the Massachusetts Bay Company put on the table for this expedition is said to have totaled what would have been forty million dollars in today's money. The ships that carried these passengers to the New World were fully stocked with everything they could ever need. They were loaded with "soap, candles, tools, utensils, steel, iron, clothing, shoes, house furnishings, sail cloth, cattle, horses, goats, hay for fodder, prayer books and Bibles."

This must have come as some comfort for folks who had to sell their homes and many other belongings to even embark on this trip to a strange new world. This was indeed a major enterprise for anyone to take. As such, the man leading the trip did not want to disappoint. John Winthrop was a middle-aged attorney, an occasional preacher, and a general Protestant crusader. Winthrop was alarmed both at the pressures that puritanical Protestants were facing at home, as well as the inroads Catholicism had been making abroad.

Catholic Spain had claimed much of the Americas long ago, taking over Mexico and Central and South America. This was certainly nothing new. But Winthrop was further alarmed to hear reports of French Catholics thriving in the North American colony of Quebec. Upon his arrival in June of 1630, Winthrop went about the difficult task of creating solidarity among the Puritan settlers, many of whom had come from different backgrounds and different regions of Britain.

Settling in the town of Salem, Winthrop told his colonial congregants that they had not only entered into a covenant with one another but also "with God." Furthermore, it was taught that the New England colony would be a "city upon a hill," one that would inspire those who saw it to imitate it. Winthrop's words were inspired from the biblical Book of Matthew, in which Christ himself told his disciples, "You are the light of the world. A city on a hilltop that cannot be hidden."

Winthrop and his Puritan followers had to forge their world from scratch, building homes and eking out an existence in an uncertain world. But despite making sure that their basic earthly needs were being met, they also had the major challenge of making sure that their spiritual beliefs remained intact as well as they created a "godly kingdom" here on Earth. Over the next few years, these colonists would forge a system of governance in which they would vote for a governor and a mock parliament, which consisted of both an upper and a lower chamber of legislators.

The local houses of worship, in the meantime, were arranged in a similar democratic process, in which church leaders were selected by members of the church. The Puritan colonies, like much of the rest of the world at the time, were ultimately a patriarch society, so when we say "members of the church," we must make it clear that it was only male members who were allowed to have a say in these affairs. And the men of the church were able to not only cast votes for church leaders but also various representatives who would make up what was known as the General Court. It was the General Court that would fashion general laws in regard to how the colony was run and how various affairs of the settlers were handled.

And in order to foster solidarity among the various churches, regular clerical conferences were held in which all of the church leaders could consult with one another about the direction of the general Puritan movement. The main leaders to arise during this time were Thomas Hooker, Roger Williams, and John Cotton. At times, these men disagreed with each other, but they were always able to do so in a fairly civil manner. But even while the Puritan congregations sought solidarity, they did not always conform to the same standard. There would almost always be a slight difference in opinion on certain matters of faith.

In the meantime, many British puritanical faithful began to view their brethren across the Atlantic with some concern and skepticism, wondering if perhaps this sect of Puritanism was drifting toward a new denomination altogether. Nevertheless, the colonial Puritans maintained that they had not changed their aim. Puritan leader John Winthrop made it clear that his intention was for settlers to enter into a covenant with one another and remain strong in the alien world that they now called their home.

As much as John Winthrop encouraged open discourse to prevent conflict, disputes would inevitably arise. Roger Williams, for example, famously caused a ruckus over oath-taking and whether or not colonial leaders had the right to regulate one's activities during the Sabbath. This Puritan was so perturbed over what was going on that he ended up moving to the nearby settlement of Providence (the future capital of Rhode Island) instead.

And the disputes didn't end there. Puritan minister Thomas Shepard had quite a bone to pick with the Protestant reformer Anne Hutchinson. Anne lived in Puritan-controlled Boston with her husband William and their fifteen children. In between taking care of all of her kids, Anne had proven to be quite a preacher. However, not all Puritans agreed with what she had to say, and Thomas Shepard, for one, was most certainly not a fan.

Shephard disapproved of Anne Hutchinson's contention that one could have a direct "spiritual connection with God." Such talked smacked of antinomianism, and Thomas Shepard and other like-minded Puritans believed that such thoughts were in error. They believed that God only directly spoke to biblical figures of the past and that his direct manifestation no longer occurred. For sticklers like Thomas Shepard, those who claimed to have a personal relationship with God were deluded at best or engaged in outright witchcraft at worst.

Those familiar with the Salem witch trials, which we will discuss in more detail shortly, realize just how quickly puritanical accusations of witchcraft can spin out of control, so such characterizations were indeed quite serious. Although most Christians today would view a personal relationship with God as being a good thing, for some of Anne's Puritan contemporaries, even one who claimed a connection to God could be accused of practicing witchcraft. And if they weren't outright calling Anne a witch, they were at the very least suggesting that she was delusional.

Anne and her followers, however, insisted that the Puritans who dismissed the spiritual connection one could have with God were the ones who were deluded. Anne believed that these particular Puritans were blinded by their emphasis on "the role of works." It's ironic that Anne would accuse her brethren of such a flaw since it was in large part due to the Catholic Church's supposed emphasis on works that the Protestant Reformation began in the first place.

Thomas Shepard and his ilk, however, felt that Anne Hutchinson seriously erred by putting too much on the "notion of free grace." Anne, on the other hand, accused her opponents of putting too much emphasis on good works and deeds rather than developing a real relationship with God. Interestingly enough, the only Puritan minister that Anne didn't accuse of being too focused on works was John Cotton, who had previously been her and her husband's personal pastor.

It seems that Anne first began to speak out on her views while working as a midwife. She and the women she regularly worked with would routinely discuss their ideas on religion, and Anne greatly encouraged these thought-provoking talks. John Winthrop would later recall of Anne "that her ordinary talk was about the things of the Kingdom of God." Having said that, most today would quite naturally ask, "Well, what's wrong with that?"

But the problem wasn't that she was talking about God but rather the subject matter she chose. At any rate, Anne was soon having regular gatherings at her house, in which she elaborated further on her beliefs and interpretation of the scripture. Initially, the attendees were mostly midwives like herself, but soon, many more began to hear of her teachings. And ultimately, both men and women regularly packed her house to hear her preach.

The two sides of this debate were increasingly at each other's throats while those caught ideologically in between, such as the more centrist John Winthrop, tried their best to find some sort of middle ground. It proved to be an impossible task. And as soon as Thomas Shepard and his hardliners gained the upper hand, they saw to it that Anne received an official excommunication and was booted right on out of the colony.

Anne, like Roger Williams before her, headed to Providence, along with her family, and created outposts in what would one day become Rhode Island. Unfortunately, Anne's life did not end very well. After staying for a time in Providence, she set up shop in the settlement of Eastchester, near the site of modern-day New York. It was here that she and her whole family met foul play at the hands of a local Native American tribe.

At any rate, internal divisions such as what occurred with Anne Hutchinson did indeed surface among the Puritans from time to time. Although the Puritans had fled from religious persecution, they were hesitant to show much in the way of tolerance when religious differences of opinion arose.

Along with these internal conflicts, the Puritan-based colonies also dealt with external conflicts as well. They faced pressures from both the Dutch, who controlled the colony of New Netherland (now New York), and several groups of Native Americans. For the Puritans settled along the Connecticut River, things became so bad that open conflict erupted with a tribe of Native Americans called the Pequot in the year 1636.

The war was basically the culmination of tensions that had been building in the region over trade, scarcity of resources, and various skirmishes that had broken out. The Puritans managed to get other local Native American tribes to side with them against the Pequot. Despite their advantage in numbers and knowledge of the terrain, the war ended up going badly for the Pequot, and once the fighting had ceased, their power was greatly diminished.

Despite the conflict, that same year, the first steps were made to establish a Puritan-backed school of learning, which would ultimately become Harvard University. The school itself was modeled after the prestigious English institution of higher learning Cambridge University. In fact, the very settlement in which Harvard was built was dubbed "Cambridge" in honor of that fact. The school originally had a heavy focus on creating ministers for the faith, but it also put a spotlight on general academia as well. At any rate, anyone who attended Harvard in Cambridge, Massachusetts, has the Puritans of the Massachusetts Bay Colony to thank for it.

The Puritans certainly had their difficulties in the colonies. But even more pressing for the American Puritans was the threat of the English Crown. At this time, the archbishop of Canterbury, one William Laud, had become practically hellbent on scaling back Puritan immigration to America. He had even openly sought to have the Massachusetts charter rescinded. The Puritans, in the meantime, feared that they would have a royal governor, who would be completely indifferent to their concerns, foisted upon them. This threat seemed to disappear when the British government became far too distracted by its own inner turmoil to bother with the Puritan colonists. For it was around this time that England would become drawn into a series of bloody civil wars. King Charles I had developed an increasingly antagonistic relationship with the British Parliament. Members of Parliament had long been skeptical about King Charles's motives, and the general public resented the fact that he was married to a woman with a Catholic background, Queen Henrietta Maria of France.

Things came to a head when King Charles attempted to throw some of his parliamentary opponents in prison. The keyword here is "attempt" since the king failed to seize his enemies. Instead, they were tipped off as to what was happening and made a break for it. It was on the heels of their escape and after the rest of Parliament learned what had happened that England turned into a country of basically two armed camps—those willing to fight for Parliament and those willing to fight for King Charles. These two sides began to face off against each other in 1642.

As the conflict heated up, King Charles I had firm control of northern England, Wales, the Midlands, and the West Country. Parliament, on the other hand, had control of London, the surrounding southeastern portion of the country, and East Anglia. They also had a trump card at their disposal, as they had the backing of the English navy. After several skirmishes, the war was essentially a stalemate by 1644. In an effort to come to a diplomatic solution, King Charles managed to hold a new session of Parliament where he was stationed in Oxford.

The results were not satisfactory, however, and the fighting continued. Oxford was then laid siege to by parliamentary forces in 1646, and the king himself just barely managed to escape. He fled to the north, where he was hidden by loyal Scots for several months. Parliament eventually managed to convince the Scots to hand him over. King Charles I was then made prisoner in January of 1647. Because religious questions played as much of a role as political ones during this conflict, many have dubbed the English Civil War as the "War of Religion."

And as it pertains to the Puritans, many leading English Puritans did indeed side with the parliamentarians against the Catholic-influenced king, whom they held in low regard. As such, some have even gone so far as to term the conflict as being a "Puritan Revolution" of sorts, in which zealous Puritans commandeered the power of Parliament to purify England of its most obvious signs of Catholic influence—the king himself.

During the course of the conflict, Puritans also made sure that they had new legislation brought to Parliament, calling for a further reformation of the English church. The Puritans of England themselves remained splintered as to the best course to follow in regard to reforms, though. One faction of English Puritans was convinced that they should emulate the popular reforms that had been carried out by Presbyterian clergy, while others were advocates of so-called "Congregationalism," which imitated that old Puritan shining city on a hill—New England.

In the meantime, all of those in Parliament were gravely concerned should any one of these factions gain dominance, lest they come to lord it over the rest. This had commonly been the case throughout the course of all reformation movements in the past. As soon as one Protestant strain became prominent, it wasn't long before they began to persecute the rest. Time and time again, the previously persecuted religious minority rose up to become the number one persecutor.

Parliament was worried about a sudden repeat of history due to a lack of "central control" when it came to matters of faith. Many today are not aware of this learned trauma of England and other European nations during the Reformation, but it was most certainly on the minds of America's later founders. It is for this reason that the concept of the freedom of religion was so important to them, as well as the concept of the separation of church and state. Many today interpret the separation of church and state to mean keeping religion out of government, but the main focus was actually to keep the state out of religion. The Founding Fathers did not want to repeat the problems caused by the Church of England, and they did not want to establish a "Church of America" that would dictate what religious rules everyone should follow. It was therefore deemed that the best approach for society was to have a complete separation of church and state, preventing the government from dictating how churches should conduct themselves.

In the aftermath of King Charles I's house arrest, a radicalized element of the king's opposition called the Levelers began to demand the "freedom of religion" for England. But before these plans could come to fruition, in 1648, King Charles escaped from his confines and managed to independently reach out to the Scotts, and he convinced them to side with him once more. This led to the so-called Second English Civil War, which erupted between the king and Parliament. This time around, the king was even less successful and was rather quickly defeated. He was then captured for a second time.

Not taking any chances, his opponents put him on trial and subsequently sentenced him to death. King Charles I's death sentence was carried out in January of 1649. This then led to Parliament attempting to forge a commonwealth, but the fickleness of the parliamentarians led to one too many disagreements, and the whole thing threatened to come undone. Stepping into this chaos was Oliver Cromwell, who seized power in 1653 and created the Protectorate of England.

Styling himself as the Lord Protector of England, Cromwell was essentially little more than a dictator. Cromwell was also a Puritan. Oliver Cromwell first came to prominence during the First English Civil War and had become a leading military commander by the time of the second one. Cromwell was pivotal when it came to reining in the Scotts and allowing for King Charles to be taken into custody. And since Cromwell was himself a Puritan, he considered it imperative to purify England of the vestiges of Catholicism. He saw himself as God's own tool in this enterprise, and he firmly believed that he was put in place uniquely for that very purpose.

Cromwell is sometimes referred to as a "reluctant" dictator. He was not an elected official and had merely seized power after the king had been deposed. Cromwell himself often spoke that he didn't want to rule England and that his reign was a reluctant one forged out of necessity.

Interestingly enough, Cromwell still remains a polarizing figure among the British public, with some likening him to an evil usurper and others insisting that he was more akin to a guardian figure. And just as his title implied, he was indeed a "Lord Protector" of the realm. At any rate, once he had power, he didn't hesitate to use it as it pertained to religious affairs.

Cromwell was also at the forefront of what had become a kind of Protestant crusade against the Catholic power of Spain. It was under Cromwell that Jamaica was seized from Spain and brought into the British fold. At home, meanwhile, Cromwell was an important Protestant reformer who sought out the help of Congregationalists and the more centrist among the Presbyterians in order to find some common ground.

In 1646, Cromwell issued the Westminster Confession of Faith, which dictated that the particular brand of Calvinist doctrine that was so pleasing to both Presbyterians and Puritans alike became the religious law of the land. Also, Puritans were politically rewarded with an increasing number of seats in Parliament.

As one might imagine, the fact that the Puritans were being treated so favorably did not sit well with those who were opposed to Puritan ideals. These opponents may have been temporarily sidelined by the new reforms, but they were just biding their time and waiting for the right time to strike. And upon Cromwell's sudden and abrupt death in 1658, yet another religious reckoning would arrive.

Chapter 4 – Puritan Paradise Lost

"In all your course, walk with God and follow Christ as a little, poor, helpless child, taking hold of Christ's hand, keeping your eye on the mark of the wounds on his hands and side, whence came the blood that cleanses you from sin and hiding your nakedness under the skirt of the white shining robe of his righteousness."

-Jonathan Edwards

After the death of Oliver Cromwell, a struggle for the control of England ensued that ultimately ended up inviting the son of Charles I, Charles II, to come to the throne in the year 1660. Interestingly, it was not the new king but rather Parliament that began to move against the English Puritans. The Church of England regained much of its authority, and the Puritans were relegated to the fringes as dissenters who refused to conform. Even as Puritans were facing renewed persecution in England, back in the British colonies in America, the opposite was the case.

The Puritans who ran the roost in the colonies were becoming increasingly intolerant to other faiths. Most notably, when the Quakers began to emigrate to America in the 1650s, the Puritans, who were often their neighbors, began to persecute them for their religious beliefs.

One of the most famous of these cases occurred when a Quaker woman by the name of Mary Dyer was given a death sentence simply for speaking to others about her faith. Despite the risks, Mary had frequently preached to others about Quaker beliefs in the Puritan enclave of Boston. She was arrested and ultimately led to the gallows as punishment for her unsanctioned evangelizing. Before her death, she was told that if she would simply swear an oath that she would desist from preaching her Quaker beliefs, she would be spared. One must wonder if this was a particularly cruel trick on the part of her Puritan prosecutors since they knew full well that as part of their faith, Quakers refused to swear oaths.

Predictably enough, Mary Dyer refused as well, and she was subsequently hanged. Many were disturbed by what had happened to Dyer, and by the time the story reached England, King Charles II was moved enough to do something about it. In 1661, he launched an official edict to all who resided in

Massachusetts Bay to cease and desist with any executions of Quakers on the specific orders of the king. In addition to this, a royal commission was dispatched to the colonies to check on colonial authorities and make sure that they were not overstepping their bounds.

Among other things, this commission made sure that the Puritans were not excluding other religious denominations from communion. This pressure to be more accepting of other religious denominations, along with the economic boom of the colonies, opened up the doors for religious settlers of all kinds to make their way to the colonial settlements in New England. This new influx led to social conflicts in many of the colonial communities. Although outright persecution of other faiths had been banned, resentment continued to simmer just underneath the surface.

Nevertheless, there would be external threats that would bring further tension to the colonists. This was the case in 1675 when Native American tribes launched large-scale attacks in the New England area in what was later termed King Philip's War. It was named after one of the main agitators, Chief Metacomet, sometimes known simply as Metacom, who had been given the nickname of King Philip.

Metacom had apparently come to the conclusion that the European settlers had simply become too numerous, and he rightfully recognized that the growing number of settlers was becoming a threat to his tribe's very existence. Despite previously friendly relations, Metacom essentially launched what could be considered a preemptive strike against the burgeoning Puritan population.

During the course of this conflict, local tribes launched several raids against the colonists, as well as the tribes with whom they had remained allied. During the course of these raids, some six hundred colonists would lose their lives, and several settlements would be destroyed. It is said, in fact, that during the conflict, which would last until 1678, at least twelve settlements were completely annihilated, and a whopping 10 percent of the total population of the colony was wiped out.

The Puritans, falling back on their beliefs during this difficult time, of course, came to consider their problems were somehow related to their faith. Many developed the firm conviction that what had happened to them was somehow a direct punishment from God. It is not hard to understand why the Puritans and other Protestants might consider a disaster such as this as being some sort of divine retribution. All they had to do was look at the Old Testament and read through the testimonies of biblical prophets who, at different times in the nation of Israel's existence, claimed that it was God's punishment being unleashed upon them when neighboring tribes attacked.

Just like the Israelites were ready to ascribe blame for hardship, the Puritans too began to openly wonder if they had committed some collective sin for which they were being punished. One of the Puritan preachers who championed this view, Increase Mather, was a native-born Puritan of the Massachusetts Bay Colony. Having "Increase" as a first name might seem a little strange to the modern reader, but there was indeed a reason behind it. His parents had been quite steeped in scripture at the time of his birth, and knowing that the Hebrew form of Joseph, *Yosef*, translated into English literally means "Increase," they decided to name their child Increase in honor of that fact. Naming kids either Yosef or the anglicized version of Joseph is common, but actually naming them the English translation of the original Hebrew is indeed a rarity in modern times. Among the Puritans, however, such things were commonplace.

At any rate, Increase Mather, whose parents arrived with that great exodus from England to the Massachusetts Bay Colony in 1630, was among the first generation of Puritans to be born in a New England settlement. He grew up during the good times of the early settlement, during which Puritan Pilgrims and Native Americans lived in relative harmony. This was then juxtaposed with the horrific experience of King Philip's War and the terror it brought about.

In the aftermath, Increase Mather was one of the Puritan leaders who did not hesitate to put forth the claim that they were suffering due to a lack of spiritual renewal. Increase Mather, whose name literally signifies an increase of blessing, sought to renew and increase the spiritual blessings of the Puritan Protestants. Increase believed that God sent various judgments upon the people in order to get them back on track, and he considered the recent hardships as a sign that the Puritans of America needed to change course.

The colonies of New England were indeed vulnerable, but it wasn't the local tribes that the colonists feared the most but rather the English government back home. After Cromwell's death, many of the gains the Puritans had made in England were rolled back under King Charles II, and when Charles II was succeeded by King James II in 1685, this new king applied even more pressure. This time, the king's efforts were directed on the New England Puritans themselves, for it was King James II who decided to completely revoke the Massachusetts Bay charter altogether. King James II then opted to establish the Dominion of New England in which all of the established colonies, along with New Jersey and New York, were combined into one overarching dominion of the Crown. This meant that there would be a royal-appointed governor general to oversee everything and that there would no longer be any democratically elected legislative bodies put in place to represent the colonists.

Even worse, and much to the chagrin of the Puritans, was the forced introduction of the hated *Book of Common Prayer*. The *Book of Common Prayer* was the official standard liturgy of the Church of England at the time, and once it was put in force, everyone was expected to adhere to it. This was most definitely not the direction that the Puritan colonists wanted to be going in. And what galled them the most was the fact that their own town meetings—the lifeblood of the Congregationalists—had been curtailed, strictly controlled, and monitored.

It was indeed particularly distressing to the Puritans that even in the New World, which they had immigrated to in order to freely practice their religious beliefs, they were not immune to the long reach of a determined enough English king. And as if all this wasn't enough, King James II was himself a practicing Catholic, which only fueled suspicions that Protestant Puritans were going to be suppressed to the point of ceasing to be a distinct body within the Church of England.

But as paranoid as the New England Puritans might have been in contemplating the machinations of their sovereign, the Puritans in England were ready to overthrow King James II outright. The incident that managed to send James II's opposition over the edge was the news that his wife had given birth to a son named James Francis Edward. Normally, the birth of a royal heir would have been a joyous occasion. But the idea of a James III on the throne, who would potentially continue on the same course as his father, was not something that was looked forward to, especially since it had been previously stated that James II would transfer power to his Protestant daughter, Mary, thereby making her Protestant husband, William of Orange, the king. It was this promise that had made things at least somewhat tolerable to the Protestants of England, and most were content to wait for that day to arrive. But when it was learned that Mary was going to be pushed out of the way in favor of a child who would be raised in the Catholic faith, it was too much for the opposition to tolerate.

Fed up with the way things were going, Parliament actually contacted William of Orange (Orange is a region in southern France) behind King James II's back and invited him to come to England and remove King James II by force. William of Orange leaped at the invitation, arriving on British shores with fourteen thousand troops at his disposal. This was enough to frighten King James into abdicating, and he sought refuge in France. William of Orange was then made the new king of England, christened King William III in 1689.

That same year, back in the New England colonies, a major revolt in Boston, known as the "Bloodless Revolution," managed to break the iron grip of New England's dominion status. In later years, Boston would become the centerpiece of many protests of English governance, culminating in the infamous Boston Tea Party of 1773. At this point in time, though, the king may have been a bit too distracted due to the fact that fighting had erupted between the British and the French in what is now the Canadian provinces of Nova Scotia and Quebec.

King William III, who came to the throne with way too much on his plate, was not willing to duke it out with the colonists as well. Instead, he readily agreed in 1691 to allow the New England settlements to break back into their various distinct identities, with the sole exception of Plymouth, which was absorbed into Massachusetts.

But although the Puritans had regained some influence, they did not have the political power that they previously did. It was still a time of great uncertainty in regard to what direction the colonies would go. New arrivals, who came with new ideas on both religion and civic life alike, were threatening to change the way things had been done.

In other words, the Puritan monopoly of New England was at an end. And it was during this time of high anxiety that a court packed with Puritan agitators in Salem, Massachusetts, would begin the most sensational court proceedings in history, known simply as the Salem witch trials.

Chapter 5 – The Witch Trials in Salem

"Let them no more say, God must do all, we can do nothing, and so encourage themselves to live in a careless neglect of God, and of their own souls, and salvation. Most certainly, although we cannot say, that if men improve their natural abilities as they ought to do, that grace will infallibly follow, yet there will not one sinner, in all the reprobate world, stand forth at the day of judgment, and say, Lord, thou knowest I did all that possibly I could do, for the obtaining grace, and for all that, thou didst withhold it from me."

-Increase Mather

If someone today were to accuse you of being a witch, you might give them a strange look and perhaps even let out a nervous laugh, but in 1692, in Salem, Massachusetts, such things were no laughing matter at all. Witches were not some cardboard cutouts from some Halloween make-believe world; for the Puritans, witches and the concept of witchcraft were quite real. They looked to none other than the biblical accounts of witchery, such as when Israel's King Saul consulted the Witch of Endor, to verify that witches were indeed a force that they had to contend with.

In the Old Testament, there is a clear account of witchcraft that takes place when a very troubled King Saul seeks to summon the spirit of the dead prophet Samuel. Previously, Samuel had been King Saul's guiding light, but after his passing, King Saul fell on hard times and sought advice. Although God had forbidden the practice of the occult, Saul, in his desperation for answers, secretly met with a witch who—according to the Bible—was indeed successful in summoning the spirit of Saul.

The prophet was none too happy that his rest was disturbed, and he chastised Saul for using the arcane arts to find answers to his problems. This biblical account indicates that sorcery and witchcraft are indeed real; it's just that God has forbidden human beings from engaging in any of it. The Bible strongly cautions against humans meddling with forces that might be too powerful to fully understand.

Having said that, the Puritans would have used the Bible as a reference when considering the possibility of a real-life witch in their midst in Salem.

The Puritans believed the scriptures, and since the scriptures indicate that witches are real and, in some instances, could even summon spirits of the dead, the Puritans, therefore, believed this was real as well. And since the scriptures clearly condemn the practice of these dark arts, the Puritans likewise condemned anyone who they suspected of witchcraft.

And in the remote, rugged world in which they lived, late at night as the wind blew through the trees and animals could be heard scurrying about, it wasn't hard to imagine that witches might be on the loose. The Puritans believed in the forces of good and evil. They believed that some were influenced by evil, but others had good on their side. Of course, such beliefs were entirely dependent on the other person's perspective. The Puritan preacher Samuel Parris, for one, thought that he was on the side of good.

Parris had founded a Puritan church in Salem Village in 1689. It's important to note the distinction between what was then known as Salem Village and Salem Town. Both areas are part of Salem, but they represent two very different sections of the settlement. Salem Town was situated on the eastern shores of Salem proper, and it had a bustling port where all manner of goods were traded back and forth across the Atlantic. Due to the commercial success of Salem Town, many of Salem's more affluent individuals began to pour into this district.

The section of Salem known as Salem Village, however, was much more backward, with ramshackle housing. After a period of decline, it became known as a haven for the poorer classes. Life in Salem Village was much harder than it was for those who lived near the harbor in Salem Town. Most of the residents of Salem Village were farmers, and when their farms failed to produce enough revenue for them to get by, they often turned to religion for answers. Was there a divine judgment at work to explain these crop failures? It wouldn't have been at all unusual for someone in Salem Village to think such thoughts.

The church founded by Samuel Parris would have been the main focal point for most of the Salem villagers. They turned to their pastor for guidance during times of hardship and difficulty, and they also looked to him for moral guidance and how they should conduct themselves.

After being installed as the new arbiter of morality in Salem Village, Samuel Parris rapidly developed a reputation of being a strict and stern disciplinarian. Some were resentful of this fact, especially some of the newcomers to Salem Village, but Parris stood firm. And for some, rather than being repelled by his preaching, they were drawn to them. These were hard, uncertain times. New England was still recovering from the rampant depredations of King Philip's War, along with the recent ravages of King

James II's war with the French, coupled with the ever-changing order of how the colonies were administrated. The Puritans still had influence, but they were no longer the sole authority.

It was in the midst of all of this uncertainty that people began to literally look for signs of the devil at work. And when Samuel Parris took to the pulpit and claimed that the devil was "in their homes," that the devil was in "their farms," and even "in their church," they believed him! Parris himself would then become the center of the evil that he so often spoke of when his nine-year-old daughter Betty and his eleven-year-old niece Abigail Williams appeared to be afflicted by an unseen force. They screamed, fell to the ground, writhed, and rolled across the floor, claiming that some unseen entity was biting, scratching, and hitting them. The whole village was on high alert for such happenings, especially after Cotton Mather—the son of Increase Mather—published his famous book *Memorable Providences*, which discussed in depth supposed signs of witchcraft.

In the centuries since these young girls erupted into these spells and fits, many have tried to figure out just what might have brought it all on. The most common explanation offered today is that the girls were simply faking their affliction to get attention. These girls lived a lonely life of drudgery. Brought up in the hard frontier country of America, their days consisted of a long list of chores and manual labor around the house and surrounding property. The best they could hope for in life was to marry well, as a man with means might be able to ease their burdens in their later years. These girls got up early, worked hard, said their prayers, and went to bed early before starting their routine all over again. Perhaps they were craving a break from the monotony and desired to be the center of attention. It's not too hard to understand why they may have felt this way; it's just mind-boggling that they would go to such extreme lengths to get it.

Nevertheless, if the whole thing really was a ploy to get attention, the girls were most likely caught up in their own game and unable to admit the truth lest they become severely punished for their deception. It very well could be that the whole thing simply spiraled out of control, and once the mischief had begun, no one—not even the ones behind it—were able to stop it.

Frantically trying to get answers from the young girls as to what was the matter, Parris learned from them that they had been engaging in superstitious activities with his servant, an old Native American woman by the name of Tituba. They claimed that Tituba had engaged in acts of divination, such as dropping an egg in a glass of water and then interpreting what the congealing egg yolk might mean. Such things probably sound silly to us today, but back then, it was a big deal. And when Reverend Parris learned that two other girls in Salem—Ann Putnam Jr. and Betty Hubbard—were displaying similar afflictions, folks began to think that the whole town was suddenly under siege by dark forces. Ann and Betty were then soon followed by another pair of girls, Mary Walcott and Mercy Lewis, who also came forward with the same exact symptoms.

The fact that so many girls came forward makes the idea that they were just lying for attention a little harder to entertain. It's not to say that the girls didn't fake it—they most certainly could have. It could very well be that they all had the same friend groups and had quietly confided in one another as to what they planned to do. The Putnam family, for one, was quite close to Reverend Parris and his family, so it wouldn't be hard to imagine these girls all getting together to discuss what they were going to do.

But nevertheless, the more bewitched girls you add to the mix, the harder it is to say with certainty that every single one of them was simply putting on a show for the villagers. With so many girls behaving in this fashion, it goes from just a couple of girls deceiving their elders to a much more elaborate plot of several girls working in tandem. Again, this very well could be the case, but it certainly complicates matters.

Then again, there are other explanations that have been offered. Because while some believe that the girls were making it all up just to get attention or even as a means to lash out at villagers they didn't like, others have theorized that perhaps they suffered from mental illness or even a common affliction brought on by some sort of food poisoning that caused them all to hallucinate. And although it's probably the least popular premise in modern times, there are those who still might consider that perhaps some supernatural force really was afoot.

At any rate, as the "bewitched" girls continued to speak to town leaders, the list of people they accused continued to grow. And by February of 1692, they had three women in their sights. Along with Tituba, they also accused a lady named Sarah Good, who was essentially a down-and-out beggar who depended on the kindness of her neighbors for meals and a roof over her head. Another woman that they claimed was a witch was Sarah Osborne, a woman who tended to stay home from church—something that was frowned upon by the villagers.

The common thread between all three of these women was that they were all on the fringes of Puritan society. The servant Tituba, due to her background and status as a servant, was an obvious outsider to the Puritans. Sarah Good was someone who didn't work and went from home to home. She was an object of scorn among her peers. She initially came from an affluent family, but after her dad—a well-to-do innkeeper—committed suicide some twenty years prior, Sarah Good fell on hard times and never quite recovered.

Sarah Osborne had a complicated and what many of her neighbors viewed as a "scandalous" past. At one time, she was a prominent member of the community, and she and her husband, Robert Prince, owned some 150 acres of farmland. After her husband died, Sarah shocked her neighbors by taking out some fifteen pounds (British money) to "buy" an indentured Irish servant by the name of Alexander.

Many today are not aware of the practice, but indentured servitude in those days was quite common. It was expensive to travel from Britain to America, so some who did not have the immediate means to pay for their trip agreed to sign a contract that would make them an indentured servant for so many years in order to pay for their trip across the ocean. Alexander had apparently agreed to just such a bargain, and he planned to work for Sarah Osborne in a state of indentured servitude until his debt was paid off. If this wasn't enough to get the Salem villagers talking, what she did once he paid his dues really got their tongues wagging. To their shock, she actually married the young man. This caused the neighborhood gossips to run wild for a variety of reasons, but most importantly, they focused on the perception that Sarah must have been intimately involved with her indentured servant before she married him. Just imagine Sarah Osborne at the local market or seated in a church pew with gossipy locals behind her, whispering of what they believed to be scandal of the highest magnitude. Just put yourself in Sarah Osborne's shoes, having to sit back and listen to people say things like, "Oh did you hear about what Sarah Osborne did? She bought a man for fifteen pounds and then married him!"

Yes, one can only imagine how difficult it became for Sarah, having to deal with this constant stream of gossip. It was so difficult, in fact, that she stopped attending church and going to many other social gatherings. But as is always the case, the more she isolated herself, the more people talked about her. This caused people to openly speculate and wonder what she did with her time. Quite frankly, the villagers simply thought she was weird. And the town gossips perhaps had already openly commented that she was a witch as it was, so it probably didn't come as much of a surprise when the "bewitched" girls proclaimed this to be the case.

At any rate, the following month, all three of these accused women were hauled off to jail so that they could be interrogated. Isolated and alone before their accusers, they were all asked the same repetitive questions, such as "Are you a witch?" "Have you seen the devil?" "What did the devil tell you?" and the like.

No matter how many times one protested that they were not a witch and did not speak to Satan, the interrogators persisted, trying to get them to crack under pressure. As for one of the women—Tituba—it wasn't hard at all to get her to admit that she was a witch. Tituba, in fact, soon openly admitted engaging in all manner of witchcraft and magic. It is important to remember that due to Tituba's religious background, which included ancestral shamanism, some of her ancestral religious beliefs would indeed equate to witchcraft in the eyes of the Puritans. And even if she did not engage in some of the things she claimed, it seems that Tituba was clever enough to realize that the more she told her interrogators, the happier they were, so she readily obliged them. And her accounts were quite incredible to hear.

She said that a tall, dark figure would visit her in the middle of the night. She claimed that he would also shapeshift into a "great black dog." This demonic entity apparently began hassling Tituba to "sign his book" and pressured her to serve him. This interaction seems to borrow from a mixture of both Christian and ancestral lore. Many Native American tribes believe in beings who are shapeshifters. The Navajo tradition of "skin-walkers," for example, is one of the more famous manifestations of this belief.

Thrown into the mix with this shapeshifting entity, at least according to Tituba's account, was a kind of evil counterfeit of the Christian Book of Life. Christians believe that all who are saved have their name written in the Book of Life. This demonic entity, however, supposedly wanted Tituba to sign her name not into the Book of Life but in a book reserved for death and the damned. A book that she said she signed with her own blood.

The most troubling thing about Tituba's testimony is the fact that she readily implicated the other accused women. If she was making things up to save herself, it would be one thing, but she also began to openly claim that Sarah Good and Sarah Osborne were her accomplices. She stated that she and the other two women had all rode through the air on wooden "poles." In other words, she claimed that she and the other women rode on broomsticks in true, classic witch fashion. Tituba went on the record to state, "I ride upon a stick or pole and Good and Osborne behind me. We ride taking hold of one another. I don't know how we go for I saw no trees nor path, but was presently there."

And fantastical as all of these claims were, it wasn't hard for the Puritans, steeped in their religious beliefs, to consider that these tales were true. All of these women were on the fringes of society, and claims of them delving into the dark arts were not too surprising to the superstitious-minded Puritans. To believe that a poor beggar, a shunned outcast, and an indigenous woman were witches wouldn't have been much of a stretch for them at all.

But on March 11th, 1692, when the bewitched young girls began to accuse Martha Corey, a well-respected Puritan woman, of being a witch, the situation became downright scary for the villagers of Salem. If Martha could be a witch, then anyone could be a witch. Now, many were beginning to take the words of the Puritan preacher Samuel Parris quite seriously, for it seemed that evil truly was lurking around every corner.

The interesting thing about Martha Corey is that she was one of the few townspeople to voice her concerns that perhaps the girls were making things up. She had openly wondered if the young women's claims were more the product of make-believe than real supernatural happenings. It was shortly after she expressed her doubts of the girls' claims that they turned their ire upon her and began to accuse her of also being a witch. This has led some to wonder if perhaps the girls made up stories about Martha Corey as a means of revenge for her lack of belief.

Upon being accused, Maratha Corey stood firm and famously declared, "I never had to do with witchcraft since I was born." However, it didn't matter how many times she denied being a witch; she was declared to be one regardless, and she ended up losing her life as a result of this false (at least most would consider it false) charge against her. In the end, despite all of her cries of being innocent of the charges leveled against her, Martha Corey was hung in the town square that September for all of the Puritans to see. This sent shockwaves through the Puritan community, and many began to fear both that their neighbors might be engaging in witchcraft and that they themselves might somehow be accused of being a witch.

Many soon realized that the best way to avoid suspicion would be to seem that they were actively on the offensive against witches. Soon, pretty much the whole community was aiding Puritan leaders in hunting for witches in Salem. Yes, the witch hunt had truly begun. Both women and men were brought in for questioning about their daily routines, with interrogators probing every aspect of their lives as they looked into the possibility that these accused just might be seeking an audience with Satan.

Incredibly enough, even little kids were accused of witchcraft, and at one point, Sarah Good's four-year-old daughter was even taken in on charges of being a witch. Soon, the local jail was so crowded that there wasn't even enough food to feed all of the prisoners. As such, some actually starved to death before their case went to trial. Others died of contagious maladies that they picked up from fellow prisoners.

By May 1692, Massachusetts Governor William Phips convened a court that would try these accused witches, which was called the Court of Oyer and Terminer. This was a Latin phrase that means "to hear and decide." It is important to note that by this time, girls were no longer the only accusers of witchcraft. Friend had turned against friend and neighbor against neighbor to avoid having accusations thrown at them. Women were not the only ones accused either, as men were not spared from the witch hunt. However, women were accused more often than men.

The first to stand before this court was a woman named Bridget Bishop. Bridget, by all means, was at odds with typical Puritan life. She was a woman who seemed to often flout Puritan rules and traditions. She was a heavy drinker, played games of chance, and liked to wear clothing that defied Puritan convention. Her accusers put forth the claim that Bridget had made herself known to them in "spectral" form. The girls claimed that Bridget would send her invisible specter to them and would hit, kick, bite, and otherwise torment them. They claimed that she was doing this even while testifying in the courtroom in front of the magistrates.

The magistrates demanded to know how Bridget was appearing before the girls in spectral form and how she was afflicting such torment upon them. All manner of accusations were heaped upon Bridget. Among other things, it was also claimed that Bridget had the uncanny ability of "transforming into a cat." As mentioned earlier, the concept of shapeshifting, along with broomstick riding, had become an established facet of witchcraft lore.

Upon hearing of the charges leveled against her, Bridget, of course, was just as confused as anyone else, and she insisted that she didn't know what they were talking about. Despite her protestations of innocence, she was given the hangman's noose all the same. In fact, she was the first person to be killed during the trials, dying on the gallows in June 1692.

The interesting thing about how the Puritans conducted the Salem witch trials is the fact that it encouraged false confessions. Those who openly confessed to being witches were often spared, whereas those who steadfastly proclaimed their innocence were often killed. Ironically, it was the very Puritan principles of honesty that led many innocent men and women to their graves. Those with less integrity readily lied about being witches and even about others being witches if it meant that their own life would be spared.

The truly honest and devout Puritans, in the meantime, would not falsely claim to be a witch even if their life—quite literally—depended on it. Bridget Bishop, for one, claimed her innocence up to her last breath, proclaiming, "I have done no witchcraft. I am as innocent as the child unborn." Yet, as much as we today tend to sympathize with these victims of the Salem witch trials, it is important to note that their prosecutors often believed just as firmly in their cause, no matter how deluded we today might think it may have been. This is evidenced by a letter sent from Cotton Mather to his uncle, John Cotton Jr., which seemed to extoll the virtue of what was happening at the time. As the witch trials heated up, Cotton Mather wrote, "Our good God is working of miracles. Five witches were lately executed. Immediately upon this, our God miraculously sent in five Andover witches." Miracles indeed.

Chapter 6 – The Salem Witch Trials Continue and a Puritan Witch Hunt Ensues

"It is absurd to think that anything in us could have the least influence upon our election. Some say that God did foresee that such persons would believe, and therefore did choose them; so they would make the business of salvation to depend upon something in us. Whereas God does not choose us for faith, but to faith. 'He hath chosen us, that we should be holy' (Ephesians 1:4). Not because we would be holy, but that we might be holy. We are elected to boldness, not for it."

-Thomas Watson

As the Salem witch trials progressed, it soon became clear that literally no one was safe from being accused of witchcraft. This was evidenced when a minister of the Puritan faith, George Burroughs, was accused of being a witch. And he was not only accused of being a witch but also of being a so-called "ringleader of witches." It would have been bad enough to be a witch, but to be their ringleader?

George may have had some among the Puritans who did not care for him, but he was an upstanding citizen by their own standards. This made the accusations being leveled against him all the more shocking. George Burroughs was brought in for interrogation before Puritan judges in April of 1692.

The signs of enchantment that his accusers presented were a bit bizarre, to say the least. One claimed that George had recently exhibited "inhuman feats of strength" due to the fact that he was able to lift up a musket by "inserting his finger into the barrel." He was also criticized for his failure to baptize his kids, among other things. Some also even claimed that Burroughs had the decidedly witch-like ability of flying. All folks had to do was picture Burroughs perched on top of a broom or with his finger in a musket, and they believed that he could be a witch.

In the end, George Burroughs was marched to the gallows and hung on August 19th, 1692. Just prior to his killing, he was heard reciting the Lord's

Prayer. The fact that he did so successfully was important, as the witch hunters claimed that someone who was a witch would be unable to do so. Some in the crowd were dismayed by this and openly wondered if perhaps Burroughs was innocent after all. Firebrand Puritan preacher Cotton Mather was on the scene, however, and he was quick to remind everyone that Burroughs had been, in his words, "convicted in a court of law."

The Salem witch trials serve as a reminder that a "court of law" heavily skewed by public opinion and mob-like instincts is not always a court of justice. In at least one case, when an accused woman by the name of Rebecca Nurse was found to be not guilty, the judge actually overruled the jury and declared that she was guilty. Rebecca had been accused by a powerful Puritan family who held a grudge against her, and apparently, their word was deemed to be better than hers. Or, for that matter, even the word of some thirty-nine people who put their names on a petition, demanding her release. The petition contained a statement, which read, "We never had any cause or grounds to suspect her [Rebecca Nurse] of any such thing as she is now accused." Nevertheless, she, too, was executed.

The fact that the presiding Judge, William Stoughton, intervened tells us a few things. It shows us that this trial by jury was not fair in the least, but it also indicates that those in charge knew that if Rebecca Nurse was found not guilty, it would serve to delegitimize many other cases. This was due to the fact that the bewitched girls had carried on with their antics, claiming that Nurse was spectrally attacking them just as they did with all of the others. If the girls who accused Nurse were somehow wrong, mistaken, or worse—flat-out lying—what did that mean for all the other people they had so dramatically accused prior to Nurse?

Those in charge knew that if Rebeca Nurse was let off the hook, it would spread doubt as to whether or not others had been wrongly accused. They knew that this would create a domino effect of doubt, and they did not know how they would be able to handle it. Obviously, they realized what they were doing was not right, but they themselves were stuck in the trap just like everyone else and did not quite know how to dig their way out of it. Although Nurse would be hanged for her supposed crime, her name would be exonerated not even twenty years later.

And as it pertains to George Burroughs, Cotton Mather, sitting on his high horse, declared that even the devil himself was able to transform "into an angel of light" and that it would be prudent, therefore, not to be persuaded by an accused man's proclamations of innocence. Despite Mather's insistence, however, it was soon quite clear that a grave injustice had been committed. In fact, the government of the Province of Massachusetts Bay (the successor of the Massachusetts Bay Colony) later cleared Burroughs's name and gave Burroughs's widowed wife some fifty pounds as compensation.

Cotton Mather would never apologize for his role in all this. Mather himself was perhaps just as caught up in the hysteria of the times as everyone else. In many ways, Mather was an incredibly insecure man. He spent most of his life trying to live up to the high standard of success and respect that both his father, Increase Mather, and grandfather, the famous preacher John Cotton, had been garnered during their lifetimes.

The Mather name was indeed a well-known one in New England, and Cotton Mather had developed a bit of a complex in his quest to fill those rather sizeable shoes. He also developed a pronounced stutter. His stuttering is said to have been so bad in his youth that it prevented him from immediately joining the ministry. Instead, he was steered in the direction of becoming a medical doctor. Cotton apparently gained some control over his stuttering and made his way into the ministry just like his forebearers.

Still, many felt that he wasn't living up to the standard set by his father, and Cotton Mather would be plagued with self-doubt much of his life. As many historians have pointed out, it was this mixture of a man with something to prove and the uncertainty afoot in Salem at the time that just might have been the perfect recipe for disaster.

By the fall of 1692, the Puritan residents of Salem began to have some serious reservations about what was happening. The aforementioned Cotton Mather's own father, Increase Mather, even spoke out against the witch trials. That October, he boldly stated, "It were better that ten suspected witches should escape, than that one innocent person should be condemned [executed]."

Many began to suspect that some of the wild accusations being made were due to nothing more than petty grudges. And in some cases, they were made just to get land from those that they accused. Sarah Osborne, in particular, was targeted by Ann Putnam in part because her family desired to take some of Osborne's land. The Putnam family apparently had an outstanding dispute with Osborne over their property lines and believed that Sarah Osborne had encroached upon their land. The excuse of witchcraft then conveniently presented itself as a reason to take the old lady's land from her.

It was only when Governor Phips himself became concerned enough to personally oversee the trials that things began to change. On October 12th, 1692, Governor Phips finally intervened and put a stop to what was happening. After bringing the trials to a grinding halt, Phips insisted that there must be clear evidence of someone committing witchcraft in order for them to be prosecuted. Phips stated that hearsay evidence of one person making up claims about another would no longer be admissible in court. There would no longer be wild claims of "spectral evidence." Now, only clear, concrete proof would be admissible in the Salem witch trials. Under this new standard, it was soon obvious that just about everyone who was being held was being incarcerated without any proof of any wrongdoing whatsoever.

As such, when the trials reconvened in 1693, almost all of the prisoners of the Salem witch trials had to be released. Governor Phips then made sure that anyone still remaining behind bars on account of charges of witchcraft was officially set free by May of that year, declaring that a grave injustice had occurred in this Puritan colony. Considering the fact that at least twenty people died as a direct result of this travesty of justice, this was by no means an exaggeration.

And even those who were released and survived the tumult ended up scarred for life, both by what they had gone through and the lingering suspicion that hung over them. Although many survived the trials, it is believed around two hundred people were accused; that is two hundred people who have been released back into the community, wondering why their neighbor turned on them. It is very possible that some neighbors still thought the freed could have been witches and spent the rest of their lives looking for more evidence. As mentioned earlier, some of the families who fell victim to the Salem witch trials were later financially compensated. However, for the families that were directly affected by this puritanical purge, all the pounds in the world were likely not enough when it came to the lives of the loved ones that had been lost.

The frenzied fanaticism of the Salem witch trials seemed to showcase all of what critics had long felt was wrong with the Puritans. They wanted to be a pure, shining city on a hill set apart from others. But at least as it pertains to Salem, in their quest for self-righteous purity, instead of standing out as an example of what others should do, they stood out as an example of what a society should not do.

Even now, the Salem witch trials and, of course, witch hunts in general have become synonymous with persecution and the unfair targeting of groups and individuals. If someone today were to claim that an investigation had turned into a "witch hunt," they mean to say that it is a biased and unfair inquiry. And the meaning of that phrase comes from the Salem witch trials.

Famed playwright Arthur Miller wrote his own rendition of the Salem witch trials with his classic work *The Crucible*. The piece was written in the 1950s when the panic of the Red Scare (the fear of the rise of communism that mainly found a home in the United States) was at its height. The Iron Curtain had descended across Europe, and the two superpowers of the US and the Soviet Union stood on each side of the divide with world-destroying nuclear weapons aimed at one another.

Those living in the United States in the 1950s lived in very uncertain times, much like the Puritans in Salem. No one knew when the bomb might drop, and along with this external threat, there was a considerable fear of the enemy taking root within. These fears were not entirely unfounded since Russian spies were indeed uncovered in various espionage plots aimed at the United States. It was these Russian spies that became the new bogeyman.

Just like in Salem, there was suddenly a witch around every corner. In much of America in the 1950s, just about anyone and everyone could be suspected of being a communist or a communist sympathizer. And once the House of Un-America Activities Committee (a group created to hunt out communist subversives) got through with them, they could have had their reputations ruined for life.

Those who merely got their reputations ruined were actually the lucky ones since others paid with their very lives. Critics like Arthur Miller felt that the communist scare and this rush to convict suspected subversives were very similar to what had happened in Salem. The Salem witch trials had become a standard for critical-thinking individuals to point to when they felt that the horrors of history were repeating once again.

This was a definite turning point, and the Puritans of New England would never be quite the same again. It wasn't until January 14th,1697, that the Massachusetts legislature felt enough guilt to declare a day of mourning for those people of Salem who had fallen. In a kind of memorial service, townspeople fasted and prayed for both those who were victimized and those who had preyed upon their victims.

It was in the middle of this outpouring that former witch trial judge Samuel Sewall issued a public apology. Incredibly enough, the firebrand puritan preacher Samuel Parris, who had stirred up so much of this drama, showed no remorse. Many held him accountable, however, and facing pressure from disgruntled members of the flock, Parris chose to leave Salem altogether.

Still, the scarred collective of Salem needed some sort of closure. There had to be a final reckoning, a coming to terms with what had happened. And in 1702, the Puritan survivors actually submitted a formal petition to ask the colonial courts to grant them "formal restitution" so that they could clear their name. Just like those blackballed for communism in the 1950s, folks who had been labeled as a witch in the 1690s had been made into social pariahs. Even after being released, their reputation was in tatters. Survivors felt that someone needed to finally clear the air.

The most the local courts would do was to introduce a piece of legislation that expressly forbade spectral evidence. Phips had already forbidden its use during the Salem witch trials, but now, it was in official legislation for all to see that so-called spectral evidence was no evidence at all. It was hoped that this declaration would serve to retroactively vindicate those wrongly accused since the form of "evidence" that had been used against them had been rendered null and void.

Perhaps the greatest vindication came in 1706 when an older and wiser Ann Putnam admitted to falsely accusing fellow Puritan residents. As hard as it may have been for them, these wronged Puritans utilized the most important Christian principle of all—forgiveness—and were able to come to terms with Ann, despite the fact that she had so spitefully used them.

Old Tituba, who survived her own charges of witchcraft, also expressed remorse in her role of accusing the other women. In later testimony, she claimed that she was threatened and coerced by the Puritan preacher Samuel Parris. At the behest of the girls who accused Tituba of practicing witchcraft, Parris had demanded to know all about her dealings with the devil. Tituba claimed that it was the threat of physical force that caused her to give false testimony.

Even this terrible episode, when seen through the Puritan lens, was a learning experience and a matter of faith.

Chapter 7 – Puritans in a Period of Decline and a Moment of Transformation

"God is the highest good of the reasonable creature. The enjoyment of him is our proper; and is the only happiness with which our souls can be satisfied. To go to heaven, fully to enjoy God, is infinitely better than the most pleasant accommodations here. Better than fathers and mothers, husbands, wives, or children, or the company of any, or all earthly friends. These are but shadows; but the enjoyment of God is the substance. These are but scattered beams; but God is the sun. These are but streams; but God is the fountain. These are but drops, but God is the ocean."

-Jonathan Edwards

The Puritans of England proved to have a much shorter shelf life than the Puritans of the New World. The Puritans had reached their height under Oliver Cromwell, but after Cromwell's demise, they faced backlash for what was perceived as their role in not only the death of King Charles II but also the subsequent tyranny of Cromwell. After the restoration of 1660, Puritan Protestants in England were on life support as a movement. The popular will was against these Puritans like never before.

Really, it can be said that the end of the Puritans as a definitive movement in Britain can be traced back to the year 1662, for it was that year that the British Parliament ratified the so-called Act of Uniformity. This act stipulated that all churches in England must adhere to the officially sanctioned forms of prayer, worship, sacraments, and other rituals as stipulated in the *Book of Common Prayer*. After this declaration was made, well over one thousand Puritan ministers made it known that they would not follow the Act of Uniformity. All this managed to accomplish for them was their immediate removal from their churches. From here on out, all ministers had to show evidence that an officially sanctioned bishop had given them proper ordination. There was no way around it. In the immediate days after their removal, many ministers broke down and came back to England's state-run church, ready to conform.

Those who decided to continue their dissent (called Dissenters) would remain shut out of official church business for a century and a half. Not only that, but they were also shut out of the two major institutions of education—Oxford and Cambridge—as well as other branches of public education. It makes one wonder if the Puritans who remained on the fringes like this viewed themselves as being persecuted by the "Beast" from the Book of Revelation. Every century, there seem to be Christian groups that come to believe that they are being ostracized and, as the Book of Revelation says, are unable to buy or sell or do much of anything without taking the mark of the beast.

For the Puritans of the late 1600s, that "mark" may very well have come to represent the call to conform to the state's prayer book. However, as much as they were shut out of the government's discussions, the disenfranchised Dissenters received some aid when the British Whig Party moved to oppose these court religious policies and instead made the argument that the so-called Dissenters ought to be able to have their own worship services held separate from the Church of England.

These efforts ultimately led to the Toleration Act of 1689. This allowed the Dissenters, who would ultimately be called Nonconformists by the 1700s, to have churches of their own. But Puritanism as a movement in England by this time was practically nonexistent. In America, on the other hand, after the debacle of the Salem witch trials in 1692, the Puritans underwent a dramatic transformation.

During the 1690s, the Puritans were increasingly known as Congregationalists. These congregations centered around clerical associations, which were used "for fellowship and consultation." The Cambridge Association in Massachusetts was among the first, which was founded in 1690. Here, Puritan ministers met and consulted with each other right on the campus of Harvard University. It was here that they would hold debates and consult with one another over the latest developments among their congregations. By that fateful year of the Salem witch trials, 1692, two more congregations were founded, and then a fifth was created in 1705.

By the 1700s, America was in the grip of the new, more rational line of thought that was a trademark of the so-called Age of Enlightenment that was being embraced on both sides of the Atlantic. This embrace of logic led to a downturn in religious interest, which caused many Puritan leaders to long for a revival. Congregational church leader Jonathan Edwards managed to spark one with his flock in Northampton, Massachusetts, in 1735, and he later wrote of the local surge in religious zeal in his *A Faithful Narrative of the Surprising Work of God in the Conversion of Many Hundred Souls in Northampton.*

Jonathan Edwards came from a long line of hardworking men of the cloth. His great-great-grandfather was a British preacher who perished during an epidemic in London in 1625. His widowed wife eventually married a man named James Cole, who took her and her son, William, to the newly founded colonies that were sprouting up in New England. William Edwards grew up and put his roots down in Hartford, Connecticut, where his son Richard came into the world in 1647. Richard then went on to marry and have six kids, one of whom—Timothy Edwards—was born in 1669.

Timothy would go on to become a Puritan preacher in May of 1694, and he wed a woman named Esther the following fall. It was from this union that Jonathan Edwards was born on October 5th, 1703. Johnathan was closely educated by his father Timothy, who, as well as being a Puritan preacher, also ran a kind of elementary school for local children. It is from Johnathan Edwards's school papers as a youth that we get an idea of just how brilliant of a mind he had. From an early age, he was writing whole treatises on everything from the color spectrum of rainbows to the nature of the soul. His paper on the refracted light of rainbows was apparently inspired by his studies of one of the great minds of the Enlightenment, the British scientist Isaac Newton, whose groundbreaking work *Opticks* changed much of what the scientific world understood at that time. It was Edwards's academic paper on the nature of the soul, however, that showed that he could delve into matters of the spirit just as easily as matters of science.

It was on the strength of both of these twin intellectual drives that Johnathan Edwards entered into Yale in September of 1716. Edwards finished up his collegiate course with the university in the fall of 1720 before embarking upon a career in the ministry in 1722. His first gig as a minister actually came at a Presbyterian church in New York. As noted previously, the Presbyterians and the Puritans always had much in common, and the fact that this preacher of staunch Puritan stock would preach at a Presbyterian church is not at all unusual. In fact, Edwards did not see anything in the Presbyterian doctrine that went counter to his own convictions and faith as a Puritan. Again, it is important to realize that Puritanism is not exactly defined as a denomination as much as it was a movement and mindset dedicated to keeping Christian beliefs "pure" of the vestiges of Catholicism. Having said that, if one were to view Puritanism as being a denomination, it would be the Presbyterians who would have had the most in common with them. After all, Presbyterians at this time shared the same Calvinist beliefs as the Puritans. Both Puritans and Presbyterians believed in predestination and what that belief entailed, so Edwards no doubt felt he was in good company. Jonathan Edwards's stint at this Presbyterian church would be brief, however, and he would end up leaving the Presbyterian parish in April of 1723.

His next major assignment would be preaching at a church in Northampton in 1726, where he received his ordination in the spring of 1727. Edwards soon endeared himself with his flock, and through good times and bad, he managed to captivate them through his sermons. In 1733, during a particularly bad year in which the colony was plagued both by locusts in the summer and an epidemic of influenza in the fall, Edwards's keen insight managed to galvanize them like no other.

His sermons were so thought-provoking, in fact, that he was convinced to write them down and have them published. It was these rousing sermons that found their way to the printed press in 1734 under the title of *A Divine and Supernatural Light, Immediately Imparted to the Soul by the Spirit of God, Shown to Be Both a Scriptural and Rational Doctrine*. This is admittedly a wordy title, but it is one that serves to sum up Jonathan Edwards's own traditional puritanical beliefs in juxtaposition with the trend toward more rational, logical thought brought on by the Enlightenment. Here, Edwards makes the case that rational reasoning alone is not always sufficient. At one point in his dialogue, Edwards states, "Experience shows things in a different light from what our reason suggested without experience."

From all his time studying rainbows and refracted light, Edwards knew that even though when staring at a rainbow head-on, one might reasonably conclude that it was a solid structure descending from the heavens. However, experience would make one quickly realize that this is simply not the case. This is why a four-year-old just might run across a field in search of the end of a rainbow, whereas a forty-year-old would know from experience not to waste their time.

In other words, reason isn't infallible, and logic only takes us so far—it's our experience that can lead us the rest of the way. In the aftermath of the Salem witch trials, a time when superstition seemed to run amuck, many turned away from leaning on their faith. But in many ways, Edwards, with his unique approach, managed to make it okay once again to be a Christian thinker. This seemed to open up the floodgates for a much more involved flock at his church in Northampton.

But this small-scale revival in Northampton proved to be just a mere prelude to the Great Awakening to come. The religious movement known as the Great Awakening was led by an Anglican preacher by the name of George Whitfield (sometimes spelled as Whitefield). Whitfield had already been a firebrand preacher in England when he left the British shores for America in August of 1739. After arriving in America, Whitfield proceeded to tour the New England colonies in 1740. He preached for several days on end to thousands of people in multiple locations. Like a religious rock star performing for sold-out concerts, Whitfield galvanized those who came to listen to him with his passionate, often theatrical preaching of the Bible. Whitfield was not only a great orator, for he was also good in print, and he made sure that newspapers wrote about him and that his sermons were widely distributed on the printed page.

Many Puritans were drawn to Whitfield's sermons, but it must be noted that Whitfield's style and the context of his preaching often differed from most Puritan ideologies. Old-school Puritans valued modesty and a life of outward good work, one in which they set a good example (just think of the city shining on a hill), whereas Whitfield focused on inner feelings, was passionately emotive, and encouraged his listeners to express themselves on an emotional level.

As it pertains to the Puritans who accepted this new mode of religious expression, they were referred to as the "New Lights" (as in the new lights on the hill, perhaps). And the ones who wished to hang on to the old ways were called the "Old Lights." Over the next couple hundred years or so, these two ideological camps would square off against each other in consideration of what the true Puritan ideal should be.

It was in the aftermath of the Salem witch trials, when logic seemed to be lacking, and the Enlightenment, in which logic and reason became the centerpiece, was on the rise that these two poles of Puritan thought emerged. Whitfield's sermons served as an alternative to the logic and human reasoning of the Enlightenment while steering clear of unbridled fear and superstition. Whitfield's sermons often stressed the need for God's help when it came to our corrupt human nature, as well as God's fury over sin and the human need to repent.

Many Puritan leaders supported the movement, but some of the Old Lights were critical, feeling that the theatrics of Whitfield simply went too far. There was now a significant wedge between the Old Lights and the New Lights, and this division would not be rectified until 1758. It was the very year that Jonathan Edwards's *Original Sin* came out, the same year that this old Puritan standard-bearer passed on, that the Puritans began to move on as well.

Chapter 8 – The New England Puritans and Patriots

"We must delight in each other, make others conditions our own, rejoice together, mourn together, labor and suffer together, always having before our eyes our commission and community in the work, our community as members of the same body."

-John Winthrop

In many ways, the Puritans had always been on the front lines in the struggle for American independence from England. In fact, the first colonists of what was then known as New England made greater independence from the mother country a common objective. The pilgrims who arrived on the *Mayflower* entered into a social compact with each other, as they were determined to uniquely define their role and exactly how they wished to live. John Winthrop came a decade later in 1630 with many more like-minded Puritan souls and went so far as to declare that the Massachusetts Bay Colony that they were establishing was going to be nothing short of a shining city on a hill. One that not only England but the whole world could look upon with admiration and wonder.

Instead of toeing the line, the Puritans sought to forge a shining example. Many argue that these words were the beginning of what has become known as American exceptionalism, that rugged individualism that sets America apart from the rest of the world. The Puritans had all of this in mind centuries before anyone dared to officially break with England. It was the Puritans who set the standard that the Sons of Liberty and other independence-minded groups of the mid-1700s followed in their eventual struggle for independence from the British Crown.

Jonathan Edwards, in particular, voiced the need to be free from the burden that the British might had placed upon the religious concourse in America. Denominations loyal to the Church of England quite obviously had a problem when the American Revolution erupted. The Quakers also had issues since they were committed to being pacifists. The Puritan-based faith, on the other hand, had no problem at all in putting its members behind the rebellion against the British.

In fact, the Puritans had practically been in a state of rebellion with both the Church of England and the English government all along. All of the previous Puritan stands against British governance served to work as a perfect template for those who were willing to take things to the next level and break from England outright. For those of a Puritan bent, there was nothing to lose and everything to gain when it came to finally freeing that shining city on the hill from English authoritarian aggression.

And it wasn't just on an ideological level that the Puritans inspired those poised for revolution, for they also aided and abetted on a real-world level by putting many Puritan boots on the ground. But it was no doubt the Puritan boots in the church who continually prayed for God's help in beating the British oppressors that had the greatest impact on the American Revolutionary War, for it was this continued ideological presence of the Puritans that would serve to inspire continued resistance to the Crown.

Boston, of course, served as the center stage for the infamous Boston Tea Party in which American Patriots dumped English tea into the harbor in protest of excessive taxation. The city of Boston itself was founded by Puritans. The Boston Tea Party, which took place in December of 1773, was mostly attended by God-fearing men who wished to shake the bonds of what they believed to be British tyranny. There were, of course, a few among them whose motives were a little less than pure. Some no doubt enjoyed smashing open the chests just for the base thrill of vandalism, and a few even helped themselves to some expensive tea leaves, stuffing them into their trousers. But for most, it was not anarchy and brazen theft that they were after that night but rather a catalyst to inaugurate in clear and concrete change on the part of their British overlords.

The British Empire had not only been trying to tell folks how to spend their money and subjecting them to high taxes but also telling them how they should worship God. This was where Puritan-minded folks drew a line in the sand and decided to rise up against their oppressors. The Puritans knew from their own collective experience that if such transgressions went unanswered, the transgressor would simply take it as a license to transgress even more.

It was the day after the Boston Tea Party had run its course that a lawyer by the name of John Adams declared that what occurred was not a travesty. To him, it wasn't a waste dumping tea into the harbor but rather "the most magnificent movement of all time." He further stated, "There is a dignity, a majesty, a sublimity, in the last effort of the Patriots, that I greatly admire."

John Adams was a Founding Father of the United States, and he would one day go on to become a US president. He also just so happened to be from a strong Puritan background. Adams later contended that his mentality had been developed from birth, citing the fact that he was born in 1735 when the colonies of New England were gripped between two ideological poles, that of the Enlightenment and that of the Great Awakening, which largely espoused Puritan ideals.

The Great Awakening also served as a demarcation line between the Old Lights and the New Lights, of which John Adams's generation was a part. Adams made the switch to a more progressive, New Light version of Puritanism when he was just a young teenager. He had come to dislike what he saw as irrational dogmatic views of earlier Puritans and instead embraced a more liberal approach, which was led by the teachings of the New Light dynamos Lemuel Briant and Jonathan Mayhew.

It was Mayhew who perhaps had the most influence. Mayhew championed the rights of citizens to rebel against unjust laws. He made these views quite clear in 1750 when he gave his famous sermon, "Discourse Concerning Unlimited Submission and Non-Resistance to the Higher Powers." In this sermon, Mayhew insisted that it was the common citizen who should be the proper judges of government officials, not the other way around.

The concept of a nation run on democratic principles, in which the common citizen would elect representatives, would end up sticking with John Adams. He later recalled the power of this particular sermon, stating that it "was read by everybody; celebrated by friends, and abused by enemies." And Founding Father John Adams, for one, would most certainly remember it when he helped draft the Declaration of Independence in 1776, which opened with the phrase, "We the People."

The United States was built upon the principles that Puritans, such as Mayhew, espoused. It was meant to be a republic designed by the people and for the people, and it drew heavily upon these Puritan values as a result. Later historian and 19th-century writer J. W. Thornton proclaimed that it was Mayhew's Puritan-infused sermon that served as "the morning gun of the revolution." It was as if Mayhew, in his great oratory and intellectual introspection, had issued a call to arms, and the British taskmaster didn't even realize it.

But nevertheless, those keen to keep and even expand upon their liberties in America took note. Just prior to Mayhew's discourse, Puritans of the Province of Massachusetts Bay were already in an uproar with the Crown over the ability of Anglicans to have part of their taxes redirected toward the building of churches and other monuments for the Church of England. Although the Toleration Act had forced Puritans to accept other religions, these developments clearly indicated the favored status of the Church of England. In 1749, one angry Puritan fired off a pamphlet in which readers were reminded that the Anglican bulwark of King's Chapel had been literally built upon the bones of Puritans since its foundation had been carelessly laid over old Puritan burial grounds. The pamphlet decried the fact "the ashes of the dead were inhumanely disturbed, in order to build the King's Chapel." The writer then pointed out that renovations had been scheduled that very year, and it was likely that even more of the Puritan dead would most likely be disturbed in the process.

However, more pertinent for Puritan Congregationalists were the growing calls from Anglicans to have a colonial bishop appointed with a direct line to the king of England. In the wake of all of this Anglican intrigue over King's Chapel, both the Puritan dead and living were indeed disturbed—disturbed enough to help start a revolution.

Puritans and Patriots alike were inspired not to sit back and complain about their lot but to actually do something about it. Men like John Adams took what they had learned from the Puritan tradition to heart and employed these principles in the founding of the United States of America. It may have been a shining city on a hill, but it was not the possession of some foreign crown; no, the Puritans had decided long ago that it was the common man who would call the shots.

And even as the opening salvos of the first guns of the revolution began to ring out, these Puritan-minded Americans were determined to make these principles a reality. Mayhew promised in his speeches that it was indeed possible to be loyal and yet still reach for freedom. And as the Puritans and the Patriots readied for the Revolutionary War, their conscience was clear in the knowledge that they were serving a higher calling. Both Puritans and Patriots, the inheritors of that original New England Charter, were ready to fight for what they viewed to be their God-given freedoms if need be.

Chapter 9 – Puritans, the Civil War, and Opportunities for Expanded Outreach

"Be not so set upon poetry, as to be always poring on the passionate and measured pages. Let not what should be sauce, rather than food for you, engross all your application. Beware of a boundless and sickly appetite for the reading of poems which the nation now swarms withal; and let not the Circean cup intoxicate you. But especially preserve the chastity of your soul from the dangers you may incur, by a conversation with muses no better than harlots."

-Cotton Mather

By the early 1800s, the Puritans and their congregational churches were again subjected to a period of change. Many had lost their tax privileges, as was the case in 1818 for the Connecticut Congregationalists and then again in 1833 for the Massachusetts Congregationalists. At this point, many other denominations had moved onto the scene, such as Baptists, Methodists, and, of course, the ever-present Presbyterians, who had only increased in number.

Puritans of Congregationalist churches, however, didn't fit into a nice and neat category, and they often opted to simply name their houses of worship as "First Church." If one lived in Ipswich, it would therefore be the "First Church of Ipswich"; if a Puritan flock set up shop in Townsend, it would then be the "First Church of Townsend." It was a simple yet ultimately confusing logic that left the Puritan churches with such sublime monikers.

For the Puritans of this period, the most important thing was the structure of their congregational model. Just as was the case in the past, they eschewed having to answer to any centralized authority. The proto-Puritans broke from the Pope in Rome, then the first generation of Puritans broke from the bishops of the Church of England. The later Puritans of the 1800s likewise refused to have centralized "synods, conferences, or assemblies." Although the congregations were loosely affiliated through doctrine and tradition, they were authorities unto themselves and insisted on handling their own internal affairs.

From the Pilgrims all the way to the 1800s, the Puritans held fast to the notion that each church had its own founding compact, a constitution, if you will, that created a "covenant" between church members and their particular church leader. As much as churches wished to remain free of outside control, inside the church, matters were often rigidly prescribed in advance. It wasn't uncommon, for example, for a Congregationalist church to actually have assigned seating.

However, these rigid internal controls often made the Congregationalist churches seem rather unwelcoming to newcomers who had to figure out where they would be in the hierarchy. And at times, they even had to figure out where they might be able to sit! As such, the expansion of these churches proved to be slow. For a while, these Puritan churches remained mostly in the region of the former New England colonies where they had originated. Meanwhile, after the American Revolution, Methodists, Baptists, Presbyterians, and the like managed to expand to just about every corner of the newly forged United States of America.

Despite their shrinking influence, the Puritans who remained leaned heavily on their history and tradition. In the former New England region, Puritans focused on the guiding moral compass of their Puritan forefathers and their robust faith in the "divine providence" of God. They harkened back to their Pilgrim ancestors, who believed that they weren't merely travelers to a new world but God's own actors chosen to fulfill his great commission. Their trend toward Calvinism did indeed lead them toward a belief in the preordained, and they believed that in God's divine plan, He had chosen them long ago to carry out what He needed them to do. They were also convinced that history repeated itself, and they looked to the Bible to see this cyclical cycle of events at work. All they had to do was look at the biblical Book of Exodus and how the Hebrew people were launched on a pilgrimage from Egypt to Israel. As one might guess, this story struck a chord with the Puritans, for they too saw their own exodus across the Atlantic from England in a similar way.

This melding of the past and present was also often convenient fodder for Puritan "jeremiads," which shined a light on the current folly of others through parallels with those who had gone astray in scripture in the bygone past. The biblical prophet Jeremiah was where much of the jeremiads were derived since it was that particular prophet who often preached to Israel to repent or face the wrath of God. Jeremiah was known as the "weeping prophet," in fact, and prior to his eventual martyrdom, he persistently proclaimed that God's judgment was coming upon Israel.

The Puritan preacher Jonathan Edwards, who was mentioned earlier in this book, was well known for his jeremiads. In fact, he could have been said to have written a whole treatise of these comparisons and exhortations in his famous sermon, "Sinners in the Hands of an Angry God." Edwards, just like Jeremiah before him, stressed that God placed his believers in a covenant relationship with him, but if those said believers were to go astray, that covenant could be removed.

To the Puritans, the jeremiads both expressed their unique relationship with God as well as warned them that if they did not do their part, they could ultimately lose their "continued blessing." The Puritans of the 19th century were constantly worried about losing not only their blessing but also their entire way of life. Not so much from outside oppression, as their forefathers had once faced, but from just sheer complacency on the part of their own parishioners.

And Puritan leaders began to warn their flock of this. Pastor William Lunt had just such a message for his Puritan flock when he delivered a stern warning to them in 1840. Lunt reminded them of all the Puritans who had lived and died for their faith in the years gone by, dramatically referencing their graves "in yonder burying ground." He also mused on what it might be like to have these deceased saints rise from the grave and walk right through the church doors "in ghostly procession."

After imagining the dead paying the church a visit, Lunt then asked the question, "What think ye would be the lessons that would be uttered by those ministers of Christ? Would they not say to you; Preserve the institutions which we, in our day, exhorted men to honor. Desert not the sanctuary of your fathers. If you must renounce our dogmas, do not—oh do not—renounce our principles. Or fall from a life of piety and Christian righteousness." This is some pretty powerful imagery, to say the least, and it was used in an attempt to bring home the importance of keeping the traditions of their Puritan ancestors alive, lest the dead themselves were forced to come back and remind them to do so.

At this point in time, two distinct wings of the Puritan Congregationalists rose up: those who believed that a kind of Christian perfectionism could be established and those who held fast to Calvinist doctrine that stressed the inescapable pull of original sin. This would be important in the years leading up to the American Civil War since it was those seeking this "moral perfection" that began to seriously consider the evils of slavery. They understood that neither they nor America as a whole could be morally justified until the scourge of slavery was eradicated. This determination was on full display in 1852 when a total of forty-four congregational churches met in Mansfield, Ohio, to sign a doctrinal statement against slavery.

Nevertheless, as the Civil War erupted in 1861, the Puritans stayed mostly silent. Christians, in general, found themselves torn between the opposing sides. Some Christians were quite vocal about their support of the North's quest to end slavery in the South. Quaker churches, for example, even those located within the Deep South itself, were steadfastly against the practice, and they found themselves at odds with their own fellow Southern residents.

Christians on both sides of the ideological divide tried to use scripture to justify their viewpoints. When the war came to a close in 1865, the Puritan Congregationalists sought to reorganize their congregations. In order to stave off their dwindling numbers, many embarked upon church-building programs. Part of this outreach was aimed at the Southern states that had just been defeated by the North. The South, of course, was in great turmoil and upheaval in the aftermath of the Civil War. Even in the midst of this turmoil—or perhaps even because of it—the Congregationalists sought to expand their reach.

Indeed, some Congregationalists felt that the aftermath of the Civil War would provide new opportunities for ministry, which was demonstrated in the previous year at a Congregationalist conference for the General Association of Illinois. According to writer and Puritan researcher Margaret Bendroth, this conference, which took place in April of 1864, focused on the theme of "shackles being 'struck from millions of slaves' and 'vast regions and populations' opening up to 'free thought, speech and free missions.'" In other words, they thought that the South might just be ripe for the Puritan ideals of the Northeast to take hold. After this conference concluded, Puritan preacher Will Patton was remembered to have boasted about "the many Congregational churches that will soon dot the South, now that the gospel and the polity of freedom can have unrestricted access to those fertile regions, from which slavery has hitherto shut out Puritan influence."

They say that God works in mysterious ways, and the Puritans, for one, believed that the trauma of the Civil War would actually serve a greater good and open the door to the hearts and minds of Southerners so that they could consider Puritan ideals. After the assassination of Abraham Lincoln in 1865, however, many Puritans, just like many other Americans in general, took a harder line against the Southerners and began to rethink having any outreach with them at all.

At the Boston Council of Congregationalists, which met shortly after Lincoln's death, Puritan Alonzo Quint famously not only railed against Southerners but also the British. This ire was provoked by the fact that the British, who still viewed America largely as an enemy, had tacitly supported the Confederacy. This support was never in an official capacity, but it was quite obvious that the British wanted to make the war as hard and costly on the North as possible. Alonzo pointed this fact out right in front of a British delegation of Puritans at the conference, charging that it was the British who were "always ready to follow the powerful, and always ready to crush the weak–robbing in India [and] plundering Ireland."

Britain, which had already outlawed slavery several decades before in 1807, was most certainly not aiding the Confederates because they agreed with them but rather did so as a means of weakening and wreaking revenge against the US itself. This aid was always on an unofficial level since the British officially remained neutral during the course of the war. Nevertheless, there were Puritans, such as Alonzo, who were ready to disown the South and all those who had ever supported them, whether that support was official or unofficial. Such fiery rhetoric could more or less be ascribed to the passions of the moment. A costly war had just been concluded, and the president, who many Puritans had looked toward as a great role model, had been cut down. There were many, of course, who were deeply upset by all of these things. This fiery indignation would cool down over the next few years, though.

And by the so-called Pilgrim Jubilee of 1870, which celebrated the 250th anniversary of the arrival of their Puritan forefathers on the *Mayflower*, Congregationalists were pushing toward what they termed to be a denominational unity. Many critics, however, pointed out that the trend toward a denominational unity would lead to too many compromises, with the overall doctrine of these Puritan inheritors becoming much more liberal as a result. And after the so-called Creed of 1883 was introduced as a unifying statement of faith, many felt it gave far too much away in the name of that said unity. One Massachusetts Congregationalist by the name of William Deloss made this very argument. In 1883, when the new creed was introduced, he mused that "[even a] professed Christian man who believes that we are descended from monkeys" would be deemed acceptable under the charter.

The debate over Darwin's theory of evolution, of course, was a major hot-button issue in the late 1800s. Those who held Puritan-based traditions close to their heart often used it as a wedge to separate themselves from those who simply called themselves true believers. For an old stickler like Deloss, it would have been anathema for a so-called Christian-believing evolutionist to be allowed into the flock.

William Deloss was just one of many conservative Old Lights who were trying to slow the change of pace in the Puritan faith. With time, however, the descendants of the Puritans would indeed become much more free-thinking and liberal in scope.

Chapter 10 – Modern-Day Puritans and the End of an Age

"The gospel brings tidings, glad tidings indeed. To mourners in Zion, who want to be freed. From sin and Satan, and Mount Sinai's flame good news of salvation, through Jesus the Lamb. What sweet invitations, the gospel contains, to men heavy laden, with bondage and chains. It welcomes the weary, to come and be blessed. With ease from their burdens, I Jesus to rest. For every poor mourner, who thirsts for the Lord. A fountain is opened, in Jesus the Word. Their poor parched conscience, to cool and to wash. From guilt and pollution, from dead works and dross. A robe is provided, their shame now to hide. In which none are clothed, but Jesus' bride. Though it be costly, yet is the robe free. And all Zion's mourners, shall decked with it be."

-William Gadsby

At the dawning of the 20th century, the descendants of the Puritan faith had reached a crossroads in their religious journey. Rather than insisting that their way was the only way, Puritans began to develop a decidedly more liberal approach. Suddenly, there was a push among Congregationalists to refrain from judging the faith of others while still holding fast to their own doctrines and traditions. One of the more famous writers and researchers of Puritanism, Margaret Bendroth, pulled up a quote from a Puritan Congregationalist, dated 1925, that seems to sum up this sentiment well. In her book, *The Last Puritans*, she documents the words of a Puritan descendant who had gone on the record to state, "We are ready to let the other fellow have his belief [but we] refuse to give up the faith of our fathers." Outsiders also seemed to soften their views of the Puritans a little bit, and the 300th anniversary of the Pilgrims landing in Plymouth was rang in with great fanfare all across the United States in 1920.

The summer of Massachusetts in 1920 was especially filled with parades, pomp, and circumstance. At one point, a parade boasted over one hundred costumed figures, which then participated in a massive and elaborate reenactment. Puritan Congregationalists in the years between the two world wars also developed a stance that has been likened to being somewhere "between blind patriotism and blind pacifism."

Unlike the Quakers, who were often conscientious objectors, the Puritans never sought to keep their youth from going off to war, but at the same time, they taught them to think very carefully as to why they were doing so. The Congregationalists had indeed maintained that fierce independent-minded spirit, and realizing they only owed their allegiance to their creator, they encouraged their members to be critical thinkers who could decide for themselves whether or not the wars their earthly government fought were worth fighting for or not.

It was in between the two world wars that an activist arm of the Congregationalists emerged, known as the Council for Social Action (CSA). This group took it upon itself to address the social issues of the day, such as fascism, racism, and economic difficulties. By the 1930s, of course, there were a lot of these social ills to take on, considering the rise of the Nazi Party in Germany, fascism in Italy, racial tensions at home, and the aftermath of the Great Depression.

This heavy focus on social issues, especially the idea of leveling the playing field as far as the economy was concerned, may have been popular in the 1930s, but after the end of World War Two and the fear of communism began to seep in, it was thought that the CSA was nothing more than a socialist or communist front. Some Congregationalists grew wary enough of the organization to create a counter group in 1952 called the Committee Opposing Congregational Political Action (COCPA). This group charged that the CSA was really nothing more than a "materialistic and immoral" organization, attempting to present itself as a Christian one.

The COPCA insisted that rugged individualism and not collective socialism was the true spirit of their Puritan forbearers and that the measures that the CSA called for were complete anathema to Congregationalist ideals. In this atmosphere, the Congregationalists began to go into decline. They ended up holding what would be one of their last main gatherings in the year 1956.

The following year, in 1957, the two factions of the Congregationalists—the Evangelical and Reformed Church and the General Council of the Congregational Christian Churches—actually merged together to become the United Church of Christ or, as it is otherwise simply known, the UCC. It was the UCC that, in great fanfare in November of 1970, celebrated the 350th anniversary of the Pilgrims' landing at Plymouth.

The UCC ran a piece in one of their publications, *The United Church Herald,* in which they praised the Pilgrims and their Puritan ways. The publication gushed over how these seekers of religious freedom had "practiced democracy, independence and congregationalism [even] before they had been defined." However, not all old-school Puritans were happy with the UCC, and its formation would lead to the establishment of the National Association of Congregational Christian Churches, which was essentially put together in protest of the UCC's founding. It was here that the hardliners of the old Puritan ideals sought to find a place for themselves. Those that were a part of the National Association of Congregational Christian Churches believed that they were the true heirs of both Puritan beliefs and spirit.

The UCC, in the meantime, became increasingly liberal in its views and found itself welcoming a wide range of religious thought, as well as accepting folks who hailed from a wide range of social backgrounds. For a church whose ancestors frowned upon something as simple as dancing and singing, the liberal amount of acceptance that the UCC congregants now espoused was quite a transformation. As the UCC continued its more liberal bent, they would give rise to controversial pastors, such as Reverend Jeremiah Wright.

Jeremiah Wright was the pastor of a United Church of Christ congregation in Chicago. He gained media scrutiny during the 2008 presidential election due to his connection to candidate Barack Obama, who used to attend Wright's church. During the presidential campaign, several old video clips of Wright's preaching began to surface in which Wright seemed to be making anti-Semitic and other controversial remarks. Obama quickly denounced Wright's words, and Wright himself went on the record to say that he "misspoke." Some clever pundits in the media recognized that Wright's church had Puritan roots and began to joke that perhaps his tirades were simply his version of the old Puritan "jeremiad."

The UCC church from which Jeremiah Wright hailed was called Trinity United Church of Christ, which was founded in 1961. It was actually the first predominantly African American UCC church. Reverend Wright saw the church through plenty of turbulent times, and by his own admission, he had developed a mindset of not holding anything back. He believed in speaking truth to power or at least his version of the truth.

As controversial as someone like Wright had become, he was from the tradition of Congregationalist churches, which itself was founded by the Puritans. Those folks who wanted to establish a shining city on a hill for the world to see probably had no idea that that one of the inheritors of their tradition would be a man who would be seen openly cursing America from the pulpit. So much for that shining city on a hill!

But then again, it would be wrong to say that Wright completely strayed from Puritan ideals. It was the Puritans, after all, who stressed the need for a pastor to be able to speak freely to his congregations without the oversight of regional authority figures. The fact that Wright was speaking his mind and independently attending to his flock is indeed in line with the general Puritan drive for freedom of worship and religious expression being unhindered within church walls.

The United Church of Christ is a liberal-leaning congregation, and its progressive nature, in many ways, does seem to be in stark contrast to the ultra-conservative roots of the Puritan movement. It is hard telling what some of the originators of the movement would think of these changes. The UCC has been criticized in recent years for focusing too much on social justice and being "too politically correct." In 2011, this so-called political correctness was on full display when the UCC decided to go gender-neutral in references to God. Instead of saying "Heavenly Father," for example, it was decided that God would be referred to as simply "Triune God." This move was somewhat backtracked since even some congregants of the UCC were uncomfortable with it. But if you really get down to it, it's perhaps a little perplexing that we envision God to have a gender at all. Even Jesus seemed to discount this notion when he seemed to remark on the genderless nature of heavenly beings. Angels, although described as having a male appearance in the Bible, are generally viewed to be genderless in the literal sense of the word. At one point in his ministry, Jesus was asked a rather witty question about who someone with multiple marriage partners would end up with in the afterlife. Jesus told them, "For when they shall rise from the dead, they neither marry, nor are given in marriage; but are as the angels which are in heaven." (Matthew 12:25)

The UCC comes from a long line of thought-provoking theologians such as Anne Hutchinson, Cotton Mather, and Jonathan Edwards. Having said that, it shouldn't be all that surprising that their descendants continue to push boundaries, even if it were something that their own forebearers may not have necessarily approved of.

Today, the UCC likes to set itself apart from its peers by proclaiming that it is a church in which the "Lord is still speaking." The founding fathers of the Puritan movement may not agree with all of the efforts taking place within the UCC, but they would have to agree with the general spirit behind it.

Chapter 11 – A Day in the Life of a Puritan

"Feelings come and feelings go, and feelings are deceiving; My warrant is the Word of God—Naught else is worth believing. Though all my heart should feel condemned for want of some sweet token. There is one greater than my heart whose word cannot be broken. I'll trust in God's unchanging word till should and body sever. For, though all things shall pass away, his word shall stand forever."

-Martin Luther

In the Puritan tradition of today, you may be surprised to find congregants having a wide range of viewpoints on key aspects of religious doctrine. This is in stark contrast to the way that the Puritans began their existence.

The Puritan belief system was centered around one's identification of God as the sole authority in one's life and the perfection of obedience to God. Puritans, as was evidenced during the Salem witch trials, truly believed that unseen forces were at work in their lives. They took to heart the words of the Apostle Paul, who stated that we "look through a glass darkly." They held firm that even those who clearly understood the scripture could not fully come to grips with the spiritual world since they themselves were still chained to the world of flesh and blood by virtue of merely being alive. As an Anglican peer of the Puritans once declared, it might be "possible to apprehend God"; however, it's not quite so easy "to comprehend God."

Nevertheless, the Puritans knew that some aspects of God could be understood simply by looking out at the world that He had designed and created. Just by pondering the cut-and-dried facts of creation, one can find evidence of a divine designer. The moon, for example, which is considerably smaller than the sun, just so happens to be, at times, positioned in just the right place in space to appear to cover the sun's solar face, rendering a solar eclipse for those of us down here on Earth. It's certainly a rather convenient coincidence, isn't it? People around the world have enjoyed total solar eclipses since the dawn of time, with most completely unaware of how unlikely such an event actually is. Many scientists have also agreed that the odds of this occurring at random are too incredible to fathom. The sun is over 93 million miles from Earth, and it has a diameter of about 864,948 miles. The moon, on the other hand, is much closer at just 238,900 miles away, and it has a diameter of just 2,158 miles. In other words, the sun is really big, while the moon is much smaller in comparison. Yet, somehow or other, when we look up at the sky, from our vantage point, we get to see two celestial objects that appear roughly the same size, and when they cross paths, they have the potential of creating a total eclipse. It would seem that these two completely different objects were put in place just for us to admire it all. Or as King David of the Bible once wrote in one of his many Psalms, "The heavens declare the glory of God; the skies proclaim the work of his hands" (Psalm 19:1).

This is indeed one of the signs a Puritan would have pointed to as it pertains to the obviously intelligent design of the universe. But as it pertained to the spiritual nature of the universe, which could not be fathomed, the Puritans turned to the Bible for answers. If, for example, someone suddenly became ill and rapidly perished, it wouldn't be unusual for a Puritan to ascribe some divine meaning behind it. Was there a reason that this person perished like this? What was God trying to tell us?

They also applied such questioning to themselves collectively as a whole. This was done with the infamous jeremiads, in which, like the prophet Jeremiah, current hardships were interpreted as being a judgment from God and a warning for the flock to turn "from their wicked ways."

Interestingly enough, however, as it pertained to the Puritans, as much as they sought to set themselves apart with their own brand of puritanical beliefs, they too suffered from eventual divisions, schisms, and theological splits. The truth is there never really was one single unified Puritan approach to religion other than the notion of striving to set themselves apart from the religious mainstream of the time, which they collectively disdained. It is precisely this lack of unified doctrine that leads most scholars to point to Puritanism as being more akin to a movement rather than a static denomination of Christian religion.

One of the fascinating aspects of puritanical beliefs was that although they held firm to the doctrine of predestination, they still stressed living as faithfully as possible. The idea that whoever goes to heaven or hell has already been predetermined might make one tempted to slack off a bit, as no amount of good works would ever change that fact. But not the Puritans! Even though they believed that it was all predetermined, they were sure to do their best, to be the shining city on a hill that John Winthrop so fondly spoke of. Despite their belief in predestination, the Puritans did everything they could to live what they believed to be a godly life.

One might wonder if Puritans believed that it was all preordained, why were they trying so hard to live out their own personal version of what constitutes a pure life? The Puritans believed that they were supposed to be examples to others, and they saw themselves as fulfilling God's will by the lives that they lived. Whether it was preordained or not, the Puritans were more than ready to play the part. Puritans also wanted to reassure themselves that they were indeed preordained for salvation.

It might sound a little convoluted, but they felt that since the fruits of their works bore witness to their overall state of being, they wanted to make sure that their fruit was good. This was a witness not only to their neighbors but also to themselves of God's goodness and, by extension, this goodness at work in their own lives. If they were doing good and generally enjoyed doing good, then they could rest assured that it must have been preordained by God that they would be saved.

Despite the stereotype of Puritans being a bunch of dour-faced people who hated to have a good time, the Puritans actually had a healthy sense of fun. They weren't all work and no play; they just insisted that their joyful activities be highly regimented. They felt that there was a time and place for everything, and they believed that their lives should follow a specific organizational structure. While it was okay to have time at the end of the day to joke around with your family in the house, it would have been viewed as highly inappropriate to be cutting up like this in the middle of a church sermon. It wasn't that the act of goofing off was really that bad; it was more that it would be inappropriate in a church setting.

For the Puritan Pilgrims, their greatest sense of enjoyment came from their time spent with nature. For a Puritan back then, a typical Sunday would have involved church service in the morning and then an afternoon spent communing with nature. Picnics would have been in order, and fishing and berry picking in the surrounding area would have been quite common.

But even in these endeavors, it was viewed that they should only be done if they served a general purpose. Fishing and then wasting the fish you just caught, for example, would have been frowned upon. So whatever fish were kept undoubtedly would have ended up on the fire later that night for dinner.

The needless bloodshed of an animal was always considered wrong, which was evidenced by the fact that the Puritans banned cockfighting. Most today would agree with the Puritans that cockfighting, which entails a crowd of people watching two birds peck each other to death, is rather cruel. But at the time, the Puritans were more the exception than the rule, as other colonists wouldn't have thought much of it. The idea of watching animals fight each other for entertainment is wrong on many levels, and the Puritans preached as much, letting it be known that there would be no room for anyone of the Puritan faith to include any so-called "blood sports" in their recreational lives.

It was for this same reason that the Puritans would refuse to take part in a game like football, which, especially in its more primitive era, would indeed have been labeled a blood sport. Another pastime that the Puritans frowned upon was the enjoyment of theatrical productions. When Oliver Cromwell came to power in the 1650s, under heavy Puritan influence (the heaviest England would ever have), he put a stop to the popular production of plays outright. This was a temporary setback for theater lovers and thespians in England, but the Puritans of the New England colonies maintained this rigid ban of the theater for several more decades to come.

When it came to the pastime of music, Puritans were a little more ambivalent. While they disliked the traditional chorus and instrumental-based music that the Church of England had inherited from the Catholic Church, they encouraged the singing of psalms, and within Puritan households, the playing of musical instruments was eventually quite common.

One of the most treasured pastimes of the Puritans, as was experienced by the first Thanksgiving, was feasting. Basically, this was the idea of setting aside a day to bring a bunch of food and have communal fellowship with friends, family, and neighbors. It was at these great feasts that Puritans shared the latest developments, joked around, and generally enjoyed the company of one another.

This was always the greatest strength of the Congregationalists—their strong sense of community. Even before they stepped foot on land, their Pilgrim forebearers were sure to forge a tight social compact, right there in the quarters of their ship. With this, they were armed with a tight social protocol of how they would deal with not just themselves but also anyone else whom they might encounter.

The Puritan gift of good food and open dialogue proved itself to be highly successful when it came to negotiations with the local Native American population already living in New England. The fact that the first few decades of the Puritan settlement were virtually unmarred by any violence between these two very different peoples is a testament to this strong social compact at work.

The Puritans, you see, were pioneers in every sense of the word. Yes, they were literal trailblazers who burned a path through the wilderness, but they were also pioneers in the sense of just how far-reaching their diplomatic relations were. They were ready and willing to meet others halfway. When dealing with a native delegation, for example, it wouldn't be uncommon for a group of Puritans to travel all the way into the middle of a wooded area that was patrolled by roving bands of tribal warriors. The Puritans were indeed bold, and this boldness was no doubt a boldness inspired by their strong belief in God.

Many Puritans felt they were on a divine mission of providence. They furthermore believed that God had preordained their ultimate success. This was their true wellspring of courage. The Puritans figured that God was on their side, and with the creator of the very universe looking after you like that, what's there to fear? This was indeed the general mindset that most New England Puritans tended to have. And the sheer audacity and courage they put on display every day of their lives bore testament to that fact.

Conclusion: They Let Their Light Shine

Although the Puritans were a powerful movement and a direct result of the Protestant Reformation, most today likely don't know a whole lot about them. Perhaps they make the connection that the Pilgrims from the *Mayflower* who dressed funny and ate turkey on Thanksgiving had something to do with them, but it usually doesn't go too much further than that. Then again, some might consider the Salem witch trials and realize the Puritan connection there.

Either way, both of these associations paint the Puritans in larger-than-life and entirely stereotypical portraits that do not quite reflect reality. The Puritans were indeed on the *Mayflower*, and they did host a series of witch trials in Salem, but this doesn't tell anyone the full story of the group. In order to best understand the Puritans, one first has to consider what drove them to set themselves apart in the first place. It was their deep ideological longing for something greater than the typical religious trappings they had experienced.

The Church of England, from whence the Puritans had originally sprung, proved itself to be far too stifling and retroactive of a vehicle for English Protestants who wished to truly reform the way that their religious services were carried out. Even though the British had broken with the Catholic Church, in many ways, it seemed that England was merely Protestant in name only since so many trappings of the Catholic Church remained in place. It was these last vestiges of Catholicism that the Puritans sought to purge. They wished not so much to create a new religion or denomination as much as they simply wanted to purify the brand of faith that they already had. By the time of Oliver Cromwell, the Puritan-friendly Lord Protector of England, many Puritan-minded believers felt that they had finally been given their chance to truly transform their religion.

But when Cromwell perished, much of this hope died with him. England then went through a series of rulers who, at times, were somewhat open to reform but also routinely backtracked on measures that were viewed as being of the utmost importance to the Protestant faithful. It was when the situation was no longer tolerable in England that many Puritans began to look toward the Americas as a permanent refuge for their flock.

The Pilgrims of the *Mayflower* in 1620, followed by John Winthrop's major wave of Puritans in 1630, proved that the Puritans could not only survive in the New World but also—just as Winthrop had described it—set themselves up as a "city on a hill." They believed that even if the situation may have been unfavorable in Britain, if they could just provide a good enough example in the American colonies, they might be able to change the minds of those who had previously opposed them. All they had to do was let their light shine.

Part 3: Anne Hutchinson

A Captivating Guide to the Puritan Leader in Colonial Massachusetts Who Is Considered to Be One of the Earliest American Feminists

Introduction

Her steps were determined and steady, even though the plank of the wooden ship bobbed up and down in the glittering but frigid water that splashed against the wet dock. In the first light of day, these were the times tinged with the hues of promise shadowed only by the vague unknown. Anne Hutchinson was just a follower, or so she thought, but she had many queued up behind her as she followed her spiritual mentor to Boston in the early days of the Massachusetts Bay Colony.

An older grave man in grey stood at the door of a roughly-hewn white-washed church. Reverend John Cotton spoke only in muted tones of love and encouragement. The people smiled and nodded as they gleefully filed past him and entered the solace of his church. With the pitter-patter sounds of the little feet of Anne's children and her husband's warm body beside her, Anne Hutchinson feels as if she's home.

The unity of their faith was like a light that guided these fervent Puritans. It was comforting to note that one's long-held religious beliefs were united with the towns that now welcomed them. Back in their homeland of Europe, their stiff, pompous church prelates couldn't handle any deviation from their staunch and ancient ways. There was no room for flexibility in England, which included thought-provoking religious reforms. However, the Puritans reproduced all the trappings of the Old World into the New World they now resided in. It was a world in which both the civic and religious government blended together in an awkward way. This was the virgin soil into which was planted the theological factions—the free grace advocates, the Antinomians, and the reformed theologians of the Protestant Reformation.

Although sometimes labeled as a feminist, Anne Hutchinson didn't blow her trumpet about women's issues. She played the horn about issues that meant something to those with eternal passions and who had tasted the victories rendered by their steadfast theological beliefs. When the hoary heads of the prejudiced jerked up with fits of venial words like "seducer," "whore," or "temptress," she heard them not. Who should pay heed to such meaningless prattle? Like her father, Francis Marbury, Anne Hutchinson was logically practical.

Only in the darkness of the unexplained shadows that had crossed various parts of this land before her and her followers were those who trod before, like John Winthrop and Thomas Dudley and about one thousand Puritan settlers. They had a charter to found the land and fashion a system of beliefs that matched those they had left behind in England, claiming they wanted religious reform. John Cotton eventually flowed with the tide, but Hutchinson didn't. She spoke for herself without parroting others, and other religious leaders wanted to understand the value of her words and compare them with the doctrine they had learned. No woman had ever related to them on their own level. However, the conservatism of the times couldn't handle her daring, incisive thoughts or her ambitions. She trudged nearly sixty miles on foot to her trial in near-freezing weather and was made to stand in the center of an assembly of men in pointy hats and black cloaks. The judges were supposed to test and judge her for the integrity and purity of her beliefs, but they, who had claimed to have come to America to escape religious persecution, persecuted her. They battered her with questions designed to entrap. Perhaps it was the fact that Anne had a depth of theological knowledge that Puritan society wasn't yet ready to accept from a woman. Or perhaps it was because Anne's beliefs were an aberration of their firmly held doctrines. Yet Anne came to serve and granted her listeners insight. In that lamp-lit, make-shift courtroom, she was made to defend the principles she taught to the members of her little meeting groups, which were modest groups composed mostly of women that the ordained and well-trained clerical judges found to be a threat. In turn, she was banished from her own countrymen and made to walk through unfriendly forests and fields in search of a welcoming refuge. Hers was a journey of determination and love, as she and her flock moved to two colonies. The peace that she finally found was all too briefly felt. Her ending was a bad and bloody one, as she and her family were victimized by the forces of unrelenting history "because there was no place for them at the inn."

This book tells the story of Anne Hutchinson's life—a life with a mission. Strict chronological sequence isn't adhered to because the content of Hutchinson's message is more thematic. The people in her life didn't appear as if in snapshots but kept reappearing over and over again. Thus, the book is split up into sections to make it easier for the reader living in a different time and place.

Chapter 1 – Ramifications of the Reformation

During the 16th century, the role of religion was intertwined with politics in Europe. For example, kings were expected to get papal permission to marry, and children were baptized by church-sanctioned clerics. Wars were fought (and are still fought) in the name of religion. In 1534, due to a dispute with the pope over permission to marry Anne Boleyn, King Henry VIII broke England's ties with the Catholic Church and founded the Church of England (the Anglican Church). No longer were the British subject to the pope and his mandates in matters of religion. Henry VIII's bold move triggered the English Reformation. In Europe, a parallel movement arose by virtue of the efforts of Martin Luther in Germany. This movement was called the Protestant Reformation. People eschewed being fed doctrine like porridge and began to think for themselves, although within limits. In doing so, people began to analyze and critique the traditional religious teachings uttered from the pulpits, which some felt were mindless drivel and primitive regurgitations of clerical syllabi. That applied not only to the people themselves but also to members of the clergy and even religious scholars.

King Henry VIII's daughter, Queen Elizabeth I, continued his efforts to purify the land of "papist" practices. However, to some, it appeared that she had not cleansed the Anglican religion of many of the vestiges that were still Catholic in appearance and function. Within the umbrella of Anglicanism, movements arose. One was propelled by John Calvin, a French theologian. His belief set was called Calvinism, but it soon took a foothold in Scotland under John Knox, who developed it into Scottish Presbyterianism. It slowly spread southward to the rest of England.

Puritanism wasn't a separate religious sect at that time; it was a movement within the Church of England. Puritans regularly attended religious services at the Anglican churches. Some of those churches were headed by ministers trained in Calvinistic theology, and their homilies and teachings reflected that. During the era of reformed theology, there arose a radical movement called Puritanism. Puritans were critical of some of the extraneous practices and leftover vestiges that could remind congregants of Roman Catholicism. They eschewed the wearing of ornamental vestments by the Anglican clergy, stained glass windows, and the like. Puritans were more stoic than the Anglicans, wore dark clothing, and disapproved of frivolous pastimes that were normally allowed by the Catholics. They also maintained a stricter adherence to the Bible.

Anne Hutchinson's father, Francis Marbury, was a minister who eschewed the use of ornate vestments and the wearing of surplices—a torso-length white cotton garment sometimes bordered in lace and worn over a minister's clothing. He also abandoned many of the ceremonial accouterments that the Anglicans had. Marbury felt that such embellishments were too "Catholic" or "papist." Although he claimed he was "no Puritan," Marbury was very much like a Puritan in his everyday behavior, though he lacked the solemnity they displayed. He was a quick wit with a sarcastic tinge—a characteristic that antagonized the Anglican authorities time and time again.

Marbury ranted for years against the religious prelates for their failure to educate the members of the clergy. He bemoaned the fact that people in the congregation hadn't even learned the Lord's Prayer. Furthermore, he indicated that very little preaching was actually done, and the ignorant clergy members even permitted chickens and pigs to wander around the church during the service! Marbury was a practical man who felt it was ludicrous to permit ministers to preach from a Bible they could barely read. He also criticized the traditional Anglican church, saying it was a "kind of charm" and that people were sometimes persuaded to believe they could "buy" salvation if they could afford to make the donations.

Francis Marbury under Arrest

Marbury bitterly complained about the lack of education of the clergy members and the poor quality of their primitive preaching practices. In 1578, he was taken into court and interrogated by the Bishop of London, John Aylmer, as well as Sir Owen Hopton and Archdeacon John Mullins. Marbury was bold and accused local prelates of the Church of England of having clergy members who were inadequate and ill-prepared when it came to preaching. Like Marbury, Bishop Aylmer was also a "hot-head" and is said to have retorted, "You have taken upon yourself to be a preacher, but there is nothing else in you. You are a very ass, an idiot, and a fool." Because of his non-conforming church practices and his belligerence, Francis Marbury was convicted of heresy and went to Marshalsea Prison for two years. Following his imprisonment, he was assigned a ministry at St. Wilford's Church in Alford, England.

In 1582, he married Elizabeth Moore and became a school teacher. About four years later, his wife died, and within a year, he remarried, this time to Bridget Dryden. History indicates that he had about twenty children. Many of the Marbury descendants were famous figures and include the poet John

Dryden, US senator Mitt Romney, and three American presidents—Franklin Delano Roosevelt, George H.W. Bush, and George W. Bush. In 1590, Marbury spoke up again, publicly criticizing the Anglican clergy members for its neglect of clerical training. As a result, he was placed under house arrest and spent many of his days in his garden since he was forbidden to preach or work while his family was struggling to survive. Most likely, they were supported by his in-laws, the Drydens. This was an age when family bloodlines meant the difference between poverty and wealth. After his suspension was lifted, Francis didn't publicly complain about the weaknesses of his Anglican overlords.

His daughter, Anne, was born while her father was under house arrest. There's no record of her birth, but she was baptized in July 1591. Like her father, she was outspoken, opinionated, and courageous. Francis Marbury homeschooled Anne along with her many siblings, which was quite a challenge. Nineteen of his children survived their childhood, despite the presence of the Black Plague. The education of women was just becoming acceptable in the 16th century, as the Queen of England herself spoke six languages. Marbury firmly believed his children should all have a solid education, regardless of their gender, so that they could contribute to society and help their communities progress into a new age. He taught his children using many techniques, including an amusing allegory in which he related his views about the inflated use of power by using the make-believe voice of an ignorant buffoon.

Once Anne's father was allowed to preach again, he and his family moved to London. He moved there because the stricter Puritan beliefs were better tolerated in the city since the population was more heterogeneous. Francis Marbury became a minister at two churches there, as there was a shortage of clergy members at the beginning of the 17th century. He had the ultimate honor of delivering a sermon upon the accession of King James I to the English throne in 1603. Marbury was well-known in his time, and some of his writings have even survived to this day. His name was mentioned by Sir Francis Bacon, a respected scientist who would one day become the Lord Chancellor of England. Bacon affectionately called Marbury "The Preacher," as if there were no others in England.

Role of Women

During the 17th century, women were relegated to tasks such as raising children and cooking. In addition, women were expected to organize the household, sew clothing, take care of the animals, clean, do some outdoor work like picking berries or help to harvest the vegetables, and "keep the home fires burning" in every meaning of the phrase. Men did the heavy work outside the house, helped with the crops, took care of ordering seeds and supplies, organized their businesses, and were expected to wrestle with intellectual concepts related to politics, religion, and affairs of the state. The latter duties were much more than social in nature; they were essential, as they were needed to influence the civic authorities in such a way that it would benefit their families. The world was now beyond the era of depending upon physical prowess for basic survival. Building and maintaining civic and religious communities were essential in reducing the stress of living. The clan mentality no longer propelled society. With regard to politics and religion, most women veiled their opinions in letter writing or confined their speculations within the walls of their homes, like turtles hiding inside their shells. Anne would turn out not to be like that. She would grow to be outspoken and even brutally frank on occasion.

Wisdom in an English Country Town

Anne grew up in Alford, a quaint and humble town that hosted weekly markets in the square and had just a handful of little buildings and shops, like the apothecary, the fabric store, and the church. That was where she met young William Hutchinson, who became the churchwarden in 1620. William Hutchinson, who was described as being gentle and soft-spoken, worked as a clothing merchant. When he moved to London, he prospered extremely well in the business.

When Anne's father was transferred to London, she renewed her friendship with William Hutchinson. It was heartening to find a friendly face and someone who had a common background. When women reached marrying age, they were encouraged to seek out men who could financially support them as well as any children from their union. Women in 17th-century England, particularly those who ascribed to Puritan values, married for love. There were no pre-arranged marriages among the Puritans. They had seen royal families subject themselves to pre-arranged marriages and spend miserable lives together, only to visit their unhappiness upon those whom they ruled.

Most importantly, it was essential that women marry young because society was male-dominated, meaning females could rarely find suitable and sustainable employment by themselves. When Anne's father suddenly died in 1611, she turned to her childhood friend, William Hutchinson, for support, and they married the following year. Marriages weren't elaborate affairs like they are today; they were simple—especially among the Puritans. Since Alford was warm and friendly to Anne and William as children, they moved back there shortly after they were married. Anne's husband was also a devout Christian, and so, the two of them kept abreast of religious matters in the area.

At St. Wilfrid's parish church of Alford, the people chatted about a charismatic preacher by the name of John Cotton, who served in the nearby town of Boston—not to be confused with the city by the same name in the United States. Cotton was a Puritan like Anne and her father, and he was critical of the ostentatious tendencies on the part of the clergy, as they wore ornamental robes and paraded about under the light cast from stained glass windows.

John Cotton's beliefs deviated somewhat from traditional Anglicanism because he emphasized the role of faith and conversion to Christ as opposed to the exclusive reliance on a life of good works for personal salvation. This religious framework is called covenant theology. John Cotton placed his primary focus on the "covenant of grace." "Grace," in a religious context, means that the unmerited favor of God is freely poured upon those who have faith. The "covenant of grace" means that God will freely welcome a person into heaven (salvation) if they profess a belief in Jesus Christ as their savior. On the other hand, some religious scholars felt that salvation was only attainable by a life of good works, known as the "covenant of works." Good works consist of acts performed by a person, such as 1) a belief in Jesus Christ as the son of God, 2) Bible reading, 3) listening to sermons, and 4) praying for the Holy Spirit to come personally to someone. Most mainstream Christian religions teach that salvation is attainable through a combination of grace and good works.

The "Puritan Bible"

Although most sermons had to do with the words in the Bible, it was the interpretation of those words that made the difference from one pulpit to another, as well as from one Protestant sect to another. In the same year that King Henry VIII established the Church of England, Reverend Martin Luther translated the Bible into the German language. Translation into the vernacular horrified many, as they found security and comfort in the more traditional but remote Latin version, known as the Vulgate, that was approved by the Catholic Church. Luther wanted the people of Germany to be able to read it in their homes and understand it. For his translation, he didn't use the Vulgate. He stepped back to its preceding languages, Hebrew, Aramaic, and Greek, and used those for his translation. It was called the Luther Bible, or as it was known in German, the *Lutherbibel.* In England, William Tyndale translated the New Testament into English. Myles Coverdale, who compiled the first authorized edition of the Bible in English known as the Great Bible of 1539, based his work on Tyndale's Bible. The Great Bible was revised again and succeeded by the Geneva Bible. This Bible was completed in different stages, with the New Testament being completed in 1557 and the Old Testament in 1560.

John Calvin was involved in the production of the Geneva Bible, as was John Knox, a Dutch theologian. John Cotton, Anne Hutchinson, and other Puritans used the Geneva Bible, also known as the Puritan Bible. The Geneva Bible showed the influence of John Calvin's religious philosophies because many of the annotations in this version of the Bible were Puritan in nature. The Geneva Bible offended Anglican clerics, who didn't care for its Calvinist flavor. Regardless, it was approved, and it was required by all the churches in Scotland until the Anglican Church received the Bishops' Bible, also known as the Queen's Bible, in 1568 That was later followed by the King James Bible in 1611. That Bible, along with later revisions, is still in use today.

Due to pressures from the Catholic Church and the emergence of diverse religious beliefs during the Protestant Reformation, Queen Elizabeth I created a settlement called the "Elizabethan Religious Settlement" in 1559 in order to maintain uniformity of religious practices. The queen saw to it that the English *Book of Common Prayer* was the catechism for English Protestants. The Geneva Bible and the 1549 edition of the *Book of Common Prayer* were carried over in 1607 to the British North American colonies in their first settlement at Jamestown, Virginia. As a matter of fact, Anne Hutchinson's father was the tutor of John Smith, the explorer and first leader of Jamestown.

Chapter 2 – Her Father's Daughter

The Religious Emigrations

Since its founding in 1534, the Church of England was led by powerful prelates. In 1633, William Laud was appointed to the mighty post of archbishop of Canterbury. It was he alone who determined the flavor and practices of his Anglican flock at that time. When some new movements developed within the umbrella of Anglicanism, Laud went on tirades to obliterate the splinter groups that sprouted from them, designating them as heretical. To a milder degree, Laud subscribed to Arminianism, named after Jacobus Arminius. Arminianism was a branch of Protestantism that was against the belief of predestination promoted by John Calvin, which had accompanied the printing of the Geneva Bible. Although the colonies first started off using the Geneva Bible, the King James Version was considered to be the official Bible by the mid-1600s. Not only did it incorporate the articles within the *Book of Common Prayer*, but it also embraced the structure of a church hierarchy, including its ritual practices, definitions of its theological concepts, and a uniform liturgy as an essential aspect of the religion.

Archbishop Laud wanted all the churches to be absolutely uniform and strictly Anglican in nature, according to his own interpretation. As such, he objected to Puritanism, which was one of the movements within the Anglican Church. Laud was extremely petty when it came to determining whether or not a religious community conformed specifically to those mandates and the doctrinal definitions as they were published in the *Book of Common Prayer*, and he meticulously monitored the churches in England to ascertain their adherence.

Since Laud was vehemently anti-Puritan, he overtly expressed his displeasure if a Puritan-leaning minister failed to scrupulously abide by the Anglican teachings and practices. If any church wasn't conforming to his orders, he could censure the minister, fine him, banish him, or, in some cases, put him in prison. In order to escape the religious persecution by Anglican extremists such as Laud, many of the Puritans planned to move to British America and set up their churches according to their own beliefs. Although John Smith had played an important role in the establishment of the first successful colony in the New World in Jamestown, Virginia, he also discovered a promising territory in the northern region, which he called "New England." The first wave of emigrants to this rugged area settled in Plymouth in the Massachusetts Bay Colony, which was at the time called Plymouth Colony, in 1620. These people were known as the Pilgrims, and religiously, these people were Puritans, that is, people who wanted to "purify" the beliefs and practices of Anglicanism. The Puritans were critics of the new Protestant beliefs that they felt merely mirrored those of Catholicism. Those who were called Pilgrims were even more extreme. They were referred to as "non-conforming" Anglicans and officially separated themselves from the Anglican Church.

In 1629, King Charles I of England dismissed Parliament and ruled on his own. He was very much an Anglican, and his wife, Henrietta Maria of France, was a Catholic. This marriage increased the power of Archbishop Laud and helped put a Roman Catholic slant on church services. At that point, the Puritans were far less comfortable than before. As a result, more English settlers embarked on the arduous journey across the Atlantic Ocean to the territories around Boston, Massachusetts. Primarily, they pursued religious freedom, but they also wanted to look for economic opportunities in the new land. It was a huge territory encompassing lands around modern-day Boston, Salem, Providence in Rhode Island, Connecticut, and New Hampshire.

In 1629, the population of the Massachusetts Bay Colony was a mixture of people under the reformed theological tradition and was mostly Calvinistic in nature. The direction and precepts of each individual church followed the teaching styles of the ministers leading each church but still fell under the umbrella of Anglicanism. More flexibility was permitted in the New World, and the people were free to apply to a church whose practices and ministers appealed to them. Once people were engaging in independent thought, they continued to develop their understanding of religious matters through clergy who were engaged by a church as its teachers.

Unlike many of the clerics of the day, Reverend John Cotton had attended three colleges, Trinity College, Cambridge University, and Emmanuel College. Like Anne Hutchinson's father, he believed in the need for education. Cotton once said, "Who dares to teach must never cease to learn." He despised the elaborate protocols attached to saying Mass and eschewed the wearing of fancy vestments like the surplice. He dismissed them as being prideful and devoid of religious meaning. In addition, he simplified his manner of saying Mass.

The Anglican authorities became enraged at his rejection of those practices. The context of his teachings on revelation and the covenant of grace likewise came to the attention of William Laud, the archbishop of Canterbury. Laud called Cotton definitively anti-Anglican, and Cotton was threatened with possible imprisonment. Consequently, he was forced into hiding and could no longer preach. Now deprived of following his vocation, he emigrated to the New World in 1633, and he was amongst the second wave of emigrants to New England.

Upon his arrival in the Massachusetts Bay Colony, which was officially established under that name in 1628, John Cotton was appointed as the teacher for the First Church of Boston under Reverend John Wilson. Wilson made frequent trips to England, and Cotton used to fill in for him. Cotton's services were extremely well-attended. He believed in preaching plainly and not given into flowery rhetoric, as he wanted both the well-educated and those who came from simple backgrounds to understand the word of God. His love of the Gospels was very obvious, and his sermons were alive with meaning and relevance.

Cotton saw his role within the church as very important, considering the politics and current events of the day. As such, he prepared his sermons carefully. They weren't negatively slanted, as he understood the challenges that his flock faced in life. John Cotton focused upon the relevance of the scripture and its application to the world in which people lived. He became deeply distressed by what he felt was the deviation of religion from the words of the scripture and the abuse of the pulpit to promote a personal agenda. He also disagreed with the Anglican interpretation that there was an absolutely causal relationship between the performance of moral obligations ("good works") and salvation. He emphasized that the grace of God was freely given. Cotton was also a firm believer in the "indwelling" of the spirit, in which each person would be given the means to achieve salvation. Anne Hutchinson particularly related to Cotton, as he was a practical person but glowed with spirituality and wasn't given to the ostentatious frills that sometimes distanced the people from the clergy who served them.

The Great Griffin

Anne and William Hutchinson's favorite clergyman was John Cotton. They had attended his services when he was at the English port of Boston near their hometown. When Cotton departed England, Anne and her husband were distressed because they favored his approach to Puritan doctrine. Anne, in particular, was a fervent Puritan and realized that she also needed to travel to Massachusetts to avoid religious persecution and, additionally, to escape the Black Plague, which was raging through Europe at that time. The Hutchinsons were very concerned about that because they had twelve children, two of whom had already died of the plague.

Anne adopted herbal remedies to prevent the plague, as did many other British people. Many of the British made masks with "beaks" on them and filled them with chopped up dried flowers, mashed wild onions, mint, and crushed minerals. It was their version of natural medicine.

Anne was devoutly religious. Like Reverend Cotton, she believed that God freely imparted his grace upon those who had faith—that is, the covenant of grace. She also believed in divine revelation and held the belief that God could and would impart insights to people individually outside of the Bible. Despite the fact that she wasn't formally schooled in theology, she learned such information from her father, who attended Christ College in Cambridge. From him and from his extensive library, Anne developed an understanding of theological principles. Anne Hutchinson was quite brilliant herself and easily grasped even the most advanced concepts.

Anne was pregnant when Cotton left England, so in 1633, she sent her oldest son, twenty-year-old Edward, on the *Griffin*, a double-masted clipper ship. It was actually the same ship that carried John Cotton. Anne, along with their children, had plans to reunite with their son as soon as her husband could make financial arrangements and wind up his business in London. His fabric business in Great Britain had been prosperous, and his reputation was bolstered by the fact that he came from a prominent family in Lincolnshire, which was the province where he grew up.

In 1634, when she was 34 years old, Anne and the rest of her family set sail aboard the same ship that John Cotton had taken the prior year, the *Griffin*. While aboard, she had a long discussion with Reverend Zechariah Symmes, in which she spoke extensively about her beliefs about God's gift of grace. She also met with a number of women and told them that they themselves could get answers from God through private inspiration, rather than always having to depend upon their ministers. Shortly after their arrival, the Hutchinsons settled in Boston. She and William aspired to become congregants at the First Church of Boston—the church at which John Cotton was a teacher. Most of the churches then had senior pastors, deacons, and teachers. The senior pastors were ordained clergy, as were the teachers. John Cotton was extremely popular in Boston, as he had a gentle way about him and was good at relating to people.

There was a specific procedure for admittance to an Anglican church. Prospective members were questioned about orthodoxy and their related beliefs to see if they conformed to Anglican standards. William was accepted after his first meeting with the church elders, but Anne's admittance was delayed due to her unique views about grace and inspiration. Her views were the same as those of John Cotton, but she was a woman who didn't fit the stereotype, and that alone gave rise to questions. In addition, it was rare to be presented with a woman who seemed to be so knowledgeable about theology.

The issue first arose when Anne discussed her views with an English minister, Zechariah Symmes, a hard-core traditionalist of the Puritan persuasion who also sailed to Massachusetts on the *Griffin.* In those days, the ministers discussed new applicants who contemplated joining the Massachusetts Bay Colony. After further questioning, Anne was admitted to the church, though many nursed reservations about her.

Anne and William Hutchinson lived in a two-story home on a small lot on the Shawmut Peninsula (modern-day downtown Boston), which juts into the Charles River. She and William had a large family, and the colony was thirsty for new inhabitants. They needed manpower to tame this raw, new, unpredictable land. Shawmut Peninsula was an idyllic setting for the family. Anne was very active in the community. She had a great deal of experience with children, and she became a midwife for other women in Boston, while her husband was in the city proper engaging in his mercantile trade. Her familiarity with herbs was an asset as she tended to the pregnant women in the community. It was said she assisted well over twenty women in childbirth. Women in those days had many children throughout the course of their life, perhaps as many as twenty.

As part of the requirements to join the Massachusetts Bay Colony, William Hutchinson had to take the Freeman's Oath, in which he swore that he was a "free man," that is, not an indentured servant. Among its terms, the oath required that new colonists pledge allegiance to the British Crown, which was headed up by the appointed governor of the colony, and that they were members of a duly-recognized church. The privileges extended to the signatories of the oath included the right to hold public office, and so, William served as a town deputy and as a selectman the following year. A selectman was someone who was on the executive board of the colonial government. Because women were considered to be subservient, they didn't hold public office but were expected to follow the lead of their husbands and weren't required to take such oaths.

The establishment of a productive civilization had now become the goal for those living in the New World, as it had entered an era when survival was extremely important. Thus, it became more desirable to tap all members of a community, including the women, so that the American experiment would work. So, the importance of the role of women in society became a threat to many men, who were already being confronted with having to contend with an untested country. Men tended to protest when females expressed themselves openly in society because they looked upon women as more competition. Enlightened men were open to the contributions of women, but this adaptation was difficult for many who preferred the status quo. Men sometimes felt that women weren't intelligent enough to comprehend more complex or sophisticated concepts and needed "protection." Protecting the less physically strong is natural to the paternal figures of any species. However, with that came the inevitability of intellectual snobbery. Everyone, women included, fear the harsh reality of losing control. Back then, though, it was the men who feared this loss. To control the reputation of their families, some men felt they had an inalienable right to mandate the behavior and curb the speech of women, particularly that of their wives and daughters.

Acceptance or rejection of a new settler, whether they were male or female, was a highly sensitive point for the founding fathers of the Massachusetts Bay Colony, like John Winthrop. He arrived in Massachusetts in 1630 to escape the rages of religious crackdowns heralded by Archbishop Laud. John Winthrop treated Massachusetts like a foster child and examined the rosters of newly arriving ships to assess the new entries into the colony and expel undesirables. Winthrop also wanted political control and ruled on the governing board of the colony for most of the time he lived there.

Anne Hutchinson's reputation had preceded her, and John Winthrop, who was overly cautious about new inhabitants, had heard about her sharp tongue and mental acuity. He didn't directly address that issue in 1634 when she arrived, though, as he was competing with Thomas Dudley and John Haynes for total control of the colony. These two men were wealthy and knowledgeable in how to administer effectively and wanted the governorship of the colony for themselves.

Although Winthrop was the first governor, Haynes and Dudley served under him as magistrates. In their positions, they exhausted a great deal of time arguing points of governance related to taxation, voting, aspects of the original colonial charter, the judiciary, and eventually became involved in analyzing the nature of the religious beliefs of the newcomers in town like Anne Hutchinson. After having spoken to her, Winthrop felt that "she was a woman of haughty and fierce carriage, a nimble wit and active spirit, a very voluble tongue." In many ways, Anne Hutchinson's personality and, indeed, her life mirrored that of her father. She was her father's daughter.

Chapter 3 – Religion and Rivalries in a Raw Land

Political Problems

Henry Vane the "Younger" came over to Massachusetts with John Winthrop the Younger, the aforementioned John Winthrop's son, and Reverend Hugh Peter, a preacher and a political advisor. Vane was elected as the governor of the Massachusetts Bay Colony in 1636, succeeding John Haynes. Both William and Anne Hutchinson were supportive of the new governor because he was an advocate of religious tolerance, something that was lacking in England. Vane was an active member of John Cotton's church in Boston and was a man ahead of his times in terms of his persistent adherence to the non-conforming Puritan values. His religious viewpoints lay closest to those of Anne Hutchinson, who was his vocal supporter. Cotton recommended Vane also, as he was an independent thinker during an age that encouraged conformity. Historians think of him as a gifted administrator and politician. Because of his intelligence and cleverness, he was seen as a threat by those who preferred utter conformity to the adherence of religious laws. Politically, there was friction among his magistrates, John Winthrop (who used to be the governor) and Thomas Dudley over the set-up of the judicial court. Vane mediated the issue, and they arrived at a compromise.

Pequot War

Although the Pequot War didn't impact Anne's life tremendously, the animosity between the Native Americans and the colonists did not improve with time, as one will notice later when discussing the events of Anne's death. Thus, it is important that this war is briefly talked about.

The southwest area of the Massachusetts Bay Colony adjoined northeastern Connecticut and southern Rhode Island. Offshore lay Block Island, which was isolated from the mainland. The Niantics, who inhabited Block Island, which they called "Manisses," was a tribe that spoke Algonquin. Over time, the Niantics split into two factions, the Western Niantics, who would join with the Pequots in the upcoming war, and the Eastern Niantics, who would ally with the Narragansetts. The Narragansetts, another Algonquin-speaking tribe, shared Rhode Island with other tribes as well as the English colonists under Roger Williams. Even though relations between the tribes and the English settlers were usually amicable, sometimes violent conflicts erupted. Back in 1634, the Western Niantics murdered an English trader, John Stone, by the Connecticut River over a dispute about fishing rights. Despite the deed being done by a different tribe, the Pequots, who controlled much of Connecticut, were blamed. No action was taken against the Pequots at that time, particularly since the people didn't care for Stone, but the colonists became very wary of them.

In 1636, toward the end of Governor Vane's term as governor, the body of John Oldham, an English trader, was found on his ship. From all appearances, he had been slaughtered by natives. Governor Vane then called upon Colonel John Endicott to rally his militia in Massachusetts to prepare to exact revenge upon the troublesome Pequots. Alarmed, Roger Williams, the leader of Rhode Island, immediately contacted Vane, telling him that the crime was most likely committed by the Narragansetts, not the Pequots. Disregarding Williams, Vane sent Endicott ahead to Block Island to invade it, as he was concerned about incursions from the indigenous people on their farms and villages. He also commanded an invasion of the Pequot territory in southeastern Connecticut. To prevent any spread of hostilities, Roger Williams was able to convince the Narragansetts to break their ties with the Pequots and go to war against them as well. Even the Mohegans, who once formed a single faction with the Pequots, joined the fight against the Pequots. Hutchinson and her followers were vehemently opposed to this escalation of violence.

The Pequots fought courageously despite the fact that they didn't possess firearms. They were experts at strategy and knew the terrain well, using it to their advantage. Many English soldiers lost their lives in the early stages of the war. In 1637, the Pequots attacked an English village at Wethersfield, Connecticut, and mercilessly slaughtered men, women, and children. Then the Pequots moved to northeastern Connecticut, along the seashore near today's town of Mystic, where they had a large village. Soldiers from Connecticut under Colonel John Mason rushed into the village and set all the structures on fire. As the Native American warriors tried to escape, they were killed by the Narragansetts and Mohegans waiting outside. Stragglers and survivors from this massacre retreated southward to Fairfield, Connecticut. They were pursued by the English, and the fighting went on until nearly all of the Pequots had died.

The Conventicles

While the Pequot War was going on, the deeply religious Hutchinson held weekly religious meetings, called "conventicles," in her house. Conventicles weren't unusual in England, and the practice continued following the years after the Protestant Reformation until 1648. At the conventicles, the attendees discussed the sermons they heard at the church services as well as the scriptures from which they were drawn. Anne was a gifted and charismatic teacher. It was written by an unnamed woman that she "was wonderfully endowed with the indescribable quality known as magnetism." Thus, her gatherings became very popular, and she developed a following. Several years later, Anne held the meetings more often. Even Governor Vane used to attend the conventicles when he was in office. Most of the members of the meetings were female, but sometimes men even attended, often merchants and seamen. The less structured and informal setting of these sessions interested them, and they were free to openly discuss economic and practical issues and reflect on the ethics they engaged in when conducting business. Because of their business schedules, many of these men weren't available for Sunday services, so the conventicles were opportunities for them to tend to matters of the spirit. There, they discussed the minister's sermons, the Bible, and the covenant theology that Anne espoused.

Conventicles were common in the religious communities of England, and the practice was carried along to America. They not only served the purpose of fortifying religious beliefs but had social functions as well. Colonial women in America were often confined to their homes on weekdays in order to raise their children and take care of the house, excluding trips going to the market. Therefore, they appreciated the company of other adults.

When the men of the area heard about these meetings, more husbands began accompanying their wives. In fact, Hutchinson's audiences swelled in numbers to sixty or seventy, and she began having two sessions per week. As word circulated, a minister of Newton, Massachusetts, named Thomas Weld, noted that "some of the magistrates, some gentlemen, some scholars and men of learning" attended the meeting. Weld felt that the spread of the conventicle movement might make the clergy lose control of their congregations, as they wouldn't be the ones guiding the people in the "right" interpretation of doctrinal beliefs and practices. Therefore, Weld grew suspicious of Hutchinson and portrayed her as being a "conspirator" of sorts, intent on infecting the community with her "venom." In fact, Weld looked upon any woman who led a community such as Hutchinson did as "having stepped out of her place" as a woman. Furthermore, he felt she was being devious and was "a dangerous instrument of the devil raised up by Satan to raise up among us divisions and contentions to take away the hearts and affection for one another."

Puritan Attitudes toward Women

Some of those who lived in the 16th and 17th centuries in America believed that each person was composed of an immortal male half and a mortal female half. The woman in a marriage was perceived to be equal to the man, but the woman was still the "weaker sex" who needed protection. Women weren't permitted to vote or attend civic meetings, not only because of their perceived lack of intelligence but because of an inherent "weakness in their brain fibers." Men preferred they use their time to keep their homes running smoothly and raising children. Contrary to popular belief, women could own property and sign contracts, mostly related to their own property. In some households, husbands asked their wives if they could act on their behalf if they weren't able to be present. It was clear that many men came to realize that their wives were astute, and many sought their advice, although they kept it a secret from other men for fear of ridicule. Some, like Anne Hutchinson, held private power, the power to educate the young and the power to lead other women in religious pursuits.

Puritan women were sometimes seen as potential "Jezebels," not because of some inherent wickedness but because of their powers of persuasion. If they operated outside of the specified female parameters of wife, lover, and mother, they could be seen as seductive. Many sociologists indicate that a female miscreant in colonial times was seen as worse than Eve being tempted by the snake in the Garden of Eden. Instead, she was thought of as the snake itself.

Other sociologists claim that Puritan men had great respect for women. They write that although the Puritans firmly believed in the distinction of the roles of the sexes, women were more than capable of scholarship. This wasn't a commonly held belief, however, and many women were relegated to expressing their thoughts, philosophies, and insights through the medium of letter writing.

Anne Hutchinson observed the fear and anxiety within the Puritan community because of the harshness of their rules. It was recorded by historians that one day, "a woman of Boston...took her little child and threw it into the well and then came into the house and said now she was sure she would be damned because she drowned her child." It was an irrational solution, but it demonstrated the extreme stress many felt because they could never measure up to the insurmountable goals the clergy placed on them. Women, in particular, were made to live in fear and terror of the authorities in New England because religious behavior and civic behavior operated together. Patriarchal inflexibility was traumatic for many of the female congregants. There are historical anecdotes of women who were penalized for infractions of parental obedience, such as in the case of Sara Scott, who was presented in front of the colonial enforcers for "reviling and striking her mother...for undutiful abusive and reviling speeches and carriages to her natural mother." As written in Nathaniel Hawthorne's *The Scarlet Letter*, women who were accused of being adulteresses (whether true or untrue) were made to walk about the town with the scarlet letter "A" sewn upon their outer clothing. This punishment was more common in the colonies later on, and although this penalty was mostly reserved for women, even men had to submit themselves to the same humiliation. For the most part, however, it was as if the male-dominated society in New England feared a female coup d'état. A descendant of Anne Hutchinson, Eve LaPlante, indicated that Hutchinson was derided by one of the Massachusetts governors as an "instrument of Satan," "an enemy of the chosen people," and "an American Jezebel."

Tensions Arise

Before Anne and William Hutchinson became well known in the colony, John Wilson was the senior pastor at the First Church of Boston. Wilson had arrived in Massachusetts along with the earlier emigrants, including John Winthrop, and he was a powerful minister who forcefully emphasized the need for good works in order to achieve salvation. He was away when Anne and her husband first attended the Boston Church, so the congregation became accustomed to their gentle teacher, John Cotton, who promoted the covenant of grace primarily. When Wilson returned, however, Hutchinson and the members of the congregation found Wilson's approach disagreeable. Wilson imparted his message in an authoritarian and strict manner, and his speaking style stood in stark contrast to that of the mild-mannered speech Cotton used.

Wilson's message was also far different from the viewpoints that Hutchinson expressed at her conventicles.

During the course of his homilies, some congregants used to interrupt Wilson and try to initiate theological arguments. Although there were traditional question periods held after the sermons, the orthodox faithful were just expected to ask for elaborations or clarifications of the content of the sermons. The ministers were unaccustomed to being questioned about the religious basis for their sermons. Anne herself was horrified that Wilson would stress that good works were needed to attain salvation and approached Wilson about it. On one occasion, Hutchinson herself actually walked out of Wilson's church, followed by many other women. While leaving during a church service wasn't forbidden, this was an enormous exit of women. Men usually attributed such exits by women as being caused by their "infirmities," but that group was too large to be ignored.

Without a blush, Anne Hutchinson took Wilson's messages home and contradicted him at her weekly conventicles. She was a zealous firebrand and went so far as to say that Wilson lacked the "seal of the spirit," a direct reference to divine inspiration where the Holy Spirit speaks to his elect. The Holy Spirit was seen as a facet of God himself.

In 1636, Anne's brother-in-law, John Wheelwright, also came to Massachusetts. He was an Anglican minister who preached at a church in South Boston. Like Anne, he agreed with John Cotton's theological stance that grace was freely given by God and didn't have to be "earned" through a life of good works. Wheelwright, like many of the non-conforming Puritans, focused upon the covenant of grace, stressing the fact that God gives his grace freely to those who seek it.

Although they had come to the New World in search of religious freedom, some clergymen started repeating the criticisms once levied at the Anglicans in England by Archbishop Laud. Hence, a number of the Anglican ministers in the environs began to question the orthodoxy of John Wheelwright, John Cotton, and Anne Hutchinson. Word raced through the ministerial community about their preaching, comparing it to the prescribed precepts in the *Book of Common Prayer* and reformed theology.

Reverend Thomas Shepard, a scholarly expert, was notified about the deviancy of this group of leaders in the Massachusetts Bay Colony. Having studied at Emmanuel College at Cambridge University and then becoming a minister of the highly respected First Church in Cambridge, a minister at Harvard University, and an instructor of clerics in New England, Thomas Shepard was considered a theological expert of renown. When he heard that these preachers promoted the covenant of grace almost exclusively, he and more local ministers became alarmed. They felt that Anglicanism was becoming polluted with these non-conformist schools of thought, which seemed to be more extreme than their own non-conforming views. They were particularly incensed that Anne Hutchinson—a woman—was bold enough to participate in theological debates, such as the ones she had with Reverend Wilson. Another minister, Reverend Hugh Peter from Salem, said Anne "had better been a husband than a wife; and a preacher than a hearer, and a magistrate than a subject." The tenor of Hugh Peter's response was no longer directed at the content of her messages but rather at her as a person. Not only that, but the fact that Reverend Peter brought up the term "magistrate" had political ramifications as well. After all, in the British American colonies, men—and only men—were permitted to be magistrates.

In the Puritan world of the Massachusetts Bay Colony, the line between civil power and religious power was blurred. In the Massachusetts Bay Colony, the designated religion was Anglicanism, and it was assumed that the people in the colony would support their governors and magistrates along with their religious beliefs. Reverend Peter, in fact, was involved in the civil administration of Salem, where he preached. Like many of the other ministers in Massachusetts, he adhered to strictly orthodox precepts, like those espoused by the archbishop of Canterbury back in England.

One of the local ministers, Peter Bulkley, was a very stiff Puritan minister who had differed with many of the prelates in England because he believed that the ornamental "frills" many of the Anglican ministers displayed in their church vestments resembled that of the Catholics. In fact, he refused to wear the surplice or utilize the ornamental embellishments that the papists and the traditional Anglicans wore. He also taught the covenant of grace, giving it the same weight as the covenant of works. For those reasons, he was called a "non-conformist" and had sometimes run into conflict with the infamous Archbishop Laud in England. However, in many ways, he displayed the same rigidity as the English archbishop and that displayed by Reverend Thomas Shepard because he was horrified that a woman would express herself so openly about religious issues. As one might be able to tell, the issue of Anne was evolving past religious differences; it was instead becoming an issue about women holding a more powerful role in society.

Chapter 4 – Controversies Abound

The Free Grace Controversy

Because of their many sermons about the covenant of grace, John Wheelwright and John Cotton became known as the "free grace advocates." Anne Hutchinson was a "free grace advocate" because she taught the same approach as Wheelwright and Cotton. John Winthrop gave a public voice to this controversy between the covenant of grace ("free grace") and the covenant of works. Politically, Winthrop saw the popularity of John Cotton and his ilk as a threat to his own influence, saying, "In the six months following John Cotton's admission to membership...diverse profane and notorious evil persons came and were accepted into the bosom of the (Boston) church." Then theological tirades began to be shouted from the pulpits Sunday after Sunday from church to church, so Winthrop decided to intervene.

Some reformed theologians felt that teaching about "free grace" would lead to the heresy of Antinomianism. The term "Antinomianism" was coined by Martin Luther during the 15th century, a view that Luther called heretical. The derivation of "Antinomianism" comes from two Greek words meaning "against the law," indicating that one could still be Christian without adhering to moral or church laws. Luther advised that a person did not need to be so overly concerned about keeping the law that they lose sight of the Christian motivation behind the deed they performed. He later felt that would lead to a misconception, so he clarified the issue. Luther admitted that he had been extreme in the beginning by the use of "excessive rhetoric against the law."

The free grace theological movement started during the 1st century but developed during the Protestant Reformation in the early 16th century. People who believed in this movement posited that eternal life is a free gift given by God, demonstrated by the death and resurrection of Jesus Christ on the cross. They believed that the gift of grace is freely given to those who believe that Christ is the Son of God. In other words, faith alone gives a person eternal life.

The Puritan church leaders saw this belief, taken alone and at face value, as a tool for creating passive Christians, who may not necessarily go to heaven without doing good works. Anne Hutchinson was raised as a Calvinist, as were most of the other Puritans. John Calvin promoted the concept of "predestination," which he interpreted as meaning that God has foreknowledge of all events that happen to individuals. Calvin believed not only in free grace but also in the fact that those who truly have faith will persevere throughout their lives in doing good works since faith and good works are intimately bound. However, some non-Calvinistic clergy members misunderstood the concept, perceiving it as being an assertion that God has decided who shall go to heaven and who shall go to hell and that this godly decision was irreversible. Others explained that those who were condemned to eternal damnation were never "true believers" in the first place.

In the religious sense, a "covenant" means a promise made between God and his people. In the case of Adam and Eve, humans broke the covenant. Upon the salvation of Christ, a new covenant was made. In the 17th century, the Puritans went two steps further with the establishment of a social covenant and the establishment of a church covenant.

The "social covenant" referred to the obligation of fellow Puritans to see to it that their families and neighbors kept the law and performed good works. This wasn't an effort to harass others but was rather an attempt to keep society as pure and holy as possible and to unify all within the community. It was believed that keeping the social covenant would facilitate predestination (or prove to others that one was destined for eternal salvation).

The "church covenant" referred to the obligation of attending church and church functions, studying the scriptural texts, and carefully listening to the homilies.

When Anne Hutchinson was conducting her conventicles, she stressed free grace, as did John Wheelwright and John Cotton. They rejected the notion that those who practiced good works and obeyed the law are saved by that alone. They believed it was by faith that one was saved and that the grace of God was freely given. Free grace allowed for the presence of flaws within the human being. A person cannot take pride in deserving eternal salvation, no matter how many good works they did, because all men are flawed. There is no checklist for the number of good works a person has to do.

As a result of their discussions, the group of ministers was satisfied with John Cotton's responses about the covenant of grace and the covenant of works, so they saw no reason to question him further. However, they were still somewhat uncomfortable about Wheelwright's position, and they urged him not to put too much weight upon the covenant of grace but rather to emphasize good works through obedience to the law. John Wheelwright, at least temporarily, agreed with the position of the more powerful clerics in Massachusetts. They next instructed Anne about the role of good works and obedience to the law, saying that both are needed to attain "justification," that is, eternal salvation. Anne claimed, however, that it was through grace alone that one was saved. Good works and adherence to the law, she indicated, are performed for the glory of God, not as a means of attaining salvation.

The ministers were horrified by that and accused Hutchinson of subscribing to "Antinomianism," the aforementioned heretical viewpoint that good works and the law were unnecessary for salvation. That wasn't what she said, but they were convinced that this untrained woman was teaching heresy to the people of the Massachusetts Bay Colony. She was also accused of being a "Familist," which was a 16th-century Dutch belief in the freedom of religion within a community.

The Antinomian Controversy

As mentioned above, the word "Antinomian" is derived from Greek words, and it means "against the law." The term frequently came into the religious jargon during the early days of the Protestant Reformation. However, during the later 16th century, the term Antinomian assumed different shades of meaning.

Antinomians were people who felt they were not obligated to abide by the tenets of a uniform religious code of law. They are saved, that is, they are "justified" by faith alone, without any moral obligation to do good works. Reformed theologians believed that faith would create obedience to the law and ecclesiastical regulations espoused through their congregations. The reformed tradition indicated that faith and good works were both essential in order to obtain salvation. Antinomians believed that the divine indwelling of the Holy Spirit of God spurred righteous behavior on the part of the believer. This state of freedom from the law resulted from the fact that a Christian was "reborn" in Christ, and the Antinomians cited the biblical passage in Romans 7:6, "But now we have been delivered from the law, having died to what we were held by, so that we should serve in the newness of the Spirit and not in the oldness of the letter." Prior to the coining of the term "Antinomianism," the early Christians such as Augustine of Hippo in the 5th century stated, "Love God; do what you will; you won't sin." He saw the integral relationship between the love of God and good works as something that did not need to be spelled out in the law. His view and that of the free grace advocates was the "spirit of the law" rather than the "letter of the law."

The Antinomian Controversy arose following the comments made by one of Martin Luther's students in 1525, and people erroneously began to equate licentiousness with Antinomianism. Anne Hutchinson and the free grace advocates, like John Cotton, became linked with Antinomianism around 1636 shortly after their arrival in Massachusetts. During those days, Christians were scrupulously observant, and it was practically a grievous sin if one didn't adhere to the proscribed beliefs they heard in their church. In most reformed sects, the term was a devastating accusation of heresy.

John Winthrop and the other ministers who took the credit for having founded the colony of Massachusetts Bay were threatened by what they perceived as distortions of their religious beliefs. Although they weren't theologians themselves, they wanted the colonists to strictly adhere to what they said. It was a subtle means of control. Any deviation, however slight, from the pronouncements of the governor and his magistrates was seen as divisive. It could result in banishment from Christian society. Critics of Antinomianism were convinced that any suggestion of it would create chaos within the community, with the more ignorant, barbaric heathens rushing around their communities committing crimes. They reasoned that if there was no legitimate secular or religious authority that people needed to follow in order to reach salvation, there would be no reason to behave morally.

Anne didn't believe that, but more recent commentators leap to the conclusion that she did. It is an easy mistake to make. People of the 17th century were oversensitive to anyone who seemed to stray from the word-for-word interpretations presented from the Sunday pulpits. The real weakness of Antinomianism is the fact that it is too ambiguous a concept. Those who do not examine it thoroughly would understandably leap to the conclusion that Antinomianism totally rejects moral law. It doesn't. Instead, Antinomians rejected the role of good works *alone* in achieving eternal salvation. Many of the Puritans of the 16th and 17th centuries believed exclusively in the necessity of performing good works, and so, Antinomianism was one of the most hated and feared philosophies. The Puritans indicated that there was no way to determine whether people were justified or "saved" except by demonstrating it through obedience to religious law by being willing to "work out their salvation with fear and trembling," according to the words of the scriptures and the Gospels. The "law" they spoke of was derived from the scriptures as interpreted by the clergy and the intellectual fathers of their faith.

The Antinomians of the 17th century, like Anne Hutchinson, were very liberal in hurling the term "crypto-papist" at their contemporaries, an insult to those who believed in the reformed traditions as it meant that they were Roman Catholics at heart. They accused many Puritan clergy members and scholars of being primarily "legalists." In the 17th century, accomplished theologians with international reputations such as Thomas Shepard, who questioned Anne Hutchinson, realized that the issue was far more complex than had at first been anticipated. They taught that men were by nature depraved and that they needed to earn their way into the good graces of God. According to Reverend Thomas Shepard, "...you do not only deserve, but are under the sentence of death and curse of God, immediately after the least hair's breadth swerving from the law by the smallest sin and accidental infirmity."

Even Peter Bulkley, the well-known minister and writer, had been attacked by Archbishop Laud back in England for his non-conformist attitudes toward Anglicanism. Bulkley wrote the book called the *Gospel Covenant* for his followers and forcefully said that the covenant of grace brings salvation. He said, "We are saved by grace, and not by works." He had noted the arrogance and pride of those within the colony who boasted about their good works, and he reacted negatively to their pompous behavior. In the end, Bulkley didn't forcefully support Hutchinson, but that appears now to be more of a case of self-preservation than belief.

In colonial times in Massachusetts, it was important that a preacher keep his reputation in good standing. Hence, ministers, like Peter Bulkley, who could have supported Anne, didn't do so. The people who ran the colony were intolerant of theological viewpoints that appeared to differ even slightly from their own. In effect, they repeated the very behavior that drove them out of England.

Those who failed to parrot the religious viewpoints of the favored clerics risked being forcibly ejected from the colony. In the untamed territories of New England, that was dangerous. However, those who permitted themselves to be vulnerable became strong. Anne Hutchinson wasn't going to compromise her convictions because they were questioned. That wasn't the way of her father before her, and it wasn't her way either, regardless of her gender or status.

Hutchinson's Unique Interpretation

The Puritans who were trained in Calvinism were taught to believe in "predestination," which means that God plans from the very beginning of a person's life whether he or she is to be "saved," that is, go to heaven, or be condemned to hell. Hutchinson rejected that interpretation, at least when presented in that form. She believed and taught that a person could be saved through faith and God's grace, which was freely given. The person then had God dwelling within them. She downplayed the role of good works to an extreme degree. People, Anne believed, would engage in good works to purify the world around them and spread the goodness of God.

Anne also didn't find it necessary to refer to the scriptures by regurgitating what they said; she believed God himself made divine revelations to a person privately within their own soul. It was said that Anne had a revelation of her own while aboard the ship that took her to Massachusetts, as she was able to predict the exact date of her arrival. According to Anne, focusing on one's own personal inspirations eliminates the necessity of scrupulously adhering to sets of regulations and laws. Her viewpoint reduced self-doubt and worry about whether or not a person measured up to moral expectations as expounded by God's earthly ministers. For her, goodness flowed from the grace of God through a person, which would then be reflected in a good life.

The difficulty posed by her views lay in the implication that the law in and of itself was useless to those with true faith. One of the other pitfalls of such an approach lay in the fact that some viewed it as being self-centered, as there was no external evidence that one was, indeed, truly an outstanding moral person. After all, there was no proof that the revelations and inspirations that one might receive were really from God, and there was no evidence that one's behavior was in accordance with moral law. Another pitfall that resulted from this controversy was the fact that this antipathy toward the law opened up the temptation for some to criticize those clergy who taught the covenant of good works.

Reverend Thomas Weld was of the opinion that anyone who taught anything that resembled Antinomianism was motivated by a "spirit of pride, insolence, contempt of authority, division and sedition." He and other members of the clergy felt that Antinomianism was an epidemic that could place the future of the Massachusetts Bay Colony at risk.

Anti-Hutchinson Campaign in Formation

Magistrate John Winthrop went on a campaign to rid Massachusetts of people such as Wheelwright and Hutchinson, as well as the more liberal governor Henry Vane, by accusing them of being Antinomians. Winthrop saw the Antinomian Controversy as a means by which he could eject those who disagreed with his political and theological approaches. As a matter of fact, he spearheaded the passage of a law forbidding residency to new settlers whose beliefs didn't coincide closely with his own. He said that the colony had the right "to refuse to receive such whose dispositions suit not ours." If the people walked in lock-step with his own theological beliefs, Winthrop could continue to hold power over the colony.

Winthrop labeled the Antinomian belief as dangerous heresy, as did many of the Protestant reformists, including the Anglicans. While it's difficult to conclude that Winthrop's political ambitions outweighed his theological positions, it is certain he saw Anne Hutchinson as a woman who would "split" the colony. There was no tolerance for female activism there.

Justification and Sanctification

Justification, according to Christians, was God's removal of the guilt of sin and the release of the soul from what was called the "original sin," which was originally committed by Adam and Eve when they chose not to listen to God and took a bite of the forbidden fruit. The first stain is washed away in baptism, but justification must be reinforced through nurturing one's continued faith in Christ. That way, a person is considered "saved," that is, they will go into a state of heavenly bliss upon death. While on earth, their good actions are holy as long as they are done through faith. Those acts are, therefore, sanctified, meaning they are "made holy." Sanctification can further be explained as the restoration to the holy image people held before the fall of Adam and Eve.

Anne Hutchinson and John Wheelwright indicated that people did not need to look in their own lives for evidence of one's election to those of the faithful, the saved, and the justified. The opposition, however, felt that wasn't the case. They indicated that one needed to look at their own lives to see evidence of one's justification by comparing their own lives with the words of the Gospel. Those who criticized Antinomianism insisted that the law (religious law) bound all believers, and they felt that the Antinomians denied the usefulness of the law. Antinomians asserted that they didn't need to appeal to the Gospels to know what is right; they simply needed to listen to the "spirit within."

As mentioned before, some of the more traditional reformed traditions like Anglicanism put the proverbial "carriage before the horse," so to speak, by teaching that the kind of grace that engenders faith could only be achieved by the performance of good acts. That way, a person can have their acts sanctified, be justified, and earn salvation.

Anne Hutchinson's approach was more positive. The only way one could lose the grace that God freely gave was to reject it. The unfortunate choice of rejecting that grace could result in a failure to be saved.

The Anglicans and more traditional reformed sects taught that this grace, which brings about justification and salvation, must first be earned. Hence, church members who were judged to be deviating from the religious law must make reparations and beg to be readmitted into the body of the faithful.

The Covenant of Works and Preparationism

This concept was based upon the belief that people who were "reborn" or who "convert" to a belief in Jesus Christ needed to "prepare" for such a life change by performing a series of spiritual steps. Many of the Puritan ministers in the Massachusetts Bay Colony promulgated the view that there was a cause-effect relationship between good works and grace. They further taught that a period of preparation was essential in order to be "born again in Christ" and be made ready to receive the gift of grace from God. In other words, people had to "work" for it, or grace wouldn't be given. Reverend Thomas Shepard, in particular, looked upon himself and other men as being defiled, unclean, and totally unworthy of God by nature. He believed in and taught the vital importance of preparation in order to receive the infusion of the Holy Spirit into one's heart and soul. Others believed that good works were an outgrowth of faith and a consequence of grace.

The difficulty of "Preparationism," as it was defined by some in the Puritan world, was the fact that this period of preparation was totally directed by the minister and the way he interpreted the Bible and religious laws. That approach shifted the control of salvation to the minister—a human agent—and away from God as manifest in the Holy Spirit.

The Covenant of Grace

The Puritans furthermore believed that the people of their faith were redeemed from their innate imperfections through God's divine favor. In other words, humankind could attain heaven if they were "reborn" in Jesus Christ and kept their faith in him. They believed, as the Bible said, "Sin shall not be your master because you are not under the law, but under grace" (Romans 6:14). Anne Hutchinson believed that salvation was attained through faith alone. Reformed theologians, for the most part, taught that the gift of grace was unconditional. Many of the Puritans in New England diverted from that viewpoint by making the performance of works and the keeping of the law a prerequisite for grace.

The strictest of the Puritan churches were like unyielding systems of checks and balances. In the Puritan churches, a pastor would preach, a teacher would see to it that the teachings adhered to the doctrine of the church, the elders would see to it that there were rules to guide the congregants, and the deacons would manage the day-to-day tasks of making everything flow smoothly—that is, financially and practically. Lastly, the churches would see to it that their congregants obeyed.

The Puritans had enforcers within their communities who punished people for breaking some of the most minor rules. Putting people in the pillory or flogging them for slight infractions was a common practice. Women, in particular, had to be careful, as there were many regulations against them, such as making one's opinion known or speaking out of turn. They also needed to keep their children well controlled. If they failed in that, mothers were penalized and humiliated. Colonial punishments could even be sadistic and violent. One could have their ears cut off for eavesdropping or their tongues pierced with hot irons for lying. Banishment from a colony was often used to prevent enlightened ideas from being promulgated. Some of the Puritan communities even forbade a special celebration of Christmas! In one of the newspapers in Boston, it said, "The observation of Christmas having been deemed a sacrilege, the exchanging of gifts and greetings, the dressing in fine clothing (is forbidden). Feasting and similar celebrations are hereby forbidden." There was even a monetary penalty for any infractions of this ordinance, and people were encouraged to report offenders to the authorities.

However, there were differences among the churches. Some of the ministers forbade their people from partying or dancing, while others didn't. Puritans could drink wine and alcoholic beverages but never to excess.

The Massachusetts Bay Colony eschewed change. Gifted leaders with new ideas were seen as too challenging to the status quo and the fail-safe predictability of everyday life.

The Covenant of Works vs. The Covenant of Grace

John Cotton disagreed with prioritizing the covenant of works above the covenant of grace. Many New England ministers preached that the covenant of works was synonymous with legalism and ascribed to it. John Cotton, on the other hand, referred to it with disdain.

Anne Hutchinson agreed with Cotton and, furthermore, realized that guilt was non-productive and deleterious to growth within a community. The precepts hollered from the pulpits of many a dark and somber church frightened the women of Boston in particular, and they felt as if they were under the constant shadow of eternal damnation.

The belief that good works culminate in salvation was appealing to many because people had control over their behavior. If they performed good works, they could then claim they were God's chosen people because they were godly, which could be seen by their actions. The covenant of grace was seen as more passive because no one could "earn" their salvation following that belief.

The Puritan oligarchy either believed in or relied upon the outward evidence of holiness, as would be seen in the observation of the covenant of works. The women, though, were expected to do the opposite–to appear nearly invisible to the male community and be demurely devout.

Anne Hutchinson, John Cotton, John Wheelwright, and Peter Bulkley were concerned about the exaggerated reliance upon good deeds to bring about salvation. It sowed fear, doubt, and even despair among the people of New England. One could get bound up in logistical concerns like counting up one's good deeds to see if one had performed enough of them to qualify as a good person.

Familism

Familism was a branch of religious belief in which the "family of God," or the "family of love," outweighed the personal preferences of an individual member, and all members were equal regardless of religious persuasion or gender. Many Familists were anticlerical and tended to reject the patriarchal domination of the church. Because of the belief in the covenant of grace, the responsibility of salvation was placed upon the individual, with the role of the male clergy being minimized. Reverend Thomas Shepard, in particular, indicated that familism was popular among the "community of women." Clerics like him in the male-dominated church felt that well-intentioned women might discuss matters of religion, but they still needed to consult with the male clergy so as not to be led astray. Both Anne Hutchinson and John Wheelwright espoused an individual's freedom of belief. What's more, it was believed by many in the colony that Hutchinson's conventicles were almost like a cult.

The religious philosophies of the Antinomians and the Familists differed from each other. That is because Antinomians felt that the moral law didn't apply to them, while the Familists felt it only applied to the members of the group or family. Regardless of the differences between those views and that of the free grace advocates, the clerical establishment believed that Hutchinson was an Antinomian and possibly even a Familist. The Familists of the 16th century believed that the community should take priority over the acceptance of a prescribed set of religious doctrines. In other words, Familists were inclusive rather than exclusive.

Banishment of John Wheelwright

In January 1637, John Winthrop called for a day of fasting and praying in order to resolve the divisiveness within the colony created by the discussions of Antinomianism. He wanted to remind the people that he had met with these "free grace" advocates and was protecting the community from any compromise of the religious principles that motivated them to come to the New World in the first place. To reinforce the importance of the issue for the everyday citizen, Hutchinson's brother-in-law, John Wheelwright, was invited to give a sermon. The sermon was later called the "Fast-Day Sermon." He preached the doctrine of free grace and often used offensive imagery, such as "firebrands" and "swords," which–it was said–was atypical language for interpreting biblical passages. It was customary that ministers condemn those who were immoral, but Wheelwright made it quite clear that he rejected those who prioritized the covenant of works over that of grace, as those "sort of people who are to be condemned" and "do set themselves against Jesus Christ: such are the greatest enemies to the state that can be." The language he used was quite inflammatory, and he had occasionally used the term "antichrist" to refer to those who held different opinions. His homily was cited as disrupting the peace within the colony.

Because this was a colony that mixed religion with governance, charges were filed against Wheelwright for sedition. In March of that year, the court convened to discuss his case. It became an issue between those who promoted the covenant of grace and those who promulgated the covenant of works. The court then leaped to the conclusion that Wheelwright's emphasis on the covenant of grace meant that he rejected the emphasis that the orthodox ministers placed on the covenant of good works. Although Wheelwright denied he had rejected their approach, they insisted that it was his intention to reject the orthodoxy of the church. Wheelwright was a fiery minister at any rate, and it is on the court record that he said, "We must lay upon them [the anti-Puritan orthodox ministers] and we must kill them with words of the Lord." The court then found Wheelwright guilty of sedition and contempt of civil authority. When the verdict was read to the populace, there was consternation among the community over the loss of their minister. He had many supporters within the community who were critical of the nearly tyrannical attitude of the ministers in the colony.

Afterward, Governor Vane read a petition in favor of Wheelwright to the people. It said that Wheelwright wasn't guilty of any sedition and that he was like the Apostle Paul because he forcefully opposed those whom he saw as being unchristian. The petition nearly set off a riot because Wheelwright's forceful speaking style tended to pit people against each other. Wheelwright had lost his support, and—by association—so did Hutchinson and Governor Vane, for that matter. Most preferred the status quo.

Wheelwright was banished from the Massachusetts Bay Colony, and the authorities, who feared a revolt, were called into court and questioned thoroughly. John Coggeshall, one of the founders of Massachusetts and a supporter of Hutchinson, did not sign the petition. Regardless, he was questioned. Later on, he was dismissed from his post as the town deputy and banished. Another supporter who spoke up for him, William Coddington, didn't sign the petition. Even though he was a known advocate for Hutchinson and Wheelwright, he wasn't banished, most likely because he was one of the wealthiest men in the colony. If Wheelwright's supporters didn't recant their testimony regarding their support for him and his theological position, they were ordered to surrender "all such guns, pistols, swords, powder, shot and match as they shall be owners of, or have in their custody, under the pain of ten pounds for every default."

One of the predominant factors that influenced the outcome of the court verdict was the fact that Wheelwright was Hutchinson's brother-in-law. It is a reasonable assumption that it was his connection to Anne Hutchinson that may have drawn attention to his sermon. The condemnation of Wheelwright, a relative of hers, was deleterious to Hutchinson, and her gender also helped place her under the shadow of suspicion.

The Political Implications

Anne Hutchinson's meteoric rise and her enduring charisma appealed to Governor Vane. He wholeheartedly supported her, and the legalistic Winthrop couldn't gain a foothold with the population. Other than encouraging the meeting of the clerics with Hutchinson, Wheelwright, and Cotton in 1636, Winthrop couldn't make a move against Hutchinson as long as Vane was the governor and remained popular. Winthrop craved the governorship of the Massachusetts Bay Colony once again. He had been governor before but wanted to be elected again. In order to influence the outcome of the election, he manipulated and conspired to have the election moved from Boston, where Vane was popular, to Newtown (currently Cambridge), where the majority of the population were legalists. "Legalists" refers to clerics and congregants who obsessively adhered to the exact interpretations of Puritan and Anglican beliefs when it came to the law as elucidated by scholars. Legalists believed that the diligent practice of religious law would assure people of salvation. Legalists also emphasized the covenant of works and gave mere lip service to one's dependence upon faith for salvation, that is, the covenant of grace.

In addition to the fact that the voters in the Newtown area would be more predisposed to vote for Winthrop, an election held there would also cause an inconvenience to Boston voters because they would have to cross the Charles River in order to access voting sites. As expected, there were fewer Bostonians who voted in the election, and John Winthrop became governor in 1637.

Henry Vane moved to Providence Plantations, Rhode Island, a colony founded by Roger Williams, another Puritan minister. Williams was sometimes seen as being a Familist because he felt that members shouldn't have to depend upon the state to dictate the moral principles by which they should live. Instead, religious sects needed to care for their own people in terms of upholding moral behavior among their members. He, therefore, believed in the separation between the church and state. Vane didn't entirely favor the separation of church and state as espoused by Williams and eventually became uncomfortable there. He then decided to give up his American experiment and moved back to England.

Chapter 5 – The Hutchinson Trial

The free grace advocates who held public office under the former Governor Henry Vane were voted out during the course of the election cycle. All eyes now focused upon the true source of their discontent—Anne Hutchinson.

On November 7th, 1637, she was asked to appear before the court, which was being held in Newtown, Winthrop's new base. It was a four-mile trip. Winter had come early that year, so the weather was frigid, but Anne and her family made their way there, despite the freezing temperature. Because horses could break their legs on ice, the Hutchinsons had to make their way on land after crossing the Charles River. Anne's son Edward was specifically required to attend because he had signed the petition supporting John Wheelwright prior to his trial and banishment. Four of William and Anne's male children were now of age and, as freemen, were entitled to vote at the trial, so they were in attendance as well.

The trial took place in a cramped colonial meetinghouse. Windows spanned only one side of the room, but deep plunging shadows draped over all the walls. There was no fireplace there, and the low-ceiling room was merely lit by waning candles, giving it an ominous appearance. Anne wore a black dress of serge, a type of twill fabric, and had wrapped herself in a cloak against the chilly wind that occasionally whistled through the cracks of the walls. As was customary, she had a white neckerchief on her shoulders and the traditional coif. Forty magistrates filed into this building, which was known as the Great and General Court of Massachusetts. The court staff alone was large. There were nine magistrates, thirty-one deputies, a whole team of assistants, and fourteen freemen representing the towns in the colony.

The court was deliberately stacked against Hutchinson, as Winthrop had dismissed the judges who were known to favor her. Among the magistrates, called "divines," were Reverend Zechariah Symmes, with whom Anne had carried on a contentious discussion on the ship over to America, and Reverend John Wilson, the pastor in Boston whom Anne had criticized at her conventicle meetings. Reverend Peter Bulkley was one of the most prominent attendees there, as he was admired for his extensive knowledge in the field of theology, but he was known to be very critical of women. Reverend Thomas

Dudley, who had been a former governor of the colony, was a known legalist, and he was appointed to serve as the deputy judge. The men of the court wore thick greatcoats, leather gloves and hats, linen shirts, knickers, and thick stockings. They took their places on a long bench facing the people in the court. With a flourish, Governor John Winthrop marched in and took his place in the center. He was to serve as both judge and prosecutor.

Although the court was stacked against Anne, the audience contained many people who supported her. Her husband, William, of course, was there, along with many of his colleagues in the mercantile business. There were traders, merchants, sailors, and brokers—in other words, there were many respected businessmen from the community and those who came from all walks of life. Many of them had, in fact, attended Anne's conventicles.

Winthrop called out officiously, "Mistress Hutchinson!" A cheer went up from the crowd, after which Winthrop impatiently slammed down his gavel. "Miss Hutchinson," he called out again. From the back of the room, she rose and took her place in the center of the room, where the accused was required to stand for the entire proceeding. "Mistress Hutchinson," he continued, "You are called here as one of those that have troubled the peace of the commonwealth and the churches here. You have been known to be a woman that has a great share in the promoting and divulging of those opinions that are causes of this trouble, and...you have spoken diverse things as we have been informed is very prejudicial to the churches and ministers thereof." Winthrop wanted to fortify his position of power by eliminating any infighting or disagreement on religious issues because he felt he would be seen as weak.

To that diatribe, Hutchinson responded straightforwardly, "I have been called here to answer you, but hear no things laid to my charge...what have I said or done?"

Winthrop responded that he had already told her of some of the charges levied against her, but it is clear from the above dialogue that he hadn't. He didn't produce any compelling charges or evidence and seemed to be saying no more than the fact that he and some of the other clerics and congregants simply didn't like what they thought she had said. His entire presentation was based on hearsay evidence and what they had heard by way of gossip. Hutchinson had never written anything down related to the content of her theological beliefs, nor had she presented her opinions in public, other than at her conventicles.

The governor attempted to implicate her guilt by association. She had supported John Wheelwright, who was banished by the community for his fiery sermon, and Winthrop attempted to infer that she was a "co-conspirator" in the "sedition" that Wheelwright was convicted of. Then Winthrop asked why she had supported him and others of the same mind. To this, Anne boldly proclaimed her freedom of choice. "That is a matter of conscience, sir," she replied. Anne firmly believed that the law should be interpreted according to his or her own conscience rather than precisely as the ministers would tell the people. Everyone in the room fell silent, as she was stating one of their dearest principles and using that as grounds for defense—the sacredness of one's individual conscience.

The Conventicle Issue

The deputy judge, Thomas Dudley, then stepped in and brought up the topic of the conventicles she held in her home. He went on to say that the general assembly in the city considered such meetings neither tolerable nor "comely in the sight of God, nor fitting for your sex." Although conventicles were permissible in private, once the size of the meetings became too large, it was understood that a religious representative would come in to approve and monitor them. At that point, they were considered to be "public." However, Anne was unaware of that.

In 17th-century New England, words were considered to be of the utmost importance. According to Puritan thinking, words carried special power but also danger. Although the weight of their words was vital, men—not women—were given full freedom to give any word of advice, cast a vote, and pronounce a verdict in any court or civil assembly as long as it was spoken courteously. The men urged women to "govern" their tongues, and the clerics even quoted the psalmist who said, "take heed that thou not sin with the tongue." Women were admonished to always use "godly speech."

Hutchinson's conventicles were meetings where its members—mostly women—discussed aspects of the weekly sermon and the Bible. However, no member of Winthrop's court had ever attended one of them. The only man with influence who attended her conventicles was Governor Henry Vane. Although the clerics were welcome to attend, they felt that they didn't need such meetings as they had far more religious education than Anne or the attendees. Leaping up, Winthrop forcefully said, "You show not in all this by what authority you take upon yourself to be such a public instructor."

The court then questioned Anne as to why she would teach women at her meetings. She responded with a biblical passage from the Epistle of Titus, "Elder women should instruct the younger." Winthrop then boldly responded with a quote from the First Epistle of Timothy, "I permit not a woman to teach, but to be in silence." Both Winthrop and Hutchinson proceeded to rebut each other by using passages from the Bible. Barb for barb, both the Trinity College graduate Winthrop and the home-schooled Hutchinson were evenly matched.

Anne Hutchinson did believe that women in a private group had the right to discuss and even argue theological principles. She eschewed the viewpoint of the men who wanted women to remain silent about such issues, and she felt that such discussion groups were appropriate marketplaces for ideas. Conventicles had not only been permissible in Christian communities, but it had also been encouraged, and there was no gender preference stated for such meetings. Therefore, it was difficult for the court to contradict this point.

Another problem that the court addressed regarding Hutchinson's conventicles was the fact that she placed tremendous emphasis on the covenant of grace.

The Covenant Issue

Deputy Judge Thomas Dudley questioned Hutchinson regarding her opinions on the traditional teachings of the ministers, which indicated that salvation was won through good works. That specific issue was taken up in a question-and-answer dialogue:

> Dep. Gov. Thomas Dudley: When they do preach a covenant of works do they preach the truth?
>
> Anne Hutchinson: Yes, Sir. But then they preach a covenant of works for salvation, and that is not truth.

The dialogue above directly addresses the point Anne was trying to make. That is, salvation cannot be attained through the performance of good works; it is freely given through faith. One doesn't have to struggle for one's whole life hoping to earn it because it is freely given from God.

The Authority Issue

Winthrop indicated Anne Hutchinson had broken the Fifth Commandment ("to honor one's father and mother") by disobeying the "fathers" of the British Commonwealth, who were her spiritual parents, by holding these meetings at her home. Winthrop believed that the men in authority were there for the outworking of God's grace, which originated from above.

As her meetings had become so well attended, the court questioned her right to hold such meetings. Anne questioned them mockingly, asking them if her name had to appear in the Bible in order for her to be permitted to do so. "Must I shew my name written within?" she asked. Winthrop also accused her of making disparaging comments about the ministers of the colony. He then went on to say that if she was to say erroneous things, they would officially reprimand her so that she would become a "profitable member" among them, and he reminded her that he and the members of the court were her judges.

She said, "You have no power over my body, neither can you do me any harm—for I am in the hands of the eternal Jehovah, my savior."

In hindsight, it is clear that John Winthrop felt threatened by her popularity. Even though it might be said that Governor Winthrop had secular political ambitions, it is also true to a great extent that he felt men who were in authority in the colony were placed there by God to be good rulers to keep peace and unity. He saw this incoming influx of Puritans as weakening a frontier community in an untested New World. The Puritans were so God-fearing that they primarily focused on life after death and might put aside practical considerations for their physical survival in the coastal colony.

Winthrop was sincerely convinced of his own importance within the community and felt that the eminent people within the colony were divinely charged with the religious and civil obligations to hold the community together. Therefore, they had been elected by these God-fearing people to direct their lives in accordance with both religious and secular directives. What Winthrop imagined was that any acceptance of the Hutchinson philosophy would open the gates to a mob of radical anarchists. The English of the 17th century greatly feared a society in which many different viewpoints were tolerated because factions that were too disparate created friction and sometimes even civil wars. The English had been brought up on a "sameness" that dictated, in essence, what everyone believed in: how they behaved and the penalties for deviation. That dedication to uniformity created a peace of sorts because it was a predictable way to live.

In 1630, John Winthrop had a sermon published called *A Model of Christian Charity* in which he warned people that they must follow the direction of their political and religious leaders because their community was "a city upon a hill, and the eyes of all people are upon us." He drew a phrase from the Sermon on the Mount in the Bible, which stated, "You are the light of the world. A city located on a hill cannot be hidden." He then went on to write that if citizens fail to follow the directives of their leadership, God will withdraw his help from them. Anne indicated that she had abided by religious leadership. She was a member of Reverend John Cotton's congregation and supported his approach to understanding justification. Like her, he expressed the belief that God freely gives his grace to the elect, those who were chosen to enjoy eternal bliss. Since Cotton was an influential and eminent member of the community, the court conducting Anne's trial couldn't find any adequate reason to reject her for being among his followers. However, there were other ways to attack her character, and they next discussed the content of her messages.

During the trial and in Anne's presence, the governor addressed some of the ministers about what Anne had said or done that they found offensive. Reverend Hugh Peter spoke up, saying that he had once asked her what difference there was between her John Cotton and him. Then he went on to elaborate: "Briefly, she told me there was a wide and broad difference...He [Cotton] preaches the covenant of grace and you the covenant of works, and that you are not able ministers of the New Testament and know no more than the apostles did before the resurrection of Christ. I then put it to her, 'What do you think of such a brother?' and she answered he 'had not the seal of the spirit.'" Peter and the other ministers were astounded at her response and, not coincidentally, her brutal frankness.

Winthrop was among those shocked at this recollection from Peter. It was Winthrop's firm belief that political power and ecclesiastic authority were inseparable. To monitor the religious beliefs of the residents of the community would result in the control of their political preferences. Thomas Weld, who was active in subduing Hutchinson and the free grace teachers, felt the same way. They wanted full control over the community and didn't want to jeopardize their positions, either religiously or politically. No women had ever challenged them quite so forcefully, but they felt unsure about ejecting her due to her large following in the community. If they could continue the proceedings, they felt as if they might be able to get her to compromise and redeem their image and reputations among her followers.

So, the next day, they addressed the sensitive issue of Anne's so-called "disparaging" remarks about some of the ministers' homilies, particularly the fact that the ministers put much more stress upon the covenant of works than the covenant of grace. Deputy Judge Thomas Dudley claimed that Anne Hutchinson "has depraved all the ministers and has been a cause of what has fallen out." During the aforementioned meeting between Hutchinson, Winthrop, Wheelwright, and Cotton, Hutchinson had been guaranteed that her statements were strictly private, that is to say, "off the record," and she was taken back by this breach of confidence. She went on to say that what she herself believed or what she said in private should not be considered a crime. However, at this trial, the presiding court ignored any prior guarantees of confidentiality, and her words became known publicly.

Once that occurred, Anne demanded that the court ministers swear to the statements they made. All but Thomas Leverett, a lawyer and church elder, Deacon John Coggeshall, and John Cotton were reluctant to do so. Thomas Leverett stated that Anne didn't say the ministers shouldn't teach the covenant of works but that they didn't teach the covenant of grace as clearly as Reverend Cotton did. Deacon Coggeshall's statement indicated that he didn't feel Anne had been as critical as the court contended. The members of the court realized that Coggeshall was a fervent supporter of both the banished John Wheelwright and of Anne Hutchinson, so they paid little heed to his statement. John Cotton ducked the topic by saying that he didn't recall Anne's words exactly, adding that he never heard her teach anything against the ministers with regard to the covenant of works, nor diminish the importance of good works as necessary for salvation. He then shied from giving Anne any appreciation for her having preferred his church to those of others. It was a betrayal in a sense when he said, "I was very sorry that she put comparisons between my ministry and that of others."

John Cotton was one of the clerics questioned by Winthrop in October when the issue first came to a head in 1636. Unlike Anne, he was soft-spoken and conciliatory. Anne was a woman, and John was a man, and that seemed to make all the difference in this case. The central theological matter had to do with the doctrine of free grace, or covenant of grace, which Cotton had been a forceful promoter of. In fact, he was seen by some as having sparked the Antinomian Controversy, which became a bone of contention between the legalistic Puritans and those who believed in the power of grace freely given by God. Cotton, as a mild-mannered and likable man, managed to escape censure during the infamous October meeting held at Winthrop's residence between himself, Wheelwright, and Hutchinson.

With regard to having made some negative statements about Wilson and other ministers, Anne didn't deny the charges levied against her but said that she was reluctant to explain her statements in open court. She relented, however, indicating that the truth bound her to do so. She stated that she felt some of the local ministers did their congregations a disservice by failing to explain the covenant of grace. However, she was somewhat embarrassed at the brashness of her words, which is why she preferred to speak about this in private rather than in open courts.

The Revelation Issue

Anne was extensively questioned because she said that she was led by God in her interpretation of the scriptures and the accompanying inspirations she said she received from God. She said that "I could not open the scripture; he (God) must by his prophetic office open it unto me." Following that, the court assistant and Mr. Dudley carried on another dialogue:

> Mr. Nowell, court assistant: How do you know it was the spirit?
>
> Anne Hutchinson: How did Abraham know that it was God that bid him to offer his son, being a breach of the sixth commandment?
>
> Dep. Gov. Dudley: By an immediate voice?
>
> Anne Hutchinson: So to me by an immediate revelation.

Dep. Gov. Dudley: How! An immediate revelation!

Governor Winthrop and the other deputies objected to Hutchinson's use of the term "immediate revelation." They feared that she recommended that a type of religious anarchy would prevail in which individuals would become passive in religious observation and act upon their own spiritual impulses, whether they were true or untrue.

The last statement wasn't intended as a question. It was rather an exclamation of disbelief. It was clear by this point that Anne wouldn't be given the benefit of the doubt. Hutchinson continued after that by way of clarification:

> Anne Hutchinson: By the voice of his own spirit to my soul. I will cite another scripture, Jeremiah 46:27-28—out of which the Lord showed me what he would do for me and the rest of his servants. But after he was pleased to reveal himself to me. Therefore, I desire you to look to it, for you see this scripture fulfilled this day and therefore I desire you that as you tender the Lord and the church and commonwealth to consider and look what you do. You have power over my body but the Lord Jesus has power over my body and soul.

With regard to what she said at her conventicles, Anne stated she felt she received direct inspiration and revelations from God that she was to be saved, along with those who likewise believed in the covenant of grace. Hutchinson stated that she herself was directly inspired by God, stating that her mystical experiences were "inward convictions of the coming of the spirit." Furthermore, she indicated that anyone could communicate directly with God without the assistance of a minister reciting biblical passages or their own prayers. This sentiment ran counter to the Puritan belief that the scriptures should only be interpreted by the church's duly ordained ministers. By saying that she had been directly selected by God to deliver some of God's messages at her conventicles, many concluded that she was blasphemous. Thomas Shepard taught that no one simply hears the voice of the Holy Spirit. It is "heard" through the reading of the Gospels and meditation.

This claim was especially offensive to the colonial and religious authorities. If Anne's attitudes about personal revelations were accepted, then there would be no need for ministers or civil authorities because they were viewed as one and the same. It could result in the "utter subversion of both churches and the civil state," in Winthrop's words. In order to preserve the unity of their orthodox beliefs, the Puritans firmly held that confession of one's faith is the role of the organized church, not the individual.

What's more, personal communication from God through the Holy Spirit might be perceived as a substitute for the words in the Bible. While

Hutchinson believed and taught from the words in the Bible, others in the community might feel that they didn't need to refer to the scriptures. In its extreme, it might encourage moral laxity.

Anne said that, through the words of the Bible, "God can communicate directly to one through those words." However, she stretched the concept of revelations by God by indicating that a person could receive a revelation from God *outside* the Bible. This offended the male sensibilities of the ministers, as it threatened their control over people's behavior. They stipulated that it was *their* interpretation of the words of the Bible as pronounced from the pulpits that would help lead the freemen of the Massachusetts Bay Colony to salvation.

Also necessary was a process of rigorous instructional preparation led by church elders, in which they addressed the basic doctrines their churches promulgated and the outward behavior they expected of all colony inhabitants. This became a way in which the Puritan elite could control the people, as they were all required to attend church services and follow the directions of the religious establishment.

Hutchinson collided with the theologians of the times when she said she was "in direct communication with the Godhead" and was "prepared to follow the promptings of the voice within against all the precepts of the Bible, the churches, reason, or the government of Massachusetts." This was disquieting to Puritan ministers and even the men in the community who prided themselves as the protectors of their wives in terms of biblical understanding.

Toward the end of her trial, Hutchinson felt a divine revelation within that pumped her full of courage that was powerful but foolhardy. Without trepidation, she spoke out loudly, announcing, "The Lord gave me to see that those who did not teach the New Covenant had the spirit of Antichrist."

Thomas Dudley questioned John Cotton with regard to that. Although the ministers had questioned Cotton several months prior to this trial, they were somewhat ambivalent about his standing, and Cotton knew that. So, he became uncomfortable and even a tad annoyed that he was being drawn out on the revelation issue. However, he did admit that there was some rationale for Hutchinson's remarks.

Some of the deputies were hesitant on what to think about Anne, including William Coddington, who said, "I do not see any clear witness against her, and you know it is a rule of the court that no man may be a judge and an accuser too," ending with, "Here is no law of God that she hath broken nor any law of the country that she hath broke, and therefore deserve no censure." Winthrop, anxious to tie up this ordeal, drove the court to consider a verdict. Putting aside the theological impact of Hutchinson's message, Winthrop considered her revelations, in particular, as seditious and in contempt of the court. "If therefore," he said, "it be the mind of the court, looking at her as the principal cause of all our trouble, that they would now consider what is to be done with her." He then made a move to have Anne Hutchinson banished from the colony.

The Verdict

Some of the court deputies voted against banishment, but the majority of the court members voted in favor of it. There were two phases to Hutchinson's sentencing: her right to remain in the colony and her membership of the church itself. She wasn't allowed to go home, so she was detained under house arrest with Joseph Weld, the brother of Reverend Thomas Weld. Governor Winthrop even had the audacity of referring to her as a "prisoner." Anne became ill during her four-month detention and wasn't allowed to see her family. William, her husband, and some of the older children spent the time scouting out some areas along the coast where they could move.

After her detention, Anne was called back before the court again. Many of Hutchinson's supporters didn't attend the session this time. Some had retreated back to their homes, but there were many who traveled with her family in search of another church and community that would suit their spiritual needs. Even after all of this, Anne still had her faithful following.

Unfortunately, this became a time when the orthodox ministers could have their vengeance on her—vengeance cloaked in the religious garbs of the various major or minor theological points of doctrine. They discussed the issue among themselves, and many of their conversations were nothing more than the "mincing of words." Then they met with Anne at her home church in Boston to go over a list of errors that Anne had committed. It was a nine-hour session, in which she elucidated her thinking on those topics. At the end of this very grueling session, they managed to zero in on two "dangerous" errors - that the Holy Spirit dwells in a justified person, and that no sanctification can be used as evidence of justification, that is, that they had been saved. The other so-called errors were merely listed. Most of them were basically opinions that arose from the ministers without a foundation in Anne's testimony. Anne was approached privately by many of the ministers who wanted to discuss the issues, compose retractions, and reform her teachings. In March 1638, Hutchinson read some retractions. Some had to do with her highly contended views of the sermons of the legalistically inclined ministers, what she said about sanctification and justification, and her prophecy about the demise of the colony.

Toward the end of the session, John Cotton made a double-handed statement. He said, "I would speak it to God's glory that you have been an instrument of doing some good amongst us...he hath given you a sharp apprehension, a ready utterance and ability to express yourself in the cause of God." He then made some references to the notion that she believed in the Antinomian philosophies and then betrayed her in the cruelest of terms by saying her opinions "fret like gangrene and spread like leprosy, and infect far and near, and will eat out the very bowels of religion."

Cotton's soft approval of Anne's actions might have possibly satisfied the ministers until Reverend Thomas Shepard, who had called her "very dangerous" even before hearing all of the evidence of the case, let out a tirade in which he called her a "Notorious Imposter" and a "Heinous Liar." Reverend Joseph Wilson, the first pastor Anne criticized, jumped into the verbal foray and stated the final sentence on March 22nd, 1638:

> Forasmuch as you, Mrs. Hutchinson, have highly transgressed and offended... and troubled the Church with your errors and have drawn away many a poor soul, and have upheld your revelations; and forasmuch as you have made a lie...Therefore, in the name of our Lord Jesus Christ...I do cast you out and...deliver you up to Satan...and account you from this time forth to be a heathen and a Publican...I command you in the name of Christ Jesus and of this Church as a leper to withdraw yourself out of the Congregation.

Although she wasn't required to speak in her own defense, Hutchinson did so. She leveled a shriveling retort intended as a prediction, uttering loudly, "You liked to put the Lord Jesus Christ from you, and if you go on in this course you will bring a curse upon you and your posterity, and the mouth of the Lord has spoken it."

Governor John Winthrop then said, "I am persuaded that the revelation she brings forth is delusion."

Her dire prediction regarding the fate of the colony was incongruous to her typical nature. Although she didn't prevail at the trial, her defense was brilliant. However, one might come to the conclusion that her spirit was broken by the overwhelming trauma of the experience.

Whatever the case might have been, that last statement of hers was tantamount to blasphemy. Whether those words were spoken by an arrogant woman who had deluded herself into believing she was a prophetess or the cry of a weary soul that felt abandoned by the Holy Spirit within her, one shall never know.

Chapter 6 – After the Trial

Anne Hutchinson was 47 years old when her trial concluded. In addition, she was pregnant and in frail condition, so Weld housed her for about a month until new arrangements could be made. While there, she was visited by Reverend Hugh Peter and Reverend Thomas Shepard on a number of occasions to attempt to persuade her to recant her "errors." They had hoped that her sentence could be lifted and felt that her admission would justify their actions.

As happened in the case against John Wheelwright, Hutchinson's supporters were given a choice to recant. Those who didn't were told to surrender their pistols, powder, and ammunition. There were 75 men from whom weapons were confiscated.

Two of Anne Hutchinson's supporters, William Coddington and John Clarke, along with William Hutchinson and a few courageous followers, came together and embarked on a torturous journey toward current-day Rhode Island. They had heard about a preacher named Roger Williams, who had literally been chased from territory to territory in Massachusetts because of his religious views. He eventually ended up in Rhode Island and was trying to establish a new church settlement there.

Anne Hutchinson in Rhode Island

Roger Williams was a Puritan who came to New England back in 1631—just a few years earlier than Anne. In some ways, he was a man ahead of his times. He had seen the negativity generated by state-run religions and was looking toward providing people with more liberty to choose their faith. In Europe, there were already burgeoning religious sects that were distinctly different in their beliefs, and Williams wanted to avoid conflict among any new settlers over the freedom to practice their religion. Such conflict constantly interfered with the running of state and foreign affairs in other colonies. What's more, it deleteriously affected the economy.

Williams was particularly interested in being a clergyman for the church in Salem, as he had heard they tended to have separatist views and did not want to strictly model the Church of England. The people of Salem invited him there, but the clergy at Boston had heard of his separatist views. As a result, Salem withdrew their invitation.

Plymouth, Massachusetts, which had been founded by the Pilgrims, had declared themselves as being separate from the Church of England, so Williams went there to explore the possibility of coming there in a clerical capacity. He encountered two difficulties with Plymouth: 1) the churches there didn't display much of the separatism from the Church of England that Williams had expected, and 2) Williams discovered that the Pilgrims had just occupied the area without making any recompense to the tribes that lived in the area. He wrote to King James I in that regard, and he also accused the king of a "solemn lie" when the king claimed he was the first monarch to have a colony in the New World. Roger Williams was right; Elizabeth I was the first English monarch to claim the new land, but one wonders why he felt it necessary to bring that uncomfortable point out in the open. Williams was, in some ways, a rebel.

After this, the First Church of Salem invited him to replace the late Reverend Samuel Skelton, despite the earlier protest by leaders in Boston. Williams was well-liked there. In 1635, Salem wanted to expand their territory and applied to the General Court of Massachusetts to take over some land in Marblehead Neck. Of course, Williams' reputation was widespread, and the civil authorities disliked him, claiming he had "dangerous opinions." The Massachusetts Bay Colony was anxious to rid themselves of free thinkers like Roger Williams, so they held up Salem's application for Marblehead in order to seize the opportunity of charging him in General Court on counts of treason and sedition. That was the same technique they used for Hutchinson and Wheelwright just two years later. Like Hutchinson, Williams, too, was banished. Williams weathered many journeys seeking a territory where he and his flock could settle and practice their faith in freedom.

In spring 1636, Williams arrived at an area in Rhode Island ideally suited for his followers, who were mostly planters. The settlement Williams helped them find was located around current-day Providence, Rhode Island. The Narragansett tribe welcomed them there, and Williams himself invited other dissenters from the Massachusetts Bay Colony to join him.

In 1638, William Coddington, John Clarke, and William Hutchinson met with Roger Williams. Although Williams had control of the land, which he bought from the Narragansetts, he was determined to separate religion from the colony's government. Hutchinson's group was pleased with that and formulated the Portsmouth Compact in order to establish their own church. John Coggeshall, who had supported Anne at her trials, was one of the main signatories. Hutchinson's adult male children also signed it, as did her husband, of course. Twenty-three men signed it in all, followed by five more newcomers a few months later. After the initial signing of the Portsmouth Compact, which took place in March 1638, they awaited the arrival of Anne

Hutchinson. Roger Williams officially established the Colony of Rhode Island, and his own settlement was called Providence Plantations.

The month of April in 1638 was bitter. Yet Anne was a tough pioneer woman who would never let the weather interfere with her objective, so she walked sixty miles in the snow to get to Rhode Island. Anne was deathly ill from her late-in-life pregnancy by the time of her arrival. Because of her age, the fetus was badly malformed when Anne delivered the baby in May, and it resulted in a "hydatidiform mole," which is a badly malformed stillborn infant. A young minister who had been traveling back to Massachusetts heard about this and described the fetus to Governor Winthrop, saying it looked like "a bunch of transparent grapes." The minister, though, overlooked the fact that Hutchinson nearly died of blood loss during the unfortunate event.

Dissension in Rhode Island

William Coddington then settled the Hutchison group in an area they called Pocasset, currently called Aquidneck Island. However, he wasn't a wise administrator and became too autocratic. In 1639, a citizen of Pocasset, Samuel Gorton, spoke up for the discontented populace. He organized a "civil body politic" that ousted Coddington. The tumult was just limited to the civil government because of the separation of church and state, so, therefore, it never accelerated to theological debates. The matter was handled civilly, and the people of Pocasset elected to change the name of the settlement to Portsmouth. They created a code of laws and created stipulations for a trial by jury. Anne Hutchinson's husband William was elected as its new magistrate.

John Winthrop of Massachusetts kept track of the events in areas near Massachusetts, such as Rhode Island, and was very quick to insult Anne Hutchinson again, along with her husband this time. He wrote about the dissent in Portsmouth, saying,

> The people grew very tumultuous and put out Mr. Coddington and chose Mr. William Hutchinson only, a man of very mild temper and weak parts (weaknesses), and wholly guided by his wife, who had been a beginner of all the former troubles in the country and still continued to breed disturbance.

As a result of the political dissent, Coddington, with his supporters, moved to an adjacent area and called it Newport. His followers included some very strong politicians such as John Coggeshall, who had traveled with Anne from Massachusetts. Other prominent men such as Reverend Nicholas Easton, William Brenton, Jeremy Clarke, and Henry Bull settled in Newport as well. John Winthrop lost no time in insulting Reverend Easton of the newly created Newport when he said, "Other troubles arose in the island by reason of one Nicholas Easton, a tanner, a man very bold, though ignorant."

Within a short period of time, amends were made between the two groups, and Newport united with the Portsmouth group. Coddington, having learned his lesson from the rift, modified his ways and was elected as governor. William Hutchinson agreed to become his assistant. The name of "Newport" was dropped, and the town became known as Portsmouth.

Anne Hutchinson and Roger Williams kept in touch for a while. In fact, Anne's sister, Katherine, married Richard Scott and lived in the Providence settlement. Williams had a civic non-sectarian government there, and a number of people from other denominations—Quakers, French Huguenots, and Jews, among others—lived there as well. Through Roger Williams, Anne Hutchinson formed relationships with the Narragansett tribe there. The women of the tribe often traded goods and furs with the colonists.

Late in 1638, Roger Williams was interested in the Baptist faith but didn't become an official member. John Clarke, who had accompanied William and Anne Hutchinson to Rhode Island, exercised the freedom of religion permitted in Rhode Island and established the First Baptist Church in Newport.

Winthrop Strikes Again

In the time that had passed since the trial, Winthrop continued to be obsessed with the experience he had with Hutchinson and what he may have considered to be a failure in the Puritan experiment in New England. Winthrop was, as a matter of fact, one of the founders of this community, and the Hutchinson trial and its aftermath took its psychological toll on him.

When he heard of the birth of Hutchinson's deformed fetus, Governor John Winthrop lashed out at Anne Hutchinson by sending a missive to Rhode Island. In the cruelest of terms, he said that the unfortunate birth was a punishment from God. As he spoke about his doubts, he was told of a similar incident that took place during the course of Anne Hutchinson's trial.

Anne, who was a midwife, had assisted a member of her conventicle, Mary Dyer, in childbirth. The child's brain didn't develop normally, and the infant died shortly after birth. In the 17th century, unsuccessful births were superstitiously associated with evil or seen as a punishment from God. The mothers were always blamed for them. Once they saw the pitiful condition of the fetus, Anne and her assistant midwife, Mary Hawkins, contacted John Cotton. Cotton rushed over, saw the condition of the fetus, and buried it secretly. Regardless of the fact that Cotton attempted to protect the reputation of the mother, word got out. Winthrop found out about it when people told him the rumor of Mary Dyer's "monstrous birth." In an attempt to justify his actions during the trial of Anne Hutchinson, Winthrop had the body of the baby exhumed and wove a wildly fabricated story about it. In his journal, he wrote that when the body was removed from the grave, women vomited violently and their children had convulsions. In describing the fetus, he wrote:

> It was a Satanic mix of a woman-child, a fish, a beast and a fowl all woven together into one, and without a head. It was much corrupted and holes in the back misshapen as the like had never been heard of. The back parts were on the sides and some scales were found. It was so monstrous and misshapen. The ears were like an ape's and grew upon the shoulders; the nose was hooking upward and the breast and back were full of sharp prickles. The back parts were on the side and, instead of toes, it had three claws with talons like a young foal. Above the belly it had three great holes like mouths and out of each of them a piece of flesh. It had no forehead, but in its place there were four horns.

Winthrop then stated that Mary Dyer had been an upstanding member of the Puritan community in New England until she came under the influence of Anne Hutchinson. He then blamed that misfortune on Anne Hutchinson, saying that she "brought forth not one, but thirty monstrous births or thereabouts...None of them was of human shape." It seems that the content of a woman's uterus had become a theme for religious debate and hasty judgment.

The Puritans held the odd belief that the soul of a male escaped the body and was resurrected after death to have a heavenly life with the angels in eternity. There was no mention of women, though. Typically, women were seen as temptresses sent to test men's faith by trying to lure them away from salvation.

Anne's husband may not have believed that women were temptresses, but he did believe in life after death. And at the age of 55, his beliefs provided him much comfort, as he passed away in Portsmouth in 1641 when Anne was fifty years old. She felt insecure after that, especially because the Massachusetts Bay Colony was now right on the southwest border and clamoring to expand. She was concerned that they would incorporate the area where she lived at that time.

For her health and well-being, Anne decided to travel to New Netherland with a group of people she had met in Roger Williams' settlement. Her oldest son, Edward, decided to return to the Massachusetts Bay Colony, and he reconciled with the ministerial authorities there. He moved back to the family homestead in Boston and became a lieutenant in the Military Company of Massachusetts. While in Rhode Island, Edward had purchased a tract of land near Providence and held on to it.

New Netherland

New Netherland was a Dutch colonial settlement that encompassed a large segment of today's New York City, the state of New York, and New Jersey. It was established in 1614 and administered by the Dutch West India Company. The principal function of the Dutch West India Company was trade, and they used the Hudson and East Rivers, along with its tributaries, to transport goods from the New World to Europe. Willem Kieft was the director of the Dutch West India Company in 1641 and wanted to possess various large plots of land to expand the colony. Therefore, he negotiated with the Algonquin Native American tribes, also known as the Wappinger Confederacy, who occupied parts of New Jersey, Connecticut, and New York. The deal was laid through a series of smaller contract purchases from this confederacy of Native Americans who dwelled on the coastal lands alongside today's Pelham Park Bay and Eastchester Bay–all of which fed into the Long Island Sound and the Atlantic Ocean.

The Dutch West India Company bought it for axes, beads, and knives, which would have been the equivalent of around four thousand dollars. That figure breaks down to less than two cents per acre. William Kieft was a greedy man who shortchanged the Native Americans for their land. He also simply stole more plots alongside the purchased land.

Dissension between the Dutch and the Native American Tribes

To the Native Americans, the "purchase" of a plot of land by settlers meant that the colonists were allowed to occupy the land, farm it, and build villages and towns. For their part, the tribes believed that they retained the right to use the land seasonally but were expected to respect the property rights of the colonists. The native people of the Americas were nomadic, so that understanding suited their lifestyle well. Thus, they often hunted on colonial farmlands and fished in the waterways of the colony. By virtue of these purchases, the tribes felt they had agreed to share the land with the settlers. Of course, that occasionally produced friction, and there were violent outbursts.

On one occasion, in the summer of 1641, members from the Raritan tribe, an Algonquin-speaking people, were accused of stealing a canoe from a trading vessel and some pigs from David de Vries, whose tobacco farm was located along the Hudson River. Kieft interfered and demanded the return of the canoe and payment for the pigs. As tempers flared up and hostilities were kindled, Kieft dispatched Cornelis van Tienhoven and seventy men to exact payment. As it turned out, the Raritans hadn't stolen the pigs (other colonists had), but they were still blamed for it. Because the Puritans were innocent of stealing the pigs, they paid nothing. The whereabouts of the canoe remained unknown. However, the Dutch soldiers attacked the Raritans anyway and killed several of them. The Raritans then burned de Vries' farm and destroyed his tobacco sheds.

Willem Kieft was inexperienced and unskilled in dealing with the native peoples, and it did not help that he saw them as inferior. When Willem Kieft noted that the native peoples continued to use the waterways for fishing, he took that opportunity to propose that the tribes pay tribute to the colonists who were using the land. A number of Dutch settlers who had lived in the area with the native people in peace for nearly ten years warned against such an arrangement, realizing that it would lead to problems. Kieft ignored their advice and made a proposal to the tribal elders that they could license the use of the area for fishing. It was rejected, as would be expected. Kieft ignored the pleas of some of the Dutch settlers and tried to extort payments nonetheless.

Manhattan, at the time, was cohabited by both the Native Americans and the Dutch settlers. On Manhattan Island, a young Weckquaesgeek lad murdered a Dutchman named Claes Swits, a bartender, as an act of revenge for the murder of the boy's uncle. Kieft and the Dutch authorities demanded that the tribe hand over the teenage Weckquaesgeek boy, but the tribe refused to do so. The issue of revenge arose in New Netherland, but the older settlers still didn't want to stir up the native peoples.

Noting the ambiguity of the colonists to generate hostilities, he appointed a Council of Twelve Men to decide whether the settlers should make war upon the tribes or not. To garner interest in war, Kieft presented the case of poor Claes Swits as an example of the dangers of having Native Americans living among the settlers. After much finagling and persuasion from two of the more powerful members, Kieft was able to convince his Council of Twelve Men to move ahead with a plan to attack the tribal nations in the area.

When Anne Hutchinson arrived there in 1642, she wasn't entirely aware of the growing antipathy of the Native American tribes in the region. The Weckquaesgeeks and Tappans dwelled just north of her home. They were being threatened by the more powerful Mohegans and Mohawks, who were encroaching on their territory. So, to protect themselves, they asked Kieft to aid them. However, he refused. Thus, they fled to southern Manhattan and eastern New Jersey and camped around the area of "Pavonia" and "Communipaw" in current-day Jersey City. Kieft, on the other hand, was on a campaign to rid the entire Dutch settlements of Native Americans. He then rallied his troops to attack them. De Vries, the man whose farm was attacked just a year prior, took pity on the plight of these displaced tribesmen and attempted to draw up a truce.

Neither de Vries nor many of the settlers who had lived peacefully among the Native Americans until Kieft arrived, wanted a war, but Kieft was determined. It was a matter of urgency because the tribal nations along the East Coast, specifically the Lenape, were increasing in number.

Kieft's War and the Death of Anne Hutchinson

At the beginning of 1643, Kieft ordered his troops to preemptively attack the tribes in Pavonia. De Vries described the attack, which was tantamount to a heartless massacre of Native Americans:

> Infants were torn from their mother's breasts, and hacked to pieces in the presence of their parents, and pieces thrown into the fire and in the water, and other sucklings, being bound to smallboards, were cut, stuck, and pierced, and miserably massacred in a manner to move a heart of stone. Some were thrown into the river, and when the fathers and mothers endeavored to save them, the soldiers would not let them come on land but made both parents and children drown.

While Kieft's War was being waged in small battles and skirmishes throughout New York, Joseph Sands, a young man related to Anne Hutchinson's husband, agreed to build a fine house in a wooded area, strewn with large rocks that had formed there in the glacial age. They selected an area on higher ground near Split Rock, a huge craggy boulder that is located in today's Pelham Bay, New York, near the city of New Rochelle. Other historians place her original homestead in today's Co-op City, New York. Both cities would have been located in the Bronx, a borough of New York City today. There was a wide but shallow river there along with two creeks nearby, which would have been a good source of water for them, as well as for their crops, chickens, a few head of cattle, and pigs. The river that inundated that plot is called the Hutchinson River today, and it was, of course, named after Anne.

As Joseph Sands was constructing Hutchinson's new home, a collection of Native Americans from the Siwanoy tribe came by, shouting loudly before sitting down. Sands was confused by that but continued to work. After all, the Hutchinson plot lay to the east of acres of woods where the Siwanoy people hunted and fished. The Siwanoys were a part of the Wappinger Confederacy and spoke an Eastern Algonquin language. Hutchinson's settlement was located in this wooded area of Pelham. So, after Anne and her family moved into the dwelling, she and her family were on friendly terms with their Native American neighbors. The Dutch people who lived in the vicinity, however, came to her and explained the hostilities that had already occurred in other places. Anne, though, was unafraid.

The Siwanoy people were among those who fought in Kieft's War. And it did not matter that Pelham was an English settlement and not a Dutch one; the Native Americans drew no distinction between the different settlements.

On August 20th, 1643, Chief Wampage and his group of Siwanoy warriors came up to Anne's house, requesting that she tie up the dogs. Thinking there was nothing unusual about that, she did it. According to Eve LaPlante:

> The Siwanoy seized and scalped Francis Hutchinson, William Collins (her son-in-law), several servants, the two Annes (mother and daughter), and the younger children—William, Katherine, Mary, and Zuriel. One of the Hutchinson's daughters, "seeking to escape," was caught as she was getting over a hedge, and they drew her back again by the hair of the head to the stump of a tree, and there cut off her head with a hatchet.

Then they dragged the bodies of the Hutchinson family into the house and burned it to the ground. One of Anne's daughters, nine-year-old Susanna, wasn't there, as she was off in the woods picking blueberries. Upon her return, she was kidnapped. The warriors admired her for her red hair, and she was taken to their encampment. It was said that Susanna was renamed "Autumn Leaf" and lived with the tribe for anywhere between two to six and a half years. Once Chief Wampage discovered that Anne Hutchinson was famous, he took on the name of Chief "Anhõõke" for Anne Hutchinson, a custom among Native Americans for when one personally kills a well-known figure.

This was a merciless and brutal way for Anne Hutchinson to be torn away from this earthly world, but it also must have been puzzling to her. After all, Anne had spent her life spreading the hope of grace and love to an ungrateful people in an unforgiving land.

Chapter 7 – And What Became Of?

It is interesting to note that only one of the people who featured prominently in Anne Hutchinson's life died because of religion. Geopolitical motivations appear to have freckled the lives of the others after Anne Hutchinson died, and many were caught up in the dark and dirty webs of their own weaving.

Archbishop William Laud

In 1640, the great migration to New England ceased. The people began to focus once more on England because the political scene there promised hope and change. Archbishop Laud, who had been ejecting non-conforming ministers and their followers, merited the wrath of King Charles I by creating too much divisiveness within the Anglican Church by stringently executing that policy and was imprisoned. There was no legal basis for eliminating Laud as a future threat to England, so they levied a charge of treason against him without solid evidence. His trial ended without a verdict, but the king hadn't forgotten a cloaked insult Laud had levied against him when he called Charles "a gracious Prince who knows not how to be great or be made great." King Charles I, with the aid of Parliament, passed a bill of attainder, which would allow for a person to be found guilty without a proper trial. On January 10th, 1645, Laud was beheaded.

John Winthrop

In 1640, John Winthrop was forced out of office as governor because the economy of the Massachusetts Bay Colony suffered a severe setback when a lot of the colonial religious and civic leaders exited along with their followers.

In 1644, a book was released in London called *A Short Story of the Rise, reign and ruin of the Antinomians, Familists & Libertines that infected the Churches of New England* about the Hutchinson trial and its implications. Although the author of the work was never explicitly stated, it is assumed that John Winthrop wrote it. In the book, the author labels the errors of those "heretics" as being the result of a conspiracy primarily promulgated by Anne Hutchinson, who, along with her "fomenters," had attempted to manipulate the clergy and magistrates of the colony. He spoke of the "lamentable death of Mrs. Hutchinson" but retracted any trace of pity for her by calling it a "remarkable judgement of God." The author goes on to explain how the ministers and magistrates of the colony drew attention to the errors of Hutchinson and the Antinomians at her trial, as if somehow warning others that doctrinal deviations would not be tolerated.

Reverend Thomas Weld wrote the preface to that book, in which he spent three and a half pages placing Anne Hutchinson at the center of the controversy, saying that she used "sleights" and "tricks" to influence the people who attended her weekly lectures. Weld used numerous gendered terms to denounce Anne, with remarks that referred to her opinions as "brats," who were "hatched and dandled." He also referred to Hutchinson's miscarriage as a judgment of God, as Winthrop had done before.

An opposing viewpoint to *A Short Story* was expressed by Reverend John Wheelwright from exile in New Hampshire. He indicated that those who were banished from the colony were disenfranchised for what could only be minute "theological lapses." He went on to write that some of the more studious members of the colony stood up to what amounted to the abuse of authority. Wheelwright railed against Winthrop's use of Hutchinson's miscarriage as evidence that she had acted wrongly.

John Winthrop was elected to the governorship once again in 1642, but he was ousted in 1644 after having cost the colony a lot of money by failing to provide military support to a French trader who had been bringing a lot of business into the colony.

While John Winthrop was busy attempting to get reelected, he wasn't taking care of his lands, and they fell into ruin. He then needed to ask people to bail him out financially. He died of natural causes in Boston in 1649.

Reverend John Wheelwright

After his banishment, Wheelwright had been invited to go to New Hampshire. He spent some in the town of Exeter preaching at a church there, then moved to Wells, Maine, where many of his parishioners followed him to a small church. Wheelwright had been deeply distressed by his banishment and wrote several treatises defending his position.

Due to the time it takes for publishing, his treatise, *Mercurius Americanus*, was published in 1645, but his banishment had been lifted the year before, and the court issued a document to that effect, saying that "Mr. Wheelwright has his banishment taken off and is received as a member of the Commonwealth." He went to Hampton, Massachusetts, where he joined Pastor Timothy Dalton.

In 1654, a petition was developed by many of his supporters requesting that Wheelwright not only be permitted back in the colony but also be permanently vindicated. It was received favorably by the court, and

Wheelwright was vindicated by the religious authorities in the colony. However, after his experience with banishment and his ambivalent reception back into the community, he became disheartened and returned to England a year later. Since he had been vindicated, though, he was free to continue preaching.

Wheelwright remained in England when Oliver Cromwell was the head of state, and Wheelwright preached in his old home town of Allford, as well as in Belleau. However, after the death of Oliver Cromwell, who usurped and executed King Charles, conditions became difficult for the Puritans, so Wheelwright returned to New England and was installed as a minister in Salisbury, Massachusetts.

In 1677, Wheelwright and one of his church members became embroiled in bitter arguments over several issues regarding the boundaries of Salisbury and a new subdivision of Amesbury, as well as Wheelwright's objection to a Quaker presence in the town. Usually, there weren't disagreements over boundary lines, but Wheelwright's opposition to the wealthy Major Robert Pike reached a fever pitch. Wheelwright appealed to the court, and Pike vociferously objected when the court ruled against him. Soon after, Wheelwright excommunicated Pike. The feud didn't end there; instead, it persisted for months until a special committee of respected people from the congregation were tasked with the job of resolving the dispute peacefully. Even though the strident Wheelwright fanned the flames of hostility, it was agreed that both would accept equal blame and that Pike would be restored as a fully recognized member of the Church. The chroniclers at the time said that this was done in deference to Wheelwright's advanced age of 85. There was no further contention between Pike and Wheelwright after that. When Wheelwright became feebler, he was given an assistant to share his church duties. He died of a stroke in 1679.

Reverend Thomas Weld

Weld was one of the most vociferous ministers who presided over the trial of Anne Hutchinson. In 1641, he and Reverend Hugh Peter, another one of Hutchinson's opponents, tried to ingratiate themselves to Governor Winthrop by offering to alleviate the economic downturn incurred by the colony, which had started a year earlier. He, along with Peter and a businessman by the name of William Hibbens, sailed to England for two purposes: 1) to raise funds for maintaining and expanding Harvard College (later Harvard University) and 2) to obtain ownership of a portion of current-day Rhode Island to expand the colony and therefore increase its revenue. They were somewhat successful in obtaining donations from the British people for Harvard, but there was a serious legal issue that arose due to their efforts to acquire the Rhode Island territory. Roger Williams, a religious leader who had been banished from Massachusetts, had a rival claim for the same territory based upon an agreement with the Narragansetts who lived there.

In 1643, Weld, in order to bolster his right to lay claim to that land, wrote a fundraising book called *New England's First Fruits*, in which he asserted that he had made inroads into evangelizing the native people of New England and that they were anxious to become members of the colony. To strengthen his claim, Weld sent an agreement called the Narragansett Patent, which was a contract granting British settlers ownership of the land. However, the document he sent turned out to be a total forgery. Roger Williams made a strong case for his side of the issue by discrediting Weld's and Peter's claim, as well as the fabricated information in the book *New England's First Fruits.* Williams was ultimately given the charter for his colony in 1663 and won the right to settle in Rhode Island. Anne Hutchinson was welcomed into his colony, as indicated earlier.

Because of his fraudulent claim, Thomas Weld was charged in the General Court of the Massachusetts Bay Colony, but he ended up staying in England and never showed up for his trial. Even if he had wanted to return, he couldn't because he spent what money he had and became impoverished. Rumor has it that he hid out near London. According to his family records, he died in 1661 or 1662 in England.

Reverend Hugh Peter

Hugh Peter, who was one of Anne Hutchinson's accusers and voted for her banishment, went over to England with Reverend Thomas Weld in 1641 to solicit money for Massachusetts for the expansion of Harvard College and to lay claim to a segment of Rhode Island for the New England colony to expand. Unbeknownst to Peter, Weld stepped over the legal line when he forged a document trying to prove ownership of the land. Peter was, in the meantime, raising money for the upcoming English Civil War in Holland, and he continued to involve himself in the civil war that was brewing between Parliament and King Charles I. Peter sided with Parliament against the king and was assigned to recruit troops and be their chaplain in the upcoming battles. In 1645, he wrote to General Sir Thomas Fairfax, "Sir, one of the greatest comforts I have had in this world next to the grace of God in Christ to my poor soul, has to a member of your army, and a spectator of his presence and you of it." After the war, Oliver Cromwell seized the throne from King Charles I and beheaded him. Hugh Peter participated in that execution himself.

After that, Peter had an eminent position under Cromwell himself, making proposals for legal reforms and similar treatises. Under Cromwell, Peter became a chaplain who accompanied Cromwell's troops when they annexed Ireland and invaded Scotland. Peter spoke with fervor against the Irish, but downplayed his support for Cromwell in Scotland because those people had fought in the earlier phase of the English Civil War and shared a similar religion—Presbyterianism.

Hugh Peter had his wealth of lands and lived a lavish life at the castle at Whitehall, where Cromwell also resided. However, upon Cromwell's death, Peter was ousted from his position by Cromwell's son and successor, Richard. Richard was a weak leader and was soon usurped by the restoration of the Stuart monarchy, which had been sheltered in Scotland. In 1660, in order to gain the good graces of the heir apparent, King Charles II, Peter traveled to St. Albans near London to greet the newly restored king and his military entourage. General George Monck, who led the military escort, ignored him. Every dignitary knew who Peter was, as he had a very distinctive voice. As soon as the royal parade had entered the palace, Hugh Peter was arrested on the charge of regicide. It had been said that Peter heavily disguised himself and acted as one of the executioners of King Charles I. Peter was sentenced to be hanged, drawn, and quartered—one of the most gruesome and horrible forms of public executions.

Peter left behind two contradictory reputations. Some indicate that he was a jocular man, honest, kind, and a victim of circumstance. Others, though, said he was an adulterer, an embezzler, and a drunk, reeking with cruelty and verbal venom. Peter was maligned as much as Anne Hutchinson was and, like her, suffered a brutal, frightful, and bloody fate.

Mary Dyer

Mary accompanied Anne Hutchinson after Anne was banished in 1638, and—like Anne—was humiliated when Governor Winthrop found out that she had also given birth to a deformed baby who was stillborn. This occurred during the course of Hutchinson's days' long trial. Winthrop blasted Mary's reputation, and people gossiped about it for quite some time. Mary stayed in Rhode Island at the Newport settlement Coddington ran. Her husband, William, was the general recorder for the colony and took Mary with him in 1651 when he went to England on business. After her husband sailed back to New England, Mary stayed behind in England for about six years. History has not recorded why she stayed there. It seems odd because she had six children at home in Rhode Island.

While in England, she came into contact with a religious group of Quakers, which was known at the time as the Society of Friends. The religion appealed to Mary even more than the version of Puritanism taught by Anne

Hutchinson, John Wheelwright, and the free grace advocates. The Society of Women actually permitted women to act as ministers and proselytize.

In 1657, Mary Dyer returned to Boston, Massachusetts, now as a Quaker. The Quakers wore a recognizable headscarf, and she was shocked when she was immediately imprisoned. William Dyer rushed over to the jail and bailed her out. He wasn't permitted to allow her to live in Boston, so she had to travel to Weymouth, another town in Massachusetts.

In Boston, and in other parts of New England as time went on, the Puritans were even less tolerant of the Quakers than they were with Anne Hutchinson. They hated the Quakers, especially for their proselytizing efforts, and banished them from the colony. If the Quakers didn't comply, the leaders of the colony dealt out harsh punishments to both men and women, like severe whiplashings in public. For other offenses, they physically tortured them and sometimes even cut their ears off. Anne Hutchinson's younger sister, Katherine Marbury Scott, was also a Quaker and was made to endure ten lashes. She and her husband then moved to Providence, Rhode Island, in 1658. It was said that they were the first Quakers in Roger Williams' Rhode Island.

In the meantime, Mary Dyer and her Quaker associates traveled from Weymouth, Massachusetts, to New Haven, Connecticut, preaching and trying to convert people to Quakerism. The magistrates of many of the Puritan towns in Massachusetts were becoming more alarmed by the increasing numbers of Quakers, and many were imprisoned. In 1659, they passed a new law indicating that they were banished from the Massachusetts Bay Colony "upon pain of death."

Mary Dyer heard that many of her Quaker friends had been incarcerated in Boston and went there to visit. As soon as they arrived, Mary Dyer and the two other Quakers who came with her—both men—were imprisoned. Governor John Endicott brought the men before him, stating,

> We have made many laws and endeavored in several ways to keep you from among us, but neither whipping nor imprisonment, nor cutting off ears, nor banishment upon pain of death will keep you from among us. We desire not your death. Hearken now to your sentence of death.

Then, Governor Endicott brought Mary Dyer before him and said, "Mary Dyer, you shall go from hence to the place from whence you came, and from thence to the place of execution, and be hanged till you are dead." She then bowed her head and said, "The will of the Lord be done."

Her companions were all hung from an elm tree, while Mary waited her turn. She was led up the ladder, and a noose was placed around her neck.

Then, suddenly, a reprieve was announced. Her husband and son had been working vigorously for her release, and the General Court had granted the appeal and gave Mary a reprieve on the basis that she was a woman.

Dyer then returned to Rhode Island but continued to be grieved by the deaths of the other Quakers, especially those who hung right before her very eyes. It was a cruel and devilish law that had been written by those who called themselves sanctified and holy. She then considered a way in which she might attempt to force the authorities in Boston to change that law. In 1660, she decided to scapegoat herself and traveled to Boston in deliberate defiance of their ban against Quakers. Ten days after her arrival in Boston, she was brought before Governor Endicott. Her husband desperately tried to secure another reprieve for her, but it was denied. Mary was hanged from the old elm tree on June 1st, 1660.

Reverend John Cotton

Once considered to be Anne Hutchinson's mentor, John Cotton distanced himself from her once she awarded herself the gift of prophecy by the Holy Spirit. Cotton believed that people could find the truth in the scriptures but that they should not separate themselves from the law.

Cotton was opposed to the separatist view held by Roger Williams, so he tried to lure him back into the fold. He also urged Williams to persuade the older sects of Puritanism and the budding religious sects of Quakers, Presbyterians, Baptists, and Anabaptists to rejoin the Church of England and set up self-governing entities while still upholding the basic doctrines of reformed theology. To promote Congregationalism, a system that promotes local churches to be self-governing, he proposed that each church take responsibility for guiding their own congregations and uphold the religious laws approved by them. His best-known work was *The Way of the Churches of Christ in New England,* which was published in 1645. Because it was considered to be too stringent, the book wasn't used as a guide for the churches, but it did become a reference in setting up the legal system in Massachusetts.

In 1651, Cotton became extremely inflexible and conservative. In fact, he turned into a very strict legalist. He condemned those who held some Anabaptist views and permitted public whippings and imprisonment for other deviant views as well. A former clerical friend of his, Richard Saltonstall from England, wrote to him, saying, "It does not a little grieve my spirit to hear what sad things are reported daily of your tyranny and persecutions in New England as that you fine, whip and imprison men for their consciences." Cotton did not change his ways too much before his death. To be fair, though, Cotton died only a year later of pneumonia.

Roger Williams

Anne Hutchinson left the relative safety of Rhode Island after disputes arose over the possession of Rhode Island. After the Pequot War, which took place between 1636 and 1637, and the difficulties over Anne Hutchinson and those whom they called "heretics," the people who lived in Massachusetts and Connecticut allied with each other in an effort to rid the area of the tribes in Rhode Island—namely the Narragansetts and the Mohegans—and simultaneously expel Roger Williams and his settlers from Rhode Island. This military alliance was formed in 1643, after Anne Hutchinson had relocated to New Netherland. After the fictitious claim of Thomas Weld was dismissed, Williams rushed over to England to fortify his demand for a colonial charter of Rhode Island. He wrote a book, *A Key into the Language of America*, to demonstrate his knowledge of the tribal languages and wrote about the richness of their cultures. One of his objectives was to encourage the English to stop belittling the tribes and respect them as sons and daughters of God. He wrote:

> Boast not proud English, of your birth and blood;
>
> Your brother Indian is by birth as good.
>
> Of one blood God made him, and you all,
>
> As wise, as fair, as strong, as personal.

He also wrote *The Bloudy Tenent of Persecution for Cause of Conscience*, which defended his argument for the separation of church and state. In the text, Williams drew extensively from scriptural quotations. The book was a 17th-century "bestseller," and Williams won the official charter for the colony of Rhode Island just a month before the death of Anne Hutchinson in August of 1643.

Following that publication, Williams wrote a number of books in an effort to convince people that the separation of church and state was the best possible solution to avoid religious persecutions and to free up civic administrations. He said that there was no scriptural mandate for a state-imposed religion. Williams did, however, believe that those portions of the Ten Commandments that constituted moral law should be the basis for civil laws.

Williams never committed to just one religion, although he did lean toward Baptist teachings. At some point between January and March 1683, Williams died, although the causes of his death remain unknown.

Edward Hutchinson

Historians generally agree that Edward Hutchinson accompanied his mother to Rhode Island in 1638. He was one of the founding fathers of their settlement of Pocasset. After serving there for a couple of years, he returned to Boston. Because there were no charges levied against him as a result of Anne's trial, he was permitted to return. Edward was in his twenties at the time.

He took over the family house and made arrangements for its upkeep by hiring caretakers. It is said that he welcomed Anne's daughter, Susanna, home after her release by the Siwanoy tribe, who had kidnapped her when her mother was killed. The approximate date she arrived in Massachusetts was 1647 when she was twelve years old.

Edward saw to it that she was taken care of until she married John Cole in 1651.

Edward was a peacemaker and improved relationships with the government. He was well-liked, personable, and was an active member of the colony militia. In 1653, he was made captain of the artillery. In 1658, he was elected as a court deputy. His cousin, Patience, had married a Quaker, and he was instrumental in campaigning for the tolerance of those who practiced different religions. Up until that time, Massachusetts had been imprisoning Quakers who had emigrated into the colony. They were treated cruelly in captivity, and Edward campaigned against that kind of treatment. In 1668, those who were imprisoned were released.

Edward got along with the native people of Rhode Island fairly well, as they were very peaceful. In fact, the Narragansetts of eastern Rhode Island and the Wampanoags and Pokanokets in the province of Plymouth, Massachusetts, had workable relations with the Pilgrims. The Wampanoags served under their *sachem*, that is, their chief, Wamsutta. He was very fond of calling himself "Alexander." After the death of Wamsutta, his brother, Metacomet, who assumed the English name "Philip," took over and decided to take a more hostile stance, as the colonists were increasing in number, encroaching on their hunting and fishing areas, and becoming embroiled in minor conflicts. The Pilgrims in Plymouth avoided Metacomet, as he was a young and impulsive young man intent on making a name for himself as a hero. Colonists hastily erected garrisons and built defensive walls around their towns in both Rhode Island and eastern Massachusetts. Every able-bodied male was recruited into the militia, including Captain Edward Hutchinson, who was called to active service and given command of a company of men.

Rumors of this pending war with the tribes were leaked to court magistrates by a Native American informer, John Sassamon. Sassamon was a Harvard graduate and a recognized translator and negotiator for the colonies. Not long after he did this, Sassamon was found murdered. In Plymouth, three warriors serving under Metacomet were hauled before the colonial court and questioned. As a result of the trial, the three warriors were hanged in June

1675. Under Muttawmp, the Nipmucs of western and central Massachusetts and the Pennacooks around Massachusetts Bay then joined the Native American alliance.

The hostilities started in Plymouth when several bands of Pokanokets attacked homesteads and slaughtered the inhabitants on the night of a full moon in the summer of 1675. There was also a vicious attack on the major town of Swansea, where buildings were burned or destroyed and several people were killed. Militias in Bristol, Rhode Island, staged a retaliatory strike on a tribal encampment nearby. The war moved to Middleborough, Mendon, Northfield, Deerfield, Hadley, and Brookfield, all towns that were located in Massachusetts.

In Brookfield, Anne Hutchinson's son, Edward, was the captain of an artillery unit. He and Captain Thomas Wheeler fought vigorously to ward off the onslaughts from the Pokanoket and the Nipmuc tribes. Toward the end of the siege at the fort they were stationed in, Wheeler and Hutchinson negotiated with the sachem of the Nipmuck, attempting to pull together a truce. It was unsuccessful, though, and the two of them were ambushed. Edward Hutchinson died of his wounds the following day. His youngest sister, Susanna, and her husband, John Cole, later settled on a Rhode Island land tract owned by Edward.

King Philip's War was not over yet. In Springfield, Massachusetts, along the Connecticut River, moderately sized groups of Native American fighters attacked the town's grist mill. They destroyed nearly all of the buildings in the town, save for the blockhouse, which is a small two-story building with openings intended for rifles.

In Rhode Island, the faithful Narragansetts weren't involved in the war for the most part, with the exception of Sachem Canonchet and his band (a sachem refers to a paramount chief). The rest of the Narragansetts gave refuge to other tribes, specifically the Wampanoag warriors, along with their families who had been hiding in the Assawompset Swamp, just below Providence, Rhode Island. Despite the fact that the Narragansetts were mostly peaceful, many of the militias from other colonies didn't realize that and attacked them indiscriminately, burning their dwellings. They also attempted to take the fort alongside the Great Swamp, which was frozen at the time. The fort at the Great Swamp, near today's Kingston, Rhode Island, housed thousands of people, including men, women, and children. The indiscriminate attacks by the colonial forces of Connecticut, Massachusetts, and Rhode Island brutally wiped out nearly a thousand unarmed people. Others fled into the bitter cold across the frozen water. Those survivors who managed to make it to

Aquidneck Island in Narragansett Bay were taken care of by some kind-hearted colonists.

Mary Rowlandson, the wife of Reverend Joseph Rowlandson, who was one of the survivors of the battle, wrote:

> Now is the dreadful hour that I have often heard of in time of war, as it was the case of others, but now my eyes have seen it. Some in our house were fighting for their lives, others wallowing in their blood, the house on fire over our heads, and the bloody heathen ready to knock us on the head if we stirred out...the bullets flying thick, one went through my side, and the same (as would seem) through the bowels and hand of my dear child in my arms.

The war raged on until 1678, with many dying on all sides. However, there was only one victor of this war, and the colonists were the ones to claim that name. Although, it should be noted that this war only increased tensions between the settlers and the neighboring tribes.

Roger Williams, who was in his seventies, was there in Providence, Rhode Island, during this cruel and bloody war. Providence was nearly in ruins, as were many other cities and towns in Rhode Island due to the warring Narragansetts who didn't remain neutral. In a desperate effort to stop the war that nearly ruined his colony, Williams often shuffled over to the warriors on his weakened legs, begging them to stop. On one particular occasion, he pointed back toward his burning house and said, "This house of mine now burning before my eyes has lodged some thousands of you for these ten years." Later on, Williams lamented to his brother, "I told them they had forgotten they were mankind and ran around the country like wolves tearing the innocent and peaceable. They confessed they were in a strange way."

Conclusion

Rather than being a feminist in the sense of promoting women's rights, Anne Hutchinson demonstrated them. She was intellectually advanced and more than willing to stand up for her beliefs. Not once during her trial did she ever use her gender to solicit sympathy. Hutchinson eschewed the weakness traditionally attributed to women of the 17th century by simply not being weak. She was, in the words of her nemesis, Governor Winthrop, "as bold as a man." While much of what Winthrop said about her wasn't true, that statement definitely was.

Anne Hutchinson was a woman born before her time. The faith she imparted was a faith she lived every day. It gave her the willingness to be vulnerable in the face of adversity, and through her vulnerability came strength. She was cautious, but not to the point that she was about to surrender her convictions to please those who labeled her as a weak or subservient woman—or as someone who bent or broke like a reed in the wind. What's more, she knew who she was and what she stood for. Part of Anne's charm was that she spoke to her followers on their own level. Her language wasn't derived from a process of literal thinking and blind faith like that of other Puritans. She didn't carefully define terms like "sanctification" and "justification," which may have been her own undoing, but she knew she didn't have to. Those terms had already been inculcated in her listeners. Hutchinson instead presented an approach to religion that helped them think for themselves and develop an inner conscience.

The Anne Hutchinson affair served to highlight the main issues that plagued the New England communities, including the danger of conducting a church trial on heresy and bridging that over to indicate sedition, a civic/criminal offense; the influence of a political campaign for governorship on religious beliefs and practices; the disenfranchisement of citizens who disagreed with the religious beliefs of the majority; the right to reject people from settling in the colony without the permission of civil authorities, and; the right to banish people from the colony on the basis of theological differences or controversy.

One of the elements often overlooked by commentators about the controversy between the Puritan elders and Anne Hutchinson is one of political survival. The Puritans came over to New England to preserve their religious beliefs and way of life. However, they were immediately confronted with the harsh and unforgiving environment of a raw new world. The one major element they shared in common was their faith, and they needed that unity to survive. There was no room for heterodoxy in the Puritan world of New England because they weren't ready for it. But some members, such as Anne Hutchinson, were, and they were willing to fight for it.

Perhaps the greatest pitfall that occurred to the Puritans and people of other faiths in the New World was the combination of church and state. In Europe, the most prominent legal structure upon which to model a government was the religious establishment. It had a hierarchy, governing bodies, a set of laws, and a judiciary of sorts. It would be quite a challenge for people who grew up in that world to think of politics that could work outside a religiously flavored framework. One would have to develop a set of rights based upon moral law, the kind of law that could hold an intelligent society of human beings together in peace.

The problem of creating a colony based upon religious affiliations is the fact that its leaders had become entangled in hair-splitting theological disputes. Those dilemmas created criteria for deciding the quality of a person's religious life and their relationship with God. Puritanism also continued to be strong in the British colonies; however, it lost its original purpose, which was to "purify" the Anglican Church. Instead, it became even more repressive and gave rise to the Salem witch trials in 1692 and 1693. In many ways, it was a recreation of the struggles Anne had gone through with those who didn't permit her to be true to herself. The majority of "witches" were women, and they were labeled as being weak and evil because they didn't conform to the mandates of those who labeled themselves as strong and good—namely, men. Yet, in the world of reality, men and women are not opposites; they are two facets of "human."

Part 4: The Pilgrims

A Captivating Guide to the Passengers on Board the Mayflower Who Founded the Plymouth Colony and Their Relationship with the Native Americans along with Their Legacy in New England

Introduction

It was Thursday, November 9, 1620, when the ship *Mayflower* reached the shores of New England. It left England with 102 people on board and arrived at its destination with 101. Only one crew member died during the three-month-long journey across the ocean. The exhausted, ill, and starving passengers were finally able to leave their cramped, foul-smelling cabins. Or so they thought. The heavy winds blew them off course, and instead of landing in Northern Virginia, which was the *Mayflower*'s destination, they landed at Cape Cod, New England. Although it seems that they needed just a few more days to travel where they needed to be, they had no supplies, they were ill, and the strong winds and shallow waters wouldn't allow them to take the shortest route south. Instead, the Pilgrims decided to find a suitable spot where they could build their colony on the territory of New England. The territory where they landed was already named Plymouth by the explorer John Smith, who first mapped the area. The Pilgrims decided the name was appropriate and somewhat prophetic as their ship, the *Mayflower*, started its journey from the port of Plymouth in England.

But the Pilgrims were not the first settlers in North America. They were not the first Europeans and not the first English who came to the shores of the New World. Spanish and Portuguese already had colonies in America when Elizabeth I decided to compete with them and send her explorers. But the queen's plan ended in a disaster when the first settlers disappeared without a trace, and their first colony was later found abandoned. Less than twenty years after the Roanoke Island colony's disappearance, England finally got its first foothold in North America. The new colony was named Jamestown, and although it had many ups and downs, it became the oldest continuously-inhabited English settlement in America. This one success was enough to encourage a group of people, the religious separatists who only sought to practice their religion in peace, to set sail for the new frontier.

Even though the continent was already inhabited by the Spanish, English, Portuguese, and Dutch colonists, Plymouth was something very different. It never fit into the image of the first colonies because all of them were started as an extension of their country's economic interests. The Spanish and Portuguese south to plunder the natives and take their riches back to their kings. Others were looking into expanding their enterprises and starting a trade of fur, tobacco, indigo, and other goods native to the New World. The

Pilgrims were the only ones who started a colony out of necessity, out of the pure will to survive. The history of the Pilgrims starts much earlier than the *Mayflower* ever set sail. The history of the Pilgrims is a story of religious intolerance, separatism, persecution, and flight. The very core of the Pilgrims was their faith, and they were willing to leave behind everything dear to them to be able to worship as they saw fit.

The Pilgrims' path was a rocky one. In just their first winter in the New World, they lost almost half their people. They had to deal with the "barbarians," the Native Americans who installed fear in godly Pilgrims with their savagery and paganism. But the Pilgrims quickly learn that they could live in peace with their new neighbors and that they had many benefits from them. The Native tribes were the first teachers of the Pilgrims. From individuals such as Samoset, Squanto, and Hobomok, the Pilgrims learned how to grow new crops, how to hunt and skin animals, and how to explore their new surroundings safely. They made alliances with the native tribes and developed trade. Unfortunately, these alliances were short-lived. The Pilgrims and the Puritans who soon joined them in the New World still observed the natives as inferiors, and they tried to convert them. When that failed, they used the natives to form exclusive trade deals, which only deepened the animosity between the tribes. The results were the wars and death that took many Native Americans as well as Puritan lives. The first settlers of New England never again learned how to live side by side with the natives in peace.

The religious freedom the Pilgrims sought soon transformed itself into religious intolerance. The Puritans, a close religious community, started persecuting other sects just as they were once persecuted in England. The Quakers were pressed hard by the Puritans, but through persistence, stubbornness, and religious fanaticism, they managed to earn their right to settle in New England. More and more settlers came to colonize North America. Some were Puritans and the relatives of Pilgrims, but many were not. In fact, most of them came not out of religious aspirations but to develop their own businesses as the New World offered new opportunities. The Puritans were forced to adapt to the new order and were soon integrated into the wider culture of the new society of America. By that time, the Pilgrims had already disappeared, completely absorbed by all the new settlers of Cape Cod. However, all these newcomers would follow the footsteps the first Pilgrims left in the sands of New England. It was the Pilgrims who set the stage for them and welcomed them into the new frontier.

Chapter 1 – The Religious Background

Wycliffe and the Burning of His Work

https://en.wikipedia.org/wiki/John_Wycliffe#/media/File:Portrait_of_John_Wycliffe.jpg

The Pilgrims were a group of people who abandoned the civilized world of Europe and started a journey across the Atlantic Ocean in hopes they could find a better life. The journey was dangerous, and they were going into the unknown. Most of the tales they heard about the colonies in the New World were of disaster and failure. The only somewhat successful story about colonizing Northern America was that of Jamestown in today's Virginia. Established in 1607 as the "James Fort," the colony managed to survive and become the first permanently inhabited place in the New World. But just in the first three years of its existence, most of its inhabitants died. Over 80 percent of the population of James Fort died due to diseases and starvation. The first Pilgrims who were yet to set sail knew about these horrific stories, yet their need to leave civilization prevailed. But what was this need that urged them to continue with their plan, despite the hardships that awaited? It was the lack of religious freedom. At the time, Europe was consumed in a religious struggle known as the Reformation. To fully understand the plight of the Pilgrims, we need to learn of the religious conditions in Europe through a brief history of the Reformation.

Western Europe of the Middle Ages was a world of a single church—the Roman Catholic Church. The religious life of every individual was ruled by the pope, who was deemed greater than the lords and kings. His power was such that the church was an extremely wealthy institution. As the head of the church, the pope was considered the world's spiritual leader. But he desired temporal power, too. After all, the church did own one-third of Europe's land as well as material goods. Eventually, the pope gained temporal power over some states in Italy, known as the Papal States. He started ruling as a secular ruler, signing treaties with other kings, making alliances, and entering wars. The power of the Roman Catholic Church was immense, but with the power came earthly temptations. The Church and its leaders started indulging in corruption and immoral behavior. Everything was for sale, even the indulgences by which souls in purgatory could be released of their punishment for temporal sins. All a relative of a deceased person had to do was to buy such an indulgence from the Church. It was also very strict about how Christianity could be interpreted and was intolerant of other religions, calling them all paganistic.

Not everyone was ready to simply accept how the Catholic Church worked. One of the first to speak against the Catholic Church was John Wycliffe (1328–1384). He was a fourteenth-century priest from England and a scholar. He was one of the first protestors who didn't like the church's stance on dissent. He claimed that the bishops and clergy became too powerful and that they imposed their will on the people. Wycliffe demanded an English translation of the Bible so everyone could read it. But the church saw the dangers in this, as people would interpret the holy book on their own, and the church would lose its influence. John Wycliffe translated the Bible himself during the 1380s. Until then, the only copy of the Bible used across Europe was its fourth-century Latin translation, known as the Vulgate. Wycliffe was convinced that people across the world, no matter their social rank and wealth, should have the right to worship God as they saw fit. Because of his convictions, he is regarded as the predecessor of Protestantism.

John Wycliffe was also a part of the envoy that discussed the differences between Rome and England with the pope's representatives. He defended his country and the interests of his king, Edward III (1312–1377), but he was suspicious of any authority. He even wrote a lengthy essay about the concept of dominion, ownership of property, and authority. Wycliffe believed dominion could be granted only by God and that the rulers or institutions that sinned were working against God's will. Therefore, they had no legitimacy. Wycliff believed this was the case with the Catholic Church. He wrote that due to the sins of its members, the properties of the Church should be confiscated. All clergy should live in poverty. He believed that was God's intention. However, no one else shared his views, and he was unable to spread his thoughts. This is why he is considered a forefather of Protestantism. He laid the foundations for the Protestant Reformation, which would come centuries later.

But Wycliffe died in 1384, and by 1415, during the Council of Constance, the Roman Catholic Church proclaimed him a heretic. His work was banned from studying, and his writings and Bible translation were burned. The Church even ordered his remains excavated and moved from consecrated ground. Catholics believed a soul was vulnerable to the works of the devil even after death and that burial in consecrated ground was protection. The removal of one's remains was seen as the ultimate punishment, and in the case of Wycliffe, it served as a warning to all others who dared to protest against the Catholic Church.

Another theologian, this time from the University of Prague, had similar ideas as John Wycliffe's. His name was Jan Hus (1372–1415), a central figure of the Bohemian Reformation. Jan Hus had many followers, who became known as Hussites. They were proto-Protestants of Bohemia, and they followed his example by denouncing the corrupted Catholic clergy and even the pope himself. Hus spoke vigorously against indulgences, and he was the main influence on Martin Luther. His destiny was way worse than that of Wycliff. Jan Hus was exiled from Bohemia. In 1415, he was invited to speak in front of the Council of Constance and share his convictions with the assembly. However, he never got the chance to speak. As soon as he arrived, Hus was arrested and burned at the stake, accused of heresy. The death of Jan Hus resonated with his followers, and the consequence was the Hussite Wars (1419–1434), in which the Hussites managed to defeat papal armies and keep Bohemia and Moravia firmly under their rule.

A century after Hus died, Martin Luther started expanding on his and Wycliffe's ideas. He not only shared the ideas of his predecessors but also challenged papal authority directly. Martin Luther believed that faith alone ensured one's salvation and that the pope was not ordained by God as an ecclesiastical ruler. He also regarded the Roman Catholic Church as a massive and unnecessary bureaucracy that needed to end. According to Luther, the Church was not relevant for one's salvation; therefore, it needed to be eliminated. He based his beliefs on the writings of St. Paul in the book of

Romans. To do that, Luther wanted to "wash the Church" of corruption, which he believed came as a consequence of allowing old pagan customs to survive. One of the main pagan customs that he wanted to end was the celebration of Christmas. Although Christians celebrate Christmas as the day when Jesus was born, in reality, it is an old pagan winter solstice celebration in honor of the sun deity. This is why later, during the seventeenth century, the Puritans would start a war on Christmas. They were well aware of its connections with pagan religions and wanted to get rid of it. In the US, the Puritans managed to ban Christmas for twenty years.

Martin Luther voiced his protests against the Roman Catholic Church in 1517 by nailing the list of his complaints, known as the Ninety-five Theses, on the door of the Wittenberg Cathedral, in today's Germany. But, most importantly, his Theses were printed in several printshops in Germany so they could circulate and warn the Christians against buying the indulgences. By 1519, Luther's writings reached Italy, France, and England, making him famous. Before the pope had the chance, Luther excommunicated himself from the Catholic Church and married a nun, as he had never believed in celibacy. The pope at the time, Leo X, took his time responding to Luther's Theses. He gathered theologians and scholars who, over the next three years, crafted a heresy case against Luther. Luther was even summoned to Rome to defend himself, and although he responded to the summons, he had to escape the city in the night to save his life. But Leo X decided for a more conciliatory approach because of the ever-present danger the Ottoman Turks posed to Central Europe. As the pope had to concentrate his powers on defending Christianity in Europe, he persuaded Martin Luther to stay silent and would order Luther's opponents into silence, too.

But Martin Luther didn't stay silent as he had promised. Instead, he hid in Germany and continued to publish his writings, using an alias. He even translated the Bible into the German language, and soon the other nations followed. The holy book was translated into many languages throughout the Holy Roman Empire. A theological storm was brewing in Europe. The Catholic Church responded by organizing a series of councils in Trent, Italy, during which Protestantism was declared a heresy. The council also initiated the Catholic Revival, better known as the Counter-Reformation. The result was 150 years of violent factionalism that engulfed Europe in what are known as the Wars of Religion. The culmination occurred during the Thirty Years War (1618-1648), which was the most destructive period of European history. Modern estimations are that around 20 percent of Europe's population perished due to this war. In comparison, World War II killed around 3 percent of Europe's population. Though it lasted for a shorter time, World War II is considered one of the bloodiest European historical events. Still, the

20 percent of souls lost during the Thirty Years War illustrates the level of violence that ensued after the Protestant Reformation.

The Reformation, as well as the undermining of papal authority, went slightly differently in England than in the rest of Europe. Due to the tribulations caused by the Tudor dynasty, the break with the Catholic Church was definitive and official in England. This Tudor turmoil started with King Henry VII, who sought to form an alliance with Spain through the marriage of his son Arthur with Catharine of Aragon. But Arthur died four months after the wedding, and the pope granted her a special dispensation so she could marry Arthur's brother, Henry VIII. But since their marriage failed to produce a male heir to the throne of England, Henry wanted to remarry. He had already fallen in love with Anne Boleyn. But, when he sought an annulment of his marriage from Pope Clement VII, he was denied. The reason for this denial wasn't religious but political, as the pope didn't want to make an enemy of the very Catholic and very powerful Kingdom of Spain. At the time, England was losing its influence in Europe, and Pope Clement had to weigh which choice was politically better for Rome. He chose Spain.

But Henry VIII felt that the Catholic Church owed him because, during the early days of his reign, he prosecuted the Lutherans in England and even had several of them burned at the stake. He was outraged by the pope's response, and in retaliation, he severed all the ties England had with Rome. He proceeded to form the Anglican Church (Church of England), appointing himself as the head of the new Church in 1534. He had help from Archbishop Thomas Cranmer and lawyer Thomas Cromwell. In his first official act as the head of the Church of England, Henry granted himself a divorce from Catherine of Aragon so he could marry Anne Boleyn. Henry didn't have much luck with women, as he had, in total, six wives. Two of them he divorced, two he had beheaded, and one of them died. The Anglican Church grew strong and played a role in intensifying the problems between the Catholics and the Protestants.

The new Church of England kept all the Catholic vestiges, which angered the Protestants, who hoped that the separation from Rome would bring reform to the church in England. They hoped the struggles to purify the church would be easier without papal influence and that the whole country would take on a new religious and political direction. But the new queen of England, Mary I (1516–1558), wasn't sympathetic to the Protestants at all, and she dealt with them harshly. Her cruelty gave her the nickname "Bloody Mary," by which she would remain known in history. She died of cancer and was succeeded by her half-sister, Elizabeth. The daughter of Henry VIII and Anne Boleyn, Elizabeth was a resolute Protestant. She was also an influential political figure, and Spain wanted to use her. This could be achieved only through marriage. But Elizabeth refused any marriage proposal that came from Spain because she was eager to help the Dutch Protestants who had trouble dealing with Spanish rule. Because she was meddling in Dutch affairs, Spain tried to conquer England. When Elizabeth's navy managed to overpower the Spanish one (mainly due to the Spanish ships getting caught in bad weather), she took it as a sign that God preferred the Protestants. She hit a final blow to the leftover ties that the Church of England had with the Catholic Church, making England officially a Protestant country.

Although Protestant, Elizabeth didn't do much to reform the Church of England. She herded people into the church, imprisoning those who refused to attend the masses. They would remain imprisoned until they accepted that they must attend the church. Elizabeth's critics complained that the Church of England lacked in practicing the Christian faith. The people who read the Bible complained that they couldn't find any of the Church's rituals in it. They saw no reason for strict Sunday masses, as they were never described in the Bible. The bishops often mocked these critics and called them "precise men" for their literal understanding of the Bible, but they were never able to silence them. The critics warned that the Church was full of corruption, and they called for the return of the pure Christianity of the past. Because of their literal understanding of the Bible and their desire to purify the Church, these critics earned a new nickname. They were no longer simply known as the "precise men" but as Puritans.

There were other religious factions more radical than the Puritans, and they demanded complete abandonment of the Church of England. They were separatists, and they were also called Brownists after their leader, Robert Browne (1550s-1633). He was even expelled from Cambridge University because of his convictions that the Puritans should leave the Church of England and start their own congregation. Browne continued to call for separation, citing Saint Paul's teachings. He was soon imprisoned but was released. Afraid of persecution, he fled to Holland, which was a Protestant country at the time.

Puritanism started as a reaction to the violent suppression of the Protestants by Mary I. But radical separatists among the Puritans evolved and soon started believing they were the chosen people, the only ones who could be redeemed.

Queen Elizabeth died in 1603. Since she had never married, she left no heir to the throne. The next in line was James I, son of Mary Queen of Scots, and he took over the royal crown. He, too, was a Protestant, and it was during his rule that the Bible was translated into English. To this day, the King James Bible remains the most famous version of the translation and the official version of the Bible in the Church of England. But it was also during his reign that a group of Protestants who believed the Church of England didn't do enough to separate itself from the Catholics decided to leave. Although Protestant, James' politics often aligned with Catholic Spain, and he staunchly supported the Church of England.

Not long after the coronation of James I, around 1,000 Puritans petitioned for church reform. This number is based on the writings of contemporary scholars and cannot be confirmed, as the original document was lost. Their request is known as the Millenary Petition, and in it, the Puritans openly criticized the Church of England and expressed their hopes that the new king, a Protestant himself, would agree to conduct a reform. The petition called on the English priests to reject their lavish garments, and it also demanded more strict observation of the Sabbath. They wanted the Church to follow what the Bible prescribed and nothing more. The Puritans criticized the Church's celebration of Sunday and religious holidays such as Christmas. James I refused most of the points from the petition, as he hoped that the translation of the Bible would be enough to appease the Puritans.

Most of the English people regarded Puritans' beliefs as too strict. The Puritans thought that the Sabbath should be celebrated with silent prayer and fasting and that the Church of England should stop celebrating Sunday and stop producing the ale they sold to finance themselves. The springtime celebration and the Maypole were seen as worship of idols, which was as much a sin as the murder of one's own child. All these stern admonitions of Puritans put them in conflict with the people of England, who wanted to celebrate and be merry. The Puritans were a minority, and they quickly realized that they had no chance of forcing religious reform—even more so when King James I proclaimed in 1604 that it was forbidden to persecute Englishmen for dancing, setting up Maypoles, archery, or celebrations of any kind on Sunday, as long as they were after the church service.

The Puritans had another chance to push for reform, or at least to persuade the king to allow them to practice their faith as they pleased. This chance was at Hampton Court Palace, southwest of London, where James called an assembly of many Anglican Church representatives and only four Puritans. During the assembly, the Puritan representatives were not allowed to speak for days. King James was afraid that if he allowed the Puritans to practice their faith and ordain their own ministers, his hold over them would weaken. Instead, the king barred all private religious gatherings and ordered that his translation of the Bible be used in all religious ceremonies. Many Puritans refused to follow the king's orders, and James felt he had no other choice but to persecute them. In 1606, there were two factions of the Puritans: those who stayed within the Church of England, hoping that in time they would be able to influence it, and the Separatists. The latter, despite persecutions from the Puritans, started their own secret congregation and started calling themselves the "Saints," as they regarded themselves as martyrs. But the king kept his promise of persecution, and in 1607, the Separatists' secret congregation was exposed to the authorities. They had no other options but to go somewhere else where they could practice their religion as they saw fit. Because Holland was a purely Protestant country, it was a natural choice.

Chapter 2 – In Leiden and Onwards

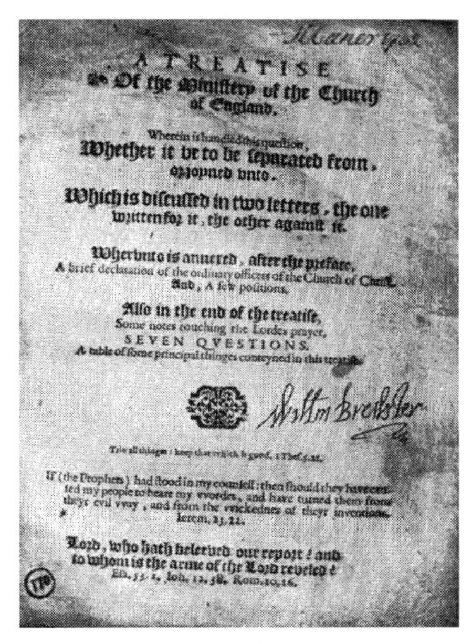
A TREATISE
Of the Ministery of the Church of England.
Wherein is handled this question,
Whether it be to be separated from, or joyned unto.
Which is discussed in two letters, the one written for it, the other against it.
Whereunto is annexed, after the preface,
A brief declaration of the ordinary offices of the Church of Christ.
And, A few positions.
Also in the end of the treatise,
Some notes touching the Lordes prayer,
SEVEN QVESTIONS.
A table of some principal thinges conteyned in this treatise.

If (the Prophets) had stood in my counsell: then should they have ... my people to heare my wordes, and have turned them from theyr evil way, and from the wickednes of theyr inventions. Ierem. 23.22.

Lord, who hath beleeved our report? and to whom is the arme of the Lord reveled? Esa. 53.1, Ioh. 12.38. Rom. 10.16.

Brewster's Pamphlet, Printed in Leiden

https://en.wikipedia.org/wiki/Pilgrims_(Plymouth_Colony)#/media/File:Brewster_COE_Treatise.png

The Puritans and the Separatist Protestants planned to leave England, but the first obstacle they encountered was the king's proclamation that all who wanted to leave the kingdom had to have royal approval and had to promise they would return. Having no other options, the Separatists had to leave in secret. In 1607, they bribed ship captains to transport them to Amsterdam. At first, the ship captains would take the bribes but report the Separatists to the authorities. The English government, and the king, didn't want to hassle the Separatists. Though they were imprisoned at first, they were released after several months. Even the ringleaders and main organizers were released and were able to plan their escape once again. The government must have realized that it was easier to turn a blind eye and let the Separatists go than to prosecute them. Their leaving might bring peace to the kingdom, as the religious turmoil would cease.

In the spring of 1608, the Separatist Protestants tried to leave England once more. To avoid captains turning them over to the authorities, they chose only Dutch ships. After all, Dutch captains were fellow Protestants and would not betray them. Finally, after several months of sailing the North Sea, the Protestants arrived in Holland. Their first stop was Amsterdam. But Amsterdam was a large city, numbering over 240,000 people. It was too large and too modern for the simple farmers from England who didn't even speak the Dutch language. They couldn't find employment in the fast-developing city, but they were finally free to worship however they wanted. They gathered in meetinghouses because they continued to despise the practices previously imposed by the Church of England. Their Sabbath started at eight in the morning, and the women and men had to sit separately. They sang psalms but with no music accompanying their singing, and they enjoyed a communal meal after the mass, again with women and men sitting separately. The second sermon would start in the afternoon, but this one was reserved only for men. During the second sermon, the men were free to discuss the Bible and exchange opinions. Women had to stay home and keep their opinions, if they had any, to themselves.

The Protestants had separated into factions back in England, and once in Amsterdam, their lives weren't what they expected them to be. At first, these factions met in Amsterdam on friendly terms, but soon they started quarreling, sometimes even violently. The first faction to land in Amsterdam was called the "Ancient Brethren," and they numbered around 300 members, with Francis Johnson as their leader and pastor. The second faction was led by William Brewster and John Robinson, and they led a congregation of 100 members, known as Scrooby Separatists, as they had formerly worshipped at Scrooby Manor, South Yorkshire. At first, the two congregations prayed together. But less than a year after their arrival, the Scrooby congregation decided to leave Amsterdam. The theological differences between them and the Ancient Brethren were too great to share the territory. The Scrooby congregation decided to settle in Leiden, a small university town, where they hoped they would be accepted and could build lives for themselves.

Once again, the English Protestant Separatists were on the move, and although they didn't call themselves the Pilgrims yet, the idea of the religious journey they had to endure was evolving. Some of them hoped they would find peaceful lives in Leiden, but others had no clear destination in mind. John Robinson became the minister of the Leiden congregation, and he was among the first to settle in the new town. The first religious meetings of English Protestants in Leiden were in their own homes. But in May 1611, the congregation finally gathered enough money to establish a formal meeting house, which was at the same time a parsonage.

The Protestants forged a life for themselves in Leiden, but it was a very difficult life. They were foreigners, unable to fit into the new society. They had to take the difficult jobs in the carpentry or cloth industry. These were such low-paying jobs that even their children had to work for a whole family to be able to support themselves. Very often, the older children would leave their families to try to integrate into the Dutch society, which would allow them better lives. But integration was very different back in the seventeenth century, and, failing to naturalize, the young English Protestants turned to become sailors or soldiers.

Although the Pilgrims had settled in Leiden for the time being, they were not satisfied with the events that surrounded them. Holland had a very turbulent relationship with Spain, and this turmoil would often escalate into open war during the sixteenth century. A new threat of war presented itself in 1619 when Dutch statesman John van Oldenbarnevelt was executed after he was convicted of treason. Van Oldenbarnevelt was an advocate of a sovereign Holland, and Spain would have none of that. Anxiety about the new war brewing loomed over the Pilgrims, and they began to think of taking another religious journey.

But the Pilgrims had yet another reason to long for a place where they could practice their religion in peace. Growing up without memories of the hardships the Protestants had gone through in England, the Pilgrim's children desired more freedoms. They thought of their Sabbath practices as too harsh and too boring. They wanted to integrate into Dutch society and have fun. The children who wanted to get an education were deprived of such privileges because modest Protestant life demanded them to labor and contribute to the congregation's wellbeing. Poverty and fear for the souls of their children stirred the Pilgrims into restlessness.

But what really pushed them to move again was the fact that Holland was just not far enough for some of them to leave their old lives behind them. In 1617, Elder Brewster stirred up trouble for the Pilgrims by printing religious Separatist pamphlets he then sent to England. He used the false bottoms on French wine barrels that were transported to England as a hiding place for his printing material. In the pamphlets, he openly attacked the Church of England, as well as the Five Articles of Perth, a religious guideline King James I had imposed on the Church of Scotland in an attempt to bring the Church of England and the Church of Scotland together. The pamphlets stirred commotion among the bishops, and the king employed the English ambassador to Holland, Sir Dudley Carleton, to investigate where the pamphlets were coming from. To discover the culprit, Sir Carleton used Dutch printers to match it to the cases of the type found in Brewster's house. To avoid arrest and punishment, Brewster fled. But the hunt England mounted on Brewster on both sides of the English Channel put all English Protestant Separatists in danger. Those in Holland decided to search for a new safe haven.

The first discussions about the new journey started as early as 1617, and they were inspired by the journey of Captain John Smith to New England in 1614. John Smith was an English explorer and sailor who was one of the crucial figures in establishing Jamestown, Virginia, the first permanent English settlement in America. He mapped the Chesapeake Bay area, but he couldn't settle. His restless spirit led him to explore the coast of New England. His writings were what inspired the first English settlers to set sail for America. But he is probably remembered the most for his encounter with the Powhatan natives. He was captured by them, and he believed his life was in danger. But the chieftain's daughter saved his life by thro wing her body over his to protect him. Her name was Pocahontas, and although the story Captain James Smith told may have been the fabrication of his imagination, Pocahontas remains one of the most respected and well-known Native American historical figures.

Smith might have imagined the story involving Pocahontas, but when it came to the colonization of the New World, he was a realist. He promoted colonization, but he also warned that it would be hard work to build a civilization in such a wild continent. He warned that America was filled with dangers and that the bored Europeans should not think of it as a vacation paradise. Unlike other explorers, Smith didn't try to find gold or precious stones in the new land. He saw America for the potential it had. The fertile land and abundant wildlife could be molded into farmland and various resources. Finally, Smith returned to London after mapping the coasts of Maine and Massachusetts, and he died in England at age fifty-one.

The Pilgrims were not the first Europeans to visit or to colonize America. In fact, as Englishmen, they had to catch up with other Europeans who had rushed to colonize the Western Hemisphere after Christopher Columbus' expedition to the Caribbean in the late 1400s. In the early fifteenth century, Amerigo Vespucci made several trips to what is now known as South America, concluding that his predecessor Columbus didn't reach the Far East as he had hoped but had indeed discovered a new continent. But the New World was neither new nor unknown to Europeans. The first contact between the continents was established much earlier, in the tenth century, when some Norse colonies were established in North America. However, these colonies were quickly forgotten, and the first permanent contact with the New World started after Columbus' travels.

Spain was the first to begin colonization of the Caribbean, Mexico, and Central America during the fifteenth century. The first permanent European colony was established in 1565 by Spaniards in what is today St. Augustine, Florida. Denmark, Portugal, France, and the Netherlands followed and established their own colonies in the Western Hemisphere. Despite the vastness of the New World, which spread across two land masses (two Americas), the colonists often violently competed with each other. As if that wasn't enough, the native people were often hostile, and disease and hunger took many lives, both indigenous and newcomers.

The first Protestant settlement, known as Fort Caroline, was founded by the French Huguenots in 1564 in northern Florida. The colony was on the St. Johns River, near today's Jacksonville, and it was the scene of one of the most horrific episodes of the sixteenth century. A year after its foundation, the colony was attacked by the Spanish naval force that was tasked with evicting the French from the area. The sea battle ended in a draw, forcing the Spanish to retreat to St. Augustine to regroup. The French followed the Spanish fleet when a storm caught them, sinking all of their ships. The surviving soldiers were stranded on the beach, unable to return home. Fort Caroline was undefended, and the Spanish took the opportunity to approach it from land. In a brutal surprise attack, they massacred all but fifty women and children. As if that wasn't enough, the Spanish soldiers found stranded French soldiers and offered them safe passage home. The French accepted, unaware that Fort Caroline had been destroyed. But as each group of the French soldiers disembarked, they were immediately executed. The inlet where the French soldiers were taken was named "Matanzas," meaning "slaughters."

The First English attempt to colonize North America came in 1584 when Sir Walter Raleigh organized an expedition party. The expedition visited Roanoke Island, in today's North Carolina. But the colonists soon found it impossible to live with the non-Christian indigenous people of the region, and hostilities broke out. When Sir Francis Drake, an English captain, stopped by to check on the colony, he picked up everyone except a small contingent of soldiers and took them back to England. Another expedition was sent to Roanoke Island in 1587, and the people expected they would meet with the soldiers left behind. But they could not find the English soldiers anywhere, and, worried they would be unable to defend themselves, they decided to turn back for England. However, their captain was already engaged in a naval battle against the Spanish, and their journey home was delayed for the next three years. When the captain was finally able to come to Roanoke Island and pick up the colonists, he found no one.

When finally a permanent colony was established successfully at Jamestown, the Separatists in Leiden were intrigued. Initially, they had no interest in the explorations of English adventurers, and they were not fascinated with the idea of New England. However, their religious needs were not met in Holland, and they started to believe they wouldn't be met anywhere in Europe. The need to move arose again, and the discussed destinations included Virginia in North America and Guyana in Africa. But none of these choices offered an easy life. The Virginia colony was on the verge of failure because the people refused to travel to it, scared by the stories of savage indigenous people and hunger that awaited them in the new land. And those who returned from Guyana would soon die of a mysterious illness.

To save Jamestown from failure, King James I offered to waive the charges against some of the English prisoners if they would depart for the colony. The Separatists hoped the king would extend the offer to them, and in 1617, they sent John Carver and Deacon Robert Cushman to petition the king. But the bishops tried to persuade the Separatists to modify their Christian practices and beliefs before departing for the New World in hopes of establishing the Church of England there. The Separatists refused, and it is not surprising that the king refused their petition. However, James I promised he wouldn't molest the Separatists who went to Virginia if they behaved peacefully, even though he had to officially decline their request for pardon and departure. But the congregation in Leiden was cautious, and this half-hearted insurance of royal non-interference wasn't enough for them. They wanted a guarantee of peace if they were to uproot their families once again and cross the ocean to settle in the new and dangerous land.

But some of them were too eager to go, and the first 200 Pilgrims were on their way to America in 1816, led by the Elder Francis Blackwell. Their losses were heavy, as three out of each four perished on their way to Jamestown. Blackwell's ship was blown off course and wandered the South Atlantic for six months. They all perished eventually due to disease and lack of water. But the Separatists back in Leiden were shocked to receive the news of some of their cousins and comrades reaching America alive. In fact, they expected them all to die on the journey. Encouraged, Robert Cushman went back to London in 1619, determined to negotiate a safe passage for the rest of the Leiden Separatists to the new colony. Finally, Cushman was successful and received a patent to set up a new colony in North America. They were offered a choice to join the already-existing Jamestown colony, but they refused. They believed that there was no returning to English society for them, as they might find their religious freedoms as repressed as they were before. They opted for creating a new settlement in Virginia, risking the wilderness and the unknown.

The London Company that first agreed to transport the Separatists was on the brink of bankruptcy and could not provide the ships, let alone the provisions needed for such a dangerous journey. The Dutch New Netherlands

Company offered a tempting proposition. They would land near the Hudson River for the Separatists to disembark, and the Separatists would be provided with free transport and cattle. As a guarantee of their safety, the Prince of Orange was to supply them with two warships that would follow them on their journey. It was a generous proposal by the Dutch, but the Separatists felt compelled to decline the offer because they still considered themselves English. The Dutch's only demand was to establish a Dutch culture in the New World, and they realized that, as Englishmen, they couldn't do that.

A third option presented itself in 1620 when a London ironmonger, Thomas Weston, promised he would ensure the loans from London businessmen to finance their voyage. He only wanted the Separatists to pay him back after they settled in the New World. The Pilgrims finally accepted this offer, and Weston came forth with seventy investors to found a new company called Merchant Adventures. A new home in which they could practice their religion freely never felt closer for the Leiden Separatists.

Chapter 3 – The Journey

A Drawing of the *Mayflower* from 1893

https://en.wikipedia.org/wiki/Mayflower#/media/File:The_Mayflower_at_sea.jpg

Fishermen

The benefactors to the Pilgrims' journey changed their lives in so many ways. They didn't just offer to pay for the voyage and the provisions; they also needed the Pilgrims as the workforce behind their own businesses. One of the investors, the Plymouth Company led by Sir Ferdinando Gorges, needed the Pilgrims to become fishermen, as they saw profit from cod fishing between Pennsylvania and Newfoundland. At first, the Pilgrims didn't know how to respond, but if fishing meant they were safe to practice their religion away from the Church of England, they were willing to try. England had a long-lasting interest in the fishing grounds off the North American coast. The fishing off the coast of Newfoundland, Maine, and Nova Scotia started as early as the fifteenth century. Even though the first English fishing colonies failed, Bartholomew Gosnold, an English explorer, discovered the abundance of cod fish off the coast of Maine in 1602. Since then, the governor of the port of Plymouth, England, had become interested in the fishing opportunities in the New World.

In 1605, a group of expeditioners under the leadership of George Weymouth docked on the coast of Maine at Monhegan Island. There they traded with the Native Americans, but once they were done, they took five of the natives as prisoners. It is possible that among them was Squanto, a native who was previously taken captive by the Spanish army and transported to Spain. This time, he ended up in England, where he learned the language and possibly even met Pocahontas. At this point, the princess was married to tobacco planter John Rolfe, who took her to England. Unfortunately, Pocahontas died under unknown circumstances in London, but Squanto would make his way back to America and play an important role as a mediator between the Pilgrims and the Native Americans.

On his way back to England, George Weymouth spread tales of the fish-rich waters of Maine and even put his money into the foundation of the Popham (Sagadahoc) Colony, at the mouth of the Kennebec River (Maine). This colony failed by 1608, but that is when Ferdinando Gorges sent John Smith to explore New England. Upon his return, Smith brought back a ship filled with fish and furs and yet another report of abundant fishing off the shore of Maine. Whoever was first to set up a fishing colony in that part of the New World would profit immensely.

The English Separatist Protestants living in Holland were no one's first choice for setting up a fishing colony, but they proved to be willing. They started their journey to America on July 21, 1620. First, they traversed the Rapenburg canal from Leiden to the port of Delfshaven, where the Merchant Adventurers set up a ship for them. Their debt to this new company was enormous, and it meant they would not be able to keep most of the money they earned, but the promise of freedom drove them forward. But the hardest part for the Pilgrims was leaving their families behind. Only one-third of the whole congregation was going to America. There were not enough funds to transport and supply all of them, and the decision was made that the young and strong should go first, and the rest would follow once the colony was up and running. William Brewster was to lead the Pilgrims to the New World, while the rest of the congregation remained behind, under the leadership of John Robinson.

Parents left their children and elderly, as the New World was hardly a place for the weak and those who depended on others. Only the ablest ones would go, women and men, although some couldn't leave their children behind. But barely any family went to America intact. Many women stayed behind with children while waving goodbyes to their husbands. But the division between the congregation didn't diminish the will of the Pilgrims to go. They found new hope in the wilderness across the Atlantic Ocean, and they had to go.

The Preparations

The group of Pilgrims who showed up on the docks of Delfshaven, Rotterdam, on July 22, 1620, numbered only sixteen men, eleven women, and around nineteen children. The ship provided for them in Holland was *Speedwell*, a small barge less than a hundred feet long, that was supposed to take the Pilgrims to England, where a bigger boat named *Mayflower* waited to pick them up. *Speedwell* was to follow *Mayflower* on the journey to North America and serve the Pilgrims as a fishing barge, while *Mayflower* would act as a ship for exploration. The crews of both ships were hired to support and help the Pilgrims for the duration of one year.

Once aboard the *Speedwell*, the Pilgrims first had to make a stop at Southampton to pick up their supplies. *Mayflower* waited there. The larger ship was first used to transport wine. It was capable of carrying 180 tons of cargo, and it was three times the size of *Speedwell*. The *Mayflower* was already loaded with people and supplies, waiting for the Leiden congregation to arrive. Some of the passengers were friends and family of the Separatists arriving from Holland, but others were new faces. Concerned that a small number of Pilgrims would fail in setting up a colony, Thomas Weston recruited more people from England. This group was called the "Strangers." Just like the Leiden group, they were commoners, former soldiers, and workers. They all hoped they would make a fresh start in the New World and didn't even dream that millions would follow them in the ages to come.

The hired crew and the Strangers were aligned with the Church of England, and together they outnumbered the Pilgrims from Leiden. But the hardship of a journey bridged all the differences, and soon they were all simply the Pilgrims. Among the Strangers was Captain Miles Standish, a soldier hired to protect the Pilgrims while they were setting up the colony. While docked at Southampton, the crews of *Mayflower* and *Speedwell* chatted, making plans for the voyage. They had enough time for all the chatter, as the voyage was delayed due to money problems. It turns out the Separatists didn't have enough money to pay for all the provisions they needed, and Weston's company denied their pleas for a loan. The company hired three agents to buy the supplies, but instead of planning together and coordinating the shopping, these three agents bought poorly. When they would come together, instead of making plans, they would only argue about the money.

But the biggest problem was the final contract Weston's company presented to the Pilgrims. The original deal was to allow the colonists to keep the profits they made two days out of every week. They were also granted the ownership of the houses and gardens they would build in the colony. But all of that was revised and pulled out of the final contract. But Robert Cushman signed this new contract without consulting the Pilgrims, claiming he had only done what the Leideners sent him to do. The future colonists were outraged. They were sure that Weston was tricking them with the sudden change of the contract. Those who had some savings among the Pilgrims had different objections: since they were all to work for the company, why did they need servants? The Pilgrims rejected the contract, but Weston informed them that in that case, they would have to provide their own supplies.

The Pilgrims were forced to sell some of the food to get enough money to buy other provisions they needed. In the meantime, they wrote a letter to the Merchant Adventurers Company, stating how Cushman had no authority to accept the changed contract. Instead, they offered a new deal to the Adventurers. If the colony failed to return a substantial profit in seven years from its establishment, the colonists would extend their commitment to the contract with the Company and would work until the profit was achieved. But the Adventurers never replied to the Pilgrims. At the time the Pilgrims set sail, their contract was still in limbo.

However, John Robinson from the Leiden congregation wrote to the Pilgrims. He was concerned about all of the last-minute changes, especially with the addition of the Strangers. But he called for his Leiden Pilgrims to be patient with the newcomers and to be fair to everyone. They were all together in this endeavor, and they need not take offense that others had joined them. He also offered advice on how to organize their colony in America. He reminded the Pilgrims about the Puritan concept of equality, which displayed the concepts of democracy. It was these principles that would become the hallmark of the Plymouth colony. He advised them to be wise when choosing the government and find a person among them who they could trust would lead all the Pilgrims with God-loving but lawful administration.

The Pilgrims continued to scramble for supplies as the summer faded away. But the manifest for both ships was set up, and the crews and their leaders were assigned to both *Speedwell* and *Mayflower*. Finally, everyone was ready to set sail on August 5, 1620. *Mayflower* was first to depart the Southampton harbor, with *Speedwell* following close behind. The larger *Mayflower* carried the majority, but together, they had 120 passengers. But the first days of the sailing presented the first troubles. The crew of the *Speedwell* soon reported their ship had leaked, and both ships had to dock at the nearest port to make the repairs. Dartmouth was chosen as the stopping point, but when *Speedwell* was repaired and the crew ready to set sail, the voyage was delayed again by bad weather.

This time, they managed to reach Plymouth, Devon, and had to make another stop, as *Speedwell* continued to have troubles. The crew was unable to find where the leak was, even though the ship was flooded with water. Finally, the Pilgrims decided that the smaller ship was not worth the trouble, and they abandoned it. Some of the passengers and the crew transferred to *Mayflower*, but others decided to quit the journey while they were still in England, as they saw the troubles as a bad omen. Out of the original 120 passengers, 102 boarded *Mayflower* when the ship was finally ready for departure. Later, it was discovered that *Speedwell* was equipped with larger masts than it could bear and that this was probably the cause of the leaks. However, Robert Cushman believed and wrote that the leak was caused by a loose board. Nevertheless, many Pilgrims believed that those who wanted to stay in England sabotaged the ship on purpose.

Mayflower was captained by Master Christopher Jones (1570–1622), who had around fifty crewmen underneath him. The identity of some of the crew members is well established, but some remain unknown. There were thirty-six crewmen and fourteen officers. Among the officers were four mates, four quartermasters, a carpenter, a gunner, a boatswain, the cook, a surgeon, and a carpenter. After landing, the whole crew of *Mayflower* remained in America for one year before turning back to England. Half of the crew died in Plymouth during the winter of 1620–21.

Among the passengers that transferred from *Speedwell* to *Mayflower* was William Bradford of the Scrooby Congregation, who had grown up under the direct influence of William Brewster. When Bradford moved to Leiden with the rest of the Separatists, he had no family of his own, and the Brewsters took him in. Only after turning twenty-one was Bradford able to claim his family's inheritance and make a life for himself. He soon married Dorothy May, his first wife, and had a son with her. The family decided to emigrate to America, where William Bradford would become the governor of Plymouth Colony. Most importantly, Bradford is the author of the book *Of Plymouth Plantation*, in which he detailed the founding of the first Pilgrim colony.

Aboard the *Mayflower*

Mayflower was finally ready to set sail, and it did so on the sixth of September (Old Style calendar)/sixteenth of September, 1620. The wind was strong, and it swiftly carried the ship away from the English coastline. Bradford wrote that the crew hired to man the *Mayflower* was often rude towards the Pilgrims, who had to endure seasickness. They mocked the passengers unaccustomed to the restless sea and often swore at them. Some even threatened Pilgrims that they would throw them overboard if they died on their way to America. But when one of the seamen suddenly got sick and died, the rest of the crew took it as a sign from God to leave the Pilgrims in peace. The rest of the journey passed without any disturbances among the people on *Mayflower*.

Although there was no more quarrel between the passengers and the crew, the journey wasn't calm. Strong winds started once the *Mayflower* reached the open sea, and the passengers were thrown back and forth. Crowded as the ship was, many people were injured from crashing against one another or the ship's walls and beams. The main beam cracked, and the crew had to connect it with an iron screw. To hold it in place, the ship's carpenters had to stick a stout timber underneath it. Events such as this one were often described in the diaries and letters some of the passengers wrote.

The people on the ship were divided by class. The *Mayflower*'s crew and the wealthier passengers took over the upper cabin. This one was much broader, as it was placed where the ship was broadest. The great cabin was twenty-five feet wide, occupying the whole sterncastle, and the people gathered there to eat and to sleep. They slept in bunks, crowded together in one wide cabin. There was little to no privacy. The crew occupied a similar but smaller cabin at the forecastle. The cramped passengers tried to divide the space by constructing makeshift cabins to provide some privacy. But these were very rudimental dividers, often made out of blankets and cloth. They provided no shelter from the noise and smells of the overcrowded ship. The food Pilgrims packed was mostly preserved, so it would last for the whole trip. They ate dry biscuits and salted beef, and on rare occasions, they would cook and treat themselves with a hot meal.

The Leiden Protestants organized communal prayers and readings of Psalms to offer consolation to anyone who needed it, and many did because the fear of drowning was real. The water constantly poured over the ship's stern, and it leaked down into the cabins. The Strangers and the crew joined the Leiden congregation in prayers, even though they were followers of the Church of England and they outnumbered the Puritans. The need for consolation and God overcame their differences, and there was peace on *Mayflower*. John Carver of the Leiden Separatists often encouraged his fellow passengers with stories of their divine purpose. He was even chosen as the governor of the *Mayflower* for the duration of the journey instead of Christopher Martin, who was put in the position by the Company back in England. It is believed that Carver started the Mayflower Compact, the first governing document of the Pilgrims, and he was chosen as the first governor of the Plymouth colony.

The sea never seemed to end, and some of the Pilgrims started wondering if America truly existed. Their journey lasted for sixty-five days, and the passengers saw land first on November 9, 1620. Everyone rushed to the deck to catch the first glimpse of Cape Cod. Relief came over the Pilgrims and the crew, and laughter and tears of joy uplifted the mood. Captain Jones tried to sail the ship south of Tucker's Terror (now Pollack's Rip) as their final destination was Virginia, not New England. But the water was too shallow for further sailing, and the *Mayflower* had to return to the northern tip of Cape Cod. By the morning of November 21, the captain anchored the ship at what is today Provincetown Harbor.

Even before setting the anchor, some of the Pilgrims insisted that since they had landed in New England and not in Virginia Colony, they were free of obligations made to the Merchant Adventurers Company. The leaders of both the Leiden congregation and the Strangers met in the captain's cabin to discuss the future of the Pilgrims. This is when the Mayflower Compact, also known as the Agreement Between the Settlers of New Plymouth, was first written. The document was devised as a social contract among the settlers, who consented to establish their government but stay loyal to the king in England. To survive, the Pilgrims needed rules and regulations to follow. Otherwise, they faced anarchy and disorder. The document stated that everyone would be treated equally by the government they were about to establish and that everyone would be obedient to the laws of the new government. The original Mayflower Compact is lost, but William Bradford wrote its text in his journal that would become *Of Plymouth Plantation.*

John Carver was the first to sign the document, followed by the Separatist men. The next to sign the document was Miles Standish, followed by traders and adventurers who made up the group called Strangers. In total, forty-one of 101 passengers of *Mayflower* signed the documents. They were all men, as women were subordinated to their husbands and had no power of decision. John Carver was unanimously chosen as the first governor of the first Pilgrim colony in America. He was a wealthy man who financed a large portion of the supplies needed for the journey. He had already proved his leadership skills on board *Mayflower*, as he was the acting governor during the two-month journey across the ocean.

The essential and extraordinary document, the Mayflower Compact, failed to uphold the equality it promised—or maybe equality wasn't intended for everyone. Women were still regarded as subordinates to men, servants still served the wealthy, and the wealthy ruled them all. Even the men who didn't own any property back in England were excluded from the government. The Separatists seized all the power, and soon, the Strangers needed the permission of the governor, or two of the governor's assistants, to cast a vote. But the document was the first step the Pilgrims undertook to govern themselves. It took power from the hands of the people who were loyal to the

Company and the investors back home and put it in the hands of the Separatists. The people chose their leader, and they could replace him whenever they were displeased. There was no king or bishops to meddle in their affairs, and the balance of power in the Plymouth colony was decided by a yearly vote. The democratic process of America was born here, among the first Pilgrims, and it would shape the future of the American republic.

At this point, the crew of *Mayflower* demanded to turn back to England immediately, but Captain Jones declined, as they didn't have enough supplies for the journey back. He was also concerned about the health of his crew. During the voyage, a strange illness had taken over the passengers of the *Mayflower*. Its first victim died while the ship was at sea, but the rest arrived safely to the shores of America. Nevertheless, they were all ill. Captain Jones didn't want to risk the wellbeing of his sailors, and he decided to spend the winter with the Pilgrims at their new colony. No modern scholar can guess what this mysterious illness on *Mayflower* was, but the records describe it as a mixture of either tuberculosis or pneumonia and scurvy. The disease was so contagious that all of the Pilgrims and the crew contracted it. They were all forced to spend winter on board *Mayflower*. Many died during that winter. Only half of the ship's crew and fifty-three passengers survived. It was not until March 31, 1621, that the Pilgrims fully disembarked the ship and started building their settlement in earnest. On April 15, *Mayflower* left Plymouth harbor, never to return. But another ship named *Mayflower* would bring new colonists to the shore of New England in 1629, and it would continue to do so in 1633, 1634, and 1639.

Chapter 4 – Contact with the Natives

Samoset's Arrival at the Plymouth Colony

https://en.wikipedia.org/wiki/Squanto#/media/File:A_popular_history_of_the_United_States_-_from_the_first_discovery_of_the_western_hemisphere_by_the_Northmen,_to_the_end_of_the_first_century_of_the_union_of_the_states;_preceded_by_a_sketch_of_the_(14597125217).jpg

The first landing on the shore of New England occurred on November 11, 1620. Sixteen men were chosen to go to shore and survey the area and gather firewood. Their report was superficial, but they felt comfortable enough to send the women ashore to wash clothes. After all, two months of the journey without washing might have been the source of the mysterious disease. The men followed the women and started the repairs on the *Mayflower*. They also constructed a longboat with two sails that they planned to use for exploration of the unfamiliar surroundings. On November 15, the Pilgrims encountered natives for the first time. A group of sixteen men, among them Bradford and Captain Standish, crossed paths with Native Americans on the beach. The natives were startled by the white Pilgrims, and they scattered into the nearby woods. The Pilgrim men spent the rest of the day trying to find them, but they had no success. During the explorations of the beach and the woods over the next three days, the Pilgrims found corn and grain that the natives had buried. They stole some of this food as hunger took over the *Mayflower*.

Ten days later, the longboat was ready for its first journey, and thirty-two people boarded it. They were led by Master Christopher Jones. Their first stop was at what they named Corn Hill, where they found more corn and even baskets filled with wheat and beans. The Pilgrims needed to take the food because their supplies were running extremely low. But they agreed they would pay the natives for the food when they made their settlement. Bradford wrote how lucky the Pilgrims were to find the buried food at that time, as only a few days later, the ground was frozen and covered by snow. At the end of November, the weather grew colder, and the ocean started freezing. But the men were determined to continue exploring Cape Cod Bay so they could find the best location for building the settlement. On these exploration outings, they would see the smoke of Native American fires or even catch a glimpse of the natives in the forest, but they never approached them.

The first aggressive encounter with the Native Americans occurred when the expedition of Pilgrims decided to spend their first night on shore. The exact date remains unknown, but instead of returning to *Mayflower*, the Pilgrims made a rudimentary shelter on the beach and fell asleep next to the fire. They were woken during the night by strange screams, and, frightened, they shot their muskets into the night. The screams stopped, and as nothing significant happened that night, the Pilgrims concluded it was the wolves. However, when morning came and the men started packing their belongings into the longboat to go back to *Mayflower*, a group of natives jumped out of the woods and started screaming and shooting arrows at them. The Pilgrims returned the fire, making the natives retreat. No one was hurt in this first exchange of fire, but the Pilgrims had to make sure they were safe. They followed the natives for about a quarter of a mile before they gave up and turned back to the longboat. They picked up the Native American arrows to send back home to England as proof that New England was not safe.

The Pilgrims had to continue their search for a suitable spot for the settlement. The group of Pilgrim explorers had set about investigating the bay when it started to snow. The sea became violent, and they concluded they could not turn back yet. They were trapped at the beach of what is now known as Clark's Island in Plymouth Harbor. They needed to spend the night there, but the Pilgrims thought they were on the mainland and that Native Americans might attack them. The next morning, they discovered they were safe on the island, and they decided to spend the day there. Only the next day did the Pilgrims dare to leave the safety of the island. On December 21, 1620, they continued their exploration of the area, and they arrived at Plymouth Rock.

They liked the terrain they saw, and Bradford noted that its discovery came at the right time because harsh winter was approaching and the Pilgrims needed to build shelters. They first investigated the harbor and concluded that the water was deep enough to bring *Mayflower* in. They headed back immediately to inform everyone that they had finally found a perfect spot for the colony.

But sad news was waiting for William Bradford back at the ship. His wife, Dorothy, had fallen overboard and drowned. The circumstances of her death are suspicious, as the ship was safely anchored and the sea was calm. Some scholars believe that she may have committed suicide. Life aboard *Mayflower* wasn't an easy one, especially for women, who were not allowed to leave yet. The dangers that awaited Pilgrims on the shores of the New World were not encouraging, either.

The Pilgrims were eager to establish their colony. All who were not sick or had recovered from illness were sent on shore to build the first huts. Able-bodied men and boys landed at the site of Plymouth three days later to start the work. However, they were caught by bad weather and couldn't do much. The second landing party was organized soon after, and the building could begin. The Pilgrims didn't celebrate Christmas or any other traditional holiday, so they continued their work. Each night the workers would return to the safety of *Mayflower*, where women, children, and the sick waited for them. The first structure the Pilgrims built was a common house. They used a wattle and daub building method, and the construction of the common house lasted for two weeks. It took them so long to build it because they didn't have enough manpower, as illness started taking more and more lives. They were also working during the snowstorm season. Once the common house was ready, it served the Pilgrims as a sickroom.

Throughout winter, they began building the rest of the settlement and chose the building site. The settlement was to be erected at the top of Cole's Hill because it was relatively flat and close to Fort Hill, on which they planned to build a wooden construction that could hold a cannon. Fort Hill served the Pilgrims as a defense point. But during January and February of 1621, sickness took most of their lives. The dead had to be buried in unmarked graves, as the Pilgrims hoped to hide their losses from the natives who were watching them from the woods. But during the same time of death and loss, the first New England baby was born. The mother was Susanna White, and the baby boy was named Peregrine. However, his father died due to "general sickness," as it was called among the Pilgrims. The first baby of Plymouth Colony was thus an orphan.

During the first winter, the Pilgrims managed to build only seven houses and four common houses out of the nineteen planned. In January, they started unloading the provisions from Mayflower, and by the beginning of March, the last of the Pilgrims came ashore. The winter was so harsh that only three families remained intact at its end. Among them was the family of William Brewster. Eighteen unmarried women started the journey, but only five survived. Ten unmarried men survived out of the initial twenty-nine who started the journey on *Mayflower*. Bradford caught the illness, but he was well enough to continue writing. In his journal, he noted that during the worst times, only twelve people were strong enough to tend to others. They had to gather wood, cook, care for the sick, and clean up after them. Bradford didn't fail to mention that the hardest-working men were William Brewster and Miles Standish. He also found it a miracle that none of these twelve people got sick, and they never complained about the work they had to perform.

During the winter, natives would occasionally approach the settlement that was being built, but they would scatter in fear if the Pilgrim men tried to talk to them. But on March 16, 1621, one brave native entered the settlement and went straight to the common house where the Pilgrims were having a meeting. First, the Pilgrims were frightened. The sentries surrounded the native but were shocked when he spoke in English. He bid them welcome and said his name was Samoset. He quickly explained he was from the Abenaki tribe and that he was a sagamore, a chieftain of one band of his tribe. He also said he came from Pemaquid Point in Maine, where he had learned English from fishermen and trappers.

The Pilgrims knew that there used to be a native village at the site of Plymouth Colony, as it was labeled on the map drawn by John Smith, the map which they possessed. The name of the village was Patuxent, and the Pilgrims wondered what had happened to it. Samoset explained that a great disease, probably smallpox, took the lives of everyone who lived in the village, and the sole survivor was Squanto, a Native American who spent some time traveling to Spain and England. He further talked about Massasoit (meaning "Great Sachem" or "Great Chief"), the leader of the Wampanoag confederacy, a loose alliance of several Native American tribes that inhabited the region. Massasoit's people were suffering an epidemic and were vulnerable to the attacks of another confederation, the Narragansetts. The great chief wanted to negotiate with the Pilgrims to gain their protection for his people, and Samoset had been sent to set up the meeting.

Several days later, Samoset returned to the Pilgrims, this time in the company of five more natives. They brought beaver and deerskin to trade with the Pilgrims, but as it was Sabbath, the Pilgrims refused to trade. The next time Samoset came to the colony, he brought Squanto with him. Squanto told the Pilgrims that he had survived the smallpox that decimated his people because he had been away. At that time, Squanto was in England, where he persuaded an adventurer named Thomas Demer to come to New England with him. Upon learning that his whole tribe was dead, Squanto approached Massasoit, who took him in. Squanto also admitted that Massasoit didn't have a love for Europeans due to an incident that occurred in 1619. A European trade vessel invited some of Massasoit's tribesmen onboard to trade. The men accepted, but as soon as they stepped onto the ship, they were slaughtered. Massasoit couldn't trust Englishmen, but he needed their alliance, and he was willing to try.

Samoset informed the Pilgrims that Massasoit was nearby, with sixty of his men, and that he wished to speak to the English people. And although Massasoit made his presence known as he rode to the top of a nearby hill, both the Pilgrims and natives were reluctant to make the first move. This is when Squanto stepped in and offered to act as a liaison between the two parties. He ran back and forth between Massasoit and the Pilgrims, carrying messages, until both parties agreed to finally meet. On March 22, 1621, Massasoit came to the Plymouth colony, where he was received in one of the common houses equipped with rugs and pillows where the chieftain could sit. Governor John Carver stepped into the house, and after exchanging greetings with the chieftain, the negotiations began. Squanto acted as their translator.

An agreement between the natives and the Pilgrims was reached, and the natives promised they would return some of the Pilgrim's tools they had stolen earlier. In exchange, the Pilgrims promised they would pay for the stolen corn, seeds, and peas they found buried in the ground. Furthermore, Massasoit and Carver agreed that punishment for crimes or offenses made towards each other's people would be decided and performed together. Weapons were to be kept out of sight when the two parties met, and if a third party were to attack any of them, they would come to each other's aid. The treaty was fair, and it was designed to keep the power between the Pilgrims and Native Americans in balance. It would last for the next fifty years or so. The natives were satisfied with their negotiation achievements, and they departed the colony the next day.

But Squanto and Samoset remained behind to teach the Pilgrims how to prepare the ground for planting by using fish as manure. Squanto also showed them how to plant corn the Wampanoag way. Edward Wilson wrote a letter to England later that year in which he praised Squanto's methods of planting. The Pilgrims successfully grew twenty acres of corn, six acres of barley, and peas. While the first year, the harvest of corn and barley was plentiful, Wilson wrote that the peas didn't grow enough since they were planted too late. Squanto also showed the Pilgrims how to hunt for eels, drawing them out of the mud with their feet. This eel hunt became the Pilgrims' yearly tradition. The Pilgrims also learned how to collect pelts, which allowed them to pay off their debt to the Merchant Adventurers quicker than they expected. Squanto and Samoset often took the Pilgrims on exploration expeditions, teaching them how to survive in their new surroundings. William Bradford developed an exceptional friendship with Squanto and listened to his advice during his tenure as a governor in later years.

March 25 was voting day for the Pilgrims, and they decided that John Carver should serve another term. He had a team of governor's advisors, which was made up of William Bradford, Edward Willson, Miles Standish, and Stephen Hopkins. On April 5, the Pilgrims said their goodbyes to Captain Cristopher Jones and his crew, as the *Mayflower* was ready to sail back to England. But the departure of the ship that had brought them to the New World came as a shock, as many remembered the death of their friends and family members that winter. Sadness took over the Pilgrims, and as if that wasn't enough, their beloved governor fell ill. Carver was working in the field on a particularly hot day in April and complained of a severe headache before lapsing into a coma. Several days later, he died. The Pilgrims, who buried their dead in secrecy, felt that they were safe now, with the alliance with the natives coming about. They wished to bury their dear governor with all the ceremonies he deserved, and they did so. William Bradford was chosen to replace Carver as the Governor of Plymouth Colony, and Isaac Allerton became his assistant.

In May came the first wedding in New England. Edward Willson decided to marry a widow, Susanna White, the mother of the first baby born in the colony. The wedding wasn't a religious event to the Pilgrims, and they celebrated the event with Bradford presiding over the civil ceremony. Everything seemed to come to life for the Pilgrims that summer. Their crops were growing, and life continued peacefully.

That summer, the Pilgrims wanted to cement their peaceful relations with the natives. They offered to help those who had suffered illness and starvation during the colder months. They shared food and provisions, and in turn, the natives looked upon the Pilgrims with kindness. When a Pilgrim boy named John Billington lost his way in the woods in July 1621, he survived by eating berries for five days. He stumbled upon natives who had their village about twenty miles away from Plymouth. The natives didn't take him in, but they sent him to another tribe. As it turns out, these were the Nausets, the tribe that attacked the Pilgrims when they first came ashore in New England, whose food the Pilgrims had stolen. Worried about the missing boy, Governor Bradford asked Massasoit to help find him. With the intervention of Massasoit, an expedition of Pilgrims with Squanto as their translator set off to meet the Nauset tribe. After a quick negotiation, the Billington boy was brought safely home. The Nausets didn't harm him in any way. Bradford learned that it was these natives from whom the Pilgrims had taken food, and he decided to pay them for it immediately. Bradford believed at that point that he had solidified peace with the Native Americans.

But when the expedition was about to return to Plymouth, they learned that the Narragansetts had attacked the Pokanokets, one of Massasoit's tribes, and that Chief Massasoit had been taken prisoner. The Pilgrims were in a panic since they had left their colony barely guarded, with so many men on the expedition to retrieve the boy. Upon returning to the colony, the Pilgrims learned that a sagamore named Corbitant had turned against Massasoit, and he actively sought to turn the Nemasket tribe against the great chieftain. At the same time, Corbitant was trying to destroy the alliance between the Native Americans and the colonists. He had his eye on Squanto, particularly, as he saw him responsible for the peace with the settlers. He also understood that if Squanto was to die, the English would lose their valuable translator. If they were not able to communicate with the natives, there would be no peace. Corbitant captured Squanto and one more native named Hobomok, who was a friend to the settlers. But Hobomok managed to free himself and run to Plymouth to warn the Pilgrims.

Bradford called for an immediate meeting to decide what was to be done. He wouldn't allow the abuse of his native friends, and he considered it to be the Pilgrims' duty to free Squanto. But he also came to realize that if the colonists did nothing to answer this situation, the natives would consider them cowards, and they would lose the natives' respect. It was decided that Miles Standish would lead fourteen armed men against Corbitant. They had the orders to behead Corbitant if Squanto was found dead. Hobomok led the way. When they reached the settlement where they believed they would find the culprit, a fight occurred, and three natives were wounded. But Corbitant was nowhere to be found. However, the Pilgrims were told that Squanto lived and that he was unharmed in one of the village houses. Hobomok convinced the Nemasket tribe that no further harm would come upon them, and in return, they offered the Pilgrims gifts and food. The Pilgrims took the injured back to Plymouth to treat their wounds. All the native tribes that lived in the area complimented the Pilgrims on their loyalty to their Native American friends, and they also noted that the Englishmen refrained from punishing the whole village. After some time, even Corbitant sought to make peace with the Pilgrims as he saw them as worthy of his people's friendship.

At the end of the summer, the Plymouth colonists established contact with the Massachusetts tribe in what is today Boston Bay. This tribe was known to be hostile towards Europeans. They were the part of Pawtucket Confederation of Abenaki peoples, and at this time, they were governed by Squaw Sachem of Mistick, the widow of Great Chief Nanepashemet, who had died in 1619.

Squanto warned the Pilgrims that these natives were evil since they had previously hunted Europeans, but the Pilgrims insisted on treating everyone with good intentions. They established trade with the Massachusetts tribe and bought all their beaver pelts. But the Pilgrims were surprised by the beauty and accessibility of the Boston harbor, and they expressed their regret that they hadn't built their colony there.

The harvest was bountiful, and the Pilgrims enjoyed the beautiful warm autumn in their new settlement. They decided to hold a harvest festival to celebrate their newfound life and freedom in America. In early October, they celebrated what is remembered as the first Thanksgiving. This celebration continued to be respected by the descendants of Pilgrims, as well as the whole North American continent. In 1863, Abraham Lincoln made Thanksgiving a national holiday, though its celebration date was moved to November. Although the Pilgrims' celebration of Thanksgiving is the most prominent one in the history of America, it was not the first celebration of that kind. Thanksgiving comes from a much older harvest celebration that many people around the world practiced. In Europe, such celebrations were known in Germany, France, Spain, and many other countries. In America, Thanksgiving was first celebrated by Spanish colonists in the sixteenth century.

The first Plymouth Thanksgivings were religious in character, and only later did this event become a secular celebration. The Pilgrims prepared a feast and celebrated for three days. Bradford sent Squanto to invite the Wampanoag tribe to join the feast. According to the writings of Edward Winslow, over ninety Native Americans and fifty-three Pilgrims celebrated for three days. The Pilgrims were worried that such a large number of guests would eat through their whole harvest. But the natives did not come empty-handed. They brought five deer, many wild birds, fish and lobsters, and wild berries. The food was plentiful, and the settlers and the Native Americans celebrated their friendship and the new beginning of life.

Chapter 5 – The Expansion of the Colony

Portrait of Governor William Bradford

https://en.wikipedia.org/wiki/William_Bradford_(governor)#/media/File:Williambradford_bw.jpg

The neighbors of the Pilgrims weren't only the Native American tribes: Pamet and Nauset at Cape Code, Wampanoag and Narragansett to the south and west, and Massachusetts to the north. In fact, there were many English fishing villages on the coast of Maine, but they were not permanent. The English fishermen came seasonally and would leave for England with their catch. To the north, in Canada, the hostile French lived, and in the area of what is today Albany, New York, the Dutch set up their trading post. Inland was the territory of the natives, a wilderness the Pilgrims were not daring to explore. Around sixty Pilgrims lived in the Plymouth colony, happy with the abundant first harvest. They were far away from England and were free. They had shelter, food, and the will to call New England their home.

A year after the Pilgrims first set foot on the shore of Cape Cod, a new ship from England arrived. It was sent by the Merchant Adventurers

Company, and it carried thirty-seven new settlers. The ship's name was *Fortune*, and it came from London under the captainship of Master Thomas Barton. Among the passengers of *Fortune* were some of the family members of the first Plymouth colonists. William Brewster's son Jonathan came, as well as John, the brother of Edward Winslow. The former leader of the Leiden congregation, Robert Cushman, also arrived in the company of his son Thomas. Philip Delano came on board *Fortune*, as well, and he is known to be the ancestor of President Franklin Delano Roosevelt. The newcomers were accepted without questions, but they did come without any supplies, which put additional strain on the Pilgrims. Not only did the harvest have to be shared among the additional people, but housing, as well.

The ship *Fortune* didn't just deliver new settlers. With it came some important documents, such as the patent signed by Sir Ferdinando Gorges and the members of the new Council of New England (previously Plymouth Company), in which they had promised the Pilgrims 100 acres of land each provided that they worked for the Company for seven years. Another document was a letter from Merchant Adventurers that scolded the Pilgrims for not signing the contract with their company and urging them to do so now. They threatened that the money and supplies would stop coming from London if the Pilgrims did not sign the contract. Thomas Weston of the Merchant Adventurers also demanded that the Pilgrims pay for the expenses of their voyage, and he bemoaned that the *Mayflower* returned without any cargo. The Pilgrims did feel guilty for leaving without signing the contract, and after deacon Cushman urged them, they agreed to do so now.

But Governor Bradford wrote a response to Thomas Weston in which he explained how the Pilgrims had worked themselves to death to uphold the contract with the Merchant Adventurers, and he notified Weston of how Governor Carver died. He also wrote that he understood how much money was invested in the journey but reminded Weston that the prospect of losses was always there. Then he proceeded to explain that the loss of money could not be compared to the loss of lives the Pilgrims had endured during their first winter in the New World. Bradford didn't want to apologize for the Company's loss of capital, as the Pilgrim's only concern during the past year had been their survival. He also addressed Weston's complaints about the *Mayflower* being sent back to England late and without any cargo. Bradford reminded him that they were blown off course and that they had to spend weeks searching for a suitable place to set up a colony. He also spoke of the disease that had decimated not only the settlers but also the crew of *Mayflower*, and he mentioned that Captain Cristopher Jones saw the wisdom in delaying the departure. He then wondered how England could complain about the empty ship that came back without taking into consideration all the hardship the settlers had endured.

But the Pilgrims started collecting fish, furs, and timber so that they could repay the Company, despite its insulting letter. In total, they managed to collect goods worth 500 pounds in total, which would be approximately 78,000 pounds today. That was almost half of what the Pilgrims owed to the company, and it would put them ahead of the promised repayment schedule. However, luck wasn't on their side. On the way back, the *Fortune* was captured by the French, and all its cargo was lost. The colony was now in an even larger deficit than before. The French stole the cargo, but they let the ship continue its journey. Bradford's letter to Winslow reached London, where it was published in 1622 under the pseudonym "G. Mourt." This was the first time people of England could read about the Pilgrim's experiences in the New World.

The new settlers were accepted by the Pilgrims, and they had to share rations to survive the next six months. The colonists hoped that the Company would send more ships carrying supplies, but that didn't happen for more than a year. However, the Pilgrims weren't cut off completely. Thomas Weston sent two more ships, the *Swan* and the *Charity*, to Plymouth in the summer of 1622. But instead of supplies, Weston sent more settlers. Sixty hungry people joined the Plymouth colony, and they brought another letter from Weston. In it, he informed Bradford that he had quit the Merchant Adventurers and was happy to be rid of the Pilgrims. He also explained that the sixty men he sent on the two ships to Plymouth were to be hosted and nourished by the Pilgrims until a new settlement was built for them. Although this was the end of the cooperation between the Pilgrims and Thomas Weston, Bradford and others often mentioned Weston in their writings, several times in a negative light.

Weston was an adventurer and a capitalist. He sought to make a quick fortune in the New World, and once he saw that the Pilgrims couldn't bring him a profit, he abandoned them. Weston came to America himself, but he broke several colonial laws and was proclaimed the enemy of the Crown. But Thomas Weston is also remembered as a man who took in the children of Katherine More, a woman accused of adultery, so he could send them off as settlers on the *Mayflower*. Under the pretense of doing good for the four siblings, he took them in only so he could give them to the Puritans, who they would serve in the New World. Three of the four siblings, between ages four and seven, died during the first winter in Plymouth. Only the boy Richard More survived. He served the Brewster family until he turned fourteen, when his indentureship expired. From that moment, he was listed in the documents as a member of the Brewster family. Thomas Weston returned to London in 1647, where he died of the Plague.

The Pilgrims had to find a way to feed the extra mouths Weston had sent, so in the summer of 1622, they renewed the trade deal with the Massachusetts natives. The Captain of the *Charity* agreed to accompany the expedition of Pilgrims to the trading post and serve as their protection in case the Massachusetts decided to be hostile. Not long before, news had reached Plymouth that the Pamunkey tribe had massacred 350 English colonists in Virginia. This caused the settlers to be uneasy. Miles Standish organized all able-bodied men into four squadrons and prepared them for the defense of the colony. He also warned that if a fire broke out in one of the houses, it could be a diversion, and the hostile natives could attack at that moment. He instructed that only half of the men should work to put the fire out, while the other half should grab their muskets and prepare for defense. That summer, the Pilgrims also constructed a "strong pale," a palisade on the perimeter of their village on which they mounted one of the canons. The people would be locked behind the palisade during the night for their safety. They also built an armory and a meeting house within the walls of their settlement. The meeting house had a flat roof and four watchtowers armed with cannons. Bradford wrote about the agony of building the defenses during the summer when the Pilgrims were starving, with so many new mouths to feed. Several men were caught stealing the crops, and they had to be punished by whipping. The news of the Virginia massacre made everyone willing to work, even though they were at the brink of their strength.

The summer of 1622 saw the second wedding at Plymouth. John Alden and Priscila Mullins, both twenty years old, vowed to each other. This couple would remain in Plymouth for years to come, and they had eleven children together. When fall came, the men Weston sent last moved away from Plymouth, burdening the Pilgrims no more. They used summertime to build their settlement forty miles to the north at Wessagusset, which later became known as Weymouth. But all this building during the summer meant that the Pilgrims had no time to tend to their crops properly, and the second harvest wasn't as bountiful as the first one. They also erected a trading post at Boston Bay to continue trade with the Massachusetts tribe, but this was still not enough to secure full bellies when winter came. Both the Plymouth and Wessagusset colonies braced for another hard winter. But they also proved to be competition to each other, as both colonies traded beaver fur. Nevertheless, they decided that an alliance was a better approach to the problem than hostility.

Squanto's End

Squanto and Hobomok remained with the Plymouth Pilgrims to serve as their translators in dealings with the Native Americans. But it seems that there was jealousy between the two, and they often fed false information to the

Pilgrims to secure better standing with them. When the Plymouth settlers wanted to trade with the Massachusetts in March of 1622, Hobomok informed Bradford that he feared the Massachusetts had joined the Narragansett's confederation and were now hostile towards Englishmen. He also informed Bradford that the Narragansetts planned to attack Plymouth. He claimed that Squanto was involved in all of this and was about to betray Plymouth. But Bradford couldn't stop the trade mission based on Hobomok's hearsay. Although worried, he was even more concerned with the lack of food that threatened his people. He also thought the natives would think of Plymouth as weak if the people remained behind walls and feared that would only inspire them to attack. He sent Miles Standish and ten other men to Massachusetts, and he ordered both Hobomok and Squanto to follow them.

But once the expedition was on its way, a member of Squanto's family came to Plymouth, obviously in distress. He claimed that the Narragansett tribe, together with Corbitant's and Massasoit's men, were coming to attack Plymouth. Bradford prepared the settlement's defense, but no attack came. Standish and his men returned immediately when they heard the warning shots fired from Plymouth, and upon hearing the claims of a possible attack, Hobomok dismissed them as false. He even sent his own wife to the Pokanoket village to ask Massasoit directly if the plan to destroy Plymouth existed. She found no evidence of preparations for war, and Massasoit sent word back to Bradford that he was disappointed in his mistrust but glad that he didn't rush to attack the Pokanokets.

Massasoit was angered with Squanto for setting up all of this commotion. He even came personally to Plymouth to demand Squanto's death. Bradford managed to appease the chief, who departed the settlement. But only a few days later, Massasoit sent a message to Bradford demanding Squanto's head. He even sent beaver fur in exchange for Squanto. But Bradford explained that it was not the Pilgrims' custom to trade people's lives. He refused to kill his translator, as he still believed this man could be useful to the colony. Massasoit reminded Bradford of their treaty and the right to punish their people for the crimes committed between them, but Bradford wanted to give Squanto a chance to defend himself. The translator denied his fault and blamed it all on Hobomok's jealousy. Squanto then said that he would honor Bradford's decision, whatever it may be.

But it was at that moment that Weston's settlers arrived, and Bradford postponed making a decision about what to do with Squanto. Massasoit didn't respond, but his relationship with the Plymouth colonists cooled off. He made sure Bradford understood that he could no longer rely on the Wampanoag's help if they came under attack by a third party. Edward Winslow wrote that, after some time, Squanto and Massasoit made peace, but he didn't offer any further explanation or a description of the events that led to this peace. Squanto continued to act as the Pilgrims' translator and guide. He even led Bradford and his men through a narrow sea passage to Nantucket Sound, where they could trade with another tribe of Native Americans.

The native villagers at Nantucket Sound told the Pilgrims that they often saw heavily-burdened ships pass through their waters. Bradford and the Pilgrims were happy to hear this news, as it meant the possibility of even greater trade. But at this time, Squanto suddenly fell ill. Bradford was shocked by Squanto's sudden weakness because he didn't want to lose the native who had been so beneficial to the colony. He lingered at the Sound, hoping his friend would feel better, but Squanto died. Bradford wrote about Squanto's last days and how he had wanted Bradford to pray to God for his soul. He also told Bradford that he was happy he would meet the Englishmen's God soon in heaven. Lastly, Squanto instructed the Plymouth governor to share his belongings among his Pilgrim friends whom he loved so much.

The Destruction of Wessagusset

The two colonies, Plymouth and Wessagusset, cooperated at first. To return the Pilgrims' hospitality and help with the building of their settlement, the men of Wessagusset helped the Pilgrims with their harvest. But the natives started complaining to Bradford that the Englishmen of Wessagusset were stealing their corn. Soon enough, the Plymouth crops started disappearing, too. The culprits were Weston's settlers. However, Bradford was aware he had no authority over the Wessagusset colony, and he could only send them a message criticizing their behavior. When the natives caught one of the Englishmen stealing, the Wessagusset men agreed to hang him to show good faith. However, rumors were spreading that they hadn't hung the culprit, but rather an old and sick man who was already on his deathbed. This became the popular story about the Wessagusset colony, but no historical records were ever found to confirm it.

When the Wessagusset colonists moved away from Plymouth, the *Charity* continued its journey to Virginia, and the *Swan* was given to the Wessagusset settlers for their use. When an English ship made a stop at Plymouth, the Pilgrims acquired a stock of beads to trade with the natives. Wessagusset settlers approached the Pilgrims, offering them a deal: they would trade the beads for an equal division of food, and the Wessagusset would give the *Swan* for transportation of the goods to the trading post. Bradford suspected that Wessagusset settlers had already burned through their provisions, and he couldn't deny them this opportunity. He agreed. The joint trade expedition was successful, and the Pilgrims and Weston's settlers divided beans and corn. But the Wessagusset colonists weren't accustomed to the harsh New England winter, and they again burned through their supplies quickly. Bradford wrote that the Wessagusset men were not well organized and that they were wasteful.

Famine struck during the winter of 1622/23, and many of Weston's men were forced to serve Native Americans—chopping their wood, building canoes, and fetching water in exchange for a handful of dry beans. The Wessagusset people started dying from hunger and cold. In February, their governor, John Sanders, complained to Bradford that the natives refused to give them more corn. He also asked for advice—whether they should take the corn by force. Bradford was firm in his response that the Wessagusset people must not attack the natives under any conditions. However, the Massachusetts had already learned of Sanders's plans from one of their traders, and they plotted how to get rid of the Englishmen. Bradford was afraid Plymouth was in danger, too, as natives often didn't see any difference between the two settlements.

In March of 1623, Massasoit was gravely ill, and Edward Winslow took in the chief to nurse him back to health. In gratitude, Massasoit extended his friendship to Winslow and even warned him that various tribes were planning an attack on the English colonies. The Massachusetts warriors influenced some of their followers, as well as the Succonet, Mattachiest, Paomet, and other tribes whose territory reached as far as what is today Martha's Vineyard. Bradford knew that Wessagusset men didn't have any weapons, so he sent Miles Standish and several armed men to help their fellow Englishmen. There are several theories about what happened next, and there is no historical consensus. Some scholars believe that the whole story about the natives planning an attack was nothing more than a fabrication of the Pilgrims, who wanted to get rid of the Wessagusset Colony since it was their rival in trade. Others believe that the Plymouth Pilgrims believed that a native uprising was indeed coming, but the attack simply never occurred.

Standish organized the defense of Wessagusset, but he was hot-headed and couldn't simply wait for the possible attack. He decided to take matters into his own hands. It was also a personal matter for Miles Standish, as one of the natives who threatened Wessagusset was Wituwamat, a warrior who had previously insulted him. Several natives were already in the settlement, among them Chief Pecksout and Wituwamat, with his younger brother. Standish planned to share a meal with these individuals in a separate closed room, where he ordered them killed. He killed Chief Pecksout personally. Soon after, all of the natives who were in the village at the time were killed. Only one survived, and he ran off into the woods to raise the alarm. Five colonists died that day. The next day, Standish returned to Plymouth with Wituwamat's head, which he then hung on the walls of the settlement as a warning to other natives.

Soon Bradford and the Plymouth people learned that Wessagusset was abandoned. Although Standish managed to kill the main Native American leaders who had plotted against the English, his actions only caused panic among Wessagusset's men. They were sure the natives would retaliate, and they sailed off to the fishing colony of Monhegan Island. The event at Wessagusset spread panic among the natives, and they moved their villages away from Plymouth and refused to trade with the English. We can learn from the correspondence between Bradford and Pastor John Robinson, who was still in Leiden, that both men disapproved of Standish's brutal methods. But Bradford also pointed out that they had no defense-capable man in Plymouth except Captain Standish and that he would leave the captain to answer to himself for his deeds.

Chapter 6 – Life Continues

Pilgrims Going to Church, George Henry Boughton (1867)

https://en.wikipedia.org/wiki/Plymouth_Colony#/media/File:George-Henry-Boughton-Pilgrims-Going-To-Church.jpg

In July 1623, two new ships came to Plymouth carrying ninety-six new settlers. The ships were the *Anne*, commanded by Master William Pierce and Master John Bridges, and the *Little James*, commanded by Emmanuel Altham. Among the passengers of these ships were some Leideners such as William Brewster's daughters: Patience and Fear. Aboard *Anne* came the future wife of governor Bradford, Alice. Other notable passengers were Roger Conant, who later founded Naumkeag (Salem), and a woman named Barbara, who would later marry Miles Standish. Some speculate that Barbara was the sister of Standish's previous wife, Rose, who died two years earlier of "general sickness." The newcomers were not happy with what they saw in Plymouth. The old settlers were wearing rags or were half-naked. The hardship they had endured could be read on their sunken faces and their thin bodies. Some of the passengers of *Anne* and *Little James* were not at all prepared for the New World and its wilderness, and they left America within a year. Others didn't want to be bound by the contract with Merchant Adventurers, and they set out to start their own colonies. The Merchant Adventurers approved special terms for the new settlers, and they were given land a mile south from Plymouth on the banks of Eel River.

But those who stayed quickly got accustomed to life in Plymouth. The *Anne* soon returned to England, and Edward Winslow departed to trade the furs and bring back more supplies for the colony. He returned six months later on board *Charity*, and he brought with him a bull and three cows. These were the first cattle the Pilgrims had seen since their arrival into the New World. Around this time, the first settlers were compelled to rethink how they were running their colony. They didn't have the concept of individual ownership; everything belonged to the community. The crops were grown on communal land, and everything had to be shared equally. Some of the people started thinking they would be better on their own, as communal sharing proved not to be enough during the winter when food was sparse. The young men who did most of the work resented sharing. It seemed unjust to them to receive the same amounts of food as those who didn't work as hard. The older men who worked slower had nothing to show off but their experience. But in the eyes of the younger men, this wasn't enough to earn them equal shares. Women were discontent, too, as they had to wash and cook for not only their own families but also for unmarried men. They felt as if they were slaves, even less than their husband's property. Governor Bradford had to take a bold step and divide the land among the families. Each family received a plot to plant their crops. Suddenly, everyone was eager to tend their corn, and the food was abundant. Bradford wrote that it was his belief the colony's famine days were over.

In 1624, the colonists demanded a change in the land distribution system. Bradford implemented a distribution system by which each family would work different pieces of land each year. But the colonists noticed that some families took better care of their plots, and they thought it would be unfair to move to the uncared ones the following year. Bradford saw sense in the demands of the Pilgrims, and he devised a new system in which each family would be permanently assigned one acre of land per member. This way, the Pilgrims were sure that everyone would have enough space to grow food for themselves. The land was near Plymouth town to make sure the colonists were always nearby the safety of the settlement walls.

Over time, more people left the colony. Some went back to England, but others left for other colonies. These were mostly Strangers and the settlers who came on later ships. But there was one occasion when people had to be exiled from Plymouth. The first man to be accused was John Lyford, a minister within the Church of England. He organized secret religious meetings with colonists who didn't want to renounce the Church of England and preached to them. Another man was John Oldham, who was in league with Lyford. Bradford managed to intercept some of the letters these two men sent to England to their Church colleagues. They were both put to trial and found guilty. Oldham was expelled from the colony immediately, but Lyford cried and begged for mercy and was allowed to stay in Plymouth for another six months.

Not all the newcomers were welcome in Plymouth. The Pilgrims simply didn't like those with loose morals. A wealthy Irishman named Fells had a maid working for him. The word got out that the girl was more than a maid to Fells and that they were sharing a bed. This was not tolerated among the Puritan Pilgrims, and Bradford had both the man and his maid questioned. They denied everything, and without any other evidence but hearsay, the Pilgrims had to leave the pair alone. This incident would probably be quickly forgotten if the maid hadn't become pregnant. Fells was afraid of the punishment they would receive from the Pilgrims and tried to move the girl somewhere safe. But he couldn't get passage for her on any of the passing vessels, so he decided to come clean before Bradford and ask for forgiveness. But the Pilgrims had no forgiveness for the sinners, and the couple was asked to leave. They managed to reach Virginia safely.

Since the downfall of Wessagusset, the Plymouth Pilgrims had trouble establishing trade with the Native Americans. Time was passing, and they started feeling pressed to expand trade so they could pay their debt to the Merchant Adventurers faster. They made contact with the Abenaki tribe on the Kennebec River, and trade was renewed. But not far from where Wessagusset used to be, a new trading post was established by Ferdinando Gorges and his associates. This post was named Mount Wollaston and was used to trade beaver fur. The post grew so fast that it threatened to establish a monopoly over the fur trade in Boston Bay, which would thwart the Pilgrims' plans. The men who lived and worked at Mount Wollaston were bondsmen, as much in debt to the Company in London as the Pilgrims were: they had paid for their transport to the New World with indentured servitude.

By the time Mount Wollaston was established, the Pilgrims had started their trading post at Aptucxet, near Buzzards Bay. Here they traded with Wampanoag and the Narragansett. The nearby Dutch colony, New Amsterdam, must have been alarmed by the presence of the Pilgrims, but they did nothing to disturb the Plymouth settlers' trade. This allowed the Pilgrims to focus on Mount Wollaston, which was led by Thomas Morton. Morton was an employee of Ferdinando Gorges, overseeing the Company's interests in the New World. He came to Plymouth in 1622 but quickly left, bothered by the Puritan intolerance that ruled there. In 1624, Morton was back in New England, but this time as one of the partners in a trading company financed by the Crown. Morton renamed Mount Wollaston "Mare Mount," which meant "mountains by the sea," but the Pilgrims called it Merrymount. Bradford despised Morton for his liberal ways and called him "Lord of Misrule," as he objected that Merrymount colonists were freely celebrating religious holidays.

The colonists set up a Maypole and drank and danced around it. They even invited natives to the celebration, much to the Puritan's dislike.

But Bradford wasn't only concerned about the merrymaking of his new neighbors. His biggest concern was that Morton traded guns to the Native Americans. This was a problem not only for Plymouth but also for all the colonies in the area, especially because the natives started trading beaver pelts exclusively with Merrymount. Arming the Native Americans was itself dangerous because of the mistrust the Native Americans and Englishmen shared towards each other. Another incident like the one in 1622 when Standish killed Native American leaders at Wessagusset, and there would certainly be an uprising of the native tribes. But it wasn't Morton who started the trade of guns with natives. It was the French explorers who taught the natives how to use guns and powder. Morton only took the opportunity to expand the business, and he even started hiring natives to hunt for him. The combination of Native American knowledge of the landscape and guns was a dangerous one. Natives quickly learned that guns were superior to their traditional weapons, such as bows and arrows. They were willing to trade almost anything for them.

Later, Bradford wrote that the Native American's use of guns was out of control. They even acquired lead molds and started producing their own bullets. They were not strangers to pistols, either, and carried them everywhere. In time, the Native Americans became better armed than the colonists of Plymouth and even some other colonies. Bradford feared that it was only a matter of time before the natives learned how to produce their own gunpowder. They always seemed to have a supply of guns and powder, even when they were in short supply among the English. This might have been the case, but only because Morton started importing guns exclusively for trade with the natives. Bradford also noted that the English and the Dutch started dying by Native American hands almost to the date when Morton started selling them guns. In his eyes, Thomas Morton was a villain.

But Morton had greater plans for the Native Americans. First, he got rid of his partner, Captain Wollaston of the ship *Unity*, by accusing him of selling servants into slavery to the natives and the Virginia tobacco plantations. He mounted a rebellion of servants against Wollaston, who was forced to flee. Once in the sole command of Merrymount, Morton founded a commune mixed with newly freed slave-servants and Native Americans willing to convert to Christianity. He planned to force the natives to settle and abandon their hunter-gatherer way of life. He even mocked the Puritan practice of setting up an intolerant colony. In response, the Plymouth Puritans called Morton's view of Christianity too liberal, little more than heathenism. They accused him of integrating the English people into the native way of life. Puritans were also discontent that Merrymount started growing faster than the Plymouth colony and threatened to take over their monopoly on both trade and agriculture.

The Pilgrims asked Morton to stop dealing guns with the Native Americans, but he refused. Bradford and the governors of several other surrounding colonies made a pact to send a contingent of men to deal with their disobedient neighbor. Miles Standish led the expedition, and they managed to capture Morton and imprison him in Plymouth. After a quick trial, Morton was exiled to a deserted island of the coast of New Hampshire, where he could wait for a ship that would take him back to England. The Puritans didn't leave enough food on the island for Morton to survive while waiting for the ship. They wanted him to starve. But Morton made many Native American friends, and they brought him plenty of food on their canoes. They offered to transport him back to the mainland, but Morton knew he would probably be put to death if he stepped on the shore of New England again. Eventually, Morton managed to find his way to England, and later he even became an attorney of the Council of New England and sued the Massachusetts Bay Company. He won the case in 1635, and the Company's charter got revoked. Although it wasn't a victory against the Merchant Adventurers, the company responsible for financing the Plymouth colonists, the Massachusetts Bay Company was founded to bring even more Puritans to the New World. In his way, Morton got revenge against the Puritans. He was now free to return to Merrymount, but he found his colony destroyed. Once again, the Puritans arrested him and shipped him back to England.

Without competition from Thomas Morton, the Plymouth colony beaver fur trade started thriving. In 1632, the Pilgrims established a new trade post deep in Dutch territory. Edward Winslow personally led the expedition to Matianuck (now named Windsor). There, the Dutch Fort Good Hope would be built the following year. But the occupation of the Dutch territory led to strained relations between Plymouth and the Dutch. New Amsterdam responded by sending seventy armed men to warn the Pilgrims that they were unwelcome. But the Dutch were unwilling to fight, and the Pilgrims refused to leave. In 1635, the elder son of William Brewster, Jonathan, took control of the post.

Matianuck was just one of many small trading posts the Plymouth colonists used to trade beaver pelts. The trade grew, and the Pilgrims were well on their way to paying off their debt to the Merchant Adventurers. However, they had many setbacks, and they managed to pay the debt in full only in 1648. One such setback occurred earlier, in 1630. The husband of Fear Brewster and Governor Bradford's assistant, Isaac Allerton, managed to cheat Plymouth for several thousand pounds. Because Bradford didn't have any business skills, he assigned Allerton to deal with the colony's debt to the Merchant Adventurers.

At first, young Isaac was honest, and in 1628, he traveled back to London, where he delivered one of the debt payments to the Company. He also managed to get a land grant in Kennebec (in today's Maine) from the New England Council. Plymouth used this land to open a new trade post under the supervision of Edward Winslow. But Allerton started his own trade business there, presenting himself not as part of the Plymouth colony but as an independent trader. He was now competition. Furthermore, he started mixing his earnings from the trade with those of the Plymouth colony and spending it all. His mismanagement of the money caused the Pilgrims to go into even greater debt.

But Allerton's financial mismanagement was only discovered in 1630 when he failed to bring much-needed supplies from England. That year, he also built another trading post near Plymouth's own, in Pentagoet, enriching himself at the expanse of the colony. That is why he was finally removed from his post as Brewster's assistant in 1631. In September of the same year, he left Plymouth and settled in Salem Harbor. In 1634, after the death of his wife Fear Brewster, Allerton was banished from Massachusetts Bay, but he made a life for himself in New Haven Colony and New Amsterdam. He traded in sugar cane in the Caribbean, which brought him more wealth and influence. He lived for two more decades in New Haven.

In 1635, Plymouth lost its Pentagoet trading post, as it was overrun by the French. In fact, that territory remained French until 1629, when the Pilgrims captured it. Bradford sent Edward Winslow, who acted as a Plymouth diplomat on several occasions, back to England to acquire a permit from Ferdinando Gorges to take up arms against the French and retrieve the post. However, at that time, King Charles (1625–1649) made the Bishop of Canterbury, William Laud, head of the Commission for Regulating Plantations. Although Laud was friends with Gorges, he despised the Puritans. Instead of entertaining Winslow's petition, Laud proceeded to argue with him on religious views. He even arrested Winslow, who spent the next four months in prison in England. Once he was released, Winslow knew there was no point in pursuing the petition, and he hurried back to Plymouth.

At this point, Ferdinando Gorges regretted ever dealing with the stubborn Puritans, and he used his friendship with Laud to devise a plan for how they would send an English army to occupy the colonies governed by the Pilgrims and establish the Church of England in Plymouth. But at that point, trouble was brewing with King Charles I and his lack of love for the Puritans. Laud and Gorges never had the opportunity to put their plan into reality.

Chapter 7 – The Rise of the Puritans

The Puritan, August Saint-Gaudens (19th century)

https://en.wikipedia.org/wiki/Puritans#/media/File:Pilgrim_Fairmount_1.jpg

Charles I ascended the throne in 1625 upon the death of his father, King James I. The same year, he married a French princess, Henrietta Maria. She was a Roman Catholic, and as such, she was never crowned in the Church of England. Because of her devotion to Catholicism, she was never loved by the people. Because of his wife, Charles I was greatly mistrusted by the Puritans and by the Parliament of England. He also fought the Parliament over his royal prerogatives. He believed in God's right of the kings to rule, and he wanted to get rid of the Parliament. He disbanded the Parliament on several occasions and tried to impose his sole rule over England, but he received strong opposition. Even his people started regarding him more as an autocrat than a monarch.

In 1642, a civil war broke out in England and lasted for five years. It was fought over the way the country was governed and the restrain on religious freedoms. Charles I had no love for Puritans, and he tried to impose the high church ideas of the Bishop of Canterbury, William Laud, on the people of Scotland, Ireland, and England, no matter their religious commitment. The king lost the civil war and was captured, tried, and convicted of high treason. In early 1649, Charles I was beheaded. Less than two decades had passed since the Pilgrims first established the Plymouth colony. But the unrest before and during the civil war created a flood of immigrants to America and the West Indies. The settlers, who were not Pilgrims, started arriving on the shores of New England. Most of them were non-Separatist Puritans. They were deeply religious but wealthier than the Pilgrims. They were business owners, middle-class merchants, and prosperous farmers.

The leader of the early Puritan settlers was John Endecott. He wanted to create his colony in Massachusetts Bay, but he was impatient and didn't wait for a charter to be granted to him. He brought his people into the territory between the Charles and Merrimack Rivers in 1628. A year later, he finally received permission for the settlement. This territory was previously known as Naumkeag, a colony founded by Roger Conant, who had been exiled from Plymouth. Conant stepped down from the governance of Naumkeag peacefully, agreeing to work with the new settlers rather than fighting them. The new settlers renamed the colony Salem, a Hellenized version of the biblical name for the city of Shalem, which is today believed to be Jerusalem. Other Puritans followed Endecott, encouraged by his successful departure from England. One of them was John Winthrop, who founded the Massachusetts Bay Colony in 1628 along with his fellow Puritans who elected him governor of the new colony. The Company would have control over the whole Massachusetts Bay area.

Four vessels came to New England on March 29, 1630. The *Arabella*, the *Talbot*, the *Ambrose*, and the *Jewel* were just a prelude to nine more ships that sailed from England that year and brought more than 1,000 Puritans to Massachusetts. Because of their numbers, it didn't take long for the Puritans to build several towns in Massachusetts Bay Colony. Among them were Dorchester, Medford, Lynn, Watertown, and Roxbury. Today, they are all a part of the larger Boston metropolitan area. The Plymouth Pilgrims suddenly found themselves with neighbors of the same religion up and down the coast. But the newcomers were not Separatists, and this bothered the Pilgrims, who had now been occupying the area for almost a decade. They wanted to convert the newcomers and infuse them with Separatist ideas.

The Pilgrims were in luck because, when John Endicott came to Massachusetts, he and his people needed help settling down. They needed medical care and religious advice. Plymouth offered to help and sent its deacon and physician, Samuel Fuller, who started spreading seeds of Separatism among the newly arrived. Fuller was sent to Charlestown as well in 1630 to help the settlers with medical problems, but he didn't miss the opportunity to preach Separatism. He was successful, as the Separatist traditions were accepted among the new settlers. This was just the first step towards the foundation of the Congregational Church.

Governor Winthrop proved to be able to lead his people, and under him, the Massachusetts Bay Colony prospered. In a short time, they surpassed their neighbors, the Pilgrims. Their experience in business and trade helped them make their endeavors a success. By 1636, everyone envied the Massachusetts Bay Colony for its prosperity. At that time, Thomas Hooker, a Puritan minister, led his family and followers to the west. There, in what is today the center of Connecticut, he founded the town of Hartford. In 1637, in the Connecticut River Valley, another town emerged and became the port of New Haven. In time, the Puritans took over the trading posts of the Plymouth Pilgrims in both Maine and the Connecticut River Valley. They took the monopoly of beaver pelt trade from the Pilgrims' hands, and consequently, the Plymouth colony struggled to pay off its debt.

In Boston Bay, life was generally good. The crops grew abundantly, and the Puritans never experienced the hardships that the first Pilgrims had to go through. Trade was also going well, and the colony grew at a rate almost double that of Virginia and Maryland. The new generation was a joy to its parents, as many children were born in the Massachusetts area. Puritan law required all the communities that had fifty or more families to have schools. This meant that the children had access to education and were likely to prosper in the future. Literacy was important among Puritans because everyone was expected to read the Bible. However, the Puritans had internal troubles and disagreements rooted in religious intolerance.

The Puritan government implemented harsh punishments for straying from God's Word. Even children who giggled or fell asleep during the sermons were beaten, and monetary fines were imposed on adults who missed church. For more serious offenses of a criminal nature, people were hanged in the Boston Common (the oldest city park in the US). Less harsh punishments included public whipping, confinement in prison, and public humiliation. It was in the Boston area that adulterers were marked with a scarlet *A* on their clothes so everyone would know their sin. In Plymouth, those who were accused of adultery wore two scarlet letters, namely *A* and *D.* Similar laws were implemented in Salem and York, Maine.

Women and their position in the society of the New World were a particular problem for Puritans. Colonials wanted to make women feel welcome, as they needed them to conceive a new generation. Because of this, women were treated more equally in the New World than back in England. Puritan women in the colonies were seen as more than their husbands' possessions. They were not servants, and they would not be treated as such. Beating women was prohibited, and those who did had to pay enormous fines. But women didn't have equal rights with men. They were not allowed to own property or to take roles in the colony's governance. Nevertheless, they were given religious freedom equal to that of a man, and in Puritan England, that was enough to attract them to America.

Anne Hutchinson was one of the many women who came to America in search of freedom. She was the wife of William Hutchinson, a London silk trader who considered that women should be equal to men in everything. He never forbade Anne to educate herself and to express her opinion. Anne was also a trained midwife and had contact with other women through her profession. She started preaching to women and claimed that God spoke to her. Puritans, in general, thought that God spoke only to men and that it was the devil who spoke through women. The Hutchinsons were followers of a preacher named John Cotton, who had emigrated to America, and they followed him. They settled in the Massachusetts Bay Colony and started building their lives. Anne started working as a midwife again, and as a female preacher.

When word got out that she claimed to speak with God, she was arrested and interrogated for days, during which she was given no food or water. She was not even allowed to go outside of the cell to relieve herself. During the final court gathering, she fainted. But soon enough, she was back on her feet, arguing her case with as much logic and exhaustive knowledge of the Bible as her accusers. She won the case, but she sealed her faith at the end by proclaiming that God told her she would win. Upon hearing that, the men of the Massachusetts Colony decided she should be banished. In March 1638, she was formally excommunicated and ordered to move out of the colony. Her husband joined her in banishment, and together they lived in a log cabin at Aquidneck Island. A year later, she was preaching again to a small congregation of women in the area where she lived.

Echoes of Revolution in the Colonies

The Pilgrims and the Puritans in America all agreed that the revolution of 1642 in England was a good thing. The Royalists, followers of King Charles I, thought that the monarch should rule over Parliament. But the Presbyterians and the Puritans, who mainly made up the middle class and were more numerous, thought that Parliament should have certain rights in ruling England, such as the levying of the taxes. The Puritan Oliver Cromwell led the armies of Parliament against the king, and they were victorious. After the king's execution in 1649, Cromwell assumed control of England. With the monarchy dismantled, England became a commonwealth. Cromwell ruled the British Islands as Lord Protector from 1653 until 1658.

Puritans in England and the New World celebrated Cromwell's victory, and the Pilgrims joined them in celebration. Edward Winslow had been elected governor of Plymouth on three occasions by 1646 when he sailed to England to deal with the colony's business. There, he became impressed by Cromwell and decided to stay and serve England's Puritans. He never returned to Plymouth, but he continued to fight for the Puritans' endeavors in the Caribbean. He died in 1655 on a mission to overthrow the Spanish who ruled Jamaica.

The Puritans had won in England and finally had the freedom to organize their religion as they wished. This was the very reason why so many of them emigrated to America. With their home country finally free, some of them decided to return. But many had established their lives in the colonies and wanted to stay. Unfortunately, they didn't count on the defeated Royalists who fled to the colonies of Virginia. After the defeat of the Stuart dynasty, those who were loyal to the king started searching for a new life in America. They were aristocrats and sought adventures in the New World. Virginia remained loyal to the king and a safe haven for aristocrats. They were wealthy, and they started building lavish manors and plantations.

The Royalists in Virginia and the Puritans in Massachusetts Bay were on the opposite sides of the revolution of 1642, but they also had different worldviews and could not get along. They never mingled, and they decided that instead of bringing the bloodshed from England to America, the best thing they could do was to avoid each other.

Two years after the death of Cromwell in 1658, the monarchy was restored under King Charles II. However, it was a different monarchy than the one ruled by his father, Charles I. Parliament became an integral part of the government, and the English people vowed they would never again allow a king or a queen to trample their rights. Charles II was a king, but Parliament had the power to oppose him in everything. It was the Puritan revolution of 1642 (the English Civil War) that allowed England and later America to develop their two-party political systems.

Chapter 8 – The Wars in the Colony

King Philip (Metacomet)

https://en.wikipedia.org/wiki/Metacomet#/media/File:Philip_King_of_Mount_Hope_by_Paul_Revere.jpeg

By 1636, The Pilgrims and the Puritans were firmly rooted in their trading posts around the Connecticut River. But the Pequot natives resented their presence. Individual skirmishes between the Pequot and the English settlers would occur, but they never really escalated to more than localized fighting. The colonists slaughtered whole Native American villages, and the natives would retaliate by slaughtering the settlers. Fear and hatred escalated on both sides, and finally, in 1636, a full-scale war erupted.

Pequot War

The Pequot War has its origins in the early 1630s. The tension between the English settlers and Native Americans was increased by a series of factors. Different native tribes sided with different groups of settlers to advance their fur trade. The Pequot sided with the Dutch colonists, while the Mohegans took the side of the Plymouth Pilgrims. At the time of the colonization of the

Connecticut River Valley, both the Dutch East India Company and the Plymouth Pilgrims had valid documents that they had purchased land from the Pequots. Both the English and the Dutch claimed the land, and it was only a matter of who would be faster to occupy it. Each tribe had its interests in helping one faction or the other. Pequots were losing their monopoly on production and trade of the wampum (beads made out of shells), and they sided with the Dutch because their competitors, the Narragansetts, were in a trade alliance with the English.

The matter escalated even more when, in 1634, the Niantics murdered John Stone, an independent English trader, and his crew members. The Niantics were the allies of the Pequot, and they claimed they killed Stone in retaliation for the murder of their leader. And although Stone had a bad reputation both among the natives and the colonists of Massachusetts Bay, he was innocent. He had sailed into the mouth of the Connecticut River and into a region that was already brewing with tension about trade rights. The Pequots, who had exclusive right to trade with the Dutch, wanted to make peace with other tribes, and they agreed to allow all of them to trade with the Dutch. However, the Dutch East India Company didn't like this, and they kidnapped the Pequot leader named Tatobem. They wanted a ransom, and after receiving it, they returned Tatobem to the Pequot, but he was already dead. It is not known if the murder of the Pequot leader was intentional or not.

The Pequot wanted revenge, and since they didn't see much difference between the Dutch and the English, they didn't mind who they would kill. Unfortunately, John Stone was the first to enter their village at that moment. They agreed to trade with him, but once he and his men got drunk and started acting violently towards Pequot women, they were all executed. The Dutch claimed justice was achieved, but the English couldn't see anything just in the Pequot actions. After all, the Dutch had killed Tatobem—why should an English man answer for their crime? The Pequots saw their mistake and tried to mend the dispute by apologizing. But the English wanted to use this dispute to their advantage. They didn't want the apology but territory to start their trade post. They also demanded that the Pequots trade exclusively with English colonists, but they refused these conditions.

Another event that influenced the tension between the Plymouth and the Dutch, as well as between the native tribes and the settlers, was the Great Colonial Hurricane of 1635. It hit the colonies of both Virginia and Massachusetts in August, and it was probably the biggest hurricane since the arrival of the Pilgrims on the coast of New England. The hurricane passed Jamestown without inflicting too much damage, but William Bradford of Plymouth Colony and John Winthrop of the Massachusetts Bay Colony wrote extensively about it. They described the winds, the swelling of the sea, and the great destruction that followed. The area between the Piscataqua River, Rhode Island, and Providence was damaged. The accounts of the destruction of the hurricane could be seen even fifty years later. Not only did Plymouth and Massachusetts Bay suffer damage but also their trading posts in the area, especially the ones to the south, where the tides were higher than usual. Farms and fields were destroyed, threatening famine. Suddenly, the people had to compete for food to avoid starvation during the winter. This competition reflected in trade, as the English colonies were badly prepared for the periods of increased need.

The final drop that overflowed the cup and started the war was the murder of another trader, the Puritan John Oldham. He was previously banished from Plymouth for supporting John Lyford, who had preached secretly to followers of the Church of England. Oldham found his fortune outside of Plymouth when he became a trader. In 1632, he even became a representative of the General Court of Massachusetts. In 1636, John Oldham sailed to Block Island, where he was supposed to trade with natives. But members of the Narragansett tribe boarded his ship and murdered him and his whole crew. The only survivors were Oldham's two young nephews. The Narragansetts tried to blame Oldham for the killing of Pequot people, but the officials of the Massachusetts Bay didn't believe them.

John Endecott was sent to avenge the death of John Oldham, and he attacked two Native American villages on Block Island. But the natives managed to escape, claiming they had only one dead on their side. Two Englishmen were injured during the raid, and Endecott claimed to have killed fourteen natives. Nevertheless, Endecott and his men came to the mainland without any prisoners. But they did steal all of the food the natives had stored for the winter and had burned the villages to the ground. Endecott stopped at Fort Saybrook, but he wasn't welcomed there, as the Englishmen who settled there did not approve of his actions. He continued to the Pequot village, where he demanded Oldham's murders be surrendered. But when the natives didn't respond, he decided to attack them. Again, he burned the village down and stole or destroyed all of their crops. Luckily most of the Pequots managed to escape into the nearby woods.

The Pequots were angry, and they started persuading allied tribes to help them in their cause against the English settlers. They managed to gain the support of some of their aliases, but not all. Their long-time enemies, the Narragansetts, as well as the Mohegans, chose to side with the English. The Pequots and the Western Niantics besieged Fort Saybrook through the winter of 1636/37. Anyone who tried to go outside was immediately killed. Meanwhile, the Pequots conducted raids on the towns in the Connecticut Valley, and they continued to do so in the spring of 1637. The towns lost around thirty people to the attacks. The leaders of the Connecticut Valley towns met to discuss a joined defense. They organized a militia, with Captain John Mason as their leader. He had ninety people under his direct control, and they were joined by the warriors of the Mohegan tribe. To end the conflict, they decided to attack the Pequot tribe directly. Another twenty men from neighboring towns joined Mason at Fort Saybrook, and together they sailed to Narragansett Bay. They planned to confuse the Pequots but also to recruit the Narragansetts, who sent 200 of their people to join the English cause. The whole alliance marched to Mystic Fort (today's Mystic, Connecticut) and launched a surprise attack.

This attack is remembered as the Mystic massacre, and it took place on May 26, 1637. The Pequot village was surrounded, but the natives managed to organize their defense by erecting a palisade, as they had anticipated that the English would retaliate for the raids. Mason ordered the blockage of the two exits from the village and then set it on fire. The Pequots were trapped among the burning wigwams. The natives who tried to climb the palisade and escape the fire were shot down. Only five Pequots managed to escape the massacre. A Pequot raiding party led by their sachem, Sassacus, was outside the village at the time of the massacre. Once they learned what had happened, they rushed to confront the English, but Mason managed to evade them. It is believed that around 700 Pequots lost their lives in the Mystic massacre, including women and children. The English and their allies suffered only two casualties and twenty injured. Sassacus was eventually found in the swamps near Sasqua village, and the battle remembered as the "Fairfield Swamp Fight" began. The colonists defeated the remaining Pequots, but Sassacus managed to escape. He ran to his allies, the Mohawk tribe, but there he was killed. The Mohawks didn't want to bring the wrath of the settlers upon themselves, and they sent Sassacus's scalp to Mason as a sign of friendship.

The Pequot tribe disintegrated after the massacre. Those who escaped and survived were integrated into other tribes and were forbidden from calling themselves Pequots. Women and children that were spared were sent to the Bermudas as slaves. Around 500 of them were sent to Barbados on the slave ship *Sea Flower*. The Plymouth Pilgrims had nothing to do with the actual fighting, but they were one of the instigators of this war. Previously so dependent on the Native Americans, the Pilgrims, and later the Puritans, became resentful of them. Governor Bradford even wrote about the massacre, praising what it achieved: the complete removal of one of the native tribes. The Pequot war had many casualties, but it was no match for the war that broke out in 1685, known as King Philip's War.

King Philip's War

Great Sachem Massasoit died in 1661 and was succeeded by one of his sons, Wamsutta. But Massasoit had two sons, who in their youth approached the Pilgrims and asked to receive English names from them. Wamsutta was known as Alexander, and his younger brother, Metacomet, as Philip. Wamsutta lived only one year longer than his father and ruled as sachem of the Pokanoket and Wampanoag only until 1662. He wanted to upkeep the peace his father had managed to maintain with the English for years. But rumors started that he was conspiring with the Narragansetts, who planned to attack the Pilgrims. Still, the Pilgrims had no evidence for this. Instead, they accused Wamsutta of independently selling the land to other colonies without consulting them. He was captured and taken to Plymouth, where he was interrogated and released. Soon after he returned home, he died of an unknown cause. The Pokanokets suspected the Pilgrims had poisoned him.

Upon becoming the next Great Sachem, Metacomet became known as King Philip among the English settlers. He signed another agreement with the Plymouth Pilgrims, vowing he would not provoke war with other native tribes. In return, Plymouth promised it would help Metacomet and advise him. But King Philip expected the Pilgrims to defend the Pokanokets if the need arose. Soon he learned that was not the case.

John Sassamot, a converted native who spoke English, served as a translator during the Pequot War. His language ability and intelligence were noted by Reverend John Elliot, a missionary who worked on converting Native Americans to Christianity. Elliot arranged for Sassamot to receive a Harvard education, but Sassamot stayed there for only one year. He became an advisor to Massasoit at one point, and he continued to serve as an interpreter between the natives and the settlers. In January 1675, Sassamot was in Plymouth. At the time, the governor of the colony was Josiah Winslow—the first governor born in America. He received Sassamot, who warned him that Metacomet was preparing an alliance of the native tribes to attack Plymouth. Winslow decided to ignore the warning and to trust the agreement Plymouth had with the Wampanoag. But the next day, Sassamot went missing. The Pilgrims found his body later in January at Assawompset Pond. They thought he had drowned, but an investigation revealed his neck had been broken. They concluded that John Sassamot was murdered.

Another converted native named Patuckson showed up, claiming he saw three of King Philip's men murdering Sassamot. It was only in June of 1675 that the colonist captured the three men and put them on trial for Sassamot's murder: Mattashunnamo, Tobias, and Wampapaquan. This was the first trial in the history of Plymouth to have a mixed jury, as the Pilgrims invited six

Native Americans to join them. They found the three men guilty and sentenced them to death. There is no known reason why King Philip would want Sassamot dead. There are speculations that he resented Christians and their efforts to convert the natives. He didn't like Sassamot because he was one of the "Praying Indians," as the converted Native Americans were called at the time. Some scholars believe that King Philip wanted to kill Sassamot because he learned that the Christian native had told the Plymouth Pilgrims about his war plans.

The tensions between the Wampanoag and Plymouth grew after the trial. Governor Winslow started believing in rumors that King Philip was preparing for war, and he organized militia. King Philip's people believed a great injustice was committed towards them, and they continued to claim the innocence of the three men who were executed for Sassamot's murder. They also believed that Plymouth had no right to exercise justice on their men, as the Wampanoag lived outside of their legal jurisdiction. The tension escalated into war when one settler at Swansea, Massachusetts shot a Native American who accidentally wandered onto his land. Even before the war officially began, the towns of Massachusetts Bay Colony (sixty-five towns in total) organized a militia, implemented obligatory military training for the men who were of age, and started mounting defenses.

On June 20, 1675, a band of Pokanokets launched the first attack. They raided several isolated homesteads of Swansea, which were the extension of the Plymouth colony itself. Five days later, they destroyed the town of Swansea and killed some of its residents. The Massachusetts Bay Colony and Plymouth responded together on these raids and attacked the natives stationed at Swansea on June 28. They also destroyed the Wampanoag village at Mount Hope, Rhode Island. The war spread quickly, and the Wampanoags were soon joined by the Nipmucs and Podunks, while the Narragansetts remained neutral. The Plymouth Pilgrims prayed for victory, while the Native Americans watched the total eclipse of the moon that occurred over New England at that time. They considered it a good omen. Encouraged by the eclipse, King Philip launched attacks on Taunton, Dartmouth, Scituate, and Middleborough while approaching Plymouth. Seeing the success of King Philip against the settlers, some of the Narragansett warriors joined the raids, but officially the tribe remained neutral because it was a long-time enemy of the Wampanoags.

The "Praying Indians" fought on the side of the English, as well as some other native tribes who believed the settlers could bring them prosperity. But King Philip's people never attacked Plymouth directly. Instead, they scorched towns such as Mendon, Brookfield, Lancaster, Hadley, and Northfield. The natives were very successful in the initial battles, and some of the colonists' towns had to be abandoned—mainly those who had less than 1,600 people, as they could not gather a force large enough to resist King Philip.

In August of 1675, a battle ensued known as the "Wheeler's Surprise." It was fought between the settlers of the Massachusetts Bay Colony and the Nipmuc tribe. The colonists were commanded by Thomas Wheeler and the Native Americans by Sachem Muttawmp. The English wanted to ensure that the Nipmuc tribe would remain loyal to them during the conflict with the Wampanoags, so they sent negotiators, but it was too late. The Nipmuc had already joined King Philip. But Muttawmp pretended he was still a friend to the English and promised he would meet with another Boston delegation to set the details of the treaty. Boston sent Captain Wheeler and Hutchinson, along with thirty other men, to meet Muttawmp. As they traveled, they fell into an ambush. The Nipmucs attacked them from two sides, blocking their escape route. They were massacred, but several men survived thanks to the leadership of their native guides. The survivors headed to Brookfield, while Muttawmp and his men followed close behind.

Wheeler was wounded, but he survived. The Nipmucs followed the survivors to Brookfield, where they besieged them. The siege lasted for two days before relief came and scattered the native forces. There were many lesser battles at the beginning of the fall, but the greatest occurred on November 2, 1675. Josiah Winslow, governor of Plymouth, led the colonial militia and their native allies against the Narragansett tribe. Although the tribe was officially neutral in the conflict, the presence of several Narragansett warriors among King Philip's band was reason enough to attack the whole tribe. The Narragansetts heard of the approaching colonial army and abandoned several villages on Rhode Island, retreating into the safety of their swamp fort. It wasn't until December 19 that the colonials managed to find this fort. Its location was at today's South Kingstown, Rhode Island. Winslow's army numbered over 1,000 colonial men and around 150 Pequots and Mohegan warriors. The Great Swamp Fight ensued, and around 600 Native Americans were slaughtered. Their fort was burned to the ground, and their food supplies were taken. But most of the Narragansett managed to escape into the surrounding woods. Winslow decided not to pursue them, as his militia was running out of supplies and winter was upon them.

Throughout the winter of 1675/76, the natives added Mohawks to their confederation. Together they destroyed more colonial towns such as Lancaster, Portland, Providence, Simsbury, and Warwick. But by the summer of 1676, King Philip's allies grew tired of raids and started longing for peace. They started abandoning him and simply surrendering to the colonists. By July, King Philip had so few supporters that he had to seek refuge in the Assawompset Pond (south of Providence). Eventually, he was killed by one of the raiding parties of combined colonial and native forces. Captain Benjamin Church and Josiah Standish (son of Miles Standish) of the Plymouth colony tracked him to Mount Hope, Rhode Island. On August 12, 1676, King Philip was killed by a native named John Alderman.

King Philip's hands and head were severed. The hands were sent to Boston as proof that the great sachem of the Wampanoags was dead. His head was sent to Plymouth, where it was spiked on the watchtower. It remained displayed there for the next twenty years. The death of Sachem Metacomet (King Philip) marked the end of the fighting. The natives were no longer a significant threat to the English colonists, but the colonists lost many men during King Philip's War. The treatment King Philip received after death was a demonstration of the Pilgrims and Puritans' intolerance towards anything that clashed with their way of thinking, anything that might oppose their way of life. But soon, the Pilgrims and the Puritans experienced the brutality of another fanatic religious group that took a foothold in New England in the 1650s. This group, known as the Quakers, the Pilgrims tolerated even less than the Native Americans.

Chapter 9 – The Last Days

The Execution Procession of Mary Dyer

https://en.wikipedia.org/wiki/Quakers#/media/File:Mary_dyer_being_led.jpg

The Quakers

The English Civil War of 1642 caused many Christian sects to emerge. Unsatisfied with the Church of England and with Cromwell's Puritanism, these small groups sought religious freedom. Among them was a young man named George Fox, who claimed that everyone can have direct contact with God, without the aid of clergy or the Church. He traveled around England, the Netherlands, and Barbados, claiming that God sent him a vision of all the places where he could gather followers. He started preaching and converting new followers, attracting them with claims that Jesus Christ had come down on earth to preach to his people. Like the leaders of so many sects before him, Fox believed that he was the founder of true and pure Christianity.

Fox was accused of blasphemy in England, and although the number of his followers rose significantly, the Church of England ordered his arrest. Around 6,000 women signed the petition for his release, but it only served as proof that the sect was a danger to the social and religious order in England. Women were especially attracted to the sect because Fox preached that a woman, who is a mother and a wife, is essential for the religious conversion of the whole family and the whole community. Women were suddenly allowed to take an active religious role in society and were seen as a pillar of the family, faith, and love. But persecutions began with the Quaker Act of 1662, and it would not stop until 1689.

Even before the Quaker Act of 1662, many followers of this sect had emigrated to America in search of religious freedom. Just like the other settlers, they wanted to build a new life for their families, and they joined the Massachusetts Bay Colony as well as Providence Plantation. However, once they started practicing their version of Christianity and preaching it to their own community, they became targets of Puritan persecution. In 1656, Mary Fisher and Ann Austin were the first women who started preaching the Quaker gospel in the Boston area. Both women were soon arrested. Their family properties were confiscated, their prayer books burned. Mary and Ann were put to trial for heresy and sentenced to banishment. The Puritans hated the Quakers, but they didn't dare sentence them to death because they were afraid of yet another military conflict. Most of the Quakers were banished or imprisoned. A small number of them were whipped and flogged publicly.

After the Civil War in England, the Massachusetts Bay Colony, Plymouth, Connecticut, and New Haven formed a mutual defense group, the United Colonies. They were afraid that the revolution back in England had left them exposed to invasion by foreign forces such as France or Spain. In 1657, the United Colonies decided that they had to deal with Quakers permanently. But the Pilgrims didn't like the Puritans' extreme approach to the problem of heresy, and they were treating the Quakers mildly. Unfortunately, the Massachusetts Bay colonists started oppressing and torturing the Quakers during the Pequot War. They started cutting their ears, blinding them, and eventually putting them to death. It was one thing to treat godless Native Americans that way, but fellow Christians, even though they were spreading blasphemy, didn't deserve such harsh treatment in the minds of the settlers. Even the people of Massachusetts Bay started feeling disgust and horror over how their officials treated other Christians. The settlers of Plymouth Colony were impressed by the bravery of Quakers who endured all the torture. It reminded them of their own struggles in England, and it reminded them why they had come to America in the first place. Many in Plymouth converted and started following the teachings of Quakers.

The government of the Massachusetts Bay Colony was pressed to ease their persecution of Quakers, and they had to stop their harsh punishments. But this didn't happen before they created several Quaker martyrs, among them Mary Dyer, Marmaduke Stephenson, and Alice and Thomas Curwen. Although the Quakers were never welcomed among the Puritan colonies, they persisted and converted people to their own religious beliefs. Quakers preached directly in churches and meetinghouses, from courthouses while they were on trial, and from jail cell windows. People were sympathetic towards them and often brought them food and paid for their release. Despite the persecution they experienced in New England, Quakers continued coming and spreading their word. They came not only from England, trying to run from much harsher persecution there, but also from neighboring colonies such as Virginia and Pennsylvania, and they came by ships from Barbados.

The Massachusetts officials had to devise new laws to stop the Quakers from coming. They couldn't punish them because of public opinion, but they tried to implement fines for ships that carried Quakers. This had some result, as the ship captains soon refused to transport members of the sect to Boston to avoid paying the fine. But the Quakers started bribing the captains and the ships' crews, and their influx to the Boston area continued. Even though they continued to be banished for heresy, they would often return. Elizabeth Hooten, a sixty-year-old Quaker, kept coming back to Boston even though she was exiled five times. By 1675, the New England settlers were occupied with King Philip's War, and they lost interest in Quaker persecution. The sect was finally free to openly live, worship, and preach in Massachusetts and Boston.

Dominion of New England

When Charles II ascended the throne, England became a monarchy once again. The king needed to ensure that the faraway colonies in the New World remained loyal to him. Although the colonies were a part of the commonwealth, they started exhibiting signs of independence, and the monarchy was afraid that the American settlers would turn from loyalists to revolutionaries. To ensure the loyalty of the colonies, the Navigation Acts were passed in 1651 by the Parliament of England. Their purpose was to restrict trade between the colonies and Europe and to prevent the development of the manufacturing industry in the New World. This way, the colonies would remain dependent on England and would have no other choice but to be loyal.

The Navigation Acts were an ideal solution for the colonies that served as plantations of tobacco, indigo, sugar, and rice. They produced the goods which were imported to England and then sold to other countries. But the New England landscape was unsuitable for plantations, and the Puritans living there mainly became traders. In fact, they developed a large trading network, and because of the abundance of animal pelts, they were able to start their own leather production industry. They also started developing textile and iron industries that presented competition to England. The Crown had to put a stop to it. Charles II had the plan to establish a new government over the colonies that would discourage people from starting their own manufacturing and trade.

In 1675, a new colonial policy was put in place. A new office, the Lords of Trade and Plantations, was created as a subcommittee of the king's Privy Council. But there was corruption among the colony's officials, both in America and in the offices in England. With bribes and nepotism, the Puritan government of the Massachusetts Bay Colony often avoided the restrictions implemented by the Navigation Acts. They also mistreated the members of the Church of England, and with the start of King Philip's War, they attracted the Crown's attention.

The Massachusetts Bay area had received a royal charter in 1629, given to the joint-stock company to colonize. This ended the land dispute between the companies that wanted to settle their people and start their businesses in the area, but it also meant that Massachusetts never had a royal governor. Charles was about to establish the Dominion of New England in 1685, and he even chose a court official, Percy Kirke, as its governor. The first Dominion was to include Massachusetts, Plymouth, the disputed Narragansett territory, New Hampshire, and Maine. But before he could approve the commission of Percy Kirke, King Charles II died.

When King James II (1685-1688) came to the throne, he wanted to continue the plans of Charles II to incorporate the American colonies under the direct control of the Crown. On June 3, 1686, King James II chose Edmund Andros, a soldier and former governor of New York, to be the Governor in Chief of the Dominion of New England. His jurisdiction included Massachusetts, Plymouth, New Hampshire, the Narragansett territory on Rhode Island, Maine, and Connecticut.

The Dominion had its headquarters in Boston, and it was modeled after the Spanish system of viceroyalty. This meant that the king ruled the Dominion through appointed officials and a council. In December 1868, Governor Andros arrived in Boston, and with him came sixty soldiers tasked with helping him establish a viceregal office. The office consisted of the governor and his council. However, it did not have a representative assembly. The local elected officials were replaced by the governor's appointees. The government restricted the rights to a jury, trial, and bail; the press was heavily censored, and people couldn't leave the Dominion without the government's approval. The official appointees were always chosen from the members of the Church of England, as the goal of Governor Andros was to dislodge the Puritans' hold on governmental power. He went so far as to force the Puritans to allow the Church of England to hold sermons in their meetinghouses.

In March 1687, Andros imposed new taxes and land policies without legislative consent. And even though the general population was glad to see the Puritans losing their power, they were eager to unite with them and form opposition to these taxes. Soon, the Dominion claimed the right to all the Massachusetts Bay Colony's undistributed land. This land was previously held by the communes, treated as common land between individual towns.

In 1688, the Dominion included New York and East and West Jersey, but these towns were so far away from the power center in Boston that there were not many events there. More interesting events occurred on the diplomatic plans the Dominion had to deal with the Native Americans. In 1687, the governor of New France attacked a Native American village of Seneca people that was located in what is today western New York. He wanted to stop the trade of English settlers with the Iroquois confederation (Five Nations, as the English called them). Governor Andros appealed to King James, and the Crown stepped into negotiations with French King Louis XIV. The results were the cease of tensions in northwestern America and the continuation of trade with the natives. But to the northeast, where the Abenaki people lived, the natives resented the English settlers. In early 1688, they started attacking the colonial towns, forcing Andros to send an expedition to Maine. Governor Andros chose to personally lead the expedition, and he raided several native villages.

Andros spent that winter in Maine, but in spring, the rumors of the revolution in England reached him. Afraid that the revolt could spread to the Massachusetts Bay Colony, he rushed back to appease the situation. The Glorious Revolution started in November of 1688 when the Protestants wanted to secure the Crown for a Protestant successor of James II. The king himself was a Catholic, and by the age of fifty, he had no male heir. His daughter, Marry II, was married to William III of Orange, the stadtholder of Holland. He was a Protestant, and as such, a perfect candidate for the English Crown. The revolution was quick and bloodless, but it managed to send ripples and echoes to the New World.

The population of Boston, affected by the events in England, rose in revolt against the governance of Edmund Andros in April 1689. The royal governor was extremely unpopular in New England, where the Puritans made up the majority of the population. His restrictions on land grants, implementation of new taxes, and favoritism of the Church of England angered the citizens of New England. The leaders of the revolt in the Massachusetts Bay Colony were Increase and Cotton Mather. They were father and son and were both Puritan clergy. In 1688, Increase traveled to England to complain to King James II about the way Andros governed, and the king was promised that the issue would be taken care of. However, the revolution in England thwarted whatever plans James II had for the colonies. When William of Orange became king, the Puritans sent him a petition asking for the restoration of the Massachusetts charter. They were granted the charter once again, but back in Boston, Andros was already preparing for unrest.

On April 18, 1689, the Boston militia started gathering outside of Charlestown and Roxbury. They took boats and crossed the Charles River, entering Boston. First, they confiscated the arms and powder reserves of the Boston guards, and then they continued to take Fort Mary, where Andros barricaded himself. They were joined by a crowd of people, common citizens who offered their support. By 10 a.m. the same day, most of the Dominion officials were arrested, and the rest begged Andors to surrender to preserve the peace. But Andros refused. He tried to escape Fort Mary but was forced to retreat. Finally, he agreed to meet with the council, but once he left the safety of the fort, he was immediately arrested. Fort Mary surrendered the next day. All of the Dominion officials, including Governor Andros, were imprisoned and taken to Castle Island, south of Boston. After ten months of imprisonment, they were all sent to England for a trial. Andros was acquitted of all accusations and later became governor of Virginia.

After the fall of Governor Andros, the colonial authorities of Massachusetts moved to restore the governmental institutions that were in place before his royal appointment. The charters were renewed for Rhode Island and Connecticut, as well as the Massachusetts Bay Colony. New Hampshire was left without a formal government, but Massachusetts Bay had jurisdiction over it. The Pilgrims of Plymouth Colony resumed their self-governance. They never received a royal charter, and their restored government was illegal. The solution came when the Lords of Trade decided to issue a charter for Plymouth, but it would be combined with the one given to Massachusetts. The result was the creation of the Province of Massachusetts Bay, which included Plymouth, Martha's Vineyard, Elizabeth Island, and Nantucket. The proclamation date of the Province of Massachusetts was October 17, 1691. The Pilgrims lost their self-governance and never managed to return it. Plymouth Colony was no more.

Conclusion

The first Pilgrim who settled in Massachusetts, and the much more numerous Puritans, were the ones who shaped the American values still practiced today. Every fourth Thursday in November, Americans commemorate one of the most important events in their history—a Thanksgiving Day in honor of the Pilgrims' survival of their first winter in 1621. However, historians point out that the Pilgrims were just one of the groups of settlers who inhabited North America at that time. They were a small group, very religious, and maybe even more of a cult than a community. The Puritans who came after the Pilgrims came in greater numbers. But still, they represented the minority. The Virginia colonies and the loyalists who inhabited them, and later Quakers, left more influence on what American society is today. Nevertheless, the Puritans did leave something extraordinary in the legacy. They left not a model but an ideology for American culture.

Aside from the Thanksgiving celebration, the Pilgrims didn't leave much influence on America. They were a very small community, and very soon, they were outnumbered by the Puritans who settled in the Massachusetts Colony. In only one generation, the Pilgrims were absorbed by the Puritans. Aside from tourist attractions, there is little to nothing left behind by the Pilgrims. The idea of a religiously fanatic community of early American settlers comes from the Puritans, not the Pilgrims. But even they weren't the force that shaped American society. Other colonists of North America during the seventeenth and eighteenth centuries lived in unorganized and disorderly places, homesteads. But the Puritans formed tight-knit communities on land that was the property of their church. They would share the land between themselves, but it was all done for the betterment of the whole community, not individuals. But the Puritan communities didn't last long. The towns grew, and naturally, they connected to the world outside of their communities. This led to a divide among the residents, who no longer looked upon their elites as role models. It took only one century for the Puritans to start exploring individuality through trade, export, and even manufacturing. The religious diversity helped dilute the communities, and the Puritans expanded their world views and started integrating into the new American society.

Because the Puritan communities were so short-lived and were a minority on a continent that was being colonized rapidly, they were not a prototype for the America that emerged later. Yet they did leave their ideology of community, free choice, and the social contract. The Puritans were well aware that individuals who obeyed the social and religious laws of their own free will were much more productive for the community than the coerced ones. Thus, they strongly believed in free choice and voluntary consent. Even being born into a Puritan family didn't guarantee membership in the community. Individual choice did. But in the eighteenth century, a new type of Puritans emerged. They were no longer looking inwards, towards their community. They were open to the world, new ideas, and self-reliance. These new Puritans were much closer to the culture of other colonists of North America. But they brought with them the ideology of choice and a social contract, which became one of the staples of American culture. Modern Americans perhaps don't practice anything the Pilgrims and the Puritans did, but they certainly follow their ideology.

Part 5: The Mayflower

A Captivating Guide to a Cultural Icon in the History of the United States of America and the Pilgrims' Journey from England to the Establishment of Plymouth Colony

All great and honorable actions are accompanied with great difficulties, and both must be enterprised and overcome with answerable courage.

– William Bradford, Governor of Plymouth Colony

Introduction

The story of the *Mayflower* is a tale of extraordinary circumstances that made ordinary people into the founding fathers of an entire nation. And although the Pilgrims were far from perfect, with their condescending attitudes to non-Separatists and for Native Americans, it is difficult not to admire the sheer tenacity that it took to bring them all the way across the Atlantic.

Many of the *Mayflower*'s passengers originated from a small community in Scrooby, Nottinghamshire, where a radical group of religious reformers broke off from the Anglican Church and tried to establish a new way of life. Driven from their homeland by a vengeful king, they found themselves in the Dutch Republic, but even that couldn't be home to them. They needed to go somewhere entirely new, a place where they could build new lives and live as they pleased.

That place turned out to be North America. And so, the Pilgrims began their impossible quest to journey across the Atlantic, a voyage that would be as expensive as it was dangerous. There, they would start a new life on unexplored shores.

The story of the *Mayflower* is one of hope in the face of relentless difficulties. It's a story of survival, of fighting back against insurmountable odds. It's a story of sorrow, of thieving from an innocent nation, of invasion into a once-free world.

But most of all, the *Mayflower*'s story is a story about home: being driven from it, defending it, and seeking it. And you can read it right here.

Chapter 1 – The Pilgrims

The little ship climbed the wave gallantly, even though the towering wall of water loomed ahead of her like an impassable mountain peak. The sails were rolled up and tethered to their masts; to hoist those great rolls of canvas would be suicide in a wind like this. The wind drove directly into the eyes of the sailors as they frantically scooped buckets of water from the deck, hurling each one back into the ocean, only for another wave or blast of wind to send a shower of spray hurtling onto the deck.

It wasn't the spray that worried Master Christopher Jones as he wrestled with the wet and slippery whip-staff, which was a stick that helped to control the rudder. It was the wave they were climbing. The tiny ship's bow seemed to be pointing directly toward the stars or at least where the stars should be; instead, there was nothing but roiling clouds and darkness and the crest of the wave, white and terrifying, somewhere high above.

Master Jones clung to the helm. He wanted to cry some kind of warning to the sailors, but there was no time. They had reached the top of the wave, and with a sickening shudder, the ship's every timber creaking as though she would simply fly apart, the ship began to tip. Suddenly, they were plunging down, down, down into the black and inky heart of the ocean, into a trough that seemed so far below them that the ship was flying through the air instead of sailing on the water.

She couldn't make it. Surely not even this brave little ship could survive, Master Jones was convinced, as he clung to the whip-staff for balance as they plunged down toward the deep. She would strike that water and shatter into matchsticks, killing every soul on board. Those who didn't die on impact or drown in minutes would freeze in hours, slowly and in agony.

The ship hit the water again with a thump that knocked Master Jones from his feet. Sailors slid all over the deck, crying out in panic. Water slapped over the deck, washing icily around Master Jones's limbs as his feet scrabbled for purchase, but he had kept his hold on the whip-staff. He struggled back to his feet and squinted into the driving rain. Somehow, his sailors were still there. Somehow, the tiny ship had made it.

But even as a rush of relief filled Master Jones's veins, he looked up, and there was another wave, bearing down upon them, the little ship being driven onward toward it. Master Jones gripped the helm and gritted his teeth.

He wasn't sure how much more of this the *Mayflower* could take.

* * * *

The *Mayflower*'s journey brought her into an icy winter storm somewhere in the Atlantic in 1620, but its journey truly began more than a hundred years before, with a Roman Catholic monk who was tired of the church.

Martin Luther had long since dedicated his life to the service of the church and his God. Yet, even though he now wore the monk's habit and had taken the monk's vows, what he truly found in the belly of the Roman Catholic Church displeased him and smacked little of his idea of God. He saw the pope as corrupt, growing fat on the people's sins instead of helping to absolve them. In 1517, few people read the Bible for themselves, but as a monk, Luther was one of those few. He had copied passages of the scripture and dreamed of translating the Bible into German decades before it was ever translated into English. He wanted to make it more accessible.

Many of his fellow monks and priests, however, had other priorities, which were far less spiritual.

Luther's study of the Bible had led him to believe that sins had to be confessed, forgiven, and repented of. However, many priests of his time had other ideas. They believed that sins could be paid for in cold, hard cash instead. And since they were representatives of Christ on Earth, these priests believed that that money could go to them. As a result, they sold indulgences: certificates that stated that churchgoers' sins had been paid for instead of repented. While the ruler of Germany at the time, Prince Frederick III the Wise, had prohibited the sale of indulgences in parts of Germany, Luther was still confronted with members of his flock who would come to him with indulgences instead of repentance.

By October 31st, 1517, Luther could bear it no longer. He sat down to pen his *Ninety-Five Theses*—a series of demands upon the Roman Catholic Church to change some of its practices. In short, he demanded the reformation of the church, and so, the Protestant Reformation was born.

Outrage exploded across the European continent. The Roman Catholic Church was more than a religious organization at that time. In fact, its pope was one of the most powerful figures in the whole of Europe, wielding power on the same scale as emperors and kings. The church had a powerful alliance with and had crowned many Holy Roman emperors, who ruled over vast tracts of land, from Italy to the borders of Denmark. To allow a mere monk to change the church was for a ruler to kowtow to a peasant. Neither the pope nor many of the higher-ranking clergymen were going to bow to this lowly heretic, and in 1521, Luther was formally excommunicated from the Catholic

Church. The same year, he was brought before the Holy Roman emperor himself, Charles V of Germany, who demanded he recant.

Luther would do no such thing. As a result, Charles V issued the Edict of Worms. Luther was formally labeled a heretic who could be murdered on sight by anyone who pleased.

Conflict broke out across Europe. Luther's supporters began to call for change; many of them were powerful men in high positions. A rift was torn in the very fabric of 16th-century European politics. This became known as the Protestant Reformation, and it sent ripples through time that we still feel acutely today.

One of those ripples was the Separatist movement in England—a movement that would lead to one of North America's very first European colonies.

* * * *

In the 1530s, the pope's power was crumbling all around him. Luther had issued his *Ninety-five Theses* more than a decade before, and he was still alive, well, and translating the Bible exactly as he had hoped. This gave rise to a shocking idea that was almost unheard of in Europe at the time: the pope could be challenged. And it wasn't long before kings began to stand against him too.

It was Henry VIII, King of England, who brought the Reformation to his green and pleasant land, but not in the way that many of its citizens had hoped.

Henry VIII, strangely enough, had once been a favorite of the Roman Catholic pope. Like most of his successors, he enthusiastically waged war with France over the province of Aquitaine, which had once belonged to England and had been won by France during the Hundred Years' War in the 15th century. The pope had given Henry his blessing for the war; in fact, if he could defeat the French, the pope had promised to crown him as the "Most Christian King of France."

All that changed with Henry's first of six marriages, which was to Castilian Princess Catherine of Aragon. Originally, Henry had not wanted to marry her, but his father's dying wish compelled him to do so, and they married just a few months after he ascended the throne in 1509. Henry was only seventeen at the time.

Like all kings of that era, it was absolutely important to Henry that he should produce a male heir—a prince who could bring not only continual power to the royal family but also the promise of stability to the entire kingdom. Having a well-trained crown prince waiting in the wings made a nation far stronger and more stable.

For the first ten years of their marriage, it seemed promising that Catherine might eventually produce a male heir. Her first child, a little girl, never took her first breath; she was stillborn. She produced a son in 1511, but the child only lived a little less than two months. This was followed by two more stillborn babies until finally, in 1516, she gave birth to a surviving child. But the baby, Mary, was of no use to Henry. She was a girl and could never carry the crown.

By the early 1530s, Henry had become desperate. Despite two decades of marriage, Catherine had failed to give him a son to bear his crown after his demise. With friction boiling across Europe, which was not helped by the Reformation that was steadily gaining ground all over the continent, Henry knew that to be a king without an heir was to place a target upon an entire nation. He needed a son, and if Catherine couldn't give him one, he needed to find another wife.

The trouble was that in 16th-century England, divorce was no simple task. In fact, divorce, as we know it today, did not exist at all. The only way for a married couple to be separated was annulment, which essentially meant that the marriage had never been valid in the first place. Henry needed to get his union with Catherine annulled, and the only person who could do that was the Roman Catholic pope, Clement VII.

Clement, however, refused. Not only was there no real reason for him to annul the marriage, but he was also firmly in the pocket of Holy Roman Emperor Charles V, who was Catherine's nephew. Even after Clement died in 1534 and was succeeded by Pope Paul III, Henry still had no luck with the Roman Catholic Church.

Many a man would have given up by that point. But Henry was a king of England, and he believed himself more powerful than some pitiful pope. If the Roman Catholic Church wouldn't help him, there was only one solution: he would have to create a church of his own, a church that would do exactly as it was told. And so, the Church of England was born, and instead of a pope, it had a monarch. And that monarch was Henry VIII.

While the split with Rome was undoubtedly a purely political move on Henry's part, it drew enormous attention from those with more spiritual motives. Reformers saw this as a chance to establish a new church that aligned more closely with their philosophies, one with a figure as formidable as the king of England behind it. For the English people who considered themselves "reformed," it was a chance to be able to openly worship the way they believed was right.

Unfortunately, for the Protestants living in England, it was not to be. Henry had little interest in changing much of the liturgy or philosophies of his church. He just wanted it to annul his marriage to Catherine so that he could marry the second of his six wives. As a result, the Church of England was similar in many ways to the Roman Catholic Church—a fact that many Protestants could not forgive. They believed that the Church of England needed to be dramatically reformed or purified, and thus, the English Protestants became known as the Puritans.

The brand-new church soon found itself under unrelenting pressure, and not only from the Puritans. Now that it was controlled by the king of England instead of a Roman pope, the church was considered his fiscal property, and Henry quickly set about plundering its coffers to fund his ongoing wars with the mainland. Monks and nuns found themselves hopeless, as churches were stripped of their finery, not only by Henry but also by Puritans who believed that worship should be a far simpler thing, one requiring no stained glass windows or golden statues.

But it was not the Puritans who would become the people who are the main focus of this book. The Puritans were moderate compared to the second group of people who opposed the Church of England. These were the Separatists, and one of the first among their number was a young man by the name of William Bradford—a young man who would become one of the very first men to be called "governor" on the soil of the modern United States of America.

* * * *

William Bradford was born to a wealthy yeoman family in either 1589 or 1590. His father, William Bradford Sr., owned vast farmlands in the beautiful countryside of Yorkshire, and little William was set to grow up with everything he could ever need. He even had some noble blood running through his veins, which came from his paternal grandfather's side.

In fact, William could have had a very cushy life as another rich English yeoman who presided over vast tracts of land farmed by serfs—peasants who were little more than slaves. But it was not to be.

Tragedy struck very early on in young William's life. He would never remember his father, as William Bradford Sr. died when his little son was only one year old, leaving his wife, Alice, alone with a tiny toddler. Nonetheless, Alice was still young and still the heiress of her husband's vast estate, and so, remarriage was not an impossibility. One-year-old William was barely aware of his father's demise. But three years later, after a suitable period of mourning, four-year-old William's world was turned upside down when his mother remarried.

The name of William's stepfather is lost to history, but it can be assumed that there was no love lost between him and his new little stepson. As soon as the stepfather moved onto the vast Bradford farm, he wanted nothing to do with William, whom he must have viewed as a rival of sorts when it came to the question of the inheritance. Little William was unceremoniously packed off to live with his grandfather. He was a little child with no concept of what was happening, knowing only that he had been torn from his mother's arms, from the only home he knew. It would not be the last time.

William lived with his grandfather for two years. It can be assumed that some form of education was provided to the boy while he was with his grandfather; perhaps his life even improved a little. If he was living with his paternal grandfather, William Bradforthe, he might have even been in the court of nobility. Nonetheless, he didn't stay with his grandfather for long. When he was only six years old, his grandfather, too, passed away.

Confused and grieving, the little boy was sent back home again since he had nowhere else to go. His stepfather reluctantly welcomed him back into his home, and for a time, William was finally in his mother's arms again. This, too, was short-lived. It seems almost impossible to believe that yet more tragedy could afflict such a young life, but when William was only seven, his mother passed away.

His stepfather had tolerated William's presence in the home only to humor Alice. Now that she was gone, he had no reason to keep William anywhere near him. The boy was sent away to live with his uncles in Nottinghamshire. While the journey south was not a long one, it was still a whole new world for William.

To make matters worse, little William was a sickly child. Perhaps as a result of the grief that had so cruelly assailed him, he suffered from a chronic illness that has gone unidentified by history. It confined him to his bed and rendered him far too weak to work on his uncles' farm.

Instead, William began to read. In 1560, thirty years before William was born, the Bible had been translated into Early Modern English in a version known now as the Geneva Bible. This was the first mass-produced English Bible, and it fueled the Protestant movement that was sweeping through England, as people found themselves accessing the scriptures themselves instead of through the medium of priests. Most Geneva Bibles were destroyed in 1611 after the King James Bible was published, but that was still years in the future. During William's early life, the Geneva Bible was one of the most readily available books in the country.

Even though William was only about eight years old, he was quick to reach for the Geneva Bible in his boredom when he was confined to his room by his illness. Even at his tender age, he quickly found himself absorbed in the contents of the book. Soon, he began to grow interested in other classical works, and he began to grow more and more fascinated by Christianity.

At the same time, change continued to sweep across England, even during the reign of Queen Elizabeth I, who has long been lauded as one of England's most astute rulers. Her rule brought peace to much of England, and while the Church of England was still integral to her government, Puritans soon found that some lenience was extended to them. They began to cautiously build small churches in the countryside, and soon, they had preachers of their own. The Protestant movement was gaining a real foothold in England, spreading like wildfire over the green hills of Yorkshire.

It was inevitable that a child as intelligent and curious as young William Bradford would eventually come into contact with reformed beliefs. William had been bounced from home to home and church to church, and he had never found himself feeling quite at home in the Church of England. What was more, the uncles who were caring for him were not particularly interested in religion of any form. They were interested in farming, and as soon as William was well enough, they put him to work on their farm just like any other boy his age.

It was around 1602 that one of William's friends came over and told him that someone was going to be preaching new and radical ideas in a nearby town. This was a Puritan preacher, one Reverend Richard Clyfton. Clyfton was a Puritan minister who was determined to bring his preaching across rural England. William's interest was immediately piqued. He agreed to go with his friend and hear Clyfton's preaching, and it changed the course of his life almost instantly.

Despite the fact that his uncles expressly forbade him from attending any more Puritan meetings, William was fascinated by them, and he continued to attend them anytime he could. Soon, he was becoming a firm part of the Puritan congregation in Nottinghamshire, and it was among them that he found the first real father figure in his life: William Brewster.

More than twenty-five years William's senior, Brewster first tasted the Reformation in the Netherlands during his travels with his employer at the time, an ambassador to the Dutch. His convictions grew increasingly Puritan when he returned to England, where he worked as a postmaster and, later, as a bailiff in Scrooby, Nottinghamshire.

By the time little William Bradford went to hear Richard Clyfton preaching in Scrooby, Brewster was a firmly established figure of the Puritans. He took pity on young William; the boy always came to the services alone, and it was clear that he had no real parental guidance in his life and had already suffered much and lost many of those closest to him. Brewster was kind to him, and he became a friend, mentor, and paternal figure to young William—one that would prove indispensable in the many trials to come.

The trials grew abruptly worse with King James I's ascent to the throne in 1603. Unlike the moderate Elizabeth, James was determined that the Church of England should control the religious lives of every soul in his kingdom. By this time, there were many small, independent Puritan churches throughout England. For James, this was a dangerous prospect. The Church of England was intricately linked with his kingdom's government, and to defy the Church of England was to defy the king too. His solution was the same as that of political and religious leaders across Europe. If the Puritans didn't worship the way he wanted them to, they would be punished. Accordingly, he directed his archbishops to crack down on the still-illegal Reformation activity that was rapidly spreading across England.

While many English Protestants continued to believe that the Church of England could yet be purified, another radical sect of Protestants—among whom Reverend Clyfton was chief—began to realize that the Church of England was never going to change. Fellow Puritans were suffering deeply at the hands of that church, and these people began to believe that it was beyond saving. This wave of religious persecution saw Puritans labeled as traitors. They could be punished by utterly crippling fines; the penalty for failing to pay these fines was imprisonment. To make matters worse, there were rumors spreading among the Puritans that their brethren imprisoned in London were not executed. Instead, they were left to starve to death.

By 1607, all Puritan activities were forced underground. Instead of preaching in a church, Reverend Clyfton was forced to hold secret meetings. As always, William Brewster rose to the occasion by offering the manor house where he worked at Scrooby as a venue for these meetings.

Sometime during this period, the Scrooby congregation was joined by a most unlikely new friend: a former curate for the Church of England. John Robinson, a young man in his thirties, had served the Anglican Church faithfully until he was asked to accept King James I's request to stamp out the Reformation within his country. He refused to do any harm toward his Puritan counterparts, and as a result, he was thrown out of the Church of England. Feeling absolutely lost without a church to call his own, Robinson eventually wound up finding the congregation at Scrooby. While there must have been some tension between Robinson and his new brethren at first, he very quickly became one of their most valued, respected, and loved members.

During the secret meetings at Scrooby, the congregation decided that the Church of England could never be purified. They became Separatists and were determined to split from the Church of England forever and form their own church.

Young William Bradford, then sixteen or seventeen, had little interest in what his new congregation wanted to call themselves. All he knew was that he had finally found a real family in this group of people, people far closer to him than his two uncles, who still disapproved of his religious activities. The more persecution the Separatists faced, the closer William drew to them and the more he attended to their teachings. No threat of chains or fines would dissuade him from his convictions.

It was in the same year as the Separatists were formed that disaster struck. The archbishop of York found out about the secret meetings at Scrooby Manor. William Brewster, young William Bradford's close friend, was arrested and fined. Others were not lucky enough to be able to pay their fines; many members of the Scrooby Separatists were imprisoned for some time. Seventeenth-century English prisons were no pleasant place, and when these people were eventually returned to their congregation, they told terrifying stories about life behind bars and more rumors of Puritan prisoners being starved to death.

While the Separatists had hung on for years despite persecution, it was starting to become obvious to them that religious freedom was no longer an option in England. If they wanted to worship freely, they would have to leave their country behind. Accordingly, they began to consider emigration. But with the archbishop of York breathing down their necks, this would be no mean feat.

Chapter 2 – Searching for a New Home

Ninety years after Martin Luther wrote his *Ninety-five Theses,* the Reformation was still dividing kingdoms and countries all over Europe. Perhaps none were divided quite so literally or dramatically as the area then known as the Netherlands. For centuries, the people of the Netherlands, which consisted of modern-day Luxembourg, Belgium, and Holland, had been passed from one ruler to the other, from Holy Roman emperors to the duke of Burgundy and finally to the king of Spain.

In 1581, however, a vast rift was torn in the fabric of the country. Spain was still profoundly Roman Catholic at the time, while many Dutch people were growing more and more Protestant. This and other issues caused tensions to boil over in 1566, and the northern Netherlands battled their southern neighbors for fifteen long and bloody years until finally succeeding in gaining independence. This independence would only become *de jure* in 1648, but by 1607, the secession of the north and south was solid. The southern Netherlands—modern-day Belgium and Luxembourg—were still under the Catholic control of Spain. But the northern Netherlands, then named the Dutch Republic and what would eventually become the modern-day country known as the Netherlands, was very much Protestant.

At the time, few European countries could claim full religious freedom for Protestants. That made the Dutch Republic a huge attraction for many Protestant families and congregations displaced by all kinds of religious persecution. The Scrooby Separatists were no different. This influx of people from all walks of life was a small part of what would eventually catapult the Dutch into a position as one of the most wealthy and influential nations in the colonial era.

* * * *

Even though Reverend Clyfton and John Robinson had decided on a destination for their emigration, their troubles were far from over. In fact, they were only just beginning.

As William Bradford would soon find out, escaping to the Dutch Republic was no mean feat. For one thing, passage to the Netherlands cost money—money that many of the members of the Scrooby congregation just didn't have. After all, these were ordinary, rural people, farmers, and tradesmen; most of them were low on the social totem pole. For another, the English authorities were not going to simply allow these criminals to simply slip out of the country. The Separatists would have to be smuggled across the sea to the Dutch Republic at considerable cost and danger.

Nonetheless, the danger of staying in England quickly began to outweigh the danger of planning an escape. For young William, this was a monumental decision, but it appears it was one that he made without a second thought. Leaving England behind would mean the loss of many things that must have been dear to him: the few family members he had left, the countryside he knew and loved. It would appear that no other members of the Bradford family had joined the congregation.

Yet, in the five years that William had been with the Separatists, they had become closer to him than his own blood relatives. He wasn't about to let them go to the Dutch Republic without him. He decided to emigrate right alongside them, a decision that set his life on a path that would later take him all the way across the Atlantic.

Now, though, he just needed to get across the British Channel. To do so, he and several others had no choice but to place their lives in the hands of a smuggler they didn't know. These upright Puritans had had little contact with the criminal underworld, but now they waded into it, having no choice but to make use of illegal methods to escape persecution. They met with a sea captain who agreed to slip them across the channel in his ship—for a pretty price, of course.

William was among the group of people who embarked on the journey across the channel with the captain. It was late in 1607, and he was no more than seventeen or eighteen years old; he must have been absolutely terrified as they were loaded into the hold of the ship. But they never left the port. Instead, the captain betrayed them, calling the Anglican authorities on them. Enforcers for the Church of England rushed into the ship, dragged William from his hiding place, and hustled him off to prison.

The terrified Separatists found themselves locked up behind bars like thieves or rapists. Even though their stay in prison was ultimately brief, it must have been a frightening experience for these ordinary husbands and wives, farmers, and craftsmen. Their only crime was what they believed and trying to escape the country that refused to let them believe it.

One would perhaps consider it forgivable if the Separatists had renounced their beliefs and turned to quieter lives in the English countryside after being released from prison. Instead, prison only made them all the more determined to escape.

Over the next two years, the Scrooby congregation slowly trickled out of England in small groups, smuggled to the Dutch Republic family by family. William Bradford would only leave Nottinghamshire in 1608. This next attempt at escape was successful. This time around, a different captain made good on his word and carried young William all the way to the capital of freedom—Amsterdam.

* * * *

While the Dutch Republic offered religious freedom to the Separatists, it proved to be anything but a paradise. Although this new land allowed immigrants to build whatever churches they pleased, it still held plenty of troubles for the English Separatists who fled there.

The first was glaringly simple. These were ordinary English folk, most of them poor, none of them wealthy, and they more than likely spent every penny of their savings to reach the Netherlands in the first place. They had lost everything: their homes, communities, and, in many cases, parts of their family. They now found themselves in an alien environment, many of them with children to feed and households for which to care. As much as they wanted to build a church of their own—now that they were allowed to do so—they were immediately confronted with the simple necessity of survival.

William Bradford was no exception. In fact, nineteen-year-old William had nothing at all in the Dutch Republic: no knowledge of Dutch, no work experience, no real skills, and no family. As always, Brewster was the one who stood up for young William and took him in. William moved in with the Brewster family in Amsterdam, and he stayed there with them for some time.

Other key members of the Scrooby congregation also made it across to the Dutch Republic, including Reverend Clyfton and John Robinson. In fact, Robinson was becoming more and more important in the spiritual lives of the Separatists. He would later become known as the "pastor of the Pilgrims," even though he himself would live out the rest of his days in the safety of the Netherlands.

Amsterdam, however, quickly proved almost impossible to navigate for the Separatists. The city was bustling with Dutch people who needed to work as well, and these English speakers were automatically at a disadvantage when it came to finding gainful employment. The work they eventually did find was, for many of them, hard. Most of them may have been skilled craftspeople back in England, but now they were forced to take whatever they could get, and much of the work was hard manual labor that paid a pittance and was both difficult and dangerous. As a result, the children had no choice but to be sent to work too; children as young as six or seven years of age could be put to work in the textile industry. These families had come to the Netherlands to worship, but it felt to them as though they did little other than work.

Many of the Separatists ultimately decided to move out of Amsterdam, with Brewster, Robinson, and William Bradford being among them. The town they chose for their new home was a picturesque small town named Leiden. They hoped that this environment would be more akin to the world they had known in the village of Scrooby and that there would be land to farm instead of factories to work in.

Even in Leiden, things didn't improve immediately. The part of Leiden to which the congregation had relocated was called Stink Alley for a reason. It was a narrow little street, lacking the gabled churches and tall buildings of the upper-class part of Leiden, and it lived up to its unprepossessing name. It was a long way from the prosperous manor and the rolling fields of farmland that Brewster and Bradford were used to. Nonetheless, it had one key quality that beautiful England didn't: Stink Alley allowed the Separatists to believe whatever they wanted. Brewster continued to keep Bradford fed and clothed, and the family struggled on together, attending regular services led by John Robinson.

Still, their troubles continued. Even though an uneasy truce had been achieved between the Dutch Republic and Spain, it was more of a ceasefire than any real peace. The Dutch continued to demand religious freedom for Protestants in the Spanish territories, while the Spanish demanded the same for Catholics in Dutch lands. Even though there was no real violence in the Dutch Republic while the Separatists were there, it was evident that tensions were still on the rise. The Dutch were steadily building up a bigger and bigger navy, and there was news of battles at sea. It was evident that a renewed war was inevitable.

One Englishman, John Carver, had managed to hold on to a significant fortune, but he nonetheless suffered during those early years in Leiden. John Carver would later become one of the most important men aboard the *Mayflower*, but there are almost no records of his early life. In fact, even his birth date and birthplace can only be estimated; he was likely born in England around 1584.

The first records we have that mention John Carver are sorrowful ones. He was living in Leiden with his first wife, a Huguenot named Mary, in 1609 when they welcomed their first child into the world. Tragically, the baby didn't live long. It was buried at the Walloon Church in Leiden in July 1609, and Mary herself followed not long after.

Now a childless widower, even though he was only around twenty-five years old, Carver was alone and grieving when he met a Separatist woman who would change his life, his faith, and his ultimate destiny. Her name was Catherine White, and she was Pastor John Robinson's sister-in-law. Catherine was as fervently Separatist as she was attractive, and it wasn't long before Carver fell head over heels in love with her and with her faith. He married her and joined the Separatist church at an unknown date in the 1610s. Even though he was a little late to the Separatist party, Carver would soon prove to be an avid believer, quickly becoming friends with Pastor Robinson and ultimately reaching the rank of deacon in the Separatist church of Leiden.

For William Bradford, things began to look up in 1611. He turned twenty-one and became eligible for the inheritance his father had left him. Somehow, despite the fact that he had left England illegally, he still managed to get his hands on the money. He was by no means rich, but it was enough for him to buy a modest house and set up a workshop on the ground floor, where he became a weaver of rough, cheap fabric used to make men's clothing. His life was perhaps a long way from his family's yeomanry, but it was an honest living. In 1613, he married a pretty English girl who lived nearby, named Dorothy May. The Separatist church had not written a marriage ceremony as of yet, so they were wed in a civil ceremony instead. Four years later, Dorothy gave birth to their first child: a little boy named John, perhaps in homage to John Robinson, who was still their pastor.

Many of the other Separatists were not so lucky. William Brewster, for one, had set up a successful Protestant press that produced anti-Church of England matter regularly throughout the late 1610s; these were proscribed in England as well, and Brewster often found himself under scrutiny from English authorities. He narrowly escaped persecution several times, most notably in 1619 when King James I's lackeys tracked him down and sought to kill him. The University of Leiden, however, was quick to protect him. Brewster had to be very careful for a while, but he was not imprisoned.

Yet, perhaps nothing was as hard for the Separatists as the change they saw in their children once they started to grow up in the Netherlands. By the mid-1610s, small children were becoming teenagers and seeking their own identity in the world. Like most young people, these children were more apt to ape their peers than their parents, and as a result, their parents felt that their English identities were slipping away. The young people picked up Dutch far more easily than the elders, and they were more accepted in the community, getting along with their Dutch neighbors more easily. It felt to the older Separatists as though they were losing their children and growing ever more alone in the world.

By the late 1610s, it was clear that a change would have to be made. The Separatists of Scrooby had no choice but to leave Leiden behind after a decade of living there. They needed to find a new home, a home where they would be allowed to live in peace. They needed to think completely out of the box. And they would have to find a whole new way of living.

What better place could there be to do this than the New World itself?

* * * *

By the time of the Scrooby Separatists, the concept of the New World was not quite so new anymore to the Europeans, but it was still largely unexplored. Even though it had been more than a century since Christopher Columbus stumbled upon the Caribbean islands in his quest for India in 1492, efforts to colonize North America had been largely unsuccessful.

Spain made short work of putting colonies in Central and South America, butchering and enslaving the native people as they went. But it was only during Elizabeth I's time that the English truly started to stake their claim in the New World, a land that had been inhabited for centuries by Native Americans. The English, like most Europeans, had no qualms about marching in and taking their ancestral homeland, and they started to found colonies there late in the 16th century. Elizabeth I had a keen interest in exploration, and her privateer, Sir Francis Drake, circumnavigated the globe in the 1570s. She also sent another courageous sailor off to North America in a bid to establish a colony for England: Martin Frobisher.

Frobisher sailed for North America, but he ended up stumbling upon Greenland instead, where he attempted to establish a small colony in a frigid bay. After this proved impossible, he headed for the coast of the modern-day United States, claiming it as "New Albion" for England in 1579. The naval powers of the Old World raced to snatch up their piece of land; England had to move fast if it wanted its part in invading North America.

Sir Walter Raleigh was the first Englishman to attempt establishing a permanent colony in North America. Sent by Elizabeth, he set sail for the coast of modern-day North Carolina in 1584. Together with a little band of 117 English people, he built a fort and named it Roanoke.

Understandably, the native people of the area—the Croatans—were less than pleased with this invasion. This group of English treated the Native Americans with arrogance and cruelty, and several skirmishes broke out between the colonists and the natives. Still, the colony held on for three years, long enough that its governor, James White, believed that it was time for more people to come to Roanoke and grow the colony.

He made the long and perilous voyage back to England in 1587 and ended up being stuck there, with absolutely no communication with the colonists, for three long years. White finally returned in 1590, and he expected to find a burgeoning colony of English people still clinging tenaciously to the wild world they'd discovered. Instead, he found an utterly empty village. Not a soul was left alive within it; there was only a single word carved into a post: "Croatan." This was the name of a nearby island as well as of the natives, and White held out hope that the colonists had moved to the island and abandoned their village. Although it is possible that is what happened, the truth is still unknown today. The colony simply disappeared.

During the rule of King James I, the first successful English colony was established. Unlike his predecessor, James was not interested in investing in land in the New World: instead, he wanted to make money off it as quickly as possible. As a result, he auctioned off strips of land on the coast of the modern-day United States, selling them to large companies in England. One was the Virginia Company of London, which was quick to stake its claim. In 1607, it sent a group of men and boys to modern-day Virginia.

They built a fort there and named it Jamestown, and almost instantly, they were assailed by countless difficulties. For one, the winter was freezing, and without the proper infrastructure, many colonists couldn't survive the cold. Another issue was disease, although it should be noted that the Native Americans suffered far more from the Old World diseases the sailors had brought with them. This was yet another reason for the Native Americans to resist the onslaught of Europeans into their land, and there were regular clashes between the Powhatan tribe and the Jamestown settlers.

To make matters worse, the Virginia Company of London was growing impatient with the lack of profits from Jamestown. There had been rumors that Virginia was rich with gold, yet miners had little luck finding any at all. Money and resources grew short as men died of disease and fighting, and the colony seemed doomed until 1612. That year, John Rolfe began to cultivate tobacco seeds from the West Indies in the rich Virginian soil, and the crop proved to be as popular as it was prolific. When the Jamestown settlers started exporting tobacco to England, the colony began to make money, and its future grew more certain.

John Rolfe would once again be an instrumental figure in Jamestown when he made peace between the English and the Powhatan two years later. In 1614, he married a Powhatan princess named Matoaka. She would go down in history by her childhood nickname, "Little Mischief," or Pocahontas.

The peace only lasted eight years, but it was all the time the colonists needed for Jamestown to grow into a successful and thriving settlement. By 1619, women were arriving by the shipload to join their husbands or marry new ones. The population began to grow, families were established, and the luckless Powhatan had to face the terrible truth: the Europeans had taken their land, and they were there to stay.

* * * *

The Separatists, like Bradford, Carver, and Brewster, knew by then that colonization was possible in the New World. Jamestown's success had proven that the English could find a foothold in the American wilderness. Still, the very thought of leaving the civilization they knew and traveling all that way into the unknown was still a fairly crazy one for many reasons.

The first was simply that this little group of English exiles was still largely penniless. Although John Carver and William Bradford both had made a fair fortune for themselves over the years, they were in the minority, and even they couldn't dream of singlehandedly funding a venture such as this one. There was a reason why James I had auctioned off the New World to the highest bidder: even the Crown didn't always have the budget for financing expeditions and new colonies. Large, wealthy corporations like the Virginia Company of London stood to lose thousands of pounds in failed colonies. Buying ships, supplying provisions for the voyage, collecting enough tools and resources to start civilization as the Europeans knew it from scratch on an entirely new continent—all of that cost far more money than the Separatists could even dream of.

Another problem was that the ordinary people of the Separatist community were not survivalists, adventurers, soldiers, or even sailors. They were just ordinary farmers and merchants; they had none of the experience required to survive in the hostile wilderness that was Virginia at the time. They would face the full wrath of Mother Nature in her rawest and purest form out there, not to mention the native peoples.

Simply put, it was unheard of for ordinary and often penniless people to simply decide they wanted to move to the New World. One only went there if one was sent by a country or a company. But the Separatists were certain of what they wanted. To them, their journey would be one of faith, and it is for this reason that they became known as the "Pilgrims" centuries after their historic voyage. They had no way of knowing that a nation would ultimately be founded on their shoulders.

Accordingly, the Pilgrims began to search for creative solutions to their problems. John Carver, now a very active member of the Separatist congregation, was one of the first to start negotiating and coming up with solutions for getting to the New World. By 1617, the same year he once again had to bury a newborn child, Carver was already starting negotiations with the English Crown for land in Virginia.

Asking an Anglican king, who had already driven them out of the country, to permit a Protestant colony on a whole new continent was already a significant obstacle. It was one that Carver ultimately overcame, but even that was less daunting than the sheer fact that the Pilgrims didn't have the money. They needed financing.

Seeking a solution, and with negotiations underway between Carver and the Crown, many of the Separatists began to move from Leiden back to England, once again living out their faith in secret in order to be in a better position to prepare for the voyage ahead.

William Bradford was among them. In 1619, he sold his house in Leiden and moved to London, taking his wife Dorothy and little John with him. Religious freedom was still a long way from coming to London, but it would seem that Bradford still managed to become a fairly successful merchant. He was one of the few Pilgrims capable of making a fair amount of money, but no matter how hard Bradford worked, he would never be able to make even a tenth of the amount of money necessary to take the Pilgrims to the New World.

Back in Leiden, John Robinson got to work encouraging and upbraiding his people for the next great step they were going to take. He considered America to be a "New Israel," a promised land flowing with milk and honey where they could build up a nation according to his beliefs. It was a fantastical idea, one that arguably never came to fruition. But it drove the Pilgrims to this historic undertaking.

Knowing that they needed the backing of some large company to finance the expedition, the Pilgrims approached numerous companies in the hopes of striking a deal. They were uninterested in profits; they just wanted to farm American soil and practice their religion in peace. While no single company was willing to take the gamble on this ragtag group of religious outcasts, a group of rich men led by Thomas Weston decided that pooling their resources would spread the risk and still have the potential for a good return. They formed a group known as the Company of Merchant Adventurers of London and agreed to fund the trip to the New World provided that the Pilgrims furnish them with resources like furs, fish, and, especially, tobacco, which they would sell in Europe at a good profit.

The Merchant Adventurers invested the equivalent of half a million US dollars in today's money, and the Pilgrims were ready to begin preparations for their voyage.

Little was known about "Virginia" and its geography at the time. The Pilgrims knew that the Hudson River existed and that it ran out into the sea at a point hundreds of miles north of the settlement of Jamestown. Even though

Jamestown was flourishing at the time of the Pilgrims' preparations around 1619 and 1620, the Pilgrims had no desire to mingle with the settlers there. The settlers of Jamestown were all loyalists to the English Crown, and the last thing that Bradford, Brewster, and the others wanted was to continue living under the thumb of the Church of England. While they would still technically be citizens of the British Empire when they moved to America, the Pilgrims knew that putting the Atlantic Ocean between them and King James' zealots would give them as much freedom as they had ever had in the Dutch Republic, if not more.

Eager to start establishing Britain's power in the New World, King James was suddenly far more amicable toward the Separatists when their plans were revealed. He finally allowed them to legally separate from the Church of England as long as they left peacefully.

Instead of settling in Jamestown, the Pilgrims elected to establish their colony at the mouth of the Hudson River, the location of modern-day New York City. That would put them at a safe distance from Jamestown and the Anglican Church's lackeys. They hoped to establish a peaceful little farming village, where they could tend tobacco crops to appease the Merchant Adventurers, build any kind of church they wanted, and raise their children to be both fully English and fully Protestant.

This dream had in large part been conceived by John Robinson, but like the biblical Moses, he would never set foot in the promised land himself. Robinson was an old man by the time the Pilgrims began their preparations, and he knew that the young and strong would have a better chance at surviving in the New World. Instead of joining the other Pilgrims, Robinson chose to stay behind in Leiden and minister to the English people who remained there. The plan was to ultimately relocate the entire Scrooby congregation to the New World; sadly, for Robinson, he would die before that plan ever came to fruition. Even though he himself never made the pilgrimage, he would go down in history as the "pastor of the Pilgrim Fathers."

Instead, a stalwart and faithful younger man would have to be selected from the Pilgrims' ranks to be their leader on the voyage and in their new home. The choice was easily made. Ever since he had lent out his manor house as the site for secret meetings back in Scrooby more than a decade ago, William Brewster had been one of the staunchest supporters of the Pilgrims' cause. From printing Protestant material in English to becoming a father figure to young William Bradford, Brewster had proven himself many times over to be a worthy leader.

Under his leadership, plans rapidly began to take shape during the first half of 1620. Now that they had procured finances, they needed two more things: ships and sailors to man them. None of the Pilgrims were particularly skilled in that regard. They would need a large ship to carry their congregants and supplies across the Atlantic, but they would also need a ship that could stay behind with them, facilitating fishing and exploration around the mouth of the Hudson. Still, even with the backing of the Merchant Adventurers, the Pilgrims' budget was still very limited. It was decided that they would lease the larger ship and purchase a tiny vessel, something barely adequate for crossing the Atlantic.

This smaller ship turned out to be the *Speedwell,* a sixty-ton English-built ship that had seen better days. Built in 1577, the *Speedwell* was already well over forty years old by the time the Pilgrims purchased her. She had been built for the English navy, where she had originally been named *Swiftsure,* and had survived plenty of action when war raged between the English and Spanish in the last few years of the 16th century. In fact, the *Swiftsure* had faced the might of the Spanish Armada and survived.

After the battles, the *Swiftsure* had been part of an expedition to the Azores, a chain of islands in the Atlantic near the coast of Portugal. She had been one of the first English ships to sail those perfectly blue waters, and she had done her country proud in exploration as she had done in war.

But that had been many years ago. She had been younger then, faster, and not in the decrepit state of disrepair in which the *Speedwell* was when the Pilgrims bought her. She had been decommissioned years ago, hence the change of name, and despite the optimistic moniker, the *Speedwell* was neither speedy nor did she go well at all. But she was all that the Pilgrims could afford. She was docked at Amsterdam, from whence she would take the Pilgrims who were still living in Leiden across to England and rendezvous with the larger ship.

The *Speedwell*'s name would largely be forgotten by history. But the larger ship's name would become recognizable all over the world, ringing down through centuries of history: the *Mayflower.*

Chapter 3 – The Passengers of the Speedwell and the Mayflower

Illustration I: A replica of the Mayflower.

Christopher Jones had no idea that his name would go down in history as the man who brought the Pilgrims to their promised land.

Jones had been born in 1570 to English parents in Harwich, Essex. His father, a trader, had been the partial owner of a merchant vessel named the *Marie Fortune*, and there may as well have been seawater in Jones's blood. The storm-tossed horizon had always called young Christopher's name, and so, when his father died and his mother remarried when he was only a teenager, there was only one place that he wanted to go: the open sea.

Jones was not yet eighteen when he first stepped aboard a sea-bound ship, and he quickly found the work addictive. With a whole new world to explore and trade bustling between England and the rest of the world, there was no shortage of ships on which a capable and driven young man could be given a job, and Jones made it his mission to making something of himself out at sea. He likely inherited his share of the *Marie Fortune* when he came of age;

combining this with his hard work, Jones was determined to become a successful trader and seaman, just like his father.

It would take time, but Jones didn't quit. There was something about those tossing waves that he just couldn't get enough of. Still, it was only after his first wife, Sara, died in 1603 that Jones really started to reap the rewards of his efforts. He married his second wife, Josian, only a few months after Sara's death; not long after that, Jones finally made enough money to have his own ship built. She was a splendid thing, too, bigger than most mercantile vessels at 240 tons. He loved and admired her, and accordingly, he named her the *Josian*.

The *Josian* became the foundation of Jones's business sailing to and fro across the English Channel, exchanging Bordeaux wine for English wool. His fortunes grew, and so did his family: the human Josian proved to be just as fruitful as her naval counterpart, and she gave birth to four children over the next few years.

Meanwhile, as Jones was sailing back and forth across the channel and as his family was growing robustly in Harwich, a ship was being built in that very same port. History took absolutely no notice, and for good reason. This ship was one of thousands of plain old merchant vessels being built all over the world. There was absolutely no difference between this ship and all the others; it was of a mediocre size at around two hundred tons, and it had a perfectly ordinary design with three masts. Even its name was a common one; in fact, twenty-five other ships shared the same name. Its owners had dubbed it the *Mayflower*.

Christopher Jones, too, was becoming a well-off but thoroughly ordinary merchant captain. The *Josian* had made him a modest fortune, and Jones was earning a reputation as a pleasant man who had perhaps a little too much disregard for the law at times; he was fined for keeping a pack of hunting dogs, an activity that was legally restricted to only the nobility. Despite this, Jones was making good money, and his family was continuing to grow.

In 1609, Jones sold the *Josian*. She had served him well, but it was time for a new venture, and that venture proved to be a 25 percent share in a new merchant vessel: the *Mayflower*. She proved to be just as lucrative as the *Josian* had been, and Jones was contracted to take longer voyages out onto the open sea, including a long trip to Norway to bring back a cargo of herring and even a whaling expedition out on the ocean.

Over the next several years, Jones would captain the *Mayflower* through many trade voyages, carrying everything from hops to hats to Spanish salt and more. In 1611, he moved his family to Rotherhithe near London; here, Josian bore him four more children.

Life was good for Jones. Yet, there must have been a part of him that hankered for the open sea. And when Thomas Weston, an unscrupulous businessman and a chief member of the Merchant Adventurers, approached him with the opportunity to take the longest voyage that the *Mayflower* had ever attempted, Jones was eager to say yes.

* * * *

As much as the Pilgrims were strictly devout, most of the Merchant Adventurers were anything but. Thomas Weston was chief among them.

Weston had been born in 1584 and grew up to become an ironmonger. He proved to be good at his trade and quickly began to expand it, changing from having a simple ironmongery business to shipping cargoes across the English Channel and cutting every corner he could to maximize his profits. He often skipped out on paying customs, no matter what kind of fraud he had to commit in order to get this done, and he also had no scruples about transporting illegal goods to England and selling them there.

Perhaps Thomas Weston would have dealt in cocaine or heroin today. But 17th-century Europe had a very different form of contraband: Protestant books and pamphlets. The Reformation was sweeping across many parts of Europe, continuing to cause division everywhere it went, and word was spreading. Much of it spread by the hand of smugglers. The Puritans in England were eager to get their hands on more Reformation material, by any means, and Weston was all too happy to smuggle it to them—at a price.

It was through his work smuggling Protestant material to England that Weston ultimately ended up meeting the Pilgrims. One of his partners in crime married a Separatist, and so, Weston was one of the first English businessmen to get involved with the Pilgrims, helping to start the Merchant Adventurers.

He was also given the task of finding a ship to accompany the *Speedwell* to America. This one would have to be far bigger, one capable of carrying the people, resources, and livestock required to start a whole new life on a different continent, but it could be returned to England when the voyage was over. Accordingly, it was decided to charter the second ship instead of buying it, and so, Weston approached Jones to lease the *Mayflower* and her crew.

It's uncertain why Jones agreed to a voyage that was so different from anything he'd ever done before. The *Mayflower* was a merchant vessel and a small one at that; it was nothing like the strong ships that had made the long journey before. This venture was far riskier than simply moving wool and wine between England and France. Perhaps Jones had been out on the open sea before, back when he was just a teenager looking for his place in the world. And perhaps there was something about those untold fathoms of water, about those distant lands and vast skies, that could never be replaced by any amount of success or fortune.

The Pilgrims had finally procured two ships in which to travel to America, and their destination was set. Still, they needed one more thing: a military man to keep them safe. That man turned out to be Myles Standish.

* * * *

The Pilgrims were well aware that one of the greatest threats they would face in America would be the Native Americans. Even though a tenuous peace still existed between Jamestown and the Powhatans at the time, there was no guarantee that the indigenous peoples of the Hudson River area would be at all welcoming—a fact for which it is impossible to blame them. Even though the Europeans saw themselves as courageous explorers who were given a divine right to claim the New World for themselves, what they were to the Native Americans was something entirely different. They were just barbaric invaders, plundering their lands.

Fearful of the threat, the Pilgrims knew they would need military support. They also knew they couldn't possibly afford to hire mercenaries for their protection, but they would ensure they had at least one military man travel with them in order to keep them safe. The first man they approached was an obvious choice: John Smith.

Smith had been instrumental in the founding and protecting of Jamestown in its early days. In fact, it may not be too much to say that he almost singlehandedly ensured its survival. An experienced soldier and reckless adventurer, Smith had explored much of Virginia, and he would undoubtedly be well suited to the difficult task ahead.

What was more, when the Pilgrims approached him in England, Smith was anything but reluctant to return to the New World. However, the price he gave them was impossibly high. In addition, the Pilgrims found themselves disillusioned with the type of man this fabled explorer had turned out to be. He was everything that they'd heard—strong, fearless, experienced—but he wasn't a Separatist. In fact, the Pilgrims found him to be arrogant and overbearing, and they feared that appointing him as their military adviser would be to subject themselves to needless tyranny.

Instead, the Pilgrims decided to turn to someone else, a man that they knew personally: Captain Myles Standish.

Like John Smith, Standish wasn't a Scrooby congregant, nor is there any evidence that he ever became a Separatist at all. In fact, he had spent his earlier years putting his life on the line for queen and country. Born in 1584, probably in Lancashire, Standish had first seen action during the Dutch Revolt that had split the Dutch Republic from the southern part of the Netherlands. Queen Elizabeth I considered it more important to fight her lifelong enemies, the Spanish, than to oppress the Protestant Dutch Republic, and she allied herself with the Dutch in order to fight Spain. Standish was one of the many young English soldiers who would have their first taste of battle in the Netherlands.

Standish likely journeyed to the Netherlands around 1603, the same year that Queen Elizabeth died. Still, he would fight there for a year, likely under the command of Sir Horatio Vere. By the time the Treaty of London was signed in 1604, Standish had seen enough of the Netherlands to know that he wanted to settle there.

It's unclear where Standish spent the next fifteen years. It is possible that he traveled back and forth between the Dutch Republic and England a few times, but by the time the Pilgrims were making preparations to leave, he was living in Leiden right alongside them. Standish wasn't a part of the Pilgrims' church; in fact, he may have been an Anglican to his deathbed. Still, he was known, liked, and respected by the Pilgrims. What was more, he had risen to the rank of captain during the war with Spain, and he was still a capable military leader.

Perhaps most crucially to the Pilgrims, when they approached Standish with the offer of making him their military adviser, he accepted a far lower offer than John Smith would have even considered. And so it was settled: Standish and the Pilgrims would be sailing to America on the *Mayflower* with Master Jones.

* * * *

By the time the final preparations were being made, the passengers of the *Mayflower* had changed become an increasingly eclectic bunch. This voyage would not only be for the Pilgrims—Thomas Weston made sure of that.

The Merchant Adventurers had only one primary objective with the voyage of the *Mayflower*: to make money. They had already made a huge investment with the purchase of the *Speedwell* and the lease of *Mayflower*, and they were eager to start making an income as quickly as possible. There was one glaringly obvious way to do so: sell tickets to the New World. While the Pilgrims had, perhaps, hoped that only a handpicked group of Separatists would be involved in establishing their new colony, their hopes were quickly shattered by the mercenary agenda of Weston and the others. Soon, the *Mayflower* and the *Speedwell* were fully booked, and not just with Pilgrims but with anyone who could afford to buy their passage across the Atlantic. Or, in the case of the four More children, anyone whose parents wanted to get rid of them badly enough that they would pay for them to be taken to a different continent.

The More children would become some of the youngest passengers aboard the *Mayflower*, and their story was a tragic one from beginning to end.

It started with two fathers who cared little for what their children felt and more for the size of their estates. Richard More of Linley and his brother, Jasper More of Larden, each owned very large and lucrative estates in the English countryside. And while Richard had a healthy eldest son who would ultimately inherit his property—Samuel More—Jasper was not so lucky. His last son had been killed in a senseless and violent duel, leaving Jasper with only a daughter, the pretty Katherine.

As Jasper grew old and faced his own mortality, he realized that the beautiful estate of Larden had an uncertain fate unless he could persuade Katherine to marry well. Yet getting her to willingly marry advantageously appeared impossible. Katherine was already in love with—and secretly engaged to—a lowly yeoman named Jacob Blakeway. He was nothing but a farmer, owning a tiny parcel of land, his birth rendering him automatically beneath Jasper More's notice, but neither he nor Katherine cared. She loved him passionately, and she was intent upon marrying him.

Yet, in 17th-century England, love mattered little when land was at stake. Jasper and Richard cooked up a scheme that would keep Larden in the family once Jasper died. Richard's son, Samuel, would be forced to marry Katherine; Richard would then become the master of both estates, and ultimately, the entire inheritance would pass to Samuel. At least then, both Larden and Linley would remain the property of the More family. The alternative was unimaginable: Jacob Blakeway would inherit Larden if he married Katherine. It was simply unthinkable for a common oaf like him to possess such a vast tract of land.

Whether Katherine liked it or not, she had no choice. She was wed to Samuel in 1611, and they moved to Larden together to begin five years of a miserable and loveless marriage. Katherine and Samuel had both been forced into this decision: Katherine by her father and Samuel perhaps by greed or by pressure from his own father. At twenty-four, Katherine was six years older than her husband; Samuel, at seventeen, was little more than a boy himself.

Nonetheless, to the joy of the two scheming fathers, Katherine bore her first child to Samuel in 1612—a little girl named Elinor. Another child followed just a year later; this time, it was a boy, an heir who would inherit the combined estates of Larden and Linley. Katherine named him Jasper after her father. The fourth child, born in 1615, was a boy named Richard after Samuel's father—little Richard's grandfather. Or at least, so Samuel thought.

As Katherine continued to bring one child after the other into the world, suspicion began to grow in Samuel's heart. The marriage had been begrudgingly consummated, yet Samuel still spent most of his time in London on business, avoiding his wife in Larden as much as possible. What was more, he was noticing that his children bore far less resemblance to him than he'd expected.

By the time Katherine gave birth to her last child, Mary, in 1616, Samuel was quite certain that the children were not his own. In fact, they strongly resembled the man to whom Katherine had been betrothed: the yeoman Jacob Blakeway.

Seventeenth-century England saw adultery as a chargeable offense, and while Samuel knew that to separate from Katherine would be to endanger the estate, he could no longer bear to look at these children who appeared not to be his own. He sued Katherine for adultery in 1616, and immediately, she found herself in deep trouble. The law and its enforcers had little regard for women, especially women who had been found guilty of infidelity, and Katherine did not deny the adultery charge. She countered by trying to have her marriage to Samuel annulled, arguing that she had been legally betrothed to Jacob Blakeway, which would make her union with Samuel invalid.

But Katherine's promise with Jacob had been made in secret. There were no witnesses, and no one could validate her claim. Katherine was found guilty of adultery, as was Jacob Blakeway. Both faced insurmountable fines.

The poor little children, with four-year-old Elinor being the eldest at the time, found themselves caught in the middle of a legal battle as ugly as any modern-day divorce. Divorce itself was as yet unheard of then, but with Katherine accused of adultery, Samuel could have the marriage annulled. He did so, and in the process, he gained control of the children. If Katherine had hoped that her beloved Jacob would back her up in this difficult situation, she was entirely wrong. Jacob couldn't pay the fines. Instead, he simply disappeared, leaving Katherine all on her own.

Elinor, Jasper, Richard, and baby Mary were torn from Katherine's arms and sent to live with Samuel's parents. They were by no means happy to be caring for these illegitimate children, but Samuel was disgusted by their presence. Katherine herself was sent to live with her parents in London. The plans of the elder Richard and Jasper had backfired badly, for they now had no heirs at all since the children were not Samuel's but Jacob's. In fact, Richard Jr had no blood relation to Richard of Linley at all.

By 1620, when the *Mayflower* was preparing to set sail, Samuel had had enough. In his eyes, the children were nothing but a burden on his parents and an embarrassment to him. When he heard that anyone could book a space on the *Mayflower* to start a new life in America, Samuel realized that it was the perfect opportunity to ship the children far away so that they could never bother him again. He bought their passage across the Atlantic.

The children, who had no comprehension of why their parents no longer wanted them, found themselves being signed over into the care of complete strangers. Even worse, the children were abruptly separated and sent to live with different guardians. Only the two littlest, five-year-old Richard and four-year-old Mary, were able to stay together. William Brewster's heart went out to their plight, and he became the guardian of the two little ones.

Still, even in Brewster's care, the children—and every other passenger aboard the *Mayflower*—had no concept of the tribulation that lay before them. They were boarding their ships to escape hardship. Yet, the hardship they would endure in the next few years would far exceed what they had suffered before.

Chapter 4 – The Sad Fate of the *Speedwell*

Illustration II: Robert W. Weir's Embarkation of the Pilgrims.

For the Pilgrims, the trip to the Atlantic began at the port of Delfshaven.

The journey to Delfshaven was not a long one from Leiden: only about forty miles. Nonetheless, the Pilgrims spent the night of June 21st, 1620, in the port town where the *Speedwell* was docked. Many of their friends came from Amsterdam to spend the night with those who were departing for the New World, and perhaps for the first time since they gathered in William Brewster's manor back in England, the Scrooby Separatists were almost all together again.

Reverend John Robinson, though he had elected to stay behind in Leiden, had made the journey to Delfshaven to encourage his flock before their departure. The only non-Separatists to be boarding the *Speedwell* were Myles Standish and his family. All the others were Pilgrims, hoping for a new life.

It must have felt dreamlike and unreal to be sleeping in Delfshaven that night. For many of the Pilgrims, this would be their last night sleeping in a real bed, on solid ground, for many weeks. They were about to embark on a journey that few had ever attempted, and they were doing it in an unprecedented manner. Many of these Pilgrims had never even seen an artist's impressions of what America looked like. In fact, many modern-day Americans are more familiar with the surface of Mars than many of the Pilgrims would have been with the coast of America.

The atmosphere must have been one of both terror and excitement. The Pilgrims had hope, for the first time, to establish a settlement on their own terms, where their religion and culture could grow unhindered. But there was also so much to fear. They were truly adventuring entirely into the unknown.

After a near-sleepless night for many of the Pilgrims, the next morning began with final preparations to board the *Speedwell.* While, for many, that meant packing up the ship and getting her ready to leave, for Reverend Robinson and the other Pilgrims, their preparations were more spiritual in nature. With a crowd of Dutch onlookers curiously watching, Reverend Robinson preached a long sermon to the assembled Pilgrims. It must have been an emotional moment for him; even though he still planned to travel to America eventually, Robinson must have feared that he might never preach to these people again. After decades of ministering to them, from the secret meetings in Scrooby to the shores of Holland, Robinson finally had to say goodbye. It would be the last time he saw many of the people who were about to board the *Speedwell,* and it would be the last time many of them heard the beloved voice of their pastor, a voice that had guided them through so many trials and difficulties.

The crew of the *Speedwell* began to grow impatient as the sermon dragged on. The tide was going to turn against them if they didn't leave soon. Finally, the Pilgrims were told that it was time to go or they wouldn't be able to go that day at all. Reverend Robinson, overcome with fear and hope, fell to his knees and clutched at the hands of his flock. They, too, knelt down beside them, and all of them prayed together for the journey that they were about to begin.

Tears poured down Robinson's cheeks when he finally said his last farewells. The Pilgrims, pale-faced and nervous, made their way onto the *Speedwell.* Even the onlookers were in tears at the soulful scene before them.

It was to the sound of quiet weeping that the *Speedwell* at last drew away from the port and sailed out onto the English Channel.

* * * *

The journey to Southampton, where the *Speedwell* was due to rendezvous with the *Mayflower,* took about three days to complete. By July 25th, the *Speedwell* was sailing bravely into English waters once more. For many of the passengers, it had been as many as thirteen years since they had last set eyes on their English homeland. There were children among them who spoke English yet had never seen England before, and it must have been with jubilation that their parents could finally show them the land that they had once loved.

Yet, the jubilation didn't last long. Once the *Speedwell*'s passengers had disembarked and gone to see the *Mayflower* and its passengers, with some Pilgrims among them, they quickly found reason to be disgruntled. Not all of the *Speedwell*'s passengers had known that the Merchant Adventurers had sold passage aboard the *Mayflower* to non-Separatists. In fact, more of the *Mayflower*'s passengers were Puritans or Anglicans than Separatists. There was great discontent among the Pilgrims over this issue, and Jones and Brewster had to smooth over some very ruffled feathers. The stark fact remained that without the money these people had paid to undertake the journey, the *Mayflower* wasn't going anywhere.

The Pilgrims were forced to accept this fact, but that didn't mean that they were happy about it. Even though many of the other passengers were simple farmers like themselves or even innocent children like the Mores, the Pilgrims still saw them as the "others" after having spent so many years in their tight-knit Separatist community. So, with considerable arrogance, they labeled the non-Separatist passengers "Strangers" and themselves as "Saints."

The next week saw the passengers spending even more of that money as they prepared to set sail. The *Mayflower* and the *Speedwell* needed to be loaded up, not only with travelers and what personal belongings they could fit aboard but also with enough food and water to supply them for many weeks. Their victuals would not only have to take them across the barren waste of the Atlantic Ocean but also last several months on the American shore itself. It could take months, if not even longer, to establish a self-sufficient colony there; food would be scarce until then. The Pilgrims brought all kinds of foods with them, as well as a handful of livestock—mainly sheep, goats, and poultry. There were also two dogs: a mastiff and a cheerful little spaniel. These animals would have to survive many long weeks in the bucking, rolling, dark hold of a ship before they would be able to stretch their legs or taste green grass again, and their suffering over the next part of the voyage is untold.

Many supplies, resources, and items of equipment had to be brought too. They needed all kinds of tools to construct homes on the new shore, and some of the building materials would have been impossible to find in America. They acquired hammers, nails, anvils, screws, and a gigantic jackscrew, a large device that could be adjusted in order to hold a load or steady a foundation. It was a small thing, but it would prove to be instrumental.

Fearing what they might face on the high seas and in the New World, the Pilgrims also brought with them some artillery pieces. The *Mayflower* wore guns, potentially for the first time, and they were a dark reminder of the fact that the Pilgrims weren't just peaceful travelers journeying to an untouched land. In reality, they were colonizers.

After spending a little over a week docked at Southampton, the *Mayflower*, the *Speedwell*, and their passengers—Saints and Strangers both—were finally ready to leave. At least, they were mostly ready. The *Speedwell* was already starting to give the Pilgrims cause for concern. She was forty-three years old, after all, and had seen much service. And although she had served her previous owners well, she was now beginning to show her age. She started taking on some water in Southampton's harbor. The local shipwrights did their best to patch her up, and the Pilgrims could only hope that she was ready for the long voyage.

On August 5th, 1620, the *Mayflower* and the *Speedwell* set sail together. For a Pilgrim standing upon the deck of one of those ships as they headed out into the British Channel, it must have been a moment of indescribable thrill and excitement, as well as great trepidation. With the wind straining the great sails, the hiss of the ocean along the bow, and the cries of the sailors as they swarmed over the rigging, this was a whole new adventure. They had left England in secret, smuggled in dark cargo holds; they left it again now on the deck of a ship they owned, in stunning summer daylight. The *Mayflower* held a reasonable load of about sixty-five passengers at that time.

Yet, that triumphant moment did not last long. Only a few days later, both ships had to turn back. The passengers had just begun to grow used to the rolling of the ships, and the open sea had just appeared at the end of the British Channel before them when disaster struck. The *Speedwell* began taking on water again. In fact, the leak was so severe that there was no possibility of making it across the Atlantic. She would have to return to England for repairs.

For Bradford, Brewster, and many other passengers aboard the *Speedwell*, this was a tragedy. The journey back to England would take time; repairing the *Speedwell* even more so. During this time, the passengers would still be eating victuals from the holds of the ships, precious food that could not be wasted. Perhaps Brewster and Bradford were already smelling disaster on the horizon. Brewster was responsible not only for his own family (his wife Mary and their two children, Love and Wrestling) but also for tiny Richard and Mary More—and, in a broader sense, for the entire community of hopeful people who had boarded the *Mayflower* and *Speedwell*.

Both ships changed direction and sailed into Dartmouth, arriving around August 15th, ten days into the voyage. Master Jones, Brewster, and Bradford had all hoped to be out on the Atlantic by now and making good progress to America, but their hopes were thoroughly dashed when Dartmouth's shipwrights told them that the repairs would take more than a week. The *Speedwell*'s timbers were pulling apart all over the hull, allowing so much water into the ship that it could ruin her cargo and even sink the ship.

For nine long days, the *Speedwell* and the *Mayflower* lay at anchor. For all that time, the passengers were still living in their bunks. "Our victuals will be half eaten up, I think, before we go from the coast of England," William Bradford wrote dolefully in his journal. Their situation was growing more and more perilous.

Finally, on August 24th—more than a month since the *Speedwell* had set sail from Delfshaven; the Pilgrims had hoped to be more than halfway across the sea by that time— Dartmouth's shipwrights at last finished their repairs. Once again, the *Speedwell* and the *Mayflower* left England and sailed down the British Channel toward open waters.

And after several days, it seemed at last that they were making good progress. The green strip of Land's End, located on the Penwith Peninsula in Cornwall, England, faded behind the ships; the wind drove them out upon the churning waves, and with every mile that slipped past under the speeding hulls, the Pilgrims drew nearer to the land that they had long dreamed of. The *Speedwell*'s creaking old timbers were holding together, if barely. The *Mayflower* was skimming along, with Master Jones at the helm, enjoying the feeling of sailing his own ship across the open ocean. For the first time, many of the passengers experienced the feeling of being surrounded by nothing but glittering miles of water in all directions. Hope rose among the passengers, and they spoke of the new world they were about to experience.

But their trials with the *Speedwell* were not over yet. Three hundred miles out on the open sea, she started leaking again.

This was disastrous. They had already traveled so far. Jones was acutely aware that time was slipping inexorably past and that the foul storms of fall were nearly upon them. They needed to get to America quickly before the summer was spent. But the *Speedwell* was endangering the lives of everyone on board. There was no other choice. Once again, brokenhearted, the *Mayflower* and the *Speedwell* had to turn back. They sailed into the nearest English port, one that would ultimately lend its name to the colony the Pilgrims would establish: Plymouth.

It was September by the time both ships sailed wearily into the harbor at Plymouth, and they were carrying a cargo of deeply disheartened passengers and crew. The Pilgrims had been unhappy at the prospect of a five-week voyage across the Atlantic in the company of the Strangers; they had now been at sea with them for a month already, and they hadn't even left England yet. The berths on the ships were cramped and crowded, the food was dry, and nothing and no one was fresh. Discontent was spreading like a plague, as was the bad blood between the Saints and Strangers. Bradford went as far as suspecting the captain of the *Speedwell* of sabotage. While it seems unlikely that any captain would willingly sign up to cross the Atlantic and then sabotage his ship, especially three hundred miles out to sea, Bradford made a good point in that the *Speedwell* had served many of her masters well since she'd been recommissioned.

Still, it would appear that the more logical explanation for the *Speedwell*'s troubles was that recommissioning. When she left the English navy, the *Speedwell* was refitted with new and far too large of sails in order to make her a faster merchant vessel. She ended up carrying far too much sail, however, and her aging timbers simply couldn't take the strain. They were pulling apart, and the shipwrights at Plymouth had to give the Pilgrims and Merchant Adventurers some very bad news. The *Speedwell* was unseaworthy. She wouldn't be making the trip across the Atlantic, no matter how much money they spent trying to repair her.

Brewster, Bradford, Weston, and everyone else involved in the voyage were absolutely horrified. It seemed as though the entire mission was thoroughly doomed. They had already spent a small fortune buying and repairing the *Speedwell*; the summer was already spent, and at this rate, they would reach America right before winter. There would be little time to establish crops, build homes, and do all the other necessary things in order to survive in a whole new continent. In fact, the Pilgrims came perilously close to abandoning their journey entirely. We may never have known the name of the *Mayflower*, and their failure might have faded into the oblivion of history.

But the Pilgrims were determined. They still fervently believed that they were destined to establish their colony in America and that it was God's will for them to leave Europe behind and build a new settlement just for Separatists. The Merchant Adventurers, too, had invested far too much money in this venture to simply abandon it now. People had paid for their passage across the Atlantic, and they were going to get that passage, come hell or high water. In the next few weeks, the travelers would experience some form of both.

Led by Brewster, Bradford, and Jones, the Pilgrims realized that try as they might, they couldn't all go to America on the *Mayflower*. There just wasn't any room; she was comfortably at capacity with sixty-five passengers aboard her already. The Merchant Adventurers, obviously, turned down the notion of leaving any of the paying passengers behind. As a result, some of the Pilgrims had no choice but to turn back and return to Leiden, their hopes dashed and deep disappointment in their hearts. We don't know how exactly it was decided which Pilgrims would go and which would stay. We do know that many children and women, including several pregnant women, would still stay aboard the ship; most families were kept together, at least in the Separatist community.

Still, it was with a sorrowful heart that many Pilgrims had to give up on their dreams—at least for the time being—and go back to Holland with their tails between their legs. Only twenty of the *Speedwell*'s Pilgrim passengers could make their way aboard the *Mayflower*. By the time all of the paying passengers and the crew were crammed on board alongside the "Saints," the *Mayflower* was far beyond her capacity, even before they added all the extra victuals that the *Speedwell* had been carrying.

The gallant little ship had 102 passengers on board—of which only a few were Pilgrims (41 men and their families)—by the time they were finished, along with all the supplies and animals they needed to keep them alive across the Atlantic and establish a new home on that distant shore. William Bradford and William Brewster, along with their families, were among them; so were John Carver and Catherine, who had seven-year-old Jasper More in their charge. Perhaps he was a substitute for the children they had wanted but who had not survived back in Leiden.

And even when the last preparations were made, the *Mayflower* still lay at anchor for one endless week. A terrible calm had fallen upon Plymouth; hardly a breath of wind stirred, and the *Mayflower* barely rocked on the mirror-smooth surface of the harbor. The days must have slipped by with interminable slowness as the passengers waited, their food ever dwindling, the winter coming ever closer. But finally, finally, on September 16th, 1620, a great wind rose up and tugged at the sails of the *Mayflower*.

As the little ship headed at last out of Plymouth, the mood on board must have been very different compared to the festive air that had surrounded the two ships when they first set sail from Southampton. The Pilgrims had hoped to be treading upon American soil already; now, they were only just setting off from England, bereft of their ship, their money, many of their resources, and even much of their community. Everything was going to be much harder now, not least because they were sailing in the fall, a time when the seas grew ever more dangerous.

If there was any hope aboard that ship at that time, it must have been very subdued. In fear and trembling, the *Mayflower*'s passengers waited silently as the little ship slid quietly onto the open sea at last.

Chapter 5 – Tossed by the Storms

Illustration III: After the Storm *by William Bradford (1861).*

Our story has now taken us back to Master Christopher Jones as he clung desperately to the helm of the *Mayflower* as she courageously butted her way up a mountain of turbulent water. Flecked with spray, the wave towered up into the storm-churned sky, robbed of the stars that were Jones's navigation. Instead, it boiled with clouds, torn apart by a great crack of lightning that ran across the face of the firmament.

The lightning illuminated the terrified faces of the sailors struggling to tame the sails, keeping them bound tightly to the masts, lest the wind take them and run the ship off the very edge of the world.

The *Mayflower* pitched violently on the crest of the wave. She sped down the tossing slope of water, her timbers squealing with the force of her speed. Jones had lashed himself to the helm; the ropes cut into his hands as the *Mayflower* thundered on. She reached the trough of the wave with a bone-shattering thud. A torrent of water washed over the deck, knee-deep and irresistible; Jones only just kept his footing as he clung to the helm.

When he regained his balance and looked up, he saw disaster had come upon them. There was a deafening crack, but this time, it wasn't lightning. It was the mainmast. It had been appallingly damaged, a terrible crack running across the great timber, and the tip of it swayed dramatically in the howling wind. (It is entirely possible that this could have been a main beam.)

But there was no time to worry about the mainmast now, even though Jones knew they'd be adrift and starving on the open sea without it. Another wave was coming—a hundred-foot monster bent on devouring the tiny ship that dared stand against it.

Jones braced himself, and the *Mayflower* once again began her perilous ascent.

* * * *

Jones had known that they were inviting disaster when they set sail from Plymouth Harbor on September 16th, 1620. Summer was the time for sailing, and thanks to the *Speedwell*'s shenanigans, summer had long since passed.

It was into the deadly fall winds that the *Mayflower* sailed, and Jones knew as they left the harbor that the strong wind that drove her now so steadily toward her destination would soon change and become the deadly nor'easter that brought howling storms crashing across the Atlantic.

Still, after leaving Plymouth, the travelers were blessed with nearly five weeks of smooth sailing. For thirty-three days, the passengers of the *Mayflower* only had the usual tribulations to contend with.

The *Mayflower* had been pretty cramped even before the *Speedwell* had had to transfer many of her passengers aboard it. In fact, with sixty-five passengers on board, the *Mayflower* had been filled to the brim. Now, she was uncomfortably full, carrying 102 passengers and a crew of 37. The ship herself was capable of carrying the weight, but relations between the passengers were considerably more strained.

The Saints and Strangers were now crammed almost shoulder to shoulder in tiny living spaces. In the tiny space called the gun decks, which were between the upper deck and the cargo hold, makeshift berths had been made for the passengers. The gun decks had a ceiling that was only five feet high. All but the shortest of people and the smallest of children couldn't even stand up straight in their rooms. Roaming around the deck was not exactly forbidden, but it was generally discouraged by the sailors, who were more accustomed to hauling wool and wine than human beings—landlubbers—who would bumble around and get in their way. There were also many fears that the tossing waves would prove too much for the Pilgrims and that someone would be thrown overboard. It was a fear that would later be dramatically justified. As a result, most of the passengers spent almost every single moment of those sixty-six days at sea in their tiny, cramped living quarters.

The entire area allocated to the passengers was 1,600 square feet: half the size of most modern-day American homes. The space was unbearably tight. To make matters worse, there was no privacy. Couples, single people, and entire families were crammed in there together, and there were no rooms. In a desperate attempt at some semblance of privacy, some passengers tried to made dividers with bits of wood or curtains with whatever fabric they had on hand.

These people had been living in these appalling conditions ever since Delfshaven back in July. However, when they were in port waiting for the *Speedwell* to be repaired, at least there was the chance of some fresh food, whether it was bread, dairy products, or perhaps even fruit or vegetables. Here on the open sea, there was no chance of that. Only preserved meats and hardtack biscuits could survive such a long voyage. Even water would no longer be potable after several weeks at sea; instead, men, women, children, and infants were forced to drink beer. The alcohol was little help for the inevitable dehydration that soon set in. The beer caused throbbing headaches, and on top of that, there was the strength-sapping scurvy from which many soon began to suffer. The beer also did not help with the seasickness.

Most of these people weren't used to sailing at all either. In fact, of every living soul aboard the *Mayflower*, only one had ever been to the New World. Stephen Hopkins had gone to Jamestown in earlier years, leaving his first wife back in England. When she passed away, he returned to the Old World and married a new wife: Elizabeth. She had given him three children and was copiously pregnant with a fourth when they boarded the *Mayflower*. While Stephen was accustomed to these conditions and long voyages, Elizabeth was not. It must have been almost intolerable for her, a heavily pregnant woman in such a tight space, trying to keep three little kids entertained as the long days slipped slowly by.

Elizabeth and Stephen had hoped that she would bring forth their next child in the New World. If things had gone according to plan, they would have been in America for almost two months already. Instead, she went into labor on board that ship—that crowded, dirty ship, where there was no privacy and no room. Assisted by Dr. Samuel Fuller, a Separatist physician and one of the Pilgrims, Elizabeth gave birth to a healthy little boy. His parents aptly named him Oceanus.

America was growing closer. Everyone aboard the *Mayflower* was starting to feel more and more optimistic; the successful birth of a new life, the shimmering beauty of the seas, and the knowledge that the New World was just days away were all heady stuff. But in mid-October, things changed for the worse.

A deadly northeasterly wind began to blow, howling the ominous tidings of approaching disaster. Soon, the beautiful blue sky and the shimmering blue sea were gone, replaced by turbulent clouds and tossing gray waves that grew higher and higher with every gust of wind.

For the next month, the *Mayflower* was buffeted relentlessly by one devastating storm after the other. On deck, Master Jones and the crew suffered as they were washed this way and that, thrown around like rag dolls on the pitching surface of the ship. But things were no better below. As the ship climbed one one-hundred-foot swell after the other, the passengers were thrown all over the gun decks while panicking animals squealed in the hold below. Children screamed, babies cried, women clung desperately to their husbands, husbands clung desperately to their families, and the lonely held on to whatever was closest.

William Bradford would describe that month of awful storms as "a long beating at sea." It certainly felt as though the passengers were being pummeled. Their belongings would have skidded helplessly across the floor of the hold while people and things smashed into one another, bruising one another. The ship creaked alarmingly all around them as though at any moment she might fly to pieces and drown them all. Seasickness was prevalent, and it would have made the stench in the hold, which was already a fog of compressed humanity, grow all the more dreadful.

When the storms were at their peak, tossing great mountains of water over the ship, there was no way to keep anything dry, even within the hold. Sheets of water gushed down over the passengers, drenching everyone and everything they owned. For Oceanus, it was a baptism in seawater; for the other children, it was a dark and terrifying ordeal as they clung to their families, the floor pitching under them, the darkness absolute, and great waves of water washing over them. Everything was soaked—the food, the people, the animals, and even the bedding.

It was in one of these storms that the *Mayflower* suffered her first and only loss of life during the voyage. Dr. Samuel Fuller's servant, a youth named William Butten, died in the midst of one of the storms. It's unclear what took Butten's life, but Bradford described it as a "grievous disease." Whatever the case, Butten became the first *Mayflower* passenger to die. As soon as it was safe to do so, he was buried at sea, and his body sank down into the Atlantic. It must have been a sober moment for all the passengers. Land was nowhere in sight, and it may have felt as though they would all inevitably share Butten's fate.

John Howland, another indentured servant (this time to John Carver), was another man who nearly met his end aboard the *Mayflower* during a storm. If it wasn't for the quick thinking of another sailor, he might have joined Butten at the bottom of the sea.

* * *

Even though Howland was an indentured servant, he was an educated man, and in later years, he would serve as an important secretary and assistant to John Carver. Born in England during the 1590s—likely in 1592—Howland may have become a servant to Carver in exchange for passage over the Atlantic.

Religious controversy was nothing new to Howland's family. Both of his brothers were Quakers, which was part of an even more radical Reformation sect that existed upon the very fringe of Christianity's traditional definitions. Howland himself, however, was a Separatist, and it seemed that servitude was a price he was more than willing to pay in order to be given the chance of a new life in a new world where he could live out the faith in which he so passionately believed.

It appears that Howland's duties as a servant were mostly bookish ones. He had brought little onto the *Mayflower* other than his Bible and some commentaries, and he would help John Carver with making notes and keeping records. Yet, even he couldn't bear the confinement of the gun decks. The unbearably close space, the stench of vomit, the unrelenting crush of people—Howland couldn't take it anymore. In the midst of a crashing storm, he pushed past the other passengers and walked out onto the deck.

That breath of fresh air must have been glorious, with no stench and no vomit, just the cool, clean spray and the refreshing rush of rain in his face. But Howland's relief didn't last long. In moments, he would find out why the captain had confined the passengers to the gun decks.

With the captain striving valiantly to control the bucking, tossing *Mayflower* on the unrelenting waves, every strong arm on the ship was needed to bail water and perform the thousand other duties necessary for everyone aboard to survive. The cracked mainmast tossed in the howling wind, the wet and slippery deck heaved underneath the feet of the crew and passengers, and screams of panic came from below deck as the passengers were drenched with rain and seawater.

John Howland was a bookish landlubber, and he had never seen the open sea before they'd left the British Channel more than a month ago. Now, however, he was forced to find his sea legs fast. The roaring waves towered over the *Mayflower*, dwarfing both the ship and everyone aboard. The whole world seemed upside down and inside out, with lightning crackling from one side of the sky to the other and spray and rain making the air feel almost as wet as the ocean herself.

A mighty swell rose over the deck of the hapless ship. There were cries of alarm, but there was no way John Howland could have escaped what was coming next. His uneducated limbs couldn't keep him upright even on a moderate swell, let alone the hundred-foot monsters the *Mayflower* was bravely climbing. The next thing he knew, a wall of water was rushing toward him. It struck his limbs with breathtaking force, and Howland knew a moment of appalling terror as he was borne off his feet, tossed helplessly on the cascade of rushing water, and then cast overboard.

It is difficult to imagine, let alone describe, the sheer terror Howland must have felt as he tumbled into the dark ocean. The *Mayflower* had been an oasis of civilization, the only proof that other humans even existed, for the many weeks that Howland and the other passengers had been crossing the open sea. Week upon week had slipped past with no sign of any other people, no contact with the rest of the world; there had just been the sea and the ship that had become their home. And now, Howland was looking up at her, at the rough timbers that creaked and whined as they were thrown hither and thither on the waters, and she was his last hope.

The roiling sea was upon him, grasping him, throwing him down into the utter darkness. Water filled his ears, reached for his lungs; noise and pressure crushed him further and further down toward the deep and whatever lay therein. With burning lungs and limbs stiffened by the unspeakable cold, Howland must have felt absolutely helpless—and then his flailing, outstretched hand found something rough and firm. A rope. It was a trailing topsail halyard that had fallen into the sea, and by sheer luck, his desperate hand had grasped it.

Still, with all the chaos on deck, it took several moments for the crew to notice that Howland was missing in the first place. For a few moments that must have felt like an eternity, Howland was towed behind the speeding, bucking *Mayflower*. He held on grimly, knowing that the rough halyard was all that stood between him and certain death. And all the while, he was sinking deeper and deeper, the flickering light of the storm growing fainter and fainter above him. He sank as many as twelve feet, and both his grip and his hope were growing feeble when, finally, there was a great tug on the halyard. A quick-thinking crew member had noticed that something was dragging on the rope and started pulling.

With a mighty effort from the crew, Howland's head was at last lifted above the water, and he clung on to the halyard—tossed all the while in the ocean, slammed at times against the rough timbers of the *Mayflower* herself—as continued efforts were made to raise him. At last, a boat hook was thrown to him, and Howland was pulled from the deadly clutches of the ocean to the comparative safety of the *Mayflower*'s deck.

The ordeal had been terrifying, but Howland was mostly unharmed. He was soaked to the skin, exhausted, and frightened to his very bones, but he was alive, and he would go on to become one of Plymouth Colony's most important figures.

Amazingly, no one else fell overboard during the devastating storms through which the *Mayflower* so suffered. And apart from the luckless William Butten, there were no deaths.

* * * *

Even when the worst of the storms had passed, Master Jones knew that the danger was still intense. It was with grim dismay that he showed the leaders of the Pilgrims, including William Bradford, the extent of the damage to the *Mayflower*'s mainmast.

Bradford, Brewster, and the other Pilgrims felt both helpless and terrified as Master Jones pointed out the terrible crack. The *Mayflower*'s mainmast was her principal method of propulsion. As it was now, it would never be able to take the strain of the wind filling the mainsail, meaning there would be no way for the *Mayflower* to continue her journey to America.

To have come so far and survived so much to be crippled for want of a mainmast—it was too heartbreaking for words. What was worse, Jones wasn't sure where exactly they were at that point. The winds and storms had driven them wildly off course, pushing them much farther north than they had planned, and provisions were running low. It was almost November by then; the passengers had been aboard the ship since leaving Delfshaven in July, and they were exhausted and hungry. Many of them had grown sick thanks to the cold and wet conditions inside the *Mayflower*'s hold.

Now, without a mainsail, even arriving at any form of land would be impossible. Jones and the others had to face an utterly appalling fate: drifting helplessly on the open ocean until madness or thirst killed them all.

In fact, that would have been the end of the *Mayflower*'s story had it not been for the fact that one enterprising colonist had found room in the hold for a tool that many others would have considered a luxury. This man—whom history does not name—knew that building a home in the New World would be challenging enough, so he brought a jackscrew with him: a large tool that could be used for adjusting the foundation of a home.

In a pinch, though, it could also be used to hold the ruined mainmast together. The colonist brought it out, and the men exacted a tenuous repair. It was unorthodox, sure enough, but at least the *Mayflower*'s mainsail could be unfurled once more and billow in the rising wind, allowing her to propel the passengers once again toward their destination.

After all that they had survived, it must have been an emotional moment to see the mainsail once again fill up with wind. The hearts of the men watching must have swelled and lifted just as that expanse of white canvas did.

The storms had subsided at last. Bradford had managed to save his diary despite the wet conditions below deck. He had been writing in it for nearly four months now, and he wrote his first November entry with hope in his heart.

Yet, that hope began to wear thin for everyone on board as one fair day after the other passed, with the *Mayflower* sailing ever on and with no sight of land. The voyage should have taken five weeks. More than seven weeks had already passed, and yet every morning, the Pilgrims rose and saw nothing but rippling ocean in every direction.

Days slipped past. The *Mayflower* butted on resolutely. Master Jones doubted his own navigation skills, wondering if he was reading the stars correctly. At night, silence and darkness spread in all directions, the stars reflecting in the water, making it feel as if the ship was floating in a sphere of endless sky.

Hope was waning in the *Mayflower*'s hold when the glorious cry rang at last through the crisp, still air: "Land ho!"

It was daybreak on the morning of November 19th, 1620, more than three months after the *Speedwell* had first left Delfshaven with those hopeful Pilgrims on board. Their number had been thinned by the loss of the *Speedwell*, and they were all hungry and cold and battered as they ventured on deck in the slowly growing morning light. But hope rose in them all as their eyes finally rested on the most blessed sight any of them had ever seen.

The sun was rising, not over rippling ocean but over solid land.

* * * *

If the Pilgrims believed that their voyage was at an end at last when they finally set eyes on land once more, they were sadly disappointed.

As the *Mayflower* drew nearer to the green strip of land that beckoned to them from the horizon, Master Jones's suspicions were confirmed. They had reached North America, all right, but there was no sign of the Hudson River's mouth, the place the Pilgrims had legally claimed and the only part of the continent to which they had any right in the eyes of Europe.

Instead, the Pilgrims were looking at modern-day Cape Cod, hundreds of miles northeast from the Hudson River.

Although they could see land at last, they had no permission to reach it and feel solid ground beneath one's feet and see real trees and birds and animals and dirt and grass and rocks again—it must have been unbearable. But the *Mayflower*'s passengers felt that they had to honor the agreement they had made with King James, not only to avoid persecution but also to appease the Merchant Adventurers, who had already put a considerable amount of money into this venture and would be highly disgusted to discover that the ship had failed to reach its intended destination and landed on some arbitrary stretch of the American coast instead.

Despite the fact that the nor'easter was still blowing the *Mayflower* ever farther north, Master Jones had no choice but to prolong the terrible voyage. He swung the *Mayflower*'s nose to the south, keeping the land ever on his right, and began to attempt a laborious trek along two hundred miles of unexplored coastline, hoping to find the Hudson River.

The attempt proved absolutely futile. Not only was Cape Cod unmapped, but it was also littered with rocks, and every fathom that the *Mayflower* sailed risked shattering her tired hull on some unseen rock. With provisions running low, many of the passengers sick or starving or simply exhausted by being at sea in those cramped conditions for so long, and the risk of a shipwreck rising with every rock that grated at the bottom of the *Mayflower*'s hull, Master Jones and the other leaders decided that enough was enough. They had risked their lives for long enough, and they would risk them no further. The captain turned the *Mayflower* around and headed back to the last useful bay they had passed.

And so, finally, on November 21st, 1620—122 days after people like Myles Standish, John Carver, and William Brewster had first boarded the *Speedwell* at Delfshaven—the *Mayflower* finally sailed into a small bay and lay at anchor at last. Its passengers gazed out upon solid ground again, and it was a beautiful land, with tall trees all decked out in their autumn colors, soft golden-green hills rising up to meet the horizon, and the bay gleaming like a mirror between the warm and verdant arms of the trees.

The bay would ultimately become known as Provincetown, Massachusetts. But at that moment, it was to the Pilgrims' eyes a complete wilderness.

Before the Pilgrims could land, however, there was one enormous problem to be dealt with. That was the fact that they had been assigned a specific tract of land near the Hudson River. Never mind the fact that the land had never belonged to King James in the first place—it was home to the people who had lived there for centuries. But in the Pilgrims' eyes, they rightfully owned a specific part of the North American continent. Now, though, they found themselves 220 miles northeast of the Hudson's mouth. They were far outside the boundaries of the land they had been given.

But sailing southward wasn't an option. Neither was returning home with their tails between their legs; they had already set sail too late, and they would never survive the storms of the return trip even if they had had enough provisions to make it. They were in America now, and they would have to make a home for themselves here in this bay or die trying.

Still, that left them outside of the boundaries of any European government, a terrifying thought to the order-loving Separatists. There were no laws here, no means of enforcing their religious freedom, no ways of establishing the hierarchy that had been agreed upon back in the civilization of the Old World.

The new colony hadn't even been established yet, and it was already teetering upon the brink of anarchy. There was no way of contacting King James to modify their agreement. There was no one in the world they could consult except the people upon that very ship.

For that reason, it was necessary to think of a whole new system of government and do something that had never been done before. And thus, the Mayflower Compact was born.

Chapter 6 – The First Winter

Illustration IV: William Halsall's The Mayflower in Plymouth Harbor.

During the long journey across the angry ocean, there had been comparative peace between the Saints, the Strangers, and the crew. Even though some of the passengers, like John Howland, had resented the fact that the crew was more or less forcing them to stay below deck, there had been no time for any real conflict. The passengers had been too focused on survival to argue among themselves, and any kind of interpersonal grievance had seemed trivial compared with the terrifying reality of the lurching ship and the unending sea.

But hardly had the *Mayflower* dropped anchor in Provincetown Harbor than trouble began to brew among the passengers. The Saints were still wholly focused on their original goal of establishing an entirely Separatist colony here in the New World, a "New Israel," as Pastor Robinson had called it back in Leiden. That was the whole purpose of their voyage. In their eyes, unless they could build a country upon Separatist principles, they had suffered the long voyage for nothing.

The Strangers, unsurprisingly, found the Saints' attitudes considerably stifling. Not only were the Saints desperate for the Strangers to conform to their vision of what their new colony would be, but they also considered themselves to be more important than the Strangers, as they had planned and organized the mission.

Friction rose sharply as the *Mayflower* rested in Provincetown Harbor, and tensions began to boil over. To make matters worse, now that they were technically outside of the English Crown's territory, it seemed that no one could exercise any kind of authority over the mutinous passengers, whose complaints and angry speeches were stirring up more and more discontent.

Carver and Brewster were both deeply worried about what was going on. Robinson had entrusted the leadership of the Pilgrims during the voyage to them, and they feared that here, on the very doorstep of the new land they intended to inhabit, they were about to be robbed of their hopes and dreams. Drastic action would have to be taken if the Pilgrims were going to live out their dream of a Separatist colony. Something unprecedented would have to be done. Together, the Pilgrim leaders decided to draw up a document unlike any other: the Mayflower Compact.

For most people of the Old World, the very idea of constructing a contract of self-government, a legal document for the government of an entire colony, would have been absolutely outrageous. But for Brewster, it was old news. He had helped to draft vital documents for the foundation of the Separatist church back in England, and the compact was based upon those documents, albeit with one major difference: the Mayflower Compact swore allegiance to King James I.

Brewster and Carver likely worked together on composing the compact, although, to this day, it's uncertain who authored this groundbreaking document. While its very first lines told of how the colonists promised to stay loyal to the English king, it has also been considered one of the earliest attempts at democracy and the foundation of the Constitution of the United States of America, which would follow many years later. Never before had self-government been attempted in a North American colony.

The Mayflower Compact, as recorded by William Bradford, was a short document, hastily composed and to the point. In fact, it is little more than a couple of paragraphs, but it laid the foundation for one of the United States' earliest colonies. In it, the Pilgrims promised to create and abide by "just and equal" laws for the benefit of everyone in the colony. While "justice" and "equality" sounds outrageously inaccurate to modern ears, considering that neither the women nor the Strangers were given any say in the contents of the compact, the document did save the colony from slipping into total anarchy. The compact also promised that the Pilgrims would create one society rather than separating the Saints and the Strangers.

The compact was enforced by the looming presence of Myles Standish, who may have been the only non-Separatist to sign the document. In all, forty-one men signed the Mayflower Compact. John Carver was the first, Bradford the second, and Brewster was the third. Samuel Fuller was there too, as was John Howland.

During the signing of the compact, the men also elected a governor for the colony. This turned out to be John Carver. He had likely been instrumental in composing the Mayflower Compact, had helped to finance the mission, and had been one of the first people to dare to believe in the idea that an ordinary group of people could make it to the New World. What was more, he'd always been a strong leader as a deacon in the church, and the other Pilgrims looked up to him.

It was unorthodox, but it worked. While disunion and occasional squabbles would continue to plague the Saints and Strangers throughout the long winter that would follow, the Mayflower Compact survived as the governing document of the colony for more than seven decades.

* * * *

The Mayflower Compact secured a tenuous peace among the passengers. This must have been much to the relief of Master Jones; although he had no part in constructing the compact and didn't sign it, he must have been worried about the rebellious mood aboard the *Mayflower*. Any captain fears mutiny.

Even though many of the Strangers still muttered in discontent, understandably so considering they had been given no say in the matter, the passengers were nonetheless able to turn their attention to another looming challenge: surviving the oncoming winter.

It was late November by this time, and a New England winter was setting in across the bay where the *Mayflower* lay at anchor. A bitter cold assailed the passengers as they waited in their berths. Their provisions, which had already been lower than they would have liked when they left Plymouth Harbor behind, were dwindling rapidly. They had hoped to have arrived in the New World by the end of August, with plenty of time to plant a few crops that would get them through the winter. But the ground, now, was growing cold and unyielding.

There was precious little water left aboard the *Mayflower* too, and everyone was growing tired and dehydrated from the beer. There wasn't time for dissent. It was time to focus on survival.

The day after the Mayflower Compact was signed, everyone aboard the *Mayflower* followed the Separatists' example and took a day of rest; after all, it was a Sunday. The Separatists prayed desperately that, somehow, their crazy plan would work. They believed that it was God's power alone that had brought them across that treacherous ocean, and indeed, Master Jones would have agreed that surviving the journey had been miraculous. Now, however, they knew they faced even greater tribulation. Little could they have imagined the hardship they were about to experience.

On November 23rd, 1620, the Pilgrims finally left the *Mayflower* behind and ventured onto the shore of the New World. What a blessed relief it must have been to set foot once more upon dry land! And after the bucking, wobbling, crowded, dark, and dingy gun decks of the *Mayflower*, that first breath of clean air, standing on sturdy ground, must have been an inexpressible delight. The verdant colors of the trees, the brilliance of the clear sky...it was all so good and so beautiful. William Bradford described a scene of joy and relief in his journal. The Pilgrims were cold, tired, and close to starving, all of them suffering from sickness, dehydration, and malnourishment, but they had finally reached a free land. Every hill and tree, every valley and bay they set eyes on was beyond the reach of the king who had made their lives so difficult. They could be free at last now, even if they were free only to die.

Their feeble but fervent joy did not last long. Even though everyone was exhausted and sickly, there was work to be done if they had any hope of surviving the winter that lay ahead.

The crew quickly got to work putting together a draft boat that had been taken apart back in England for storage in the *Mayflower*'s cargo hold. Known as a shallop, she was fairly small, but she would carry a few sailors or fishermen where they wanted to go. The shallop was a poor substitute for the *Speedwell*, which would have stayed behind with the colonists, but at least she was something–and she would prove instrumental in finding the bay where they would ultimately establish their colony.

Rebuilding the shallop would take time, however, and time was a luxury that the colonists did not have. Every breeze that blew was colder and tore more and more brown leaves from the trees. There was not yet snow, but hard frosts came in the night, cold enough to freeze the earth. This made everything worse, as little aboard the *Mayflower*, including clothes and bedding, had had a chance to dry out after being drenched during the storms. Finding a place to build homes would be imperative to the survival of the colony, and although the area immediately surrounding the bay was beautiful, it was too rocky and hilly for the colonists to build there.

While they were waiting for the shallop to be rebuilt, the colonists selected a group of explorers–led, of course, by Myles Standish–to venture deeper inland and search for a place where they could plant crops, build homes, and establish the lives they had so long dreamed of.

In early December, Standish and a small group of men set out. The jubilation of their arrival in the New World had given away to a quietly throbbing desperation. The men in that expedition had families waiting aboard the *Mayflower*; they had seen their wives suffer, watched their children weep for week upon terrifying week across that ocean. Their children were emaciated. Their wives were depressed. They had promised them that life would be better out here, but so far, they had gone from poverty and oppression to starvation and danger. They were desperate to help their families.

As they ventured across the countryside, heading through the woods and up and down the hills, the party grew desperate in another way too. There was precious little water left on the *Mayflower*, and the bay in which she now lay was salty. They had taken nothing with them except for a bottle of liquor. It did nothing to slake their thirst as they went onward, and they had been dehydrated enough to start with; what was more, these men had had little exercise in all those weeks at sea, and weakness soon began to overcome them.

They were starting to grow feeble with cold and thirst when they finally found it: the first freshwater spring that the Pilgrims would discover in the New World. It was just a seep of fresh water from the ground, but to those men, it was life. At last, for the first time in weeks, they could kneel down and cup their hands around that abundant freshness and drink and drink and drink until their thirst was slaked at last.

Moving onward, refreshed by their first good drink of water in weeks, the group came across their first sign of civilization: a grave. They had stumbled upon a burial ground belonging to the Native Americans in that area.

From the beginning, the Pilgrims had decided that they would avoid conflict with the indigenous peoples at all costs. For one thing, they weren't warriors; they didn't stand a chance against a group of angry Native Americans defending their homes. For another, they hoped to evangelize the Native Americans, not murder them. More than that, the Pilgrims were different from the Jamestown colonists in that they had not come to the New World for money. They weren't there to plunder the locals and murder anyone who stood in their way of colonizing the New World. Instead, these people were refugees, fleeing from a regime that didn't allow them to live the way they wanted. They were invading the homes of these Native Americans because they no longer had homes to call their own.

Accordingly, Standish and the others hoped to barter with the Native Americans for food and other goods, and they'd brought along some beads, which had historically been successful in trading, to exchange for the things they needed. But desperation and fear now clouded their earlier hopes. When they came upon the grave, they began to dig. No one knows what exactly they hoped to find, but when they uncovered a bow and arrows, it brought home to them the fact that these were people who would fight to protect their homelands. Standish stopped the men, realizing how disgusting the act of disturbing this grave would be. They covered it over with earth again but not before stumbling upon a stash of something that would be more valuable at that moment to the colonists than any amount of gold or jewels: corn.

Although corn was relatively unknown to these English farmers at the time, they knew from reports by other colonists that corn was a key crop in the New World. Native Americans had been growing it there for centuries upon centuries. Growing it would ensure the colonists' survival, and the Pilgrims were desperate.

It's unclear whether they didn't know or just didn't care that the corn hadn't been buried there to be dug up and used again later. It was a sacrificial offering, buried with the dead in order to help them in the afterlife. Standish and the others may have thought that they were just stealing, but in reality, they were desecrating something sacred in the eyes of the native people. Their actions that day would be similar to setting set fire to a church. The Pilgrims did hope, however, that they would be able to find the natives and repay them for the corn they had taken.

After some time, Standish's party came upon a Native American village. The indigenous people of the area—the Nauset—were semi-nomadic, moving from one established village to the other with the seasons. The village that Standish found was completely empty, either because the Nauset had moved southward for the winter or because the terrified inhabitants were hiding from these armed men. Once again, the Pilgrims took several items from the Nausets' homes. They had intended to leave beads behind to trade instead of just stealing, but hunger and desperation made them forget their good intentions toward anyone other than themselves, and so, they simply took what they wanted and carried it back toward the *Mayflower*.

When they returned, at least one piece of good news greeted them. Firstly, the shallop was nearly done, and secondly, another baby had been born in the *Mayflower*'s gun decks. Susanna White, the wife of William White, had hoped that she would have been safely installed in a cozy little cottage by the time her child was born. Instead, she brought him into the world in the filthy berth with no privacy or hygiene.

The little boy was named Peregrine, and he was the first Pilgrim child to be born in the New World and among the first English children born in North America. His elder brother, Resolved, was one of the children who had journeyed to the New World on the *Mayflower*. It is difficult to imagine the desperation and fear that Susanna White must have felt as she wrapped her newborn child in rags. Her boy had been born free, unlike little Resolved, free to worship in whatever way he pleased. But the future was so uncertain, the bitter winter drawing so near, and the baby's plaintive cries split the air with a note piercing enough to break any mother's heart.

* * * *

As soon as the shallop was ready, Master Jones and Standish resolved to explore more of Cape Cod's coastline. Although the land surrounding Provincetown Harbor was pleasant enough, they hoped they would find somewhere easier and more suitable to build their homes, a place with clearer fields and fewer woods.

With the shallop rebuilt, Jones, Standish, and a party of men set sail from the harbor in mid-December. By then, the *Mayflower* had been at anchor for weeks already; the Pilgrims had at least found fresh water, but they were heading toward the dark heart of winter, and they needed to start building homes if they wanted to survive. Jones knew that there was no chance of returning home himself until spring brought fairer weather. The voyage had already been more than he had bargained for, and it was going to take more still.

The shallop cautiously made its way through the treacherous, wintry waters of Cape Cod, heading southwest in search of a safer harbor. Sailing around the edge of the large Cape Cod Bay, the group soon found another, smaller bay: Wellfleet Bay. It was here that they had their first sighting of the Nauset. As the men sailed toward the bay, they saw a group of people on the beach.

The sighting must have been startling in many ways. Most of the men aboard the shallop had never seen Native Americans before except in drawings, and no one present had seen anyone other than a fellow *Mayflower* passenger in months. The people on the beach were crowded around a beached pilot whale, butchering the animal for its meat, fat, bones, and skin. When the shallop drew nearer, however, the Nauset scattered, leaving the bountiful whale on the beach.

Whales were a significant part of the Nausets' diet, as Jones and the others soon discovered when they dropped anchor in Wellfleet Bay and went out onto the beach. A brief exploration revealed more whale carcasses lying nearby. They were near to a Nauset settlement, that much was certain, and this time, Jones, Standish, and the others hoped to make contact and start trading with them. They knew that cooperation with the Native Americans would be integral to their survival.

What was more, Wellfleet Bay was beautiful. The area surrounding it was more level and welcoming than the hilly surrounds of Provincetown Harbor, and the Nausets had cleared many cornfields in the area, making it even more appealing. Standish was confident that he had found the perfect place for the Pilgrims to start their colony.

Still, even though Standish hoped that they could have peaceful relations with the Nausets, he was deeply cautious. The Pilgrims had been told scary stories about Native Americans, born from the regular conflict between the people of Jamestown and the Powhatan. Bradford, in his journal, noted how they had been warned that Native Americans would capture people and then cut off their limbs and cook and eat them in sight of their still-living victims. There is no evidence to suggest that most Native American tribes were cannibalistic; these stories were hyperbole for the most part, told to make the Native Americans seem less human.

Thus, even though Standish hoped that they could make peace with the Nauset, he also intensely feared them. He'd been told terrifying stories of scalping, cannibalism, and thoughtless killings and not the truth of desperate people defending their homes. So, when Standish and the others settled in to spend the night on the beach, they built a barricade around their camp. The men all had matchlock muskets with them, which were inefficient, especially in the hands of these ordinary people, but potentially deadly. Standish himself carried a flintlock musket, which was never far from his reach.

It turned out that he would have need of it. The group had settled in on the beach when a blood-curdling cry filled the air. "Indians!" shrieked a watchman. "Indians!"

Chaos instantly broke loose. Standish's party, clearly not warriors themselves, had left their armor and weapons lying nearer to the water. They panicked and scattered, rushing for their weapons. At once, a volley of arrows rose from the nearby woods, their hiss in the air a harbinger of danger. They punched into the sand, their deadly tips buried in the dirt, and Standish desperately aimed into the woods and fired. Gunsmoke filled the air, and the crack of the firearm echoed across the beach, shattering the peace of Wellfleet Bay.

The skirmish was a brief one. Almost before the other Pilgrims had managed to get their hands on their weapons, there was a cry of pain from one of the Nauset, likely wounded by Standish. The group of Nauset faded into the trees and melted into the landscape, disappearing from view.

Heart hammering, Standish took quick stock of his men. There were arrows all over the camp, but none of the Pilgrims had been hit. Apart from the wounded Nauset, there were no casualties of what would become known as the "First Encounter."

Nonetheless, Standish knew that things could have gotten ugly. The Nauset in the area had clearly had contact with Europeans before, likely with fishermen who had come to the area for its cod or, even worse, with some Europeans who had made a business of kidnapping Native Americans and selling them as slaves in the Old World. The Nausets knew that Europeans brought only danger with them: disease, murder, kidnapping, and theft. They wanted nothing to do with these Pilgrims, no matter how hungry and desperate they looked. And while this skirmish had ended well for the Pilgrims, it appeared that the Nausets' attack might have been little more than a warning.

It was a warning that Standish took seriously as he looked down at the arrows still jammed into the sand. His men weren't warriors; that much was abundantly clear. They could have all been killed, and the Nauset clearly weren't interested in trade. Beautiful as Wellfleet Bay was, the passengers of the *Mayflower* weren't welcome there, and they would have to move on.

Once again, the shallop set sail, following the curving bay of Cape Cod toward the mainland of North America. Buffeted by winter winds, the tiny boat struggled on through the harsh waters, and everywhere Standish looked, he saw unfamiliar territory. They traveled for two cold, hungry days, sleeping on the shallop under the stars.

Standish was starting to despair of ever finding a new home for his people when, on December 10th, they came upon the most beautiful bay that he had ever seen.

The moment the shallop sailed into the bay, Standish knew that it could be home. Unlike the rest of the densely wooded coastline, there were clear fields here, dusted with frost but ready and waiting for the spring. The curves of the bay welcomed the shallop like open arms, and when Standish and the others landed and started to explore, they found more and more good things—and more and more hope. Fresh water was plentiful; there were springs and streams everywhere. The fields had obviously been cleared by human hands, but there was no sign of human habitation.

Standish had found a home for his people at last, a place where they could build something new, something free. They returned to the shallop and set sail back toward Provincetown Harbor to tell everyone aboard the *Mayflower* the good news.

What Standish didn't know was that the area wasn't uninhabited. Its people were just too weak to fight back.

* * * *

Massasoit, Sachem of the Wampanoags, knew better than most that the Europeans were nothing but trouble.

The Wampanoag had many sachems—local rulers or chiefs—but Massasoit was the leader over them all, a high king of an area spanning much of modern-day Massachusetts. His people had been vast and powerful only a few decades ago when Massasoit was a boy in the 1580s in his birthplace of Montaup (modern-day Bristol, Rhode Island). The Wampanoag was not a single tribe but rather a confederacy of Algonquian-speaking people, and it included tribes such as the Mashpee and Pokanoket. Massasoit himself was a Pokanoket, and he rose to power with the cooperation of the lesser sachems.

With Massasoit at the helm, the Wampanoag prospered. Numbering close to seventy thousand people, they had made a tenuous peace with their more warlike neighbors, the Narragansett. The Wampanoag were a peaceful people, building permanent villages and establishing beautiful farmlands. Like the Nauset, they moved from time to time, living in temporary shelters known as birchbark houses in the summer but constructing winter villages with communal longhouses. While they hunted and fished for their food, they were also farmers and grew beans, sweet potatoes, and the all-important corn, among other things. They used dugout canoes for fishing and wore warm, sturdy clothing made with fur and leather.

The land was bountiful, and the Wampanoag thrived. While there were no colonists in Massasoit's area, there were cod fishermen in the bays, and several of the local sachems began to trade with them. While there were some kidnappings, in general, there was peace between Massasoit and the handful of Europeans that came to his lands.

Yet, what no one knew was that the Europeans had unknowingly brought with them a weapon far deadlier than any gun or blade. They had brought Old World diseases—sicknesses against which the Wampanoag had absolutely no immunity. Illnesses such as tuberculosis and smallpox had killed millions of people in the Old World, but the robust sailors who had survived to cross the ocean were thoroughly immune to them. Still, they carried those deadly diseases to the New World with them, and they spread through the susceptible native population like wildfire.

In just a few years, Massasoit had seen his people relentlessly decimated. The illness killed without thought, without purpose. Entire villages were destroyed, vibrant communities turned into graveyards of rotting corpses with no one left alive to bury their dead. Children became orphans, wives were widowed, and chaos reigned.

Massasoit could have tried to fight off an invasion. However, this plague was something that no one could stand against. It spared the sachem himself, but it tore his domain to shreds and crushed his people in an iron fist.

When it was all over and the dying finally stopped somewhat, the Wampanoag were a thin shadow of the thriving people that they once had been. Where there had been bustling villages and well-tended farmlands, there were now ghost towns and empty fields. Where there had been laughing children, there were grieving parents. And where there had been a strong and prosperous people, there was a shattered remnant, grieving, sickly, and afraid. Over forty-five thousand people were dead—two-thirds of the population.

Massasoit had survived the epidemic, but now, the Wampanoags' troubles were far from over. Their neighbors, the Narragansett, had fared better during the plague, and they sought to take advantage of the Wampanoags' weakness and attack them to expand their territories. The threat of invasion loomed over the Wampanoags' heads, and Massasoit knew that his people in their weakened state would never be able to fight it off.

Things only got worse when one of the sachems near the coastline, an Abenaki named Samoset, reported the bad news. More Europeans had come to the nearby bay, in an area surrounding one of the villages that had been abandoned after its people were killed by diseases. They had disappeared after a short while, but now they were returning—and this time, they had brought an enormous ship with them. There were women with them, children even.

The news was grim for Massasoit. If these Europeans had brought their families with them, then they weren't just hunters or fishermen passing by to trade and then go back to the Old World. They were colonists.

Massasoit now faced invasion on two different fronts.

* * * *

The *Mayflower* sailed into the pleasant bay on December 18th, 1620, nearly five months after the Pilgrims first departed from Delfshaven. They had been living in the cramped quarters of the gun decks for 149 days, but now, at last, they had reached the place that would become their new home.

As they began to further explore the area, they saw neither hide nor hair of the native people who had cleared these fields. There was an abandoned village nearby; the Pilgrims appear not to have disturbed it, but they must have wondered where all the people had gone. Perhaps they guessed at the gruesome truth: that Old World diseases had rendered two-thirds of the Wampanoag settlements as empty as this one.

In any case, the Pilgrims didn't see any Wampanoag that winter, and they were grateful that there were no attacks such as there had been from the Nauset. Between the lack of resistance from the indigenous people and the clear farmlands, the Pilgrims knew they had finally found a place to call home.

Like many other colonists, they wanted to name their new home after their old one. They would never have left the English shores they treasured if James's anti-Separatist campaign hadn't forced them to go. Ultimately, they decided to name their new bay after the last English shoreline they had seen:

Plymouth. And so, Plymouth Colony was born—and it was born into struggle and strife.

The European diseases that had wiped out Massasoit's people did not spare the Pilgrims either. Malnutrition and the cold New England winter—a cold for which the Pilgrims were woefully unprepared—cooked up a deadly concoction of disease aboard the *Mayflower*, which was exacerbated by the cramped and unhygienic conditions. As the Pilgrims began to cut timber and put together the first wattle-and-daub cottages, disease swept through them, and it would devastate them nearly as bad as it had devastated the Wampanoag.

Standish's men were among the first to be affected. On several occasions, as they spent the night on the shore during their expeditions, the temperatures had grown so cold that their wet socks had frozen on their feet. Frostbite was inevitable, and the cold was so terrible that some of the men fainted due to it. They were weak enough as it was. A terrible cough and a raging fever followed close on the heels of that cold.

With every cough, those men were expelling droplets of infection into the air. It spread to the rest of the *Mayflower*'s passengers. Before long, the entire ship was echoing with the sounds of illness, and the Pilgrims had to face the fact that they had lost their race against the cold weather. They would be struggling to build their homes in the very depths of a New England winter.

The extent of that struggle for survival is difficult to comprehend. The cold, the starvation, the unrelenting sickness—it must have been too miserable and frightening and depressing to describe. The colonists had left Delfshaven with so much hope. They had just been looking for somewhere to live out their faith in freedom and peace. Instead, they were struggling to cut wet timber, to dig foundations in frozen ground. The men worked as hard as they could when they were well enough to stand, but they struggled on with burning fevers, with chests ablaze with disease because they had no choice. And when they were no longer able to walk, they tossed and turned in the same uncomfortable bunks that had been their unhappy lot since the summer.

It wasn't long before people started to die. People who had made it through that terrifying voyage were now succumbing quickly to the dreaded disease that stole their breath and ravaged their emaciated bodies. Children were dying as their mothers lay suffering beside them. Men watched their wives melt away before their eyes. Women who had loyally followed their husbands across the stormy ocean were now watching as their last hope of security, their last symbol of normality, faded away.

Bradford's description of that dark time is tragic and sobering. Once people started dying, they died at a terrifying rate. As many as two or three people were dying every day. Burying them was nearly impossible in the frozen ground, and it took up time and energy that was so desperately needed in order to build warm homes to save the ones who were left.

The suffering of the sick was appalling. According to Bradford's account, it was bad enough that many Strangers refused to go near their sick fellows, abandoning them to care for themselves. For the Saints, however, it was time to set their differences aside and tend to whoever needed it, whether they were a Separatist or not. Many Strangers who had joined the *Mayflower* expedition in a bid to give themselves and their families back in England better lives now lost the only lives they had, suffering and alone among people they hardly knew.

There were times when so many of the *Mayflower*'s passengers were sick that only six or seven people were left to tend to the ill. Construction of the settlement ground to a halt for days at a time as the handful of healthy people struggled to care for the dying. The sick were so incapacitated that they couldn't bathe or feed themselves. These patient few, themselves still malnourished and cold even if they weren't sick, were forced to feed the sick, turn them over, strip them of their soiled clothes, clean their filthy bodies, and try to keep them warm.

For the Separatists, too, the losses were absolutely devastating. This congregation had survived so much together. They had attended secret meetings in Brewster's home back in Scrooby. They had smuggled one another across the British Channel to Leiden, risking fines and imprisonment all the way. In Leiden, they had stuck together despite the poverty and alienation that they found there. And they had even survived the trials of the *Speedwell* and the harshness of the open sea. But now they were losing friends and family members. For the Separatists, their congregation had been the one constant through all the trials since King James I first started his campaign against them. And now they were losing the people they loved at an incomprehensible rate.

For Susanna White, the mother of little Peregrine, it meant the loss of her husband. She herself survived and found herself alone to raise her baby boy on a foreign continent. And for Governor John Carver, though he and Catherine both survived, it meant the loss of little Jasper More, the child they'd adopted. Carver had already buried two children back in the Old World; now, in the frigid ground of Plymouth, he laid Jasper to rest too. Young Jasper's two sisters, Ellen and Mary, also perished. They had been the last family that Richard More had left. The boy's parents didn't want him, and now, his siblings were all dead.

Myles Standish and William Bradford also suffered incomprehensible losses. Both had brought wives to the New World, and both lost their wives that dark winter. Dorothy Bradford had drowned back in Provincetown Harbor, her body disappearing into the depths of the sea without a trace. And Rose Standish, who had stood so staunchly by her husband for so long, died aboard the *Mayflower* in late January.

Despite the appalling deaths that continued all around them, the able-bodied colonists continued to work away at building their settlement, desperate to have somewhere to live away from the death ship that the *Mayflower* was fast becoming. Slowly, the settlement began to take shape between two hills. Cole's Hill would become the location for most of the buildings of Plymouth Colony. They were primarily wattle-and-daub cottages, but as time went on, timber buildings began to take shape.

On the other side, Fort Hill, a wooden platform was built overlooking the tiny colony. Here, five cannons were taken from the *Mayflower* and stationed on top of the hill. Peaceful though the Pilgrims hoped their relations with the natives would be, Standish wasn't taking any chances, especially after the "First Encounter."

By the end of February, the buildings were still woefully inadequate. The colonists had planned to finish at least nineteen buildings by that time. Instead, only eleven small buildings clustered miserably around Cole's Hill, with a growing collection of graves lying beside them. Yet, those eleven buildings were almost enough to house the remaining Pilgrims, for of the 102 passengers that had boarded the *Mayflower* in England, only 45 survived that terrible winter.

March brought the first thaw, longer days, and a breath of hope. The disease stopped at last, its deadly work done. The grieving people were able to look forward to their first summer in the New World. But even now—even after financing the voyage, surviving it, and living through that awful winter—trouble still loomed on the horizon. The Wampanoag had noticed the cannons on Fort Hill. And they were desperate to protect themselves against this European threat.

Chapter 7 – The First Thanksgiving

Illustration V: An artist's impression of Tisquantum, who was nicknamed "Squanto" by William Bradford, presumably because his real name was difficult for Englishmen to pronounce.

Massasoit was worried, and he had reason to be.

Spring was coming to Massasoit's domain. The plague had finally stopped attacking his people, but now that the thaw had come, he knew that the Narragansett would soon be planning their next move. And now that the Europeans had built a settlement on the shore, Massasoit's people were caught between two enemies.

None of the Wampanoag had actually spoken to the Europeans yet, but Massasoit had heard the stories. He knew how people had been stolen away by the Europeans and were sold as slaves, of how these barbaric invaders had raped women, desecrated holy sites, and taken land. In fact, one of Massasoit's own subjects, Tisquantum, had been kidnapped by Thomas Hunt and sold as a slave in Spain; he had only recently been able to return to America.

The Europeans' disrespect and their unrelenting savagery had shocked Native American leaders all over the continent. And now, with his people weakened and the Narragansett at their backs, Massasoit knew that they were facing that same terrible threat themselves.

Every report that reached his ears from Wampanoag who had ventured nearer to the European settlement worried him more and more. His fears were confirmed: the Europeans had built a permanent home, and, worse, they had erected a platform with cannons on top of the hill. Massasoit had heard of what cannons could do to a troop of men, how it could rip them to pieces and tear great holes in the earth. Those ugly black cannons on the hilltop were, to Massasoit, a statement of war. These colonists were going to ravage his people just like their diseases; the struggling remnants of the Wampanoag would be butchered and kidnapped, sold and destroyed.

Before March, the Wampanoag had still not yet made real contact with the settlers. They had observed them from afar, always bolting in fear whenever the Europeans came too close; one bold party had stolen some tools left at a worksite and brought them back to their people. As the March days lengthened, however, Massasoit knew that it was time to act.

Even with their small numbers, the Wampanoag could have attacked the colony. They had suffered, thanks to the disease, but there were still several thousand of them; they could have beaten the Pilgrims in battle, even if that meant angering the English Crown itself. But two Native Americans changed Massasoit's mind, two men who would become instrumental in saving the colony: Samoset and Tisquantum.

Samoset was the first Native American to make contact with the Pilgrims. He himself was not native to the Pokanoket region where Massasoit lived. Although Samoset was a minor Abenaki sachem, he was nonetheless part of the Wampanoag confederacy, and he had come to Montaup on a diplomatic visit to Massasoit. Unlike Massasoit, however, he had had direct contact with the English. His domain included the Gulf of Maine, where English fishermen often came to fish the rich and abundant waters. These fishermen had little interest in what happened inland if they were allowed to fish in peace, and so, they had no hostility toward the Abenaki.

Samoset, a fearless young ruler, had spoken with the English on enough occasions that he could speak some of the language. He had also traded with them and enjoyed a friendly drink over a campfire with the fishermen. He suspected that the colonists in the area where the Patuxet lived were more like the fishermen than like the bloodthirsty men of Jamestown. He had a feeling that the Pilgrims were just ordinary people trying to survive. He encouraged Massasoit to talk to the colonists and try to establish peace with them.

The other native was Tisquantum. Tisquantum was either a captive or a refugee among the Wampanoag, and he himself was Patuxet—the last living Patuxet, in fact. The very village that the Pilgrims had discovered was the place where he had grown up; it had once been a thriving community of around two thousand people. Tisquantum's fate took a sad turn when he was only a young man.

If anyone had reason to hate the Europeans in general, and the English in particular, it was Tisquantum. Born around 1580, he had been a young man in his twenties when he was kidnapped in 1605 by Captain George Weymouth. Weymouth was exploring the northern New England area, where Tisquantum and some others happened to be on a hunting expedition. He wanted to kidnap some "Indians" in order to show them to the owner of the company that had sent him to the New World: Sir Ferdinando Gorges. To Weymouth and Gorges, these native people were nothing more than a fascinating novelty.

Tisquantum was among the unlucky number that was forced into a ship and carried across the Atlantic, an experience that had been terrifying enough for the Pilgrims, who had boarded the *Mayflower* voluntarily. Tisquantum was thrown around in a dark hold, treated as something inferior, and never told what was happening to him.

Traumatized and malnourished, Tisquantum arrived in England later that year, only to be given to Gorges as though he was nothing more than a trinket from the New World. Gorges made it his mission to turn this fascinating novelty into a "civilized" member of society, and Tisquantum learned to speak fluent English when he was held captive by Gorges.

Nine years after being dragged to the Old World, Tisquantum finally had an opportunity to return home. John Smith recognized Tisquantum's value as a guide and interpreter in the New World, so he took him back across the Atlantic—this time as a free man—in order to help out near Jamestown in 1614. Sadly, for Tisquantum, he had only a bare taste of freedom and no contact with his home tribe. Thomas Hunt, another explorer, had determined to add to his cargo of fish by taking some Native Americans back to the Old World to sell as slaves. He deceived some members of a local tribe by inviting them aboard his ship to trade furs; Tisquantum likely came aboard as an interpreter. But no trade took place. Instead, Hunt closed up his ship and sailed to Spain, taking the Native Americans with him—including Tisquantum—to sell at a handsome profit.

Hunt was hoping to feather his nest at the expense of these innocent people, and he sold several of them at the Strait of Gibraltar on his return to Europe. A group of Spanish monks, however, were determined to foil his nefarious plans. When they saw the terrified and confused Native Americans being sold off helplessly to uncertain fates, they refused to stand by and watch.

The monks intervened, putting a stop to Hunt's schemes by bringing Tisquantum and a handful of others back to the monastery with them. These monks were powerless to send Tisquantum home, but they did continue his English education, and they also gave him the freedom to do as he pleased.

Only five years later, in 1619, Tisquantum managed to get himself hired again as a guide and interpreter, traveling back to the New World with an enterprising adventurer. This time, he made it back to Cape Cod at last.

Fourteen years after he had been abducted, Tisquantum finally walked back into the village of Patuxet, the homeland he had been longing for ever since that dreadful day. But if he had been dreaming of being welcomed home by friends and family, his dreams were horrendously dashed.

It is difficult to imagine just how tragic that moment must have been for Tisquantum. He had suffered so much and endured such hardship in order to come back home. And now, even though the fields were as green as he remembered, the water as perfectly smooth, and the woods as coolly shaded, Patuxet had changed. The very heart of the land had been torn out, its soul ripped away.

Everyone was dead.

Tisquantum walked into an abandoned village. There were no people. No animals. No crops. Only some bones—the remnants of a plague so vicious that no one had been left to bury the dead. Smallpox had destroyed the entire village, Tisquantum's whole family, his tribe, his people, even his identity. The moment was meant to be one of a joyous homecoming, but instead, it was the day that Tisquantum learned that he was the very last Patuxet.

And so Tisquantum found himself in Massasoit's court. The Europeans had essentially ruined his life in every sense of the word: they had kidnapped him twice, enslaved him, passed him about like a mere object, and then brought disease to the New World that had wiped out his entire family. Yet, for whatever reason, Tisquantum pleaded on behalf of the colonists. He asked Massasoit to give him the grace of meeting with them first to attempt to establish a peace.

It was not only for compassionate reasons that Massasoit agreed with Samoset and Tisquantum. He knew that he could not afford to be fighting a war on two fronts. What was more, if he could make peace with the

Europeans, perhaps they could be persuaded to help him if the Narragansetts attacked.

Massasoit agreed to try to make a treaty with the Europeans, and he sent Samoset to speak with them.

The young sachem was all too happy to be entrusted with this task. He was absolutely fearless, and he harbored less resentment of the Europeans than Tisquantum did, so he set out for Patuxet with a swagger in his step.

* * * *

Spring had brought hope to Plymouth Colony but also fear.

The surviving colonists, about fifty in all, were half-amazed, half-relieved that they had made it through that unbearable winter. Their sick were recovering, with most of them finally able to get to work again, and they had started to till the empty fields surrounding the mysteriously abandoned village. Governor John Carver, albeit not in good health, had succeeded in keeping order between the Saints and Strangers.

The great threat that faced them now was the Native Americans.

Myles Standish, grieving though he was, knew that the cannons alone would not be enough to ward off a full attack by some outraged tribe. He would have to convert this batch of ordinary people into warriors.

Accordingly, Standish selected a handful of men and started training them in the art of war. They were a motley bunch, but he was determined to make it work.

The colonists were, in fact, in the very middle of their training when a tall, young Native American man came swaggering right into Plymouth Colony. He came so boldly that they might have fired the cannons on him if it wasn't for the fact that his hands were empty (although he had a bow and two arrows in his quiver) and that he was alone. As it was, the women and children ran, panicking for their homes, while the male colonists gathered warily around him, nervous but hoping that their plan of making peace with the natives would finally be given a chance to succeed.

To their shock, the Native American greeted them in broken English and introduced himself as Samoset, a lord of a nearby area—and then asked them if they had any beer. The request put them instantly at ease. The colonists were running short on beer, but they offered him water, butter and cheese from the cow that had survived the journey, some biscuits, and some duck. When the wind rose, they also offered him a coat—a well-meaning, if perhaps unnecessary gesture. Samoset cheerfully accepted these and started to tell them all about the new land they had come to.

Something that had been concerning the colonists was the abandoned village. They wanted to know who this land belonged to. Samoset put their minds at ease, telling them about the plague and the death of the Patuxet. In the colonists' eyes, that made this land their own.

They visited with Samoset all afternoon and into the evening. Although the colonists remained wary, Samoset's cheerful, free manner started to put them at ease. He spent the night in Stephen Hopkin's home—albeit under some guard.

Samoset had told Governor Carver that Massasoit wanted to make peace with them. This was a massive relief, and Carver sent him back to the sachem with a few small gifts.

A few days later, Samoset returned, bringing with him a few other men and also the tools that had been taken from Plymouth Colony. This gesture of goodwill served to put the colonists even more at ease. Samoset also brought some furs in the hope of trading with the colonists. Carver was delighted by this. Another threat that had been looming over Plymouth Colony was their mounting debt to the Merchant Adventurers, and the trade in furs would be their only real hope of paying the company back. However, it happened to be a Sunday, and Carver couldn't accept the furs on a day he considered to be holy. Instead, he offered the men something to eat and encouraged them to come back later.

When Massasoit and his delegation arrived on March 22nd, 1621, Carver and the others were ready and relieved to be friends with their new neighbors. Massasoit's impressive group, which arrived with considerable pomp, dwarfed the pitiful scrapings of the trumpet and drum that announced the arrival of the sickly Governor Carver. Still, Massasoit saw potential in the colonists and the potential for an alliance that could ensure their mutual survival. After sharing a meal together and exchanging some gifts, Carver and Massasoit signed a peace treaty that would last for fifty years.

The peace itself was a gift that contributed to Plymouth Colony's survival. But Massasoit also left behind another gift, one that would finally ensure that the colonists could make a home for themselves in the New World: Tisquantum.

It's unknown whether Tisquantum willingly went to live with the colonists or whether Massasoit made him do it. Perhaps he joined them hoping to be free of Massasoit, or perhaps his motivation was a deeper one. Tisquantum had walked the hills of Patuxet, his homeland, and heard only silence after the terrible plague. He had known unutterable grief and loneliness. He had been robbed of his entire family, his whole people.

But now, there were people in Patuxet again. There were children, dogs, women, livestock, and fishermen. They were far from perfect. They weren't Patuxet. They weren't even Native American. But for Tisquantum, they had the potential to be a family for him, despite their white skins. And so, after the celebrations had died down and Massasoit and Samoset had returned to their domains, Tisquantum threw himself wholeheartedly into the task of helping the Pilgrims survive.

Bradford would later call Tisquantum "an instrument of God." His presence in the colony was nothing short of miraculous. The Pilgrims had been trying to grow the corn they'd stolen from the Nauset, but it wouldn't come up, no matter what they did. It was Tisquantum who showed them how to plant and fertilize it with the abundant fish they could catch in Plymouth Harbor. He showed them how to trap and skin beaver for their lucrative fur. He showed them how to grow all the vegetables that his tribe had always grown, and so, thanks to one man's compassion, Plymouth Colony began to thrive at last.

* * * *

Almost a year had passed since the Pilgrims came to Plymouth, and the air was thick with festivity.

Fall had come to New England, all green and gold and breathtaking scarlet. The gathering of houses that formed Plymouth Colony had grown; the cannons on Fort Hill were dusty with disuse. The storehouses were full to the brim. The fields were empty, their abundant crops gathered safely for the winter. Livestock grazed on the hillsides, thriving and well. And in the middle of the colony, a great feast was underway.

Everyone was there—everyone who had survived, anyway. There was William Brewster, who had now become the pastor of Plymouth Colony, with Mary and little Richard More by his side; the widowed Susanna White, one of only four married women who had survived the winter and who had been faced with the challenge of cooking a vast feast with only a handful of people to help her; John Howland, now an important figure in the colony and one who had been instrumental in negotiating peace with the Wampanoag; Myles Standish, stalwart as ever; Tisquantum, the hero of Plymouth Colony; Massasoit, with a huge delegation of Native Americans, which outnumbered the colonists almost two to one; and William Bradford.

Sadly, John and Catherine Carver had died in the spring of 1621. It was as though Carver had held on for just long enough to see peace between the colonists and the Native Americans. He was not there to see this great harvest celebration, but William Bradford had become the governor of Plymouth

Colony in his stead, and he would lead the colony for nearly thirty years to come.

It was with a full heart that William Bradford looked out over the great feast that Susanna White and the other women had prepared. There were vegetables and grains from the colonists' fields, fish and shellfish from the bay, fruits and nuts from their orchards, and venison from their new friends, the Wampanoag. Everywhere Bradford looked, he saw smiling faces. Laughing children. Happy couples. Cheerful men.

He was a long, long way from Nottinghamshire now, and his faith had taken him a long way from home. But now, at last, the Separatists had a home of their own.

That was enough reason to be thankful. And so, hundreds of years later, a harvest festival a little like this one would become an annual American tradition: Thanksgiving.

Conclusion

The name *Mayflower* would become one of the most famous in history. In fact, it is debatable whether any other ship is as well known across the world. She was a very ordinary ship, an underdog, honestly, compared with the other vessels that had to make their way across the Atlantic. Yet her voyage was a historic one.

Perhaps it was the *Mayflower*'s mediocrity that made her voyage so extraordinary. The Pilgrims, too, were just ordinary people. They weren't adventurers, sailors, or wealthy merchants. They were just farmers and fishermen with families to feed, people who wanted nothing more than to practice their faith in peace and who were willing to do whatever it took to make that happen.

As for the *Mayflower* herself, she would only become famous many years later, after Plymouth Colony had endured for decades and the Pilgrims had all died and been buried on Cole's Hill, along with the victims of that deadly plague in the winter of 1620. Her end was tragically ignominious.

In April 1621, once most of Master Jones's crew had recovered from their illness, he was finally able to set sail toward home. This time, the journey was an easy one. Only a few weeks later, on May 5th, 1621, the weary *Mayflower* finally sailed back into her home port of Rotherhithe. But neither Jones nor his ship was the same as they had been when they had left England. The journeys had taken a terrible toll on them both. The *Mayflower* was all but falling apart, her timbers creaky, her mainmast cracked, and her crew racked by disease.

Josian Jones hardly recognized her own husband when he returned to her arms at last. The once-sprightly captain was a mere sickly shadow of the man he had once been, and his health would continue to fail. He was home for only ten months before the sickness finally won out. He died in March 1622, leaving the *Mayflower* to his grieving widow.

At first, Josian wanted little to do with the ship. Her other owners, too, appear to have more or less forgotten about her. She lay neglected in port until Josian finally had her appraised in 1624, hoping to settle her husband's estate. Sadly, there was nothing more to be done with the *Mayflower*. She would never sail again, and although her ultimate fate is not known, she was likely broken up and sold as scrap lumber.

It was a tragic ending for a ship that had carried the founders of a nation across the Atlantic. But although the *Mayflower*'s timbers have likely long since rotted into nothing, her story lives on. It has endured for generations, and it will endure for many, many more.

Part 6: The Pequot War

A Captivating Guide to the Armed Conflict in New England between the Pequot People and English Settlers and Its Role in the History of the United States of America

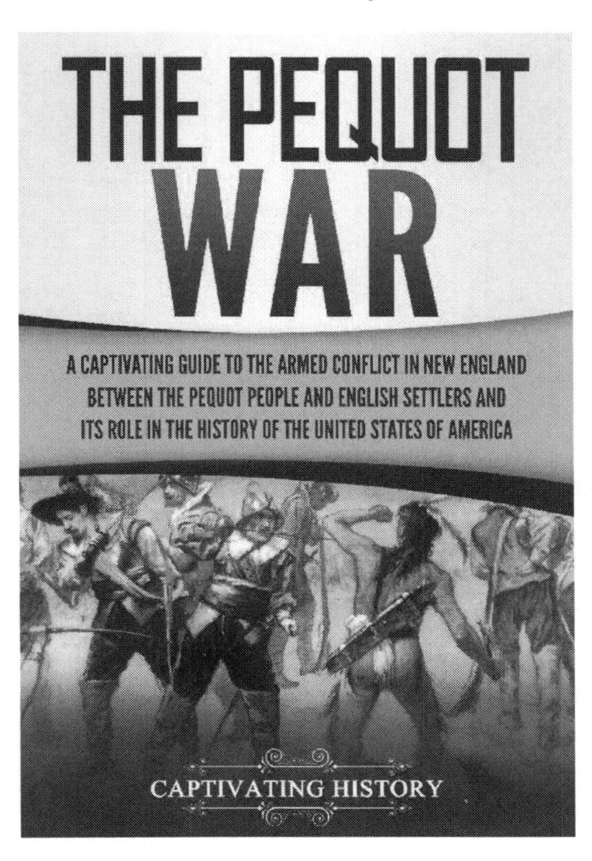

Introduction

The Pequot War (1636-1638) was a short-lived but extremely violent and bloody episode in United States history. This event represents one of the turning points in the entire history of North America, as the war changed the balance of power. The Dutch colonial authorities lost their status of being the dominant economic and political force, while the English took over this epithet. The end of the war also represented the first stage in England's intensive expansion in that part of the world.

This historical event demonstrates the insurmountable antagonisms between two opposing cultures and perceptions. It was just the beginning of the conflicts between the European settlers and the Native Americans, as the Pequot War allowed the Puritans to have a testing ground so they could examine their military capabilities in the New World and observe the capabilities of the Native American tribes.

The book is composed of several chapters that examine various aspects of the Pequot War. In the beginning, the reader will have the opportunity to get acquainted with the Europeans' views on the people who inhabited the New World. The average European image of the indigenous "savage" who lived in North America is one of the key elements essential for understanding the enormous amount of violence recorded during the Pequot War, as well as other conflicts that later took place. In this book, one can also find information on the Pequot tribe and their importance to the wider Connecticut area, as well as their customs, way of life, and religion. The conditions in which the Puritans left their homeland, the process of settlement and colonization, the organization of the colonies, and the ambitions of the leaders of New England are also elaborated upon.

This conflict was the product of extremely complex events, and one of the broadest chapters of this paper talks about the events that led to the war. This book also provides details about the military capabilities of the warring parties. Both sides' combat tactics are presented in detail, including the military arsenal that the Puritans and Pequots had at their disposal. There will be an inside view of the military maneuvers, initial war operations, and conflicts between the warring parties. The central and most extensive part of the book talks about the organization of the largest military operation during the Pequot War: the English Mystic River campaign, which was also the conflict's final stage.

The Pequot War contains racial and religious issues that allude to the genocidal actions of Europeans in North America. This dimension of the war is still the subject of controversy among the academic community, and one will understand why. Finally, there will be a discussion of the consequences of the Pequot War and the historiographical approach to this event.

Throughout this book, we will expand our understanding of the main protagonists of this historical episode. These individuals made their mark on one of the most significant episodes in the history of the United States.

Chapter 1 – The European Conception of the Native Americans

Suppose we start looking for the factors that led to the Pequot War and other mutual conflicts between the Native Americans and Europeans. In that case, it is necessary to look at the European man's understanding of the indigenous tribes of North America. The earliest records of the newly discovered world and the natives of North America significantly led to the formation of stereotypes. These records depict Native Americans as blasphemous savages who drink blood and sacrifice boys. The partial occurrence of cannibalism among Native Americans had a considerably negative effect on the European understanding of the natives of North America, and texts about ghost worship and witchcraft had a very negative impact on Catholic Europeans. Records of incest, sodomy, and witchcraft are also common elements found in these early texts.

Intensive contact between Europeans and natives from the beginning of colonization led to the appearance of infectious diseases among North American natives, who had not developed immunity to certain illnesses, such as smallpox, tuberculosis, influenza, and malaria. Europeans viewed this pandemic through the prism of religion. Namely, the established opinion was that God was punishing the Native Americans for blasphemy and, in general, for their way of life, one that was unacceptable to Europeans. The Puritans believed that, in this way, God "purified" the earth for them and gave them space to settle. The Church also did not make any provisions for the Native Americans; on the contrary, the Church propagated Christianity among the natives at all costs. This ubiquitous view of Native Americans resonated among Puritans as well. It is undoubtedly one of the elements that led to the unprecedented brutality during the Pequot War.

From the beginning of the 17th century, the New World became synonymous with the incarnation of Satan. Because of such attitudes, it is not surprising that the Puritans were skeptical about coexisting with the Pequot and other tribes in the neighborhood. Information about such attitudes of the Puritans is brought to us by the Massachusetts Bay Colony's chronicler,

Edward Johnson, who served as a soldier in the Pequot War and was one of the founders of Woburn, Massachusetts. Europeans believed that by colonizing, they brought peace and civilization to the Native Americans; however, the Europeans were, in fact, only imposing their politics, religion, economics, and universal understanding of life upon them. Europeans believed in moral superiority over others and sought to pass those values on to others at all costs.

Because of this European vision, Pequots and other American natives certainly aroused fear in the Europeans, and therefore, it was inevitable that the settlers would believe the natives posed a threat. One of the principles of the Puritan ideology of the time was the battle against evil. As mentioned above, the Native Americans were the devil incarnate, and the English believed that one of their main missions was to wage war against Satan. The English were also furious because their persistent efforts to baptize the native tribes were unsuccessful. The English colonists did not understand coexistence and tolerance, for they believed that if they allowed such a thing, in time, they would become such themselves.

Sadly, due to the lack of written sources, there is not much data on the Native American understanding of the Europeans. Apart from oral traditions, there are no other sources that tell us how they perceived Europeans and their ways. We know that the Native Americans at the beginning of colonization were pleased with their mutual trade cooperation. Through trade, Europeans introduced Native Americans to iron and specific technical achievements that made their daily lives more comfortable. Thus, the tribes developed good trade relations with the Dutch at the beginning of colonization and cooperated with them for years to the general satisfaction of all.

The problem arose when there was a mass migration of Europeans to North America. Disagreements arose among the European immigrants themselves, which greatly affected the indigenous population. According to the available oral traditions that have been preserved to this day, it is clear the Native Americans did not fully understand why the Europeans went to such lengths to impose their way of life upon the tribes. The natives observed the technological achievements of the more advanced European civilization with interest and curiosity. To them, the large European ships didn't look like boats; instead, the Native Americans called them "Moving Islands." It was not clear to Native Americans why Europeans wore so much clothing, given that they were mostly covering their intimate body parts. After arriving in North America, the first European researchers recorded how some natives began to worship metal axes and firearms after becoming acquainted with these objects. The Europeans' way of life and manners were utterly unknown to the natives, so these "white people with beards" were considered by some to be a new species. The interpretation of infectious diseases among the natives is also interesting; namely, they viewed this phenomenon as a terrible and deadly power that the white man carried with him. Over time, the Native Americans began to view the Europeans as occupiers who wanted their country no matter the cost.

Chapter 2 – Who Were the Pequots?

The Pequots were a sizeable Native American tribe. According to the first historical sources dating back to 1600, the Pequot tribe had about 4,000 members. They inhabited the southeastern bank of the Connecticut River, as well as around the banks of the modern-day Thames River. The area they settled was about 250 square kilometers. According to the latest sources, the word "Pequot" comes from PAQUATAUOQ, WHICH LOOSELY TRANSLATES TO "destroyers." Most likely, that name was the product of fierce wars with other indigenous tribes. The Pequots were reputed to be aggressive and brave warriors. They are also believed to have migrated twenty years before the arrival of the English from the upper New York area.

Some believe their arrival in the Connecticut area was turbulent. It affected the entire region, as they displaced the smaller tribal communities that inhabited the area. By migrating, they showed their belligerent attitude toward others. However, this might not have been the case, as historical and scientific teachings regarding the migration of the Pequot tribe are quite divided. Some archaeological results indicate that the Pequot had inhibited the territory of Connecticut for much longer. Some linguistic studies also suggest a more established presence of the Pequot in the Connecticut area.

It is assumed that before the arrival of the Europeans, the Pequot was a community of clans. Each clan represented a different political entity, in which similar beliefs still prevailed. The establishment of trade relations with European immigrants changed certain social currents of the Pequot tribe. Before these first commercial connections, the Pequot tribe's dwellings were temporary. As their involvement in trade became more and more intense, the Native Americans became more attached to trading points and changed their nomadic habits. Under such circumstances, native settlements gained importance, as many became important trading places. To some extent, these economic changes affected the natives' attitude toward the environment, as the Pequots began to produce and exploit more natural resources.

In the early 17th century, the Pequot and Mohegan tribes were united, and they were led by Chief Sassacus. Soon, there was a split between these two tribes, and they began to act independently. Uncas, a former member of the unified Pequot tribe, separated with his like-minded people and formed the Mohegan tribe. Even though the Mohegans and the Pequots were identical in cultural characteristics, their different outlooks and interests in leadership led to the split between the two.

The Pequots engaged in agriculture, hunting, and fishing. The most important crops grown by this tribe were corn, beans, and pumpkins. It is interesting that women, with the help of children, were exclusively engaged in agriculture, except for the cultivation of tobacco, which was solely grown by men. The Pequots' diet was varied, although crops, meat, nuts, and fruits were regularly on the table.

The tribe lived in permanent dwellings, and during the hunting season, the men would leave their homes and form temporary settlements called "wigwams." These were shelters made of trees in a pyramidal shape, covered with tree bark, leaves, and animal skins.

The Pequots had an organized tribal hierarchy. The tribe's representative was the chief, but the shaman also had an important part in society. The tribal council played a pivotal role in decision-making. Between ten and fifteen men were on the council, and these men had to prove themselves in a certain way, whether on the battlefield or in another leadership role. The great chief, or sachem, was the most influential individual of the tribal community. The sachem's function oscillated according to the tribe, meaning that some sachems had greater and some lesser influence than others. As an interesting side note, women were equal members of Pequot society. They even had the right to run their own businesses.

The Pequots did not use money; instead, they relied on barter. Their trading currency was wampum, a highly coveted string of beads. This jewelry was not only a means of trade, as it also symbolized status in society and spiritual power. Wampum was valued not only by the Pequots but also by many other North American indigenous tribes. It should be noted the Pequots did not work for material gain. The notion of economic benefit did not exist; instead, the Pequots lived in the community and only used what natural resources they needed to survive.

The Pequots are generally known to have been extremely skilled hunters. The primary weapons used by the Pequots in both war and hunting were batons, axes, knives, and bows and arrows. They also used canoes made of wood for transport. The Pequots often deliberately caused controlled fires, thus maintaining the forests' passability, which made it easier for them to hunt. Before the Europeans' arrival on North American soil, the Pequots were already well organized in military, economic, and political terms. In primary sources, they mention the Pequots as a wealthy tribe compared to others.

The Pequots made their first contact with the Europeans at the end of the 15th and the beginning of the 16th century. Rigorous contact with the European immigrants continued during the 17th century, which was when the mass colonization of North America took place. The Pequots established intensive contact primarily with the Dutch, with whom the Pequots traded leather, decorative jewelry, and wampum. Like with many other indigenous tribes of North America, this more intense contact with Europeans was fatal to many. Namely, various contagious diseases were transmitted to them by the Europeans, decimating the tribes and somewhat changing the structure of North American tribal communities.

The beginning of the 17th century led to more mass migrations of European immigrants to North America, which led to an increase in the number of infected. The only way to fight infectious diseases was to leave the territory, after which the Europeans then seized the region for themselves. In 1616, in the area where the Massachusetts Bay Colony would be established later on, the bubonic plague broke out. The second wave of this disease occurred three years later, and it was even more intense than the first. In 1633 and 1634, an epidemic of smallpox occurred in the same area. These events greatly affected their native neighbors who were settled near the newly formed English colony, which was established in 1629. Among the closest were the Pequots. According to some sources, about 1,600 members of the Pequot tribe died from the bubonic plague and smallpox epidemics.

The interaction between the natives of North America and the Europeans had extremely tragic outcomes from the very beginning. The epidemics destroyed entire villages and families and attacked all sections of the population, including the Europeans. Although the Europeans had a higher immunity, 17th-century medicine was underdeveloped, which led to greater deaths. These diseases destroyed traditional social connections, especially in those tribal communities where the Europeans were in the "neighborhood." The coast of New England was very densely populated, and intensive trade contact between European immigrants and natives accelerated the spread of the epidemic. These epidemics were reported by English colonist Thomas Morton, whose account dates back to the 17th century. Morton is most notable for founding the colony of Merrymount, modern-day Quincy, Massachusetts. The Nauset tribe (also known as the Cape Cod Indians), who inhabited the Cape Cod area, captured a European colonist, who then transmitted the virus to the entire community. Morton writes the following about this event:

> One of these five men, outliving the rest, had learned so much of their language as to rebuke them for their bloody deed, saying that God would be angry with them for it, and that he would in his displeasure destroy them; but the savages (it seems boasting of their

> strength), replied and said, that they were so many that God could not kill them. But contrary-wise, in short time after the hand of God fell heavily upon them, with such a mortal stroke that they died on heaps as they lay in their houses; For in a place where many inhabited, there had been but one left to live to tell what became of the rest; the living being (as it seems) not able to bury the dead, they were left for crows, kites and vermin to prey upon. And the bones and skulls upon the several places of their habitations made such a spectacle after my coming into those parts, that, as I travelled in that forest near the Massachusetts, it seemed to me a new found Golgotha.

There is an obvious religious "overtone" in Morton's understanding of what occurred to the native tribe. This allows the reader to see how most of the Europeans observed the epidemics that raged against the native populace.

The elements of antagonism between European settlers and indigenous tribes were multiple, but one of the biggest barriers to mutual understanding was religion. Rigid Puritan beliefs were the biggest obstacle to any interaction between the natives of North America and the Europeans. The only fragment in which the two dogmatic narratives could be reconciled was the belief in the afterlife. The Native Americans, unlike Europeans, did not have colossal buildings intended for performing prayers or other forms of spiritual ritual. Religious symbols and texts were also not integral elements of the religious practices of the natives. The natives' religious beliefs were intertwined with their tradition, so fragments of their dogmatic beliefs permeated in their folklore. Through dance, the Native Americans sought to connect with the spiritual; it was one way in which they could become closer to a higher entity.

The Native American tribes that lived nearby the colonies of New England, among whom were the Pequots, believed the human soul existed on three levels. The first level of these beliefs involved people's spirits or souls. The Pequot believed that in certain states, the human soul separated from the body and could travel and communicate with the world around it. The second level implied guardian spirits; they, according to native beliefs, could exist in various forms and even take the forms of plants and animals. The highest degree implied a supreme entity, which could be compared to the Christian concept of God. As in many other religions, the Native Americans of North America believed in the intrusion of evil spirits (similar to Satan). Tribal shamans sought to drive such spirits out of the tribal community or reduce their appearance through various rituals.

The colonial census from 1774 showed about 151 members of the Pequot tribe on the Mashantucket Pequot Reservation, which is one of the oldest reservations in North America. The next census, which dates to the beginning of the 19th century, was even more devastating, as it showed only 35 members. By 1960, most Pequot on the reservation left for economic reasons. Those who remained were tied to the land of their ancestors. Local authorities sought to turn the Mashantucket Pequot Reservation into a state park. However, three half-sisters born and raised in the area, Alice Brend, Martha Langevin, and Elizabeth George, tried to obstruct this attempt at all costs. Thanks to their perseverance and efforts, and despite not having financial resources and adequate legal assistance, they managed to keep the reservation intact.

However, even during the 1970s, the situation was not significantly better, as the members of the reservation had many financial problems. During this period, the tribe survived on nature, their main food source, and minimal financial support. The tribal community also built a large greenhouse facility and raised domestic livestock. Today, the tribal community is governed by seven men over the age of fifty-five, who are elected for a term of three years. The tribal council manages all affairs but also maintains contacts with state and local representatives and authorities. Today, the tribal community takes special care of the youngest members of the community. Healthcare is regulated for everyone, and a significant emphasis is placed on education. The tribal community seeks to encourage as many people as possible to pursue higher education, no matter their age. The youngest community members learn about the history, culture, and traditions of the Pequot tribe.

Chapter 3 – The Massachusetts Bay Colony of New England

In the northeastern region of America, settlements were established in the early 17th century by two major religious groups: the Pilgrims and the Puritans. The Pilgrims settled the Atlantic coast in present-day Plymouth, Massachusetts. The Pilgrims were separatists from the Church of England, and they established Plymouth Colony in December of 1620, which was the first permanent European settlement in New England. It was also the second permanent settlement in North America, with Jamestown, Virginia, being the first. One of the major characters in this group of Pilgrims was William Bradford, who helped organize this venture for religious freedom. Bradford proved to be vital for the growth of Plymouth Colony because he, among others, helped frame the Mayflower Compact. The Mayflower Compact was the first governing document of Plymouth Colony, and it was also the first document of self-governance in the New World.

The other religious group to settle in America was the Puritans. Many Puritans first migrated to the Netherlands, but the liberal Dutch society was in complete contradiction to their beliefs. Therefore, they decided to move to the New World. The Puritans left England en masse, not only for religious reasons but also for economic ones.

There were two factions among the Puritans at the time: separatists and non-separatists. Separatist-minded Puritans believed that the Church was too corrupt and that reform was out of the question. In their opinion, the only solution was the complete separation from the Anglican Church. The other faction believed that an internal reorganization of the Church was possible. Such attitudes posed significant adversity among the Puritans. Namely, it was impossible to separate the Church from the state in England because that act would be considered high treason. Their only option was to leave their home country.

In 1628, John Endecott and a group of about 400 people and 200 cattle sailed to New England. At the time, it was one of the most participated overseas trips. When they arrived, John Endecott and other leaders founded the settlement of Naumkeag, which would later be renamed Salem. John Endecott was unofficially elected as the first governor of the newly formed colony. He would go on to become the longest-serving governor of the Massachusetts Bay Colony, serving for a total of sixteen years.

The Massachusetts Bay Colony was one of the first English colonies founded in North America. To formally found the colony, though, a charter was needed. In 1629, King Charles I granted the charter to the Massachusetts Bay Company, licensing the company to colonize and trade. It is more than likely that Charles did not realize this colony would harbor Puritan emigrants; rather, King Charles I intended to form an English-controlled company in the New World. However, in time, all business would be in the hands of the colonists.

Another wave of colonists soon settled in the same area. In 1630, a group of around 700 people in 11 ships came to the region. Due to the influx of colonists, new cities were founded. In September 1630, Boston was established, which would become one of the most important cities in colonial America due to the people who populated it and the ideas that emerged from there. Most of these early immigrants engaged in agriculture, while others were ordinary workers; these people represented around 95 percent of the population. The remaining 5 percent were shareholders, who ran the colony as well as church affairs. The founders of the colonies were men whose beliefs were contrary to the Church of England's teachings. These were the followers of the reform movement that erupted throughout Europe during the 17th century.

To fully understand the religious landscape, one must go back to the 16th century when there was general discontent in the Church of England. The pope's interference in church relations aroused great dissatisfaction among many inhabitants. The influence of Protestant philosophers and thinkers, who advocated living after the example of Jesus Christ, was beginning to permeate society. Also, a large number of people protested against the enrichment of the clergy. The selling of indulgences, which was a way to reduce the punishment for one's sins, enraged the people and brought even more dissatisfaction. Some reformists felt that separation from the Vatican was not enough and believed that the Church of England, the prominent religion in England, needed to be cleansed of all traces of Catholicism. This large group of like-minded people was called the Puritans.

One of the main notions of Puritanism was the theory of predestination, an outlook borrowed from Calvinism. This doctrine challenges the idea of free will by stating that one's destiny is decided upon birth. The Puritans also believed that all Protestant followers had a greater chance of salvation and that they would enjoy paradise in the afterlife. Puritan dogma did not require tolerance toward other religions. Puritan religious teachings indicated that all people were believed to be born innately evil and sinful, so it was necessary to live by strict beliefs to cleanse one's sinful nature and avoid eternal hell.

The early colonists in the Massachusetts Bay Colony mostly came from middle-class families in England. In most cases, complete families moved. Puritan families migrated to North America from every corner of England, yet most colonists came from eastern and southern England. A healthy environment and favorable living conditions were, in addition to the migrations, huge elements that resulted in population growth. Stable economic conditions led to more marriages and, subsequently, more offspring.

The initial stages of settlement of the New World brought many temptations and tribulations, so it was important to have strong leadership. In the Massachusetts Bay Colony, the idea of political organizing was first realized during the mid-1630s, leading to an elected assembly and a municipal court. The assembly consisted of representatives from each city of the colony, and voting was a luxury, as only adult men could vote. The governor and the representatives of the municipal court were elected every year.

One of the most prominent and politically significant characters of that time was John Winthrop. John Winthrop was born in Edwardstone, located in Suffolk, England, in 1588 into a well-to-do family. His grandfather was a wealthy man who made his fortune by producing textiles. Winthrop spent most of his youth working on a farm in Suffolk. He was a man of strict Puritan beliefs, striving to incorporate biblical practices into every segment of his life. Winthrop attended Trinity College for law, and by 1628, he had made much progress in his career, having obtained several important positions. Due to his religious beliefs, Winthrop lost more and more hope for his home country over time. Things worsened in England with Charles I coming to power in the 1620s. The Puritans were much closer to the English Parliament in terms of political activity. But the moment the king dissolved Parliament, a huge problem arose for the Puritans. The Puritans considered the king to be a dictator and sought to leave the country. As the situation became more and more complicated, the Puritans decided to leave England once and for all and head for the New World.

Before arriving in North America, Winthrop was appointed the governor of the Massachusetts Bay Colony by the Massachusetts Bay Company in 1629. He would land a few months later in June 1630, taking over the governorship from John Endecott. Winthrop had a natural gift for politics and management, and he successfully led the newly formed English colony. For Winthrop, going to North America was not an escape but a way to fulfill God's will and to "properly" organize the Church of England in a new territory. After becoming the governor, he organized several expeditions that brought Puritan migrants from England.

Winthrop pointed out to his people that their success lingered solely on mutual respect and appreciation. He loathed consumerism and pointed out that people should only spend what they needed and leave the rest for others. He encouraged gentleness, patience, and mutual understanding in the Puritan community.

Winthrop's mission was to essentially create a "perfect society." However, the first years in the New World were not easy. There was evident fatigue on the people's faces. Many decided to give up and return to England. Although the situation was exceptionally trying, Winthrop did not give up on his goal. He worked hard to prepare the colonists for the coming winter. Despite the hardships he faced, he never regretted his departure from England, which is evidenced by the letter he sent to his wife, Margaret, who had stayed behind along with the rest of his family. In the letter, Winthrop points out, "I thank God, I like so well to be here, as I do not repent my coming: and if I were to come again, I would not have altered my course, though I had foreseen all these Afflictions: I never fared better in my life, never slept better, never had more content of mind."

The first year brought extreme difficulties; the winter was long and harsh, and since the colonists arrived late, they failed to sow enough crops. As a result, food shortages were inevitable. Under such circumstances, there was a sharp jump in food prices. About 200 colonists died during the winter due to the difficult circumstances, and in the early spring, about 80 left the Massachusetts Bay Colony and returned home.

Once the winter was over, Winthrop sat down to work. His extensive education was of great importance for the formation of the colony's government. Various institutions were formed that were vital for the general organization of the newly formed colony. Winthrop surrounded himself with quality collaborators to sort out the situation as soon as possible. He was often able to calm tensions among the colonists by using his social skills, which allowed him to maintain harmony throughout the colony. John Winthrop was elected as the governor of the Massachusetts Bay Colony twelve times. He was fully committed to the colony's development until his death on March 26th, 1649.

The Massachusetts Bay Colony existed and operated as a joint-stock company; namely, the elections of authority figures operated on the principle that only men with sufficient capital or shares could elect other men to office. The name "Massachusetts" comes from the tribe who inhabited the area before the English arrived: the Massachusetts. This native tribe was almost extinct by the time the English permanently settled in the area. During the great pandemics of 1616 and 1619, the tribe was severely affected by infectious diseases. It is believed that the tribe initially had 4,000 members, and their numbers dwindled down to around 500 by the 1620s.

The settlements formed on the coast of New England had the potential to greatly expand, which was one of the reasons why massive migrations to this area took place. Rapid expansion was possible due to its favorable geographical position. The colonies of New England differed from others in the homogeneity of the population. Namely, in time, the area would be inhabited almost in full by only English. New England's population engaged in various activities, such as fishing, trade, and agriculture. Those who engaged in manufactory production were the most affluent stratum of society. The people produced everything, including food, clothes, shoes, and even furniture.

The river-rich area of New England was ideal for the development of trade. For centuries, the colony would be an unavoidable route for merchant ships. Since roads were almost nonexistent, trade mostly took place by the sea. The number of ships in New England continuously grew throughout the years, and the main raw material that was exploited was fish. Many of these ships were built by the fishermen themselves, and the Massachusetts Bay Colony became a very important shipyard over time.

In the colonies of New England, religion and education held a special place. The Puritans viewed the pastor as an intellectual and religious leader. The religious class was composed of willful and discerning leaders. These were the people who were "shod" by knowledge and contained all the characteristics that a true leader should possess. Crime and poverty in New England's colonies were a much rarer occurrence compared with other English colonies. This was the result of organized, capable leaders.

The fact that the life expectancy of the Puritans living in the New World eventually became significantly higher than that of their associates in England also speaks volumes about life quality. It must be noted that this took time; at the very beginning, the Puritans struggled to survive. One interesting phrase points out that the Puritans invented grandparents. Of course, they didn't invent grandparents, but given their longevity, many were fortunate enough to experience life with their children's children. Education and literacy rates in the colonies of New England were immensely high. Schooling was an obligation imposed by law, and every settlement that numbered over fifty people had to have a school financed directly from the tax system. Every Puritan wanted a child who knew how to read the Bible, which was one reason for the high literacy rate among the colonists.

In the end, the rise of the standard of living and the permeation of luxury into everyday life did not benefit the sophistication of the people, as strict religious rules still prevailed. Attending church sermons remained the obligation of every Puritan, and avoiding these obligations caused financial punishment. During church rites, a priest with a wooden stick patrolled the congregation. At one end hung feathers, which would tickle the chins of sleeping older men; at the other end was a wooden ball, which served as punishment for boys who laughed or were restless during the sermon.

It was previously pointed out that Winthrop worked intensively to settle the colony and form institutions to organize the new living space better. These institutions were imbued with religious elements, and in addition to the church and the governor, an important administrative body of the colony was created: the Court of Assistants. This institution was in charge of administering justice in the colony. The penal code in the colony was not clearly defined, so the people who held office made assessments as to how to mete out punishments. Bible guidelines were used in almost all court proceedings. In some cases, the intervention of clergy was required if the court had a more demanding case. At times, the population's dissatisfaction grew since all decision-making was in the hands of a few people. Over time, the colonists would receive written laws, which were still almost entirely imbued with religious elements. The code that was eventually drafted was called the "Body of Freedom," and it included about a hundred civil and criminal laws. The civil laws in New England's colonies were considerably more advanced than the laws in England. As for the penal laws, despite displaying more cruelty, they were more lenient than those in England. However, all legal regulations were based solely on the Bible.

The Puritans could not make wooden houses upon their arrival, so they inhabited dwellings that were covered with clay and moss with earthen floors. This form of housing construction was no innovation; rather, it was characteristic of Scandinavia and medieval Germany. The only wooden dwellings in these early colonial settlements were buildings formed to protect against possible attacks by the Native Americans. Years after the first migrations, the first wooden homes would be built.

These homes would not have been ostentatious, as that went against their beliefs. This can also be seen in the clothing they wore. Leather was one of the basic materials from which clothing was made. Workers and servants dressed in garments that were mostly made of deerskin. Socks were made of various materials, and almost all shoes had exclusively wooden soles. Hats were both modern and popular, and leather gloves were an almost indispensable clothing article. As the population became richer and as imports and exports of goods in Boston stores increased, so did clothing made from various materials imported from England. The permeation of modern clothing among Puritan settlers led to a ban on silver, gold, and silk lace. These fashion standards imposed from the mother country were difficult to control. Thus, many colonists were taken to court for disobeying these laws. Lace, short sleeves, short socks, and clothing items that revealed body parts were strictly forbidden.

Unnecessary entertainment was forbidden in the Massachusetts Bay Colony, as everyone was supposed to focus on the community. Since Puritans were devoted to strict biblical rules, they made sure their children followed them, instructing them about the beliefs and rules they must follow to live a good life at a young age. Puritans followed the Bible almost literally. There were even cases of executions of children if the child hit a parent.

Puritan society was strictly patriarchal, which is most evident in their treatment of women and children. Women were allowed to attend religious ceremonies in the church, but they were forbidden to engage in politics, whether it was church- or government-related. Those who "deviated" from God's path were punished severely, and members of other religions were often hanged at Boston Common. Therefore, religious tolerance did not exist, and those Puritans who fled Europe due to religious persecution ironically endorsed these practices themselves. All those who strayed from the Puritans' religious dogmas were called nonconformists or dissidents, and the punishments were extremely brutal. Besides hanging, other forms of punishment were applied, such as flogging and imprisonment. For instance, adulterers in the community were severely punished, and they were often subjected to a public lynching. During the late 17th century, there were several trials of people accused of witchcraft. During this time, the Puritans condemned not only women but also men. Puritans often resorted to public lapidations of people accused of witchcraft.

Chapter 4 – The Events That Triggered the Pequot War

The Pequot tribe had strongly developed trade ties with the Dutch colonists, as the area around the Connecticut River (modern-day Thames River) was a central trading hub. Near the Pequot tribe lived their greatest rivals: the Narragansett tribe. The rivalry was present in various areas, but it was primarily a trade or economic rivalry. While the Dutch traded with various indigenous tribes, the Pequots claimed the right to trade relations with the Europeans, as they were the most powerful tribe in the area.

The Dutch, who began settling in North America in the 1610s, controlled the Hudson River, which was their most important stronghold. The most popular item for trade among the Dutch population was leather, primarily beaver, which was mainly used for making hats. On the other hand, the Pequots demanded metal objects from the Dutch, such as teapots, buckles, and hooks, which the Native Americans removed and sharpened as arrows. The Pequots also made amulets and different jewelry from these metal objects. The Native Americans, especially the Pequots, were an essential factor when it came to trade, laying the basis for the formidable economic war to come. The English believed that the Pequots were detrimental to trade, namely because the English sought to take the business into their own hands.

This attitude became more prevalent as the English began to colonize New England more intensively. But even before the establishment of colonies like the Massachusetts Bay Colony or the Colony of Connecticut, the English was in geopolitical competition with Spain. The famous British geographer Richard Hakluyt wrote as early as 1584 that settling in the Americas should be one of England's top priorities. He believed this was the only way to prevent the Spanish from settling the entire continent. And the English acted on this by first settling a colony on Roanoke Island, located off the coast of North Carolina, in 1585. Although this colony was not a success, the first permanent English colony, Jamestown, was soon established in 1607. After that, the English colonization of America intensified, and the number of English migrants grew steadily year after year.

King James I sought to intensify the English colonization of America. In 1606, the English Parliament founded the Plymouth Company to help settle

America. In time, England would establish dominance over North America, while Spain directed its colonization efforts to South America. The establishment of English colonies meant a struggle for the commercial supremacy of North America. Soon, with its influence, the British colonial empire would completely oust the Dutch from New England. The number of British colonists grew so much over time that their actions began to threaten the main Dutch trade garrison called House of Hope or Fort Good Hope, which was built in 1633. Several houses were built next to the garrison, and two cannons were installed at the checkpoint, which provided additional security. A small number of soldiers stayed in the newly built trade facility, securing the checkpoint's goods. By doing this, the Dutch made their presence in the Connecticut area official.

Jacob van Curler, a representative of the Dutch West India Company, was in charge of obtaining the land for Fort Good Hope. He purchased it from the Sequins, a tribe that inhabited Connecticut. Although the peaceful acquisition of land took place several times in North American history, the prevailing European belief was that the land belonged to them, not the natives, and oftentimes, the land was acquired through more violent methods. Also, when purchasing land, Europeans often used alcohol in negotiations to honor the Native Americans in an attempt to reduce the price of the land.

Part of this violence stemmed from the fact that the Europeans, especially the English, viewed the Native Americans as savages who needed to be civilized. The texts of Captains John Mason and Underhill, who were major players in the Pequot War, abound with derogatory labeling. Through the prism of religion, they call the Pequots barbarians and savages. John Underhill wrote about the Pequots before going to war, saying that God himself sought to punish the Pequots for their sins. Underhill often refers to religion in his texts and quotes biblical passages to justify the English colonists' actions. The Church itself supported colonization, emphasizing that every being should feel the "grace of Christ," i.e., be saved from hell.

As time went by, philosophers and thinkers criticized such beliefs, although it should be noted this kind of viewpoint was not prevalent among people at the time. Denis Diderot, who was active over a hundred years after the Pequot War, stands out as one of the men who advocated for better treatment of the natives. Diderot points out that Europeans were the ones who were uncivilized. He believed that culture imposes morality and strengthens the norms of respect. Yet, in the example of the European colonization of the Americas, Diderot states that these norms were not present because the individual was so far from their home country. The French philosopher further says that the American colonies became places of brutal clashes, primarily because the colonists were so far from their home countries and were not within the radius of firmly established organized, legal institutions. In this way, the habit of restraining one's instincts for violence was weakened.

However, in the beginning, the interactions between the colonists and the Native Americans were fairly peaceful. With the formation of the colonies in New England, the British came into contact with the Pequots and Narragansetts. The Narragansett tribe was the first of the two to enter into trade relations with the English. In 1632, they sent their envoys to the English, who expressed a desire to establish trade relations with their new neighbors, the Massachusetts Bay Colony. At first, the Pequots were not very interested in intensive cooperation with the English. In the same year (1632), they proposed to the Dutch that they set up new trading points on the Connecticut River to intensify their trade cooperation, primarily the "Good Hope" trade point. This proposal reached the prominent people of Plymouth Colony, who thought this move could potentially endanger their trade interests in the area. The English, therefore, sought to form their own trading post north of the Dutch one, thus devaluing the importance of the Dutch trading post. The leaders of Plymouth Colony presented their plan to the people living in the Massachusetts Bay Colony, as well as other smaller New England colonies. However, the first governor of the Massachusetts Bay Colony, John Winthrop, rejected the plan, pointing out that they did not want to interfere in these affairs. However, Winthrop lied when he said this, for he soon sent scouts to reconnoiter that territory, with John Oldham leading the mission. The reason Winthrop refused to cooperate was that he did not want to share the profits with others. After returning from his brief mission, Oldham brought great news to his governor, noting that it was a vibrant area and an excellent trading location. Plymouth, meanwhile, was forming its own trading base, ignoring the possible danger from the Dutch.

During this time, the Pequots continued their cooperation with the Dutch, but they were not the only tribe to do so. Other smaller tribes inhabited the same territory and also dealt with the European settlers. The Pequots considered them competition and, on one occasion, liquidated several members of a rival tribe after they ignored the warning of the Pequots to stop trading with the Dutch. The Dutch did not appreciate this act. Jacob Elkins, who ran Dutch trade in the New World, was furious since he had good trade relations with other tribal communities, and with this move, the Pequots threatened their trade with the Dutch.

In 1632, the Dutch captured the Pequot's sachem, Tatobem. As one might expect, these events completely halted trade between the Dutch and the Pequot tribe. For Tatobem's release, the Dutch demanded a large ransom, and the Pequots collected a large amount of wampum to pay it. However, after the Pequots paid the ransom, the Dutch killed Tatobem anyway. The Pequots were furious about this, saying that they would seek revenge for the murder.

The Pequots, intending to avenge their tribe, attacked a European merchant ship, killing crew members and the ship's captain, John Stone, on August 8th, 1634. However, John Stone was not Dutch but rather English. Stone was a merchant who traded goods from various parts of the world, including India, Britain, and the Americas. Yet, at that moment, no one really cared about his death. Stone's behavior had long damaged his reputation, for heled an extremely tumultuous life. Alcohol, blasphemy, and violence were the cornerstones of his life, to the point that the governors of the English colonies wanted no association with him. The Dutch even rejected Stone as a potential business partner. A few months before his death, Stone was accused of attempted piracy in Manhattan but managed to escape certain death. After that, Stone acted as a free trader.

There are several versions of what happened to Stone on that eventful day in August. The first version says that Stone sailed with a crew to a Native American village. After drinking alcohol, the crew became very violent, so the Native Americans killed them. Another version points out that the Pequots killed Stone by mistake, thinking that he was a Dutch colonist.

In the months that followed, serious problems began to rise up for the Pequots. Soon after, the Narragansett tribe declared war on the Pequots. Their sour relations were primarily due to the trade rivalry between the two tribes. The Mohegan tribe also joined the war alliance against the Pequots. Under such circumstances, the Pequots set out in search of allies.

At the time, the leader of the Pequot tribe was Sassacus, the son of the murdered tribal leader Tatobem. Sassacus decided to look for allies in the Massachusetts Bay Colony. In October 1634, he sent a delegation to the Massachusetts Bay Colony's headquarters to establish trade ties and friendship with the English. The English accepted this olive branch but only on the condition that Captain John Stone's killers were arrested so they could put them on trial. The Pequot envoys informed the English that Captain Stone's violent death was retribution for kidnapping several members of their tribe, as Stone had allegedly demanded that the prisoners be his guides on the Connecticut River. Another problem cropped up when the English leaders in Boston demanded more wampum than the Pequot had offered them. Some sources even state that the Puritans asked the Pequots to trade exclusively with them. The Pequot envoys informed the English that before the treaty was finalized, they wanted the English to meet with Sassacus. However, some sources say the Pequot envoys engaged in an oral agreement with the English, although there is no written evidence of this actually occurring. The only thing we can be sure of is that the English acted as peace mediators between the Narragansetts and Pequots, restoring peace for a short period of time. After this agreement, the English established three trading cities on the Connecticut River, which was one of the main trading points in the region.

Soon after these cities were built, the leader of the Mohegans informed the English that the Pequots intended to attack the newly formed English cities on the Connecticut River. The warning was taken seriously in Boston, the capital of the Massachusetts Bay Colony. The English soon organized a new meeting with the Pequot envoys, repeating the same demands as before, with a particular emphasis on obtaining the assassins of Captain John Stone. The meeting did not go as expected, and the situation continued to spiral.

After the meeting, the English decided that the possibility of any negotiations with the Pequots no longer existed. Just days after the event, on July 20th, 1636, John Oldham, an important figure in the Massachusetts Bay Colony, was killed by Native Americans. What further infuriated the colonists was that John Oldham's body was found completely naked. They interpreted this act as an attack on Catholicism. English Captain John Mason wrote extensively on the events of the Pequot War. In his notes, he pointed out that the Pequots were a barbarian tribe and that this would not have been the first assassination of English colonists by them.

The English learned about the murder of John Oldham from Narragansett envoys. While the Narragansetts admitted that some of their men were involved in the murder, they claimed that the Pequots had organized the entire operation. The details provided by the Narragansett envoys were probably a lie, and to this day, no one is sure who should be held responsible for the death of Oldham. Most likely, Oldham was killed by members of the Narragansett tribe, as their age-old rivalry over trade with the Pequots, at times, targeted colonists who traded with the enemy.

The assassination of John Oldham was probably the tipping point. Although John Oldham had some disagreements with the authorities in the English colonies, he was a highly important community member. He played a significant role in trade, and the colonies of Plymouth and Massachusetts relied on his services. Oldham transported highly valuable goods, such as corn, which was one of the most important raw materials in the New World. He worked with the Native Americans as well, first coming into contact with them in around 1633. His death aroused concern among the colonists. Not only was Oldham their contact with other Englishmen in the area, but they believed this kind of brutality could happen to anyone—even their own families.

Although his murder is still largely a mystery, some accounts exist that help piece part of the puzzle together. John Gallop, a Boston merchant, discovered the boat in which John Oldham's body lay. As he approached Oldham's ship, Gallop saw a large number of Native Americans on the deck. At that moment, he hurried to get to the boat as soon as possible because he immediately suspected that something was wrong. When the Native Americans spotted him, they panicked and began to flee the ship. Several natives were caught and overpowered by Gallop's crew. A search of John Oldham's ship resulted in Gallop's crew finding the mutilated body of the unfortunate merchant. Gallop, highly infuriated and in fear of an impending rebellion on his own ship, tied some of the prisoners together and threw them overboard. Gallop first headed to Fort Saybrook to spread the news of the English merchant's death and immediately sailed to Boston afterward, where he submitted a detailed report on his colleague's death. The captured Narragansett said that members of the Narragansett tribe and their allies were behind Oldham's murder. John Winthrop concluded that Oldham had been killed because he found himself at the center of turmoil among the tribes.

There is another version of Oldham's death, in which the murder resulted from a transactional dispute between Oldham and the tribes with whom he collaborated. The third version, which was mentioned earlier and is the least plausible, was the one put forward by the Narragansetts, of how the Pequots killed Oldham. Winthrop also claimed that most of the evidence pointed to the natives living on Block Island. The small tribe that inhabited Block Island had close ties to the Narragansett and Eastern Niantic tribes.

There is much evidence to point to the guilt of the Narragansetts, yet the British chose to listen to their version of the events. Truthfully, the British could not afford to wage war against both the Pequots and the Narragansetts. Instead, they decided to wage war against the stronger tribe, the one that controlled larger territories and had more wealth. Also, the British had to take into consideration that the Pequots were responsible for the deaths of several members of rival tribes that traded with the Dutch, so the possibility that they may have been the culprit for the murdered merchant could not be completely ruled out. On top of this, the British still had a fairly fresh memory of the murder of John Stone. While Stone might not have been greatly loved by the community, his death could have been used as an additional impetus for war. Thus, the British colonists decided to launch a punitive expedition against the Pequots.

Although the English later made an alliance with other native tribes to fight against the Pequots, they at first targeted whoever they could get their hands on. The first move of the English was an expedition to Block Island. John Endecott was placed in charge of ninety men, and their goal was to punish the killers of John Oldham. Many of the soldiers led by Endecott (about 40 percent) were experienced fighters who had fought on European soil. Captain John Endecott himself is mentioned in historical sources as an experienced soldier with exceptional courage. He is said to have been an unyielding Puritan who showed intense intolerance of Roman Catholics.

John Underhill, an English captain in the Pequot War, made several reports of this event. His texts represent the most extensive material regarding the attack on Block Island, and he was also one of the commanders of that operation. Underhill points out that the effort to access the mainland of Block Island was initially impossible. After realizing the English were approaching the coast, the Native Americans showered the colonists with many arrows. Underhill also states that the Native Americans shot firearms, with some of the shots hitting the soldiers. A group of about fifty Manissean warriors offered violent resistance to the English, but their resistance was in vain. The English colonists soon reorganized, and the Native Americans began to flee. Most of the natives were able to flee, and the English, likewise, did not suffer much damage.

During this punitive expedition, the English set fire to several villages and cornfields on the island to send a strong message to the Native Americans. This action was a severe blow to the natives on the island, as the English destroyed large quantities of their food supplies and burned their crops.

The next stop of this punitive expedition was the territory under the control of the Pequots. The Pequots were oblivious to the English operations on Block Island, so they welcomed the English warmly from the shore. After the colonists did not respond to their greetings, the Pequots sent one of their elders by canoe to talk to the English. The demands of the colonists were exacting. Firstly, they once again insisted that the Pequots must hand over the assassins of Captain John Stone. The tribal leader who paddled out to speak with the English pointed out that the Pequots could not hand over Sassacus, noting that he had no choice and that he had to avenge his father's death. The tribal leader also expressed regret over the death of John Stone, reiterating once again that the Pequots thought he was a Dutch colonist and not an English one.

Underhill noted some more details during the negotiations between Endecott and the Pequot elder. He pointed out that the Pequots delayed the negotiations, which the English interpreted as a means to gain time for their warriors to organize. Also, it was noted that there were no women and children on the coast that day. Despite the warm welcome, this detail aroused suspicion among the Puritans, as the English interpreted this as a willingness to engage in military action. Also, Sassacus was not present that day; the tribal elder who spoke to the English colonists said that he had gone to visit one of the neighboring Pequot tribes. Endecott informed the elder that if the Pequots did not meet the conditions imposed from Boston, then the English would take twenty Pequot children as hostages. Such conditions would be difficult for any tribe to accept, especially the Pequots. The tribe had been decimated by epidemics, and they could not agree to further reduce its population by giving the English hostages. Also, the English demanded some material compensation from the Pequots, as paying tribute to the English would create a subservient feeling among the Pequots, which would hopefully help guarantee their future good behavior. The Pequot elder was finally allowed to return to the coast and talk to the other members of the tribe about what the English had said.

In Underhill's account, the English became more and more impatient as time passed. Many believed the Pequots were readying themselves for war, as they could no longer be seen on the coast. Eventually, Endecott decided to attack first. The attack did not meet with significant resistance, and apart from the burning of homes and the looting of crops, nothing significant happened. Lion Gardiner, who was the captain of Fort Saybrook, and his men were the most active during this campaign, as there was a famine among his crew at Saybrook. Once the English dispersed, the colonists in the Connecticut area and at Fort Saybrook had to spend the winter alone, without support from Boston. In other words, they were left at the mercy of the enraged Pequot warriors. After this event, the Pequot War officially began.

Chapter 5 – Military Capacities, Organization, and Tactics of the Warring Parties

To better understand the course of the Pequot War, it is vital to get acquainted with the Puritans' and Pequots' military capabilities.

Pequot warriors had a lot of combat experience since they consistently fought with other tribes. These encounters involved a direct showdown on the battlefield, meaning there wasn't much use of tactics. The Pequots mainly relied on bows and arrows, with the occasional use of firearms. Some indicators show that the Pequots had dozens of rifles, but they seldom used them during the Pequot War. According to some information, the Pequots had slightly more than 1,500 warriors before the Pequot War broke out. This information is based on the number of warriors who died at the end of the war, which was around 1,500. It is logical to assume that not all the warriors were killed and that a small number of them managed to escape.

When the first battles with the English broke out, the Pequots had to completely change their approach to warfare because of the Europeans' armor and firearms. The Pequots were well aware of the fact that if they launched a massive attack, it would result in a complete catastrophe. So, the Pequots initially led small raids, which often ended fatally for the English. The natural surroundings and local environment allowed the natives to camouflage themselves more easily, allowing them to surprise the English. The Pequots also knew the disadvantages of European armor, and during the battles, they often aimed for the weak points, such as the neck, legs, head, or shoulders.

The structure of the attacks used by the Pequots in some situations is quite interesting. Namely, during the attack, several warriors fired arrows, after which they would throw themselves on the ground backward, thus leaving space for the archers behind to fire a new round of arrows. The arrows used back then had a range of about thirty meters (around ninety-eight feet). On the tips of the arrows, the Pequots placed sharpened bones, eagle claws, or metal heads made of brass. These metal tips posed the greatest threat to English soldiers, so the English sought to obstruct the Dutch trade with the natives early on, as this was one of the items that were often traded. Interestingly enough, the Pequots learned information about the European way of warfare from the Dutch, such as the importance of armor and the firearms they used.

The Pequots knew that the English needed time to reload their muskets, so they tried to use that period to attack. On average, a soldier took one minute to fire two shots, which meant about thirty seconds to reload. More experienced soldiers were able to fire up to three shots. An English soldier could easily hit a target in combat at a distance of between 50 and 75 meters (164 and 246 feet) in favorable conditions. During the fighting in the Pequot War, English troops mostly fired at the enemy from close distances. There are some indications that the Pequots asked English prisoners to show them how to make gunpowder, but this information is not entirely reliable.

The bow and arrow came to the forefront during the Pequot War. The Pequots tried to inflict damage on the English troops from a safe distance by firing from farther away. This was usually a distance of between 100 to 150 yards (between 91 and 137 meters). The Pequots used other weapons as well, including war clubs, tomahawks, hammers, axes, and knives, some of which were made of stone, bone, or iron. The use of European firearms was never fully utilized by the Pequots, which was to their disadvantage, as they posed a greater danger to the colonists. The main obstacle to the use of European weapons lies in the fact that the natives did not know how to service them, as they often broke down and were unreliable. The nature of Native American warfare before the Europeans' arrival also did not involve the use of heavy armor and protection, which the Europeans widely practiced.

Commanders, known as *pniese*, led larger groups of Pequot warriors. They were not sachems, but they were highly regarded in the community because of their knowledge and abilities. In 1623, Edward Winslow, who was the governor of Plymouth Colony three times, described his experience during an encounter with one of these *pniese*.

> The Pnieses are men of great courage and wisdom, and to these also the Devil appeareth more familiarly then to others, and as we conceive maketh covenant with them to preserve them from death, by wounds, with arrows, knives, hatchets...yet they are known by their courage and boldness, by reason whereof one of them will chase almost an hundred men; for they account it death for whomsoever stand in their way. These are highly esteemed of all sorts of people, and are of the Sachems Council, without whom they will not war or undertake any weighty business. In war their Sachems for their more safety go in the midst of them. They are commonly men of the greatest stature and strength, and such as will endure most hardness, and yet are more discreet, courteous, and humane in their carriages

> than any amongst them scorning theft, lying, and the like base dealings, and stand as much upon their reputation as any men.

Also, among the Native Americans, there were cases of conflict resolution by two tribal fighters fighting each other. For that purpose, those warriors who were known as the best and the bravest in the tribe were chosen.

Such a situation was witnessed by English colonist Thomas Morton, who immigrated from Devon (England) to North America. Morton describes this struggle as follows:

> The two champions prepared for the fight, with their bows in hand, and a quiver full of arrows at their backs, they have entered into the field, the challenger and challenge-ed have chosen two trees, standing within a little distance of each other, they have cast lots for the chief of the trees, then either champion setting himself behind his tree, watches an advantage to let fly his shafts, and to gall his enemy. Then they continue shooting at each other, if by chance they espy any part open, they endeavour to gall the combatant in that part, and use much agility in the performance of the task they take in hand. Resolute they are in the execution of their vengeance, when once they have begunne, and will in no wise be daunted, or seem to shrink, though they doe catch a clip with an arrow, but fight it out in this manner till one or other be slaine.

As one can ascertain, the Pequots had one of the most respected military forces in the New England area. However, this partially led to their downfall in the war. The Pequots underestimated the European way of warfare, which meant observing the opposing forces, organizing troops, utilizing the appropriate tactics, and patiently waiting for the right moment to strike. These techniques were usual for European battlefields, which the English then transferred to North America.

Although this played a role in the outcome of the war, the main reason for the defeat of the Pequots was the technological supremacy of the Europeans, i.e., their use of muskets and armor. The musket first appeared in the 16th century, and it evolved over time. By the 17th century, the musket was the most used weapon. One would have to light a wick, which then lit the gunpowder and spat out a projectile. This projectile could be a round metal object or a stone. Muskets had a range of up to 140 meters (around 153 yards), but at a greater distance, they were useless. It was impossible to use muskets during the rain, and soldiers often experienced accidents due to the weapons malfunctioning. In any case, muskets were one of the factors that brought dominance to the English in the Pequot War.

Colonial soldiers were also armed with pistols, but this type of firearm was not very popular during military operations at the time. The reasons are multiple. These guns were used more often for close combat and not for military campaigns that required long-distance shooting. Also, the range of pistols during the 17th century was considerably less than that of the musket. A pistol could fire a projectile within a range of 35 meters (around 38 yards). The pistols were designed to insert two bullets at once, and when fired, both would be ejected. However, there is one similarity between pistols and rifles: the type of ammunition they used.

During the fighting at Mystic Fort, the use of firearms was not particularly stressed, as the settlement was densely populated. The fighting took place too quickly, and during the fighting, the English mostly used swords. The mandatory equipment of the European soldier during the 17th century included not only swords but also knives. Therefore, New England's colonial army had a wide range of weapons at its disposal. When we talk about armaments, it should be noted that English soldiers during the Pequot War used, to some extent, war axes, which were more characteristic of the arsenal of native warriors.

The colonists of New England sought to create a strong militia even before the Pequot War broke out. To this end, the English hired several experienced European soldiers, such as John Underhill, Daniel Patrick (a captain in the Massachusetts Bay Colony), and John Mason, who quickly adapted to the conditions in the New World. These were not the only experienced soldiers in the colonies, as a good chunk had taken part in the Thirty Years' War (1618–1648), a war that pitted the countries of central Europe against each other. These hired men intensively trained troops, showing them how to handle firearms and swords efficiently. They were well received into the Puritan community even though they were not members of their church. The Puritans accepted them as professionals who were there to do their job.

Another important factor contributing to the Pequots' defeat is that the English made a military alliance with the traditional enemies of the Pequots: the Narragansett and Mohegan tribes. In addition to gaining more men to fight in the war, the warriors of these tribes were also familiar with the terrain on which the battles took place and the military capabilities of the Pequots.

English colonists wore armored iron vests or heavy, long leather coats. At that time, this type of protection was excellent, and it allowed the English to significantly reduce the number of victims in their ranks. These coats were extremely expensive because the leather was of high quality and was produced in England. Hence, the colonists imported a large number of these coats as mandatory equipment for soldiers. The protection of soldiers also included helmets, which were of vital importance, and metal covers above the knees. And even though that kind of equipment was quite heavy and greatly restricted movement, it provided soldiers during the Pequot War with security. This equipment was produced throughout Europe; therefore, different models were available to the Puritans. John Underhill once pointed out that it was this protection that saved him from certain death.

The English tactics used during the war were reflected primarily during the Mystic campaign, which was the main campaign of the war. The troops were divided into two groups, which coordinated attacks, leaving the defenders with no chance of victory. The perimeter was encircled by assisting units that had a dual role. They "guarded the backs" of the majority of the troops, but they also captured all those who tried to escape from the fort. According to estimates from Mystic Fort, only a dozen Pequot survived, which speaks volumes about the efficiency of this type of organizing. The English tried to use the element of surprise several times during the Pequot War. These surprise attacks diminished the possibility for a quick and proper reaction by the Pequot warriors. It also prevented the Pequots from consolidating their troops, which gave the Europeans a better advantage since the Pequots had superior numbers.

During the Mystic campaign, the English worked intensively to gather intelligence, a technique unknown to the Pequots. For instance, John Mason constantly sent Native American scouts ahead of the bulk of English troops and their allies. These scouts consisted of warriors and guides of the Narragansett tribe, who updated Mason continuously about the situation that awaited him on the field. Mason was also given information about the Pequots' position by scouts who carried out daily activities during the advance of the English troops.

In addition to the tried and true tactics, the English also used newer techniques during the war with the Pequots, as they had to adapt to the Pequots' way of warfare. This was especially reflected during Endecott's punitive expedition to Block Island. On these occasions, the Puritans could not make full use of their military capabilities. They had to take longer breaks to attack at intervals, as their enemy was constantly on the move. Certainly, the experiences gained during Captain Endecott's expedition were later analyzed by the English and used against the enemy.

Chapter 6 – Conflict Escalation

The war came at an exceptionally trying time for both sides. The year before, the region had been hit by a hurricane, which devastated crops and demolished homes. The situation worsened because of the flooding, which took many lives and caused substantial material damage. As a result, the winter of 1635/36 was immensely harsh, and the lack of food led to the deaths of many animals, which subsequently caused another shortage of food for the people. The colony's distressing situation can be confirmed by a letter from a certain Edward Trelawny, who conveyed the events to his brother in England. "Currently, the country is in general poverty, a large number of people have arrived in the country." This period was also accompanied by the mass migration of English to North America, meaning there were more mouths to feed but not enough food to do so. Diseases also caused a demographic catastrophe among the local inhabitants, so there were not even enough people to cultivate the land. Another problem for the English was that they did not fully adapt to the North American sowing conditions. This new situation, according to some historians, hastened preparations for war.

The situation in the English fortress of Saybrook, where many actions of the Pequot War took place, was also complicated. Some sources point to the general dissatisfaction among the Saybrook inhabitants. Namely, the people residing in the fort wrote to the colony leaders about starvation and the shortage of clothes. The biggest problem the people faced was the lack of corn. This commodity was valued not only among the natives but also the European immigrants. Corn was easy to grow and fed both humans and livestock. It could also be consumed in many ways, such as dried, cooked, and baked in bread.

There was some dissatisfaction among the Puritans over the decision to go to war with the Pequots. Lion Gardiner, the commander of Fort Saybrook, pointed out that his crew was starving in a time of peace. He secretly hoped that the Native Americans would accept Boston's demands for fear of escalating the conflict. The crew at Saybrook had good reason to fear the oncoming war. Namely, the fortress was located near the Pequots, and there was the logical possibility that they would be the first to be attacked. However, over time, Gardiner changed his mind about the war because the opportunity arose for the English to gain the rich fields owned by the Pequots.

No matter what some of the Puritans might have thought or wished, a war was coming. The punitive expedition to Block Island, which was led by the experienced Captain John Endecott, was just an overture to the bloody war between the Puritans and the Pequots. However, the Block Island campaign itself did not result in significant human casualties on either side, although Endecott burned several villages and looted supplies.

After Endecott's campaign, the Pequots began looking for allies. They contacted the sachems of the Narragansetts and Mohegans, asking them to join in the war against the English. If the Pequots had gained this alliance, the war would have very likely turned out to be in their favor. First of all, they would have eliminated the enemy "from their doorstep," and the English would not have one but two powerful tribes against them. However, those tribes would decide later on to fight on the side of the English. In this way, any possibility of the Native Americans joining together to war against the European immigrants was suspended. It seems that the long history of internecine conflicts between the Pequots and the Narragansetts was an insurmountable obstacle. Nevertheless, the Pequots were still an exceptionally vigorous opponent, with as many as twenty-six sachems of smaller tribes on their side. However, most of these alliances were not of great importance to the Pequots when the war began since most of the tribes remained neutral.

The Pequots were furious over the actions of the English; the burning of their villages and the destruction of crops aroused great disdain and hatred toward the European settlers. Lion Gardiner, who was in charge of Fort Saybrook, and Edward Winslow, the governor of Plymouth Colony, wrote to the leaders in Boston because of the reckless actions that had been organized there. These leaders pointed out that the problems had been solved, at least for a while. Therefore, Winthrop did not think that the Pequots would respond with military intervention. He considered the punitive expedition led by Endecott to be a warning to the Pequots, who he assumed would realize that they were facing a powerful enemy.

For the Boston leaders, this opinion turned out to be a mistake. At the beginning of 1637, the Pequots began planning more intensive military operations. They directed their first actions against the colonists living around the Connecticut River. Their guerilla-style attacks caused immense damage to the English. The beginning of 1637 was essentially revenge for Endecott's actions in the previous summer. During this period, around thirty English colonists lost their lives. Those who were captured alive by the Pequots suffered a worst fate: torture and a slow death.

There were occasional raids on Fort Saybrook, which was designed by Lion Gardiner and built at the mouth of the Connecticut River. In addition to its importance as a military base for the Puritans, it also had a large mill. The attacks on Fort Saybrook were intense, but the Pequots carried them out in smaller groups. Lion Gardiner provides some information about these events. *"One day members of the saybrook crew had to leave the fort to procure supplies. During negotiations with the pequot, they were allowed to pass safely through their territories. Upon our return, our three men were ambushed by an indian. The pequot tribe's warriors organized the ambush, and all three were killed, and the goods intended for the crew in the fortress were looted."*

Soon, a conflict would take place that the English could not easily ignore. In April 1637, about 200 Pequot warriors attacked the small settlement of Wethersfield, which was stationed south of Hartford. On April 23rd, the Pequots carried out a sudden and fierce attack on the English colonists while they were carrying out spring planting. Among the Pequots' ranks were members of the Wangunk tribe. Six men and two women lost their lives in the Pequot attack. The Pequots and their allies also killed twenty cattle. The killing of these animals created additional problems for the colonists because it reduced their food supplies when there was already a food shortage going on.

In that swift raid, the Pequots captured two girls, who belonged, incidentally, to the richest man in Wethersfield. Sources state that the Pequots, as they canoed by Fort Saybrook, mocked the colonists living there. They showed them the bloody clothes of the slain colonists and ridiculed the captured girls. The two girls were eventually returned after a ransom was paid. Dutch traders mediated the exchange.

Many historians believe that this Pequot attack was an effort by the natives to destroy English supplies and create additional problems for them in an already difficult year. By doing this, the Pequots essentially told the English they were not welcome.

The events of April 23rd, 1637, made things irreversible. It can certainly be considered one of the turning points in the Pequot War. Instead of the surprise hit-and-run tactics, Sassacus and his tribe began openly showing aggression toward the Europeans. These actions served as an indicator of what was to come. A few days after the attack on Wethersfield, on May 1st, 1637, the Colony of Connecticut officially declared war on the Pequot tribe. The General Court in Hartford had no argument over this ruling; a war with the Pequots was the only option for the colonists.

Philip Vincent, a soldier at Saybrook, provides information about the actions of the Pequots in the area of the Connecticut River and their attacks on Fort Saybrook. His descriptions of the Pequot warriors are very captivating. He points out that they had an imposing physique and that they were extremely adept warriors. Vincent also describes the Pequot as a savage barbarian tribe that no one dared to go against in open battle. These descriptions help show why many of the other tribes feared the Pequots and how they posed a threat. According to Philip's testimonies, even many English soldiers were fearful of the Pequot warriors.

The actions of the Pequots around Fort Saybrook and the Connecticut River area lasted for months. In the early spring of 1637, the English officially made a war alliance with the Pequots' traditional enemies, the Narragansetts and the Mohegans. The English had learned of the Pequots' attempts to ally with these two tribes, and such knowledge was not at all pleasant to them, as a native alliance would have certainly crushed the colonists. This was just one of the reasons why the English were in a hurry to gather allies in this war. However, gaining native allies could, at times, be rather difficult. Some tribes distrusted the new settlers, and they didn't want to help the colonists only to be betrayed later on. In addition, the Puritans viewed the natives with some disdain.

During the Pequot War, an extremely bizarre practice took place, namely the exchange of body parts of a killed enemy. In occasional battles with the Pequots, the Mohegans and Narragansetts cut off body parts and wore them around their English allies, who, in turn, ridiculed their native allies. However, a similar practice was prevalent among the English settlers, as they often beheaded their enemies. The exchange of these war trophies was a form of strengthening the war alliance between them. This mechanism, that is, the gift between the different cultures and peoples of the time, displays a notion of authority. Anthropological observation of such phenomena indicates the flow of power.

The Puritans did not apply this process of desecrating a dead enemy's body; they only did it to prisoners of war. A large number of heinous offenders and thieves in Puritan society suffered a similar fate. In Puritan society, during the beheading process, the rest of the desecrated body was chopped up and divided into quarters. Persons convicted of high treason inevitably went through that kind of punishment. Throughout Puritan history, there have been cases where top government officials experienced such a fate.

In England, a person convicted of high treason would have their head decapitated in front of an audience, and the head would later be publicly displayed as a warning to others. The English would often boil the severed head to slow down the deterioration of the tissue. In this way, the heads remained "fresh" for days, which gave the impression that the head had recently been cut off, which, in itself, is a highly morbid act. The cheeks on the severed head were sometimes painted red, which gave an additional effect of freshness. This form of desecration of an enemy's body is present in the

Puritans' religious texts. Since religion had an immense impact on every sphere of life, this phenomenon was frequent.

The Puritans justified their actions by religion. In the holy texts, King David launched a campaign to punish all the unbelievers of the world for creating a new Canaan. In a way, the Puritans identified with this act, as they sought to create a place in the New World that was purified of nonbelievers. It was with these elements of religion that the Puritans sought to silence critics after the Mystic River massacre, which will be covered in the next chapter.

However, the practice of profaning the body of a dead enemy was also present among many native tribes of North America. In addition to written sources proving this, there is material evidence of these practices. Namely, archaeologists have found bodies that lack limbs or skulls. Such customs were deeply rooted in many Native American communities. Warriors often carried home body parts of their slain opponents from battles. They then showed these body parts to their families, other members of the tribe, and tribal chiefs. In this way, they proved they had emerged victorious from the war. It also demonstrated a warrior's courage, as he had protected his community by putting his life on the line.

Many tribes practiced brutal torture, which was done in public. The captured warrior was expected to endure this physical torture bravely while being observed and scrutinized by his enemy. These bloody customs primarily involved cutting off the prisoner's hands or feet. The final act in this process was beheading or scalping the prisoner of war. Given that the Pequots often captured colonists alive during the Pequot War, it is safe to say that many of them suffered various forms of torture.

Many Native American tribes had an extremely peculiar view of such a public, bloody act. They believed that a captured warrior had a chance to redeem himself, as he had not died an honorable death on the battlefield but had rather fallen into the hands of his enemy. That is precisely why the tribes of North America expected courage from the warrior who went through these tortures.

Similar to the English, Narragansett warriors publicly hung the limbs of slain enemies, and they did the same with the Pequot warriors. During the Pequot War, Uncas and other warriors from the Mohegan tribe captured five Pequot men. After torturing them, they were decapitated, and the severed heads were taken to their Puritan allies. The severed heads were publicly exhibited in Fort Saybrook. In this way, Uncas strengthened his alliance with the European colonists. These actions were fairly common during the war.

The English often rewarded their allies during the Pequot War for bringing in body parts of the slain Pequots. After the Mystic River massacre, the practice of beheading and mutilating body parts of fugitive Pequot warriors continued. On one occasion, a sachem of a smaller tribal community visited Fort Saybrook to try to arrange a trade with the Puritans. Captain Lion Gardiner told him a trade was possible, but he had one condition. He asked the sachem to bring the severed heads of those Pequot who sought refuge in their tribe. All those who brought the limbs or heads of Pequot warriors were rewarded. This move allowed the neutral parties of the war to become more involved and assist the English.

The act of exchanging body parts, torturing, and beheading was not just characteristic of the Pequot War. Throughout history, similar examples can be found in many cultures and parts of the world. Today, in the 21st century, there are countries in which certain serious criminals and political dissidents are punished by cutting off body parts, desecrating a man after death, or being killed in public executions. For the most part, these are countries whose laws are based on totalitarian political principles and whose laws are derived from religious texts and beliefs. In other words, these are mostly societies that are not familiar with democratic principles and basic human rights and freedoms.

Chapter 7 – Mystic River Campaign

In the literature, the Mystic River campaign is also known as the "Mystic Massacre." We draw most of our knowledge about the largest and most massive military operation of the Pequot War from the notes of the direct protagonists of that event. Much of this information is provided to us by Captain John Mason. In addition to Mason, some information about the Mystic campaign is provided by John Underhill and Lion Gardiner. Historiography agrees on one thing; while all these sources can be considered reliable, they were all written by the victors of the Pequot War. Some oral history of this event survived, which was primarily transmitted by the Mystic River campaign participants and the small number of surviving Pequots, who then passed on their terrible experiences to future generations. In addition to these sources, historians can look at the archaeological evidence. Douglas D. Scott led several archaeological expeditions to learn more about the most significant battle of the Pequot War. Douglas Scott is considered to be one of the most renowned American archaeologists today. He has been awarded numerous recognitions by respectable institutions, such as the United States Department of the Interior, the National Park Service, and the Archaeological Institute of America. The owners of plots in the neighborhood selflessly ceded certain sites so they could be surveyed, and metal detection clubs have, in some small part, also contributed to the research of the Mystic Fort site. Thanks to this research, today, we have a lot of data to utilize to better understand the Mystic River campaign.

The Puritan campaign in Mystic River represents the first major action in the Pequot War. Indigenous raids during the months-long siege of Saybrook allowed the English to gain some insight into the fighting capacities, habits, and movements of the Pequot warriors. The Mystic River campaign lasted from May 17th to May 27th, 1637. The campaign's culmination was the battle at Pequot Fort, better known as Mystic Fort (also spelled as Mistick Fort in some sources), which lasted over an hour.

The whole campaign was excellently organized by experienced English military personnel. The Puritans undertook extensive observation measures, mapped their approach, organized the men, and figured out how best to withdraw troops from the scene. Until the battle at Mystic River, all the other

English military maneuvers, such as the action on Block Island, can only be viewed as punitive expeditions; the same goes for the Pequots, whose actions are often seen as raids.

The Mystic River campaign was primarily the result of the Pequots' attack on the colonial settlement of Wethersfield in late April 1637. A colonial court in Hartford indicted the Pequots for killing English colonists in the Connecticut River area and appointed Captain John Mason to lead future military actions in the war against the Pequots. In addition to the experienced Captain Mason, Robert Seeley, William Pratt, and Thomas Bull joined the operation. These three men served as lieutenants. Eight sergeants were also involved in the Mystic River campaign, and local authorities made their own contributions as well. They were ordered to procure twenty sets of armor, weapons for the soldiers, and other necessary equipment for the military operation. While local authorities were given detailed instructions on how much to procure, each soldier was required to bring one pound of gunpowder, four pounds of shot, and twenty bullets. The settlements that made the highest contribution to the Mystic River campaign were Hartford, Windsor, and Wethersfield. In addition to the allied Mohegan and Narragansett tribes, warriors from the Suckiaug (also spelled as Saukiog or Sickaog) tribe also joined the action.

The Puritans were resolute about sending troops seventeen days after they declared war, which speaks volumes about their determination to deal with the Pequots once and for all. The troops sailed from Hartford on May 10th, 1637, and the journey to their first destination took about seven days. The winds were blowing against them, so the journey took longer than anticipated. They finally arrived at their desired destination of Fort Saybrook on May 17th, 1637.

Mason received clear instructions from his superiors regarding the attack on the Pequots. After arriving at their destination, he met with Captain John Underhill and Lion Gardiner, with whom he discussed the plan of attack and other instructions dictated from the council in Hartford.

The original proposed route dictated from Hartford involved advancing along the Connecticut River and using the typical combat formations. But although this action relied on standard military formations and tactics, there was something novel about it: the support of allied Native American tribes. The English troops numbered about 77 men. The allied tribes contributed around 250 warriors, who were, for the most part, Mohegans and Narragansetts.

Underhill suggested they reject the original plan of attack. As it has already been pointed out, the Pequots had changed certain habits and approaches to war to better fight the English. Underhill knew this. In fact, Underhill understood the Pequots perhaps the best of the three campaign leaders because he had more experience with their war capabilities and resources. The plan presented by Captain Mason implied direct conflict, and Underhill knew the chances of such a skirmish were minimal or nonexistent. Since the Pequots knew the advantages of European armaments, it was almost certain that they would avoid a direct clash with the British.

There was another problem as well. The English were fighting on foreign ground. Although some men had lived there for a few years, their knowledge of the terrain paled greatly in comparison to the Native Americans. It helped the English to have some of the tribes on their side, but Underhill and Gardiner were skeptical of including them in their ranks. To many, the fact that the natives had recently been allies of the Pequots raised doubts. Gardiner wrote the following, "How they dared to trust the Mohegan Indians who themselves descended from the Pequot." There was an established opinion among the colonists that the natives were generally a volatile factor; such an attitude had been formed during the first years of colonization.

However, they had no better choice; native allies during the Mystic River campaign were necessary. Captain Mason understood this and spoke up in defense of the Native American allies. Mason recognized that the campaign could not succeed without people who possessed knowledge of the terrain. Also, the Mohegans and Narragansetts were able to provide information on the movements of the Pequot warriors and the deployment of enemy troops.

During the negotiations of the Mystic River campaign, Dutch merchants arrived at the fort. They returned with the two girls who had been kidnapped by the Pequot warriors during the attack on Wethersfield on April 23rd, 1637. Around that same time, the leaders of the campaign came to an agreement. The frontal attack that was supposed to be carried out along the Connecticut River was unanimously rejected. Instead, the Puritans decided to sail outside Connecticut territory to make the Pequots think their troops were leaving. Underhill's men joined the military operations, while Gardiner decided to ensure the surgeon at Saybrook provided medical assistance to the wounded soldiers.

On Thursday, May 18th, 1637, the expedition set out to attack fortified Pequot areas, with the first target being Mystic Fort. To get there, the English decided to go across Narragansett territory, as it was located near where the Pequots resided. The expedition arrived in the Narragansetts' territory on May 20th, but the troops had to wait a little longer for the attack, as bad weather occurred and the army's leaders had to meet with the sachem to discuss the plan of attack. The Narragansetts suggested that the best chance for success was to launch a surprise attack during the night. They also gave detailed information about the enemy's position and the locations they were about to attack. It was agreed that the Narragansetts would organize themselves outside the settlement and ambush those Pequots escaping from the attack. Miantonomi (also spelled as Miantonomoh), the sachem of the Narragansetts, offered the English their best guides.

In the end, it was decided that the English and their allies would continue through the territory of the Narragansetts, then through the enemy's territory until they reached Mystic Fort. The English commanders considered speed, secrecy, and efficiency to be the keys to the campaign's success, so any further delay was unacceptable. Time was of the essence, as any prolongation could lead to the possibility of detection.

Once the Mystic River campaign leaders concluded that the operation was already behind, they decided not to wait for reinforcements from the Massachusetts Bay Colony. On May 24th, the expedition embarked on a journey of thirty-five miles (fifty-six kilometers) and soon reached the Niantic fort. This fort was not one of the planned targets, but the English knew the Niantics were on fairly good terms with the Pequots. If the Niantics spotted the colonists' movements, they could then inform the Pequots, which would jeopardize the entire operation. Since they could not enter the fort, their only option was to surround it and prevent the Niantics from leaving.

Mystic Fort was around fifteen miles (about twenty-four kilometers) away from the Niantic fort. On the morning of May 25th, the bulk of Mason's troops continued their journey. During the day, the forces covered a huge distance, which took a great toll on their physical endurance.

Before the attack, Mason decided to hold a war council, where they once again went over all the details. This break allowed the soldiers to rest before the great clash with the enemy. The expedition soon learned that several other well-guarded strategic sites were in the immediate vicinity of Mystic Fort. However, at no point did such knowledge discourage Mason and his troops. Although the soldiers did not have enough time to rest from their long journey, it was decided they would attack the fort. Before the attack, the Puritans joined in prayer, which was something they typically did before an immediate battle.

The English counted on the surprise factor. The ideal scenario would be to catch the Pequots asleep. It is not known when exactly the English attacked, as the sources differ. According to some information, the attack started one hour after midnight, while other sources state the English attacked four hours after midnight.

The troops were divided into two groups, with one led by Captain John Mason and the other by John Underhill. The plan was devised in this order:

Mason would attack from the east entrance, while Underhill led the attack from the west. Tall wooden pillars surrounded the fort, and the entrances were camouflaged, yet that didn't prevent the guides from discerning the paths to the entrances. Mystic Fort covered about two acres of land, and the attack was supposed to be coordinated so that both groups attacked simultaneously.

However, things rarely go as planned. As the English approached the fort, dogs began to bark, revealing the presence of the English soldiers. One member of the Pequot tribe saw the English and began to alarm the others. At that moment, the English decided to attack, even though the troops were not in the agreed positions.

Mason's force met with fierce resistance from the natives, especially when he entered the settlement, for the fighting had intensified. The interior of the fort was densely populated. Mason's group suffered some losses but continued to suppress the Pequots. The Pequots, who had many of their best warriors in the fort, fought bravely. It is believed between 100 and 150 Pequot warriors were inside the fort. Testimonies say it took five soldiers to defeat just one Pequot warrior. At one point, Mason realized that if the fight continued at that pace, the operation could end unsuccessfully, as it would be too difficult to eliminate all the natives in the fort with the number of soldiers he had left. There were also many wounded among the English ranks, which made Mason's position even harder.

Due to these circumstances, Mason was forced to rethink his strategy. He decided to set fire to a dwelling inside the fort, and his soldiers followed his example. John Underhill describes the details of Mason's move as such:

> Captaine Mason and my selfe losing each of us a man, and had neere twentie wounded: most couragiously these Pequeats behaved themselves: but seeing the Fort was to hotte for us, wee devised a way how wee might save our selves and prejudice them, Captaine Mason entering into a Wigwam, brought out a fire-brand, after hee had wounded many in the house, then hee set fire on the Westside where he entred, my selfe set fire on the South end with a traine of Powder, the fires of both meeting in the center of the Fort blazed most terribly, and burnt all in the space of halfe an houre; many couragious fellowes were unwilling to come out, and fought most desperately through the Palisadoes.

This move is considered to be one of the main actions that led to the success of the Mystic River campaign. There are certain indications that the English would have failed if Mason had not decided to utilize fire. As one will shortly see, the Pequot War is characterized by unconventional military maneuvers, which further reflects the brutality of that short-lived but bloody war.

When the fire broke out, Underhill and his troops attacked immediately, demonstrating his experience and quick wit in battle since none of this had been planned. Underhill's men entered the fort armed with firearms and swords. The northern part of the fort was already on fire, and Underhill and his men followed the example of Mason and continued to set fires. When Underhill noticed Mason's troops had advanced, he decided to withdraw his contingent to outside the southwest entrance to the fort and continue fighting there.

Many Pequots tried to escape the fortress, especially in moments when the intensity of the English attack was too great. Thankfully, for the English (and unfortunately for the Pequots), one thing went according to plan. Several troops, mostly composed of native warriors, had surrounded the fort to prevent the escape of the Pequots. Thus, most of the people who managed to escape from Mystic Fort fell into the hands of the Mohegans, Narragansetts, and Suckiaugs and were killed. Sources indicate that the warriors of the Pequot tribe fought bravely to their last breath.

The end of the battle showed all the destruction and devastation that had been wrought. Sources differ, but between 400 and 700 members of the Pequot tribe lay dead in or near Mystic Fort. Most sources indicate that a little more than 400 people lived in the fort before the attack, and since almost everyone lost their lives that day, the estimate of a little over 400 people is the most likely. The largest number of casualties were women and children. It is estimated that the majority of the victims died in the fires caused by the English. The English casualties, on the other hand, were incomparably smaller. Two soldiers were killed, while a large number were wounded. Over 30 percent of the Puritan soldiers were seriously or lightly wounded in this battle, which lasted for over an hour. The native allies also suffered casualties; however, the exact number of how many died or were wounded is not known. Many of them suffered at the hands of the English themselves since they could not distinguish their native partners from the Pequots. As a result, the English shot their allies.

The returning journey posed an even greater challenge to the English and their Native American allies than the battle at Mystic Fort, as they had to carry a large number of wounded soldiers through enemy territory. Immediately after the battle, a temporary military camp was formed since they expected a Pequot counterattack. Hundreds of Pequot warriors from neighboring villages gathered on the nearby hills. Fear reigned among the English and their allies, but they didn't have much time to dwell on it, for the Pequot response was so quick that the English had no real time to rest. The Pequots kept out of reach of English firearms, so Underhill sought to mobilize the Mohegan and Narragansett warriors to form a defensive formation, which managed to repel the Pequots.

Some warriors of the Narragansett tribe feared that the English would run out of ammunition and decided to leave the campaign and return to their territory. This move shows how the allied tribes relied on the English and their technological military achievements. About fifty Narragansett warriors decided to leave the campaign. On their return home, they were attacked by the Pequots. However, Underhill decided to help the allies, jumping to their assistance with about thirty soldiers and saving the runaway Narragansetts from certain death. At that moment, the rest of the English troops were endangered, considering that Mason was left with a large number of wounded and without the thirty soldiers that Underhill took with him.

The Pequots were unsuccessful in their first two attempts to attack the English and their allies, and to make matters worse, they lost even more warriors. The counterattack lasted about an hour. The English decided to retreat to the designated point, the Thames River Harbor, which was accompanied by a series of counterattacks by the Pequot warriors. Mason states that about 300 warriors participated in the largest Pequot counterattack. Most of these counterattacks were successfully repulsed, which inflicted heavy losses on the Pequots.

Mason and Underhill formed a column with their wounded and descended Pequot Hill from the west slope. Mason led and guarded the wounded column with his soldiers, while Underhill was at the back of the column with his units. About 100 Pequots attacked the back of Underhill's column. A large number of them directly attacked the English, so they were easy targets for muskets. Part of that group attacked from the sides but without success.

The return journey was exceptionally trying and exhausting, and danger lurked constantly. Since the Pequots were trying to attack from all sides, protecting the wounded from the front and rear was not enough, so the English reinforced the sides as well. Most of the Pequot counterattacks were carried out from nearby swamps, and the English soldiers would occasionally open fire preventively in the direction of the swamps they encountered.

The attacks continued until the column was about two miles (just over three kilometers) from Thames Harbor. Sources indicate that the Pequot lost more warriors in these counterattacks than in the battle for Mystic Fort. This information is reported to us by Underhill, who talks about the Native Americans' disorganization in the military sense. To get revenge on the

English as soon as possible, the Pequots had pushed forward without a concrete plan of attack, inflicting much damage on themselves in the process.

Underhill continued to advance toward the ships with the wounded and soon sailed for Saybrook. In the meantime, Mason continued to march to the east coast of Connecticut with the remaining troops on May 27th, 1637. Mason's troops encamped for another night, and early in the morning, they set out for Saybrook. There are certain indications that Sassacus tried to retaliate with fifty warriors, but this information must be taken with a grain of salt since it is not completely reliable.

On June 2nd, 1637, the General Court provided Mason with another thirty men to continue his fight against the surviving Pequots. Sassacus found himself on the run with about 200 members of the tribe, which included both warriors and civilians. Several military units were organized in the Connecticut area to hunt down the runaway Pequots. Some of the soldiers even came from the Massachusetts Bay Colony. In the meantime, Plymouth Colony declared war on the Pequots. The hunting and killing of the Pequot tribe that had managed to survive continued for a week after the Mystic River campaign.

In the area around Fort Saybrook, no attacks were carried out by natives, attacks that had been occurring almost every day, which speaks volumes about the devastation in which the tribe found itself. The Mystic River campaign inflicted incalculable damage on the Pequots, and every attempt to recover was unsuccessful. Some sources indicate that the allied tribes of the English, who, as we saw above, were an extremely important factor in the battle, agreed to cooperate with the Puritans on the condition that women and children be spared. If this actually took place, the Puritans most certainly ignored this deal since most of the victims in Mystic Fort were women and children.

The members of the Pequot tribe from nearby areas who came to Mystic Fort after the English departed were appalled by the sight; they had not seen anything like it before, nor was it clear to them how men could carry out such an atrocity. Even some English soldiers were disgusted by the scale of the massacre that had ensued in Mystic Fort. Still, Underhill pointed out that it was God's wrath against the ungodly savages, which was a belief most Puritans held.

The killing of the fleeing natives continued almost daily. Sources from that time indicate that some colonial cities, such as Hartford, were flooded with the limbs and heads of runaway Pequots, which, as mentioned above, were often brought in by other natives, whom the English then paid. This practice lasted for weeks after the Mystic massacre.

The end of the Mystic River campaign also led to the enslavement of a large number of Pequots. Most of them were sold to colonies outside of the

New England area so that they could not easily return to the territory that their ancestors had inhabited for hundreds of years. A large number of women and children were sent to live with the English allies. These unfortunate women and children typically ended up as servants in the Narragansett and Mohegan tribes.

As one can tell, after the Mystic River campaign, the Pequot tribe, which had once been mighty and strong, was put into the unfortunate position to fight for its survival overnight. There are certain indications that Sassacus and his surviving warriors sought to attack the English; however, he did not have enough men to carry out that plan. The survivors eventually set fire to their settlement out of helplessness and eliminated all the Mohegans in their ranks. Sassacus fled the Connecticut region, as he and his members were wanted by the English. He found temporary refuge with the Mohawk tribe.

The Mohawk tribe soon learned through merchants' stories of the extent of the brutal English attack on Mystic Fort. Fearful of the English attacking for providing refuge to the Pequots, the Mohawks liquidated Sassacus and all those who came with him. His head was first sent to Hartford, and by August, it was in Boston.

The last battle between the English and the Pequots took place between July 13th and 14th,1637. It was a shorter episode known as the Fairfield Swamp Fight or as the Great Swamp Fight. After the Mystic massacre, a group of Pequots escaped to what is today Fairfield, Connecticut, where the Sasqua tribe lived. In that skirmish, there were members of the Sasqua tribe, besides a few dozen Pequot warriors.

Around 160 soldiers from the Massachusetts Bay Colony managed to locate the Pequots, who were hiding in a swamp near modern-day Fairfield, Connecticut. The English surrounded them, preventing any attempt to escape. According to English estimates, there were between seventy and eighty warriors and several children and women inside the circle made by the Puritans. The children and women were taken as prisoners, while the tribe's warriors offered their last resistance to the superior Englishmen.

Initially, there was a constant fire of English muskets and Native American arrows. Sources point out that the Pequots also owned several firearms by this time. After the English consolidated the ranks, secured the circle, and made sure that the enemy had nowhere to run, on the foggy morning of July 14th, a proper attack was carried out.

The last resistance of the Pequots was broken. It is believed all the Pequot warriors who fought in the Great Swamp Fight died. The British suffered no casualties, but there were several wounded soldiers. This military operation and the assassination of Sassacus ended the Pequot War.

The Treaty of Hartford between the English and the tribal leaders of the Mohegan and Narragansett tribes was finalized on September 21st, 1638, officially ending the Pequot War, although the fighting had pretty much ended over a year ago. The territory previously controlled by the Pequots came into the hands of the English. The allied tribes that had participated in the war received a large number of Pequots as slaves. In return, they had to declare loyalty to the English.

By 1638, the subjugation of the survivors and the elimination of the Pequot tribe was complete. The trade that had previously been in the hands of the Pequots in the Connecticut territory fell into the hand of the English. The Treaty of Hartford banned the tribal name of "Pequot." From that point forward, any Pequot would be referred to as either a Mohegan or a Narragansett. Thus, the Pequot tribe was almost wiped off the face of the earth.

It can be easy to judge the English for what they did based on our modern understanding of right and wrong. The Mystic River campaign and the terms in the Treaty of Hartford would be entirely unacceptable in this day and age. However, back then, this kind of warfare was typical. While the Native Americans in New England engaged in massacres, which rarely included the killing of women and children, although it most certainly happened, they were not used to this scale of brutality, but many of the colonists were more than familiar with it back in the Old World. What drove the English in the Pequot War was not the thirst for blood but rather the thirst for victory. And to achieve such a victory, the leaders of the colonists used tactics that had already been established in Europe. The conflicts in England, the wars with other European countries, and the wars in Ireland show the same intensity of violence demonstrated during the Pequot War and other wars with the natives of North America.

And in addition to the many experienced soldiers who took part in the war, there were also many recruits who had a strong desire to prove themselves in battle and eventually advance in military service. They believed that by following their leader's orders and winning a decisive victory against their foe, they were on the best path to making a name for themselves in the New World.

Religion also played a major role in the decimation of the Pequots. To the English, war was much more than killing enemies; it was understood as a struggle for higher, divine goals. This was not a new concept to them either, as it had been deeply rooted in European society for many, many years. The involvement of the Church made things even more complicated, as violence became the subject of propaganda of the state and the Church. Soldiers who fought in wars believed their engagement was derived from a higher purpose; it was not just a mission to defend their state and family, nor was it a way to gain fame, material rewards, or decorations from rulers.

The English saw this fight as a matter of life and death. They were new to this land, and being overrun by the natives, who they considered to be inferior, would not only be insulting but would result in their own demise. If the English won, not only would they prove themselves to all the Native Americans, but they would also gain the wealth the Pequots had, allowing the English to prosper.

The Native Americans, on the other hand, had no religion-based goals to achieve during the Pequot War. Their understanding of the spiritual world had a completely different outlook from the European one. And the Pequots also did not fight for economic or political reasons. Although the natives were more than accustomed to warring with other tribes, many of the tribes in the New England area lived fairly peacefully together. At the same time, though, their battles could be incredibly brutal and bloody. However, Native American war practice in New England did not involve the mass killing of women and children of an enemy tribe. Very rarely were women and children killed by the New England tribes, and it definitely never happened on such a massive scale before the attack on Mystic Fort. For the most part, the New England tribes generally took prisoners. In this way, they sought to increase their numbers and compensate for any losses during the war.

Chapter 8 – The Mother of All Crimes

The Convention on the Prevention and Punishment of the Crime of Genocide was the international legal instrument that codified the crime of genocide for the first time. It was adopted by the United Nations on December 9th, 1948. The Convention defines genocide as the intent to destroy a national, ethnic, racial, or religious group in whole or in part. Genocidal acts include killing members of a group, violating the group members' physical or mental integrity, deliberately subjecting group members to living conditions that could lead to the complete destruction of the group, measures to prevent the group's birth rate, and forcible relocation and deportation. This is why genocide is known as the "crime of all crimes" or as the "mother of all crimes." However, the definition of genocide itself is problematic for doctrinal and material reasons and often arises from disagreements and controversy to prove genocidal acts.

This short overture on the character and definition of genocide is important to understand. Modern historians are conflicted as to what happened in the Pequot War, particularly during the Mystic massacre. Some believe the aggression of the English was justified, while others believe it was more akin to genocide. It is important to consider both views so one can gain a fuller understanding of what is being discussed in the academic community. In this chapter, we will look at the possible genocidal acts of the Pequot War, examine other factors, and present the thesis and antithesis of the "mother of all crimes" in North America.

One of the most common definitions of genocide in use is the one given by Polish lawyer Raphael Lemkin, who was of Jewish descent.

> Generally speaking, genocide does not necessarily mean the immediate destruction of a nation, except when accomplished by mass killings of all members of a nation. It is intended rather to signify a coordinated plan of different actions aiming at the destruction of essential foundations of the life of national groups, with the aim of annihilating the groups themselves. The objectives of such a plan would be the disintegration of the political and social institutions, of culture, language, national feelings, religion, and the

economic existence of national groups, and the destruction of the personal security, liberty, health, dignity, and even the lives of the individuals belonging to such groups.

As we will have the opportunity to see in this chapter, the Mystic River campaign depicted many elements of Lemkin's definition. This definition is used by many scholars to prove genocidal acts took place in North America. Raphael Lemkin's definition of genocide was also adopted through a United Nations resolution.

Genocide, as a legal norm, is relatively "young." However, its practice has been in use since the dawn of the first civilizations. Mass torture and deaths were not only unique of the Second World War. Still, the scale of suffering in that war was so massive that the United Nations legally passed a convention on genocide at the international level. The resolution was also passed to prevent future mass casualties, as well as to prevent wars. Violations of basic human rights have been reflected throughout all historical epochs and are characteristic in almost all world cultures. As a legal term, genocide is mostly the subject of law, but genocide is also present in historiography, political science, anthropology, sociology, and philosophy. It can also be observed from a psychological point of view.

In the context of the international law passed in 1948, the campaign on Mystic Fort had elements of genocide. The Puritans' actions in what was essentially the final phase of the Pequot War were aimed at the systematic destruction of an entire tribe. The actions at Mystic Fort included killing civilians and forcibly deporting the survivors with the purpose of exterminating an entire group. The Europeans gave themselves the exclusive right to sovereignty in the New World and extinguished all elements of the Pequots' autochthony.

Proponents of genocidal action against the natives point out that the Pequot War's biggest battle was just an overture to what followed decades after the war. In the years after the Pequot War, the natives of North America experienced a demographic collapse, with some tribes being completely exterminated.

Some sources indicate that the Europeans deliberately transmitted infectious diseases to the Native Americans through the trade of blankets. However, there is no real evidence to point to a systematic plan to infect the Native Americans with disease. However, proponents of the thesis of genocidal actions have a stronger argument when it comes to population demographics. Through the decades of European domination of North America, the number of native peoples was brutally reduced. Over time, the

Europeans viewed the people who had lived in the country centuries before they came as a hindrance.

Certain high-ranking people in politics indicate the extent of the indifference toward Native American tribes during colonization. The first governor of California, Peter Burnett, called for a war of extermination against the Native Americans, one that would continue "until the Indian race became extinct." Burnett called for this war because he believed that Native American tribes were preventing expansion and progress in the exploration of mineral resources in the area of California. In the following period, the authorities eliminated thousands of members of the Yuki tribe, who had inhabited the northern parts of California. Like the Pequots, there are not many members of the Yuki tribe left today. Unlike the Pequots, the Yuki might never be able to recover their language.

Later on, many Native American children were forced to attend boarding schools, where they were taught lessons in English and learned English customs, which helped contribute to the demise of their own languages and traditions.

These events have a distant echo that one can still hear today. In the modern era, there is still a certain amount of prejudice against Native Americans. Such an attitude toward the natives results from centuries of unfounded stigmatization of the indigenous peoples of North America.

However, it is important to examine why historians believe what took place was not genocide. Many scholars state that the Europeans' attitudes toward Native Americans can be defined as a crime but not genocide. To defend their thesis, they look at the vague figures of Native American demographics that anthropologists have presented to the public. And indeed, so far, scientists have not come close to agreeing on an exact figure or even an approximate figure. In the 1920s, it was reported that about 1.5 million Native Americans lived in America during the arrival of the Europeans. In 1987, it was believed that the figure was about 5 million natives. Finally, it was stated that before the arrival of the Europeans, the number of Native Americans was 18 million people.

While no one can argue that many Native Americans died in wars with the Europeans, many also died in battles with each other, as the natives did not always get along. Also, as mentioned above, an incredibly high number of Native Americans suffered and died from various diseases. Smallpox caused the most damage, for this disease did not discriminate based on age. Therefore, many adults fell ill, so there was no one left to fully cultivate the land and to hunt. Thus, many tribes died of starvation.

Considering that "intent" is one of the key elements of the definition of genocide, many scholars think that the Europeans who transmitted infectious diseases to the natives had no intention of doing this. There were some occasions where the Europeans deliberately contaminated blankets, but those are isolated cases and not a common practice; therefore, it did not represent the official attitude of the colonial governments.

As one might expect, the crime perpetrated against the Pequots, whether it was genocide or not, contains elements of racial and religious intolerance toward the natives. The Puritans lived according to their religious beliefs, which were deeply ingrained in their everyday life. They believed that Jesus Christ was sent to Earth to save several people or the "chosen ones." Their dogmatic beliefs implied rigid adherence to certain rules; they valued cleanliness and were wary of the forest, as the forest was, according to their beliefs, Satan's home. The natives were deeply connected with the forest and nature, which was incomprehensible to the English. The sources that are generally used to reconstruct the Pequot War are flooded with elements of religious intolerance. Underhill, Mason, Gardiner, and Winthrop all characterize the Pequots as atheists, savages, and Satan's servants who need to be destroyed. To this end, after the Mystic River campaign, John Mason wrote the following:

> Let the whole Earth be filled with his Glory! Thus the Lord was pleased to smite our Enemies in the hinder Parts, and to give us their Land for an Inheritance: Who remembred us in our low Estate, and redeemed us out of our Enemies Hands: Let us therefore praise the Lord for his Goodness and his wonderful Works to the Children of Men!

These elements of religious extremism were directed at all the Native American tribes of North America equally.

Elements of racism were the product of several different factors. Religious persecution, the birth of a national identity, and geographical discoveries are all factors that led to the formation of racial intolerance. And although some of these factors brought about progress and a shift in humanity, such as geographical discoveries, racism emerged as a negative result. The initial contacts between the European immigrants and the Native Americans did not allude to open racial intolerance, but as their contact intensified over time, racial discrimination against the natives became more pronounced. Eventually, the natives were seen as racially and politically inferior in the Europeans' eyes. Contributions to science and technology and the birth of a national entity laid the fertile ground in which racism could blossom.

The development of a national identity meant the people shared a common language and culture, as well as racial and religious unity. While this brought together one group of people, it created intolerance toward others. When we talk about the development of science and its impact on the emergence of racism, one can look at the advancements in biology. During the early stages of the Enlightenment, which began in 1715, the classification of flora and fauna took place. This classification would eventually be raised up as an example of one group's racial inferiority over another. Developments in technology brought about practices that one can equate with capitalism. For businesses to perform at the highest level, the enslavement of certain peoples for economic gain became a common practice.

However, the first stage of English colonization of the New World was conceived in a completely different way, as the English believed they would bring justice and religious enlightenment to the Native Americans. Since the Spaniards were ruthless toward the natives, the English tried to prove that they were superior to the Spaniards. These initial efforts soon turned into the struggle for supremacy over North America.

Chapter 9 – Analysis and Comparison of King Philip's War and the Historiography of the Pequot War

The Pequot War was the first conflict in New England between the Native Americans and the European colonists, and it permanently changed the relations between the Europeans and Native Americans. The balance of power changed quickly, and the numerous but disorganized natives of North America came to be subordinate to the Europeans. By destroying one of the most powerful Native American tribes in New England, one obstacle to the Puritans' intensive spread on North American soil was removed.

After the war, British authorities established complete domination over the economy and trade in that part of North America, as the Pequots were no longer able to provide a buffer to their expansion. In the years after the Pequot War, that area of North America was intertwined with global economic trends, as the Puritans involved the New World in the European mercantilist system. A more intensive penetration of capitalist ideas began to flow into North America. Some tribes adopted these economic patterns, and even the monopoly over wampum came into the hands of the English.

The Pequot War showed the English settlers' determination for territorial expansion at all costs. In the 1630s, there was a mass migration of Puritans to North America. Statistics show that the end of the Pequot War significantly increased the influx of new people to New England. Thus, one can conclude that the colonists' victory in the war influenced the mass migration of Puritans to the New World since all obstacles to English domination had been removed.

After the Pequot War, the Native Americans and Puritans lived in relative peace. While there was the occasional raid, for the most part, things had settled. This all stopped when King Philip's War broke out in 1675. Many historians consider King Philip's War to be the continuation of the Pequot War, as it was necessary to "jump over" another barrier to expand English influence. While the English pursued economic interests during the Pequot

War, King Philip's War was a battle for territory. After the Pequot War, the Puritans saw all tribal communities as subjects who had to abide by the colonies' instructions and imposed laws. It was extremely difficult for the natives to submit to the colonists' laws, as they opposed their traditional patterns, notions, and belief system.

When we talk about the causes that led to King Philip's War, most historians agree that the main factor was the usurpation of tribal land by the Puritans. The mass migration of English settlers to the New World had created the need for expansion, which came at the expense of the native tribes. The English tried to take over the natives' land, which eventually resulted in a bloody war.

The name of the conflict is related to the name of the sachem of the Pokanoket and the grand sachem of the Wampanoag Confederacy, Metacomet, who took the English name of Philip to become more closely tied to the English. Metacomet sought an alliance with Plymouth Colony, and although they entered into an agreement, he soon realized they wouldn't help the tribe as much as they had promised.

In late January 1675, a corpse of a Native American was found in a pond in southeastern Massachusetts. However, this wasn't just any ordinary person. This man was John Sassamon, and he was what was known as a praying Indian. These were Native Americans who had converted either willingly or unwillingly to Christianity. It is estimated that over 1,600 Native Americans in the Massachusetts Bay Colony and Plymouth Colony had accepted Christianity prior to the war. It seems that Sassamon, who was from the Massachusett tribe, was a willing convert, as he spread Christianity to nearby tribes. Sassamon was also of import to the English because he could read and write in English and also served as an interpreter. Before his death, he warned the English that Metacomet was planning an attack. Initially, when the Puritans found Sassamon's body, they thought he had an accident. But upon closer inspection, they realized his neck was broken. Many thought that John Sassamon had been killed under the sachem's order, who was seeking vengeance on John for adopting English customs and religion. It is also possible that Metacomet found out that John had revealed his plans. In June, three Wampanoags were tried by a jury on suspicion of participating in the murder of the baptized John Sassamon. Interestingly enough, this jury was the first mixed jury in Plymouth Colony, as it contained six Native American elders. The three men were convicted and sentenced to be executed.

Soon after, Pokanoket warriors attacked Swansea, a small settlement in Plymouth Colony. They destroyed the small town, then came back later to kill and pillage some more. This was most likely done without the approval of

Metacomet, but it is hard to know for certain since the Native Americans did not keep extensive records. Either way, Metacomet got the war he was looking for, as the attack on Swansea is considered to be the opening act of King Philip's War. After the attack, the Massachusetts Bay Colony's and Plymouth Colony's governments decided to send a military expedition to a Wampanoag settlement in Rhode Island.

Just like the Pequot War, the colonial authorities sought the support of Native American tribes. In fact, during this war, the Pequots helped the Puritans, as did the Mohegans. This time around, the Narragansetts remained neutral, although a few of them did help out the Wampanoag Confederacy in some raids. The English sought more alliances, such as from the Nipmucks, but to no avail. When the colonists arrived at a Nipmuck village outside of Boston, all they found were empty wigwams, for the Nipmucks had already left to join Metacomet. Although the Wampanoags had a fairly large union of Native American tribes on their side, they were not truly united, and a number of Native Americans continued to cooperate with the English.

The initial military operations on both sides were spontaneous, and there was no organization. In the beginning, the war mostly involved the destruction of crops and the killing of cattle, but the clashes intensified in September 1675. This was perhaps due to the fact that the colonists officially declared war on September 9th, which would have undoubtedly kicked off more serious actions than punitive expeditions and raids.

Although comparisons can be drawn between King Philip's War and the Pequot War, there were some major differences. Unlike the Pequots, the Wampanoags had several fairly successful military actions, and they engaged in tactics that were more reminiscent of the English during the Pequot War. For instance, the Battle of Bloody Brook, which was fought on September 12th, saw a group of Native Americans attack a wagon train carrying food and supplies. The natives reportedly killed around forty soldiers and seventeen civilians. In October, right before winter, the colonial settlement of Springfield, Massachusetts, was burned to the ground, and although most of the people survived, the attack destroyed much of the saved food for the winter months.

In December, one of the harshest battles of King Philip's War was fought. Back in October, Plymouth Colony authorities had decided that some sort of action had to be taken against the Narragansett tribe. Although they hadn't truly participated in the war, they had given refuge to members of the Wampanoag Confederacy. The Puritans might have feared that the Narragansetts might join with the Wampanoag, which would have made the fighting even harder for the colonists. They also didn't quite understand which tribe was involved in the war efforts and which ones were not. Whatever the case might have been, the colonists decided to take preventive measures and burned several Narragansett villages in early November. In mid-December, Narragansett warriors attacked a Rhode Island garrison and killed around fifteen people. This prompted the largest military operation in the war to date. Like the Mystic Fort campaign, this campaign was reminiscent of those battles organized and fought on the European continent.

On December 19th, 1675, around 1,000 colonial soldiers and 150 Native American warriors marched toward Rhode Island to retaliate against the Narragansetts' attack. There, in the biting cold, the colonists and allied Native Americans surrounded the Narragansetts completely, without any possibility for escape. When they entered the fort, a great struggle began. Unlike the Pequots at Mystic Fort, the Narragansetts knew about the advance of the English troops, so they were ready to welcome the attackers. But they perhaps weren't prepared for the brutality that was about to be unleashed.

It is interesting that the crucial battles of both the Pequot War and King Philip's War involved the burning of a major fort. Just as at Mystic Fort, women, children, and warriors perished in the flames of the Narragansett fort. The exact number of causalities is not known, but it is believed that around 97 warriors and between 300 and 1,000 civilians died. However, unlike Mystic Fort, the Narragansetts were able to inflict some damage on the English ranks. Many Narragansett warriors fled the burning fort, and in the subsequent battle, around 70 English were killed and 150 wounded.

Throughout the winter, the Native Americans continued to use similar tactics as the ones used during the Pequot War, mostly employing guerrilla attacks. Unlike the Pequot War, most of these attacks were carried out on villages, meaning women and children were often victims. The natives avoided direct confrontation with the English troops rather skillfully. Due to the terrain, the British often did not have enough space for larger military maneuvers, with which they were most familiar. Most of the actual battles took place in areas like swamps.

The English tried to retaliate against these hit-and-run attacks, which led to one of the most brutal moments of the war, and this time, the English were not behind it. The Puritans had received information about the movement of Native American troops, and on March 26th, 1676, Captain Michael Pierce took about sixty colonial soldiers and twenty native allies to pursue the Narragansetts, who had just burned down several villages. Captain Pierce knew that the Native Americans favored ambushes and sudden attacks, but he must not have put too much significance on it. Even though he was an experienced soldier, Pierce made the mistake of acting hastily and abruptly mobilizing his troops without first observing the situation and sending a reconnaissance team ahead. As a result, the Narragansetts ambushed the English troops. The English and their allies formed defensive formations, but the number of English troops decreased as the battle progressed. The Narragansetts attacked in short intervals, which meant they preserved their energy while not giving their enemy enough time to take stock of the situation. The battle lasted a little less than two hours, and during it, nearly all the English soldiers were killed, including Captain Pierce. The Narragansetts, on the other hand, only lost a few warriors. The slaughter alone is brutal enough to place it in the history books, but the Narragansetts took it one step further. They took ten colonists as prisoners and then proceeded to torture nine of them to death. The site where the torturing took place is known as Nine Men's Misery, and one can still visit the plaque that marks the spot today.

King Philip's War continued throughout the summer of 1676, with the Native Americans being increasingly pushed back, although they did strike some severe blows. For the most part, though, they were on the retreat, looking for the perfect opportunity to gain a better foothold in the conflict. Unfortunately for them, that opportunity never arrived. In July, the female Niantic sachem, Quaiapen, went to retrieve food with a band of about 100 Native Americans. Around 300 colonists and 100 native allies attacked Quaiapen's force. Her men were destroyed, and those who made it out alive were sold into slavery. Quaiapen herself was killed in the clash, and many historians believe this was the point of no return for the Narragansetts, not just in the war but in general. After this, they would be unable to reorganize themselves efficiently, which led to the loss of many of their members. The Wampanoags also suffered, as they began losing allies left and right. It didn't help that the natives did not have the capacity or resources to continue the war against the English, who were much more sophisticated in terms of warfare.

The Native American alliance was dealt another great blow that summer when the sachem of the Narragansetts, Canonchet, died. He was captured by the English-allied Mohegan tribe and was executed. By August 1676, King Philip, or Sachem Metacomet, was constantly on the run. He was shot and killed by a man named John Alderman. Like John Sassamon, Alderman was a praying Indian. English tradition dictated that Metacomet's body be beheaded and then drawn and quartered. According to some sources, his severed head was placed on a stake, which remained in Plymouth for decades. Sources say that Alderman received Metacomet's head, as well as one of his hands, for killing the sachem. He later sold the head to Plymouth Colony for thirty shillings.

Metacomet's death signaled the end of the fighting in the main theater of the war, but the fighting continued in New Hampshire and Maine, the latter being a place where the Native Americans saw more success. The Treaty of

Casco, which was signed in 1678, saw friendly relations being reestablished between the colonists and Native Americans, namely the Wabanaki. The English retained their right to the lands, but in return, they had to pay an annual tribute of a peck of corn for each family settled on them. Of course, since the Wampanoag had lost their war, they never saw a treaty that dictated friendly terms like this. However, many who had fought in King Philip's War in the southern theater made their way north to the Wabanaki. Today, one can find the descendants of these refugees living there. Some eventually returned to Massachusetts during the Seven Years' War.

Since the colonists were successful, they were able to acquire the land they had been seeking without too much resistance, at least for the time being. There wouldn't be another major war in New England between the colonists and Native Americans until 1722, with the outbreak of Dummer's War. However, massacres and raids still occurred, with both sides being the instigators. King Philip's War was important to the colonists in other ways, though. It marked the first large-scale conflict where the settlers acted on their own without any support from Europe. One could consider this the first stepping stone to the colonists realizing they could thrive on their own without European interference, although true independence wouldn't come to the colonists until a little less than 100 years after King Philip's War officially ended.

King Philip's War had dire consequences for the region. A large number of people were killed on both sides, and statistics show that when we look at the total population and size of New England, this was the most devastating conflict in the country's history. It is believed that around 5,000 Native Americans and 2,500 colonists perished. This equates to 40 percent and 5 percent of their population, respectfully. Many believe that, at the very least, it was the most devastating conflict in American colonial history.

In many ways, King Philip's War was reminiscent of the Pequot War. Both wars shared the same intensity of brutality, although the statistics are somewhat different. However, King Philip's War was a much larger conflict than the Pequot War, so it makes sense that the causalities would be higher. Many tribes took part, and this time, most of them sided with the offended Native Americans, unlike in the Pequot War, where the Pequots, for the most part, fought by themselves. However, like the Pequot War, many of these tribes suffered to the point where they couldn't find their feet again. For example, the Wampanoags were nearly wiped out to the point of extinction. After the war, it is believed there were only 400 of them left.

A key difference between the Pequot War and King Philip's War lies in the fact that King Philip's War was not a localized affair. The war took place in

Massachusetts, Rhode Island, Connecticut, and even Maine. The war also caused enormous material damage. According to available information, by the beginning of the war, the British had founded about ninety cities in New England. The Native Americans carried out attacks on over fifty of them, seventeen of which were burned to the ground. The fact that King Charles II of England was aware of the graveness of the situation speaks volumes about the scale of the conflict, as the war significantly drained the financial resources of the colonies.

King Philip's War was novel in its own way, though. During the war, the English effectively disseminated propaganda. Bulletins appeared throughout England, especially London, showcasing the atrocities and brutal methods the Native Americans carried out against the colonists. The press closely followed the events in New England. For instance, an attack on an English family was carefully described. In this instance, a group of natives killed a family of six: a father, a mother, a son, the son's wife, and two young children. The details of that massacre were appalling to those who read about it, which further developed antagonism toward the natives.

However, like the Pequot War, there is a lack of written Native American testimonies. When scholars examine the events of the Pequot War, they are forced to use the narratives of the direct participants in the war, such as John Mason, John Underhill, and Governor John Winthrop, as Native American sources are almost nonexistent. The problem is these sources only reflect one side, so, inevitably, bias and distorted perceptions tint the writing. In such a situation, it isn't easy to make an accurate reconstruction of the events that took place, and the same was true of King Philip's War.

Early historiography transmitted information from the primary sources without a serious interpretation, ignoring the bias that might be present. After the Second World War, a new approach to the history of the Pequot War, as well as other colonial conflicts, was formed. Many newer-generation historians view wampum as the basic economic factor that led to the Pequot War. Several historians have also emerged who advocate the thesis that the English actions in the New World were directed against the indigenous tribes because of their greed; historians believe this was an effort to confiscate the natives' land and control the wampum, of which the Pequots had large stores. In addition to this, historians point to the cultural and social factors that led to the war. Religious factors, without a doubt, played a role in the outbreak of the conflict.

During the Vietnam War, there was a glorification of values, such as morality and the strengthening of liberal currents, in the United States. This was also reflected in the sciences and the interpretation of events in history.

During this period, some American historians, such as Laurence M. Hauptman and Barbara Alice Mann, directly characterized the Puritans' actions, primarily the Mystic River campaign, as genocidal acts.

A more accurate insight of the Pequot War would be possible with the Pequots' testimonies, but unfortunately, none of those survived. In this way, history has been deprived of a complete picture of the Pequot War and the centuries-old relationship between the Native Americans and European immigrants.

Chapter 10 – Where Are They Today? A Look at the Pequots

By 1683, those Pequots who remained in the New England area were moved onto reservations. There weren't many of them left, as the vast majority had either been wiped out due to disease, the war, or had been made into slaves, with many of them being owned by those tribes who had helped the English. However, as time passed, some managed to make their way back to their ancestral home, and the government of Connecticut established two reservations: the Eastern Pequot Reservation and the Mashantucket Pequot Reservation.

It seemed as if the Pequots were losing the battle to keep their tribe intact as the years went by. As mentioned in an earlier chapter, a census in 1774 showed that there were 151 Pequots on the Mashantucket Reservation; by the early 1800s, that number had dropped to around 40. Many moved off the reservation, looking for work, and thus engaged in traditions that were more European in nature, such as attending English schools or converting to Christianity.

Take the efforts of Samson Occom (1723-1792) as an example. He was one of the founders of the Brothertown Indians, which was a Native American tribe composed of former members of the Pequot and Mohegan tribes, and they were firm believers in Christianity. Occom himself wasn't a Pequot; rather, he belonged to the Mohegans, and it is believed he might have been the descendent of Uncas, the chief who separated the Mohegans from the Pequots. Occom's faith was unshakable, and he spent his life helping tribes like the Pequots assimilate into English culture, which included not only religion but also clothing, buildings, and food. However, even though Occom was a believer in assimilation, he was still treated wrongly by the English. For instance, around 1765, Occom reached an agreement with a minister named Eleazar Wheelock over the founding of a Native American school. Wheelock persuaded Occom to travel to England to gain more funds, and while Occom was overseas, Wheelock turned the school into Dartmouth College, one of the most prestigious universities in the United States today. But although Occom's dreams for a Native American school were dashed, his beliefs stood firm, and he continued to spread the message of Christianity throughout the area.

Occom's work was just one of the many factors that led to the dwindling numbers of the Pequots. In 1856, the state of Connecticut sold off a large part of the Mashantucket Pequot Reservation. The Pequots once lived in a space that consisted of 989 acres; now, they were reduced to eking out a living on a 213-acre-reservation. It is no wonder that many moved away, as the vast majority of the tribe migrated to the newly formed urban areas nearby, such as Westerly, Rhode Island. A census from 1910 states the Pequots on the Mashantucket Reservation only numbered around sixty-six.

In the 19th and early 20th centuries, many surviving Pequot members were forced to adapt to the new way of life that had sprung up in the country. Industrialization had transformed the country into a powerhouse, and these changes would not simply pass the Native Americans by. A large number of Native Americans were attached to the sea, engaging in the fishing and shipbuilding industries. Some of the Pequots earned their money from setting sail on fishing and whaling expeditions, which could last for months at a time. Besides fishing, the Pequots were also responsible for making sails and ropes to be used on the many ships docked in the harbors of New England. The practice of hunting whales had also intensified during this period. Whale fat, which would then be rendered into oil, was used for a number of things, including soap and cosmetics. It was a very demanding and complicated process to extract the desired whale fat, but some Pequots specialized in this business. Native Americans also helped produce harpoons and other equipment, and some of them even used their harpoons to earn a living. George, a Christianized Pequot, ran a specialty store in Mystic Harbor in the 1930s that manufactured barrels containing whale oil. In addition to this, there was an increase in trade, and the local ports formed by the English during the 19th century were a gathering place for not only the Pequots but also other members of descendants from the Pequot War, namely, the Narragansett and the Mohegan tribes. Women from the Pequot tribe were also involved in business practices, as they often rented out boarding houses to sailors from all over the world. Such circumstances allowed the Pequots to pass down their businesses and skills to future generations, which means that those who lived off the reservations would have no plans on returning anytime soon.

However, things wouldn't remain so bleak, although it took many decades for a resurgence to happen. During the 20th century, the Pequot community continued to be displaced from the Massachusetts area, mainly due to economic factors. The remaining Pequots in the area, whose numbers continued to fall, sought to live in harmony with the environment; to them, the land represented a crucial element of their tribal and individual identity. The 1970s was a decade of hope and promise for the Pequots, who began to move back to the Mashantucket Reservation. They realized that to have any hope of saving their culture, they needed to go back to their homeland and demand their rights. By restoring the land that had been illegally sold, the Pequots believed more members would come to join the tribe, and over time, they would be able to provide for themselves and develop their culture, which had been practically lost. If it wasn't for the efforts of these people, it might have been lost entirely.

The 1950s, 1960s, and 1970s proved to be a pivotal time for the Native Americans in general. Throughout history, there were many who spoke out about the injustices that had been done to them, but it was as if a switch was flipped in the late 1950s. More and more people engaged in activism to demand respect and recognition of their tribes be given to them. Militant groups also sprung up, demanding change, although this happened more in the late 1960s. And change definitely needed to be taken. In 1970, the Native American unemployment rate was ten times the national average, and around 40 percent of Native Americans lived below the poverty line. Life expectancy for a Native American was only forty-four years, and many of those lives were spent in squalor. The conditions on the reservations had deteriorated so badly that they resembled third-world countries rather than a part of the United States.

Different movements sprung up, and although each had different goals, a common ambition was the federal recognition of the lands that had been taken from them. They also wanted to be able to exert more control over their lands and have more of a voice in government. Although Native Americans had been designated as citizens in the 1920s, they weren't allowed to vote unless the state approved it. Their fight to vote carried on into the 1960s, and even then, this was hampered by poll taxes and literacy tests. This movement for Native American rights happened alongside the African Americans' civil rights movement, and both sides seemed to respect and champion each other's causes. Both African Americans and Native Americans wouldn't be guaranteed the right to vote peacefully until the Voting Rights Act of 1965 was passed.

The Pequots would join this movement for more civil rights. In 1973, the last remaining Pequot on the Mashantucket Reservation, Elizabeth George, died. Since no one was left living on the land, it was reverted back to the state of Connecticut, which happened according to the law. However, Elizabeth's family believed the land belonged to the Pequots, not the state. In 1975, Elizabeth's grandson, Richard A. Hayward, met with the Coalition of Eastern Native Americans, also known as CENA, and they helped him begin the steps to reclaiming the land. Richard also began campaigning for federal recognition of his organization, and a year later, Connecticut recognized his group, which he named the Western Pequots.

Richard and his group weren't alone in their fight. In 1976, the Pequots filed a suit against the landowners of the land that had been illegally sold in 1856 by the government of Connecticut. To help them win this battle, the Pequots gained the assistance of the Native American Rights Fund and the Indian Rights Association. They would fight in the courts for seven years until the land was finally given back to them. In the meantime, Richard Hayward and the Western Pequots were given a grant to develop an economic plan for the reservation, and they steadily rebuilt the small reservation so it met better standards.

In 1982, Hayward and his group sought federal recognition for a new tribe, which would come to be known as the Mashantucket Pequot Tribal Nation. However, in order to do so, they needed to get the Bureau of Indian Affairs involved. The problem was that the Western Pequots had no paperwork to prove their lineage, which they needed. In fact, American author Jeff Benedict believes the Mashantucket Pequots are not actually Pequots; his opinion is that they are actually descended from the Narragansetts. The Pequots have come out and stated that Benedict's assertion is false, especially since he fails to take into account the lineages of early 20th-century censuses, which shows the lineal descent of eleven Pequot families (this was used in the court case to prove their lineage). To push their claim through, the Western Pequots teamed up with the Pequots who were seeking to gain the illegally-taken land back. Although the bill passed the Senate, US President Ronald Reagan vetoed it, as he believed it would set an alarming precedent for the creation of tribes. However, members of Congress thought that Reagan had just passed over a bill that was of the utmost importance to saving Native American tribal communities. Reagan saw reason and came to a compromise, and the bill was passed later on in 1983. In addition to becoming federally recognized, the tribe was given enough money to buy back their confiscated land. It was a great moment for the Pequots because they were able to independently organize self-government and obtain certain legal powers. The federal recognition of the tribal community also granted the Pequots certain benefits in the form of healthcare and economic assistance for education.

The Pequots settled on the reservation and began finding ways to earn a living. Many became involved in selling maple syrup, cordwood, and crops. They also invested in pigs, a hydroponic greenhouse, and a sand and gravel business. Richard Hayward had grand plans of his own to revitalize the economy of the reservation, and one of the first things he looked into was building something that would make the reservation some fast money. He thought the best way to do this was to invest in a high-stakes bingo venture, which was opened in July of 1986. Two years later, it had generated over thirty million dollars.

That same year, the Indian Gaming Regulatory Act was passed, which set the framework for legalized gambling on reservations. Hayward realized that having a casino on the reservation would attract even more people, who would be encouraged to help the economy by supporting small businesses while in the area. However, many experts thought that this move was not financially viable because the Connecticut area was not a popular destination. Tribal representatives sent a letter to Wall Street, asking them to support their efforts financially. This request was not accepted, but the Pequot community did not give up. They sought financial help from a Malaysian investor named Lim Goh Tong, who was once the richest man in Malaysia. In 1992, Hayward opened the doors to the Foxwoods Casino, a world-renown casino today.

The casino didn't start out big, though. In the beginning, there were only table games, but slot machines were added about a year later. Although it wasn't a large enterprise in its early years, it held a monopoly on gambling in the region, which would allow it to expand even more since it had no other competition. Initially, the casino was intended to be opened for between eight and twelve hours. As time passed, and as the crowds continued to come, the owners realized they could stay open 24/7. Today, Foxwoods Casino has over fifty table games, almost 1,500 slot machines, a huge hotel, a 4,000-seat theater for concerts and the like, four restaurants, and four outlets. It earns billions of dollars in revenue, and it is the fourth-largest casino in the world.

In the Connecticut area, the Pequot tribal community is the largest private employer. In addition to the casino, there is a post office in that area called the "Pequot Post," which employs mostly members of the tribal community. The post office was opened in 1993, and since then, it has been performing standard tasks related to the mail. In regards to the post office, the tribal community repeatedly sought to obtain its own zip code, and their efforts finally bore fruit in 2002.

Today, the tribe can look back at its long history and see the tremendous strides they have made. Where they used to be only one member on the Mashantucket Reservation, there are now over a thousand. And instead of living in a territory that consisted of 213 acres, the Pequots now live on a reservation that covers a whopping 1,200 acres. It must be noted that there are more Pequots in existence than those living on the Mashantucket Reservation, although the exact number is not known.

Modern Pequots are constantly seeking to bring their history closer to the American people and their own traditions and culture closer to their own. They launched an initiative to increase the number of lessons about their history in educational institutions. To this end, they donated a large amount of written material, which is still waiting to be consolidated into one large study of the Pequots. The Pequots have also undertaken efforts to regain their language through these documents and through the analysis of closely related languages. They have reclaimed one thousand words so far, which is not enough to truly have a language of their own, but it is the start of something promising.

The Pequots managed to survive the turbulent times of history. It is a community that, at one point in its existence, almost faced extinction. But in the end, they survived the hardships that were placed before them.

Conclusion

The Pequot War represents one of the most significant episodes in the history of the United States. Before the war, the Pequots were a large community with thousands of members. They were the most powerful tribe in the wider Connecticut area, but with the arrival of the English, a new power would come to the forefront. But even before a shot was fired, the Pequots were decimated, like other tribes, by the infectious diseases the Europeans brought.

The Puritans' settlement of North America intensified during the 1620s. In the beginning, though, people got along peacefully enough. The English tried to be actively involved in trade, and due to this, they interacted intensively with the Dutch colonists and indigenous tribes, of which the Pequots were one of the most significant. In their search for commercial domination, the Puritans came into conflict with everyone. However, the Pequots also came into conflict with everyone as well in their quest to be the most dominant force, to the point where they alienated other tribes.

During the dramatic events of the 1630s, the Pequots killed English colonist John Stone. Almost no one was interested in the event at the time, but eventually, the Puritans would use his death as one of the reasons to start a war against the Pequots.

About two years later, John Oldham died, although who his murderer was is still unknown to history (although it is very likely it was the Narragansetts, who then framed the Pequots for Oldham's death). With these reasons in mind, the English felt they had no other course but to declare war upon the Pequots.

Many factors influenced the outcome of the Pequot War. The English won mainly thanks to their use of more modern warfare, their technological superiority, their organization, and their military tactics. The Pequots were inferior compared to the English when it came to those things, and since the English were still fairly new to the continent, the Pequots had not yet had a chance to study and learn the Europeans' way of fighting.

Without a doubt, the most important battle of the Pequot War was the battle of Mystic Fort. At Mystic Fort, the English killed between 400 and 700 Pequots, half of whom were burned alive. Most of the victims were children and women. With this campaign, the English prevented any recovery of the Pequot tribe.

John Mason sought to justify the massacre at Mystic Fort by using religion, which was a common justification back then. According to Mason, "But GOD was above them, who laughed his Enemies and the Enemies of his People to Scorn, making them as a fiery Oven: Thus were the Stout Hearted spoiled, having slept their last Sleep, and none of their Men could find their Hands: Thus did the LORD judge among the Heathen, filling the Place with dead Bodies."

Despite disagreements among historians about whether genocide took place or not, it is clear the war nearly wiped the Pequots off the face of the earth. The survivors were sold into slavery or given as gifts to the allied tribes. As a result, the English established total dominance in the Connecticut area. It was the first phase of the English expansion in North America.

In 1889, a monument to Captain John Mason was erected at the Mystic massacre site. Over time, initiatives have been launched to remove the memorial. This dispute became a long-standing problem for local authorities, and it was eventually removed and relocated to Windsor, Connecticut. The wider territory of the Mystic Fort is today in the National Register of Historic Places. It was added to that list on August 24th, 1979.

Part 7: The Quakers

A Captivating Guide to a Historically Christian Group and How William Penn Founded the Colony of Pennsylvania in British North America

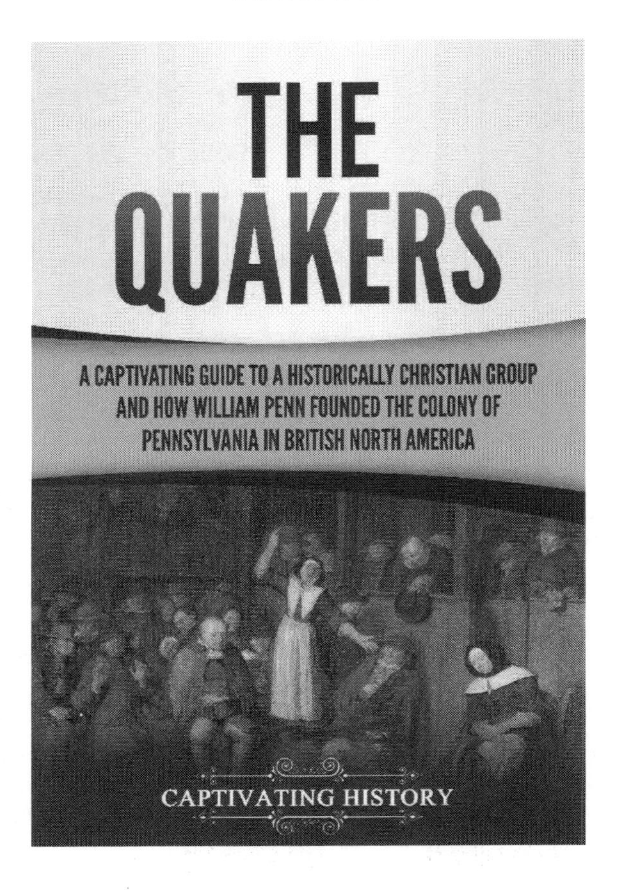

Introduction: The Origins of the Quakers

The Quakers, known for their austere religious beliefs and strong social convictions, were very much a product of the English Civil War. It's important to note that the "English Civil War" was a series of three large uprisings against English governance that took place between 1642 and 1651. The origins of this upheaval can be traced back even further, to the year 1625.

For it was in 1625 that Charles the First came to the throne in England, and he brought considerable discord to the kingdom. Much of this discord had to do with religion and state. Charles didn't feel that he should be questioned by Parliament since he believed he had a God-given right to reign over his people. But ever since the signing of the Magna Carter in 1215, which limited the English monarch's power, the days of absolute authority over the kingdom had long since passed.

By 1640, King Charles had developed an increasingly antagonistic relationship with the British Parliament. Charles was fed up with members of Parliament, whom he viewed as obstructionists to his policy, and he was also irked at what he felt was longstanding resentment for his choice of marrying a woman of Spanish Catholic background. England had become increasingly Protestant, and a virulent strain of anti-Catholic sentiment ran rampant throughout the British Isles.

King Charles was attempting to put down a rebellion in Scotland at the time, but he needed members of Parliament to approve the taxation required to raise money for the enterprise. Parliament dithered and began to insist that King Charles further limit the scope of his authority. For a king like Charles, who believed that it was God's will for him to rule, this, of course, did not sit well. He lost his patience and tried to have some of his opposition arrested instead.

These Parliament members were notified ahead of time and managed to make a break for it before the king could put them in irons. Shortly after, two factions rose—one loyal to the king and the other loyal to Parliament—and faced off against each other. English society was about as fractured as possible, with regular citizens and the military splintering into the two sides.

While the British factions of the Parliamentarians and Royalists battled it out over just what kind of constitution and governance Great Britain was going to have, another argument was taking place in religious circles. Previously, the Church of England had dominated all religious affairs, but with the iron-fisted monarchy's downfall, England's first real religious reformation took shape.

It was out of this tumult that the Quakers were born. The first Quakers can be traced back to the East Midlands of England. And the first well-documented instance of Quaker happenings seems to have occurred in 1647. For it was that year that a Quaker firebrand by the name of George Fox came into his own. George Fox was one of the many individuals who became disillusioned with the official doctrine of the Church of England during this period.

Fox also allegedly had some visionary experiences in which he was persuaded that a "direct experience of Christ" outside of the official doctrine of the Church of England could be achieved. Taking his beliefs to the people, Fox began to preach his message all over England, as well as in Holland and even as far as Barbados, which was a British colony at the time. For his efforts, Fox was eventually arrested and made to answer charges of "religious blasphemy."

It was during his interrogation by authorities that George Fox quoted scripture from the Book of Isaiah and advised his accusers to fear God and "tremble and quake at the word of the Lord." Fox was roundly ridiculed for his words and was subsequently dubbed a "Quaker" for this advice. The term began as a pejorative against the movement's leader, but Fox's followers soon embraced the term and made it their own. They would later rebrand themselves as the "Society of Friends," but the moniker of "Quaker" would remain their ultimate calling card.

By early 1562, the group had gained significant momentum and had acquired some powerful emissaries in the form of James Nayler and Richard Farnsworth. Richard Farnsworth would become Fox's right-hand man when it came to evangelism. However, Fox parted company with Farnsworth in the summer of 1652, for this was the year Fox engaged in a renewed campaign across northern England. He was a tireless evangelist, and even when he was "pelted with stones on Walney Island," a region off the west coast of England, in September of 1652, he faithfully soldiered on.

In 1654, after spending two years roaming the countryside, Fox made his way to London, where he was ready to spread the Quaker faith to those that flocked to the city. The faith would greatly expand from here, and as a result of the many ministrations of Fox and his friends, by the end of the decade, the

Quakers numbered in the tens of thousands. However, as their popularity grew, so did their persecution.

Many other mainline Christians viewed the Quakers as a dangerous sect, so much so that they pressured the British Parliament to pass the Quaker Act of 1662. This act set forth in law the "prescribed form" of prayer and worship as designated by the state. It was a formula that specifically left the traditions of the Quakers out. Unable to gain acceptance in England, the Quakers would soon leave the place of their origin altogether and try their luck in a brave new world on another continent.

Chapter 1: The Quakers Arrive in America

The Lord showed me, so that I did see clearly, that he did not dwell in these temples which men had commanded and set up, but in people's hearts. His people were his temple, and he dwelt in them.

-George Fox

The first wave of Quakers reached America in the 1650s. The first documented arrival of a Quaker in America was a woman by the name of Elizabeth Harris, who arrived in the Chesapeake Bay area around the year 1655. It's said that she had "left her husband and son behind in England" in order to "evangelize the Puritan remnant" that remained in the region. This outreach was not always something the Puritans would take too kindly to. As the years passed, these two religious worlds would continue to collide, as one would try to convince the other of their ideological superiority. And in this struggle, it must be said that it was the Puritans who bared their teeth.

While the Quakers sought to persuade their Puritan neighbors with their preaching, the Puritans sought to curtail the Quakers through sheer force. There is a reason why the phrase "puritanical" has come to refer to someone or something that is unbending in their beliefs.

Ironically, the Puritans were initially persecuted back in England for breaking away from the Anglican faith. Yet as soon as they reached the New World and set up their own little puritanical enclaves, the persecuted Puritans quickly became the persecutors. They attempted to stamp out any beliefs that they had come to view as being "heretical" to their particular brand of Christianity.

However, early American Quakers, like Elizabeth Harris, were not going to be steamrolled by the Puritans quite so easily. Harris turned out to be a rather convincing evangelist, and despite any puritanical oppression sent her way, she developed many strong converts. She even managed to persuade a notable man of the community by the name of Thomas Marsh to join the Quakers, who, in turn, brought his entire family into the religion's fold, creating a bastion of Quakers on their little settlement of Marsh's Seat. But perhaps the most significant of her converts was William Fuller, who was a member of the governor's council in Maryland. It was this conversion of prominent members of the community that created a backlash against the nascent Quaker community.

In 1656, while Elizabeth Harris was having much success in evangelizing to the locals, two new Quakers arrived from Britain and began to try their luck. They were Mary Fisher and Ann Austin. These two ladies preached all over Massachusetts, hoping to win hearts and minds over to Quakerism, but the prevailing authority figures of Boston, Massachusetts, shut them down rather quickly.

The women were taken into custody for their efforts. They had their "Quaker books" burned and were closely examined to see if they showed any signs of being witches. After all, this was Massachusetts, the colony in which the infamous Salem witch trials would take place between 1692 and 1693. The idea that someone was a witch and working for the evil one was no laughing matter for the Puritans, and almost anyone preaching a different doctrine than what they were used to was immediately suspect.

It's unclear whether they believed the women were witches or not, but shortly thereafter, they were both shipped off to Barbados—an island in the Caribbean—seemingly banished to the most remote British settlement in the Western Hemisphere at that time. Soon, the provincial legislature even went so far as to pass a law refusing to allow Quakers access to their territory. They also fined ship captains who had the audacity of simply bringing a proselytizing Quaker to their shores.

New converts among the colonists were equally mistreated. If a fellow neighbor found out about one's conversion to Quakerism, they faced having their land taken from them and being exiled from the community. Sometimes even their children were at risk of being confiscated. In one instance, a couple of Quaker kids were threatened with banishment to Barbados, where they would be forced into indentured servitude. The only reason this punishment wasn't meted out was simply that the colonial authorities were unable to procure a ship willing to do their bidding. As all of these draconian measures taken by colonial leadership would seem to indicate, the Quakers were now officially *persona non grata.* And by 1660, the same persecution the Quakers had left behind in England came home to roost in the British colonies of Maryland and Massachusetts, this time with a vengeance.

It was in Massachusetts that the Quaker evangelist Mary Dyer was given a death sentence for her faith. On June 1st, 1660, she was executed on the authority of the Bostonian government for daring to proselytize in Boston. Right before she was executed, Mary was told that she would be set free if she simply gave her word that she would leave and never return.

There were two problems with this request. Number one, Quakers don't swear to do anything, and number two, Mary Dyer would rather die than give up preaching to the folks of Massachusetts. She readily replied, "Nay, I cannot, for in obedience to the will of the Lord God I came, and in his will I abide faithful to death." Even in death, Mary would manage to send shockwaves throughout the colonies, bringing greater attention to Quakerism than if she had simply been left to preach in peace.

So much so that, in 1661, this action would eventually provoke a response from none other than the king of England, Charles II, who, in a sudden show of compassion, made it expressly forbidden for anyone in the Massachusetts Bay Colony to hand out death penalties to those "professing Quakerism." Nevertheless, despite efforts to enforce toleration, non-Quakers often viewed Quakers with absolute contempt. Quakers were roundly criticized for their refusal to show deference to authority figures, as well as for having religious beliefs that others in the community felt were heretical.

Meanwhile, back in England, George Fox and his fellow British Friends began to use Britain's legal law to further ensure their freedom of religion. This was done through appeals and pointing out loopholes in the law as it pertained to the cases of Quakers who had been imprisoned. Quakers would even seek audiences with the king himself, so they could request pardons for those Quakers being detained.

Even though more tolerant measures had been achieved, there was still great suspicion in British society that the Quakers were an alien presence among them. British society had already undergone many upheavals in recent years, and it didn't take much for fringe groups, such as the Quakers, to be perceived as a potential threat to the social order. It was for this reason that George Fox wrote down his famous "Peace Testimony" in 1661.

This epic testimony laid out the Quaker intention to live peaceably with their neighbors and sought to clear the Quaker name of any "accusations of plot and fighting and demonstrate their innocency [sic]." The testament then went on to state the following affirmation: "All bloody principles and practices, we do utterly deny, with all outward wars and strife and fightings [sic] with outward weapons, for any end or under any pretense whatsoever."

Not only did this document help to calm some British nerves, but it also set forth the prime directive and charter that the Quakers would follow in the centuries to come. Here in this treatise, George Fox made it absolutely clear to his followers that Quakers needed to be above the fray when it came to violence of any kind. If there was any doubt among the Society of Friends over whether or not pacifism would reign supreme, it was as good as written in stone now.

Pacifism wasn't the only thing the Quaker Peace Testimony enshrined. It also represented a turning point in Quakerism, as they were moving away from the more radical Quaker past. Previously, the Quakers, galvanized by a younger George Fox, had enthusiastically preached of the imminent arrival of the end times. And like any religious group thinking the end was near, they sought to get their message across at all costs, even if it meant belligerently interrupting a service or two.

Yes, one of the oddest things about early Quakers was their penchant for bursting into the church of another denomination to proclaim their gospel while the Presbyterians, Methodists, Lutherans, Puritans—or whoever they might be—were in the middle of their sermon. This move certainly didn't gain Quakers very much sympathy from the leaders of other denominations, but this radical aspect of Quakerism seemed to suddenly come to an end with George Fox's Peace Testimony.

The Quakers who came after Fox's guidelines were laid out became much more pragmatic in their approach to ministry. Just like other religious sects that went from a cult-like status to becoming part of the mainstream, the Quakers moved away from a take-no-prisoners approach to a more organized outreach. They no longer expected an imminent Armageddon and instead focused on a long-term and strategic plan for evangelism.

It was during this period the Quakers first hammered out the official shape of their own religious gatherings. It was determined that the Quakers would meet on a "monthly, quarterly, and yearly" basis. These gatherings would be referred to as "meetings." The concept of having monthly, quarterly, and yearly meetings is one that is still practiced among the faithful Quakers to this very day.

Back in the states, the Quakers continued to maintain a strong presence in southern Maryland, as well as Salem, Massachusetts. The Quakers were also present in the Dutch colony of New Netherland (later New York) as well. Quakers initially faced persecution from the Dutch, but by the early 1660s, the Dutch government ordered the people to leave the Quakers alone as long as "they remained peaceable." This policy was then continued by the British when they took over the colony in 1664.

Since this general acceptance continued, the founder of the Quaker faith, George Fox himself, set sail for the Americas on August 11th, 1671. Although it was styled as a grand tour, Fox was basically there to check the pulse of these satellites and make sure the various Quaker organizations were foundationally solid. Fox, along with his right-hand man, William Edmundson, first arrived at the Caribbean island of Barbados in October 1671.

It was here that Fox once again played the role of a Quaker apologist. Since tensions between the slaveholding populace and the Quakers of Barbados had begun to erupt, Fox fired off a letter to Colonel Christopher Codrington, the governor of the island, assuring him that the Quakers were not intentionally inciting slave rebellions. The animosity the plantation owners felt toward the Quakers was largely due to the fact that Quakers had made it their practice to preach to both the free and slave populations of the island.

Fox ended up meeting with the governor in person, and the meeting is said to have gone well, with Fox later reporting that "they were treated very civilly and kindly." Nevertheless, Fox refused to stop preaching and reaching out to the enslaved Africans on the island. While seeking to soothe the nerves of the island's governor, he instructed the Quaker faithful to continue to "take the enslaved to meetings to educate them." He also urged slave owners to "deal mildly and gently with them [slaves] and not use cruelty."

It wasn't long before the folks running the plantation began to complain that Fox and his Friends were "rabble-rousing." Fox soon left Barbados, and after a brief stint in Jamaica, he went to the mainland of what would become the United States, sailing all the way up to Maryland. As mentioned, the Quakers already had a strong presence in Maryland, and George Fox was intent on capitalizing on it.

Here, he gathered up all of the local Quaker leaders and engaged in a series of meetings that took place over the course of four days' time. George Fox's grand tour came to an end in the summer of 1673 when he finally boarded a ship and returned to Great Britain, confident that the many seeds he had planted in the New World would take root.

Chapter 2: William Penn Comes to the Quaker Faith

Did we believe a final reckoning and judgment; or did we think enough of what we do believe, we would allow more love in religion than we do; since religion itself is nothing else but love to God and man. Love is indeed heaven upon Earth; since heaven above would not be heaven without it. For where there is not love; there is fear. But perfect love casts out fear. Love is above all; and when it prevails in us all, we shall be lovely, and in love with God and one with another.

-William Penn

As powerful as the Quakers had become in Maryland, Pennsylvania would become the true bastion of the faith. Pennsylvania was founded by William Penn, who took charge of the region through a royal grant awarded to him in 1681. With this royal mandate, Penn would go on to create a government in Pennsylvania that would not only embrace the religious freedom that the Quakers craved but also many of the other essential American freedoms that the United States would someday hold dear.

Penn himself came to the Quaker faith as a young man. His first encounter with the Quakers occurred when he was just thirteen years old when his father Admiral Penn had a Quaker friend named Thomas Loe come over to his home and preach to his family. This seems to have been a spur of the moment decision, but it would have lasting consequences for the admiral's son.

Like most British people at the time, Admiral Penn was a member of the Church of England. Yet he was still openminded enough to hear other people's points of view and beliefs. During this session, Admiral Penn's son, William Penn, first got a taste of Quakerism and came to admire the faith. His eyes were opened to the possibilities that day, and he would never forget the words that Mr. Loe had preached.

He learned of the inner light Quakers claimed inhabited all human beings, which allowed them to have a direct channel of communication with God. According to the tenants of Quakerism, we all have this divine light within us that we can tap into it at any time. This concept was mind-blowing for someone who grew up believing that there was a distinct separation between man and his creator.

Loe taught that this direct line of contact made preachers, churches, sacraments, and any other ritualized service completely unnecessary. There was no need for an intermediary of any kind. According to Loe, all one had to do was quiet themselves down and consult the inner light within. By doing this, they would be in direct communion with their very creator. William Penn was absolutely spellbound by what he had heard, and thus, the seeds of Quakerism were planted in the young boy.

The idea that one could have such a rock of stability within themselves was certainly appealing considering the tumultuous times in which they lived. England was in the throes of severe political instability. The nation had suffered a civil war, and from 1653 to 1658, it was being controlled by a former general turned dictator: Oliver Cromwell.

Officially known as the "Lord Protector," Cromwell had usurped power from the deposed King Charles II, with whom William Penn's father had been on good terms. Nevertheless, despite the loss of this royal benefactor, Admiral Penn found his footing under Cromwell, who made him "Rear Admiral of the Irish Seas," as well as "Vice Admiral in command of England's Third Fleet." By 1653, the older Penn was made "General at Sea," a role he carried with distinction.

Nevertheless, the thin ice underneath Admiral Penn's feet began to crack shortly after, and in just a few years' time, he was tossed into the horrid dungeon known as the Tower of London. The reason? He was believed to have somehow been in cahoots with the deposed King Charles II. Admiral Penn was only imprisoned for about five weeks, but the incident would leave a lasting mark on both him and his family.

It was after his release and his return to his homestead in Ireland, called "Macroom Castle," that the admiral invited Quaker minister Thomas Loe to say a word or two. Considering the circumstances, the Penn family was perhaps well dispositioned to hear the stirring message this Quaker conveyed. The idea that God's inner light rested in everyone and could not be taken away by tyrannical despots must have been appealing. And the younger Penn certainly never forgot the sermon delivered by Loe that day, as he held this precious moment dear to his heart.

Several years later, in 1667, after Cromwell had been removed and King Charles II restored to the throne, the now grown-up William Penn heard the same Quaker minister was back in town holding a meeting. William Penn's heart must have been stirred with fond memories of that day back at Macroom Castle, for he didn't hesitate to attend.

Penn apparently stood out from the outset due to his aristocratic dress. All the Quakers wore plain clothing, whereas Penn was decked out in the best finery of the day. Who was this wealthy looking young man who dared to attend a meeting of the Society of Friends? Quaker meetings at this time were illegal, and anyone in attendance was subject to arrest. It was a dangerous prospect for Penn just to attend.

William Penn had a lot going for him at the time. As the son of a British admiral, he was groomed for the finer things of British society. The idea that he would visit such a fringe group would have struck most of his peers as madness. He had a lot to lose being associated with the Quakers, yet William Penn still couldn't help but feel compelled to revisit the Quaker doctrine that had stirred his soul as a child.

William Penn was indeed taking a risk, and the precariousness of his situation was soon proven when the local authorities decided to break up the gathering. Someone must have tipped off the locals because this particular meeting was interrupted when one of the king's soldiers came barging right in.

It is interesting to note that only one man was initially tasked with shutting down the meeting. Since the Quakers were known to be nonviolent, this lone enforcer counted on the fact that the Quaker faithful would not resist his efforts. The Quakers who did indeed eschew violent action of any kind did not do anything to impede the intruder's advance.

Penn, who was not yet a Quaker, didn't hesitate, and he rushed to greet the interloper. This authority figure was no doubt shocked to see a finely dressed young man—someone who appeared to be of nobility no less—suddenly rush forward to greet him. William Penn seized hold of the man and appeared to be ready to do his worst, before some of the Quakers managed to convince Penn to let him go.

But if William Penn or his Quaker friends thought the government enforcer would simply shrug off the incident and forget about it, they were mistaken. The man took off only to return a short while later with more troops. This time, there was nothing Penn could do. He and all of the Quakers who were at the meeting were taken into custody and made to answer to a court magistrate.

After being released from jail, William was summoned by his father to explain what was going on. When Penn showed up with a Quaker friend in tow—one Josiah Coale, a man who was a known rabble-rouser among non-Quakers—Admiral Penn only became more agitated. Wishing to speak with his son alone, Admiral Penn took William to the side and began to question him as to what he was doing.

Even the manner of William Penn's speech offended his father, as William had since adopted the Quaker habit of referring to everyone as "thee" and "thou." Quakers did this in order to deny any acknowledgment of rank or status among people. The Quakers believed (and still do believe) that all were equal, as everyone had the same spark of divine light within them, and they refused to reference any sense of superior status.

In the Old English vernacular of the day, the terms "thee" and "thou" were used when speaking to commoners or the young, whereas the term "you" was used when addressing elders, especially those who had high-ranking social positions, as was the case with Admiral Penn. Taking umbrage to what he felt was a blatant show of disrespect, Admiral Penn chastised his son's speech, telling him that he "must use 'you' in speaking to older people or persons of high ranks."

His son was in his twenties at this point, but Admiral Penn must have felt that he was suddenly correcting a five-year-old. After all, everyone in English society knew better than to disrespect their elders like this. But William Penn's choice of words was not due to a lack of education or an intent to willfully disrespect anyone; he had simply been enlightened by the Quaker view that all should be equal under God, with no distinction showed whatsoever.

William Penn explained as much to his father. As his frustrated old man listened, William preached about how God was "no respecter of persons," and since God did not recognize status or rank, he and his Quaker brethren showed no such distinction either. Admiral Penn, however, was not too pleased by the sudden spiritual epiphany his son was having.

When Admiral Penn surmised that his son wanted to become a Quaker, he was immediately opposed to it. It's rather ironic that Admiral Penn was the one who had introduced his son to the Quaker faith in the first place yet was so displeased when the seed he had planted finally came to take root. Admiral Penn, who wished for his son to be a successful nobleman and not a Quaker fanatic, told his son of his displeasure in no uncertain terms and bid him to leave the family estate. William was essentially kicked out of the house.

Undaunted, Penn continued to pursue his beliefs. In fact, his father tossing him off the family estate only drove him further into the arms of the Quakers. From this point forward, William lived and breathed Quakerism. He not only went to Quaker meetings, but he also lived with Quakers. If necessary, he was willing to go to jail with them. During this period, William Penn even wrote religious tracts for the faith.

One of these, a tract entitled, *The Sandy Foundation Shaken*, landed him in some real hot water with the Church of England. The tract criticizes basic tenants of the Church of England's' doctrine, and when the Bishop of London got a hold of it in 1668, he was absolutely indignant and asked for William Penn to be arrested. For this simple little tract, which criticized the Church of England, William Penn was thrown into the Tower of London.

The Tower of London had served as a jail for all manner of dissenters. These people were cruelly tortured and, at times, executed. As such, it was certainly not a good place for William Penn to be in, by any stretch of the imagination. Nevertheless, when William Penn was given a chance to denounce Quakerism and be set free, he held firm, proclaiming, "My prison shall be my grave before I will budge a jot."

But very much in the tradition of George Fox who had come before him, William finally wrote an apologist treatise, in which he clarified his views and denied ever willfully hurting the Church of England, rejecting Christ, or disparaging the king. This was apparently enough for King Charles II, who was on good terms with William's father, and he had William Penn released from the Tower of London on July 28th, 1669.

The year 1669 was a pretty significant one for King Charles II, for he forged his infamous "CABAL" during this time. King Charles's cabal was a special council he created that consisted of his most trusted advisors. The name "cabal" actually comes from the first letter of each of the members' first names. The men on his cabal council were Clifford, Arlington, Buckingham, Ashley, and Lauderdale.

It was with this group of advisors that King Charles II would seek to further his policies. Due to the British government's tumultuous nature at the time, he needed this special council to help him push forward his aims. Yes, even though Charles II was king, he still had to strategize and finagle just like anyone else to get things done.

Charles II, who himself was secretly a Catholic, was constantly viewed with suspicion by his Protestant peers. Just about any move he made was held with equal suspicion. Even the simple act of setting William Penn free was met with harsh words and sniping criticism behind the king's back. Many undoubtedly felt the king was wasting his time with a religious reprobate who would never change his ways.

And sure enough, scarcely a month later, Penn ran afoul of the authorities once again. On August 14th, he was found preaching on the street in front of a closed meetinghouse to a large group of people. The sermon was quickly disrupted when the "sheriff and soldiers arrived" on the scene. William Penn was arrested by the sheriff and charged with "preaching seditiously and causing mayhem."

During this stint in jail, William's chief complaint was apparently over an interview the mayor made, in which the city leader made disparaging remarks about his father, Admiral Penn. From his prison cell, William wrote his father, explaining that while he "could bear harsh words about himself," he would not stand for verbal abuse being hurled at his dad. The mayor had apparently trudged up old criticisms, such as his father was a poor ship captain and that he "had starved his seamen," among other insults.

Such petty remarks were no doubt meant to rile up William Penn rather than actually injure the old admiral. And it seemed to work. Out of all the indignities William Penn suffered, nothing seemed to agitate him more than seeing his father being denigrated like this. Perhaps his knee-jerk reaction to defend his father's legacy inspired him to reach some sort of reconciliation with the admiral.

In his letter, Penn wrote his dear old dad the following: "Be not displeased or grieved. What if this be designed of the Lord for an exercise of our patience? I am very well and have no trouble upon my spirits, besides absence from thee."

Considering the fact that Admiral Penn had witnessed quite a transformation in his son, it was still hard for him to wrap his head around what was happening. Penn, a young man who previously seemed to have a promising future ahead of him, was suddenly being thrown in and out of jail and becoming associated with those considered to be on the margins of society. His son asked him to "exercise patience," and Admiral Penn probably was indeed having to pray for more than a little patience when it came to dealing with what he perceived to be his wayward son.

And it was probably with a heavy sigh that Admiral Penn read the last sentence of this letter. Because even though his son affirms his love for his father, he ends the missive with that ever so troubling pronoun of "thee." If it wasn't clear before, it must have seemed absolutely certain now to the old admiral that his son would never leave the Quaker faith.

Chapter 3: William Penn's Holy Experiment

We are inclined to call things by the wrong names. We call prosperity happiness, and adversity misery, even though adversity is the school of wisdom and often the way to eternal happiness.

-William Penn

William Penn languished in prison for two weeks before he was sent to trial on September 1st, 1670. He was tried on charges of holding an unlawful assembly and otherwise disturbing "the peace." Penn pleaded not guilty to all charges. As the trial convened, Penn and his fellow Quakers became ensnared by the prosecution in their refusal to remove their hats. In those days, it was common courtesy for someone to take off their hat when inside a courtroom, but for the Quakers, who refused to recognize any distinction of rank or authority other than God, this proved to be an impossible feat.

The prosecutors took note of this fact and used it as a means of attack every chance they could. Pretty soon, the Quaker defendants were being threatened with heavy court fines if they continued to insist upon wearing their hats. By the time Penn was called to the stand, he was defiant. He stated that he "would not recant" and would not even "validate" the charges against him since he believed they were unjust.

Penn then went on to state that he and his Quaker colleagues had the right to "preach, pray, or worship the Eternal, Holy, Just God" completely unhindered. He then advised that it was their "indispensable duty to meet incessantly upon so good an account; nor shall all the powers upon Earth be able to divert us from reverencing and adoring our God who made us."

The prosecution seemed to feel that this was simply grandstanding on Penn's part and insisted that he was not "on trial for worshipping God, but for breaking the law." Penn denied breaking any law and stated that the jury needed to have it explained to them just law he had supposedly broken so they would "know by what law it was that he was [being] prosecuted."

Not wanting to play this game, the court recorder simply snapped, "The Common Law!" He was unwilling to elaborate any further, stating that he would be unable to "run up so many years, and over so many adjudged cases which we call Common Law." Penn then shot back with the canny reply, "If it be common, it should not be so hard to produce."

Infuriated, the recorder resorted to name-calling, shouting, "You are a saucy fellow, speak to the indictment!" However, Penn was insistent, and he said, "You are many mouths and ears against me. I say again, unless you show me and the people the law you ground your indictment upon, I shall take it for granted and your proceedings are merely arbitrary."

The court recorder still continued to ignore Penn's argument and rejoined with "The question is whether you are guilty of this indictment." But William Penn continued to argue. "The question is not whether I am guilty of this indictment but whether this indictment be legal. Where there is no law there is no transgression." A heated back and forth followed before the recorder finally rebuked Penn, telling him, "Sir, you are a troublesome fellow, and it is not the honour of the Court to suffer you to go on."

Finally reaching his limit, the recorder eventually called for Penn to be confined to the back of the courtroom while the proceedings continued without him. Still, Penn would not be silent, and shouting from the "bail dock" where he was being held, he challenged, "Who are my judges?" Directing his remarks to the jury, he then shouted, "You of the Jury take notice that I have not been heard."

Fed up, it was at this point the court officials decided to have Penn and his associates taken out of the courtroom entirely and placed in a separate holding cell while the proceedings commenced without them. The jury was then asked to render a verdict, but when four of the jurors refused to find the Quakers guilty, the court began to threaten and use abusive language against them. Nevertheless, no matter how many times they were threatened, those four jurors would not buckle, they would not break, and they would not find Penn and his Quaker brethren guilty of any crime.

For this reason, the infuriated prosecution decided to hold Penn and his comrades for their failure to pay the fines leveled against them for refusing to take off their hats in court. William Penn knew his father would most likely pay this fee so that he could be released, but William wrote him a letter, specifically asking him not to do so.

William wrote his father, saying, "I intreat thee not to purchase my liberty...I would rather perish than release myself by so indirect a course as to satiate their revengeful, avaricious appetites. The advantage of such freedom would fall very short of the trouble of accepting it. Let not this wicked world disturb thy mind, and whatever shall come to pass, I hope in all conditions to prove thy obedient son."

Admiral Penn, of course, would not stand by and allow his son to rot in jail, so he indeed came to his son's rescue. The admiral not only bailed William out but also all of his Quaker associates as well. This would prove to be the last act of benevolence that the admiral would show toward his son since he was seriously ill and already close to death at the time, a fact the old admiral stoically acknowledged when he wrote his reply to William.

His father's letter read: "Son William, if you and your friends keep to your plain way of preaching, and keep to your plain way of living, you will make an end of the priests to the end of the world. Bury me by my mother. Live all in love." Time was indeed short for Admiral Penn, but his son was released just in time to be by his father's side when he finally passed on September 16th, 1670.

William would get in and out of trouble due to his Quaker beliefs quite frequently in the first few years following his father's passing. During this time, he also met and fell in love with a woman who strongly believed in the Quaker faith: Gulielma Maria Springett. She was the stepdaughter of a prominent Quaker by the name of Isaac Penington. As the son of the former mayor of London, Isaac Penington held great influence, and he used this to shape the early Quaker faith. William Penn and his new bride would likewise follow his lead, first in England and then in places much farther afield.

William Penn would first become involved in the New World when he was approached in 1675 by a couple of Quakers who had large property holdings in what was then known as "West Jersey." Penn, who was knowledgeable of the law by training, was tapped to forge a constitution for the region, which he called "Concession and Agreements." This document outlined the religious freedoms the Quakers desired and the kind of democracy they craved.

In many ways, this charter for West Jersey (later to become Pennsylvania) was a forerunner of what the actual United States Constitution would entail. "Concession and Agreements" contains general guidelines for the community, with an additional listing of allowed civil liberties, which are very much in line with what would eventually become the US Bill of Rights. William Penn, who lived one hundred years before the founding of the United States, is not usually considered a Founding Father, but there are those who would argue that he very well should be.

After forging this document, events unfolded rather rapidly, which put William Penn into a position of not just writing out legal charters for land but rather gaining land himself. Some of the original landholders began to sell off portions of their land, and Penn received some of them since he was one of the acting trustees. In 1680, the Duke of York (who would one day become

King James II) gave even more holdings to Penn and some of his Quaker associates. On March 4th, 1681, none other than King Charles II himself granted William Penn some 46,000 square miles of colonial land in America.

It was King Charles II who decided to change the name of the colony to Pennsylvania. The appellation came from the Penn family name, with the notable addition of "sylvan," which is Latin for "forest land." According to some accounts, it was William Penn who initially came up with the idea to call the place "Sylvania," but it was King Charles II who added Penn in front of the term, rendering the name to be Pennsylvania.

Not surprisingly, William Penn, a modest Quaker, immediately rejected having his name attached to the colony. Upon hearing of it, he complained to King Charles II, telling him, "I feared lest it would be looked upon as a vanity in me and not as a respect in the King, as it truly was to my father whom he often mentions in praise." Attempting to pacify the Quaker's concerns, the king artfully deflected the perceived accolades, informing him, "We will keep it, my dear fellow, but not on your account, do not flatter yourself, we will keep the name to commemorate the Admiral, your noble father."

So, Penn had expressed reservations about having a colony named after him only for the king to basically tell him, "Oh! You thought I was naming the land after you? No way! It's being named after your dad!" Whether the king sincerely was naming the property after Admiral Penn or just wishing to present the matter in a way that would be more palatable to William Penn is anyone's guess. Perhaps it was a little bit of both. Admiral Penn was, after all, a well-respected man, and even William Penn would find it hard to refuse the colony being named in his honor. So, it was with this little change of perspective that William Penn agreed to allow Pennsylvania to be born.

Penn had called the land "Sylvania" due to the massive forests that blanketed the region. And in those rugged frontier days, Pennsylvania was indeed little more than a wooded forest. It was in this vast, untamed wilderness that Penn wished to conduct a "holy experiment," as he wished to plant and cultivate the full fruits of religious freedom.

Now that William had this land, he had to figure out how to govern it. In the charter for Pennsylvania, he was determined to create a bastion of liberty and tolerance. Unlike the surrounding colonies, in which someone could be summarily executed on the flimsiest of grounds (Mary Dyer was executed in Massachusetts simply for being a visiting Quaker), Penn made sure that the death penalty would only be enacted for those who had been convicted of murder or "high treason."

In April 1681, Penn sent his cousin, William Markham, to preside as the region's deputy governor, while he stayed behind to tie up loose ends in

England. Markham washed up on the shores of Pennsylvania that summer, but he didn't come alone. He came armed with a rather long-winded epistle from William Penn, which set out in exact detail what he expected the future of Pennsylvania to be. To understand Penn's frame of mind better, here is his written directive in full:

My friends: I wish you all happiness, here and hereafter. These are to let you know that it hath pleased God, in his providence, to cast you within my lot and care. It is a business that, though I never undertook before, yet God has given me an understanding of my duty, and an honest mind to do it uprightly. I hope you will not be troubled at your change and the King's choice, for you are now fixed at the mercy of no governor that comes to make his fortune great; you shall be governed by laws of your own making, and live a free and, if you will, a sober and industrious people. I shall not usurp the right of any, or oppress his person. God has furnished me with a better resolution, and has given me his grace to keep it. In short, whatever sober and free men can desire for the security and improvement of their own happiness, I shall heartily comply with, and in five months I resolve, if it please God, to see you. In the meantime, pray submit to the commands of my deputy, so far as they are consistent with the law, and pay him those dues (that formerly you paid to the order of the Governor of New York) for my use and benefit, and so I beseech God to direct you in the way of righteousness, and therein prosper you and your children after you. I am your true friend. -William Penn

If the settlers in the region had worried over who would take control, this statement undoubtedly did much to allay their fears. In furtherance of this sentiment, Markham was given a prime directive by Penn to maintain healthy relations with those who already called Pennsylvania home, meaning the local Native American populations and the European settlers who were already maintaining a presence in the region.

Penn was especially mindful of not offending the Native Americans, instructing Markham "to be tender of offending the Indians." This approach was certainly fairly unique, setting Penn apart from his colonial contemporaries. Pennsylvania's constitution was also quite different from others, as it allowed many of the liberties that the future US Constitution would have, such as freedom of the press, trial by jury, and freedom of religion. Of course, the latter was crucial for the Quakers, as they had been terribly persecuted for their religion for many years. So, it is perhaps no surprise that Penn purposefully instituted a governance framework that would be friendly to the Quakers. Pennsylvania, which was noted in particular for its tolerance of Quakerism, would also become known as a haven for freedom of religion in general, and it would become fertile ground for a wide variety of religious expressions in the years to come.

Although he initially governed from afar, William Penn finally arrived in Pennsylvania on October 27th, 1682. Almost as soon as he arrived, he made it his priority to enter into peace talks and negotiations with the local Native American populations. The Native Americans were naturally suspicious of the newcomers and with good reason, considering that so many other European immigrants had been deceptive in their aims.

However, Penn wanted to make his good intentions clear, and he entered into the so-called "Great Treaty" with Native American leaders, in which he expressly stated that "no land could be taken away from them." Not only that, but he also made it a point to actually become friends with the local Native Americans who lived in the area. Penn would come and visit their homes, eat with them, speak with them in their own tongue, and even attend Native American festivities in an effort to show that he meant no harm.

King Charles II cautioned Penn, telling him that he needed to allow for an "armed force to protect the Quakers from the Indians." William Penn steadfastly refused. Penn resolutely told the king, "I want none of your majesty's soldiers." The king is then said to have asked, "But how will you get your lands without soldiers?"

This statement is indicative of what was really going on in Pennsylvania. Although the British had claimed the territory, and the king had given it over to Penn as if he was the owner of the land, both the king and William Penn knew that others already laid claim to it. It was for this reason that King Charles II suggested armed troops were needed to solidify the British grip on the territory and allow for further expansion as desired.

But the fact that the Native Americans had been there first was certainly not lost on Penn. And his response demonstrates how he viewed the whole situation. Without blinking, Penn answered, "I mean to buy their lands of them." Buying lands from Native Americans? This was certainly not what King Charles II was expecting to hear. And he practically shouted in response, "Why man—you have bought them of me already!"

Penn did not dispute the British concept that the Pennsylvanian wilderness had been titled, deeded, and handed over from the monarchy, but he didn't discount the Native Americans either. Penn thus replied, "Yes; I know I have, and at a dear rate too. I did this to gain thy good will, not that I thought thou hadst any right to their lands—I will buy the rights of the proper owners, even of the Indians themselves: by doing this, I shall imitate God in his justice and mercy, and hope thereby, to insure his blessing on my colony, if I should ever live to plant on in North America."

Penn demonstrated the perfect example of both Quaker humility and the Quaker sense of fairness and justice. If settling Pennsylvania had been wrong,

William Penn was more than willing to make it right. And his efforts produced some rather immediate results because shortly after Markham explained his aims to the local Native American leaders, they declared that they would "live in peace" with the Quakers "as long as the sun and the moon shall endure."

The colonization of Pennsylvania ran its course at a fairly steady rate. It is said that between 1681 and 1682, some 23 different ships, each carrying around 2,000 passengers, arrived from England. On the ground, Markham had done well to fulfill William Penn's wishes in peacefully purchasing property from the Lenape. He made sure the purchases he made were contiguous, and with them, he slowly extended the range of the Pennsylvania Colony both north and south alongside the natural boundary of the Delaware River.

As soon as William Penn arrived on the scene, he began to handle the land purchases himself, and he negotiated several acquisitions. In the summer of 1683 alone, he managed to secure three huge tracts of land from various representatives of local tribes. These acquisitions were then followed by even more valuable territory nestled in the Brandywine River, which was acquired on November 19th, 1683. William Penn attempted to be as cordial as possible in his relations with the tribal groups and even went so far as to learn the language of the Lenape (also known as Delaware).

In the ensuing years, events made life harder for the British Quakers. British Parliament had been actively contesting the authority of King Charles II. They also decried the king's closeness with non-mainstream religious groups like the Quakers. This resulted in a backlash from the king, which led to tightening constraints on groups such as the Quakers. This overreach only ended when King Charles II abruptly died from a massive stroke a few months later. After his death, Charles's brother, James II (the former Duke of York), was crowned king in February of 1685. Although King James II was a staunch Catholic, he would become one of the greatest benefactors the Quaker faith had ever known.

Chapter 4: William Penn, Pennsylvania, and Its Quaker Legacy

I expect to pass through life but once. If therefore, there be any kindness I can show, or any good thing I can do to any fellow being, let me do it now, and not defer or neglect it, as I shall not pass this way again.

-William Penn

King James II was inaugurated as Britain's new monarch on February 6th, 1685. As it turns out, King James II would be the last Catholic king of England, yet despite his preference for Catholicism, he would be rather friendly to the Quakers. In fact, he had been a good friend of Admiral Penn's, and by extension, he was on good terms with his son as well. Although James was a Catholic, it was due to the words of his good friend William Penn that he came to understand and respect the Quaker faith, despite its differences from mainstream Christianity.

Penn was the one who convinced King James II that the values of the Quakers would not upset the social order but actually benefit it. James, though by no means thinking of converting to the faith himself, soon came to believe that the British government had nothing to fear from the Quakers. George Fox may have begun this trend when he penned his famous Peace Testimony, which explained the peaceful nature of the Quaker's intentions. But as far as King James II was concerned, it was William Penn who made these words a reality.

It was with this new understanding that King James II, who enacted sweeping religious reforms in the spring of 1686, began the process of pardoning those who had been thrown into jail over their religious beliefs. During this general amnesty, it is estimated that over 13,000 Quakers were given their freedom. But despite all of this goodwill toward other religions, the English elite feared having a Catholic monarch on the throne, and it wasn't long before courtiers began to grumble against him.

Due to the resistance Catholic King James II faced due to his faith, he could, in some sense, relate to the difficulties of the Quakers. This empathy added yet another layer to the mutual understanding between the king and William Penn. This understanding was evidenced by King James II's "Declaration of Indulgence," which went into effect on April 4th, 1687.

This declaration that did away with the enforcement of "penal laws," which had previously demanded adherence to the Church of England's orthodoxy. It also finally gave British subjects the official right to pursue their own religious inclinations, even if it went against the mainstream practices of the Anglican Church.

By helping religious minorities such as his Quaker friends, King James II was actually helping himself, for he saw greater religious tolerance in general as a means of making Catholicism more palatable in Britain. Penn was very close to the king around the time of this declaration, and some have suggested that Penn was the principal "instigator" in bringing it about.

Of course, the closeness between these two men would not go unnoticed, and it wasn't long before the king's enemies became William Penn's enemies.

Some of the other Protestant denominations, which despised the fact their reigning monarch was Catholic, began to deny Penn's Quakerism and made William Penn out to be a Catholic himself. Some even went so far as to call him "William, the Papist," indicating that Penn was under the sway of the Roman pope. Of course, this was not only ridiculous but absolutely false.

In fact, most people who lived in England at the time were probably aware of Penn's staunch Quakerism, yet this lie was propagated all the same. Back then, as is still the case today, falsehoods were sometimes actively promoted to bring down someone who a certain group did not like. And William Penn himself was unfortunate enough to fall into the crosshairs of such malicious liars.

These detractors actively sought a way to take Penn's benefactor, King James II, off the throne. Their opportunity came in the form of William of Orange, who was a Protestant from the Netherlands. British Parliament actually sent out a request for William of Orange to come and seize the kingship for himself. He accepted the offer, showing up with about 14,000 soldiers. King James II did not like his odds and fled to France.

This turn of events caused a lot of trouble for William Penn, who had made his way back to England by this time. Since he was on such good terms with King James II, he was suddenly viewed as being on the wrong side of history. Any friend of the deposed King James II was perceived as an enemy of the state, and this resulted in William Penn's arrest on December 10th, 1688, just as William of Orange was securing power for himself.

Made to answer for his past association with the now-deposed James II, William Penn stood strong and spoke his mind. Instead of groveling for mercy, he clearly stated his case. He told those who would listen that he "loved his country" and would never do anything to betray it. Penn denied the charges that he had been in league with the Catholic Church, and he also proclaimed his solidarity with the Protestants. Even though the Quakers were considered a fringe group, they were indeed counted as one of the many products of the Protestant Reformation.

However, Penn refused to renounce James II, not because he believed that all of his actions had been right, but because he simply viewed him as a trustworthy friend. Penn told his accusers that if he was loyal to the king, it was out of gratitude for how good he had been to him and his family. This only increased some of the calls for Penn's immediate execution, but luckily enough, Penn's honest, forthright answers won over the only person that really mattered—William of Orange.

The new king was not a fan of groveling, and so, he was impressed with Penn's bold stand. William of Orange, now King William III, had Penn released, and the charges against him were dropped. And to the horror of Penn's enemies, he ended up in the good graces of yet another British monarch. It was partially due to Penn's influence that William III presided over a Parliament that managed to pass the Act of Toleration, which ensured a relative degree of religious freedom in Britain.

In the meantime, Penn was routinely harassed by his pollical enemies, who were constantly looking for some reason to have William Penn hauled off to jail. This constant scrutiny led to Penn's arrest once again in 1690 when he was brought in on charges of having carried out correspondence with the dethroned James II. Once again, the charges didn't stick, and after a short time, Penn was released.

George Fox, the founder of Quakerism, passed away in 1691. Penn attended the funeral, where he gave a rousing speech. Immediately after the funeral service, he was alerted about plans for his arrest on charges of treason. This forced Penn to lay low for a while. However, Penn's low point was still to come, and it arrived in the spring of 1692. This was the year that William Penn lost control of Pennsylvania. King William III appointed a royal governor to preside over Pennsylvania instead.

The everyday persecution of Quakers had intensified greatly in the meantime, with random acts of violence and vandalism becoming commonplace. Unlike during the benevolent tolerance of King James II, the Quakers suddenly seemed to have no quarter. Seeming to voice the abrasive, intolerant sentiment of the times, a priest from Glasgow even went so far as to call Quakers, "Heretics, blasphemers, possessed with the devil and as dangerous to converse with as those that have the plague."

Considering that England had recently been struck with a terrible case of bubonic plague, for a preacher to label all Quakers as bad as the virulent strain of pestilence that was killing people left and right is pretty inflammatory, to say the least. And as might be expected, this kind of language only incensed those who opposed the Quakers. During this period, there were actually cases of mobs spontaneously gathering to "throw stones" at Quakers.

Despite this fierce opposition, the Quakers, who lived and breathed the New Testament, no doubt felt that this only showed they were living out the ideals of Christ. They cherished the words of the Good Book and saw direct parallels between the persecution of the saints of the Bible and the persecution they themselves faced. Biblical figures, such as Stephen, were stoned to death, Apostle Paul was stoned to death, and even Jesus himself was nearly stoned at one point. It is no wonder the Quakers thought they were in good company.

In fact, the Quakers were following a familiar script that has played out ever since the writing of the New Testament in the 1st century CE. Until religious tolerance was the norm in the Western world, every time a new religious mode of Christian thought popped up, the orthodoxy rose in opposition to stamp it out. This began with the first Christians themselves, and it continued with every new movement that emerged throughout the years.

George Fox, Martin Luther, and other early Christian thinkers, such as St. Thomas Aquinas and St. Augustine, were all inspired by the radical nature of the New Testament (after all, there is nothing quite as radical than a book that asks one to love their enemies), and they had visions of a better way to approach a personal relationship with God. They also had their own orthodox detractors who quickly rose up against their vision, crying out that those who dared to try a new approach to mainstream religion were "blasphemers."

The Quakers were indeed a part of this same religious cycle that had been repeating since Christianity's inception. They had become the new martyrs of the age, willing to die for their faith just like the heroes they had read about in the scriptures. But fortunately for the Quakers (or unfortunately, if some among them truly did have their hearts set on being martyrs), the political winds of Britain would shift once again, and the persecution would wane.

And as for William Penn himself? In 1693, some of William Penn's connections in the king's court managed to convince him to reinstate Penn's status. Penn was then given a "new charter" for Pennsylvania and was sent to be the governor of those Pennsylvanian woodlands once again. But there were a few strings attached to this reinstatement. For one thing, Penn was required to supply troops for Pennsylvania.

The king feared an imminent French invasion. King William III claimed he had reason to believe that French King Louis XIV, who just happened to be shielding his predecessor, James II, had designs on New York and Pennsylvania. Of course, this was quite a conundrum for a Quaker like William Penn, who abhorred violence. Whatever troops he gathered, they would have to be non-Quakers.

Before William Penn could sail to Pennsylvania, his life was disrupted by the death of his wife, Gulielma Maria Springett, on February 23rd, 1694. While he tried to handle his remaining affairs in England, he once again made William Markham governor in his absence. It wouldn't be until five years later that Penn would have his affairs well enough in order to set sail for Pennsylvania. Within that time, Penn had actually met and married another woman by the name of Hannah Callowhill, whom he wed in 1696.

It was with Hannah that he would return to stake his claim in Pennsylvania in the fall of 1699. By that time, William Penn was just about bankrupt after years of having to foot the various bills of Pennsylvania through his own pockets. The situation was so bleak that he considered selling his holdings back to the king. But before he did any such thing, Penn wanted to make sure that the state he left behind had remained strong.

The Quaker haven of Pennsylvania would become known for its fair and just treatment of the Native American tribes who lived nearby. This created much goodwill in the region, and it was this lasting legacy that granted Pennsylvania relative peace over the next several decades while other states faced routine skirmishes with nearby tribes. In fact, William Penn was so revered by the local Native Americans that they actually used him as a peace broker when fighting broke out between two different tribal groups.

William was definitely rare for the times he lived in, and his public policies proved it. In the spring of 1701, Penn held a meeting with the governor of Virginia and the governor of New York to brainstorm ways they could strengthen the ties between the states. Even though states like Pennsylvania, New York, and Virginia were basically separate entities, each with their own separate charters and beholden to the king, Penn argued for creating more unity and uniformity among them. He believed the colonies needed universal court practices, currency, and even a police force that could operate from colony to colony. Of course, this was what would happen one hundred some years later after the colonies gained independence, but when Penn championed these ideas back in 1701, his colleagues mostly just humored him. No one took it too seriously at the time.

Shortly after this conference, Penn found cause for alarm when he received word that the king of England planned to turn the colonies into "royal provinces." This would mean the colonies would be under the king's direct control, and the king would be able to arbitrarily appoint his own royal governors. Penn wasn't going to stand for that, so he left his Quaker brethren behind to head back to England once again. Before he left, he made sure the legislative body made an updated Pennsylvanian constitution that further enshrined the Quaker principles of peace, fair dealing, and benevolence.

Once this was settled, Penn set sail for England. William Penn showed up on the last day of the year—December 31st, 1701. When he arrived, he received word that the king had actually passed away during his voyage. This made James II's daughter, Queen Anne, the new reigning monarch.

William Penn and some of his Quaker entourage made their way to the queen's court to check the pulse of where the Quakers currently stood with the regime. The meeting apparently went well, and Queen Anne duly informed Penn, "You and your friends may be assured of my protection."

But even with Queen Anne's support, Penn's situation was rather grim. He learned that his old "agent," Philip Ford, had passed away. As it turned out, Ford had mishandled Penn's finances, made bad investments, and created a lot of debt. Ford's family then demanded Penn pay the leftover debt. Unable to pay it, Penn was actually sent to a debtors' prison in 1708. This was indeed a time in which people with outstanding debts could be sent to jail, and Penn would languish in a jail cell for the next several months.

Penn, of course, wasn't a stranger to confinement, but the fact that he was imprisoned over debt rather than religious persecution must have been quite a matter of embarrassment. It's one thing to go to jail fighting for what one believes in; it's another matter entirely to do time for failing to pay your bills. However, Penn was vindicated by his old Quaker friends, who managed to go through the financial records of the late Ford and found evidence of just how much Ford had swindled Penn out of money.

Taking this into consideration, the legal counsel strongly urged Ford's surviving family members to scale back on their demands. Finally, they accepted a settlement of 7,600 pounds. The same friends that uncovered Ford's corruption raised the money to pay off this settlement, and William Penn was freed.

Penn would live out the rest of his life in England. After suffering a stroke in 1712, his health would deteriorate, and he would finally die, some say "penniless," in 1718, at the age of seventy-four. But what he didn't have in money, he more than made up for in faith and the great legacy he left behind.

Chapter 5: The State of Quakerism after William Penn

Be patterns, be examples in all countries, places, islands, nations wherever you come; that your carriage and life may preach among all sorts of people, and to them; then you will come to walk cheerfully over the world, answering that of God in everyone; whereby in them you may be a blessing, and make the witness of God in them to bless you.

-George Fox

William Penn would pass away in 1718, but the example that William Penn had set for religious toleration would be continued by his further successors, who kept a steady social compact over the next few decades. It was his sons, Richard and Thomas Penn, as well as his grandson, John Penn, who would inherit the stewardship of Pennsylvania from William.

Immediately after William Penn's death, his wife Hannah took over the administration of Pennsylvania—a role she would serve until her own passing in 1726. After Hannah's death, Thomas, who was Hannah and William's son, would run the colony for nearly forty years in an arrangement that had him named as the "managing proprietor." Thomas proved to have the same knack for management that his father had, but his religious views differed. In fact, Thomas would opt to leave the Quaker church altogether and join up with the Church of England instead.

This would have been completely abhorrent to his father since William had struggled so hard to be free from the Church of England's grip for most of his life. But where his father attempted to stand his own ground and set himself apart from the status quo, Thomas seemed more inclined to go with the flow. He was described as "prosperous, accomplished, sensible," and a "cool-headed gentleman."

Thomas was not the firebrand that his father was, as he would much rather polish his social skills and fit into conventional norms than go against the grain as his dad had. Thomas was also much more pragmatic and careful with his finances, whereas his father William Penn didn't hesitate to spend large amounts of his own money, often to his own detriment.

To his credit, Thomas attempted to keep much of his father's social policies intact in the colony. He did his best to maintain the liberties set down in Pennsylvania's charter while struggling to make sure the British monarch in power was happy with the results. This was certainly not an easy balancing act.

It also must not have been easy to make sure that the settlers and Native Americans didn't rub each other the wrong way. Thomas, who upheld his father's pledge for fair dealings with the Native American tribes, tried his best to make sure that land deals were appropriate and that tensions never boiled out of control. Initially, the policies of William Penn were continued, but dishonesty and malfeasance, especially as it pertained to the local Native Americans who had dealings in the region, eventually began to seep in.

This can be seen in the infamous "Walking Purchase of 1737." In this dreadful episode, the trickery employed by greedy settlers who wanted Native American land was at its worst. The purchase revolved around a group of local Delaware, who measured their land by the "walking distance" of one day. They apparently agreed to sell some of their property along the Delaware River based on these measurements, and this was where settlers saw an opportunity for deception.

They used their own surveyors to walk the distance and apparently had their "fastest walkers" halfway run up the river so that the distance traveled would equal more land than the Delaware intended to sell. When the incredulous Delaware balked at the measurements, the settlers, instead of admitting their trickery, called in a militia from New York, who forcibly made the Delaware leave their property. The Delaware tribe would not forget this treachery and would become a bitter nemesis to the Pennsylvanian settlers after that.

By the 1750s, the pacifism that had been so carefully fostered by the Quakers began to give way to naked aggression. Outright conflict emerged in 1755, most notably with the Penn's Creek massacre, in which settlers were slaughtered by the Lenape (also known as the Delaware) tribe. This led many nonviolent Quakers in the legislature to openly renounce their positions. And without the Quaker influence, Pennsylvania fell into open warfare.

However, even as Quakers left positions of power, they proved themselves to be powerful activists, standing up for Native Americans' rights and being among the first to call for the abolition of slavery. One of the most powerful advocates for the abolition of slavery was a man named John Woolman. Woolman was born in 1720 and developed a passion for justice and equality from a young age.

He was in his early twenties when he experienced something that would change his life. Woolman was working for a man who was selling a slave, and he was asked to personally arrange the transaction. It was his job as a clerk to compile any bill of lading his employer requested, but Woolman immediately knew in his heart that this particular sale was horribly wrong. And not only did he think it—he acted upon it. Woolman stood up to his boss, resolutely informing him that slavery was wrong and that he would not play any part of such an evil transaction.

From that day forward, he became a staunch advocate for abolition. He also became a dedicated Quaker minister, who ceaselessly preached about the "truth and light" within everyone. This is still a major Quaker theme today, one that had been developed by the Quaker founder George Fox.

Woolman was a sensitive man who truly cared about others. Even animals were not exempt from his compassion, as was indicated when he decided to shun the use of horses for transportation since he felt the animals were often treated cruelly. Yes, long before animal cruelty was even really a concept, this sympathetic Quaker became a passionate advocate for animal rights.

Woolman traveled far and wide, spreading his views on Quakerism. He also spread his views on the evils of slavery. He continued to denounce slavery in both his words and his actions. It's said that whenever he visited someone's home that had slaves in the household, he always made sure to pay the slaves for whatever services they rendered, and he made sure to confront the slave owners about the practice.

And for Woolman, these things usually went hand in hand. For example, if someone in bondage served John Woolman dinner, he would hand them money for their work. And if the slave owner questioned him about it, which they often did, this opened the door for Woolman to condemn the practice to the slave owner's face. With the help of Woolman's tireless crusade against slavery, Quaker minds began to shift and become much more resolute on denouncing the practice.

By 1750, they were more or less convinced of the evils of slavery and began proactive measures to stem the tide of the practice. The Quakers began to see slavery as not only detrimental to those who were in bondage but also to those who held them there. First and foremost, they saw enforced servitude as not only a denial of the rights of the enslaved but also a covering up of their "inward light." Again, the Quakers believe that we each have an inward manifestation of God that needs to be allowed to shine bright. Just think of the kid's song, "This little light of mine–I'm gonna let it shine!" The Quakers believe that God's light dwells within all of us and should not be hindered. Therefore, they believed it a terrible travesty that the darkness of slavery covered up the inward light of the enslaved.

The Quakers also saw the practice as dimming the inward light of the slave owners as well. How could God's light shine through a person when they were engaged in such a horrid enterprise as slavery? The Quakers believed that the slave owner's light was greatly diminished by exploiting the labor of others. That's not to say the Quakers themselves never had slaves, as some among them most certainly did. From the Caribbean island of Barbados to the Southern United States, there were Quakers who ran plantations. And besides the Quakers who actively took part in slavery, there were also those who didn't own slaves yet indirectly benefited from the practice. Cotton merchants, for example, would have been less likely to find fault in slavery since their income partially depended upon it.

As it pertains to universally condemning the practice, real progress was made in 1758 when the Quakers launched an official edict stating that any Quakers who had slaves needed to "to be labored with." In other words, they needed a stern dressing-down. This meant that even though slave-owning Quakers would not be kicked out of the Quaker faith outright, they would not be allowed to attend meetings and would be excluded from many other aspects of church life. Some might have seen this as the Quakers shunning others of the same faith, while others might have viewed it as common decency that would help pave the way for a better, more tolerant future. Either way, slave-owning Quakers were ostracized for their participation in slavery.

The next major milestone in the Quakers' quest to rid slavery from their ranks occurred in 1770 at the "New England Yearly Meeting," when it was determined that any Quakers who had slaves had to take steps toward their emancipation. This then culminated into a Quaker-wide declaration being made in 1784, which demanded that all Quakers take immediate measures to free their slaves. If they did not, they would lose their membership in the church.

So, less than a decade after the American Revolution, the Quakers were staunchly opposed to slavery. And their efforts bore immediate fruit, as they were able to not only convince some slave owners to free their slaves but also aided runaway slaves in gaining freedom. These efforts would culminate in the Quakers participating in the Underground Railroad.

Up until the abolition of slavery, the Underground Railroad served as an active conduit for the transportation of runaway slaves to the North. However, this "railroad" did not depend on railroad tracks or train cars. It depended on dedicated men and women who agreed to transform their homes into secret "stations," at which runaways could stop and rest while they were on their trek to freedom.

The Quakers' role in this elaborate system of sheltering and stewarding runaway slaves to the North cannot be understated. The Underground Railroad gave African American men, women, and children, who lived in bondage in the Southern states, hope that they could find deliverance if they just made their way to the North. Not only that, but the continued stream of runaways helped to eat away at the entire slave system of the South. The Southern slave system could have no sense of security as long as groups like the Quakers actively aided and abetted runaways.

It was out of desperation to stop this migration to the North that Southerners pushed for the so-called Fugitive Slave Laws of 1850, demanding that they had the right to bring runaways who made their way north back to the South. It was this draconian measure that would increase tensions between the abolitionists of the North and the slaveholders of the South until an all-out civil war finally erupted to settle the score once and for all.

Along with these general contributions to the eventual abolition of slavery, it is also said that the Quakers were integral in ensuring slavery did not exist any farther north than Maryland. The Quakers had quite literally drawn a line in the sand when it came to slavery, and they rose up in deliberate action to make sure the terrible practice of bondage would not be allowed to propagate itself any more than it already was.

The Quakers having such a strong voice in these matters speaks volumes to their influence. This once little-known sect from England now made a substantial impact in the United States. Although the years after Penn's death were filled with plenty of ups and downs, Quakerism was still a strong force to be reckoned with, both in North America and beyond.

Chapter 6: Quaker Life during the American Revolution

All that dwell in the light, their habitation is in God, and they know a hiding place in the day of storm; and those who dwell in the light, are built upon the rock, and cannot be moved, for who are moved or shaken, goes from the light, and so goes from their strength, and from the power of God, and loses the peace and the enjoyment of the presence of God.

-Edward Burrough

The American Revolution was a time of radical reorganization of thought as it pertained to society and how people should be governed. Many Protestants were supportive of these efforts from the beginning, as they were under the idea that putting distance between their own ideologies and the dictates of the Church of England would most likely be in their best interest.

On the other hand, the Quakers faced their most difficult period in America during the American Revolution, which lasted from 1776 to 1783. As pacifists, the Quakers were against war in all forms, and so, they were quite naturally against an armed uprising against the British Crown. This refusal to side with the American freedom fighters put the Quakers under immediate suspicion.

They were sometimes cast as Loyalists, even though, at least for the Quakers, it was much more complicated than that. Most of them simply eschewed violence and bloodshed of any kind. The idea of an armed revolt was out of the question for most of them. Although the Quakers were against the war, some did side with the American revolutionaries, at least on an ideological level. They recognized the freedom the Founding Fathers promised would be much greater than anything the Crown had ever offered them.

Still, most Quakers were shunned and viewed as "security risks." And due to their peaceful and friendly disposition, they sometimes were. For instance, in the winter of 1777/78, some Quakers rendered aid to the British forces in Philadelphia. The Quakers undoubtedly felt they were doing their Christian duty to aid the struggling British, but this led to at least one of these collaborators being executed by the American revolutionaries.

In some instances, Quakers were held indefinitely without any clear charges other than vague accusations of "treason." This happened to a Quaker man by the name of Henry Drinker. He was arrested and detained in the fall of 1777. Drinker was held behind bars and told to swear allegiance to the American government. When he refused, he was then shuttled off in a wagon and dumped in Virginia, where he was an unwanted exile as punishment.

This treatment of the Quakers seemed to harken back to the puritanical 1650s when colonial authorities routinely banished Quakers from their communities. Despite its best intentions for a more equitable society, the American Revolution was most certainly a time of hardship and uncertainty for the Society of Friends. Whether they admitted it or not, many of the Quakers remained essentially loyal to Britain and simply did not see revolt and revolution as a good course of action.

Of course, this sentiment would lead to much friction with their fellow Americans, but it was a decidedly complicated situation. For one thing, the Quakers in America still had strong ties to the Quakers in England, and their British counterparts always advised their colonial brethren not to stir up trouble, lest they jeopardize these fraternal ties.

There was also a little bit of petty grudge-holding involved in the decision among some Quakers to stay neutral. Many of the American Quakers were not always treated the best by the local American Revolution leaders, which led to a natural wariness of being involved in any uprising engineered by those who had been less than kind to them.

Despite all of the reasons not to encourage fighting, a few Quakers were involved with the American Revolution. One of them, a man named Stephen Hopkins, even signed his name on the Declaration of Independence. To be fair, Hopkins was a former Quaker since he had actually been kicked out due to his refusal to emancipate his slaves.

There were also the rare Quakers who ignored the Quaker tenants of nonviolence and suited up with the Continental Army. One such Quaker was a young man by the name of Charles Darragh. Darragh was from a notable Quaker family in Pennsylvania; his father, William, was a teacher, and his mother, Lydia, was a midwife. Despite any misgivings these stalwart Quakers may have had, their son joined the Continental Army to serve under the 2nd Pennsylvania Regiment.

Although Charles was the one to enlist, it was actually his mother who would prove to be the most invaluable. When the British began to occupy the region, Lydia, who kept a line of communication open with her son, began to provide him with invaluable intelligence as to the movement of British troops.

In the fall of 1777, the Brits took over all of Philadelphia, and British General William Howe set up shop right inside Lydia Darragh's home. The British were indeed an occupying force, and if they wanted to make use of someone else's living quarters, there wasn't much the residents could do about it. The British most likely felt they had nothing to fear from the Quakers since they were known to be avowed pacifists.

But little did General Howe know that one of the Quakers he had barged in on—Lydia—was quite adept at gathering information! Soon, the staff meetings General Howe regularly hosted in Lydia's abode were subject to a major leak of vital intel, which was siphoned off by Lydia herself and fed directly into the ears of the men fighting in the American Revolution.

The British seemed to be blithely unaware of this fact, and General Howe continued to hold planning sessions in her home. At one point, in December of 1777, he even went so far as to tip Lydia off that a "major meeting" was about to take place, advising her to go to sleep a little early that night, lest she be disturbed. It seems General Howe wasn't very worried about being spied upon; rather, he was just trying to be polite.

Well, Lydia was not about to sleep through all of this chatter from the enemy and instead stayed up. Unbeknownst to the general, she sat right by the closed door so she could listen to every single word. From this session, Lydia learned the British were planning a sneak attack on the Continental Army arrayed outside of the city, which was led by General George Washington.

Lydia certainly knew she had discovered something of major import, and she was determined to let the revolutionary soldiers among know about it. As soon as she was sure the meeting was about to come to a close, Lydia carefully made her way back to bed. The next day, Lydia sought and was given permission to leave British-occupied territory so she could purchase some groceries. But she was determined to do more than shopping that day. She ended up dropping off her "empty bag" she used to shop with at a local mill and made a bee-line for the camp of General George Washington instead. Lydia was then able to impart what she had learned to the revolutionaries.

Thanks to Lydia's intel, when the British tried to launch their surprise attack on Washington's troops, they were prepared. Instead of being surprised, the Americans were able to launch a ferocious counterattack of their own and send the British running for the hills. And all of this was thanks to one meek and mild Quaker woman who decided to intervene. The British actually questioned Lydia later on when they discovered their operation had been compromised, but in the end, they never believed her to be a spy. Nevertheless, it was due to Lydia's heroics that many American lives were saved that day.

Another Quaker woman who found herself in a very similar position during the war was a North Carolinian by the name of Martha Bell. Martha and her husband owned a gristmill that specialized in making flour. As the war heated up between the Americans and the British, her gristmill was overrun by British troops, which began to regularly seize ground corn flour and other supplies from the mill.

Although Martha and her husband supported the revolutionary cause, they didn't hesitate to help the enemy British troops occupying their property. For a Quaker, all life is precious, even those with whom you ideologically may disagree. Martha frequently tended the wounds of the British troops, while her husband helped grind corn into flour at the mill.

During this time, the Bells seemed to gain the favor of the occupying general, who promised them that "no harm would come to their property." Martha would later use this assurance to her advantage when she went to visit the British encampment later on. By this point, the Brits had moved on from the mill, but Martha visited the British camp anyway, pretending to be concerned over some damage done to her property.

However, this was just a ruse. Martha made up this scheme so she could take note of enemy positions, troop numbers, and armaments—all vital intelligence information she hoped to gather for the revolutionaries. She was then able to take all of this valuable data back to the revolutionary troops, giving them astoundingly accurate information about the capabilities of this British regiment and where they were most likely to head next.

All of this Quaker cloak and dagger activity was certainly helpful for the cause of the American Revolution. But most of these efforts were virtually unknown to the rest of the population. Besides these unsung Quaker heroes, the most notable Quakers who decided to throw in their lot with the revolutionary cause were the so-called "Free Quakers" of Philadelphia, Pennsylvania. They were founded in 1781. The most well-known member was a woman by the name of Betsy Ross, who would go on to allegedly design the first American flag.

But Quakers like Betsy were the rare few, and the rest of the Quakers mostly just tried to keep their heads down. Some were even forced to lay low. Quakers wanted to avoid fates of being shunted about, as was the case with many Philadelphian Quakers. They were relocated to Virginia's backwoods since they were deemed untrustworthy and potential "security risks."

The Quakers also naturally got into trouble when revolutionary authorities began to request "oaths of loyalty" from citizens. The Quakers had long sworn off any kind of oathtaking, so they, of course, fell short whenever they were called upon to pledge their allegiance to the American war effort. In some instances, Quakers were fined for failing to participate with local militias, which many other local citizens were doing. Such things became increasingly hard to avoid, as many of the key battles fought in the Revolutionary War occurred in places heavily populated by Quakers.

And for those Quakers who did join militias and take up arms for the cause of the American Revolution, they faced immediate repercussions from their local Quaker meeting house. Since Quakers were supposed to uphold nonviolence, many of these Patriot Quakers were excommunicated for their actions. Those who were shunned by their local Quaker leaders often found an accepting place in the Society of Free Quakers, which had been formed in Philadelphia. Here, Quakers who actively supported the war effort could support one another.

It was indeed a difficult and confusing time to be a Quaker. Nevertheless, by the time the war came to its conclusion, most of the Quakers were able to reconcile with both the newly established United States of America and with each other. Quakers also had to reconcile the fact that much of the power they had held over state legislatures and other colonial power structures had mostly been demolished.

For those that longed for the glory days of William Penn, this was a dispiriting situation. But for the hardcore orthodox Quakers who wanted to get back to their roots and be free of the burden of politics, this severance of political ties came as a relief. They believed it was a means of moving the Quakers "away from the world and its enticements."

Even as their temporal power began to recede, the spiritual power of the Quakers entered into a great awakening all of its own. Soon, there was a renewed interest in what it meant to be a Quaker and how Quakers should respond to the larger world around them. Were Quakers a part of this world but not of this world? Just how would Quaker beliefs fit within the context of the newly christened United States of America? Themes such as these would be routinely debated in Quaker meeting houses all across the land for many years to come.

Chapter 7: A Time of Great Adjustment

I believe there is something in the mind, or in the heart, that shows its approbation when we do right. I give myself this advice: Do not fear truth, let it be so contrary to inclination and feeling. Never give up the search after it; and let me take courage, and try from the bottom of my heart to do that which I believe truth dictates, if it leads me to be a Quaker or not.

-Elizabeth Fry

By 1800, the Quakers were a strong, unified force that had spread across the nascent United States. This expansion continued as the United States gained territory farther west. In particular, the Quakers established enclaves in the newly established states of Ohio and Indiana, where slavery was illegal. Of course, this better suited the Quakers' sensibilities since they were completely against the abhorrent practice.

One of these enclaves was in Henry County, Indiana. By the year 1828, the Quakers had been in Henry County for about ten years. Here, they established a regular meeting organization known as the "Duck Creek Friends." The matters discussed among this group primarily pertained to the church. There were frank discussions of doctrine, as well as internal matters that needed to be hammered out, such as wayward Quakers who had broken the rules.

Although this was just one microcosm of Quakerism, the Duck Creek Friends of Henry County, Indiana, were fairly typical of what the Quaker experience was like during this period. At this point, the Quakers still firmly believed in a set of universal truths that every Quaker was expected to follow. The two main focal points for instruction were still Philadelphia and London, but the Quakers looked more to their own local leaders than to anyone else.

One of the great controversies to erupt during this period came from a Quaker minister from Long Island, New York, by the name of Elias Hicks. Hicks was a devout Quaker, but some of his beliefs differed from the traditional Quaker faithful. In particular, Hicks was assailed as having denied the "divinity of Christ." This criticism came from arguments Hicks had made in which he theorized that Christ was not born divine. Instead, Hicks believed he had become divine by living a sinless life and that he was in tune with the "Divine Light that was within him."

Again, one has to realize that the Quaker belief in which everyone has a "divine spark" or manifestation of God within them seems to verge on pantheism at times. Hicks apparently took this idea a step further by saying that Christ was no different than anyone else; he was just someone who suddenly woke up and realized that this spark—this manifestation of God—was within him and was then able to utilize it to its utmost perfection.

The implication that Hicks suggested was that anyone could emulate Christ if they simply chose to do so. This went against the doctrines of most Christian denominations, which clearly stress that all "fall short of the glory of God" and all need Christ as their intermediary in order to be saved.

Interestingly enough, even though Hicks seems to portray Christ as an ordinary figure who suddenly woke up to realize nirvana, he didn't deny all of the superhuman feats attributed to Christ. For example, even though Hicks downplayed the idea that Christ was born divine, he did not downplay the doctrine of the virgin birth. Hicks accepted that Christ had been born of a virgin, and basically every other miracle attributed to Christ, Hicks wholeheartedly believed. All the same, he still held fast to his theory that Christ's divinity was not achieved at birth but had manifested later in his life.

While some were drawn by Hicks's unique teachings, the traditional Quakers were disgusted by them, and they sought to end any further mention of what they viewed to be outright heresy being preached among their ranks. Those who were distressed by Hicks and his so-called "Hicksites" eventually found powerful backers in England, who came to visit the states in the 1820s. In this contentious debate, those who positioned themselves to be against Hicks came to be known as the "Orthodox Friends."

Hicks, however, was quick to point out the so-called "Orthodox Friends" were often more interested in "political power" and "material gain" than anything else. Those in the Orthodox faction insisted that the thing they were most interested in was simply sticking to the same doctrinal truths that most Christians held dear, namely that Christ was perfect from the beginning, as he was born the son of God, and that he was placed in this world for the sole mission of saving us by paying the price of human sin through his crucifixion.

However, the Orthodox Friends seemed to agree with Elias on his view that the scripture itself should not be elevated above the light of God. For Elias and apparently many other Quakers, the scriptures were viewed as a tool. But at the same time, the Orthodox Friends felt that Elias's teachings were dangerous because he veered too close to actually "diminishing" the Bible in a way that wouldn't be proper.

The friction between Elias, his supporters, and the more traditionalist Quakers would continue throughout much of the 1820s. This split seemed to also often fall along city and country lines. Most of the Quakers who lived in the cities often followed the Orthodox beliefs, whereas the rural, more remote Quakers were more likely to gravitate to Hicks's unorthodox teachings. The more urbane Quakers of Philadelphia, for example, often looked down their noses at the "prattling" teachings of Elias Hicks.

Hicks often ran afoul of the Orthodox Philadelphia leadership, no more so than Samuel Bettle and Jonathan Evans. Evans would become a common foil to Elias Hicks whenever he came to Philadelphia to preach. There were several noted instances in 1826 in which Hicks spoke at Quaker meeting houses in Philadelphia and was roundly rebuffed by Jonathan Evans. Every time Hicks would speak his peace in the meeting house, Jonathan would offer the Orthodox counterargument.

It was around this time that the so-called Hicksite/Orthodox separation became the most evident. The Hicksites were increasingly at odds with the world around them and called for reform, whereas the Orthodox were comfortable with business as usual and sought to maintain the status quo. It was in this fight that Hicks became an unlikely champion of reform. He was an obscure farmer, who used rural speech to get country Quakers interested in his ideas. But for many, his reforms weren't really new practices, as they were merely a call to get back to the Quaker roots that many felt had been lost.

In that sense, you could almost call the Hicksites throwbacks and conservatives to an earlier Quaker era. Along with this harkening back to the past, the Hicksites were also quite notorious for eschewing many modern conveniences. Hicks was known, for example, to speak out against the railroads, canals, and turnpikes, among other things. He even once criticized the building of Pennsylvania's Erie Canal by flatly stating, "If the Lord had intended there to be internal waterways, he would have placed them there."

But probably the thing that set the Hicksites and the urban Orthodox apart the most was Hicks's general disdain for city life. He viewed cities where people crowded around together as inherently corrupt and "centers of worldliness" and "lazy luxury." Or as he himself once put it, "What a vast portion of the joys and comforts of life do the idle and slothful deprive themselves of, by running into cities and towns to avoid laboring in the field."

Things would come to the point of no return in 1827 during the Philadelphia Yearly Meeting. Several Hicksites were determined to break away from the Orthodox hegemony of Philadelphia and form a yearly meeting of their own. And this was no small move. About "two-thirds" of the original membership actually left to join up with this new yearly meeting, creating two focal points of Quakerism right next to each other. This would lead to a domino effect, in which other meeting houses in places such as Baltimore and New York would follow suit, with the Hicksites separating themselves with their own meeting houses. As this veritable civil war between Hicksites and Orthodox Quakers erupted, the ideological lines between the two were starkly drawn.

But although the lines between the Orthodox and Hicksite Quakers were clear, the ranks of the Hicksites themselves were soon blurred and then fractured into several other groupings. The most numerous of these factions was one that could be considered to be conservative in its leanings, and they held the opinion that the Orthodox Friends had strayed away from the true path of Quakerism. Another strain rejected some of the ideas of Hicks and was instead more in step with the Orthodox Quakers. A third group was more liberal and actively involved in movements that were "radical" at the time, such as antislavery and women's rights. They were also keen on religious ideas outside of the Quaker faith, such as Unitarianism. The Unitarians were part of an early Christian movement that denied the Trinity and promoted the idea that God was one person.

Part of the reason the Hicksites fractured so early on could be attributed to outside pressure from society. For example, women's rights and the abolition of slavery were picking up steam, and Quaker activism in these two areas would lead to a refinement of many core Quaker beliefs.

Lucretia Mott was a Hicksite Quaker who played an integral role in the first summit for women's rights, which was held at Seneca Falls, New York, in the summer of 1848. Another social movement that attracted many Hicksites during this period was the American Anti-Slavery Society, which was formed in Philadelphia in December of 1833. Much as the name implies, this was an abolition group dedicated to the eradication of slavery, and it was the Quakers who led the charge.

Another focal point of activism/idealism that took hold of the Quakers during this period was that of the so-called "nonresistant movement." Quakers had long been against violence, and for those who considered themselves "nonresistors," the end goal was to create a society in which no coercive force was necessary.

This led to much experimentation in the 1840s with utopian-styled communities, which, in many ways, reflected upon William Penn's "holy experiment" with Pennsylvania about 200 years prior. Just like Pennsylvania under William Penn, the nonresistors attempted to create a society in which people could live in peace and harmony, without any military, police, or other coercive agent dictating how people should live.

The idea that humanity could live together without coercive measures in place to make sure citizens follow the rules has floated around for thousands of years. As recently as 2020, advocacy groups have tinkered with the notion that citizens can live without police enforcing the laws and have called for police departments to be defunded or perhaps even abolished outright. But such plans rarely—if ever—succeed.

Nevertheless, for these Quaker communes, the goal was to simply live a life based on the tenants of the New Testament and trust the other Quakers who participated in this experiment to keep themselves within the bounds of common decency, meaning no outside coercion was necessary. These nonresistor settlements began to pop up all over the place throughout the 1840s. As one can see, the first half of the 19th century proved to be a time of much experimentation and adjustment for the Quakers.

Chapter 8: The Quakers the Civil War and Its Aftermath

But in the central innermost region of our minds there shines one pure ray of direct light from the very throne of God. One ray which belongs to each one individually; which is for that one supreme and apart. The ray which shining from the heavenward side of conscience, and so enlightening and purifying, it must of necessity dominate the whole being.

-Carline Stephen

The Quakers were arguably one of the most proactive advocates for the end of slavery in the lead-up to the American Civil War. Along with advocating for the abolition of slavery, the Quakers were also quite busy during this period championing the cause for equality between the sexes, fair treatment of Native Americans, and the establishment of humane jail systems for prisoners, among other things.

Having said that, however, as forward-thinking as most Quakers may have been, they were a complicated group, and they were not always uniform in their march for justice. As mentioned previously in this book, not all Quakers supported freeing the slaves; in fact, some may have been direct beneficiaries from the enterprise. And even if Quakers weren't involved in the slave trade, many merely rendered lip service during discussions on abolition.

At the same time, there were some deeply sincere abolitionists among the Quakers who would eventually leave the Quaker faith to more effectively pursue abolition. This segment of the Quakers often felt torn when it came to what they felt was expedient for religion and what they knew was most expedient for the social justice issues of the day.

A Quaker by the name of Amy Kirby Post found herself in just such a position. Kirby hailed from Long Island and grew up hearing all of the rumblings of Elias Hicks and the Hicksites. She became a regular at Hicksite gatherings by the late 1820s and would remain so over the next couple of decades. In the 1840s, however, she began to pull back from the Hicksites, who shunned the world, and she began to take a bold stand against what she saw as the evils of humanity.

Post still believed in core Quaker principles; she just sought to channel them into a more activist approach when it came to righting society's wrongs. This formula would lead Post to help form an offshoot of the Society of Friends, known as the Congregational Friends, which was formed in 1848. This group would then morph into the Progressive Friends before finally moving on to become the Friends of Human Progress.

Those involved in this organization were fully focused on racial and gender equality throughout the 1850s, leading right up to the American Civil War, which began in 1861. Amy Post was an interesting character. Although she was considered a progressive Quaker, she also had a deeply spiritual side to her, which can be seen in what were essentially "seances," which were conducted at her residence in Rochester, New York.

At first glance, the Quaker faith and the spiritualism movement may seem like strange bedfellows, but the ideologies merged among certain Quaker circles. After all, both the Quakers and the spiritualists gathered together in meetings in which they would sit in silence until supernatural forces moved them to speak, write, sing, or otherwise act. Of course, the big difference was that the Quakers believed they were being prompted by the spirit of God, whereas the spiritualists thought they were channeling disembodied spirits.

At any rate, Amy Post was just as dedicated to forging her own path in the spirit world as she was to finding justice in the physical realm. It seems that for a Quaker like Post, the Society of Friends only went so far when it came to righting America's wrongs, leading her to embrace more progressive blends of belief and activism. On the other hand, more traditional Quakers thought she had taken things further than she should have. At one point, the local meeting house she attended in Rochester, New York, actually chastised her for being "too worldly" due to her active involvement in the abolition movement. Worldly or not, Post pushed on.

One of the most effective ways she created change was to become involved in a little something called the Underground Railroad. The Underground Railroad was a clandestine route that slaves took when seeking to escape Southern plantations to the freedom of the north. The Underground Railroad actually had nothing to do with trains and railroads; it was simply an overland route that slaves were directed to take on their journey north. On this route were "stations," at which the slaves would stop at.

These "stations" were actually secretly designated safe houses, where abolitionists would take in the runaway slaves and give them food, shelter, and supplies before they headed back out onto their journey north. Amy Post and her husband, Isaac, maintained a station on the Underground Railroad and personally sheltered many slaves during their exodus to freedom. Another

Quaker who was famous for conducting runaway slaves north during this period was Levi Coffin, whose home in Newport, Indiana, was an important stop on the Underground Railroad.

Coffin was such an integral figure of the Underground Railroad that he was sometimes known as the "President of the Underground Railroad." Coffin himself estimated that he helped steward about one hundred slaves a year during his station's operation on the railroad. He was also noted for his cordial relationship with the freed African American community that lived in and around Newport. Coffin would regularly consult and organize efforts to aid further runaway slaves with this community. He treated his freed black neighbors as his friends and made them a part of his operations.

Sadly, Coffin was an exception rather than the rule. Many of the Quakers, even those who participated in the abolition movement, viewed segregation as a necessary component of life. This could obviously be seen during Quaker services. If African Americans were allowed to attend, they were almost always placed in segregated pews, and these separate pews could be pretty sternly enforced, as one Quaker activist discovered after being chewed out by a Quaker pastor in Philadelphia simply for sitting in the "colored" section of the meeting house.

Nevertheless, despite such internal prejudices, the Quakers soundly rejected slavery as a whole. And by the 1850s, the rejection of slavery was just about universal among the Quakers. They held firm on this, even as the faith fractured into more and more sects, for it was around this time that the Orthodox Quakers split into what would become known as the Gurneyites and the Wilburites.

The source of this split was due to a British Quaker by the name of Joseph John Gurney. Gurney came from an affluent background and had strong familial ties to the Quaker faith; he even counted the Quaker leader Robert Barclay among his ancestors. Gurney was a great speaker and an excellent scholar, who was quite gifted at arguing the finer points of what it meant to be a Quaker. He was also a passionate abolitionist and energized the Quaker base on this front as well.

In addition to all of this, Gurney was an advocate for what was known as "unprogrammed worship." This referred to a worship service that didn't follow any particular routine or "program." Members would simply arrive at the meeting house and do what the spirit moved them to do. Some would sing, some would pray, some would speak, but much of the time, they would just sit in silence and listen—listening for that still small voice they knew to be God's.

In 1837, John Gurney came to spread his message to the United States, gaining many followers in the process. And by 1840, he gained his largest critic, a Quaker pastor from Rhode Island, by the name of John Wilbur. As one might surmise, the followers of Wilbur would become known as the aforementioned Wilburites.

One of their chief complaints was the fact that Gurney and his followers depended heavily on scripture. It must be noted with some irony that these Orthodox Quakers were distressed that Gurney put so much emphasis on scripture, whereas a couple of decades prior, the Orthodox Quakers were mad at Hicks for doing just the opposite. The Wilburites, it seems, sought a happy medium of not placing too much emphasis on scripture yet not denying its importance outright, as Hicks seemed to be on the verge of doing.

At any rate, the Quakers were even more ideologically divided by the time of the 1860 presidential election—a contest in which Republican abolitionist politicians stood to gain from the Quaker vote. Even though the Quakers were divided over internal doctrine, they were at this point in virtually complete agreement that slavery needed to end. The subsequent election of Abraham Lincoln that November, who actively courted the Quaker vote, would lead to several slaveholding Southern states seceding from the Union.

Although the election of Lincoln triggered the Southern states to rebel, the lead-up to the Civil War had been decades in the making. And if one event precipitated the Civil War more than any other, it would have to be John Brown's daring—and some might say dastardly—raid on Harper's Ferry. John Brown was a radical abolitionist who believed that slavery had to be stomped out at any cost, even if it meant taking violent action.

Even before Brown launched his raid on Harper's Ferry, which would lead to several dead and wounded, he had already murdered at least five people in cold blood in Kansas, allegedly in retribution against harassment carried out against abolitionists there. Surprisingly enough, for a group that was against nonviolence, there quite a few members of the Society of Friends who not only approved of John Brown's actions but also applauded them.

Perhaps most notable were the remarks of Levi Coffin, a stalwart abolitionist and Quaker conductor of the Underground Railroad. At the time of the raid on Harper's Ferry, Coffin, stated his belief that the condemned killer, John Brown, had been "an instrument in the hands of the Almighty to commence the great work of deliverance of the oppressed." As long as they could sit on the sidelines, the Quakers supported people as radical as John Brown. If it meant putting a dent into slavery, many Friends were all for it.

However, once the Civil War broke out in earnest, the Quakers would face a stark decision when it came to their principles. Once the guns began to fire, the Northern Quakers were the ones being drafted into the Union Army to take on the Confederates in the South. In the state of Indiana alone, it is estimated that about 25 percent of Quakers enlisted to serve in the Union Army. This meant the Quakers had to decide whether to hold firm to their commitment to nonviolence or temporarily put their pacifism aside to partake in a fight that nearly all Quakers viewed as just.

For the first time in the religion's history, many Quaker leaders quietly allowed their young men to pick up arms and join the army. A Quaker named Daniel Wooton was among those who took up the charge. Wooten described the sentiment at the time, saying, "We all know the Bible says thou shalt not kill: but what are we to do with those persons that rebel against the law of our country? Did God sit down and let the Devil take the uppermost seat in heaven when he caused the rebellion there? No Sir!"

Quakers like Daniel Wooten were ready to fight, and they felt the cause was just enough that God would be on their side. This was an opinion that was seconded by the likes of Captain Benjamin Nields, a Quaker who directed the 1st Delaware Light Artillery unit, which had amongst its ranks several Quakers. But it was another Delaware brigade—the 4th Delaware—that would boast one of the most dedicated Quaker soldiers.

His name was Henry Gawthrop, and at the outbreak of the war, he signed on with the 4th Delaware Regiment Volunteer Infantry. This brigade was put into action by Union Colonel Arthur H. Grimshaw in 1862. By the spring of 1864, Henry Gawthrop and his company were sent out to the front lines. During his time with the 4th Delaware, Gawthrop had to directly come to grips with the horrors of war and what it meant to his Quaker faith.

After surviving an early skirmish, Henry wrote home to tell his family all of the details:

We have been under fire on picket and in the trenches since 9 o'clock yesterday morning at which time we marched from our camp of night before and took possession of the 2nd line of works. We were fired on by sharpshooters but no one hurt except private Ruth, pioneer of Co H, who was wounded in the right breast. Towards evening the rebels opened on us from their batteries and we had our first experience of shelling, and I can say that it was about the hardest of my life. Heaven's artillery was playing at the same time and the rain pouring down. Later we were marched more by the right. As we advanced in line through the woods the rebels opened on us and we poured in a volley and rushed for the breast works we were to occupy. Our fire drew that of their artillery and sharpshooters. We passed a very miserable night without rest. A constant fire from the rebels across the woods, and the rain pouring down.

Here, Henry highlights the incessant dread of open battle. The enemy was camped out just "across the woods" from them and was intermittently firing through the rain. Despite the hardship, Henry still looks toward God, likening the thunder and lightning he heard in the distance to "Heaven's artillery."

Henry Gawthrop would go through quite a bit during his service for the Union. He would be injured several times and end up having one of his feet amputated. But even through all of this trauma, he was thankful that, to his knowledge, he still hadn't broken the cardinal rule. As far as he knew, he hadn't actually killed anyone.

Or as Henry himself described it:

I had been in great danger—three times wounded, horse shot, a bullet through my blanket roll and from shots striking objects near me, in different engagements. These experiences gave me a dislike of firearms, and (after leaving the arm) an uneasy feeling when one was handled near me. Except firing at a mark or firing the novel breech loading guns already noted, I made no use of firearms. I believe I have never killed anything in my life larger than a rat and I am glad of this though, of course, I shared fully in the responsibility, as I did the parts assigned to me. I was quite a success as a target. There was rarely any personal feeling on my part against the rank and file of our opponents and I think it was the same with my comrades. Whenever opportunity offered on picket line, we established, as it is shown in this narrative, friendly relations, though it was a dangerous practice, as someone higher up might end the parley without due notice.

Quakers were supposed to shun and abhor war, and it seems the actual experience of armed conflict only made Gawthrop detest the practice all the more. It's hard to believe that none of the bullets he fired while serving in the Union killed anyone, but this is what Henry Gawthrop maintained. He went through all the motions and participated in the charges, yet his bullets never killed anything "larger than a rat." Perhaps this was a miracle in itself, as it allowed Henry to participate in the fighting and keep his conscience clean.

It may have worked for Henry, but others would hold firm to their nonviolent stance and seek a way around the general call to arms the Union had made.

Fortunately for those in the latter camp, President Abraham Lincoln was willing to accommodate conscientious objectors. Unlike during the American Revolutionary War, when Quakers were sometimes thrown in jail for their refusal to participate in the war effort, Lincoln acknowledged religious objections to fighting and made an exception for them. This is the first known instance of conscientious objectors being accepted during wartime.

Though not a Quaker, Lincoln sympathized with their views on equality, as they were views he shared. Lincoln valued the Quakers' abolitionist sentiment and their votes, for he knew that a heavy Quaker voting bloc in Pennsylvania had been crucial for him in winning the state during the election of 1860. Lincoln knew the Quakers placed a high standard on the freedoms he held dear.

Just prior to his inauguration as president of the United States in 1861, Lincoln cited the Declaration of Independence as his compass when it came to the inherent freedoms that belonged to any man. The Declaration of Independence declared that all men were created equal, although it took the Civil War for America to finally recognize that creed, and it took even longer for the creed to finally benefit all citizens. Lincoln stated he "never had a feeling politically that did not spring from the [Declaration of Independence], which gave liberty, not alone to the people of this great country, but hope to the world for all future time."

President-elect Lincoln, full of passion and conviction, then made an ominous prediction, declaring, "If this country cannot be saved without giving up that principle—I would rather be assassinated on this spot than to surrender to it." As history can attest, Lincoln indeed died for his principles when Southern radical John Wilkes Booth assassinated him in 1865.

The Civil War came to a close on April 9th, 1865, when Confederate General Robert E. Lee signed the Confederate Army's surrender to the presiding Union General, Ulysses S. Grant. Although this was the official end of the war, hostilities would certainly linger, as was so tragically evidenced when Abraham Lincoln was hit by an assassin's bullet just five days later on the evening of April 14th.

Lincoln, sustaining mortal injuries, would cling to life before finally passing on the morning of April 15th, 1865. Much of the nation was sent into a state of shock and mourning at the news, especially the Quakers. After all, it was through Lincoln that the Quakers had finally achieved the abolition of slavery, for which they had fought so long and hard.

The Quakers had been such staunch abolitionists for so long that once the end of slavery was achieved, many Quakers wondered where their advocacy should be placed next. It didn't take them long to find it. It was just a few years after the war, in 1869, that President Ulysses S. Grant commissioned a group of Hicksite Quakers to engage in "humanitarian work" with the Native Americans.

Francis T. King, a notable Quaker, also led efforts during the Reconstruction era, helping to build up the educational systems of North Carolina. It was King and the Baltimore Association that established public schools in the region for both recently freed African Americans and European American residents. It is said that Quaker schools like this were used as a template for many of the public schoolhouses across the country.

Laura Haviland was another Quaker of this time period who played a prominent role in aiding freed slaves. When newly freed slaves were rendered refugees due to the rescinded former promise of forty acres and a mule, they migrated up to Ohio, Indiana, and Illinois in search of food and shelter. Laura made sure that Quakers were there to meet them. In Illinois alone, she managed to aid tens of thousands of newly freed African Americans. Despite the fact they arrived penniless, most became completely self-sufficient after being given this little bit of help. Haviland also would go on to work at the Freedmen's Aid Bureau in Washington, DC, where she ran educational workshops for newly freed African Americans.

The nation changed much after the conclusion of the American Civil War, and the Quakers changed just about as much as everyone else. The war had the effect of shaking up the faith and causing Quaker leaders to reconsider what they previously believed to be an excommunicable infraction among their members.

This was due in large part to the many young Quaker men who had broken the cardinal rule of holding fast to nonviolence so they could fight in the war. Previously, such things would have led to their dismissal from the church, but after the war, most Quaker meeting houses welcomed the young men back with open arms and no questions asked. This seeming willingness to bend the rules would lead to a general relaxation of others.

Most notably, it became more acceptable for Quakers to marry outside of their faith; for the last two centuries, such a thing was sternly frowned upon. At this point, the Quakers, who for many years had been known for their "peculiarity," began to become a widely accepted member of the mainline Protestant denominations. As such, the old Quaker meeting houses began to look more and more like traditional Protestant churches. In the aftermath of the Civil War, the Quakers, who had typically belonged on the fringes of Christianity, began to enter into the modern organization by which the Friends are known today.

However, with the abolition of slavery, the Quakers had lost the main unifying factor that had bound all of the Quaker factions together. Now that abolition had finally been achieved, Quakers wishing to create social change would have to find new modes of doing so.

Chapter 9: Some Modern-Day Quaking in the Making

There is something of God in every man, let us affirm it more certainly than ever. But surrounded as we are by millions of new-made graves and with the voices of the hungry and the dispossessed in our ears, let us not easily accept the impious hope that the natural goodness of ourselves is sufficient stuff out of which to fashion a better world.

-Gilbert H. Kilpack

The first decade of the 20th century was perhaps one of the most active for the Quakers. During this time, you could see Wilburites, Hicksites, and Gurneyites all holding regular meetings in search of how they could bring unity to Quakerism at large. It was during this period that the Wilburites began to go by the name of Conservative Friends.

As the name might imply, this sect of Quakers was the most traditional. In 1913, this group proclaimed their "common doctrinal statement." They became known for their insistence of eschewing all "religious symbolism," such as communion and all forms of water baptisms. People mainly attended gatherings in rural meeting houses, but these began to decline in the next few decades and would never quite recover.

The Hicksite strain of Quakerism in the early 20th century dropped the name Hicksite in favor of the "Friends General Conference," or just "FGC" for short. Despite the rebranding, Hicksite membership began to decline. It is estimated that by 1900, the Hicksites had been reduced to a number of somewhere around 17,000 members. Such low membership was certainly not encouraging, and by 1919, the trend was even more pronounced, with attendance at meetings in Illinois, Indiana, and New York only reaching into the hundreds.

Around this time, a little-known town just north of Indianapolis, called "Westfield," became a Quaker hot spot of sorts. Nestled in the middle of cornfields and country roads, Westfield, Indiana, was the "Union Bible Seminary." This seminary became actively involved in overseas missions, and in 1919, it launched mission trips to the South American country of Bolivia.

However, a shift began to take place by the end of the 1920s, with larger Hicksite (FGC) gatherings emerging in major urban areas, such as Ithaca, New York, and Cleveland, Ohio. With these newly established urban centers, the FGC managed to even itself out over the next couple of decades. 1926 was an especially pivotal year for the FGC since a new charter was developed to foster "uniform discipline" among all their members.

The Gurneyites, on the other hand, were initially not very well-organized and continued to have trouble uniting their base. By the 20th century, much of this base actually centered around Richmond, Indiana. Eventually, they got their act together and would become great missionaries, taking the Quaker doctrine as far afield as Kenya, India, China, and even Alaska. Their work in Kenya would have the most lasting legacy. Kenya, to this day, has more Quakers than anywhere else outside of the United States.

In the 20th century, the Quakers almost universally stuck to their guns when it came to nonviolence, refusing to participate in either World War One or World War Two if it meant they had to take another human being's life. This doesn't mean the Quakers weren't involved in the world wars. While some Quakers refused to aid in the war effort at all, as they were outright conscientious objectors who preferred to sit on the sidelines, other Quakers participated in the world wars in assisting roles, becoming medics or ambulance drivers. British Quakers streamlined this service even further by creating their own ambulance service, which they called the Friends' Ambulance Unit.

This worked well enough for most, but for those who considered themselves to be so-called "absolutist conscientious objectors," even participating in an ambulance service was going too far. According to the sentiments of these absolutist Quakers, war was an all or nothing enterprise, and you were either helping the war effort or were not. For them, driving an ambulance for the Allies was just as bad as picking up a gun since it was aiding in the overall war effort.

A Briton named Wilfrid Littleboy was one of these absolutist conscientious objectors. As soon as the war began, he held fast to his Quaker principles and refused to have any part in the war effort. He didn't know what would happen to him or what kind of punishment he might receive for shirking his marching orders, but he just couldn't bring himself to compromise all he held dear.

Initially, officials took a light-handed approach with Wilfrid, and in his first hearing, which was presided over by none other than future Prime Minister Neville Chamberlain, he was given a wide range of options as it pertained to non-combat roles. Wilfrid remembered Neville as being quite kind, considerate, and accommodating. The meeting ended with Neville Chamberlain simply asking Wilfrid to "think about it."

But at Wilfrid's second hearing, those who met with him were not quite so kind. Neville Chamberlain was gone, and in his place was a presiding officer who took on an adversarial tone from the very beginning. This man had neither the respect nor the patience to hear about Wilfrid's Quaker beliefs, and he instead lambasted the young man for failing to sign on to any of the non-combat roles that had been offered to him.

Wilfrid Littleboy was once again directed to sign on with the Non-Combatant Corps. Wilfrid, however, had no such intention of doing so. This wasn't a flippant decision on Wilfrid's part since he knew he could be apprehended and hauled off to jail for failing to report to duty. As Wilfrid described it, "One almost got used to the fact that you might go into town one day and be picked up without any warning."

That day came in 1916 when Wilfrid went to a Quaker meeting one night only to find the police camped out, waiting for him to leave. The police informed Wilfrid that he would have to report to court and answer for his evasion of service. He faithfully attended the hearing the next day and was then promptly placed into military custody.

The military authorities basically tried to force Wilfrid to enlist. They tossed a soldier's uniform at him and ordered him to put it on. Wilfrid refused, and in doing so, he was immediately court-martialed. He now went from Quaker conscientious objector to Quaker inmate, and he was sent to a military jail—all because he simply didn't want to take part in the war.

Wilfrid would remain incarcerated for the duration of the war. World War One came to a close on November 11th, 1918, but Wilfrid Littleboy would not be released until the following year, in 1919. Wilfrid didn't hold any grudges for his internment, and upon his release, he immediately got back to work and back to the Quaker meeting house. Wilfrid's experience was fairly typical of what many Quaker conscientious objectors went through during the war.

After the war was over, the Quakers showed they didn't take any sides when it came to the needy, as they immediately rendered their services to Germans who needed assistance just as they would to their own countrymen. While Germans struggled under a bankrupt and broken economy, the Quakers rushed forward to render aid through food supplies and whatever else they could muster.

World War Two would prove to be the most pivotal for the Quakers, as it brought those of the Quaker faith together from all over the globe, forging bonds that had been loose into a much tighter knot. It was this wartime solidarity that brought about the Friends World Committee for Consultation.

The Quakers during World War Two would render much-needed relief to both troops and civilians during the war. But the most heroic Quakers were behind enemy lines. In both Germany and Italy, Quakers were present on the ground helping to aid civilians, even under the threat of being arrested and sent to a concentration camp. Despite such terrible repercussions, the Quakers refused to stand idly by while others suffered.

In fact, the Quakers played a vital role in rescuing Jews from being sent to the death camps. In what was essentially an "underground railroad" in Western Europe, the Quakers created a series of safe houses that allowed them to conduct Jewish refugees to freedom, with many of their charges seeking asylum in America and Great Britain. These efforts led the Quaker branches of the American Friends Service Committee and the British Friends Service Council to receive a Nobel Peace Prize after the war.

As confusing as all of the Quakerism sects can be, it was shortly after World War Two that yet another brand of Quakerism hit the mainstream, which would become known as the Association of Evangelical Friends. This was founded in 1947.

That same year, a prominent Quaker named Clarence Picket announced at a conference of Quakers that the tensions between the Soviet Union and the US had become so dangerous that the Quakers should do what they could to stem the aggression. So, on the eve of the Cold War, the Quakers decided to become more politically involved than ever before.

In fact, it was under the auspices of this reenergized Quakerism that a young man by the name of Richard Nixon would come to prominence. Yes, not many are aware of it, but tricky Dick Nixon–the US president so often scorned for his actions at Watergate–was indeed a Quaker. Nixon began his life in Yorba Linda, California, where he grew up as a Quaker throughout the 1920s and 1930s. Nixon graduated from the Quaker-founded Whittier College in 1933. The school was named after a famous Quaker abolitionist by the name of John Greenleaf Whittier.

Vice President Richard Nixon discussed the sad state of America's race relations in the 1950s with Martin Luther King Jr., lamenting how racial disparities at home were absolutely devastating for the nation's reputation abroad. How could the US tout itself as the leader of the free world and a better alternative to communist Russia if everyone in America were not being accorded the same rights?

Martin Luther King was apparently convinced of Nixon's sincerity, and he walked away with a favorable view of the Quaker politician. Martin Luther

King later went on the record to state, "Nixon happens to be a Quaker and there are very few Quakers who are prejudice [sic] from a racial point of view."

Others would later contend that Nixon was simply a good actor and that he was often able to manipulate his conversations well enough to appear to be whatever anyone wanted at the time. And since the Republicans of the 1950s were actively supportive of the nascent civil rights movement, some would say that Nixon was simply trying to play that angle up for all it was worth. But nevertheless, when Nixon spoke of his Quaker values when it came to equality, Martin Luther King believed him to be sincere.

And if anyone knew the Quakers, Martin Luther King Jr. did. King was actually very involved with Quaker organizations throughout the 1950s and 1960s. Martin Luther King's relationship with the Quakers dates back to 1955, the year that Rosa Parks famously "sat down for her rights" by refusing to stand when a white patron wanted her seat. This event led to widespread bus boycotts in Montgomery, Alabama, which were led by King. The Quakers heard of these happenings and began to debate whether this was a social issue they should become involved in. In the spring of 1956, the civil rights movement was a matter of intense discussion at the Philadelphia Yearly Meeting.

The Quakers were finally moved to action after the secretary of the "Yearly Meeting Peace Committee" spoke with King on the phone, who agreed to send a group of Quakers to Alabama. These Quakers worked like a fact-finding mission to determine just what was happening on the ground. They soon saw firsthand the oppression African Americans were facing. At the same time, they were greatly impressed by the skillful, nonviolent resistance Martin Luther King Jr. led.

Around the time Nixon first ran for president in 1960, the Quakers saw their next major surge in growth, which would lead to the formation of the Evangelical Friends Alliance. This movement would lead to the founding of several more churches in places like Nixon's Yorba Linda, California, as well as Ohio, Virginia, North Carolina, and Florida.

As action heated up in a little-known place called Vietnam in the 1960s, the Quakers entered into a new and decisive phase of activism, in which they dared to defy their own government in order to help the Vietnamese. The Vietnam War was a complicated affair from the very beginning. Vietnam had previously been a French colony, but after the French had been shaken loose by the Japanese during World War Two, the Vietnamese sought to establish their own independence.

However, the French weren't quite willing to relinquish their possession and sought to regain control. In their struggle, the Vietnamese made the mistake of embracing communist ideology as the avenue for their deliverance. This provoked the ire of the United States government, which was increasingly wary of the spread of communism during the Cold War. So, after the bloodied and beat French gave up and pulled out of Vietnam, the United States stepped right in, in order to prevent a communist takeover of Southeast Asia.

The US backed a pro-capitalist government in South Vietnam and actively aided them in their fight against the communists of North Vietnam. When the South Vietnamese were on the verge of defeat, the Americans put their thumb on the scale and decided to intervene directly. This war, fought on the basis of correcting the ideology of a foreign land, led to tragic outcomes in regard to civilian death and destruction, as American warplanes began to hammer the North Vietnamese and US troops burned down villages, seeking to put a stop to the communist advance.

This carnage inspired the Quakers to go against their own country and aid average Vietnamese civilians on the ground. The Society of Friends mailed "relief packages" to North Vietnam in 1966. However, these efforts were halted by the post office, which refused to deliver aid to an enemy combatant of the United States. The Quakers also attempted to send aid in the form of cold hard cash through the Red Cross Society located in North Vietnam, but this, too, was seized by US government officials before the North Vietnamese could use it.

If that wasn't enough to make sure those troublesome Quakers knew the federal government meant business, the Friends were then threatened with a possible ten-year prison sentence from an old bit of legislation from 1917 called the "Trading with the Enemy Act." The act grants the authority to an American president to prosecute anyone conducting any kind of trade with enemies of the United States.

It wouldn't be the first time that Quakers were viewed as enemies and potential communist collaborators. When Richard Nixon was vice president of the United States in the 1950s under the Eisenhower administration, he alerted his associates that he believed communists were manipulating the sympathies of Quaker groups. Although Richard Nixon himself was a Quaker, he was ready to lay down the gauntlet against them in spite of his beliefs.

Nevertheless, even with the threat of jail time, the Quakers weren't willing to simply give up, and in 1967, the Quaker Action Group took the audacious step of sending a yacht loaded with supplies to North Vietnam. On March 22nd, 1967, the yacht left, and it would ride the waves for five days from a Quaker enclave in Hong Kong to enemy territory in North Vietnam.

The captain, an anthropologist and explorer by the name of Earle L. Reynolds, suggested they should be armed in case they got into trouble. The Quakers, of course, refused, citing their nonviolent beliefs. For this trip, they weren't going to put their faith in guns; they were going to put all of their faith in God. And they would need it. Because as soon as they docked in the Gulf of Tonkin, they were greeted with a volley of artillery fire.

This burst of artillery was not meant for them, though; it was for those who were lurking in the skies above. Soon after, they would discover that an American fighter craft had just been shot down. Most Americans wouldn't appreciate the fact that Quakers were aiding the North Vietnamese—especially since they were aiding them while they were in the process of killing Americans—but the Quakers were indeed a rarified bunch. Due to their wide-ranging views of morality, they felt the North Vietnamese needed their help, and they would do so whether anyone else agreed with them or not.

The Quakers were indeed well received by the North Vietnamese, who were grateful for the medical supplies as well as the kind gesture it represented. They gave the Quakers a grand tour of their stomping grounds, taking them to lavish banquets that had been prepared in their honor, as well as having them visit the sick and injured Vietnamese in their hospitals. By the time word of this reached the American press, the reactions were understandably mixed and matched the polarized sentiment of the time.

By the late 1960s, about half of the American public was against the war, while the rest still deemed it a necessary struggle against the creeping advance of communism. Those who were against the war, predictably enough, applauded the Quakers' efforts. In contrast, those who supported the struggle against the communist North Vietnamese deemed the Quakers' aiding of enemy combatants a travesty and an outright betrayal of all the blood America lost fighting them.

The Quakers just wanted to help people, and to show they were not taking a side in the conflict, they sent supplies to South Vietnam on their next voyage. However, the South Vietnamese didn't want anything to do with them and refused to let the boat land. At one point, they even threatened the Quakers with artillery. The Quakers were finally forced to sail to Hong Kong and have some of the supplies shipped through anonymous freight.

The Quakers then made their final trip to Vietnam in January 1968, this time returning to North Vietnam. They were indeed successful in once again dropping off medical aid packages, but due to the ramping up of the Tet Offensive, they had to make a quick getaway lest the Americans "bomb the port to ashes." Predictably, those who were against the Vietnam War supported the Quakers' efforts, and those who were for it were aghast, calling them unpatriotic at best and downright traitors at worse.

In the 1970s, the Society of Friends would wade into perhaps even more tumultuous, polarized political waters when they weighed in on the Israeli/Palestinian conflict. Seemingly siding with the Palestinians, the Quakers demanded that all US aid to Israel cease at once. In 1973, during the Yom Kippur War, the Quakers pushed for the United States to enter into an arms embargo with Israel. The US, of course, wasn't about to do any such thing.

The Quakers were persistent and decided to take matters into their own hands. They opened up shop right in Israel and began to send Quaker counsel to any Palestinians standing trial in Israeli courtrooms. The Quakers continued their activism throughout the 1980s, regularly taking a stand against such things as nuclear proliferation and South Africa's apartheid, just to name a couple of the Quaker movements at work.

They had the most grassroots success in South Africa. In the 1980s, during the height of the resistance to apartheid, the Quakers founded their Peace Centre in Cape Town in order to take in refugees who had been expelled by the apartheid regime. The Friends also rendered much-needed monetary assistance to apartheid activist Steve Biko's Black Communities Programmes, as well as Winnie Mandela's home industries for black women.

The most arguably influential Quaker in the struggle against apartheid in South Africa was Nozizwe Madlala-Routledge. Nozizwe ceaselessly led protests for the end of apartheid all throughout the 1980s, ending up in jail for her efforts. Nevertheless, she would rise above the adversity and become an active participant in the ending of apartheid. In 1999 when Nelson Mandela was president, Nozizwe was made deputy minister of defense. In this role, Nozizwe took on the task of spreading awareness on South Africa's greatest enemy at the time—AIDS. She spearheaded a movement to bring the epidemic to the public's awareness.

Meanwhile, Quakers in the United States were busy with relief efforts throughout all kinds of catastrophes and incidents of civil unrest, from the Los Angeles riots of 1992 to Hurricane Katrina in 2005. Their relief efforts during Katrina were particularly memorable, with Quakers literally sending out truckloads of food and other much-needed supplies to aid the hurricane survivors. Leading this charge was the Friends Disaster Service (FDS). The FDS was founded in 1974 after a tornado struck the Quaker-friendly town of Xenia, Ohio. During Hurricane Katrina, the FDS was crucial when it came to helping those who weren't able to help themselves.

The FDS was again on the scene when a major earthquake hit Haiti. There, they not only supplied food and medical supplies but also played an active role in rebuilding much of the devastated infrastructure. Perhaps their greatest relief effort is still unfolding. Since the COVID-19 pandemic erupted in the spring of 2020, the Quakers have been on the frontlines, helping to fight this terrible scourge of humanity. The Quakers have been instrumental in their efforts to send food, supplies, and personal protection equipment to areas hit hard by the coronavirus. They also raised substantial funds to help out those facing eviction or in need of a little bail money to get out of overcrowded COVID-19 infested jails.

Whatever and wherever they thought they could make a difference, the Quakers have always done their best to make the world a better place. The jury is still out on whether they were always on the right side of history, but the Quakers have at least made an effort to maintain William Penn's original vision. "Right is right, even if everyone is against, and wrong is wrong even if everyone is for it."

William Penn was a man who was shaped by his revelatory experiences, and he knew that the divine love he experienced, if harnessed properly, could change the world. If we would just utilize the divine light—the innate good in all of us—we would never be led astray. As we harken back to the words of William Penn all those years ago, one can't help but feel that some modern-day quaking might yet still be in the making.

Conclusion: The State of Quakerism

History is full of religious sects that broke away from their main religious body in order to express new fundamental truths and insights to the masses. After all, Christianity was originally an offshoot of Judaism that proclaimed a new means of salvation was at hand. In a similar fashion, George Fox had a revelation of what it meant to be a Christian and how one should approach God. During the time of the first Quakers, the Church controlled much of the religious experience of worshipers, dictating when to arrive, where to sit, what to sing, and what to pray.

Prior to the Reformation, many were not even allowed to read the Bible for themselves, and they were forced to only hear scripture through the interpretation of their local priest or pastor. Martin Luther, the Reformation leader who rocked the Catholic Church in the early 1600s, railed against the fact individuals were not allowed to seek God on their own terms but rather through the lens of the clergy.

The likes of George Fox and the Quakers took this much further, and they not only decided they didn't need a pope and a bunch of cardinals in distant Rome dictating their relationship with God, but they also didn't need religious finery, icons, or ceremonies. The Quakers taught that each of us has the inner light of God inside of us, and in order to commune with Him, we don't need pieces of bread and grape juice—we just need to sit quietly and get in tune with the consciousness that resides inside.

As excited as the Quakers were about their perceived revelation, many were not too pleased with the notion that the Church or even the Bible might not be necessary for salvation. Even Martin Luther himself might have objected to some of these teachings. Nevertheless, the Quakers believed they had stumbled upon a cosmic secret that few others had realized. They believed that the light of God could shine bright in humanity if they would only come to realize that God didn't dwell in churches made of stone but within human beings made of flesh.

Those who came to understand and appreciate this teaching often felt as if they had been struck by lightning at the realization. This was precisely how William Penn felt all those years ago when he heard a poor and humble old

Quaker minister preach at his dad's castle. Upon hearing the words of Thomas Loe, William Penn felt as if he had just uncovered the greatest secret of the universe. God wasn't in some faraway dimension somewhere; he dwelled deep within our souls and could be tapped into at any time!

The concept the Quakers developed had far-reaching social ramifications. They came to realize that if everyone had the inner light of God within them, that must mean that everyone was equal in the eyes of God. This concept of equality was already backed up by scripture. After all, Apostle Paul famously declared, "For ye are all the children of God by faith in Christ Jesus. For as many of you as have been baptized into Christ have put on Christ. There is neither Jew nor Greek, there is neither bond nor free, there is neither male nor female: for ye are all one in Christ!"

This statement of equality comes right out of the New Testament, but for the Quakers, it was their revelatory experience with the divine light within that made the equality of God all the more real to them. And once they came to believe it, it made them value all human life as precious. How could they harm someone who had the light of God dwelling within them? How could one look down upon, abuse, enslave, or otherwise mistreat a vessel that God works through? To them, it would be like maliciously burning down a church or tearing down an altar!

This understanding led the Quakers to refuse the recognition of ranks, titles, and distinctions. This great vision of equality guided the Quakers to treating others with respect. This could be seen early on, with the Quakers treating Native Americans with dignity and denouncing slavery centuries before most other Christians would even dare to approach the subject. The Quakers' strong convictions and beliefs made them stand out, and they were persecuted early on because of it.

As the trials and tribulations of a young William Penn can attest, even something as innocuous as not taking the hat off one's head could land a Quaker in jail. Nevertheless, they persisted, and the more they were persecuted, the more they persevered. So much so, that someone like Penn, who had spent time in the dreaded Tower of London, would later be commissioned to found the American Colony of Pennsylvania.

William Penn himself did not take this great reversal in fortune for granted. On the contrary, he made sure he remained humble and faithful to the tenants of Quakerism for the rest of his days, as he was determined to leave behind a legacy of Quaker values long after he passed from this earth. All one has to do is look at a copy of the US Constitution to find Penn's values of freedom of religion and freedom of speech since they are enshrined in the nation's Bill of Rights.

Most would say a Quaker like Penn was a true visionary, but William Penn would probably humbly admit that it was not his vision but God's that allowed him to fashion such an epic charter of human rights in the first place. This was indeed the state of Quakerism then, and as long as we hold fast to the great legacy and principles that Quakers like William Penn left behind, it will continue to be the state of Quakerism for the foreseeable future.

Here's another book by Captivating History that you might like

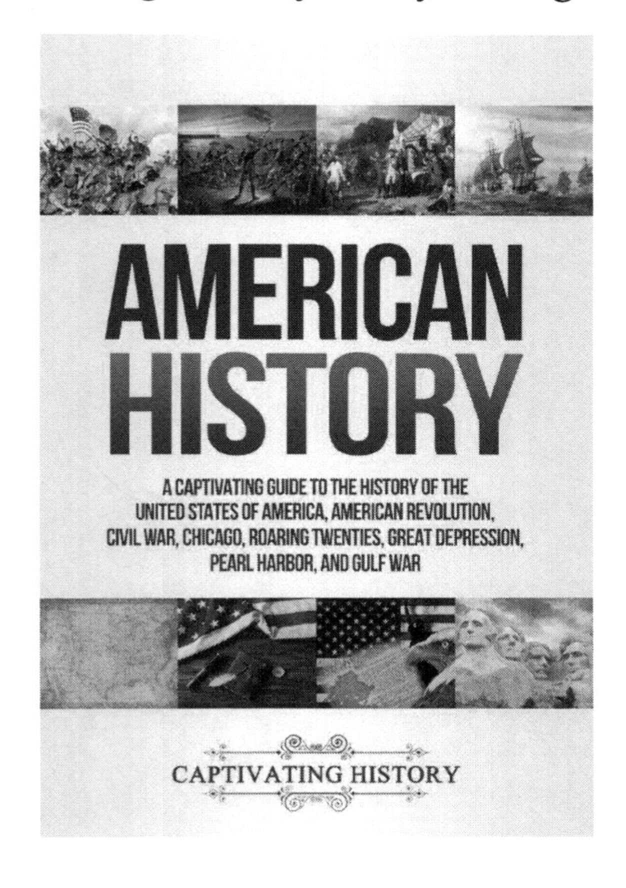

Free Bonus from Captivating History (Available for a Limited time)

Hi History Lovers!

Now you have a chance to join our exclusive history list so you can get your first history ebook for free as well as discounts and a potential to get more history books for free! Simply visit the link below to join.

Captivatinghistory.com/ebook

Also, make sure to follow us on Facebook, Twitter and Youtube by searching for Captivating History.

Appendix A: Further Reading and Reference

Here is a list of some of the reading and reference materials that helped make this text possible. All of these sources cover a wide-ranging variety of the Quaker story. Feel free to look through them on your own.

Radical Friend: Amy Kirby Post and Her Activist Worlds. Nancy A. Hewitt

The Quaker Colonies. Sydney G. Fisher

A Quaker Officer in the Civil War: Henry Gawthrop of the 4th Delaware. Justin Carisio

Abraham Lincoln, the Quakers, and the Civil War: A Trial of Principle and Faith. William C. Kashatus

The Rich Heritage of Quakerism. Walter R. Williams

The Quakers in America. Thomas D. Hamm

The Light in Their Consciences: Early Quakers in Britain, 1646-1666. Rosemary Moore

The Quakers, 1656-1723: The Evolution of an Alternative Community. Richard C. Allen and Rosemary Moore

A Lenape Among the Quakers: The Life of Hannah Freeman. Dawn G. Marsh

Nixon's First Cover Up: The Religious Life of a Quaker President. H. Larry Ingle

The Worlds of William Penn. Andrew R. Murphy, John Smolenski

Gary Anderson Clayton, "The Native Peoples of The American West: Genocide or Ethnic Cleansing?" WESTERN HISTORICAL QUARTERLY, Volume 47, Issue 4, Winter 2016

Michael Brown, *Shared History: Understanding the Impact of the Pequot War*, May 2016.

Bethany Berger, *Red: Racism and the American Indian,* University of Connecticut, 2009.

Alfred A. Cave, *The Pequot War,* University of Massachusetts Press Amherst, 1996.

Katherine A. Grandjean, *New World Tempests: Environment, Scarcity, and the Coming of the Pequot War,* Omohundro Institute of Early American History and Culture, 2011.

Denis Diderot, *Thoughts on the Interpretation of Nature,* France. 1754.

Raphael Lemkin, *Axis Rule in Occupied Europe: Laws of Occupation, Analysis of Government, Proposals for Redress,* Washington, DC: Carnegie Endowment for International Peace, 1944.

Philip Jenkins, *History of the United States,* originally published by Palgrave, Houndmils, Basingstoke, Hampspie, Beograd (Serbia), 2002, Translated by Filip Višnjić.

Jacobs Jaap, *Dutch Colonial Fortifications in North America,* New Holland Foundation, Amsterdam 2015.

Andrew C. Lipman, *Murder on the Saltwater Frontier: The Death of John Oldham,* University of Pennsylvania Press, Spring 2011.

John Lazuk, *Cultural Perception in Early New England: Europeans, Indians, and the Origins of the Pequot War of 1637,* University of Montana, 1983.

George Francis Dow, *Every Day in Massachusetts Bay Colony,* First Published in Boston, 1935 Reissued in 1967, by Benjamin Bloom, Inc. Reprint Edition 1977 by Arno Press Inc, November 2013.

Brenden Rensink, *Genocide of Native Americans: Historical Facts and Historiographic Debates,* University of Nebraska, Lincoln, 2011.

Group of authors: Kevin McBride, Douglas Currie, David Naumec, Ashley Bissonnette, Noah Fellman, Laurie Pasteryak & Jacqueline Veninger, "Battle of Mistick Fort, Site Identification and Documentation Plan," Public Technical Report National Park Service American Battlefield Protection Program, Mashantucket Pequot Museum & Research Center.

Group of authors: David Naumec, Ashley Bissonnette, Noah Fellman & Kevin McBride, "Technical Report Battle of Pequot (Munnacommock) Swamp, July 13-14, 1637," September 2017.

Group of authors: Allan Nevins & Henry Steele Commager, *The Pocket History of The United States*, Pocket Books Inc, New York, August 1992.

Primary Sources

Lion Gardiner, *Relation of the Pequot Warres* (1660), University of Nebraska - Lincoln, Editor: W. N. Chattin Carlton.

John Mason, *A Brief History of the Pequot War*, University of Nebraska-Lincoln, Editor Paul Royster, August 2007.

John Underhill, *Newes from America; Or, A New and Experimentall Discoverie of New England; Containing, A Trve Relation of Their War-like Proceedings These Two Yeares Last Past, with a Figure of the Indian Fort, or Palizado*, University of Nebraska-Lincoln, Editor Paul Royster, August 2007.

Philip Vincent, *A True Relation of the Late Battell fought in New England, between the English, and the Salvages: With the present state of things there* (1637), University of Nebraska-Lincoln, Editor: Paul Royster, 2007.

Anonymous 2017, *New World Economics: How the Pilgrims Financed Their Journey*, New Era Debt Solutions, viewed May 2021, <https://neweradebtsolutions.com/new-world-economics-pilgrims-financed-journey/>

Anonymous 2011, *Church of England*, British Broadcasting Commission, viewed May 2021, <https://www.bbc.co.uk/religion/religions/christianity/cofe/cofe_1.shtml>

History.com Editors 2020, *Martin Luther Posts His 95 Theses*, A&E Television Networks, viewed May 2021, <https://www.history.com/this-day-in-history/martin-luther-posts-95-theses>

Petruzzello, M. 2016, *Separatist*, Encyclopedia Britannica, viewed May 2021, <https://www.britannica.com/topic/Separatists>

Voiland, A. 2016, *Holland: First Stop for the Pilgrims*, NASA Earth Observatory, viewed May 2021, <https://earthobservatory.nasa.gov/images/91317/holland-first-stop-for-the-pilgrims>

Pruitt, S. 2020, *Colonists at the First Thanksgiving Were Mostly Men Because Women Had Perished,* A&E Television Networks, viewed June 2021, <https://www.history.com/news/first-thanksgiving-colonists-native-americans-men>

Biography.com Editors 2020, *Squanto,* A&E Television Networks, viewed June 2021, <https://www.biography.com/political-figure/squanto>

Siteseen Limited 2012, *Wampanoag Tribe,* Siteseen Limited, viewed June 2021, <https://www.warpaths2peacepipes.com/indian-tribes/wampanoag-tribe.htm>

History.com Editors 2020, *Mayflower Docks at Plymouth Harbor,* A&E Television Networks, viewed June 2021, <https://www.history.com/this-day-in-history/mayflower-docks-at-plymouth-harbor>

Brosnahan, T., *Massasoit, Wampanoag Sachem,* New England Travel Planner, viewed June 2021, <https://newenglandtravelplanner.com/people/massasoit.html>

Gillo-Whitaker, D. 2020, *Biography of Chief Massasoit, Native American Hero,* ThoughtCo, viewed June 2021, <https://www.thoughtco.com/profile-chief-massasoit-2477989>

Britannica, The Editors of Encyclopedia 2013, *Nauset,* Encyclopedia Britannica, viewed June 2021, <https://www.britannica.com/topic/Nauset>

Seay, B. 2019, *Reframing the Story of the First Encounter Between the Native Americans and the Pilgrims,* GBH News, viewed June 2021, <https://www.wgbh.org/news/local-news/2019/11/28/reframing-the-story-of-the-first-encounter-between-native-americans-and-the-pilgrims>

Harrigan, S. 2012, *First Encounter,* HistoryNet, viewed June 2021, <https://www.historynet.com/first-encounter.htm>

History.com Editors 2019, *Plymouth Colony,* A&E Television Networks, viewed June 2021, <https://www.history.com/topics/colonial-america/plymouth>

Bradford, W. 1656, *Of Plymouth Plantation,* excerpts by National Humanities Center, viewed June 2021, <https://nationalhumanitiescenter.org/pds/amerbegin/settlement/text1/BradfordPlymouthPlantation.pdf>

Beyond the Pilgrim Story 2012, *John & Catherine Carver,* Pilgrim Hall Museum, viewed June 2021, <https://pilgrimhall.org/john_catherine_carver.htm>

History.com Editors 2020, *Mayflower Compact,* A&E Television Networks, viewed June 2021, <https://www.history.com/topics/colonial-america/mayflower-compact>

Roos, D. 2020, *The Pilgrims' Miserable Journey Aboard Mayflower,* A&E Television Networks, viewed June 2021, <https://www.history.com/news/mayflower-journey-pilgrims-america?li_source=LI&li_medium=m2m-rcw-history>

Klein, C. 2019, *Did the Pilgrims intend to land at Plymouth?,* A&E Television Networks, viewed June 2021, <https://www.history.com/news/did-the-pilgrims-intend-to-land-at-plymouth>

Harris, D., *The More Children's Story,* Shropshire Mayflower, viewed June 2021, <http://shropshiremayflower.com/the-four-more-children/>

History.com Editors 2019, *John Smith,* A&E Television Networks, viewed June 2021, <https://www.history.com/topics/colonial-america/john-smith>

Spencer, A. 2019, *New Evidence: Was Thomas Weston, Seventeenth Century London Merchant among the First to Sail Fish to Virginia's Starving Colonists?,* Global Maritime History, viewed June 2021, <http://globalmaritimehistory.com/thomas_weston_merchant/>

Mark, J. J. 2020, *Mayflower Passengers & Crew*, World History, viewed June 2021, <https://www.worldhistory.org/article/1631/mayflower-passengers--crew/>

Mullane, J. 2017, *The Speedwell, forgotten ship of the Pilgrims' voyage*, Courier Times, viewed June 2021, <https://www.buckscountycouriertimes.com/news/20171122/speedwell-forgotten-ship-of-pilgrims-voyage/1>

Britannica, Editors of Encyclopedia, *John Robinson*, Encyclopedia Britannica, viewed June 2021, <https://www.britannica.com/biography/John-Robinson-English-minister>

Moffitt, D. 2020, *Myles Standish: The Lancashire man who founded modern America*, LancsLive, viewed June 2021, <https://www.lancs.live/news/lancashire-news/myles-standish-lancashire-man-who-18048918>

Worrall, S. 2006, *Pilgrims' Progress*, Smithsonian Magazine, viewed June 2021, <https://www.smithsonianmag.com/history/pilgrims-progress-135067108/>

History.com Editors 2018, *William Bradford*, A&E Television Networks, viewed June 2021, <https://www.history.com/topics/colonial-america/william-bradford>

History.com Editors 2019, *The Pilgrims*, A&E Television Networks, viewed June 2021, <https://www.history.com/topics/colonial-america/pilgrims>

Illustration I: By wikitravel:user:OldPine, CC BY-SA 1.0, https://commons.wikimedia.org/w/index.php?curid=986647

Illustration II: https://commons.wikimedia.org/wiki/File:Embarkation_of_the_Pilgrims.jpg

Illustration III:
https://commons.wikimedia.org/wiki/File:After_the_Storm,_by_William_Bradford.JPG

Illustration IV:
https://commons.wikimedia.org/wiki/File:Mayflower_in_Plymouth_Harbor,_by_William_Halsall.jpg

Andrews, C. M. (1934). *The colonial period of American history.* New Haven: Yale University Press.

Collier, C., & Collier, J. L. (1998). *Pilgrims and Puritans, 1620-1676.* New York: Benchmark Books.

Floyd, C. (1990). *The history of New England.* New York: Portland House.

Gill, C. (1970). *Mayflower remembered: A history of the Plymouth Pilgrims.* Newton Abbot: David & Charles.

HALL, D. D. (2021). *PURITANS: A transatlantic history.* S.l.: PRINCETON UNIVERSITY PRES.

Hubbard, W. (1848). *A general history of New England, from the discovery to MDCLXXX.* Boston: C.C. Little and J. Brown.

Morison, S. E. (1965). *The Oxford history of the American people.* New York: Oxford University Press.

Philbrick, N. (2006). *Mayflower: A story of courage, community, and war.* New York: Viking.

Robertson, W., & MIntosh, D. (1817). *The history of America: Including the history of Virginia to the year 1688, and New England to the year 1652.* London: Published by Richard Evans ... and John Bourne ..., Edinburgh.

Streissguth, T. (2018). *The Mayflower story.* Minneapolis, MN: Essential Library, an imprint of Abdo Publishing.

"The Problem with Anne Hutchinson," Retrieved from

https://theimaginativeconservative.org/2019/10/problem-anne-hutchinson-michael-connolly.html

Belknap, M. R. (1994) *American Political Trials* Praeger (2nd edition)

Bradford, W. & Bradford, J. A. *Of Plymouth Plantation, 1620-1647* Retrieved from
https://scholarworks.montana.edu/xmlui/bitstream/handle/1/4676/31762100116936.pdf;sequence=1

Burnham, M. "Anne Hutchinson and the Economics of Antinomian Selfhood in Colonial New England," Retrieved from https://scholarcommons.scu.edu/cgi/viewcontent.cgi?article=1008&context=engl

"Colonial Presbyterianism: Old Faith in a New Land" Retrieved from http://www.centerforcongregationalleadership.com/uploads/6/0/0/9/6009825/woodward_richard.pdf

Dale, E. (2018) *Debating and Creating – Authority: The Failure of a Constitutional Ideal* Routledge

Hofstadter, R. & Ver Steeg, C.L. (1969) *Great Issues in American History, Vol. 1: From Settlement to Revolution: 1584-1776* Vintage

Glover, J. (2014) *Paper Sovereigns: Anglo-Native Treaties and the Law of Nations, 1604-1664* University of Pennsylvania Press

Jones, M. (2013) *"Antinomianism" Reformed Theology's Unwelcome Guest* R&R Publishing

Kamensky, J. (1999) *Governing the Tongue: The Politics of Speech in Early New England* Oxford University Press

LaPlante, E. (2005) *American Jezebel: The Uncommon Life of Anne Hutchinson, the Woman Who Defied the Puritans* Harper One: Reprint ed.

Leight, J. (2001) "Anne Hutchinson: A Life in Private," The Concord Review, Inc. Winter, 2001

Rowlandson, M. A. (2013 repr.) *True History of the Captivity and Restoration of Mrs. Mary Rowlandson* Alejandro's Libros

Shepard, T. (1853) *The Works of Thomas Shepard: First Pastor of the First Church Cambridge, Mass. With a Memoir of His Life and Character, Vol 1* Doctrinal Tract and Book Society

"Wappinger History," Retrieved from http://www.dickshovel.com/wap.html "Wappinger History"

Winship, M. P. Making Heretics: Militant Protestantism and Free Grace in Massachusetts Retrieved from http://people.ucls.uchicago.edu/~pdoyle/bustlesandbeaux.wordpress.com-Mrs_Hutchinson_by_Nathaniel_Hawthorne1830.pdf

Winship, M. "Times and Trials of Anne Hutchinson," Retrieved from http://historicalsolutions.com/the-times-and-trials-of-anne-hutchinson-by-michael-winship/

Killing England: The Brutal Struggle for American Independence. Bill O'Reilly, 2017.

As a City on a Hill: The Story of America's Most Famous Lay Sermon. Daniel T. Rodgers, 2018.

The Puritan Experiment: New England Society from Bradford to Edwards. Francis J. Bremer, 1976.

The Last Puritans: Mainline Protestants and the Power of the Past. Margaret Bendroth, 2015.

The Puritans: A Transatlantic History. David D. Hall, 2019.

Pilgrims and Puritans: 1620-1676. Christopher Collier & James Lincoln Collier, 1998.

Who Were the Accused Witches of Salem? And Other Questions about the Witchcraft Trials. Laura Hamilton Waxman, 2012.

Reformation: A World in Turmoil. Andrew Atherstone, 2015.

A Delusion of Satan: The Full Story of the Salem Witch Trials. Frances Hill, 2002.

Alan Taylor. *American Colonies: The Settling of North America.* 1955.

Charles C. Mann. *1493: Uncovering the New World Columbus Created.* 2011.

William Bradford (Editor: Harold Paget). *Of Plymouth Plantation.* 2016.

David Hackett Fischer. *Albion's Seed: Four British Folkways in America.* 1989.

William Cronon. *Changes in the Land: Indians, Colonists, and the Ecology of New England.* 2003.

Stephen Brumwell. *White Devil: A True Story of War, Savagery and Vengeance in Colonial America.* 2006.

Don Jordon & Michael Walsh. *White Cargo: The Forgotten History of Britain's White Slaves in America.* 2008.

William Dalrymple. *The Anarchy: The East India Company, Corporate Violence, and the Pillage of an Empire.* 2019.

Cokie Roberts. *Founding Mothers: The Women Who Raised Our Nation.* 2005.

Marilynne K. Roach. *Six Women of Salem: The Untold Story of the Accused and Their Accusers in the Salem Witch Trials.* 2013.

James Horn. *1619: Jamestown and the Forging of American Democracy.* 2018.

Made in United States
Orlando, FL
11 August 2022